PREACHING THROUGH
THE CHRISTIAN YEAR

PREACHING THROUGH THE CHRISTIAN YEAR

Year B

A Comprehensive Commentary on the Lectionary

Fred B. Craddock
John H. Hayes
Carl R. Holladay
Gene M. Tucker

Trinity Press International   Valley Forge, Pennsylvania

First Edition 1993

Trinity Press International
P.O. Box 851
Valley Forge, PA 19482-0851

Cover design by Brian Preuss

Library of Congress Cataloging-in-Publication Data

Preaching through the Christian year. Year B / Fred B. Craddock . . .
  [et al.].
    p.   cm.
  Includes index.
    ISBN 1-56338-068-4 (v. 2)
    1. Bible—Homeletical use. 2. Bible—Commentaries. 3. Common lectionary
(1992) 4. Lectionary preaching. I. Craddock, Fred B.
BS534.5.P7272 1992
251—dc20   92-25860
                                                              CIP

Printed in the United States of America on acid-free paper.

97   6   5   4   3

Contents

PROPERS AFTER PENTECOST

Introduction

The Consultation on Common Texts issued the *Common Lectionary* in 1983, inviting the churches to use it and then offer suggestions for amendments and modifications. That trial period is now ended, and in December 1991 a final draft of the calendar and table of readings was completed. No further changes in this lectionary are anticipated.

The present volume—the second of three to appear in a series—is based on the newly revised *Common Lectionary: The Lectionary Proposed by the Consultation on Texts* (1992).

The now finalized *Common Lectionary* more fully converses with the lectionaries of the Episcopal, Lutheran, and Roman Catholic churches than did the 1983 edition. Readers will notice the influence of these three traditions in both calendar and readings. For example, Holy Saturday with its appropriate readings is offered for those who observe liturgically the Saturday between Good Friday and Easter. At some points, this greater inclusiveness has meant embracing the selected texts in the Roman, Lutheran, or Episcopal lectionaries. In other instances, the texts of these three traditions are offered as alternate readings. In every case, it has been our decision to comment on all the texts, hoping to make this commentary useful to as wide an audience as possible and as helpful to as many pulpits as possible.

In 1989, the New Revised Standard Version of the Bible was published. The present work follows the NRSV as its primary translation. In addition, two other widely used translations, the New English Bible and the Jerusalem Bible, have been used in their new revisions. Other translations are also quoted occasionally.

This commentary series will treat all the readings for each year in a single volume. Having in one volume a full year's calendar, table of readings, and commentary gives the preacher and others who work with the liturgy a clearer sense of continuity and greater ease of reference within a year and of cross reference among the three years. A commentary is a reference book, most at home on a study desk.

As an aid for focus and direction, each of the volumes in the series will provide a brief introduction to the readings for each service.

We think it important that the reader understand the perspectives and convictions that will inform our work throughout the three volumes. We offer these under the following three headings.

The Scripture. There is no substitute for direct exposure to the biblical text, both for the preacher in preparation and for the listener in worship. The Scriptures are therefore not only studied privately but also read aloud as an act of worship in and of itself and not solely as prelude to a sermon. The sermon is an interpretation of Scripture in the sense that the preacher seeks to bring the text forward into the present in order to effect a new hearing of the Word. In this sense, the text has its future and its fulfillment in preaching. In fact, the Bible itself is the record of the continual rehearing and reinterpreting of its own traditions in new settings and for new generations of believers. New settings and new circumstances are properly as well as inescapably integral to a hearing of God's Word in and through the text. Whatever else may be said to characterize God's Word, it is always appropriate to the hearers. But the desire to be immediately relevant should not abbreviate study of the text or divorce the sermon from the biblical tradition. Such sermons are orphaned, released without memory into the world. It is the task of the preacher and teacher to see that the principle of fidelity to Scripture is not abandoned in the life and worship of the church. The endeavor to understand a text in its historical, literary, and theological contexts does create, to be sure, a sense of distance between the Bible and the congregation. The preacher may grow impatient during this period of feeling a long way from a sermon. But this time of study can be most fruitful. By holding text and parishioners apart for a while, the preacher can hear each more clearly and exegete each more honestly. Then, when the two intersect in the sermon, neither the text nor the congregation is consumed by the other. Because the Bible is an ancient book, it invites the preacher back into its world in order to understand; because the Bible is the church's Scripture, it moves forward into our world and addresses us here and now.

The Lectionary. Ever-increasing numbers of preachers are using a lectionary as a guide for preaching and worship. The intent of lectionaries is to provide for the church over a given period of time (usually three years) large units of Scripture arranged according to the seasons of the Christian year and selected because they carry the central message of the Bible. Lectionaries are not designed to limit one's message or restrict the freedom of the pulpit. On the contrary, churches that use a lectionary usually hear more Scripture in worship than those that do not. And ministers who preach from the lectionary find themselves stretched into areas of the canon into which they would not have gone had they kept to the path of personal preference. Other values of the lectionary are well known: the readings provide a common ground for discussions in ministerial peer groups; family worship can more easily join public worship through shared readings; ministers and worship committees can work with common biblical texts to prepare services that have movement and integrity; and the lectionary encourages more disciplined study and advance preparation. All these and other values are increased if churches share a common lectionary. A common lectionary could conceivably generate a communitywide Christian conversation.

However, to the nonlectionary preacher also we offer this commentary as a helpful tool in sermon preparation. An index of Scriptures on which comments are made is provided in each volume. By means of this index, any preacher or teacher will find easy access to commentary on hundreds of biblical texts.

This Book. This volume is not designed as a substitute for work with the biblical text; on the contrary, its intent is to encourage such work. Neither is it our desire to relieve the preacher of regular visits to concordances, lexicons, and commentaries; rather, it is our hope that the comments on the texts here will be sufficiently germinal to give direction and purpose to those visits to major reference works. Our commentary is an effort to be faithful to the text and to begin moving the text toward the pulpit. There are no sermons as such here, nor could there be. No one can preach long distance. Only the one who preaches can do an exegesis of the listeners and mix into sermon preparation enough local soil so as to effect an indigenous hearing of the Word. But we hope we have contributed to that end. The reader will notice that, although each of us has been aware of the other readings for each service, there has been no attempt to offer a collaborated commentary on all texts or a homogenized interpretation as though there were not four texts but one. It is assumed that the season of the year, the needs of the listeners, the preacher's own abilities, as well as the overall unity of the message of the Scriptures will prompt the preacher to find among the four readings the word for the day. Sometimes the four texts will join arm in arm; sometimes they will debate with one another; sometimes one will lead while the others follow, albeit at times reluctantly. Such is the wealth of the biblical witness.

A final word about our comments. The lections from the Psalter have been treated in the same manner as the other readings, even though some Protestant churches often omit the reading of the psalm or replace it with a hymn. We have chosen to regard the psalm as an equal among the texts, primarily for three reasons. First, there is growing interest in the use of psalms in public worship, and comments about them may help make that use more informed. Second, the psalms were a major source for worship and preaching in the early church, and they continue to inspire and inform Christian witness today. And third, comments on the psalms may make this volume helpful to preachers in those traditions that have maintained from earliest times the use of psalms in Christian services.

A brief word about the relation of this commentary to our earlier work, *Preaching the New Common Lectionary*. From the comments above, it is already apparent why those volumes could not be given a new introduction and offered again to you. Changes in appointed texts, revised translations of the Bible, additions to the liturgical calendar, and attention to texts appearing in Lutheran, Episcopal, and Roman Catholic lectionaries necessitated much new writing. The new writing in turn called for a reappraisal of the comments on texts that remained unchanged, prompting additions, deletions, and modifications. The result is a new, larger, and, we hope, improved commentary to aid those who preach and teach.

Fred B. Craddock (Gospels)
John H. Hayes (Psalms and the Old Testament)
Carl R. Holladay (Epistle and Acts)
Gene M. Tucker (Old Testament)

First Sunday of Advent

Isaiah 64:1–9;
Psalm 80:1–7, 17–19;
1 Corinthians 1:3–9;
Mark 13:24–37

On this First Sunday of Advent, the church is called to longing for God's redeeming presence, to the sorrow that is not sentiment but repentance, and to expectation. Both Isaiah and the psalmist lead in a lament by the believing community and a prayer for God to come in saving power. Mark offers a description of how it will be, and is, when God's Christ comes to perform God's final work of judgment and redemption. In the epistle, Paul reminds even a troubled church such as Corinth that God's coming in Christ is the formative act for the Christian community.

Isaiah 64:1–9

As part of a communal lament, this passage constitutes a powerful plea for God to intervene in history in a decisive fashion to bring redemption to the people. As a special petition for divine redemption, the passage embodies the central themes of the Advent Season—the sense of a need for redemption, the feeling of unworthiness before God, a longing for God to act, and the assurance that as Father, God is also Redeemer.

Two background issues should be noted about this text, one historical and the other literary. First is the historical context of the pericope: the passage belongs to a part of the Book of Isaiah (chaps. 56–66) that had its origin either among the Jewish exiles in Babylon after the fall of Jerusalem in 586 BC or after the initial phase of the return under the Persian king Cyrus (in 539). The people, here praying for redemption, if they were in the exile were alienated from their homeland, living among foreigners, suffering for their sins, and estranged from God. Their wrongdoings were understood as the source of their condition.

In the second place, Isaiah 64:1–9 is one component in a larger literary unit, namely, a lament offered by or on behalf of the community (for similar communal laments, see Pss. 44; 74; 79). The larger unit begins in 63:7 and ends in 64:12. A lament is a prayer to God for help in time of need. As such, laments contain typical features: a description of the trouble or distress of the worshiper(s) as well as a plea for God to redeem the one(s) praying from the destitute condition that produced the turmoil and the anxiety. Isaiah 64:1–9 contains such a description of the distress situation along with the plea for redemption. In the text there is a movement from the plea for redemption to a description of the distress. These two components are concluded by

1

a statement of confidence in God, who is addressed as Father, and a final plea. Thus we have the following outline in the pericope: a plea for God's redeeming activity (vv. 1–4), a description of the distress (vv. 5–7), a statement of confidence (v. 8), and a concluding request for divine favor (v. 9).

Let us first examine how the text talks about the distress. In an earlier description of distress but in the same unit (63:17–19), the focus is on the people's alienation and estrangement from, and their loss of contact with, God. Three aspects of this condition are emphasized. (1) In verse 17, the community declares that it is God himself who makes them err and sin and who hardens their hearts so that they do not fear the Divine. Old Testament faith was quite willing to claim what makes moderns cringe, namely, that the Divine could bring evil upon God's own people and harden their hearts so that punishment was inevitable (see Isa. 6:9–13, 45:7; Deut. 32:39). (Honesty in our proclamation should prevent us from toning down such an emphasis, for frequently our misery seems God-sent and the Deity appears as our enemy!) (2) The temple, representing God's presence, has been destroyed, and adversaries occupy God's holy place (v. 18). Foreigners are in the place where God's people made contact with the Divine. (3) Verse 19 declares that the sense of alienation from God is so great that it is as if God had never been their ruler and they had never borne and confessed the divine name. They feel as if they had never belonged to God.

A second description of distress, in today's text (vv. 5–7), focuses on the sinful state of the people and their sense of absolute lostness. Numerous metaphors are used to describe such a condition. The people feel unclean and thus ostracized from normal life (see the condition of the leper in Lev. 13:46) or like a polluted garment, contaminated, fit only to be destroyed. Like a withered leaf or wind-blown trash, the people find that their iniquities have destroyed the substance of life (v. 6). The human condition is so bad that no one anymore seems faithful—they live, not in God's hand, but in the clutches of their iniquities (v. 7).

The petition for redemption (64:1–4) pleads for God to act, not in some normal way, but with decisive force as before when God caused mountains to quake and fire to blaze forth (see Exod. 19:16–18; Ps. 114:3–6). Isaiah 64:4 concludes the plea for divine intervention with a statement of confidence—God can so act for those who wait because neither ear nor eye knows of any God so great!

The opening and concluding statements of confidence affirm the people's trust in God, whom they call Father. To be able to address God as Father is a claim to be children of the Divine in spite of all the evidence. The people may feel as if they cannot claim the patriarchs Abraham and Israel as their fathers (63:16) and that they are merely clay (64:8); yet it is faith in God as Father, which supplies a confidence transcending any other relationship, that is the ultimate basis of their hope.

Advent, like Isaiah 64:1–9, is concerned with human alienation from God and with the drastic consequences of human sinfulness; but like this text, it looks beyond these to God's intervention from heaven (64:1) through the incarnation, when Christians affirm that the alienation is transcended and human sinfulness is overcome.

Psalm 80:1–7, 17–19

Like the reading from Isaiah, Psalm 80 is a communal lament. Such prayers were frequently offered by the community in the context of a national fast after some calamity had threatened its existence, drained its physical and psychological well-being, or dissipated its life.

On such occasions, the people broke with the normal routine of life, assembled at sanctuaries, offered sacrifice, lamented their distress, and entreated the Deity to intervene on their behalf.

The first seven verses of this psalm have been selected for Advent reading because of the material's description of distress and the plea for restoration. Verses 17–19 contain a petition on behalf of the "one at God's right hand" and a vow of devotion in the future. These verses ought to be studied and understood in light of the entire psalm, or else they will appear as only a truncated part of the whole. The integral relationship of the entire psalm, which is addressed to the Deity, is substantiated by the threefold repetition of the refrain (in verses 3, 7, 19), which is almost identical in all three. Perhaps in the service of communal lamentation, these refrains represent the part of the liturgy spoken by the entire congregation, whereas the rest of the psalm was voiced by the priest or person in charge on behalf of the community.

An outline of the entire psalm makes for a better understanding of the opening verses. The following are the component parts: (a) address to the Deity with an initial plea (vv. 1–2), (b) the initial refrain (v. 3), (c) a description of the distress (vv. 4–6), (d) the second refrain (v. 7), (e) a second description of the distress (vv. 8–13), (f) a plea for God's help (vv. 14–17), (g) a vow or promise of loyalty to the divine if salvation is forthcoming (v. 18), and (h) the concluding refrain (v. 19).

Two primary images of the Deity appear in the psalm. At the beginning, God is addressed as the Shepherd of Israel (v. 1), a very common way of speaking of the Deity in the ancient Near East, where sheep raising and the importance of shepherds were widely understood. In verses 8–13, God is portrayed as the viticulturist, or vineyard keeper. Both images imply a God who must oversee the items under his supervision with great care, concern, and tenderness.

Now let us focus more closely on the verses of today's lection. The opening address to the Deity would suggest that the psalm originated in the Northern Kingdom of Israel. The use of the name Joseph for the people as well as the reference to the northern tribes of Benjamin, Ephraim, and Manasseh (the last two were names of the sons of Joseph; see Gen. 48:1) point in this direction. Also, the reference to God as "you who are enthroned upon the cherubim" was a divine epithet used of God's sitting enthroned upon the ark, which contained cherub decorations. (Cherubs were considered semidivine figures probably depicted with an animal body, human head, and bird wings; in the ancient world, they were not depicted as little fat winged angels!) This epithet was used at the old ark shrine in Shiloh (see 1 Sam. 4:4). All of this implies that the distressful situation requiring a lament had to do with a calamity involving the northern state of Israel. What the calamity was is unknown, perhaps defeat in some military campaign.

In the description of the distress, the people complain that God is angry with their prayers, that is, unresponsive to their pleas for help (v. 4). Unlike a good shepherd who provides the flock with sustaining food and good water, God is depicted as feeding them with the bread of tears (associated with burials and times of mourning) and giving them tears to drink in full measure. That is, God is accused of bringing misery and suffering on them and of failing to function as a good shepherd (v. 5). Instead of protecting them from their enemies, God becomes their enemy. Their plight is so bad that their neighbors make fun of them and their adversaries hold them up to ridicule (v. 6). It is, indeed, the dark side of the Divine (the *Deus absconditus*) that the people have experienced. Just as they see that their hope is in God, so they attribute their misery to the same source.

The refrain in verses 7 and 19 is an appeal for God to help; if only God's face would shine forth—that is, if the divine disposition would change—then the people would be saved.

Verse 17 is an intercessory prayer on behalf of "the one at your right hand, the one whom you make strong for yourself." This reading would suggest that Israel is described as the one at God's right hand, that is, the one who occupies the choice place and, thus, a special relationship. The right hand, even in ancient times, was considered the good hand and the left hand the sinister (from the Latin *sinistrum*, meaning "left"). The Hebrew really reads "Let thy hand be upon the man of thy right hand, upon the son of man whom thou madest strong for thyself" (KJV). This could suggest that the text refers to the king who sits at the right hand of God (see Ps. 110:1). (For other possible references to the ruler as "man" or "son of man," see Ps. 146:3; Mic. 6:8.) If this be the case, then this portion of the psalm is apropos of Advent, because the work of the Son of Man (Jesus) brings comfort and strength so that we like the ancient community can speak of forthcoming, faithful devotion (see v. 18).

Just as Israel gave thought and expression in this psalm to its need for God's help and saw its situation as desperate without divine aid, so we in the Advent Season think of the misery of human existence and look forward to the shining of God's face in the coming of the Redeemer. Advent, like Israel's lamentation services, should be a time to ponder the conditions of life under the anger of the Divine and life's futility without the presence of God's shining face.

1 Corinthians 1:3–9

This passage embodies two of the formal features with which Paul typically opens his letters: the greeting and the prayer. Because the letter was written to be read aloud to the congregation assembled as a house-church, probably in the home of Gaius (cf. Rom. 16:23), both elements were appropriate for a worship setting—the one as a congregational greeting, the other as an opening prayer. As one would expect, the prayer was crafted to fit the special needs of the hearers as they awaited their founding apostle's advice and instructions contained in the letter that was to follow.

The invocation of grace and peace combines the standard forms of greeting commonly used by Gentiles and Jews, but here they have become thoroughly Christianized. They are in no sense ordinary greetings. The source of both grace and peace are seen to be in God the Father and the Lord Jesus Christ.

The opening prayer of thanksgiving can be profitably compared with similar prayers in Paul's other letters (cf. Rom. 1:8–17; Phil. 1:3–11; 1 Thess. 1:2–3:3; 2 Thess. 1:3–12; also 2 Cor. 1:3–7). Such prayers normally have two functions: to set the mood and overall tone of the letter that follows and to serve as a "table of contents" by telegraphing in advance some of the main concerns to be unfolded in the letter.

The tone of the opening prayer is one of confidence and reassurance. Paul begins by recalling the decisive event in which all Christian experience is anchored—God's gracious gift of Christ. It was this that provided the fundamental reference point for all future orientation and the basis on which Paul provided further instruction and exhortation. This in itself is instructive, for it shows us how Paul the pastor anchored his teaching and instruction in that which his readers had already received and experienced (cf. 1 Cor. 15:1–11).

Paul reassures his readers that they are rich in speech and knowledge, that they are not deficient in any spiritual gift, and finally that the commitment which they began as Christians will be sustained through the assistance of God until the day of Christ. As is well known, each of these becomes a major theme that is developed later in the letter (cf. 8:1–3; 13:1–13; 15:1–58).

As the remainder of the letter makes clear, a situation had developed within the church that caused some of the members to become painfully aware of their deficiencies. Some of the weaker members, probably newer converts, were being intimidated by some of the stronger, more experienced members who claimed greater and more impressive spiritual accomplishments. As a result, some of the members were anxious about their own status before God and apparently confused about the coming of Christ. Consequently, much of the letter is written to strengthen the whole church collectively. On the one hand, Paul insists that the better side of "knowledge" is love (8:1–3), and that every member, regardless of the gifts one has received, is a vital member of the body (chap. 12).

Given this level of anxiety and uncertainty—not at all uncommon for newer Christians—Paul's stress on the fidelity of God is well directed. "God is faithful," he asserts, reminding them that the God who had called them into the fellowship with Christ could, and would, sustain them until the end. That God can be trusted unconditionally is reiterated later in the letter (1 Cor. 10:13) and is frequently asserted by Paul (cf. 2 Cor. 1:18; 1 Thess. 5:24; 2 Thess. 3:3; cf. Heb. 10:23; 11:11; 1 John 1:9; Rev. 1:5), although it is the one axiom of Christian faith consistently called into question by many of life's experiences.

The strong eschatological emphasis in the passage, seen especially as the prayer moves to a conclusion, can be profitably explored during Advent. It is worth noting that there was considerable confusion within the Corinthian church concerning the last days and that this elicited from Paul his most extensive set of systematic comments about the resurrection (chap. 15). Moreover, eschatological misunderstandings had ethical implications. The belief that some had already experienced the second resurrection led to spiritual arrogance and resulted in open immorality. Accordingly, Paul's remarks here serve as a reminder that the resurrection is still future and that the interim need not be spent in anxiety. Instead, Christians may live in full confidence that God is faithful and that God can sustain to the end those who have committed themselves to the life of faith and trust. Even the least gifted can live in the assurance that the God who calls also sustains.

Mark 13:24–37

A nd what I say to you I say to all: Keep awake" (v. 37). It may be disconcerting at first that the Gospel lection to begin Advent is from Mark, who has no birth narrative, and that the particular reading from Mark is from a discourse about the end of time. But the appropriateness not immediately apparent becomes clear upon reflection. Advent, after all, has to do with the coming of the Lord, the birth being but one form of the appearance of Christ. And at the center of faith's understanding of the end times is the coming of the Lord. Because God is "The One Who Comes" to strengthen, to reveal, to judge, and to redeem, the posture of the people of God is always the same: repentance, expectation, and hope.

Mark 13:24–37 concludes a lengthy discourse of Jesus sometimes called "the little Apocalypse" because of its similarity to the Apocalypse to John. The reader of apocalyptic literature is impressed through vivid cosmic images that God's coming, whether to punish or to rescue, is no small event. When God comes, the heavens break their cycle of days and seasons, and the earth convulses. The farthest star, the smallest blade of grass, everything created, is affected by the activity of the Creator. Such are the events (the end of the temple, the end of all things, and the coming of the Son of Man are interwoven themes) described here.

Upon leaving the temple in Jerusalem for the last time before his death, Jesus made the pronouncement that the temple would be destroyed: "Not one stone will be left here upon another" (v. 2). The speech itself is in response to questions posed privately by Peter, James, John, and Andrew (vv. 3–4). Scholars have long recognized the composite nature of the discourse, as evidenced by portions of it being found in other contexts in Matthew and Luke. For example, the statement that no one except God knows the time of the end (v. 32) is a pronouncement found in many places and in a variety of forms (Matt. 24:42; 25:13; Luke 12:38, 40; Acts 1:7). Because this verse contains its own truth, it can easily conclude the preceding paragraph (vv. 28–31), or it can introduce verses 33–37, a literary unit that begins and ends with the same word and contains one governing thought. Apparently, the author who drew together these sayings into one speech wanted the emphasis to fall here. The final word of Jesus prior to the passion story is a thrice-repeated word (vv. 33, 35, 37): "Keep awake."

Because of the instructional and hortatory nature of Mark 13, many have surmised that it was a portion of a catechism for new converts. But whether to new Christians or to those who already bear the burden of discipleship, these words are definitely addressed to believers who not only suffer but who also must try to interpret events that seem to contradict the expectations of those who trust in God. At the time that Mark wrote his Gospel, Jerusalem and the temple lay in ruins. Civil strife had outlived Roman patience, and the threats begun by Emperor Caligula (AD 39–40) are now (AD 70) carried out. What did this disaster mean for the purposes and promises of God? Jewish prophets had fed the war effort with messianic ideology, but how were followers of Jesus to understand the end of the Holy City and the temple? Added to the persecution at the hands of religious and political authorities and the anguish of families torn apart by differing loyalties (vv. 9–13) was the unbearable confusion created by false messiahs and false prophets (vv. 6, 22). False messiahs were claiming, "This is the Second Advent; I am Christ returned," and false prophets were turning religion into an almanac: "The signs are right; this is the end." Experiencing most heavily now the absence of Jesus, the faithful are torn between giving themselves up to despair or reaching for any flicker of hope.

To that church and to all the faithful everywhere ("And what I say to you I say to all") the word of our text is both encouraging and demanding. The believers are not robbed of their expectation of a final day, a day of relief and vindication. That time will come, but it will be at God's determination and accompanied by signs God will give. All human calculations are confusing and futile. In fact, the day of the Lord is not to be tied to any political condition or religious institution. The weals and woes of any nation, even a nation claiming to have a central place in the purposes of God, do not dictate the time or place or form of God's advent. Nor do religious institutions, even those established to serve and honor God such as temple or church, fix the calendar of heaven. God survives all human structures and institutions, sometimes having to shatter and re-create the communities that exist for God's work in the world. In other words, true hope is trust in the faithfulness of God, constant amid the rise and fall of the worst and the best of human achievement.

The clear evidence of trust in the faithfulness of God is faithfulness in our work and witness. This is the meaning of being alert and watchful. To watch is not to scan the heavens, read the horoscope, comb through obscure texts, and begin every sentence with the words "When the Messiah comes." Such uninvolved waiting for the Messiah is not hope; it is postponement and evasion. Looking upon scenes of human misery and mouthing "When the

Messiah comes" has nothing to do with this text. The brief parable in verses 34–35 (conflating themes from parables in Matt. 25:14ff. and Luke 12:35ff.) makes it quite clear what life is for the disciples of Jesus. It is as though a master, absent on a journey, had left his servants in charge, *each with work to be done,* with a keeper at the door. The message, then, is to be neither falsely optimistic nor falsely discouraged. Christ will come and with signs that no one can miss. In the meantime, appropriate Christian behavior is enduring, without trying to guess when; it is continuing the mission to the nations (v. 10) without giving up. "And what I say to you I say to all: Keep awake." To keep awake is to be faithful in our work, as though we were already in the presence of the One for whose coming our hearts are eager.

Second Sunday of Advent

Isaiah 40:1–11;
Psalm 85:1–2, 8–13;
2 Peter 3:8–15*a*;
Mark 1:1–8

Today's readings shift the mood from lament and longing to the good news of God's coming soon. Both Isaiah 40 and 2 Peter 3 remind us of conditions in the world that persuade some that salvation is nowhere near. But those same texts boldly make their announcements of comfort and redemption to waiting believers. Mark uses Isaiah 40 to say that the promise is being fulfilled in the appearance of John the Baptist to prepare the way. Psalm 85 helps us enjoy now the anticipated consequences of God's presence.

Isaiah 40:1–11

This passage opens what has been called the prophecy of Second Isaiah. Isaiah 40–55 is generally traced back to a single anonymous prophet who carried out his work in the Exile just as the Persian ruler Cyrus had begun his conquest of the Babylonian Empire (see Isa. 44:28; 45:1). Isaiah 56–66, or at least parts of this material, may have come from the same unknown prophetic spokesperson.

In its wars with the Babylonians, Judah had been overwhelmingly defeated. Its capital city, Jerusalem, had been captured in 597 BC and King Jehoiachin and his family taken into captivity in the first Babylonian deportation of exiles (2 Kings 24:1–17). Ten years later, Judah was again locked in battle with the Babylonians. This time, in 586 BC, Jerusalem was destroyed, its walls pulled down, the temple burned, the Davidic family removed from the throne, and additional Judeans deported. The crisis that these events created for the Jewish community is echoed in the Book of Lamentations, which speaks of the horrible calamities that befell the city. Second Isaiah's message should be read in parallel columns with the Book of Lamentations because the misery and destitution that Lamentations bemoans, Second Isaiah proclaims are coming to an end and salvation is at hand.

The burden of Second Isaiah's preaching was twofold. On the one hand, he had to convince the despondent exiles that events in the international scene, especially the meteoric rise of Cyrus, was the work of Yahweh, Israel's God—that God was again moving in history and had not deserted the world or the chosen people. On the other hand, the prophet had to convince his own people that Cyrus's conquest would bring a new day for the exiles and the Judeans—that God had forgiven the people and was going to inaugurate an act of salvation that would free them from exilic conditions. In both, the prophet sought to bolster the courage and hope of the desolate and despondent community.

Isaiah 40:1–11, the introduction to the remainder of chapters 40–55, has many of the features of a prophetic call to prophesy or to a special task (see Isa. 6; Ezek. 3). In this text, however, the focus is not on the one who is to be the messenger but instead on the message itself. Four voices are depicted as speaking in this text: in verses 1–2 the prophet reports what he hears God saying; in verses 3–5 another voice other than God speaks; in verses 6–8 still another unidentified voice makes proclamation; and, finally, in verses 9–11, apparently the prophet issues his clarion call for Judah to carry the good news, "the gospel," of God's coming to the cities of Judah.

The best way of getting into this text is to examine the content of the four speeches associated with the four voices. In the divine speech, God commands, first of all, that comfort be proclaimed to the people. The term translated "comfort" is a plural imperative and suggests that comfort is what is to be proclaimed by the subsequent three voices. Now it is God who, with a note of urgency, declares that comfort and tenderness are the message of the hour. Unlike the earlier Old Testament lessons for Advent in which the people lament, cry, and plead to God, the emphasis in this text falls on the initiative of God, who demands that the people be addressed. In the second place, the proclaimed comfort is based on the divine decision that the people have suffered enough, the years of disciplinary judgment are over, the price for the sins of the past has been paid. Note the threefold divine affirmation: warfare (or the compulsory time of service) is ended; iniquity is pardoned; God's demand for punishment for sin has been met because the people's suffering and affliction have paid double (or perhaps "the equivalent") for all their sins. The end of strife and the forgiveness of sin herald a new relationship.

The second voice (of an angelic messenger?) calls for the preparation of a highway in the desert, a highway for God, whose glory shall be revealed publicly (40:3–5). The imagery of such a highway probably harks back to the fact that in Babylonian religion, special processional ways were constructed along which the images of the gods were carried in an annual procession so the people could see the representations of the objects of their worship. Yahweh's highway was to lead (from Babylon) across the desert (back to the Land of Promise). Just as in the first exodus, which led the people through the desert, so now Second Isaiah has a messenger announce a second exodus in which nature is to be transformed and an unobstructed way for God is to be prepared.

The third voice proclaims the assurance of God's word, which, unlike the fleeting, fading, withering, and temporary, is proclaimed as standing forever. It is the word that is the basis of hope and certitude. It is the divine word proclaimed from the time of creation and throughout history (Isa. 40:21) that now is addressed in a new form so that the people can look forward to the "new thing" that God promises (Isa. 43:18–19) certain that the word is secure, for "the mouth of the Lord has spoken" (v. 5).

Finally, the prophet calls on Jerusalem to serve as herald, as the evangelist, of God's coming (vv. 9–11). Two factors are stressed about the coming of the Divine. On the one hand, God comes with might and strength to rule; yet, on the other hand, God comes with great tenderness as the shepherd who gathers the lambs, cuddling them in his bosom, and watching carefully over the yet unborn.

Psalm 85:1–2, 8–13

The verses in this psalm have been selected as part of the Advent cycle because they speak of some of the consequences of God's promised salvation. The reading, however, is best seen in light of the psalm as a whole. Verses 1–3 recall an earlier time when God had restored the fortunes of the people, forgiving their sins and withdrawing the divine wrath. What this section talks about specifically remains uncertain. Does it refer to the return from exile proclaimed in glorious terms in Second Isaiah? Or does it revolve around features of Israel's great autumn festival season when God was annually proclaimed as forgiving the people's sin on the day of atonement, thereby proclaiming for the people a new slate and a new fate for the coming year? Probably the latter should be seen as the context of this psalm's imagery and the phenomenon described in verses 1–3. The prayer for God to revive and restore the people in verses 4–7 would thus be a plea that God would again, in the festival, put away his indignation and anger and display instead his salvation and thus revive the people.

Verses 8–13, according to the above interpretation, would be an oracle spoken in the service of worship by some cultic official (priest? prophet?) who already envisioned and anticipated what God's response would be and what consequences it would produce. (Note that verses 1–7 are addressed to the Deity and are thus prayers, whereas verses 8–13 speak about the Deity and are thus similar to the preaching and proclamation of a prophet.) Psalm 85:8–13, like Advent, anticipates the coming and already perceives its consequences. What God will speak is peace (shalom). The consequences of Yahweh's speaking are described in a play on a number of terms—faithfulness, righteousness, peace, steadfast love. What these terms describe are all good qualities. They are depicted coming together as if they were two who meet and kiss or as if one springs from the earth and the other looks down from the sky. That is, because God speaks, full harmony and unity result. Here ideal qualities are merged.

Verse 12 returns to more mundane matters; God will give what is good, and the land will yield its increase. This again suggests the use of this psalm in the fall festival, when the old agricultural year ends and a new year begins. In Palestine, the rainy season, from October through April, is followed by a rainless season, from May through September. Thus the new agricultural year in the Bible began after the first rains in the fall when new crops could be sown. The fall festival was celebrated as the hinge between the ending of the old and the beginning of the new. Thus the oracle of verses 8–13 closes with the promise of a good agricultural year. (Perhaps verses 4–7 suggest that the previous year's harvest had not been good.) Advent, like the fall festival season in ancient Israel, is the hinge that joins the old and the new. Anchored in the past with all its failures, shortcomings, sufferings, and heartaches, it nonetheless is attached to the future and already joined in anticipation to the time when God "will speak peace to his people" (v. 8).

2 Peter 3:8–15a

This passage exhibits a twofold structure: instruction about the Parousia (vv. 8–10) and moral exhortation (vv. 11–15a). It arises in response to "scoffers" (3:3) who find the notion of Christ's second coming incredible. From their perspective, they find no pattern of divine intervention in history. They have seen an earlier generation of Christian apostles and leaders, the "ancestors" (v. 4), die before experiencing Christ's return. Living now in a later generation, they are disillusioned at the prospect that Christ will ever return. They are convinced that things now are pretty much as they always were and are likely to continue along the same course. The source of their views is not clear, but such skepticism is known to have existed among various religious groups in the ancient world.

The author of Second Peter perceives the problem as not only shortsightedness but as essentially a matter of whether one's worldview is broad enough to admit divine activity within the human arena. If God can play a decisive role in the beginning of things, it is possible to see the end of history from a similar perspective (vv. 5–7).

The scoffers are reminded not to assume that God calculates time as they do: "With the Lord one day is like a thousand years, and a thousand years are like one day" (v. 8). God does not necessarily follow a human calendar. Moreover, they should reckon with the possibility that God has delayed as a means of extending mercy and forbearance to humanity. After all, God's ultimate desire for humanity is that no one should perish but that all should respond penitently to the divine will. The final reminder is that however overdue the day of the Lord may seem to be, it will be unexpected, coming "like a thief" (v. 10). The language used to describe the final consummation reflects a Jewish apocalyptic outlook: "The heavens will pass away with a loud noise, and the elements will be dissolved with fire" (v.10). The notion that the world would end in a final conflagration was not uncommon in antiquity. Though the sentiments expressed are couched in ancient terms, they are frighteningly modern for those who have attempted to visualize the prospects of a nuclear holocaust.

However difficult it may be for Christians to conceptualize Christ's second coming—and its cruder depictions certainly strike many modern believers as naive—the fact remains that it is now possible to conceive of the instantaneous dissolution of all human life in a way heretofore unimaginable. Such thoughts always have a sobering effect.

The second part of the passage quite understandably turns to moral exhortation. In early Christian teaching, eschatological instruction was intimately connected with moral exhortation. As Christians contemplated the end of things, they were enjoined to reflect on their own style of life and conform themselves to the sobering realization that life is moving toward a purpose. Given the possibility of ultimate destruction of all human life as we know it, "what sort of persons ought you to be in leading lives of holiness and godliness?" (v. 11). The Christian hope is that beyond human depravity there is the promise of "new heavens and a new earth, where righteousness is at home" (v. 13). Accordingly, Christians are urged to practice the moral life, while regarding the Lord's willingness to delay not as a failure to be punctual but as a generous and merciful gesture toward humanity: "Regard the patience of our Lord as salvation" (v. 15a).

This text is filled with themes rich in possibility for the Advent Season. Many modern Christians find the notion of Christ's second coming difficult to comprehend. Rather than recasting this ancient article of Christian faith into terms suitable for a modern outlook, modern believers sometimes respond by abandoning any belief in God as the Omega. The method of approach in the text is itself instructive, for the author anchors his response in theological reflection. He appeals to the Christian doctrine of creation as the basis for a viable eschatology. It is also instructive that he insists on the connection between eschatology and ethics. Abandoning any real conviction about God's ultimate purpose in history all too easily translates into moral laxity or cynicism about whether there is any ultimate justice. The homiletical task here is to shape a responsible eschatology for modern believers that, on the one hand, preserves a meaningful sense of the future, but, on the other hand, neither forecloses God's role in that future nor relaxes our responsibility in facing it.

Mark 1:1–8

The Advent Season has no more appropriate voice than that of John the baptizer (Mark 1:4; Mark identifies John by function rather than by title, the Baptist, as in Matt. 3:1). John was a prophet both of anticipation and of preparation, the twin themes for beginning Advent. Our Gospel lesson today introduces John in the earliest and briefest of the four accounts.

"The beginning of the good news of Jesus Christ, the Son of God" (Mark 1:1). With these words Mark does not simply launch the story of Jesus but provides a title for his narrative. As far as we know, this is the first use of the word *gospel* (good news) to refer to a written account of the narrative about Jesus Christ. By referring to his account as "the beginning," the author may have been thinking of a Christian Genesis, but more likely he meant to say that the life, death, and resurrection of Jesus were, for all their central importance, but the beginning of the mission to bear the good news to every nation under heaven.

And where does one begin a story entitled "The beginning of the good news"? In a sense, the beginning is with the prophets of Israel. Most likely, the early church had a collection of passages from the Hebrew Bible for use in Christian preaching. Two such texts happily joined were Malachi 3:1 and Isaiah 40:3, both of which announce God's coming, preceded by a messenger to prepare the way. Mark, perhaps because Isaiah 40 is the dominant passage, refers to both as being from Isaiah, a confusion cleared up by Matthew (3:3) and Luke (3:4) by omitting the citation from Malachi. The importance of Malachi 3:1 for Mark is that it identifies the messenger preparing the way as Elijah (Mal. 4:5), and some in the early church identified John as Elijah heralding the coming of the Lord. Mark also interprets Isaiah 40:3 so that "in the wilderness" locates the messenger (the voice in the wilderness) and not, as in the original oracle, the place of God's appearing ("in the wilderness prepare the way of the LORD" [Isa. 40:3]). By so reading his sources, Mark says the prophets bear witness to this "beginning." Here we can see how the Bible understands itself. Although the coming of Christ is a new thing God is doing, it is not without a past. John's preaching is news, good news, but it has a history, a memory. Memory is the soil in which hope survives, and that which is remembered is the promise of a faithful God.

In a more immediate sense, however, "the beginning" points not to the prophets but to John himself. It is John who bursts upon the scene creating new excitement, stirring hearts, and gathering all Judea and Jerusalem to the Jordan River to hear his message of repentance, confess their sins, and receive baptism and forgiveness of sin. John is the beginning of the Gospel, for it is his dynamic ministry that prepares the people for the one mightier than he (v. 7). His popularity and influence made an impact upon political (Mark 6:17–29) and religious (John 1:19–28) leaders as well as the common people. How does one account for his popularity and influence? The curious came, of course, for he was an unusual man, and the nostalgic, too, for this image of Elijah (2 Kings 1:8) must have stirred longing for the good old days. But basic to the power of his ministry were the two themes of his preaching: the Messiah is at the door, and repentance is essential as preparation to receive him. In other words, he gave his listeners hope, and he gave them a way to enter into that hope.

But if we listen to John, "the beginning" is not the prophets or himself but Jesus Christ. Jesus is the Messiah, the Son of God; John is the voice, the messenger, the preparer of the way. Jesus will baptize with the Holy Spirit; John baptizes in water in an anticipatory rite of repentance and forgiveness. Whatever John's followers claimed for him, Mark and the early church are clear in their understanding: John is the forerunner; Jesus is the Messiah. The issue is settled: Jesus Christ is "the beginning."

But the prophets, John, and Jesus are but names, figures of the past, unless there is "the beginning" in the effective sense in the lives of those who heard. John's good news of forgiveness and the approach of the Messiah was not without demand and judgment. Most scholars agree that Matthew 3:7–12 and Luke 3:7–18 preserve original elements of John's message: an ax laid at the root of trees; baptism with fire; the winnowing fork blowing away chaff for burning. And it is to the people of God that this call for repentance comes! The very sermon that God's people had been preaching to the pagan world—repentance and submission to rites of cleansing—is addressed instead to them. Repent of the arrogant assumption that you alone are favored, that you are exempt from the moral demands put on others, that being better than your worst neighbors is your salvation, as though God grades on the curve. Repent, be honest, come clean, unload fruitless patterns of behavior, abandon clever devices for maintaining the illusion of innocence. What could be better news than this—an offer to repent, to confess, to enter into a rite of cleansing, to be forgiven.

Advent pilgrims on the way to the manger must pass through the desert where John is preaching.

Third Sunday of Advent

Isaiah 61:1–4, 8–11;
Psalm 126 or Luke 1:47–55;
1 Thessalonians 5:16–24;
John 1:6–8, 19–28

Understandably, the idea and image of the Lord's coming produces both fear and joy. Our texts today encourage the faithful to be full of joy. Such is Paul's word to the church at Thessalonica, while both Isaiah and Luke (the Magnificat of Mary may serve as the psalm for today) announce good news to the poor, the lowly, and the oppressed. A similar note is sounded in Psalm 126, where recalling God's saving work prompts outbursts of laughter and joy. The Gospel reading focuses again on John the Baptist, but this time as witness to the light and life offered to all in Jesus Christ.

Isaiah 61:1–4, 8–11

In analyzing many biblical texts, it is frequently essential to notice any changes in who the speaker is and who are those being addressed. Such a shift in speaker and addressee occurs throughout Isaiah 61. The section opens with a confessional statement about God (vv. 1–4), then God presumably speaks (vv. 5–9), and finally apparently the community communicates (vv. 10–11). Nothing is provided in any of the speeches to suggest who the intended audience is. Presumably one should think of the community of the prophet's day as the addressee. In our analysis, we will divide the text of the lection into the following units: verses 1–4, 8–9, 10–11.

In verses 1–4, a figure speaks about an endowment for a task, the objectives of the task, and the consequences of the task. The entire content of this section is very similar to the so-called Suffering Servant poems found earlier in Isaiah (42:1–4; 49:1–6; 50:4–9; 52:13–53:12). These poems speak about a particular figure assigned to a task that involved not only special functions but also severe suffering. The early church, which interpreted much of the Old Testament as predictions about both Jesus and the life of the church, was certain that these poems were prophecies and that Jesus was the Suffering Servant. Modern scholarship, doubtful that an ancient prophecy about Jesus would have meant much to a generation that lived hundreds of years before his birth, has attempted to identify the figure with someone known to the prophet's audience. Was it the prophet himself? Israel? the exiled Judean king? the Judean exiles? the Persian king Cyrus? Research has raised numerous candidates for the figure but produced no agreement or certainty on the issue.

Likewise, in this text one cannot be certain of the mold in which the figure's identity has been cast. Part of the description of the endowment, especially the anointing, suggests a royal figure, because in ancient Israel to speak of the anointed one (the messiah) was to speak of the king (see 1 Sam. 24:6). On the other hand, high priests were anointed in later times, and one text speaks of the anointing of a prophet (1 Kings 19:16). Thus the figure may have been conceived in royal, priestly, or prophetic terms or some combination of the three.

The task of the figure incorporates multiple activities. One theme, however, runs through all the descriptions: the work of the figure is to bring a reversal of fate to those in various states of destitution and deprivation. Those to be the recipients of the work of the spirit-filled anointed one are the afflicted, the brokenhearted, the captives, those bound in prison, and the mourners. As in the earlier Old Testament lessons for Advent, the imagery of the text suggests groups in desperate straits bewailing their conditions and yearning for release. The new note in this text is the assertion that God has now appointed a figure to take action that will relieve the situation primarily in the proclamation of good tidings and good news.

Much of the content of the anointed figure's proclamation is depicted in political rather than spiritual terms. One is reminded of Moses' activity in proclaiming liberation to the Hebrew slaves in Egypt. (a) Good tidings to the afflicted and the binding of the broken-hearted can only refer to the alleviation of these conditions. (b) Liberty to the captives and the opening of the prisons suggest a political act and has led many to think that the figure of the Persian Cyrus may have colored this presentation, for he freed many who had been exiled in foreign lands by the Assyrians and Babylonians. Frequently, new kings proclaimed amnesty to those enslaved and imprisoned. (c) The reference to the year of the Lord's favor is best understood as a reference to either the coming of a sabbatical year or the year of Jubilee. In the former, the sabbatical (or seventh) year was a time when slaves were freed and debts were canceled (see Exod. 21:1–11; Deut. 15:12–18). The Jubilee, the fiftieth year in a cycle, was the time when slaves were freed, debts canceled, and the landholdings redistributed to their original owners (see Lev. 25). At any rate, both were years of God's favor, when human misfortune was reversed and a new beginning proclaimed and realized. For those who benefited, either was a year of release, but to those who had subjected others, it was a day of divine vengeance.

Those mourning in Zion would possess new symbols of their status replacing the old symbols: flower garlands rather than ashes, oil to soothe the skin rather than mourning, mantles to wear rather than a fainting spirit (v. 3). The consequences for those blessed would be a new status; they would be a new planting for a new day. In turn, the new status would bring a new task—the rebuilding of the cities and the restoration of the ruins to remove the results of years of devastation (v. 4).

In verses 8–9, God declares the Divine's love of justice and dislike of the opposite, and promises the renewal of the covenant, the reestablishment of the proper relationship between the people and the Deity. This new status of the people—restored and blessed in a newly rebuilt land—would give them respect and thus grant them the opposite of their former status, which had made them the laughingstock of their enemies (see Ps. 80:6).

In the final unit, verses 10–11, the speaker is again difficult to determine. It may be the anointed figure of verses 1–4 or perhaps even the community speaking as an "I." At any rate, one can see the pattern indicated in the text. The anointed figure proclaims his task (vv. 1–4); God responds to affirm the divine activity of covenant reestablishment, that is, the return to a time like the days of old (vv. 8–9); and finally there is the enthusiastic assurance expressed by the recipients (vv. 10–11), who already see themselves as partaking of the salvation of the new age. Two things should be noted about the description of the new conditions. First of all, newness is expressed in terms of clothing—garments of salvation, robe of righteousness, and wedding attire. The new inner state manifests itself in the outer person. Second, the newness of righteousness and praise springs forth like new vegetation growing among the nations; it is only the beginning, but at least a beginning.

Psalm 126

This psalm has been selected as a companion reading to Isaiah 61:1–4, 8–11 because of its assumed connection with the return from exile, which parallels the Isaiah statements about the coming events of redemption. The association of the psalm with the Exile appears to be a secondary development, however. The psalm was probably originally written for use in the fall festival, which fell just before the autumn rains and the fall planting. The theme of the psalm—the reversal of fortune—fits nicely, however, with the Isaiah text.

The first half of the psalm (vv. 1–3) looks back to the past, probably to the preceding year's festival time, whereas the last half (vv. 4–6) looks forward with intercession to the future.

The opening verse is translated in various ways. An alternative to the NRSV is the translation "When the Lord determined the destiny [or set the fate] for Zion." Such a determination was probably considered part of the annual fall festival, which marked the end of the old year and the beginning of the new. It was believed that during the festival, God decreed what would happen in the coming year and thus set the destiny for the future. Remnants of a similar perspective can be seen in our beliefs about beginning anew with resolutions and a clean slate on New Year's Day. The past restoration or determination of fortunes is recalled in the psalm as a glorious time. The expectations of the future on that previous occasion made the people seem as if they were dreaming; that is, the expectations were uninhibited by the normal limitations of reality. Laughter and joy were the characteristics of the experience. God had done or decreed great things, things to be recognized even by the nations, the Gentiles (see Ps. 98:1–3, which also belongs to the fall festival context).

The prayer of petition and appeal in verses 4–6 requests a good future in the coming time that would reverse the status of the present. (Just as our New Year's resolutions and expectations exceed the realities of the year, so it was in ancient Israel.) The dry wadi beds, the dusty gullies of the Negeb desert, are used to symbolize the present, and the way in which these could be transformed into watercourses with growing vegetation by the coming rainy season symbolize the hoped-for future. Such imagery may have been a proverbial picture indicative of a sudden and drastic change.

Mythological and primitive concepts underlie the references to sowing with weeping, reaping with joy. The association of tears with sowing is based on several factors: tears symbolize rainfall; sowing involves death, for the seed must "die" to appear as new grain growth; planting is a gamble and a risk; and the scattering of seeds resembles the shedding of tears. Such customs as weeping when sowing are found in many cultures around the world. Significant also is the idea of performing one type of action in the present so as to achieve the opposite at a later time. Deprivation in the present, the temporary suspension of gratification, can be seen as the means to fuller realization in the future. Weep now and shout for joy later.

Luke 1:47–55

This alternate psalm for the Third Sunday of Advent is a song of praise to God, who remembers the poor and lowly and delivers them from the proud and oppressive. This psalm is not found among the songs of David but is the song of Mary, mother of Jesus. When the angel announced to Mary that she would bear the Christ Child, she was told that her kinswoman Elizabeth, barren and advanced in years, was now in her sixth month of pregnancy (1:36). So Mary went to the hill country of Judea to the home of Elizabeth and Zechariah, and after greetings were exchanged Mary burst into song.

It is important first of all to note that the song is Mary's, not Elizabeth's, as one would expect. The Magnificat is based largely on the Song of Hannah in 1 Samuel 2. The story of Hannah and Elkanah, parents of Samuel (1 Sam. 1–2), should be reviewed in preparation for understanding Luke 1:47–55. Hannah, distressed that she was barren, tarried in the temple after a festival, weeping and praying for a child. The priest Eli thought she was drunk. She made known her prayer, promising that if God gave her a son she would give the child to God. Her prayer was answered, and she named the child Samuel. When she brought the child to the temple as a gift to God, she sang a magnificat. The story so parallels that of Elizabeth and Zechariah that one would expect Elizabeth to sing as did Hannah. Both women were older; Hannah was assured of a child while at the temple just as Zechariah was; both sons, Samuel in the one case and John in the other, were given to God under special vows, and they lived as set apart for God. A few late manuscripts are so attracted to the similarities between the two families that they have replaced Mary's name with that of Elizabeth in Luke 1:46. However, "And Mary said" is the reliable, very well-established reading. But it does not fit for a young virgin to sing Hannah's song. The tradition of God granting a son to elderly childless couples is well established: Abraham and Sarah were given Isaac, Manoah and his wife were given Samson, and Elkanah and Hannah, Samuel. In that tradition of God blessing the barren, John now comes and to that history he belongs. But when a song from that tradition is sung by a young virgin, the tradition is interrupted, the old is new, and the familiar is strange. God is doing a new thing. Had Elizabeth sung Hannah's song, it would have been said that God continues to be gracious to the barren, as of old. But when the virgin Mary sings, it must be said that God's grace is not as of old, but new and strange and surprising and beyond understanding. This child will not be as Isaac or Samson, or Samuel, but will be the Son of God.

And what is it that Mary sings? Her song opens with joy and praise that God has favored a handmaiden of low estate. But only briefly does she speak of herself. She sees God's grace and goodness toward her as but a single instance of the ways of God in the world. God blesses the poor and oppressed and hungry; and in the final eschatological reversal, God will bring down the proud and rich oppressors and exalt those who have been disfranchised, disregarded, and dismissed. The most remarkable quality of the song is that the justice God will bring to pass is spoken of in the past tense: has shown strength, has scattered the proud, has brought down the powerful, has lifted up the lowly, has filled the hungry, and has sent the rich away empty. Why the past tense? According to the latest news reports, these things have not yet occurred.

Of course, these conditions are not yet, but one of the ways the faithful express trust in God is to speak of the future with such confidence that it is described as already here. Such faith is prerequisite to being a participant in efforts to achieve that future. To celebrate the future as a memory, to praise God for having already done what lies before us to do—this is the way of the people of God. Without this song of praise, the noblest efforts to effect justice in society become arrogant projects, messianic moves by one group against another, competing for camera time. God's people parade before they march; for history teaches us that without the parade, the march may soon become lockstep, and perhaps even goose step. Who, then, will remain to say, "My soul magnifies the Lord"?

1 Thessalonians 5:16–24

Though addressed to the young Thessalonian church, this concluding series of exhortations is broadly applicable to all Christians. Previously, Paul has given pithy words of advice directed at the internal life of the community (vv. 12–15). He now turns his attention to the inner life of Christians, enjoining them to "rejoice always, pray without ceasing, give thanks in all circumstances" (vv. 16–18a). Though general in scope, each of these injunctions has special force in light of the previous discussion where he addresses the anxieties within the church arising from their misunderstandings about the Parousia (4:13–5:11). Such anxiety could all too easily produce grief and gloom (4:13). The confidence that God had destined the saints not for wrath but for salvation (5:9) should come as a source of encouragement and serve as a basis for edification and hope. Therefore, "rejoice always" is not an empty cliché here.

Similarly, vigilance in prayer is appropriate behavior for the Christian who lives with an eye to the future committed to God. Giving "thanks in all circumstances" may have struck the Thessalonians as odd advice, considering the affliction they had endured (1:6; 2:14–16). Yet because of their steadfast hope (1:3), they had reason to live in gratitude, not for their affliction per se, but for the confidence that enabled them to rely on a promise-keeping God: "The one who calls you is faithful, and he will do this" (v. 24). Just as Paul could appeal to the fidelity of God in opening his letters (cf. 1 Cor. 1:9), so did he find it an appropriate note on which to conclude this letter.

The Thessalonians are enjoined not to extinguish the fire of the Spirit (v. 19). Endowments of the Spirit historically have been unsettling and unpredictable: "The wind [or Spirit] blows where it chooses" (John 3:8). Yet this prophetic energy within the church is essential for renewal. One response by the church is to "despise the words of prophets" (v. 20). Paul cautions his readers not to squelch the prophetic voices within their midst. Rather, he calls them to be discriminating. "Test everything," he urges, insisting that they be discerning as they listen to the voices of prophecy among them. The following words may be general moral exhortation, but more likely are to be understood in this context of prophetic discrimination: "Hold fast to what is good; abstain from every form of evil" (vv. 21–22). Christians are urged not to be naive in listening to those who claim to speak on behalf of God. They should recognize that prophetic words should be weighed rather than accepted blindly.

For the church living in the interim between the "already" and the "not yet," Paul's advice here retains its force. One way of preparing for Christ's coming is to resign oneself to fate, lapse into passivity, and suspend all judgment. Later, Paul addresses this tendency to adopt a stance of quiet resignation (2 Thess. 3:6–13). Yet Paul never allows such a stance to be a responsible option for the Christian who lives with the expectation of Christ's return. Accordingly, the church's role, even as it faces the "not yet," is one of confident hope balanced with vigilance in prayer and thanksgiving, as well as the exercise of an active role in discharging its prophetic ministry. Taken seriously, Paul's advice here keeps us from adopting an attitude of disengagement as the church faces the realities of life and the world, even as it looks to Christ's coming.

The final section of the passage is a prayer calling for the God of peace to bring about the full sanctification of communal and individual Christian life. Indeed, every fabric of the human personality—spirit, soul, and body—is committed to the care of God, who prepares the church for the Parousia.

John 1:6–8, 19–28

Because the Magnificat (Luke 1:47–55) may serve as the Psalm for this Third Sunday of Advent, many preachers will no doubt be attracted to that reading as basic to the sermon for the day. This may be further motivated by the fact that the Gospel lection focuses on John the Baptist, who was the subject of last Sunday's Gospel (Mark 1:1–8). Attraction to the rich and beautiful Magnificat is understandable, but John 1:6–8, 19–28 certainly should not be slighted as though its message were repetitious; it definitely is not.

All four Evangelists give attention to John the Baptist, seeking to achieve a balance between the praise appropriate to his role in relation to Christ and a polemic against the movement in John's name that grew alongside the church and in a sense competed with it. According to Acts 18:24–28, a preacher from Alexandria knew only the baptism of John, and in the city of Ephesus Paul began his mission among a group of disciples who had received John's baptism (Acts 19:1–7). Even today, a small sect in Iraq called Mandeans trace their history back to John the Baptist. No wonder, then, that the Gospels try to keep John in the role of forerunner to Jesus and only in that role recognize his greatness. Mark deals with John by being brief, citing John's acknowledgment that Jesus is "more powerful than I" (Mark 1:7) and contrasting their two baptisms. Matthew says that although John baptized Jesus he was hesitant to do so, saying he should be baptized by Jesus (3:13–15). Luke, who interweaves the stories of the births of John and Jesus, says that when Mary entered the house of Elizabeth, John leaped in Elizabeth's womb in recognition of the mother of the Lord (1:39–45).

In today's Gospel text, the Baptist is presented twice: in the Evangelist's word about John (1:6–8) and in John's word about himself (1:19–28). The first presentation is as a prose insertion into the poetry of the prologue. The prologue (1:1–18) is in praise of the eternal divine Word, agent of creation and redemption, who becomes flesh in Jesus of Nazareth. But twice (vv. 6–18, 15) the author interrupts the poem to explain quite emphatically: I am not talking about John. While it is true he was sent from God, he was not the Word, he was not the light, he was not the life of the world. John was a witness to the Word, Jesus Christ. Three times in verses 6–8 and again in verse 15 John is called "a witness." That simple word best captures this Gospel's portrait of John.

Following the prologue, the narrative begins with what amounts to a title for the account, which continues through verse 24: "This is the testimony [witness] given by John" (v. 19). John's witness consists of two parts, the one concerning himself (1:19–28) and the other concerning Jesus (1:29–34). John's testimony concerning himself was not a part of his proclamation but was in response to investigators, priests, and Levites, sent from the Jews and from the Pharisees in particular (v. 24). When asked, "Who are you?" notice how strongly stated is the reply; he confessed, he did not deny, he confessed he was not the Christ. The implication is that some people believed that he was. John claimed no title or station; in his own estimation he was not the Christ, or Elijah, or any other prophetic forerunner of the Christ. He was, he said, a voice (v. 23). When asked why he baptized, he made no claim for his baptism, neither as a means of forgiveness nor of reception of the Holy Spirit. What others claim for what one does and what one claims for oneself are often different, and properly so. John's identity, says this Gospel, was totally in relation to Jesus Christ to whom he was a witness. Even as John spoke, Jesus stood among them as one they did not know (v. 26).

Even though John came prior to Christ, as a witness he is in many ways a model for all who follow. "You will be my witnesses" (Acts 1:8). Witnessing is most difficult, not because we do not believe but because we do. The more important the subject matter, the harder it is to say the words. Speech stumbles over feelings of inadequacy and unworthiness; the words proceed cautiously to the listener's ear for fear of offending. Glib talkers who are "really good at it" seldom persuade us that they have just come from the empty tomb. And the church corporately is called to witness. During Advent, how full the church calendar is; it can be such a rich and rewarding experience. But over it all, over every song, cantata, party, gift, service of worship, act of charity, let the church first say, "We are not the light but came to bear witness to the light." The true Light is in the world, but among the people he is often One they do not know. Some miss him perhaps because they have made looking for the Messiah a way of life, preferring their own desires as to what life will be when the Messiah comes to the responsibilities that follow the confession "The Messiah has come, and it is Jesus." The first great task of a messiah is to bring to an end the search for a messiah.

Even in Advent we witness to the One who already stands among us, who has already come.

Fourth Sunday of Advent

2 Samuel 7:1–11, 16;
Luke 1:47–55 or Psalm 89:1–4, 19–26;
Romans 16:25–27;
Luke 1:26–38

Today's readings are, appropriately enough, celebrative and doxological. The narrative base is provided by 2 Samuel 7, which tells of God's covenant with the house of David, and Psalm 89, which celebrates that covenant while calling on God not to forget. God did not forget, says Luke, but remembers and sends Gabriel to tell Mary that through her the promise will be kept. Paul reflects on what that fulfilled promise of God means for Israel and for all the world, and closes his Roman letter in a burst of praise.

2 Samuel 7:1–11, 16

The seventh chapter of Second Samuel contains the fullest narrative account of the Davidic covenant. The Old Testament lection comprises only a portion of the chapter, namely, the part that focuses specifically on God's promise to build David a house. In the narrative of Second Samuel, David has finally acquired "rest from all his enemies around him" (v. 1) and decides that it is time to build a house (a temple) for Yahweh, whose ark, the symbol of the divine presence, was residing in a tent in Jerusalem (6:17). With the help of the Phoenician king, Hiram of Tyre, David constructed a great palace of cedar in the capital city (5:11; 7:1). The king felt that such difference in life-style—he in a cedar palace and the ark in a tent—was hardly commensurate with the way affairs should be.

David proposed building God a "house," and this theme forms the backdrop for the subsequent promises of God to the king. The narrator plays on the double meaning of house, signifying both temple, in the case of God, and dynasty, in the case of David. The king's plan was submitted to the prophet Nathan, who first approved the temple construction but then withdrew approval after a nighttime consultation with God (7:2–7).

With God's disapproval of the construction of a temple, the focus shifts from God's house to David's house and from David's desires to the divine promises. (According to Ps. 132:1–5, David had sworn that he would never enter his house nor sleep until he had found a dwelling place for God, but there is no reference to this promise of David in the books of Samuel.) Several features are noteworthy in Yahweh's promises to David.

1. David is reminded of his humble origins as a shepherd, from which he was elevated to become prince over Israel (v. 8). Here one finds a common motif of the Bible—God's sympathy for the powerless and divine benevolence for the humble. Another way of describing this motif is to see it as the Cinderella theme—the success of the unpromising. Over and over again this theme reappears in Scripture (see 2 Sam. 2:7–8; Ps. 113:5–9). One can recall the aged Abraham and Sarah without child; Moses as a babe afloat on the crocodile-infested Nile; motley, unorganized slaves laboring in Egypt; and, as Advent approaches, a Babe in a manger. In all of these, the meek and powerless for whom God has special concern find their ultimate status in a reversal of their original status.

2. David is reminded of his conquest over his enemies (see 2 Sam. 8). He is also reminded that his reputation will be like that of the great ones of the earth and that his name will be remembered forever (v. 9)—a theme that reappears in the emphasis on Jesus' name in the New Testament.

3. David's success and greatness would be shared by his people Israel, who would live in tranquillity in their own place (vv. 10–11a). The God who is described as constantly wandering (v. 6) promises the people a place where they will be planted—a place where the humble David, who is elevated, will have a people with whom to share the glory of the newly acquired state.

4. Above all, God promises David that his family will be established forever. There is no house for God who dwells in the temporality of a tent, but for David there is an eternal house! The continuity of David's family and the eternity of its rule are promised in general terms in verse 16, which highlights and summarizes the central promise to David—a dynasty, a kingdom, and a throne, *forever*. All subsequent Jewish expectations of a coming messiah were fed in one way or another by this text.

5. Verse 12 focuses on the immediacy of the promise. One of David's immediate offspring will succeed him; his dynasty will not be replaced like that of Saul (v. 15). Here, of course, the narrator and reader anticipate Solomon, who would come after David and build God a house (v. 13).

6. Finally, David's son will also be God's son: "I will be a father to him, and he shall be a son to me" (v. 14). The ancient Israelites probably did not think of David's son as actually being "sired" by God, that is, in terms of physical descendancy, but in terms of a relationship. God and David's son would be like Father and son. Sonship in this text, however, involves not so much special privilege as the promise of God's chastisement of the son for disobedience. Here the narrator anticipates the eventual lack of complete obedience on Solomon's part and the subsequent disruption of the kingdom at his death (see 1 Kings 11).

Second Samuel 7:1–17 thus forms the *locus classicus* for the expectation of the eternal rulership of the house of David and is the fountainhead for all messianic hopes about the revival of David's rule after the fall of Jerusalem in 586 BC. As part of the readings for the Advent Season, it looks forward to the One who is the David to come.

Luke 1:47–55

See the discussion of this text at the Third Sunday of Advent, where it serves, as here, as an alternate Psalm.

Psalm 89:1–4, 19–26

This psalm offers the fullest exposition in the Old Testament of the divine covenant with David and the promises this covenant involved (see vv. 19–37). In some respects, 2 Samuel 7 may be seen as merely a narrative adaptation of the Davidic promises celebrated in this poetic form in the royal rituals of the Jerusalem court.

Psalm 89 is in reality a lament that speaks of the divine promises to David after they have all been called into question. The conclusion of the psalm, verses 38–51, bemoans the humiliation of the Davidic ruler who is the object of divine wrath, whose covenant is renounced, whose strongholds are in ruin, and for whom all the promises of God seem to have failed. The description of the king's condition simply piles up one disappointing condition upon another. The psalm ends with a complaint about the loss of God's love and faithfulness and a prayer for God to note how the king bears in his bosom the insults of the nations roundabout and how the enemies mock the footsteps of the anointed (the messiah).

If one takes this material as reflective of some actual historical situation, then the king must have suffered a severe humiliation in battle. In fact, the psalm sounds as if it is a description of the consequences that resulted from the destruction of Jerusalem by the Babylonians.

But this week's psalm lection does not focus on the humiliation aspects of the psalm; it focuses on the positive. Verses 1–4 both remind and praise God for divine faithfulness and steadfast love, which are always the basis for confidence. Note that God is reminded that steadfast love is forever and his faithfulness as sure as the heaven. (Although the minister may not wish to highlight the point, these are exactly the divine qualities called into question in verse 49. Perhaps few psalms so stress the twofold quality of the Deity—the divine care and the divine forsakenness—as does this psalm.) God is made to recall that he swore to David that his descendants would rule forever and his throne endure for generations. The ancient Hebrews were not bashful when it came to reminding God of the divine commitments and to reiterating the promises on which they banked their hopes. (One should remember that when this psalm was read or used in public worship, the person who spoke the first four verses with their calm serenity and secure promises was aware of the trauma yet to be expressed before the Psalter scroll was rolled together and neatly tied and tucked away again.)

Verses 19–24 focus on portions of God's eternal promises to David and recall the words in God's vision in which David was chosen and exalted among his people (see 2 Sam. 7). Several factors about David and God's relationship to him are stressed, and it must be recalled that the David spoken of here is more the idealized David of messianic quality than the David of history. First, David was found by God (see 1 Sam. 16:1–4). Here the emphasis is placed on the divine initiative. The true servant is the one whom God separates out, not the one who grasps at equality or the one who strives for superiority. He who would claim to be the messiah should always be questioned. Second, as the anointed, David is set apart, set aloof from the rest, where he, like the New Testament Messiah, must know what it means to be one "apart." Third, David is promised that victory over his enemies and dominance over his foes are part of the assurance granted, for it is God who stands behind him and strikes down his opponents and foes. The interpreter here must remember that ancient Israelite life was always threatened and that survival could never be taken for granted. Although this emphasis on being constantly threatened might sound a bit paranoid, even Jesus is said to have struggled with Satan in the wilderness. Finally, the psalmist quotes God as promising that faithfulness and love for

David are certain and that in God's strength David's horn will be exalted—that is, his status will be secure.

This psalm, like Advent, calls on people to rely on the divine promises even when those promises seem to lie shattered at the feet of those who pray, but who pray for the coming redemption in spite of the realities within which they live.

Romans 16:25–27

This doxology is traditionally attributed to Paul, but its place in the manuscript tradition is disputed. In some manuscripts, it is located at the end of chapter 14, in others at the end of chapter 15, and in still others it is omitted altogether. Not only does the style appear more involved than Paul's, but the central theme of the mystery, once hidden but now revealed, is more reminiscent of the later Pauline letters.

The gospel as a mystery, formerly hidden but now revealed, is not prominent in the undisputed Pauline letters, but is not absent (cf. 1 Cor. 2:6–10; 15:51; Rom. 11:25). It is much more fully developed in the deutero-Paulines (Col. 1:24–29; 2:2–3; Eph. 3:1–13). Although the content of the mystery could focus on the Christ-event as the central feature, in its later formulation it also encompassed the work of Christ as it made possible the inclusion of the Gentiles within the messianic community. It is especially this latter emphasis that becomes more fully articulated in Colossians and Ephesians. Indeed, this appears to be the case here, especially if verse 26b is rendered literally, "to bring about the obedience of faith" for all the Gentiles.

Embodied within this doxology is what appears to have been a well-established type of early Christian preaching. This form of proclamation had as its central focus what had been present, though hidden, since eternity, but had finally been revealed in Christ. This early Christian homiletical practice is instructive and might well suggest a point of departure for appropriating the text now. As an Advent text, this passage reflects the shift that occurs in the lectionary in the Advent Season, where there is a gradual shift from the Lord's promised coming to the Lord's first coming. This theme of that which has been hidden as now being revealed dovetails especially well with the Johannine prologue in the lectionary of the Third Sunday of Advent and is a natural sequel. It might profitably be explored as a continuation of the Johannine passage, although theological reflection is taking place in a different mode.

It should also be noted that the emphasis on the prophetic writings (v. 26) anticipates the reading of the Old Testament text from Isaiah on Christmas Day. The universality of this revelation as embodied in the inclusion of the Gentiles also provides expositional possibilities.

The doxology especially highlights the strengthening capacity of the gospel and the preaching about Jesus Christ. The clear sense of the opening words is that Christian readers who begin to realize more fully the cosmic scope of God's revelation in Christ can only stand in awe. Reaching as it does from eternity to eternity, God's divinely revealed mystery encompasses the whole of human history. It is this that no doubt caused this pattern of preaching to excite early Christians. Accordingly, the structure of the doxology itself reflects this same sense of breathtaking awe, for it stops in midair and concludes with the only natural response—confessing God as "the only wise God" to whom eternal glory through Jesus Christ is given.

At Advent, in particular, is this sense of wonder elicited as one approaches the moment in the church calendar when the disclosure of God in human form again occupies center stage.

Luke 1:26–38

For the preacher who had planned to fuss at the congregation about Christmas commercialism or scold the once-a-year worshipers, it is too late. The angel Gabriel is already here with a startling announcement, and the news is totally disarming.

Angels were not a part of Jewish theology in its earlier stages, apparently entering late as an influence from Persian religions in which angels abounded. In some circles, angels were given special assignments as guards or messengers or caretakers, and certain ones had names, such as Michael or Gabriel. Coming out of late Judaism, Christianity was from the start influenced by the widespread belief in angels and demons. And so Luke tells us that the angel Gabriel came twice from God's presence with good news, first to Zechariah to say that he and Elizabeth were to have a child in their old age (1:5–25), and then to Mary to announce that in her virginity she would conceive and bear the child Jesus, son of David and Son of God (1:26–35). The child of Zechariah and Elizabeth would prepare the way for God's coming (1:17), and God's coming would be in Mary's child, conceived of the Holy Spirit (1:35).

Before trying to distill a theme or central message from this text, the preacher would do well to approach the passage in two ways.

First, the literary style and quality of Luke's composition are important for understanding what this text says and does. It is well known that the author of the Third Gospel was a conscious literary artist, and nowhere is that more evident than in the first two chapters. Many believe that here Luke is sharing materials used in the worship of the early church. Filled with songs, the liturgical character of the entire narrative is evident. Doxological texts deserve doxological sermons. Of the passage before us now, 1:26–38, two qualities should be noted. First, the form of the announcement by the visiting angel, here and to Zechariah (1:5–25), is in the pattern of such stories in the Jewish Scriptures. The angel appears (Gen. 16:7; Judg. 13:3), the person visited reacts (Gen. 17:1–3), the person is reassured (Gen. 17:4ff.), the birth is announced (Gen. 16:11; Judg. 13:3), the one to be born is named (Gen. 16:11), the child's future is predicted (Gen. 16:12; Judg. 13:5), an objection is raised (Gen. 15:8; Judg. 6:15), a final reassurance or sign is given (Gen. 17:21; Judg. 6:17ff.), and the word is accepted (Gen. 16:13; Judg. 6:24).

The second quality to be noted is the use of the language of the Jewish Scriptures: "Greetings, the Lord is with you"; "you will conceive in your womb and bear a son"; "the Holy Spirit will come upon you"; "let it be with me according to your word"; "nothing will be impossible with God." Unlike Matthew, who often tags a citation, "As it is written," in order to prove or authorize his point, Luke weaves the language and phrasing of the Scriptures into his own narrative. For example, Matthew quotes in full Isaiah 7:14 to prove the virgin birth was according to prophecy (1:22–23), whereas Luke merely echoes Isaiah 7:14 with his introductory comment about the angel visiting a virgin named Mary. Luke is no less filled with Scripture than Matthew, but the difference is important for those who communicate the Gospel materials. Matthew argues, establishes, proves; Luke tells a story. Sermons should reflect the difference.

In addition to approaching the text literarily, the passage calls for theological reflection. A visiting angel dazzles us, an obedient Mary moves us, and a virgin birth arouses our minds, but the chief character in the story is God. God is here portrayed as a God of grace and of power. Grace fills the story because God is sending a gift to the world. Gift is the correct word because all the conditions of normal human action and achievement are absent. There would have been room enough for praising God and saying, "This is the Lord's doing," had Mary and Joseph been, like Elizabeth and Zechariah or Sarah and Abraham, old and barren. How much more amazing is the announcement of the birth of God's Son to a girl, young, single, and still in her virginity! The cross speaks of grace, to be sure, but so does the manger. And the power of God? In Genesis 18, Abraham and Sarah receive heavenly messengers who promise they shall have a son. To the bewildered old couple the messenger says, "Is anything too wonderful for the LORD?" (v. 14). To the frightened and bewildered Mary, the angel says, "For nothing will be impossible with God" (Luke 1:37). This is the creed behind all other creeds. The church should recite it often, not only at the manger, not only at the empty tomb, but on any occasion of reflecting on its own life, joy, and hope.

Christmas, First Proper
(Christmas Eve/Day)

Isaiah 9:2–7;
Psalm 96;
Titus 2:11–14;
Luke 2:1–14 (15–20)

The waiting is over; the Lord has come. Luke tells the story of the Messiah's birth simply and quietly, reserving angelic announcements and songs for the shepherd's field. Isaiah 9 also sings of the birth of the messiah, but in the triumphant tones of a coronation. Such also is the mood of Psalm 96, celebrating the eternal reign of God in all creation. The epistle, in a more practical vein, reminds us that our lives are framed between "Christ has come" and "Christ will come."

Isaiah 9:2–7

The use of this text in Handel's *The Messiah* has indelibly etched it into the Advent-Christmas Season. Its references to a light amid the darkness, to the birth of a son, to the longing for peace with justice and righteousness are now intertwined with all those other sentiments that we associate with Christmas and with the advent of new hope.

Probably Handel's, and our own, use of this material has taken numerous liberties with the original meaning of the passage. In origin, the text probably had nothing to do with the actual birth of a baby, for surely no one would turn over the government to a babe still at its mother's breast. In spite of this, however, just as all great literature can be read and appreciated in a variety of ways, so this text has tended to lose its moorings in earlier history; and although not quoted directly in the New Testament, it has become an integral feature of the Christmas celebration of the Christ-story.

One way of viewing this text, which is widely accepted by scholars, is to understand it as a composition by the prophet Isaiah that draws upon the language and imagery used in the coronation of a new king, which were reemphasized on the annual anniversary of the king's accession. Isaiah used this material to address a very specific historical situation. The following historical conditions have to be borne in mind as the background for this text. (1) Israel and Judah, for over a century, had been political allies with the great power Assyria. (2) The state of Israel had lorded over the state of Judah since the time of Kings Omri (879–869 BC) and Ahab (868–854 BC) so that Judah had been a vassal to Israel (see 1 Kings 22:44; 2 Kings

3:7). (3) In the years following 750 BC, a strong anti-Assyrian coalition developed in the west. Judah refused to join this group. Israel also refused to join this group until Pekah seized the throne in Samaria in the fall of 734 BC (2 Kings 15:27–31) and threw his support behind the coalition. When Judah refused to join, Pekah with his ally, King Rezin of Damascus, marched against Jerusalem to depose its king, Ahaz, and to wipe out the Davidic family (2 Kings 16:5; Isa. 7:1). (4) When Ahaz refused to follow Pekah's policy, he declared Judah's independence from Israel and continued the policy of not fighting Assyria.

Verses 2–5 are very much filled with the imagery of battlefields and the sounds of war, and yet they open with the affirmation that a light is now shining in darkness and that a time for rejoicing is at hand. Verses 4 and 5 speak of a burden that has been lifted from the people, as in the days when the Midianite suppression was lifted from Israel (see Judg. 7:15–25). How does one best understand this portion of the text?

First of all, Assyria, the foreign aggressor, had conquered most of the Near East after about 750 BC. Judah, however, had remained neutral and an ally to Assyria. In 734 BC, Israel, Syria, and other states, but not Judah, were seeking to break away from Assyrian control. Because Judah, ruled by King Ahaz at the time, refused to go along, Israel and Syria invaded Judah and sought to depose Ahaz. The prophet Isaiah, however, encouraged Ahaz to remain true to God, to be neutral in the struggle, and to declare Judah independent from Israel. Judah was "the people who walked in darkness [and] have seen a great light" (v. 2). When war broke out and the Assyrians won, the threats of Israel and Syria were broken. Thus the pressure on Judah was relieved. The expectation of this forms the background for the emphasis on good news and the freedom from military pressure in verses 2–5. With the Assyrian suppression of Israel and Syria, Judah, for a time, was able to live again peacefully in the area. The country may have reaped some benefits from the spoils of war they were not involved in (see v. 3). Verses 6–7 would have been spoken by Isaiah, not so much about the new political and military situation as about King Ahaz. Ahaz's grandfather, Uzziah, who reigned as king until leprosy led to his abdication (2 Kings 15:5) had no doubt continued to exercise primary authority in Jerusalem. King Uzziah died just before Pekah and Rezin attacked Jerusalem, and one of Ahaz's first acts after Uzziah's death was to declare a Judean policy independent of Israel.

Verses 6 and 7 seem to reflect clearly aspects of the coronation ritual. The day of the king's accession to the throne was considered the day of his "rebirth" or adoption as the son of God. In Psalm 2:7, the reference to "today" as the day of the king's being begotten is the day of his coronation. Thus as the new son of God (see 2 Sam. 7:14), the government would be upon his shoulders. As a new son, the king was probably given a new name or set of names or titles. It may have been the function of the court prophet to help name the new children of a king as well as to come up with royal coronation titles. Nathan, for example, gave Solomon the name Jedidiah, "beloved of the Lord" (2 Sam. 12:25), and Isaiah had apparently picked out the name Immanuel for a child to be born at the royal court (Isa. 7:14). Verse 6 in the lection seems to refer to four honorific titles given the new king—"Wonderful Counselor, Mighty God, Everlasting Father, Prince of Peace." We know that the ancient Egyptians bestowed such honorific titles on new pharaohs at their coronation. Such titles were expressions of hope and of the new status enjoyed by the royalty. Kings throughout history have borne such honorific epithets—"defender of the poor, preserver of peace, defender of the faith," and others. (The late emperor of Ethiopia possessed enough titles to fill a paragraph in a newspaper story!) The prophet Isaiah was reminding the people and King Ahaz of the promises of God made to the ruler.

Verse 7 predicts that the new ruler will enjoy times of prosperity and peace on the throne of David and that he will rule with justice and righteousness throughout his reign. Such prophetic oracles at the king's coronation not only presented the new king with a set of promises but also was a way of reminding the new ruler of his responsibilities.

Although this text probably had a specific setting in the strife between Israel and Judah, it is nonetheless messianic through and through and most appropriate for Christmas Day. Just as Jesus is greeted as the Messiah, so was the ancient Davidic king. Just as the "hopes and fears of all the years" are focused on the new Messiah Jesus, so in ancient Israel, they come to focus on the new monarch whose coronation was the day of his birth as the son of God.

Psalm 96

Psalm 96 is a hymn that calls the people to proclaim the greatness of God in song and praise. Its special appropriateness to the Christmas Season lies in its universal call for all the earth to sing a new song and to worship God.

This psalm probably was used originally in ancient Israel as part of the celebration of the fall festival. One of the aspects of that festival was the celebration of God as creator and king of the world. Evidence suggests that in the festival it was believed that God re-created or reestablished the earth for the coming year (note v. 10). Though the belief that God re-created the world annually may sound a bit unusual, we must recall that every Christmas is celebrated as the birth of Jesus. So, such repetitions are commonplace in religious expression in worship.

Three emphases in this psalm are noteworthy in addition to its call for the universal praise and worship of Yahweh.

1. Verses 3–6 contrast the Israelite God with those of other peoples. The gods of the peoples are declared to be mere idols; that is, they are human products, impotent and without power (see Isa. 44:9–20). Over against the idols that are the work of human hands is Israel's God, who is not only uncreated but also is the creator—the One who made the heavens. Thus, in this psalm, the doctrine of creation undergirds the call to honor and praise God. The reference to God's sanctuary in verse 6 may not be a reference to the temple but rather to creation itself, which is conceived of as God's sacred place.

2. Just as verses 3–6 emphasize God as creator and thus as unique among the gods, so verses 10–13 emphasize God's kingship and execution of justice. In verse 10, the phrase "the LORD is king" appears. The Hebrew expression that is translated here could just as easily be rendered "the Lord has become king." Such a translation would indicate that in the fall festival, God annually reassumed the role of king. The basis for God's kingship is found in the fact that "the world is firmly established; it shall never be moved" (v. 10). It is difficult to believe that such an affirmation and its corollary that "God has become king" are based on the original creation of the world by God. Again, the text probably should be seen in its original usage as affirming God's annual reestablishment of the world and its orders. As the one who does this, God thus asserts divine rulership over the cosmos.

3. A further emphasis in verses 10–13 is God's judgment of the earth. This emphasis too probably reflects an aspect of the fall festival. Just as God reestablishes the world, reassumes the kingship over creation, so also God judges the world. In later rabbinic Judaism, the belief

that all the world was judged in conjunction with the fall festival was widely current. We can see this factor already evident in this psalm. Stress falls, however, on the fact that God judges with equity, righteousness, and truth.

Such a psalm as Psalm 96 is very apropos for the Christmas Season, for it speaks so much of divine triumph and affirms that a new situation exists in the world. God is king, the world is established, and all that exists in creation—heavens, earth, sea, field, trees, and above all, peoples throughout the world—are called to praise and worship God.

Titus 2:11–14

The pastoral epistles are noted for their interest in institutional questions and are quite often disparaged because they address overt questions of institutional form and portray stylized modes of conduct. Admittedly, they address concrete ecclesiastical concerns in a way the authentic letters of Paul do not, but they are not devoid of richly textured theological passages. This text is one such example (cf. also 3:4–7).

This text provides an excellent counterpoint for the traditional Christmas text from Luke's Gospel. For one thing, it is bifocal in its treatment of the Christ-event, linking the two themes of Advent, Christ's first and second coming, into a single piece. In this respect, it sets the Christ-event in a broader theological framework and serves as a reminder that even at Christmas the eschatological dimension of Christ's work is present. The initial manifestation of God's grace through the coming of Christ into the world, although focal in the celebration of Christmas, nevertheless causes us to look forward to "the blessed hope and the manifestation of the glory of our great God and Savior, Jesus Christ" (v. 13).

The "high Christology" expressed here is also worth noting. This is one of the few instances in the New Testament where Jesus is explicitly referred to as God (cf. Rom. 9:5; John 1:1; Heb. 1:8; also Acts 20:28). In this respect, this passage represents an advanced stage of christological reflection, as does the infancy story in Luke 2:1–20.

Another salutary feature of this text, which echoes Pauline sentiments but represents a further stage of reflection within the Pauline school, is its emphasis on the ethical implications of the Christ-event. The position of the text within chapter 2 should be noted. The preceding verses contain ethical instructions to various groups: older men (v. 2), older women (vv. 3–5), younger men (vv. 6–8), and slaves (vv. 9–10).

Although this version of the "household code" differs from others found in the New Testament (cf. Eph. 5:21–6:9; Col. 3:18–4:1; 1 Pet. 2:18–3:7), it is nonetheless a clear statement of the Christian imperative. What follows in verses 11–14 is the "indicative," which serves as the basis and motive for the ethical behavior called for earlier. This connection is seen in the introductory word "for" in verse 11.

This is seen especially well within the passage itself, where the educative function of God's grace is unfolded. We are told that the grace of God "trains," or "disciplines," us so that a definable life-style results. At its best, the grace of God disciplines us to renounce "godless ways and worldly desires" (REB) and evokes "temperance, honesty, and godliness in the present age" (REB). This is, of course, in keeping with the emphasis in the pastorals on ethical conduct as expressed in more regimented and codified form (cf. 2 Tim. 3:2–5, 10–11; 3:16). Although the liberating force of God's grace—the central thrust of Paul's gospel—

should not be forgotten, neither should its capacity to shape character be overlooked (cf. 2 Tim. 1:7; Titus 1:8; 1 Tim. 2:2).

In this respect, our text merely attests what Christians historically have experienced at Christmas. Reflection on the story of Christ inevitably prompts us to reflect on our personal story, its overall shape and general direction. The work of Christ is properly conceived as redeeming and purifying, yet a chief goal of his redemptive work is to form a people "zealous for good deeds" (v. 14). As earlier theological debates within the early church showed, an overemphasis on good works easily led to a debilitating theology of salvation by good works; and when this was the case, stressing the liberating force of the grace of God was quite appropriate. Our text, however, serves as a reminder that experiencing the grace of God is not simply an existential experience in which the individual achieves freedom from the bondage of the will; it also results in practical acts of Christian charity and good deeds.

Luke 2:1–14 (15–20)

Before looking into the Gospel lesson for today, let us pause a moment to reflect on what it means to preach on Christmas Day. Many ministers find it difficult to preach at Christmas. This is especially true of those in traditions in which the sermon is the centerpiece of Sunday morning, all else serving in satellite roles. At Christmas, however, the sermon and every other element of worship become but a part of the rich tapestry of celebration. Some preachers thus feel minimized and confess an ego problem. Others feel the wealth of the season makes even a good sermon seem poor indeed. Who is capable of rising to an occasion on which the most beautiful texts of the Bible are read, texts that can make our sermons turn pale and stammer? Nor is it uncommon for a minister to be burdened by the heavy pathos that haunts the edge of Christmas. The luxury of the season points up in sharpest relief the conditions of human misery everywhere. Frustrated by the futility of laying a heavy load of guilt on the parishioners Christmas morning, the pastor may prefer delivering a plate of food to delivering a sermon.

Then there are those whose very definition of preaching is exhorting, filling the air with ought, must, and should. Then comes Christmas when the angels and the children combine choirs to go caroling. There is nothing here for the common scold. But most of all, the familiarity of the songs and texts clips the wings of a preacher, sending some in covert searches for something novel, even if it is inappropriate, irrelevant, and has no substance. But the familiar, rather than deadening, can be the preacher's delight. To say the texts and message are familiar is to say they already belong to the listeners, and there is power, enjoyment, and an occasional "amen" when people hear what they already know. This means it is their sermon, not solely the pastor's. Sometimes we need to preach *for* rather than *to* the church. Now to our familiar text, Luke 2:1–20.

Luke's story of Jesus' birth consists of three units: verses 1–7, the birth itself; verses 8–14, the annunciation to the shepherds; verses 15–20, the visit of the shepherds to Bethlehem. The Gospel reading for today embraces the first two units with the third optional. The alternate reading for the Second Proper for Christmas offers units 2 and 3 with unit 1 optional. Perhaps it would be most helpful to provide comments here on the entire narrative (vv. 1–20) and leave to the preacher the option of using one, two, or all three units, regardless of whether the First Proper for Christmas or the Second Proper for Christmas is followed.

Luke 2:1–7 contains three elements: prophecy, history, and symbolism. Prophecy, fulfilled in Jesus, is not a thesis for Luke to establish but is rather a way of telling the story, of weaving old and new together as one fabric. Without referring directly to Micah 5:2, Luke uses all the elements of that prophecy: Bethlehem, house of David, the Davidic messiah. Similarly, Isaiah 1:3 and Jeremiah 14:8 provide the manger and the image of God lodging for the night. No characteristic of Luke-Acts is more pronounced than the author's insistence on the continuity of Judaism and Christianity. The Hebrew and Christian Scriptures tell one story, not two. God is not starting over with Christians, having failed with Jews. What God said to Abraham is coming to pass: In your seed all nations shall be blessed. The story is marked by rejection and resistance, to be sure, but God is faithful to the promise. For Luke, every Gentile believer can properly say, "Abraham and Sarah are my father and mother."

The second element here is secular history. "A decree went out from Emperor Augustus" (v. 1). Historians have had difficulty with Luke's report of the census under Quirinius (v. 2). Has Luke misplaced the census that came later after Archelaus was deposed as ruler of Judea and the country placed under the governor of Syria? The debates fill the commentaries, but regardless of the reliability of Luke's sources, his purpose is clear—to tie sacred to secular history. As God used Cyrus, king of Persia, to effect the divine purpose (Isa. 45), so God uses Emperor Augustus. The coming of Christ is not hidden in a corner; Rome is joined to Bethlehem. The world is God's, and the gospel is for God's world. The good news does not belong to the church, which may decide to share it with the world. Rather, Mary's baby is God's yes to the world, which includes us.

And the third element is symbolism. Why give attention to Jesus as a baby, wrapped, as any baby would be, in swaddling cloths, lying in a manger crib? Why not, like Mark, go straight to his ministry? Luke paints the whole picture in this small scene. God's Son, vulnerable as every infant is vulnerable, subject to all the conditions under which we all live, fully identified with every human being's need for love, lies here unnoticed, without trumpet or drum roll and without a place to lay his head. Jesus lived from crib to cross, but the teller of the story wrote from cross to crib.

Because verses 8–14 constitute an annunciation, it might be helpful to review the literary pattern common to such stories (cf. comments on Luke 1:26–38, Fourth Sunday of Advent). The annunciation here parallels the angel's visits to Zechariah and to Mary, the three accounts providing the central structure for Luke's Nativity. That commentaries on this text will refer to analogous stories of the births of emperors and kings, replete with heavenly messengers, signs, and widespread hope for peace and prosperity, should be informative to the preacher but not disconcerting. These stories from secular literature are informative in that Luke is a first-century writer, telling his story in a mode familiar enough to be a vehicle for communication. A modern reader is aided in grasping how Luke's first readers understood his Gospel. But these parallel stories should not be disconcerting. Analogies neither prove nor disprove a writer's claim, but they serve to clarify. If a story is such as to be totally without analogy, then who could understand it? Besides, Luke's theology welcomes similar accounts from other cultures. Luke's God is universally available, never without witness among the nations (Acts 14:17). Even pagan poets said, "In him we live and move and have our being" and "For we too are his offspring" (Acts 17:28). People everywhere hope and rejoice that the birth of a new leader will bring heaven's blessing of peace and joy. Luke's witness is that they brought their hopes to Bethlehem and did not go away empty.

The annunciation is to shepherds in the field. We are not sure whether the shepherds are for Luke a continuation of the focus on David, who was a shepherd of Bethlehem (1 Sam. 16), or a symbol of the poor of the earth, who are in Luke the special objects of the grace of God (4:18; 14:13, 21). Both interpretations could be correct. David is a very important figure for Luke, not only in the stories and songs related to the birth of Jesus (1:27, 32, 69; 2:4, 11) but also in the sermons related to the birth of the church (Acts 2:25–35). In Acts, David is presented as a prophet who spoke of Jesus' resurrection and enthronement at God's right hand (2 Sam. 7:12–16; Ps. 110:1; 132:11). As to the second interpretation, shepherds were not only poor but of poor reputation, treated religiously and socially almost as nonpersons. They qualify easily as the least likely to have God's favor on them, and God's favor on the least likely is a theme throughout the Bible. Israel was the least likely, as was David, and Mary, and Paul, and even Jesus himself. This text certainly provides an opportunity to deal with Jesus' birth through Luke's eyes, quite apart from Matthew, who places Jesus' birth among the wise, powerful, and rich. Matthew will speak to the church later, on Epiphany Sunday.

The heavenly host praised God and spoke of peace on earth. Peace (shalom), a quality of wholeness in life, made possible by a balance of all the forces within and without that affect us, was always the desire of Israel. The eschatological hope (Isa. 9:6; Zech. 9:9–10) was, says Luke, fulfilled in this one who would "guide our feet into the way of peace" (Luke 1:79). This peace is too immense to be confined to an inner experience, but it is also too personal to be left to the affairs of nations. The preacher will want to give careful attention to the translation of verse 14. Some ancient manuscripts read "on earth peace, good will among people," a phrase without contingency or condition. The best texts, however, make "good will" a condition for having peace. The phrase may read "among people of good will," "among those whom he favors" (NRSV), or "to all in whom he delights" (REB). One must wrestle here not only with texts and translations but with one's own theology.

A brief word about the sign given the shepherds (v. 12). In a field now radiant with heaven, the shepherds are told that the sign is a baby, wrapped as all newborn were, and lying in a feed bin for animals. In other words, the sign was as common as the shepherds themselves. Notice Luke's reversal: earth is not looking to heaven for a sign, but heaven looks to earth. The extraordinary points to the ordinary and says, "See, God is among you."

The third unit of the birth narrative (vv. 15–20) tells simply of the shepherds' visit to Bethlehem, and in this visit units 2 and 1 are joined; this is to say, the message of the angel to the shepherds (vv. 8–14) is confirmed by the manger scene (vv. 1–7). Just as the annunciations by the angel to Zechariah and to Mary proved true, so it is here. Strikingly, verses 1–7 tell a painfully simple story of political power, economic pressure, and the birth of a child away from home. There are no angels, no heavenly host, no revelations. On the other hand, verses 8–14 are filled with the extraordinary and the heavenly. In the shepherds' visit, heaven and earth meet, each witnessing to the other. But is it not strange that the holy family, the principal characters in the drama, get the good news of what their ordeal really means through the witness of others?

When the annunciation to Mary was confirmed, she praised God. When the annunciation to Zechariah was confirmed, he praised God. Not unexpectedly, therefore, Luke concludes this narrative with the shepherds returning, "glorifying and praising God."

Christmas, Second Proper
(Additional Lessons for Christmas Day)

Isaiah 62:6–12;
Psalm 97;
Titus 3:4–7;
Luke 2:(1–7) 8–20

All the texts for today remind worshipers around a manger that what we are receiving and experiencing is the work of the one God who is, after all, the subject of the entire Bible. It is God who delivers Jerusalem (Isa. 62); it is God who is enthroned over all the earth (Ps. 97); we have received the grace and favor of "God our Savior" (Titus 3); therefore, our song is "Glory to God in the highest" (Luke 2). Those of us who center faith in Jesus Christ need to recall often that Christ came to us, sent from God.

Isaiah 62:6–12

The material in this lection has Zion-Jerusalem as its focus, both in its longing for salvation and in the assurance that the city's coming salvation has already been proclaimed and is on its way.

The interpreter of this text and any who would preach on it need to recall that most of the texts in Isaiah 55–66 depict Zion-Jerusalem as still awaiting salvation, a salvation that has been proclaimed but not yet realized.

Who the ancient reader may have thought was speaking in verses 6–7 remains uncertain. The first part of verse 6 sounds like a word of God, yet the second part and all of verse 7 seem like the prophet's address. As we have noted with earlier texts from Second Isaiah, this difficulty in determining the speakers is a characteristic feature of the material.

Isaiah 62:6–7 focuses on the work of city watchmen whose task was to warn the population of danger and to proclaim any news or any change in the people's situation. Note what Isaiah 21:6–7 says of their task:

> "Go, post a lookout,
>   let him announce what he sees.
> When he sees riders, horsemen in pairs,
>   riders on donkeys, riders on camels,
> let him listen diligently,
>   very diligently."

According to Ezekiel 3:16–21; 33:1–9, the watchman was held accountable if the proper warning was not sounded. Here Ezekiel is, of course, comparing the office of prophet to that of watchman and thus highlighting the responsibility of the prophet. Although the watchman's job was important, Psalm 127:1*b* warns, "Unless the LORD keeps watch over the city, the watchman stands guard in vain" (REB).

Isaiah 62:6*a* seems to affirm that God has set watchmen over Jerusalem to function day and night. (In ancient Israel, the night was divided into three watches, but in later Roman times, four watches were common.) The fact that the watchmen are never to be silent could suggest the constancy of danger or an exaggerated emphasis of their tasks. The second half of verses 6 and 7 assign two unique functions to the watchmen. (1) They are to remind people of the Lord and to keep God in remembrance. This may refer to various blessings spoken by the watchmen, particularly if the watchmen were also priests or cultic functionaries (see Ps. 134) who served at night in the temple. (2) A second task of the watchmen is to give God no rest until Jerusalem is established and becomes an object of praise throughout the earth. Such a task for the watchmen certainly sounds abnormal. Those on duty day and night are never to let God find peace until Jerusalem has found peace. Although such statements may strike moderns as impious, the Old Testament here is quite willing to speak of the necessity to keep reminding God of the divine responsibilities and promises, even to pester the Deity (see also Ps. 44:23–26). If the watchmen were priests, then they would be merely representing the people's sentiments to the Deity.

Verses 8–9 quote an oath sworn by God that the people's crops and wine harvests will no longer be consumed by foreigners but by the people themselves who have produced them. Because Palestine was a land bridge between Africa to the south and Asia to the north, foreign armies constantly traversed its territory, looting and living off the land, to the deprivation of its people.

Isaiah 62:10–12 shifts the emphasis to focus on preparation for the coming salvation. People are to be prepared, highways cleared of stone, and an ensign set up to mark where the people should congregate. The prophet reiterates what God has already proclaimed, namely, that salvation is coming and that Jerusalem is to receive reward and recompense (see Isa. 40:1–11).

The new status that will come to the people will be reflected in a series of new names: "The Holy People," "The Redeemed of the LORD," "Sought Out," "A City Not Forsaken" (v. 12). The theme of the different names of the city also appears earlier in Isaiah 62, where the old Jerusalem and the land are called "Forsaken" and "Desolate" (v. 4). The restored city in this same verse will be called "My Delight Is in Her" (Hephzibah), and the land will no longer be called a widow (see Lam. 1:1) but instead will be known as "Married" (Beulah). In ancient Israel such a change of status was frequently embodied in a play on words or a new name reflective of the new conditions (see Hos. 1:4–2:1 and the earlier discussion of Isa. 9:2–7, for the First Proper for Christmas).

In verse 12 of the lection, one finds a variation in the use of plural and single verb forms: "they shall be called" and "you shall be called." If the single "you" refers to Zion-Jerusalem, then the plural "they" may refer to foreigners and pagans who seek out the city and thus become part of "The Holy People" and "The Redeemed of the Lord." One of the features of the second half of Isaiah (especially texts in Isa. 56–66) is the conversion of foreigners who turn to Jerusalem and find in the temple "a house of prayer for all peoples" (see Isa. 56:1–8). This could suggest that the foreigners' turning to Jerusalem is also alluded to in verse 14. If so, this makes the text even more appropriate to the Christmas Season, because in the birth of Christ we welcome the universal Savior and, like the Magi, seek out the One whose star lights up the sky.

Psalm 97

P salms 96, 97, and 98 have been called "Enthronement Songs," because they celebrate God's enthronement and the function of the Divine as king. As we noted in the earlier discussion of Psalm 96, the reenthronement of God was probably celebrated as part of the fall festival. The ceremony in which this was expressed in the cult probably involved the removal of the ark, the symbol of God's presence, from the temple. This would have symbolized the temporary "dethronement" of the Divine—a parallel to the Good Friday experience. The transference of the ark back into the temple would have symbolized God's reassumption of kingship and God's reestablishment in Zion (see Pss. 132; 47).

Psalm 97 opens with the cry "The Lord reigns," or perhaps better translated, "The Lord [Yahweh] has become king." This affirmation gives expression to the new state of affairs attendant upon God's reassumption of the role of universal king.

This psalm is divided into three stanzas in the NRSV. Stanza 1 (vv. 1–5) describes, in metaphorical terms, the awesomeness that the Israelites associated with the appearance or theophany of their God (see Exod. 19:16–18). Clouds, darkness, fire, and lightnings suggest that much of the imagery here has been borrowed from phenomena associated with the frequently violent thunderstorms that often occur in the Holy Land. All the imagery in this stanza emphasizes the shattering, abnormal sense of awe that is produced by the presence of the Deity. In spite of the awesomeness of God's presence, the divine throne and thus the divine rule are said, however, to be founded on righteousness and justice and not totally on the display of power.

Stanza 2 (vv. 6–9) stresses the reaction of both pagans and Zion to God's appearance and the manifestation of divine righteousness in the heavens. Both the pagans—idol worshipers—and their gods are forced to bow down and recognize the omnipotence of Israel's God. One, of course, does not have to assume that this actually happened in some historical event. In the cultic worship where this psalm was used, ideal, not actual, conditions were affirmed, and hopes, not full realities, were expressed. Zion, on the other hand, can hear of God's appearance and receive the good news with rejoicing, for God's judgments are given in favor of Zion. Because Yahweh is exalted above all gods, Zion and the daughters (cities) of Judah can rest in the assurance that they worship the only God who really counts. This uniqueness and righteousness of Yahweh are the basis of Zion's confidence.

Stanza 3 (vv. 10–12) concentrates on God's preservation of those who belong to the people of God. They have nothing to fear. Note the three actions of God that are emphasized: the Lord loves, preserves, and delivers. The opening line of verse 10 has no hesitancy in declaring that God loves those who hate evil. Ancient Israel had no qualms about affirming hatred if it was hatred of that which God did not condone. The righteous and the upright in heart in verse 11 are probably synonymously used terms. The righteous were those declared in the right in judgment. Because in biblical thought the heart was the center of the will and the intellect, being upright in heart was being consistent in thought and action. (The heart's association with the intellect has been preserved when we say we memorize things "by heart.") Though the psalm closes with a call to rejoice—that is, a call to let human emotions be given free rein—it also closes with a call to worship and give thanks to God.

The use of this psalm during the Christmas Season emphasizes that regardless of how God's appearance comes, in thundering cloud or whimpering babe, only those who worship idols are put to shame (v. 7). Those who belong to God can rejoice and be glad.

Titus 3:4–7

In the earlier text from Titus, it is the "manifestation" of "our great God and Savior, Jesus Christ" that is central. Here, however, it is the appearing, or dawning (cf. REB), of the "goodness and loving kindness of God our Savior" that is more prominent. To be sure, the work of "Jesus Christ our Savior" is mentioned later (v. 6), but his incarnation remains implicit within the passage. Strictly speaking, then, the incarnation of Christ is not the major focus of this passage, although it is the set text for the additional Christmas lection.

This, however, might provide an excellent occasion to remind the community of faith of God's role in the incarnation. The New Testament is a pervasively christological book, and its main concern, taken as a whole, is to unfold the life and work of Christ and their implications for the life of believers and the believing community. Because early discussion and debate in the first century focused less on the explicitly theological questions—that is, questions about the nature and work of God—many statements about God remain implicit within the New Testament. In fact, it has been suggested that God is the "neglected factor in New Testament theology." Similarly, at Christmas, Christian reflection and preaching about the work of Christ can all too easily overshadow the divine initiative and work of God.

It is striking here that God is called "our Savior," a term we more commonly reserve for Christ, at least in popular parlance. Yet in the pastoral letters, in particular, God is frequently designated as Savior (cf. 1 Tim. 1:1; 2:3; 4:10; Titus 1:3; 2:10). It was common practice for Hellenistic rulers to be called "savior," and by the late first century AD when our text was written, Roman rulers were receiving, and claiming, the title more frequently and more audaciously. It may well be that the pastorals frequently designate God and Christ as "Savior" in response to claims made of human rulers in the imperial cult. If this is the context in which these attributions to God and Christ occurred, it is clear how Christians would have forged their faith over against the competing claims of the imperial cult. Here the issue would have been one of ultimate sovereignty, and the Christian witness is clear, as seen in our text: It is God and Christ who are to be confessed as Savior, not human rulers. The latter are to be respected, indeed obeyed (cf. 3:1), but not worshiped.

Developed in this direction, in the context of Christmas, the text might easily be used to remind Christians that the Christ-story invites all persons to look beyond humanly constructed saviors and salvation systems, be they political rulers or systems, national or local ideologies and ideologues, as their ultimate hope.

As the text makes clear, the way of escape from a life of folly, disobedience, various forms of slavery, and internecine behavior begins with the recognition of the "kindness and generosity" of God our Savior. In a once-for-all act, God "saved us" (v. 5) by taking the first bold and dramatic step: God lavishly poured out his mercy through Jesus Christ our Savior (v. 6). The text also asserts that this was done as an act of unprompted and uncalculating mercy, not as an irresistible response to human achievement and progress.

As numerous saving ideologies compete for the attention of modern persons, the Christ-story, celebrated throughout the liturgical year but begun at Christmas, still provides a clear option for those attracted to a "life-story" in which acts of unprompted grace, selfless sacrifice, and mercy are the distinguishing traits of its central figure.

Luke 2: (1–7) 8–20

In the discussion of the Gospel reading for the First Proper for Christmas, the entire birth narrative in Luke 2:1–20 was treated. The reader is referred to that discussion if this alternate proper is used for the sermon.

Christmas, Third Proper
(Additional Lessons for Christmas Day)

Isaiah 52:7–10;
Psalm 98;
Hebrews 1:1–4 (5–12);
John 1:1–14

The readings before us are of two textures, both appropriate for Christmas Day. Both Isaiah 52 and Psalm 98 are expressions of praise to God who comes as king, not only of Israel but also of all the earth. The tone is triumphant. Both Hebrews 1 and John 1, although liturgical and recitative, are theological summaries of the fact and meaning of God's Son coming into the world. Quite early the church framed its faith so as to be learned, said, and passed on clearly and positively. The tone is reflective.

Isaiah 52:7–10

This lection is especially appropriate for Christmas Day, for it concentrates on two features so significant for the season: good tidings and the arrival of a king. A third element—namely, the messenger—is also stressed. As should be the case with modern ministers, the messenger's importance here derives not from his or her own person but from the content of the message.

The passage celebrates, in highly exalted fashion, two factors about the God of Israel that can be integrated into the themes of the Christmas Season: God's reign as king and the divine return to Jerusalem.

The text's description of God's reign and return is probably built on the old components of royal processions in which a triumphant monarch returned to the capital city after attaining success in battle. The first component of such an occasion would be the actual victory of the monarch, a feature noted in verse 10. The reference to the baring of God's holy arm is a way of referring to divine triumph. Note that Deuteronomy 26:8 speaks of God's triumph over the Egyptians in terms of "a mighty hand and an outstretched arm," both symbols of power. Thus the triumphal procession was preceded by a royal victory. The second component was the monarch's return home as the victorious leader. This feature is noted in verse 8, which speaks of Yahweh's return to Zion. The final component of the procession was the acclamation and greeting by the home folks. The announcement of good tidings in this text emphasizes the fact that God reigns as king and has triumphed in such a way that the ends of the earth may see the divine salvation. It is interesting to note how the text introduces or speaks about the messenger. It talks about the beauty of the feet of the one who brings good news. Of course, this is an allusion to the common ancient practice of sending messages by runners. The character of the message is what matters most: it concerns peace, tidings of good, the fact of salvation, and the proclamation that God reigns. Just as at Christmastime, it is the angelic good tidings, not the angels themselves, that are of consequence.

The voice of the messenger upon arrival in the city is pictured by the prophet as being joined by the voices of the watchers on the wall who shout together for joy to make known the good news. Finally, even the waste places of Jerusalem, the destroyed parts of the city, are called upon to break forth into singing and celebration.

In spite of this text's affirmation of good news and its great spirit of exaltation, the entire passage has a very poetic quality about it that somewhat removes it from the realm of the mundane and the ordinary. The literalist would want to ask questions about the reality of the changes wrought, but such a text as this defies much specificity if read on its own. For Second Isaiah, the triumph of God must be seen as the granting of freedom to the exiles to return home. This is clearly evident in Isaiah 52:11–12, the verses that follow today's Old Testament lection. In these verses, the prophet calls on the people who carry the temple vessels to depart the foreign land and to keep themselves ritually pure, knowing all the time that the God of Israel is their leader as well as their rear guard. The homecoming is thus both for God and for the people.

The Christmas Season can be appreciated and preached as the time when good tidings—even in the face of bad conditions—must be proclaimed. It is also to be preached as a time when God returns to the world, to God's own. As in this text, the focus of the season should be on celebration, the joyous response of even the waste places to the assurance that peace, good, salvation, and God's rule are the themes of the occasion. Christmas may also be seen as the time when we as people return home—when we return to those true essentials that make a Babe's birth a time of peace and good tidings.

Psalm 98

Like Psalms 96 and 97, this psalm celebrates and proclaims the universal establishment of God's rule and thus represents another expression of the themes found in those psalms as well as in Isaiah 52:7–10. Like Psalm 96, this psalm opens with a call to sing to Yahweh a new song. As a hymn, the psalm is celebrative, oriented to confessional praise, and speaks about, rather than to, the Deity.

The language of the psalm is poetic; and although it speaks of divine victory, it does not specify the nature of that victory. Thus many scholars associate the psalm with the annual celebration of Yahweh's kingship as part of the fall festival.

Verses 1b–3 describe the basis for the excessive celebration called for in the rest of the psalm. As part of God's victory, the divine vindication has been manifest among the nations. That is, the power, might, and reputation of Israel's Deity have been publicly revealed for the nations of the world to behold. This same sentiment can be seen in the star and the Magi of the Christmas story, for both reflect the public aspects of God's revelation. God's victory is also the divine way of expressing steadfast love and faithfulness to the house of Israel. Thus God's fidelity to Israel and divine manifestation before the nations are two sides of the same coin.

In the ancient world, a god's reputation was not a foregone conclusion. The welfare of the worshipers of that god and the status of their life and culture were taken as indication of the strength and power of the deity. When people were weak, their god also was considered weak. This is why divine vindication before the nations and divine fidelity to Israel are so closely linked. Verses 4–6 call on the earth to sing praises to God with various forms of musical instruments. Ancient Israel certainly recognized that there are times when worship and service of the Divine are best expressed in joyful sound and praise and that this is all that is called for. Perhaps the Christmas Season should be viewed as one of those occasions when song and praise are more important than homily and lecture.

In verses 7–8, the poet extends the imaginative imagery and calls on all of nature to function as participants in praise. Four contrasting entities are addressed: the sea with all that lives within it; the whole earth with all those who dwell upon it; the turbulent flood waters that lie deep in the bosom of the earth (see Gen. 7:11; Ps. 93:3); and the hills that reach up toward the heavens. Such extremes are used to emphasize that praise should be rendered by all of the created order—everything in it. (Note that we often use similar language when we speak of people coming from near and far, meaning from "everywhere.")

The celebration before God called for in the psalm is finally based on the assurance that the victorious God comes to judge the earth with righteousness and the peoples with equity. The world is not called on, in other words, to worship and praise a deity who refuses to function as judge or a deity who judges unjustly. The character of God is an important foundation and an essential underpinning of all celebration and praise.

Hebrews 1:1–4 (5–12)

Though the lection ends with verse 12, the thought unit extends through verse 14. The most natural transition occurs after verse 14, as seen by the use of "therefore" in 2:1. The following warning and exhortation (2:1–4) derive directly from the remarks of chapter 1.

This text is truly remarkable in several respects. First, it displays fine literary style, having been deliberately composed to achieve maximum effect as an opening for this impressively argued treatise. The tone of the passage is thoroughly majestic and is meant to be read by an oral interpreter sensitive to style as well as to substance.

Second, it is one of the most definitive statements in the New Testament of Christ's role as the one through whom God has finally spoken. As such, it is an important text for the Christian understanding of God's revelation. Set over against the prophetic witnesses through whom God spoke "in many and various ways," Christ is the one through whom God "in these last days" has finally spoken. The multiplicity of their witness is contrasted with the singleness of his. Many voices have now given way to a single voice; the chorus has now given way to the soloist whose appointed time has come to be heard, with the rest, but now above the rest. It should be noted here that the author presupposes that God has never been silent. What has changed is the messenger, who himself is now the message. The major theme of these opening words may be said to be the "God who speaks." If the Old Testament attests the "God who acts," as the biblical theology movement emphasized, so does it present a God who is revealed through words, the words of his prophets then, the word of his Son now.

Third, the passage is remarkable for the truly staggering set of claims it makes about Christ. The Christology here is definitely high. Several christological images cluster: Christ as the Son of God, and therefore as God's heir; Christ as creator and sustainer of the world; Christ as high priest. In particular, the preexistent work of Christ receives special attention. He is not only the one through whom God created the world (v. 2); he is also the one who "sustains all things by his powerful word" (v. 3). Similar emphasis on the creative work of Christ is found elsewhere in the New Testament (cf. 1 Cor. 8:6; Col. 1:15–20). Here, however, both Christ's work and his nature are defined with respect to God. "He is the radiant light of God's glory and the perfect copy of his nature" (v. 3, JB). Both images are drawn from Alexandrian philosophical traditions. The former image recalls the Genesis creation story and possibly the language of Exodus 24:16; in any case, as God is understood as pure, radiant light, so is Christ understood as essentially light who emanates from God and reflects similar "glory," or brightness. The latter image effectively excludes Christ as, in any sense, a counterfeit copy of God: He is through and through, both in form and substance, an exact replica of God. The reference to his having made "purification for sins" doubtless evokes the image of Christ as high priest, a theme more fully developed later in the treatise (cf. 4:14–7:28).

Fourth, the passage is remarkable for the extended midrash in verses 5–14, where Christ's superiority to angels is elaborated. The chain of seven Old Testament passages (Ps. 2:7; 2 Sam. 7:14; Deut. 32:43; Ps. 104:4; Ps. 45:6–7; Ps. 102:25–27; Ps. 110:1) are strung together to achieve maximum cumulative effect. Each in its own way shows that by comparison the angels are but "spirits in the divine service, sent to serve for the sake of those who are to inherit salvation" (v. 14). Their role is truly subordinate to that of the Son.

This deliberately composed and thoroughly majestic passage, with its singular attention to Christ, is especially well suited as a Christmas text. Even though the role of the preexistent Christ is in the forefront, Advent themes are present. This is especially the case in verse 6: "When he [God] brings the firstborn into the world." This appears to be the case in verse 5 as well, where Psalm 2:7 is cited. Ordinarily, this psalm is cited in early Christian literature in connection with Christ's resurrection (cf. Acts 13:33; Heb. 5:5; Rom. 1:4). Here, however, it appears that the generation of the Son rather than his resurrection is in view. If this is the correct interpretation, it is indeed surprising.

Clearly, this text reveals an advanced stage of christological reflection and most likely comes rather late in early Christian thinking about the work of Christ. A wide range of traditions have been drawn upon, most notably wisdom traditions, and in this respect our passage is similar to the Johannine prologue and the Christ hymn in Colossians 1. Obviously, Old Testament texts have exercised a decisive influence on this christological statement, and the catena of Old Testament texts appears to have taken shape at an early stage as the author's predecessors sought to relate the Old Testament witness to Christ. Also noteworthy is verse 8, where Christ is directly addressed as God. Such explicit christological claims by Christians appear not to have been made at the earliest stages. It seems to have taken a while for such audacity to surface in confessional form.

This text, then, striking for the boldness and clarity of its claims, is a richly textured meditation on Christ. The main stress is on Christ's superiority to the angels, at least as the passage unfolds. Whether the historical situation envisioned here is similar to that addressed in Colossians, where Christ's status has been diminished by relegating him to the ranks of all other angelic beings, is not clear. Probably not. However, the thrust of the passage is clear: Christ is presented as the preeminent Son of God, without peer within the heavenly hierarchy. This passage is remarkably full of superlatives that reinforce this position of Christ's ultimate supremacy (cf. vv. 2–3).

There is a sense in which this staggering set of claims all derive from the one claim of Christ's sonship. If Christ is not *a* son of God but *the* Son of God in an absolute, unqualified sense, the implications are vast. He is indeed God's "heir of all things" (v. 2); he quite naturally qualifies as God's collaborator in creation and the one who sustains all things by his powerful word.

If Christmas is the one time of the church year when Christians reflect seriously on Christ's sonship and his divine begetting, this text illustrates some of the far-reaching ramifications of such a claim. This point is especially worth making at Christmas, for Christians find it easy to be compelled by seasonal pressure to appropriate the Christ-story in only a limited way by celebrating the birth of Christ. It is all too easy to romanticize the story of Christ's birth without realizing the full implications of confessing Christ as the Son of God. Out text, however, illustrates the other end of the trajectory, filling out as it does the cosmic implications of belief in the sonship of Christ. Hebrews 1:1–12, therefore, may be said to represent a more mature understanding of Christ to which Christians may advance, even if they have begun with relatively simple meditations on the stories of Christ's birth.

John 1:1–14

The Gospel of John does not have nativity songs as does Luke, but John does have a hymn to Christ (1:1–18). The Gospel of John does not have a birth story, but John does proclaim that the Word became flesh and dwelt among us (1:14). The Gospel of John does not say that the one conceived by the Holy Spirit would be the Son of God, but John does say that the One who became flesh was with God from the beginning, and what God was, he was (1:1). The Gospel of John does not say that God's Son was wrapped in swaddling cloths, lying in a manger, but John does say that the revelation of God in Jesus was concealed, if not hidden, veiled in flesh (1:14). John 1:1–14 is, then, an appropriate text for Christmas.

The verses selected for today (1:1–14) are a portion of a unit only slightly larger, 1:1–18, commonly referred to as the prologue. The prologue is clearly a distinct literary unit, having a clear beginning and ending, being poetic in nature in contrast to the prose narrative that follows (1:19ff.), and focusing on a single subject, the Word of God. Because of its unusual literary form and because its presentation of Christ as the Word (Logos) appears nowhere else in the Gospel, some have suggested that 1:1–18 was not an original part of this Gospel. The issue is not a vital one for the preacher, because the theological perspective of the prologue is fully congenial with the remainder of the book. In fact, the entire Gospel is in a sense an elaboration upon 1:18: "No one has ever seen God. It is God the only Son, who is close to the Father's heart, who has made him known."

John 1:1–18 consists of three stanzas with two insertions about John the Baptist (vv. 6–8, 15). (For comments on these verses, see the Third Sunday in Advent.) The first stanza, verses 1–5, relates God to all creation through the Word; the second, verses 9–13, relates God to human life through the Word; and the third, verses 14–18, provides the divine offer of grace and truth through the Word. It is not abortive of meaning to conclude at verse 14 as does this lection, for verse 14 is John's "Christmas story" in capsule; but because verses 14–18 are the affirmation of faith (among *us*, *we* have seen, *we* have all received) concluding the hymn, the sermon properly should embrace the whole of the prologue.

A preacher may recoil at the thought of a single sermon on the entire text, and properly so. Its scope is immense: all creation, Israel, the Baptist movement, the church, preexistence of the

Word, and salvation through the revelation of the Word. In addition, the passage is not only hymnic but polemic, contending with the synagogue and the followers of the Baptist (vv. 6–8, 15, 17). But for the occasion of Christmas, one would do well to step back and see the whole of it. Sometimes enabling listeners to sense the size and grandeur of a text is of more value than detailed application to their lives.

Let us, then, allow the Fourth Evangelist to tell us the good news. A fundamental human hunger is to know God. "Show us the Father, and we will be satisfied" (14:8). In fact, to know God is life eternal (17:3). But no one has ever seen God (1:18), and even though God is the creator and sustainer of all life and available to obedient faith (1:1–12), knowledge of God does not come by observation or by the accumulation of proofs. However, because God is gracious toward the world (3:16), the darkness of ignorance and death are dispelled by the coming of the Son as revealer (1:18). In order to tell this story, John borrows a category familiar to Jewish and Greek culture—Word, or Logos (the feminine synonym often interchanged with Logos is Sophia, Wisdom). The Word, or Wisdom, through which God created and sustains the world (Gen. 1:3; Ps. 33:47; Heb. 1:3) came to be personified in late Judaism as a separate being (Prov. 8; Wisd. of Sol. 7; Sir. 24). In Sirach, for example, this Wisdom through whom God created the world asked of God permission to come dwell on earth. Permission was granted, but the earth was evil, foolish, and inhospitable. And so God made Wisdom to become a book, the Book of Moses, to dwell in the tents of Jacob (Sir. 24). But for the Evangelist, the eternal Wisdom, or Word, becomes not a book, but flesh—a person, Jesus of Nazareth.

Not all who met Jesus experienced God, nor do they today, but to all who do, God gives "power to become children of God" (1:12).

First Sunday After Christmas Day

The following readings are used on the First Sunday After Christmas unless the readings for the Epiphany of the Lord are preferred.

Isaiah 61:10–62:3;
Psalm 148;
Galatians 4:4–7;
Luke 2:22–40

In Jesus Christ, God has done a new thing, but our texts for this Sunday offer us two important reminders. First, what God has done in Jesus is a fulfillment of and not a departure from God's work in the past. Luke portrays a young Jesus being reared according to the law of Moses, and Paul concurs in Galatians 4; Jesus was born of woman, under the law. Second, God's act of redemption is still in process (Isa. 61) and calls for a response of obedience and thanksgiving (Ps. 148). This Sunday is after Christmas, but it is also before Epiphany.

Isaiah 61:10–62:3

Portions of this lection were also part of the Old Testament reading for the Third Sunday of Advent. The fact that the passage stresses salvation as already partially realized as well as anticipated makes it appropriate for an Advent reading. As a post-Christmas reading, its emphasis on the experience of salvation, its interest in the nations, and its focus on Zion make it appropriate as a text that looks forward to Epiphany.

The lection clearly breaks down into two distinct units. The first in 61:10–11 is a joyful response celebrating the salvation that God has brought about or at least promised. Perhaps the "I" of verse 10 is the prophet speaking, or probably more likely it is a personified embodiment of the community. Two images are drawn upon to give expression to the experience and anticipation of salvation. The first, in verse 10, uses aspects associated with the joy of a wedding ceremony—salvation is a garment in which the saved are decked out like the bride and bridegroom adorned in the finery and wealth of their wedding garments. The bride of God is a common emphasis in many of the books of the prophets (Hos. 1–3; Jer. 2:1–3). Many of the sayings and parables of Jesus likewise draw upon wedding imagery. The minister might think about this text in terms of a sermon on salvation as a wedding. The second image, in verse 11, draws upon agricultural phenomena. The assurance that God will make righteousness and praise spring forth before the nations is compared to how the land or a garden causes to grow what has been planted in it. The salvation and the assurance may be no more than seeds lying in the soil, but as the farmer has the certainty of growth and harvest, so the Word of God brings with it the certainty of salvation. Again, the imagery of sowing and harvesting is significant in many of Jesus' sayings and parables.

The second portion of the lection, Isaiah 62:1–3, really goes with what follows in the remainder of chapter 62 more than with the preceding chapter. The reference to the nations and the kings seeing the glory of Zion, however, can give this text a connection with the approaching Epiphany Season.

In 62:1–3, we encounter the prophet as intercessor before God on behalf of the people. Although the character of the prophetic office tended to stress the prophet as one who spoke for God and addressed Israel, the prophet also spoke for Israel and addressed God. In this second function, the prophet was the people's representative before, and intercessor with, God (see Amos 7:1–6; Jer. 7:16; Ezek. 13:1–5).

The prophet declares in 62:1 that he will not be kept silent but will pester and intercede with the Deity until Jerusalem has experienced a salvation that can be seen as clearly as a bright light or a burning torch. Obviously, the prophet seems set on overcoming some skepticism in the community about whether the coming salvation is certain or not. The prophetic promise of incessant intercession thus functions as a word of assurance to the community. The minister could focus a sermon on the importance and role of intercession and intercessory prayer, stressing the fact that intercession gives expression to the common bonds that bind all humanity together and provides a means of touching the Deity on behalf of others. Being intercessors on behalf of others also provides the ones interceding with a new perspective on themselves.

In addressing Zion, in verses 2–3, the prophet assures the city that nations will eventually see her vindication and kings her glory. (This theme can be viewed as analogous to the coming of the Wise Men at the birth of Jesus.) Jerusalem will be given a new name by God as the sign of the city's transformation from a desolate, dissipated place (see Isa. 62:4–5, 12) to become a crown of beauty and a royal diadem. The fact that God is to give the name carries with it extra significance, for it indicates that the new status and the new circumstances are divinely ordained.

Psalm 148

Psalms 146–150 constitute a small collection of hymns of praise. All begin and conclude with the cultic shout "Hallelujah" that calls upon the community to "praise Yahweh," "praise the Lord."

Psalm 148 consists of two types of genres: two extended calls to praise (vv. 1–4, 7–12) and two statements giving the reason or rationale for praise (vv. 5–6, 13–14).

The psalm is an exuberant summons for the whole of creation to join in shouting out and celebrating the name and glory of Yahweh. Practically no aspect of creation is omitted in the call to praise: angels, heavenly hosts, sun and moon, shining stars, highest heavens, waters above the heavens, sea monsters and all deeps, fire and hail, snow and frost, stormy wind, mountains and hills, fruit trees, and all cedars, wild animals and all cattle, creeping things and flying birds, kings, princes, rulers, young men and women, old and young. What a chorus!

In spite of its tone, Psalm 148 should not be faulted for a Pollyanna perspective on life. There are times when unbounded jubilation should reign and carry us to the limits of celebration, to the borders of insanity, and to the heights of self-transcendence. Few are the times when the whole world is a chorus and the music of the spheres invades every nook and cranny of existence. Their scarcity should only endear their occurrence. It is only in such moments that we can spiritually and sensually realize the truth that modern ecology has taught us. We are all—from shining star to slithering snake—in this together, and we need to sing, at least occasionally, the same song and join in a common medley.

The psalm offers two reasons undergirding such praise. The first (in vv. 5–6) declares that Yahweh is the creator of all, who has established everything and set a law that cannot pass away (NRSV margin). The created order is divine handiwork in which every part serves its function within a created natural order (see Jer. 5:22–24; 31:35–36). The second (in vv. 13–14) alludes to the rule of the Davidic monarch, the horn raised up for the people of Israel. (On the horn as the symbol of strength and royalty, see 1 Sam. 2:10; Pss. 75:4–5; 89:17, 24; 92:10; 112:9; 132:17; Lam. 2:3, 17.) The psalm thus anchors praise in the divine rule in the universe and the messianic rule over the chosen people.

Galatians 4:4–7

This text from Galatians, with its dual emphasis on Christ as God's Son and, by extension, Christians as God's sons, or children, effectively extends themes celebrated at Christmas. Paul's statement that Christ was "born of a woman" (v. 4) in one sense serves as a hinge connecting this reading with the Lukan birth narratives read earlier for the Fourth Sunday of Advent and for Christmas Eve/Day. It also fits well with today's Gospel text, which is the final section of the Lukan birth narrative.

It is worth noting that this is one of Paul's rare references to an event in the life of the historical Jesus. To be sure, the language is traditional, yet is shows that Paul was not totally uninterested in this first stage of Christ's earthly ministry. Some scholars have seen here a cryptic reference to the tradition of Jesus' virgin birth ("born of woman—not man," as both Matthew and Luke attest), which is otherwise not mentioned in the Pauline letters. However formulaic the language here, it fully conforms to Paul's insistence elsewhere on Christ's full humanity (cf. Phil. 2:5–11).

Because most of the earlier epistolary readings to this point have been drawn from the non-Pauline and deutero-Pauline letters, this might be an appropriate occasion to explore this aspect of Paul's Christology. Some of the Pauline passages treating the humanity of Christ include Romans 1:3; 7:4; 9:5; 1 Corinthians 15:21; 2 Corinthians 8:9; Philippians 2:7–8; also cf. Colossians 2:9.

In similar fashion, the phrase "born under the law" might be explored in direct connection with the Gospel lesson for today (Luke 2:22–40), where Jesus' parents are portrayed as faithful adherents to the Mosaic law (cf. Luke 2:39). The final section of the Lukan birth narrative (Luke 2:41–52) also presents Jesus as a young man being nurtured in the traditions of his parents. Naturally, Jesus' Jewishness raises critical issues concerning the relation between law and gospel. Paul's arguments in Galatia have influenced Christian thought to draw a sharp distinction between "bondage under the law" and "freedom in the gospel." Here, however, Christ's solidarity with his Jewish past is asserted, and this might be used to explore the lines of continuity between Christianity and Judaism.

In verses 5b–7, the newly obtained status of sonship is obviously the central point. The opening phrase, "because you are children" (v. 6), is emphatic and unequivocal. As confirming testimony to the reality of this new status, "God has sent the Spirit of his Son into our hearts, crying, 'Abba! Father!'" "Spirit" here is doubtless the Holy Spirit, and its close association with Christ is not unusual for Paul (cf. Rom. 8).

Paul conceives of Christ's Spirit as the catalyst within every Christian working to bring about the filial obedience that typified the work of Christ himself. "Abba! Father!" is one of the few instances outside the Gospel tradition where the literal words of Jesus are preserved in their original Aramaic form. This in itself signifies the importance of these words uttered by the historical Jesus. So memorably did they symbolize Christ's willingness to fulfill his commitment to be Son of God in an absolute sense that the early church preserved them as originally spoken. With these words we are hearing not only Jesus' own language of prayer, but also, as the text suggests, the prayers of the early Christians as they besought the Spirit of Christ to bring about in them the quality of pristine obedience they understood the death of Christ to represent. The interior quality of Christ's life of sonship is now envisioned as a reality for every one of God's "sons." No longer is such a level of sonship something for which we must wait; it is the legacy of everyone who is in Christ. The Christian's task is not to wait any longer for this legacy, but to lay claim to it now, in the "fullness of time," when God's eschatological work has already begun.

This text, then, read on the First Sunday After Christmas, might be developed profitably in several directions. First, one might wish to focus on Paul's particular way of dealing with Christ's humanity, contrasting this with the more extended narrative treatments of the Gospels. Second, one might wish to focus on Christians' status as God's children, adopted yet nonetheless full heirs. It might be noted here that in dealing with this passage, it will be more difficult to use inclusive language. "God's child/children" will usually do double duty for "God's Son/sons," but it is easy to lose the subtlety of the Pauline play on words—Christ as God's Son, Christians as God's sons—especially taking seriously the adoption metaphor. Third, the unusual occurrence of "Abba!" with all the attention it has received in recent years, offers many possibilities (cf. Rom. 8:15). One might easily develop the theme of the profile of "sonship" that results as one gradually learns to make Jesus' prayer, "Abba! Father!" one's own. Or, the role of the Spirit as the enabling agent in bringing about this life of obedience is equally suitable and homiletically productive. In either case, the liberating power of Christ's work remains a central theme.

Luke 2:22–40

Whether the Sunday after Christmas is a significant time or merely the occasion for picking up the twelve baskets of fragments depends very much on the minister. If the minister understands that the congregation does not always have to be at high tide but may experience ebb and flow in good health, then this Sunday can be anticipated as an important time for preaching. In fact, just as many welcome meat and potatoes after surfeiting on holiday goodies, so might a solid offering from the pulpit be warmly received. We are indebted to Luke for a text that speaks to us after shepherds, angels, and heavenly hosts are gone. Mary and Joseph have a son to rear, religious obligations to keep, and a trip back to Nazareth to make. Sounds familiar enough.

The Gospel lesson for today, Luke 2:22–40, serves at least four purposes for the author. First, even in his infancy, Jesus' life was characterized as being in full obedience to the law of Moses. Even in this brief text, that fact is stated no less than five times (vv. 22, 23, 24, 27,

39). The particular forms of that obedience consisted of circumcision, which Luke combined with the naming according to the angel's instruction (vv. 21; 1:31); the dedication of the firstborn to God (Exod. 13:1–2); and the purification of the mother (Lev. 12:6). Because of the family's poverty, they were allowed to sacrifice according to the law's special provision (Lev. 12:8). For the purposes of his narration, Luke has related the dedication and purification as one event. (For an earlier story of a mother giving her son to God, see 1 Sam. 1–2.) By stating repeatedly that the law was being observed, Luke was saying that Jesus was a true Israelite. Circumcision, dedication, purification of the mother, the trip to the temple at age twelve, public life at age thirty, worshiping in the synagogue on the sabbath as was his custom: these and other proofs of Jesus' commitment to the law are given by Luke. And in Acts, the church continued synagogue and temple attendance, and Paul went first to the synagogue in every city and went through vow ceremonies in Jerusalem at the request of church leaders there. In other words, says Luke, Jesus and the church are no renegade splinter movement, flaunting freedom as disobedience to the law. Rather, in Jesus and the church Judaism is properly continued and fulfilled. Jesus worked within and through his tradition; he threw no stones from a distance.

A second purpose fulfilled by Luke in 2:22–40 is the declaration of the Child's greatness. At birth the declaration was by an angel, at age twelve by the teachers of the law (2:46–47), and at the beginning of his ministry by the voice from heaven (3:22). Here it is by two aged, pious Jews, Simeon and Anna. Simeon was inspired by the Holy Spirit (vv. 25–27) to recognize in the infant Jesus the fulfillment of his hope. His waiting was for the consolation of Israel (Isa. 40:1), but he foresaw that Jesus would be a center of controversy, the occasion for the fall and rise of many in Israel (an allusion to the stone that would aid or cause to stumble, Isa. 28:16), and a cause of piercing grief to his mother (vv. 34–35). Anna, a prophetess, was a widow (the Greek is unclear whether she was eighty-four or had been a widow eighty-four years), and as such belonged to a class well known in Israel (Naomi, Judith) and in the early church, where their duties included prayer night and day (1 Tim. 5:3–10). Through these two, Luke may be saying that Israel, when led by the Spirit, righteous, and devoted to prayer and fasting, could see in Jesus the fulfillment of her longing.

A third purpose of this passage is to return the family and the action of the narrative to Galilee and to Nazareth. Luke will later present Jesus announcing the nature and purpose of his ministry in a synagogue in Nazareth, "where he had been brought up" (4:16). For now, and for the next twelve years, it is enough to say that "the child grew and became strong, filled with wisdom; and the favor of God was upon him" (2:40).

A fourth and final purpose of this text is to introduce another Christian hymn, the "Nunc Dimittis" (vv. 29–32). Like the other hymns that Luke has used in chapters 1–2, this one consists of phrases and lines from the Hebrew Scriptures, mostly Isaiah 49 and 52. The song speaks of the fading of the old before the new, the realization of hope, and God's final embrace of all peoples, Jew and Gentile.

If the preacher needs an image for this last Sunday of the year, here it is—an old man holding a baby.

January 1
(Holy Name of Jesus: Solemnity of Mary, Mother of God)

Numbers 6:22–27;
Psalm 8;
Galatians 4:4–7 or Philippians 2:5–13;
Luke 2:15–21

Celebrating the beginning of the new year on January 1 goes back to the mid–first century BC, when Julius Caesar restructured the civil calendar. Prior to that time, March 1 marked the beginning of the new year. From the outset, it was a festive celebration that easily gave way to excesses of various kinds. In response, the Roman church called on Christians to open the new year with prayer, fasting, and penitential devotions. Another way to provide an alternative to raucous festivals was to designate January 1 as a time for honoring Mary, the Mother of God. In the Roman calendar, the day was designated *Natale Sanctae Mariae*, the Feast of Saint Mary.

Even though the particular emphasis given to January 1 has shifted through the centuries, in modern times, and especially in the Roman church, this day has received a dual emphasis. First, it is a time to recall the naming of Jesus, hence the designation the "Holy Name of Jesus." This aspect of its celebration is closely related to the custom, going back at least to the sixth century, of celebrating the Feast of the Circumcision of the Lord on this day. Second, it is an occasion for commemorating Mary, hence the designation the "Solemnity of Mary, Mother of God."

The readings selected for this day echo these themes. The Old Testament reading is chosen because of its emphasis on the bestowal of the divine name on the people Israel. Psalm 8 is the response because its initial and concluding lines praise the name of the Lord. The epistolary readings in different ways pick up on both themes: the Galatians passage embodies a pre-Pauline tradition in which Christ is confessed as one "born of woman, born under the law," whereas the Philippians reading lays stress on the exalted name that God bestowed on the risen Lord. The Gospel text combines both themes: the central role of Mary as the one who pondered the divine mystery in her heart and the circumcision of Jesus as the occasion when he received the holy name.

Numbers 6:22–27

The Aaronic priestly blessing, which has become so much a part of the liturgy in Jewish and Christian worship, sits like a shining gem in a rather mundane context. It is preceded by laws related to the life of the Nazirite and is followed by an account of the elders of Israel bringing their offerings to the newly completed tabernacle. The pericope thus has no indigenous connection with its context. Nonetheless, it presents us with a classic jewel that has nurtured the faith of centuries of worshipers.

Primary among the duties of the priest was the blessing of the community at worship (see Deut. 10:8; 21:5). Generally, the blessing pronounced by the priest was in the name of Yahweh (see Ps. 134), although Psalm 118:26 contains an indication of a blessing that is less direct: "We bless you from the house of the LORD." The latter was probably a statement of welcome announced upon the worshipers.

The unit consists of the Aaronic blessing surrounded by a brief narrative framework. The narrative (6:22) simply but significantly indicates that what follows is a divine speech to Moses. The benediction as a prayer for God's blessing was itself a gift from God. In effect, God tells Moses to instruct Aaron and his sons—that is, all future priests in the line, down to the writer's day—to bless the people of Israel, gives them the words of the blessing, and then (6:27) states the meaning of the act of blessing.

The blessing itself (in vv. 24–26) contains three sentences, each with two parts and each one longer than the one before. The lines increase in number from three to five to seven words. The number of letters in each of these sentences increases from 15 to 20 to 25. The pattern thus builds in a rising crescendo pattern.

The sense of the text is probably best expressed in the NJPSV:

> The Lord bless you and protect you!
> The Lord deal kindly and graciously with you!
> The Lord bestow His favor upon you and grant you peace!

The REB translates so as to add an element of wish or hope: "*May* the LORD bless you. . . ."

Each of the lines refers both to an action of God in the first half—the movement of the Divine toward the people—and its consequence in the second half. God's blessing leads to protection, the Lord's shining face (the divine favor or smile) results in the experience of grace, and the bestowal of divine favor gives peace.

Because the form of address is second person singular, the blessing may apply equally to individuals or the group as a whole. The contents concern God's protection (v. 24), gracious care (v. 25), and gift of peace. "Peace" (shalom) is a comprehensive term, a fitting greeting, that includes wholeness. Priests are to pronounce the blessing, but, as verse 27 expressly states, the Lord is the one who blesses.

What does it mean that by pronouncing the blessing the sons of Aaron thus put the divine name upon Israel? One hardly need stress the importance of names in the Old Testament. When a covenant was made with them, Abram and Sarai were given new names (Gen. 17). After struggling through the night, Jacob was given the new name Israel, but the one with whom he struggled would not reveal his name, for in the name is power (Gen. 32:27–29). Yahweh was to be worshiped at the place where he would choose "to put his name . . ." (Deut. 12:5). To "put the name" of the Lord over the people of Israel is to indicate that they are known, and know themselves by that name. They are thereby identified with this God, and this God with them. In fact, the expression probably denotes ownership by God. Thus the NJPSV translates "Thus they shall link my name with the people of Israel, and I will bless them."

Recently, two small silver plaques, dating from the seventh or sixth century BC, were discovered in a tomb just outside Jerusalem. They contained the words of this priestly blessing. The plaques were probably worn as amulets, which suggests that the wearers took literally the statement "put my name on the Israelites" (v. 27).

Psalm 8

This hymn was composed in praise of God the creator, whose name and handiwork pervade all the earth. This is made evident in the prologue and epilogue verses (vv. 1a, 9). The second person speech—direct address to God—that appears throughout the psalm is unusual in hymns that are normally human speech to a human audience intent on instilling and enriching faith. (Ps. 104 supplies another example of such a second person hymn.) The hymn could have been spoken in worship by the Judean king who, it appears, may have referred to himself circumlocutionarily as "son of man" (v. 4b; see also Pss. 80:17; 144:3), although the NRSV universalizes this reference by translating "mortals" (see NRSV marginal note g).

Two aspects of human existence are highlighted in this psalm. There is, first, the human sense of insignificance when confronted with the awesome reality of the created order. Whoever penned verses 3–4 must have viewed the heavens on some clear, crystal, Palestinian night and wondered, like many of us who have beheld the earth as televised from some silently sailing spaceship, where humans—invisible from such heights—fit into the scheme of things. This is the feeling in the psalm that viewed matters from the human side looking upward.

A second set of anthropological affirmations center on humankind's high status in the created order—"a little less than God" with "dominion over." Humans are thus the intermediates between the heavenly and the nonhuman world. The positions in this psalm should be compared with Genesis 1, the Priestly account of creation. In the latter, humans are made, unlike any other part of the earthly order, in the image of God (1:26) and are granted dominion over the other orders of creation—fish, fowl, and land animals (1:28). As a little lower than God, humans are thus affirmed as related and akin to the divine order. The other side of this affirmation is seen in the role of humans as supreme in the world of creation. Domesticated animals, wild beasts of the field, fowl of the air, and fish in the sea are all seen as subservient and subordinate to the human world. Such a claim and understanding allowed the Israelites, with a sad conscience nonetheless, to slaughter and consume other living beings, only returning the blood (symbolizing life) in sacrifice or burial to God as an apology for killing (see Lev. 17:1–13).

In this psalm there is only a tinge of that anthropological ambivalence that has occupied the thought of philosophers, the concern with humanity's double quality of greatness and depravity. (For the Yahwist, the first human was viewed as a divinely animated clod—Gen. 3—that preserves the twofold quality of human existence.) There is little of that ambivalence one sees, for example, in the description of humankind by the French philosopher-mathematician Blaise Pascal (1623–62): "What a chimera then is man! What a novelty! What a monster, what a chaos, what a contradiction, what a prodigy! Judge of all things, feeble earthworm, depository of truth, a sink of uncertainty and error, the glory and the shame of the universe."

The elevated, exalted state of man in this psalm and its employment of the phrase "son of man" made it possible for the early church to use this text in expounding an understanding of Jesus, who as "Son of Man" reigns over God's order (see Matt. 21:16; 1 Cor. 15:27; Heb. 2:6–9) and bears the name that is above all names (Phil. 2:9).

Galatians 4:4–7

Born of a woman, born under the law." These few words are as close as Paul comes to providing a birth and infancy narrative of Jesus. Yet for all their remarkable compactness, they capture the essence of Luke's birth narrative. "Born of a woman" naturally applies to Mary's giving birth to the Son of God, and it is this phrase that especially commends this epistolary lection for the celebration of New Year's Day as the "Solemnity of Mary, Mother of God." Some scholars believe that the phrase is pre-Pauline and thus stems from the very earliest stages of primitive Christianity. If it is part of a creedal statement, we can see that quite early on Mary was the object of early Christian confession.

If "born of a woman" underscores the humanity of Jesus, "born under the law" underscores his Jewishness. For Paul, this had special significance, for he is concerned to show that precisely because Jesus lived under the Mosaic law he was able to redeem us from the bondage of the law. What Paul says here in shorthand, Luke portrays in narrative form: Jesus is circumcised according to the prescription of the law (Luke 2:21) and brought to the temple for the rite of consecration (Luke 2:22–38). He is the son of parents loyally devoted to life according to the law of Moses (Luke 2:39–51). Just as the first phrase links the epistolary text with the celebration of Mary as the Mother of God, so does this second phrase link directly with the circumcision and naming of Jesus (Luke 2:21).

Homiletically, these two motifs might be explored by showing how the devotion of Mary, as depicted in the Gospel reading, related to the devotion of Jesus. Both have in common their loyalty to the law of God. We are told that she and Joseph were scrupulously loyal, performing "everything required by the law of the Lord" (Luke 2:39). In the same breath, Jesus is portrayed in terms reminiscent of Samuel, the faithful servant of God (1 Sam. 3:19). It would be possible to trace the Lukan portrait of Mary, especially noting her favorable status (in contrast to the Markan portrait) as among those "who hear the word of God and do it" (Luke 8:19–21).

Like mother, like son.

Philippians 2:5–13

If one chooses the Holy Name of Jesus as the focus of attention on New Year's Day, this will be the more appropriate epistolary text since it draws our attention to God's bestowal of the divine name on Jesus.

If this epistolary text is chosen, it provides a strong counterpart to the Gospel reading (Luke 2:15–21), where the name given to the Son of God, according to the angel's prescription, is "Jesus" (Luke 1:31). By contrast, in the epistolary reading the "name that is above every name" (v. 9) is "Lord" (cf. 1 Thess. 1:1). This is the name bestowed on Jesus because of his resurrection (Rom. 1:4); or, in the words of our passage, because "God also highly exalted him" (v. 9). To be sure, it is the "name of Jesus" before which the universe bows in submission, but the heart of the confession is that "Jesus Christ is Lord." We can begin to see the true significance of this ascription if we remember that in the Greek Old Testament Yahweh was commonly designated as Lord. Thus, for Christians to give Jesus this title was to ascribe to him a status normally reserved for Israel's God, Yahweh.

The sequel to this part of the Christ-hymn is well worth exploring in a New Year's Day setting, because it spells out the implications of confessing and submitting to the divine name of Jesus Christ the Lord. Submission to the name implies submissive obedience that is worked out in salvation. It is not, however, the work that we do but the work that God does within us that brings about such obedience. We are reminded that "fear and trembling" accompany God's saving work within us. Not that we become feckless and craven before a vindictive, bloodthirsty God, but that we respect the exalted status and universal dominion of the One we confess as Lord. Such a perspective creates within us a healthy respect for the numinous and holy that prevents us from confessing the name of Jesus blithely and unthinkingly. This day is, after all, a celebration of the *Holy* Name of Jesus. It may be well to call the church to recover this sacred dimension as it launches into a new year.

Luke 2:15–21

The tradition that calls for this special service on January 1 carries with it a double focus, either one of which may be central to the liturgy and sermon for any given year of the lectionary. Primary attention may be given to Mary, or it may be given to the child upon the occasion of circumcision and naming. In either case, it means for the preacher a return to the Lukan text treated earlier as the Gospel (along with John 1:1–14) for the season of Christmas. Only verse 21 is added to the earlier reading. This return will be no strain either on the familiar text or on the preacher's imagination if the special focus on this service is kept in mind. We will here discuss Luke 2:15–21, with attention first upon Mary and then upon the eight-day-old child, leaving to the preacher the choice of accent. For the recovery of the whole narrative (Luke 2:1–20), the reader may wish to review the comments on the Christmas lection.

In Luke 2:15–20, Mary is in the unusual position of hearing from strange visitors, the shepherds, the testimony about her son's significance in God's gracious purpose for "all the people" (v. 10). The shepherds receive from heaven's messenger the good news of a Savior; the shepherds hear the angelic choir; the shepherds are given a sign for confirmation. Mary, the child's mother, hears all this, not directly, but through their testimony—not that there is anything wrong with hearing it the way the whole world receives it (24:47–48; Acts 1:8). But this young mother, in pain, away from home, uncomfortably housed in a stable, would surely have been cheered and encouraged by a brief return of the angel who visited her nine months earlier. Nine months is a long time; in fact, plenty of time to doubt one's own experience, plenty of time to wonder about the adequacy of one's answers to inquiring relatives and friends.

But our quiet wish for Mary is not her own wish. She keeps these things in her heart, pondering, remembering (v. 19). The witness of the shepherds confirms what Gabriel had said (1:26–38) and what her kinswoman Elizabeth had told her (1:39–45). Soon Simeon would add to this testimony, as would Anna, and the child himself at age twelve, causing Mary to ponder further the meaning of all this (2:22–51). Mary was not, however, only a ponderer. She believed God's word and was obedient to it (1:38, 45); she had strong confidence and hope in God (1:46–55); and she became a disciple of her firstborn, joining his other followers in Jerusalem as they prayerfully waited for the Holy Spirit he had promised (Acts 1:5, 14). No fear of an excessive adoration of Mary should blind us to Luke's portrayal of her as a true disciple.

Verse 21 provides the second perspective in today's lesson, the naming of Jesus. Luke, who alone among the Evangelists records this moment in Jesus' life, conveys three messages in the one sentence devoted to it. First, there is the name itself. Jesus is a form of the name Joshua, which means "salvation from Jehovah." Luke has already called Jesus "Savior" (2:11), but it is Matthew who states more directly the choice of the name: "you are to name him Jesus, for he will save his people from their sins" (1:21).

Luke's second point is that the naming of Jesus both fulfills and confirms the word of God delivered by the angel (1:31). To say the word was fulfilled is to acknowledge a pattern of promise/fulfillment very important to Luke both in the Gospel (4:16–21; 24:44) and in Acts (2:17–36). More consistently in Luke than in any other New Testament writer, the theme of continuity between the Old Testament and the New is developed. To say the word of God was confirmed is to say that the event of naming the child Jesus confirmed the divine revelation. The same was true in the case of John. The name was given to Zechariah in a revelation (1:13), and so the child was called John, much to the surprise of relatives and neighbors (1:57–63). Both John and Jesus are of families who hear, believe, and obey the word of God.

And finally, Luke wants it understood that there was nothing about Jesus and his followers that violated the law of Moses. In chapter 2 alone, Luke cites repeated observances of the law: circumcision, dedication at the temple, purification of the mother, journey to Jerusalem at age twelve for the Passover. Luke's Jesus worships regularly in the synagogue (4:16), and following his death, the disciples continue to worship God in the temple (24:53). Jesus and his disciples do not represent a breach of ancient law and covenant but rather continuation and fulfillment of God's gracious purpose as revealed in the law, the prophets, and the writings (24:27, 44–47).

January 1
(When Observed as New Year's Eve or Day)

Ecclesiastes 3:1–13;
Psalm 8;
Revelation 21:1–6*a*;
Matthew 25:31–46

These texts address beautifully but firmly those persons poised on January 1 between the old and the new. The writer of Ecclesiastes is so caught on the cycle of the seasons and the ceaseless turn of time that the only word is to try to live in harmony with time's flow. If passing time brings a sense of futility and diminished worth, the psalmist has an uplifting word about humanity's likeness to God. Matthew reminds his readers that there is such a thing as a radically new life, quite different from the old, and the apocalyptic Seer envisions a radically new created order: "a new heaven . . . a new earth . . . the new Jerusalem."

Ecclesiastes 3:1–13

It is appropriate that one of the lections for the new year be this passage from Ecclesiastes, although in many ways this is a very pessimistic text. But then, of course, so is practically the whole Book of Ecclesiastes.

This text is concerned with time and the proper occasions for doing things and also with the continuously repeated round and routine of human experience and existence. Like the content of this passage, the passing of every old year and the beginning of every new year ought to make us more time-conscious as well as more aware that both time and events have their occasion and their season, and that to act at the proper time is a matter of great insightfulness and is not the consequence of merely moving through life without thought.

The opening verse of this chapter lays out an abstract thesis: everything has its season, and there is a proper time for every matter under the heavens. The wisdom poem that follows in verses 2–8 illustrates the abstract reality by a series of concrete examples. Fourteen pairs of antithetical actions are stated in order to illustrate the general principle. The poem presents life and the routines of existence as occasions for action, though the proper type of action required is neither random nor open. Thus this text views human life as predetermined in many ways. That is, if one is to act successfully, then the timing of the act must meet the real opportunity and need of the occasion. Human action, according to this text, is not a matter of absolute freedom. The success of an action must recognize the limitations placed on the action and the necessity to fit the action to the needs and opportunities of the occasion.

The Old Testament, especially in the wisdom books, stresses the need for word and action to be appropriate to the occasion—the proper action on the proper occasion. Note the following texts:

To make an apt answer is a joy to anyone,
    and a word in season, how good it is! (Proverbs 15:23)

A word fitly spoken is like apples of gold in a setting of silver. (Proverbs 25:11)

Isaiah 28:23–29 emphasizes that in agricultural pursuits one has to perform the right tasks at the proper time. A new year's sermon could build on the theme of the proper time by emphasizing the necessity to correlate actions and occasions so that the two blend together harmoniously. For one to correlate action and occasion to produce that which is most appropriate requires close attention to all the circumstances and a weighing of the consequences of actions on the circumstances. Otherwise one may end up weeping when laughter is called for or dancing when one should be mourning.

The old poem in verses 1–8 appears to have been taken over by the author of Ecclesiastes, who then dialogues with its content by presenting an even more pessimistic reading of the human opportunities that the occasions in life present. Verses 9–13 suggest that God has predetermined everything to such an extent that humans are really rather powerless before the determinations of God. Verse 9 suggests that if things are going to happen in a divinely determined way there is nothing that the doer of an action can do to add anything that makes a difference. God has assigned humans their tasks, "made everything suitable for its time" (v. 11) (or better, "made each thing right for its time"), but humans do not have the capacity to find out what God has done or will be doing. Verse 11 in the NRSV states that God "has put a sense of past and future" into human minds, but they are still incapable of understanding God's doing. The word translated "eternity" in many translations (see RSV) might also be rendered "enigma," "obscurity," "the unknown." The NRSV refers to a sense of past and future. In spite of how one translates the word, the sense is clear: Humans may have inquiring minds, but they do not possess the capacity to understand the activity of God.

In light of this rather pessimistic reading of time and human understanding, the author of Ecclesiastes offers an evaluation or an approach to the situation: The best thing people can do in life is to be happy and enjoy themselves and take pleasure in whatever occupation or toil comes their way. Although such a philosophy produces a rather diminished vision of human achievement, it nonetheless stresses an important factor about life: Happiness and pleasure should be sought and enjoyed amid the toils and occupations of life (see Eccles. 2:24–25; 3:22; 9:7–10; 11:8). Happiness and pleasure are also gifts of God and should be enjoyed wherever they may be found in the normal course of living.

Psalm 8

The contents and emphasis of this lection are almost completely the opposite of Ecclesiastes 3:1–13. The latter presents humanity almost at the mercy of divine determinism. Psalm 8, however, stresses the exalted position of humanity in God's created order, although it too can speak of the human sense of insignificance when confronted with the created universe. Both of these emphases, the greatness and glory of humanity and yet its sense of insignificance when viewed in light of the divine might and majesty and the vastness of the universe, can be combined in a sermon, and the minister can have the two lections dialogue with each other, recognizing the truth in both positions.

Although it is true that Psalm 8 sees humanity in a more exalted status than practically any other biblical text, nonetheless, the focus of the psalm is praise of a God who created the world and conferred on humanity a position of honor and responsibility exceeding that of any other created being. (Note that Eccles. 3:19 declares that humans have no real advantage over animals in that both end up suffering the same fate—death.) This praise of God as the purpose of the psalm can be seen (1) in its hymnic quality, (2) in the fact that it is a hymn directly addressed to the Deity, which is a very rare feature of biblical hymns (for another example, see Ps. 104), and (3) in the use of identical praises in the prelude and the postlude. Thus, what the psalm has to say about both the insignificance and the status of humanity is a way of praising the Deity.

Verses 1b–2 present innumerable problems both to the translator and the exegete, although the sense of the text seems to be that babes and infants recognize and testify to the greatness of God (see Matt. 21:16) and that their testimony puts at rest any enemy or avenger. Babes see the truth that others miss; they have not yet adopted adult perspectives and prejudices.

Verses 3–4 give expression to that universal feeling of humanity's inconsequential status when confronted with the broad sweep of the night skies dotted with the moon and the stars. (One should note that in antiquity, when pollution was so much less and artificial light was nil, the skies at night must have been even more splendid and awesome than they appear today.) Confronted with the lighted canopy of the heavens, humans almost naturally sense their littleness and wonder why God could be concerned for something so small. If the ancients felt this way, how much more insignificant do we moderns feel, who have seen the earth from outer space and are aware of the vastness of the regions beyond our solar system! (With a universe so large, does it ultimately matter if we ordered English peas and instead were served green beans?)

Over against the sense of human insignificance, Psalm 8 affirms the high status of human existence. Humans are created only a little lower than God, who has placed the whole of creation under human dominion. The works of God's hands are placed beneath the feet of humankind. Humanity thus serves as God's vice-regent over the whole of creation. In preaching from Psalm 8, and especially when combined with Ecclesiastes 3:1–13, the preacher could focus on the paradoxical nature and situation of humans in the world. Opposite poles—human lowliness and human heights—are held in tension because both reflect realities of the true situation. Humankind, this mortal creation of insignificance, overshadowed by the vastness of the sky's canopy, nonetheless holds dominion over the whole of the divine creation and shares in the divine dignity.

Revelation 21:1–6a

This text also serves as the epistolary lesson for All Saints' Day for this year, as well as for the Fifth Sunday of Easter in Year C. The reader may want to consult our remarks on this text in these other liturgical settings.

The use of this text in such varied liturgical settings provides an excellent example of how a single passage will be read and heard differently in different contexts. On All Saints' Day, it serves as a reminder of the heavenly hope to which God's people aspire and for which they have lived and died. In the post–Easter Season of Year C, it serves as one of several semicontinuous readings from the Johannine Apocalypse. Bracketed by texts from the same canonical writing on preceding and succeeding Sundays, it will be heard as part of the continuous revelation of John. In its post-Easter setting, its triumphant note will be especially apparent. But heard in the context of New Year's, the same text is bound to evoke yet other responses.

What strikes us first is the recurrent refrain of the new—new heaven, new earth, new Jerusalem—all finally culminating in the bold declaration by the enthroned God: "See, I am making all things new" (v. 5). We are hearing again the voice of Yahweh, who spoke to the disconsolate exiles, urging them: "Do not remember the former things, or consider the things of old," declaring instead, "I am about to do a new thing" (Isa. 43:18–19a). If they felt locked into the slavery of exile and alienation, they are now reminded that God can break through the old and inaugurate the new. Things need not remain as they have been. Dramatic change is possible when God decides to let new shatter old.

Similar sentiments are echoed when Paul declares Christ to be the arena of new creation (2 Cor. 5:17). He too calls attention to this new reality, inviting us to open our eyes: "Everything old has passed away; see, everything has become new!" If Yahweh had broken through Israel's fixation on the past by reminding them of the divine capacity for renewing, Christ now becomes for Paul (and us) the agent of divine renewal. Through him the old era gives way to the new. In this new age, moral renewal is possible: we can now walk in "newness of life" (Rom. 6:4). Conforming our will to the divine will result in a "renewing of the mind" (Rom. 12:2), which doubtless entails both a renewal of the intellect as well as the will. How we think changes along with why we act the way we do. What ultimately matters is not how well religious acts are performed, but whether they are indicative of genuinely moral and spiritual renewal—whether they are expressive of the "new creation" (Gal. 6:15).

To be sure, the vision of the Seer in today's text is an eschatological vision, one of several visions with which the Book of Revelation closes. The collapse of the old order is seen in the passing of heaven and earth, or the world as we know it (v. 1). The vanishing of the earthly order is often depicted in apocalyptic thought as earth, mountains, and sky fleeing away (cf. 6:14; 16:20; 20:11; 2 Pet. 3:7; also Ps. 114:3, 7). Into this cosmic vacuum there descends a new order, the heavenly city of Jerusalem (cf. 3:12; Gal. 4:26; Heb. 11:16; 12:22). With its descent comes the presence of God, radically new in the way it redefines the people of God. The new presence enables the new relationship of which the prophets spoke (Jer. 31:13; Isa. 8:8, 10). To dwell with God is to know God in a radically different way. The pressures, anxieties, and pains of the old order are no more (v. 4).

Even if the vision is eschatological, it is not any less compelling. Is it not the vision of what can be that often forces us to question what is and what has been? It was the future that beckoned the exiles to forget the old and look to the new. It was the Christ-event that shattered the old with the utterly new. It is the hope of a future totally defined by God that shatters our reliance on the past and moves us along toward a new time, a new day.

Matthew 25:31–46

The Gospel reading for today prompts the observance of New Year by reflecting on rather than forgetting the past. The "new" in our text is the new age, the time of final reward and punishment launched by the coming of the Son of Man, who pronounces judgment entirely on the basis of past behavior toward persons in need.

Before looking at this lection, let us locate it in the scheme of Matthew's Gospel. Jesus' apocalyptic speech delivered from the Mount of Olives details the end of the temple, Jerusalem, and this present age, and envisions the coming of the Son of Man (24:1–36). This discourse is followed by a stern call to vigilance in view of the uncertain time of that certain event (vv. 37–44). The call to vigilance is followed by three parables concerning behavior during a possible delay in the Lord's coming: the parable of the slave supervisor (24:45–51, "My master is delayed"), the parable of the ten maidens (25:1–13, "As the bridegroom was delayed"), and the parable of the talents (25:14–30, "After a long time"). At this point Matthew places our reading, as if to say, "But when the Lord does come, late or soon, it will be as follows." With 25:31–46, an account without parallel in the other Gospels, Matthew concludes the public ministry of Jesus.

Matthew 25:31–46 is not a parable but a prophetic vision not unlike the throne scene of Revelation 20:11–15 in which the final judgment occurs. The enthronement of the Son of Man occurs elsewhere in Matthew 19:28, but the uses of Psalm 110:1 (the Lord seated at the right hand of God) are many and varied in the New Testament. In fact, the image in Psalm 110:1 lies at the base of the early Christian confession "Jesus is Lord" (Rom. 10:9; Phil. 2:11), which replaced "Jesus is the Messiah" as the church moved into cultures where a messiah was not expected.

There is no question but that for Matthew the one enthroned in power and glory is Jesus, but the passage draws upon titles from Jewish literature that Christians applied to Jesus. Daniel 7:13–14 provides a scene of one like a son of man coming with the clouds of heaven to be presented before the Ancient of Days, who grants to this one dominion, glory, and kingdom. The image is, as in Matthew, that of a cosmic ruler. The term "Son of Man" shifts to "king" (Zech. 9:9; Ps. 89:18, 27) at verse 34 as well as to "son of God" (implied in "my Father," v. 34). In addition, there is a variation, from Ezekiel 34, of the picture of the shepherd dividing sheep and goats. But regardless of the various sources for the imagery, for Matthew the scene is that of the Parousia, the coming of Jesus as Lord and judge of all people, Jews and Gentiles, church and nonchurch alike.

Several features of the judgment are most striking. First, there is the Lord's identification with the poor, lonely, hungry, sick, and imprisoned (vv. 35–36, 40, 42–43, 45). At Matthew 10:40–42 and 18:5 in the instructions about giving the cup of water and practicing hospitality, Jesus says such activity is ultimately toward himself and toward God. But there is nothing there or elsewhere in the Gospels that approaches the complete identification expressed in "I was hungry . . . , I was thirsty . . . , I was a stranger." Nor is there any indication that the text refers only to the poor and neglected within the church; before him are gathered "all the nations" (v. 32).

A second striking feature of the vision is that judgment is not based on heroic deeds or extraordinary feats but on the simple duties, the occasions for expressing care for other persons that present themselves every day. In fact, some students of Matthew have expressed concern over the absence of major Christian themes such as faith, grace, mercy, and forgiveness. That those matters are important to Jesus and to Matthew is beyond question; they are well documented elsewhere, as in 20:1–16, but not every parable or vision emphasizes every truth. To do so would blur all truth. However, it should be said that the Christian's concern for faith and grace should not replace attention to fundamental human obligations that, as this vision reminds us, are a primary concern of him who is Lord of all people of the earth. One does not cease to be a member of the human race once one joins the church.

A third and final unusual feature of the judgment is that both the blessed and the damned are surprised. Those banished to eternal punishment apparently miscalculated on what it takes to gain eternal bliss. And those rewarded had attended to the needs of others with such naturalness and grace that they were surprised that their behavior received heaven's attention. Saints are always surprised to hear their deeds recounted.

Second Sunday After Christmas Day

Jeremiah 31:7–14 or Sirach 24:1–12;
Psalm 147:12–20 or Wisdom of Solomon 10:15–21;
Ephesians 1:3–14;
John 1:(1–9) 10–18

The preacher will notice that Jeremiah 31 and Psalm 147 are similar in their praise of God's faithfulness in dealing with the weary and scattered people of faith. Ecclesiasticus (or Sirach) 24, Ephesians 1, and John 1 are likewise similar in that all three declare that God's work of redemption and revelation began before creation. The reading from the Wisdom of Solomon links the people of God with wisdom. In Sirach, God revealed, created, and redeemed through Sophia, or Wisdom, and in John through Logos, or the Word. Ephesians agrees, insisting that both Christ and God's plan for our salvation are eternal, not contingent upon the world's favor or opposition.

Jeremiah 31:7–14

In 722 BC, Shalmaneser, the Assyrian king (727–722 BC), and his forces captured Samaria, the Israelite capital city. The town had defended itself against the Assyrian siege for three years even though the Israelite king Hoshea had been imprisoned by the Assyrians before the siege began (see 2 Kings 17:1–6). Obviously, the Israelite population had strongly supported the rebellion from Assyria and saw in their efforts an opportunity to secure national independence.

Shalmaneser died shortly after Samaria was taken. Apparently, with his death the main Assyrian army returned home, where Sargon (722–705 BC) became the new monarch.

In spite of their recent defeat, the Israelites resumed their rebellion and rose up in defiance against the new Assyrian monarch. In an Assyrian cuneiform text uncovered in excavations in the early 1950s, Sargon reports the following about his handling of the old Northern Kingdom of Israel and its capital at Samaria:

> 27,280 people with their chariots and the gods they trust, as spoil I counted, 200 chariots of theirs I included in my army. . . . The city of Samaria I restored, and greater than before I rebuilt it. Peoples of other lands I settled within it; my official as ruler I placed over them; and together with the people of Assyria I counted them.

In this text, Sargon tells of capturing the city and taking away its gods (probably the items associated with religion, such as the sacred calf set up in Samaria; see Hos. 10:5–6). The city was rebuilt, partially resettled with foreigners, and the region became a part of the Assyrian Empire with a military governor.

Sargon claims to have carried over 27,000 Israelites into exile. We don't know if this number included only the males or everyone. If it were only male heads of households, then the number would be three or four times larger. From the beginning of the reign of Tiglath-pileser III (745–727 BC) to the end of the reign of Ashurbanipal (627 BC), over three and a half million persons were deported and exiled by the Assyrians.

Most of us in the Western world of today do not realize the trauma either of being exiled or of watching family and friends being deported and settled elsewhere. Many aging parents in the ancient world watched their children led away and spent the rest of their lives hoping to see them again. Many a caravan that arrived from afar must have been greeted with the hope that loved ones were returning home.

In Jeremiah 30–31, we possess what has been called the prophet's Book of Comfort, two chapters concerned with the return of exiles to their homeland. Jeremiah 31:1–22 speaks of the return from exile of northern Israelites and their renewed life in the land. Even though Jeremiah preached over a hundred years after the exile of the northerners, the hope of return still remained alive.

In verses 7–14, Jeremiah speaks of the assurance that exiles will return and of the nature of their renewed life in the land. Several matters are noteworthy in this text.

1. *Celebration as response.* Jeremiah's audience is called on to celebrate, in advance, the return and restoration of exiles. (Part of the celebration associated with Christmas is celebration in advance, celebration of Easter already at Christmas.) Note the number of verbs emphasizing rejoicing and celebrating in verse 7 (NJPSV):

> Cry out in joy for Jacob,
> Shout at the crossroads of the nations!
> Sing aloud in praise, and say:
> Save, O Lord, Your people
> The remnant of Israel.

2. *The nature of redemption.* In verses 8–9, the extent of the return is noted. Exiles will come from the ends of the earth—the north country and the farthest parts of the world. There will be a great company, even including those whom one would normally not expect on a journey: the lame, the blind, the pregnant, and the newborn (instead of the NRSV's "those with child.") The return will be characterized by weeping (for joy), consolation (or compassion), and a journey eased by refreshing brooks for rest stops and a level road (or straight path) for safe travel.

3. *Proclamation among the nations.* Ephraim's deliverance and return will be proclaimed among the nations of the world. For the Northern Kingdom, Jeremiah uses the old tribal name Ephraim, the region in which the capital was located. Firstborn denotes here "favorite" (see Exod. 4:22). Just as the firstborn who had to be ransomed (see Exod. 13:11–13), so Ephraim would be ransomed and reclaimed from the strong hands of the oppressor who had exiled him. What Jeremiah here proclaims is that Ephraim would be restored to its old status.

4. *The nature of the restored life.* In verses 12–14, Jeremiah describes the conditions that will prevail in the days of salvation to come. (a) Zion/Jerusalem will be the place where even the northerners worship, as in the days of David and Solomon. (b) People will be radiant over the blessings of Yahweh—the grain, wine, oil, and newborn of the flock. The minister, in preaching on this text, should note that the ideal future is not some out-of-this-world, miraculous existence but the return to normalcy. The blessings, however, are received with joy and thanksgiving. (c) Life will be like a watered garden, always productive and bearing. (d) Rejoicing would be characteristic of life. "Then shall maidens dance gaily, / Young men and old alike" (NJPSV). Dancing is taken in the Bible as one of the surest expressions of joy and well-being. (Like exercise, exertive dancing is the natural enemy of depression.) (e) The section closes with Yahweh's promise to reverse the patterns of past existence—mourning to joy, gladness to sorrow. Even the clergy would enjoy "their fill of fatness," for the priests would share in the people's sacrifices that would follow on their receipt of bounty.

Sirach 24:1–12

The Book of Ecclesiasticus (or The Wisdom of Jesus the Son of Sirach) was part of the Bible of the medieval church but was dropped from the canon by Luther and the other reformers. Originally written in Hebrew about 190 BC, the work was translated into Greek for the use of Greek-speaking Jews living in Egypt sometime after 132 BC (see the Prologue to the book). Only portions of the Hebrew text of the book have survived, because it formed no part of the Hebrew canon. Five fragments of the Hebrew text have been recovered from the Genizah (a depository for sacred texts) of a synagogue in Old Cairo in 1896 and following. Since then, a few verses of the text in Hebrew have been discovered among the Dead Sea (or Qumran) Scrolls.

The author of the book lived in Jerusalem (in chapter 50 he described how thrilling it was to watch the high priest Simon perform the liturgy in the Jerusalem temple). He was a schoolteacher who invited the untaught to come and lodge in his school (51:23). His book, a combination of proverbial wisdom (like the Book of Proverbs) and rudimentary philosophy, was written before the wars between the Jews and the Seleucid Greeks created turmoil in Palestine beginning in the mid-170s BC (see 1 and 2 Maccabees).

In this Sunday's lection, wisdom is the central topic. Just as the Prologue to the Gospel of John speaks of the Word (the *logos*), so Sirach speaks of Wisdom (*sophia*). Unlike the *logos*, which is described as masculine in gender and became incarnate in Jesus, *sophia* is feminine in depiction and comes to reside in Israel and Jerusalem. (Later, *sophia* was identified with the Jewish law.) The tendency to describe wisdom as feminine, even alluring and seductive, is already found in the Book of Proverbs (see Prov. 8, which closely parallels Sir. 24).

In 24:1–7, *sophia*, or Wisdom, describes herself as what might be called universal reason, cosmic order, or the sense of existence. She describes herself as the direct product of the Divine, having been immediately spoken into existence (v. 3*a*). Her presence is universal, pervading all things (vv. 3*b*–6*a*) and being found among all people (vv. 6*b*–7). Here, the Hebrew philosopher asserts that the special knowledge possessed by Israel, what may be associated with what Christians call "special revelation," is shared with all other people. All people possess a limited but true knowledge, true wisdom, a knowledge of the Divine and the way the world really is.

In verse 8 following, Wisdom declares that God ordered her to dwell in Israel and to take up residence in Jerusalem. (Some of the rabbis taught that the law sought to reside with many nations but was refused a dwelling place until Israel was willing to receive the divine Torah.) Among Israel, wisdom took root and grew. In verses 12–17, various plants are used to describe this growth, all emphasizing the luxuriance and beauty of the growth.

Psalm 147:12–20

The ancient Greek translation of the Old Testament (the so-called Septuagint) treated Psalm 147 as two psalms. Verses 1–11 were counted as Psalm 146 and verses 12–20 as Psalm 147. (In this version, some psalms that were independent in the Hebrew version were combined and some psalms were separated. This explains the variation in enumeration.) In Roman Catholic texts, this division is still observed.

Modern scholarship often assumes that Psalm 147 is composed of three independent compositions (vv. 1–6, 7–11, and 12–20). The calls to praise in verses 1, 7, and 12 are taken as introducing new units. By merely assuming that the psalm repeats a similar structure three times, however, it is possible to understand the psalm as a single composition.

The lection for today calls on Jerusalem/Zion to offer praise to Yahweh and then offers a variety of reasons for such praise. A series of ten actions of God can be seen in the descriptions: (1) God strengthens the city's defense (v. 13a), (2) gives the city offspring (v. 13b), (3) establishes peace in its borders (v. 14a), (4) provides wheat for food (v. 14b), (5) addresses the world (v. 15), (6) gives snow (v. 16a), (7) scatters frost (v. 16b), (8) makes it sleet (v. 17), (9) sends forth the divine word and melts the ice, snow, frost, and sleet (v. 18), and (10) makes known the word (the law) to Israel (v. 19).

As in the Prologue to the Gospel of John and the text from Sirach 24, the Word/Wisdom is pictured taking up residence in or being revealed in a special way to Israel. Verse 20 affirms the uniqueness of this relationship and knowledge, something granted to no other nation.

Wisdom of Solomon 10:15–21

The Wisdom of Solomon was composed in Greek, probably in the Egyptian city of Alexandria, by a pious Jewish intellectual living in the Diaspora. Its date is uncertain, although the late first century BC has been suggested by many scholars. More philosophical than most of the other wisdom books, it finds its closest parallels in Proverbs 1–9, especially chapter 8.

In The Wisdom of Solomon 10:1–11:4, the examples of eight lives are treated—seven positively and one negatively—to illustrate how wisdom, understood as a female cosmic figure, brought salvation and the good life: Adam (10:1–2), Cain (10:3), Noah (10:4), Abraham (10:5), Lot (10:6–8), Jacob (10:9–12), Joseph (10:13–14), and Moses (10:15–11:4). The last of these biographical vignettes provides the context for this lection.

In this version of the Exodus, it is Wisdom who plays the role of redeemer and guide for the Israelite people. She delivers from oppression, enters the soul of Moses, and performs the task of leading the people from bondage and through the wilderness. Wisdom tends to assume the place occupied by the Deity in the Exodus account of the events. Verse 20, with its reference to "O Lord," suggests that Wisdom and God, however, are not completely identified in this text.

That this book may have been intended for apologetic purposes in defense of Judaism in an alien Hellenistic climate is indicated by two factors. First, Israel is described in extraordinarily glowing terms: a blameless race, a holy people, and the righteous. Second, none of Israel's faults—murmuring, and so forth—that characterize the Exodus account are even referred to in this particular section.

Wisdom in this text, like the Word (*Logos*) in John's prologue, is the guiding, unifying principle emanating from and doing the work of God.

Ephesians 1:3–14

Today's epistolary lection comprises the prayer of blessing with which the epistle to the Ephesians opens. Like other prayers of blessing that serve to introduce New Testament letters (e.g., 2 Cor. 1:3–11; 1 Pet. 1:3–9), it is modeled after the Jewish *Berakah*. The distinctive feature of such prayers is that God is the focal point of attention, the One to whom, and before whom, the petitioner pours out blessings.

What prompts such an outpouring of praise in this prayer is what God has done through Christ—or, more precisely, what God began to do through Christ even before the beginning of time. Far from being an idea on the periphery of God's mind, salvation, or the process of choosing an elect people, is seen here as a central concern of God from the very outset. Looking down the corridor of history, God envisions a people uniquely set apart as the community that would embody the divine hopes and promises. Central to this people's destiny would be God's own Son, Jesus Christ, "the Beloved" (v. 6), the one whose sacrificial blood would dedicate them to God's purpose in the world.

So understood, Christ is seen as the fulfillment of God's divine purposes, the one toward whom God's intentions moved, and finally the one on whom God's hope rests. Thus the prayer blends both christological and ecclesiological elements. Christ and the people of God are closely intertwined, the one embodying the hopes and destiny of the other. It is no surprise that the prayer gives way to such excess of emotion, for Christ is seen in such all-encompassing terms. But this is the language of worship, stemming from the deepest conviction that Christ is not only a personal Savior, but also, in some fundamental sense, the key that unlocks the mystery of God's universe.

If history is viewed as a line, Christ is seen here both as the point from which it begins as well as that toward which it moves. Indeed, the line itself can hardly be construed apart from Christ.

This prayer of blessing is meditation of the highest order and properly belongs here in the liturgical year. If Christmas tends to set us thinking about the incarnation—Christ's coming in the flesh to the world we know and live in—before long we begin to wonder about the primeval origins of this profound conviction. And the perspective of Ephesians is one possibility—the thought that God, all along, had something like this in mind, that it was not an afterthought, and that it somehow encompasses more than me and my world, but all time and history. Yet precisely because it does include the one who is "in Christ," it thereby links us with people of God whom we have neither known nor seen.

John 1:(1–9) 10–18

All of today's readings proclaim God's visiting us with favor, but the Prologue to John's Gospel is of central importance to Christian history, Christian doctrine, and the understanding of the life of faith. The Gospel lesson for Christmas, Third Proper (second additional lesson), was John 1:1–14, and the preacher is referred to those comments for use here, especially if that lection was not treated in a Christmas service. We will here add to the earlier discussion only comments on verses 14–18, which constitute a unit that concludes the Prologue as a literary piece distinct from the narrative beginning at verse 19.

Before proceeding, however, the preacher will want to decide whether to treat verses 1–9 as optional. If John 1:1–14 was used at Christmas, avoiding some repetition would justify exercising such an option. Omitting verses 1–9 would also allow for moving away from the preincarnational work of God's Word (vv. 1–5) and the preparatory work of John the Baptist (vv. 6–8) in order to focus on the incarnation of the Word and its benefits for the world. Or more simply, one might use only verses 10–18 in order to attend to a more manageable portion of Scripture. Some preachers avoid John 1:1–18 altogether because its theological and philosophical sweep of thought is so intimidatingly immense. As stated above, we refer the reader to the earlier treatment of verses 1–14 and here focus only on verses 14–18.

Verses 14–18 make the following three statements:

1. "And the Word *became flesh*" is a christological affirmation of a radical nature with far-reaching implications for our thinking about God, life in the world, and what it means to be Christian. Analogies about changing clothes, as in the stories of a king who wears peasant clothing in order to move among his subjects freely, are not adequate for clarifying John 1:14. The church has always had members who wanted to protect their Christ from John 1:14 with phrases such as "seemed to be," "appeared," and "in many ways was like" flesh. Whatever else John 1:14 means, it does state without question the depth, the intensity, and the pursuit of God's love for the world.

2. John 1:14–18 is a confessional statement. Notice the use of "us" and "we." The eyes of faith have seen God's glory in Jesus of Nazareth, but not everyone has. At the time of this Gospel, the Baptist sect (v. 15) and the synagogue (v. 17) were viable religious groups, and they did not see the glory. Faith hears, sees, and testifies, but faith is not arrogant or imperialistic, as though its view were so obvious as to be embraced by all but the very obstinate. Faith involves a searching (Rabbi, where do you live? 1:38), a response to an offer (Come and see. 1:39), a hunger (14:8), a willingness to obey (7:17). Nothing about Jesus Christ is so publicly apparent as to rob faith of its risk, its choice, and its courage. Faith exists among alternatives.

3. The observation above in no way means that faith must be tentative and quiet about its central affirmation that the God whom no one has seen (v. 18) is both known and available in Jesus Christ. Jesus reveals God (v. 18) and makes God available to us (v. 14) in gracious ways (v. 16). Believing in Jesus is not simply adding another belief to one's belief in God; it is also having one's belief in God modified, clarified, and informed by what is seen in the person and work of Jesus. Jesus' statement "Whoever has seen me has seen the Father" (14:9) does not simply tell us what Jesus is like but what God is like, and to know God is life eternal (17:4).

Epiphany

Isaiah 60:1–6;
Psalm 72:1–7, 10–14;
Ephesians 3:1–12;
Matthew 2:1–12

Matthew's story of the visit of the Magi is the central text for Epiphany, which is the time for commemorating the presentation of Christ to the world. The wealth and power of the nations pay homage to the king. Undoubtedly, one text inspiring Matthew's story was Isaiah 60. Psalm 72, a psalm for a coronation, sustains the royal and triumphant language and was taken by early Christians as applying immediately to Israel's royalty but ultimately to "him who was born king of the Jews." Ephesians 3, although not employing the language of royalty, does affirm that Christ's presentation to the world certainly means the inclusion of all nations in God's purpose through the church.

Isaiah 60:1–6

This text has long held pride of place in the Epiphany Season. Its vivid imagery and dramatic language are echoed throughout the Christmas story.

These verses begin a three-chapter section in Isaiah (60–62) characterized by the unconditional proclamation of salvation. These chapters contrast drastically with the preceding section (56–59) made up of calls to repentance, strong judgments, scathing warnings, and conditional promises. This shift in emphasis has often been taken as evidence that two different authors wrote the two different sections. Probably nothing more is involved than the prophet's sudden shift to the proclamation of God's unconditional mercy for reasons now unknown.

There are three special emphases in this text that can be related to Epiphany. First, there is the call to Zion to arise and shine, coupled with the promise that the glory of God has arisen over the people. Although darkness may cover the earth and its peoples, Zion will shine forth because of the revelation of the glory of Yahweh.

Second, the scattered exiles will return home (v. 4). This motif—the gathering of the scattered, the return of exiles—is a common theme that one finds throughout the ancient Near East and in the Old Testament, but especially in the prophets. From the time Israel and Judah became caught up in the maelstrom of Near Eastern politics—beginning in the ninth century BC—her citizens were carried away to foreign lands. Palestine was located between

Asia to the north, with its civilization centers in Mesopotamia between the Euphrates and Tigris Rivers, and Egypt to the south, with its magnificent cities nestled along the banks of the Nile. Thus the land of Palestine formed a coastal bridge joining two continents with desert to the east and the sea to the west. Wars between these two civilization centers always carried foreign armies through the Israelite homeland. When such wars raged and Israel and Judah became involved, aged parents watched their youth carried away to foreign lands as booty. The hope of the return of those exiled was passed down through history from one generation to another. The prophet here promises the reversal of this old course of history: "Your sons shall come from far away, and your daughters shall be carried on their nurses' arms" (v. 4b). The sight of the returning exiles streaming home is pictured making the city itself radiant and rejoiceful (v. 5a).

Third, not only would the native exiles return but also other nations, foreigners, and their kings would be attracted and come to Zion (vv. 3, 5b–6). In the process, the wealth of the nations would flow to poverty-stricken Zion. The universal aspect of this latter movement is indicated by the geographical references to the sea (the West) and the Arabian kingdoms of the desert (the East). The prophet depicts the wealth of the sea and the exotic exports of the East (gold and frankincense) coming to Zion. Such heavy-laden camel caravans from the East would proclaim the praise of the Lord.

The content of this promise and proclamation of salvation must have been in Matthew's mind when he wrote the story of the visit of the Magi who came to Jerusalem because they had beheld a light in the East. Both this passage of Isaiah and that from Matthew give expression to the significant role that Israel and Jerusalem-Zion had long seen not only as their goal but also as their destiny—to be a light to the nations (see Isa. 2:1–4; 42:6).

Psalm 72:1–7, 10–14

This psalm, which probably was a petitionary prayer of the community employed at the coronation of a king, requests the fulfillment of the aspirations associated with the Davidic monarchs. Like other royal psalms (see Pss. 2; 110), this psalm was written to honor the human king on his accession to the throne but was kept alive even after native kingship had ceased after the fall of Jerusalem. In their preservation and later liturgical use, such psalms were interpreted with reference to the messianic king who would come in the future. The Advent Season for Christians is the time when we confess that the messianic promises witnessed their fulfillment in the birth of the Christ Child.

Verses 8–11 and 15–17 of this psalm embody the central affirmation that finds expression in Epiphany, the manifestation of Jesus to the world. Any legitimate preaching on this text, however, should make clear that the sentiments it contains were first applied to actual Davidic rulers, then reinterpreted in terms of the messiah to come, and finally applied to the birth and epiphany of Jesus.

Although a prayer, this text, like many prayers, contains a lot of preaching; that is, it reminds the ruler of the responsibilities of the royal office. This can be seen in an analysis of the psalm.

This psalm gives expression not only to the status of the king amid the external world of the nations but also to the aspirations and hopes of the people for their benefit through the rule of the king. In addition, the psalm stresses the internal function of the king within Hebrew society.

The psalm opens with a prayer that the king would be given justice and righteousness so that his rule would establish a proper social order that was both just and prosperous (vv. 1–4). The king is here presented as the guarantor of the social order responsible for the operation of justice in the community. As the defender of justice, the king bore a special obligation for the defense of the poor and needy against those who would oppress them.

The close association between the nation's well-being, health, and prosperity and the life and fate of the king appears throughout this psalm. Prayer is made for a long life for the king (v. 5) and for his reign to fall upon the nation like the showers and rain that fall upon the land, rejuvenating the crops (v. 6). Righteousness and peace, which are requested in verse 7, denote the existence of right conditions and the total well-being of the community.

The universal dominion of the Davidic ruler is the theme of verses 8–11. The mythological expressions "from sea to sea" and "from the River to the ends of the earth" are equivalent to saying "the whole world." "The kings of Tarshish and of the isles" were the Mediterranean powers to the west, and Sheba and Seba were the spice- and incense-rich states of South Arabia to the east. Both mythological and historical/geographical references are employed to give comprehensive expression to the universality of the dominion claimed by the Davidic king. The plea to God was that the king would have universal dominion over nations that would be submissive to his rule and lavish in their payment of tribute.

The responsibility of the king to protect and defend the weak members of society is the theme of verses 12–14. There were no laws in ancient Israel requiring the king to protect the rights of those members of society who were open to exploitation by the privileged, wealthy, and oppressive. In fact, the Old Testament legal material dealing with the king is very limited. The only regulations are found in Deuteronomy 17:14–20. Nonetheless, the society placed the king under the moral obligation to defend the defenseless, to aid the needy, and to pity the weak. Moreover, the prophets applied this moral imperative to the whole of Israelite society, demanding justice in social affairs as service to God (see Amos 5:10–15, 24; Isa. 1:12–23). The treatment of the poor, the fatherless, the widows, and the needy was seen as the real test of a society's commitment to divine justice. When the prophet Jeremiah wished to condemn the wicked King Jehoiakim, he did so by pointing to the king's construction of a lavish palace at the expense of the rights of the common man. When he wished to praise the good works of the righteous King Josiah, he did so by noting that this king "judged the cause of the poor and needy" (Jer. 22:13–17).

Ephesians 3:1–12

As early as the fourth century, Epiphany was celebrated in the Western church as a way of commemorating the manifestation of Christ to the Gentiles. Just as the story of the Magi in today's Gospel reading provides in narrative form excellent symbolism for the universal impact of Christ's coming, so does this vital theme of the inclusion of the Gentiles within the church form the central theme of the epistolary text.

Even though the text is generally regarded as pseudo-Pauline, it belongs within the Pauline trajectory of early Christian traditions. The language and imagery are reminiscent of the genuine Pauline letters where Paul uses the term "mystery" not only of the whole Christ-saga (1 Cor. 2:1–13) but also with specific reference to the role of the Gentiles in salvation history (Rom. 9:25). Even so, the term itself is rare in the genuine Pauline Letters, and it becomes far more fully expanded in the Deutero-Pauline letters (cf. e.g., Rom. 16:25–27). In these later Pauline letters, especially in Ephesians, the "mystery hidden for ages" has as its content the message that the Gentiles have been included as part of God's "new humanity." The mystery of Christ revealed to Paul is that "the Gentiles have become fellow heirs, members of the same body, and sharers in the promise in Christ Jesus through the gospel" (v. 6; cf. Eph. 1:19; Col. 1:26–27; 2:2).

Several features of this text are worth noting in this understanding of the Epiphany celebration. First, the inclusion of the Gentiles was part of the initial intention of God: "the plan of the mystery [was] hidden for ages in God" (v. 9). The final unveiling of the mystery came late, but this course of events was part of the "eternal purpose" (v. 11) that was finally realized in Christ.

Second, the inclusion of the Gentiles was an event of truly cosmic significance. Typical of the letter to the Ephesians is the cosmic scale on which the purposes of God are sketched. "The rulers and authorities in the heavenly places" (v. 10) are said to be witnesses to this unfolding of God's church, "the wisdom of God in its rich variety." It is the church universal, not the church local, that is in view in Ephesians. The worldview that is presupposed here is, of course, heavily indebted to Jewish apocalyptic (cf. Eph. 6:10–20), but in the author's time this was not only indigenous to Judeo-Christian thought, but provided one of the most effective sets of symbols through which he could express the universal and cosmic dimensions of the Christ-event.

What it means for the church to be genuinely ecumenical in the sense of our text—Christ's church as the one body in which hostility, alienation, and exclusivism among human beings is absent—is still an unrealized vision. The deeply rooted tradition of celebrating the universality of Christ's manifestation at Epiphany can serve as one more moment in the church's life where the people of God are called into account by the Word of God. Today's text warns us not to narrow this biblical vision of the universal church into a national, racial, regional, or even confessional church.

If one wants to develop this text in this direction, it is possible to appeal to the same warrant in calling for a truly ecumenical church, namely, that it has been God's eternal purpose for there to be "one humanity" in Christ. Today, however, now that the church is essentially Gentile, our task is not to get Jewish Christians to make room for Gentiles, but to get Gentile Christians to make room for Jews. The Jewish-Christian aspect of the modern ecumenical debate has begun to confront squarely some of the issues facing the church as it seeks to define itself and its mission over against other peoples of God, most notably Jews. An abundant literature has begun to be generated and provides excellent resources through which Christian ministers can rethink and clarify their own position even as they invite their churches to become part of this critical reappraisal.

Matthew 2:1–12

Epiphany provides the preacher the occasion for sharing some of the grandest texts of the Bible, for this is the season to declare the manifestation of the divine Son. The revelation is no longer a baby in a manger, no longer a whisper in Bethlehem, but a voice from heaven at Jesus' baptism and the dazzling light of the Transfiguration. Epiphany begins, however, with an even earlier announcement of the glory of the Son of God, the visit of the Magi to Bethlehem (Matt. 2:1–12).

Matthew 2:1–12 is not a birth story. Matthew's birth account is in 1:18–25, and to that story 2:1–12 is not directly tied. "In the time of King Herod, after Jesus was born in Bethlehem of Judea" is a chronological introduction to the cycle of four stories extending through 2:23. These texts are properly treated quite apart from Luke's nativity; trying to conflate Matthew and Luke is more confusing than helpful. The move to Matthew means a shift in the writer's purposes and the theological statements. The shift is dramatic: exit shepherds, enter Wise Men; exit stables, enter palace; exit poverty, enter wealth; exit angels, enter dreams; exit Mary's lullaby, enter Rachel's wail.

Our text, then, is better understood as an announcement story. The emphases in the story are three. First, Christ appears not for Israel alone but for the world. The Wise Men, neither named nor numbered, are probably astrologers and represent for Matthew the fulfillment of Isaiah 60:1–6, which prophesies the pilgrimage of the rulers of the nations to Jerusalem to worship Israel's God, bringing gifts of gold and frankincense. The appearance of the light of God's glory initiates the era of universal worship. In addition, Numbers 24:17 speaks of a star arising out of Jacob, as does the Testament of Levi (18:3). Likewise, Hellenistic literature was not without its stories of heavenly configurations announcing events of great importance. There were available to Matthew and his readers quite sufficient resources for making his declaration that Christ is for the world, to be worshiped by all nations. This Gospel, known for its Jewishness, must not be misunderstood: statements of the universality of the Gospel are frequent (4:15–16; 25:31–46; 28:18–20). In fact, there is not a Gospel that will provide a supporting text for those who wish to be exclusive with reference to race, nationality, or sex.

A second emphasis in Matthew 2:1–12 is that Jesus Christ is the true king of Israel. To develop this theme, Matthew uses Bethlehem (Mic. 5:2) and David (2 Sam. 5:2) materials from the Hebrew Scriptures. One might wonder why the Davidic theme would be developed when it was potentially so troublesome, creating messianic expectations that would obstruct the purposes of Jesus' ministry (22:41–46). However, Matthew wants to establish not only that Jesus is the royal shepherd of Israel (10:6; 15:24), but that his life and work were sufficiently witnessed in Israel's Scriptures to make rejection of him inexcusable.

A third and final emphasis in today's Gospel lesson is the hostility to Jesus and the gospel by the political and religious establishment. The tension is posed early in the account by the references to Herod the king and Jesus the king. To develop this theme, Matthew uses the account of the children (Exod. 2). Stories of old rulers being threatened by the birth of heirs to the throne were common in Matthew's day, but clearly the direct antecedent was the Moses story. This image of a tyrant, jealous and intimidated, screaming death warrants and releasing the sword of government against the innocent to preserve entrenched power, stabs awake the reader and abruptly ends a quiet Lukan Christmas. But Matthew must speak the truth: good news has its enemies. One has but to love to arouse hatred, but to speak the truth to strengthen the network of lies and deception. It is no mystery why One who gave himself to loving the poor and neglected of the earth would be killed; there are institutions and persons who have other plans for the poor and neglected. Of course, no one wants a hassle, much less a clash, but what shall Jesus' followers say and do? The fearful whisper, "Tell the Wise Men to be quiet about the Child."

Baptism of the Lord
(First Sunday After the Epiphany)

Genesis 1:1–5;
Psalm 29;
Acts 19:1–7;
Mark 1:4–11

If baptism is understood as a new beginning, then it is appropriate to look to Genesis 1 as background and perhaps as a source for analogies. Psalm 29, with its vivid portrayal of the union of natural storms with the voice and activity of God, moves the reader closer to the account of Jesus' baptism in Mark 1. That occasion was also one of disturbances in nature as well as a heavenly voice. Acts 19, which serves as the epistle for the day, raises again the thorny issues of John's baptism and the reasons why Jesus submitted himself to it.

Genesis 1:1–5

The selection of this text to be associated with the baptism of Jesus is based on considerations of both imagery and theology. The image of the Spirit of God moving over the waters, God speaking and thus creating, and the reference to the first day remind us, at least in the way of analogies, of many features associated with the baptism of Jesus. Theologically, baptism as new creation can be seen against the original creation. Just as the original act of God inaugurated the first creation, so the baptism of Jesus inaugurated his career, and the baptism of individuals inaugurates their new creation.

When preaching from this text, the minister should realize that its association with baptism is a secondary application made on the basis of imagery and theology; thus one should be willing to inform an audience of such secondary application.

In its primary emphasis and original intention, Genesis 1:1–5 proclaimed the Divine as the creator and all that existed as the created. Thus the world of creation is seen as dependent on the creator and as living and sustained by the continuing power of the Divine.

Some particular features in the theology and content of the text should be noted: (1) the text seems to presuppose that God's primary act is one of formation rather than creation; God gives shape and order to the earth which existed as "a formless void"; out of chaos, God acts and speaks to produce cosmos; (2) the Spirit of God, as in baptism, is given its role to play in the inauguration of creation; (3) the speaking of God calls realities and new conditions into existence; (4) creation is a process of separation and thus the establishment of divinely ordained orders in the world; (5) creation involves naming and thus declaring and identifying that which God has called into being.

Psalm 29

This psalm was probably used in ancient Israelite worship as part of the fall festival, which was both a new year celebration and an occasion anticipating the coming autumn rains. Thus Psalm 29 describes the epiphany and action of God in terms of a storm. Some scholars have suggested that this psalm was borrowed by the Israelites from the Canaanites, who first used it in connection with the worship of their god Baal, who was the lord of the weather and the storm.

The connection of the psalm with the baptism of Jesus is again very secondary and simply draws on some of the imagery of the psalm. The association is based primarily on the constant repetition of the expression "the voice of the Lord," which also has associations with Jesus' baptism.

The primary emphasis in this psalm is the kingship and enthronement of God (see v. 10), which is demonstrated in the coming of the life-refreshing rainstorms on which the ancient Israelites depended. This description of the activity of God reflects the actual path taken by most Palestinian storms. The voice of the Lord (the thunder) upon the waters (vv. 3–4) is reminiscent of the collecting storm clouds out over the Mediterranean Sea. The storm then moves into the Phoenician coastal region with great ferocity, causing the earth to reel and rock (vv. 5–6). The storm moves southward, with its flashing lightning shaking the wilderness of the desert (vv. 7–8) and making the trees shake and tremble (v. 9). The response to God's action in the storm theophany is the response "Glory!" heard in the temple. With the storm as the action of God, it is clear that the Divine sits enthroned over the chaos of the flood waters and is enthroned as king forever. The psalm concludes with a petition that God will strengthen and bless the people with peace (v. 11).

Just as the first storms and rainfall of the autumn made possible the beginning of a new planting and growing season, so the baptism of Jesus makes possible the beginning of new redemptive activity.

Acts 19:1–7

The true significance of the baptism administered by John the Baptist has always been something of an enigma. Was it a completely new practice without precedent, or was it analogous to the Jewish lustrations practiced in first-century Palestine? In looking at the Gospel account of Jesus' baptism, one can ask both historical and theological questions. From a historical perspective, one question is what it actually signified in terms of Jesus' own life and work. Presumably, submitting to John's baptism meant that Jesus himself became one of John's followers. At the theological level, one might ask about its significance in terms of Jesus' messianic status or self-understanding. In second-century Gnostic circles, the baptism of Jesus was regarded as the moment when he became "Son of God" in a real sense. Christ's epiphany was closely identified with this event in his life. Or the stress could fall on other moments in his life as the time or moment when his true divinity became manifest: his birth, his first miracle at Cana, his transfiguration, or his resurrection. Thus the baptism of Jesus came to be understood as an important moment in determining the point where Christ's divinity first became manifest.

One problem faced by the early church concerned the reason Jesus was baptized by John. As this text from Acts indicates, and as the Gospels confirm, John's baptism was a "baptism of repentance" (v. 4). It required a change of heart and life which signified that the person who received such a washing was preparing for the last days. The Gospel accounts, however, also indicate that John saw himself as the messianic forerunner who pointed beyond himself to Jesus as God's designated Messiah. It was Jesus who would truly usher in God's new age, the earmark of which would be the Holy Spirit. Consequently, Christian baptism as it was practiced in the early church was distinguished from John's baptism primarily in this respect—that it brought with it the gift of the Holy Spirit in a way John's baptism did not (Act 2:38).

In Ephesus, when Paul discovered the twelve disciples who had been members of John's movement, he asked them—to determine whether they were aware that the Messianic Age had dawned—if they had received the Holy Spirit. Clearly, they had not, and Paul responded by baptizing them "in the name of the Lord Jesus" (v. 5), after which, through the laying on of his hands, they received the Holy Spirit, spoke in tongues, and prophesied.

In the ancient church, in some areas, Epiphany was the time of the year when converts or catechumenates were baptized. Thus Epiphany became an occasion for double celebration: for remembering the baptism of Jesus and for witnessing the incorporation of new members into the congregation. Accordingly, Epiphany can have a dual focus for Christian reflection and preaching as we think of the significance, first, of Jesus' own baptism, and, second, of our own. How central to Christian life and thought is the baptism of Jesus is attested by the popularity of this event in Christian art. As one reflects on the historical and theological significance of Jesus' own baptism, it becomes an appropriate time for us to reflect on the significance of our own baptism. Similar issues of vocation arise: baptism as an expression of sonship with all the requisite obedience that it entails; repentance as both a point of departure and a continuous style of life for the one who has been incorporated into Christ through baptism; baptism as the time when one's life is intersected by the divine thrust of the Spirit of God, who both signifies, calls to, and enables genuine sonship.

Several homiletical possibilities present themselves as one reflects on this passage from Acts 19:1–7 in the context of the celebration of the baptism of Jesus: first, the relationship between John the Baptist and Jesus as that of prophetic forerunner to the expected messiah; second, significant elements of the baptismal rite that prompt Christian reflection, such as repentance and the Spirit as God's gift to baptized believers; third, the Holy Spirit as the certifying agent of genuine Christian conversion and the ways in which this can manifest itself in the contemporary church.

Mark 1:4–11

For those with the historian's mind in search of the facts about Jesus' life, the baptism of Jesus provides a certainty. This conclusion does not follow because all three Synoptics record it, but because Jesus' being baptized came to be problematic for the church. Why would the Christ, the Son of God, be baptized? Matthew is sensitive to the problem as reflected in John's hesitancy to baptize Jesus (3:14), whereas Luke, without mentioning who baptized Jesus, joins baptism and prayer in a subordinate clause, giving primary attention to the divine witness to Jesus (3:21–22). Later Christian documents glorified the entire scene with bright light and fire over the surface of the water. For Mark, the baptism of Jesus is an epiphany, but the brief account reflects no tension nor does it carry side arguments aimed at detractors. Mark apparently was confident his readers understood that among the baptisms by John, that of Jesus was unique.

Even though our text for today is Mark 1:4–11, we will give attention only to verses 9–11 because this is the account of the baptism proper and because verses 1–8 were discussed in the material for the Second Sunday in Advent. The baptism of Jesus is the second of the three parts of Mark's introduction: the ministry of John (vv. 1–8), the baptism of Jesus (vv. 9–11), and the temptation of Jesus (vv. 12–13). Mark states clearly and briefly that Jesus was baptized by John in the Jordan, but in an accent characteristically Markan, Jesus is identified as a Galilean from Nazareth (1:9; 1:24; 10:47; 14:67; 16:6). Galilee, not Judea, is home, and even after the resurrection, Jesus' disciples were to meet him in Galilee (16:7). Also in Mark, the heavens splitting, the Spirit descending, and the voice from heaven are seen and heard by Jesus alone. The event does not carry, as does Matthew 3:16–17, any public declaration about Jesus. Only Jesus and the reader receive heaven's testimony.

Mark's message here is threefold. First, Jesus' baptism and the beginning of his public life usher in the new age, the eschatological time. The signs are the splitting of the heavens (Isa. 64:1; Ezek. 1:1), the descent of the Spirit (Isa. 11:2; 42:1; 61:1–4), and the voice from heaven (Ps. 2:6–7; Isa. 42:1). The one more powerful than John who would baptize with the Holy Spirit (1:7–8) is here. The plan of God and the experience of Mark and the church join in the testimony that Jesus means a new age. Mark's second message is that Jesus is declared Son of God. Mark has already said so (1:1) and will again (9:2–8; 15:39), but here the expression, which can have any number of meanings (for example, Adam is called son of God in Luke 3:38), is given specific content. The message of the voice from heaven combines Psalm 2:7, which is God's declaration of sonship at the coronation of a king, and Isaiah 42:1, a portion of a description of the Servant of the Lord. By the union of these two very different texts, Jesus as Son of God is portrayed as both sovereign and servant. This is to state in part the third of Mark's emphases in this brief text—the commissioning of Jesus for ministry. In Mark's work, Jesus will be more powerful than John, for in the power of the Holy Spirit he will do battle against demons and all the evil forces that maim, cripple, alienate, and destroy human life. But in him will be no arrogant display of power, for he is the Servant of God whose ministry will take him to the cross.

It is clear, even in Mark's brief record, that the baptism of Jesus was not only an epiphany, a declaration of the Son of God, but was also, by Mark's time, a statement of the church's self-understanding. The church understood that as disciples of Jesus, they were people of the new age. They also had come to associate baptism with the Holy Spirit, a connection apparently widespread in the early church (Acts 2:38; 19:1–7). As the people of the new age, they shared that power made available through Jesus Christ, the Holy Spirit. For all the varieties of interpretations of the Holy Spirit, this gift was the hallmark of the Christian movement. And finally, the church had come to associate baptism and the commission to serve. By baptism, the whole church was called to ministry, the recollection of baptismal vows functioning as a kind of ordination. If Jesus was designated Servant of God and declared concerning himself that he "came not to be served but to serve" (Mark 10:45), then one definition of discipleship was and is unavoidably clear.

Second Sunday After the Epiphany

1 Samuel 3:1–10 (11–20);
Psalm 139:1–6, 13–18;
1 Corinthians 6:12–20;
John 1:43–51

Last Sunday's lections centered on the baptism of Jesus and its implications for Christian baptism. Today we are moved beyond baptism to the life that follows it. The reading from First Samuel relates the call to service that Samuel received. The selections from Psalm 139 acknowledge God's nearness to us as well as God's intimate knowledge of our inmost being. The moral implications of the life of discipleship, or as Paul says, "in Christ," are spelled out in 1 Corinthians 6. The Gospel text presents the witness to Christ by Philip. Those who hear are offered the invitation to trust, to "come and see." Trust responds by "abiding" with him.

1 Samuel 3:1–10 (11–20)

This lection constitutes what might be designated either the infancy narrative about the prophet Samuel or the account of his call into the service of prophecy by God. How Samuel had been conceived by the barren Hannah as a child of promise is told in 1 Samuel 1. As a response to the gift of a child, the mother presented Samuel to the service of God at the temple in Shiloh, then under the care and service of the old priest Eli and his disappointingly decadent sons (see 1 Sam. 2:12–17).

Samuel served in the Shiloh temple under Eli's supervision from the time of his weaning. (Hebrew children were weaned at about the age of three.) His early service was obviously that of a mere functionary during these days, for he "did not yet know the LORD, and the word of the LORD had not yet been revealed to him" (3:7).

Several points are made in this narrative about Samuel, his call, and his message.

1. Samuel's nocturnal call by God was met by an enthusiastic response on the part of the lad. The fact that God calls three times without the source of the call being recognized, that Samuel thinks it is Eli, and that the priest only slowly realizes that it might be God speaking to the lad are all dramatic touches in the story. They are not intended to condemn Eli so much as to illustrate the point made in the opening verse: "The word of the LORD was rare in those days; visions were not widespread." The fact that religion had reached this point made the old priest,

now with eyesight so dim he could not see (another dramatic touch), unexpectant about any word or vision from God. Samuel, even though he does not realize the source of the voice addressing him, responds vigorously offering himself to the priest with a hearty "Here I am" (see Isa. 6:8). Once the source of the voice is known, in God's fourth call, Samuel responds with a promise of a faithful hearing: "Speak, for your servant is listening" (v. 10).

2. The call of Samuel is the inauguration of a new state of affairs in Israel and Shiloh. God announces to the youngster that a new thing is about to be done that will startle everyone when they hear it (v. 11). Thus the prophet becomes the confidant of God, the sharer in the divine determination of events, and the spokesperson of what is about to dawn.

3. The word of God about the future is a word of judgment, a word condemning the house of Eli, and it is Samuel who must be the bearer of the word to those under whose service he has labored (vv. 12–18).

4. The inauguration of Samuel's career was followed by a stage of service in which "the Lord was with him and let none of his words fall to the ground" (v. 19). The fidelity of the prophet involved the hearing and the proclamation of the word even when the word was one of judgment on his own people and colaborers. God supported the work of Samuel by seeing that none of his words fell unfulfilled.

5. Samuel's activity and proclamation established his reputation as a prophet throughout Israel—"from Dan to Beer-sheba"—so that his work brought a reversal of affairs in Israel (compare v. 20 with v. 1). Where vision and word had been rare they now became frequent.

This text has been selected for the Season of Epiphany to illustrate the typological correspondences between Samuel's call, his response, and his nurture in the Lord, and those of Jesus (see Luke 2:52). Like Samuel, Jesus is called and designated as an eschatological prophet to his own people with a message that will establish his reputation and ultimately strike at the temple itself.

Psalm 139:1–6, 13–18

This psalm appears to be a composition produced for use in legal procedures in the temple when an individual was charged, perhaps falsely, with some particular wrong or crime. In Psalm 139, the wrong appears to be some form of idolatry or turning away from Yahweh, the God of Israel. This is suggested by three factors: (1) there is no indication in the psalm of charges about injury or wrong done to humans; (2) the "wicked way" (v. 24), or, in some readings of the Hebrew text, "idolatrous way," suggests apostasy or false worship as the problem; and (3) the plea for action by God in verses 19–24, especially verses 19–22, focuses attention on those who defy God, lift themselves up against God, and hate God, which demonstrates the concern for the proper relationship to the Deity as the focus of the psalm.

The psalm is best understood as the lament of one who feels unduly and falsely accused of infidelity to God. Verses 1–18 speak about the Deity's knowledge of the worshiper, whereas verses 19–24 are a call for God to judge and slay the wicked. Thus the latter verses would have functioned as one's self-curse if the person praying them fit the category of those upon whom the judgment is requested. At the same time, verses 21–22 are also an affirmation of the worshiper's innocence. The worshiper can claim to hate, with a perfect (or utter) hatred, those who hate God. Although such an expression may shock our sophisticated sensibilities, it was a way of expressing devotion to God, championing the divine cause, and placing oneself squarely in God's camp. Under these circumstances, such extravagance in terminology would have been expected in ancient cultures.

Verses 1–8 all speak or confess the knowledge that God has of the human/individual situation. (Note that the entire psalm is human speech to the Divine, that is, prayer.) Verses 1–6 describe the *insight* God has into the life of the individual. Verses 7–12 describe the divine *oversight* that God has of the individual life. Verses 13–18 speak of the divine *foresight* that God has over the person from conception to death. In a way, all these sections seek to say the same thing by approaching the matter from different perspectives or slightly different angles. The reason for such extensive coverage of the topic of God's knowledge of the individual is that the supplicant in the legal case was claiming innocence, and one way to do this was to point to the omniscience of God. Had anything been amiss, were there any infidelity, then the Deity would surely have known and taken action.

The insight that God is said to have into the person in verses 1–5 is expressed in a number of ways, mostly in the form of opposites: sitting down—rising up (inactive—active); inward thoughts—from afar; my path (where I go, my walking)—my lying down (where I rest, my reclining); behind—before. All these are ways of saying that persons in the totality of their behavior are known to God. Even the thought, before it finds expression on the tongue in words, is known (v. 4). The knowledge of God, the psalmist confesses, is a fathomless mystery (v. 6).

Verses 7–12 affirm that there is no escaping the Deity, whose presence (Spirit) knows no limit and who is not subject to the normal conditions of existence. A number of geographical metaphors, again in opposites, are employed to illustrate the point: heaven—Sheol; winds of the morning (to the east)—uttermost parts of the sea (to the western horizon). In all these places, the psalmist says he or she would find God (see Amos 9:2) or be found by God. The psalm, however, not only affirms the all-pervasive knowledge and oversight of God, but also the universal sustaining quality of the Divine—"Your hand shall lead me, and your right hand shall hold me fast" (v. 10).

For the Divine, according to the psalmist, normal conditions do not prevail. Verse 11 makes this point, a point best expressed in the new NJPSV which, following medieval Jewish exegetes, translates: "If I say, 'Surely darkness will conceal me, night will provide me with cover'"; then darkness does not conceal, because for God light and darkness do not determine or set limits regarding knowledge.

Verses 13–18 affirm that from conception until life's end "all things" are known by God. Verse 16 expresses a rather strong note of predestination. The psalmist claims that one's life was known by God like a book even before the first day was lived; at least, the length of one's life was already determined and recorded by God!

1 Corinthians 6:12–20

Shun [sexual] immorality" (RSV, v. 18) aptly states the gist of Paul's exhortation here. Within the young Corinthian church an elite minority of its members were pushing the Pauline theme of "freedom in Christ" beyond its limits. Paul begins by quoting their own slogans: "All things are lawful for me" (v. 12) and "food is meant for the stomach and the stomach for food" (v. 13). The one expresses their permissive, libertine outlook, the other their insistence that eating is a physical act, nothing more.

By extension, these members apparently contended that they had similar license in sexual matters (cf. 1 Cor. 5:1–2; 15:29–34). They could do as they wished with their bodies, they thought, because sexual intercourse, like eating, was a physical activity, nothing more. By making a sharp distinction between the spirit and the body, one could easily stress the importance of the former and the relative unimportance of the latter. One could nourish the spirit but do with the body whatever one pleased, confident that the one did not affect the other.

In response, Paul first insists that "freedom" as the Corinthian "gnostics" understood it was an illusion, for it not only produces behavior that is "not helpful," either to the individual or to the group (cf. 1 Cor. 8), but also produces the opposite effect—it actually results in enslavement (v. 12). Moreover, such a schizophrenic view of the human personality ignores God's sovereignty over all things—spirit and body. The body, by which Paul means the whole human personality, far from being merely physical, is "for the Lord" (v. 13), that is, the risen Lord. Thus Christian existence is only properly understood when defined by the risen Lord; in fact, the "Lord [is] for the body" (v. 13), probably in the sense that the redemptive work of Christ was after all directed toward the individual: "You were bought with a price" (v. 20). The body can hardly be ill esteemed if one considers the full import of the resurrection: just as the Lord was raised, so will all those who have been incorporated into Christ. Our destiny, indissolubly linked with Christ's, involves the whole human personality—"the body."

Another line of response is Paul's reminder of the corporate dimension of Christian existence (vv. 15–20). Three times he uses the phrase "Do you not know . . ." to introduce his instructions. The formula is typically used to introduce familiar, traditional instruction. Thus the Corinthians are being called to remember that which they should have realized already. First, that being "in Christ" has corporate implications. What the Christian does with his or her body directly involves, if not implicates, the other members (v. 15). Second, sexual intercourse with one who has not been declared of "one flesh" according to the biblical understanding of marriage (Gen. 2:24) is not merely a physical activity, but the creation of a new relationship involving the whole person. Union with the Lord results in being "one spirit with him" (v. 17), and this suggests that relationships where persons are involved with each other sexually are to be taken with the utmost seriousness because they extend to and involve the whole human personality. Entangling alliances are created even if one views the relation as casual, particularly when it involves sexual union. Third, the body is not to be understood as radically separate from the spirit, but is to be understood as the very temple of God's Holy Spirit (v. 19). It can never be understood as anything other than a sanctuary serving as a dwelling place for God's own presence.

The cumulative effect of all these reminders is that those "in Christ" are not "their own" in any unqualified sense. "Freedom in Christ" is precisely that: "in Christ." The way this phrase is used by Paul suggests that being incorporated with Christ indissolubly links the Christian with God, Christ, the Spirit, and the community of believers for whom these are all living realities. Individual behavior for those "in Christ" can never be individual per se, for it has theological, ecclesiological, and eschatological dimensions.

Paul's advice here is broadening rather than narrowing, for some Corinthians have viewed both themselves and their behavior in too restricted a sense. They are thus called to redefine their Christian perspective so that it encompasses the whole spectrum of existence "in Christ."

John 1:43–51

The biblical word central to the Season of Epiphany is "revelation," for this is the time to celebrate the revealing of the Son of God. But the companion word to revelation is "witness," for revelation in the biblical sense is never open and obvious to everyone, interested or not, believer or not. There is always about it a kind of radiant obscurity, a concealing that requires faith to grasp the revealing. One is not permitted a controlled, managed, guaranteed, no-risk response to Jesus. Those, therefore, who have beheld the glory become flesh (John 1:14) cannot prove, but they can witness. Witnessing to the revelation does not refer to lengthy self-disclosures, narrating one's feelings in response to the word, but rather to confession of what one has seen and heard. No one understands this better than the author of the Fourth Gospel who, after a prologue announcing the revelation (1:1–18), follows with a series of accounts of witnessing to Jesus Christ (1:19–51).

In the Gospel of John, witnessing to Christ begins with John the Baptist (1:29–34). Verses 19–28 are primarily John's witness about himself, that he is not the Christ. John's testimony causes two of his disciples to follow Jesus (vv. 35–42), and they in turn witness to their friends (vv. 43–51), creating an ever-widening circle of testimony, faith, and further testimony.

Our reading for today belongs, then, to this widening circle of witness and faith—a circle that, as we will see at verse 51, includes the reader of this Gospel. The author has already spoken *for* the community of faith ("we have seen his glory," 1:14), but at the close of this text, he will speak *to* the reader as a member of the community.

The record begins in a clear, straightforward way. The place is Bethsaida in Galilee, and the witness is Philip, having recently been called to faith by Jesus, and the listener is Nathanael. The word to Nathanael is faith's witness to Jesus as the promised Messiah. The response is a reasonable one: the credentials of Jesus hardly qualify him as the one promised by Moses and the prophets as the people's deliverer. Those of us who regularly evaluate strangers by place of origin, residence, family, education, and station should not find Nathanael's response unusual. The invitation to join in faith's inquiry is extended: "Come and see" (v. 46; also 1:39, 46; 4:29; 11:34). Let the preacher notice that witnessing invites, it does not argue or coerce, and certainly does not cartoon or discredit Nathanael's initial doubt. Faith sickens and dies in an atmosphere where doubt is laughed at. Nathanael encounters Jesus' supernatural knowledge and is persuaded. (Recall the Samaritan woman's response to Jesus' special knowledge about her, 4:16–19.)

Nathanael's confession of faith (v. 49) seems too elaborate, too enormous, to have been prompted solely by Jesus' words to him. Clearly, Nathanael is voicing the community's faith. In fact, as "truly an Israelite," Nathanael, who is never mentioned in the lists of Jesus' disciples in the other Gospels and Acts, could be the paradigm of believing Israel, those within Judaism who accepted Jesus as Messiah. Such a view is supported by the identification of Jesus with Jacob (who became Israel) at Bethel (Gen. 28:12). Angels descending and ascending as at Bethel (v. 51) dramatically identify Jesus as the place of God's presence. In him heaven and earth are joined; he is "the gate of heaven." In John's language, the Word made flesh reveals God's glory.

Thus a simple story of a person meeting Jesus is elaborated into a Christian proclamation. Clear evidence of this enlargement is found in the shift to the plural form of "you" in the dominical saying in verse 51: "Very truly, I tell you, you will see." That which began as private conversation is now obviously sermonic: Jesus speaks to all, including the readers. (See the same move from private to public through the shift to the plural "you" in Jesus' conversation with Nicodemus [3:1ff., especially vv. 7, 11, 12].) The observant preacher will find in this form of literary movement (from conversation to proclamation) a pattern of communication that is both effective and congenial to a Gospel that does not pound the listener into a choiceless corner. Notice also that verses 50–51 include the readers, living as they do at a time and place distant from Galilee, within the circle of Jesus' followers. In fact, rather than being at a disadvantage as though they were secondhand believers, the readers (including us) will, because of faith, see even "greater things than these."

Third Sunday After the Epiphany

Jonah 3:1–5, 10;
Psalm 62:5–12;
1 Corinthians 7:29–31;
Mark 1:14–20

All the readings for this Sunday remind the preacher and the church that with the Epiphany of God, whether that takes the form of prophetic call, a prayerful reflection, a pastoral exhortation, or an encounter with the person of Jesus, there comes a radical shift in values and life orientation. Life does not continue the same. Jonah was the instrument of that change in Nineveh. Psalm 62 affirms trust in God and immediately recognizes the transient value of material goods. Paul reminds the Corinthian church that the surpassing worth of Christ relativizes all other values. And when fishermen are called by Jesus of Nazareth, Mark says they left everything behind.

Jonah 3:1–5, 10

The prophetic Book of Jonah differs from all the other prophetic books in that it is primarily a narrative with practically no prophetic proclamation. It is a story about a prophet, his reluctance to preach repentance to the hated Assyrians living in Nineveh, and his final submission to the prophetic task and the subsequent repentance of the Ninevites.

The Book of Jonah is thus best understood as a prophetic legend that has been built around the single reference to a prophet named Jonah. He is said to have prophesied during the days of King Jeroboam II of Israel, who reigned during the first half of the eighth century BC (2 Kings 14:25). Jonah in the legend represents the staunch nationalistic, antiuniversalistic attitude that seems at times to have characterized certain segments of Israelite religion and outlook.

The first part of the book (chaps. 1–2) presents the prophet in his futile and feverish attempt to escape the prophetic task placed on him. The story of the great fish, which so often occupies the attention of preachers to the exclusion of the second half of the book, occurs in this section. The fish story and Jonah's attempt to escape his role emphasize the persistence of God in seeing that the divinely appointed tasks are carried out. Even on the occasion of the second call, Jonah still grudgingly hesitates to fulfill the obligations of the prophetic task. Eventually, however, he goes to Nineveh, whose size is also described in legendary terms. (Excavations at the site of the ancient city have revealed a town about one and a half miles in diameter—not one that would require a three-day journey to cross.) When

83

Jonah proclaims that Nineveh will be overthrown in forty days, the people believe God and manifest signs of remorse—fasting and wearing coarse-clothed garments ("sackcloth"). Both people and beasts share in the attitude (see 3:7–9).

It is interesting to note that it is not only the citizens of Nineveh who repent but also God (v. 10). For us moderns, references to God's repentance strike us as incompatible with the divine nature. The Old Testament, however, was quite willing to speak of the divine change of mind, as in this text (see Amos 7:1–4).

This lection from Jonah presents him as a type or an antitype to Jesus. Jesus is said to have compared the Son of Man (himself) to Jonah as a sign of the judgment of God. Unlike Jonah, Jesus appears as a willing proclaimer of the kingdom of God and judgment, but both Jonah and Jesus are representative of the prophetic call to repentance.

Psalm 62:5–12

This reading has been selected for the lectionary because it manifests confidence and hope in God, the proper response to the call to both repentance and discipleship. In addition, the reading stresses the fact that God requites persons according to their work, that is, according to their obedience and the character of their discipleship.

The homiletician should realize that this section of the psalm has a very complicated structure in that it contains a confessional statement of the worshiper (vv. 5–7), a call to others to trust in God (v. 8), proclamation about the delusive character of human wealth and prestige over against the power and stability of God (vv. 9–11), and finally an address to the Deity that affirms God's fidelity both in love and in just rewards (v. 12).

The psalm exudes confidence in God, who is described as a rock, salvation, a fortress, and a mighty rock, all images suggesting refuge and protection. Having such protection, especially against one's enemies and the slander of gossip (vv. 3–4), allows the psalmist to possess hope and to pledge loyalty in spite of all circumstances.

This confidence theme can be better understood in light of the possible original usage of the psalm. The text sounds very much like psalms that were prayed in a temple ritual in which a person had been falsely accused. Whenever a court case or charge could not be proven because of lack of evidence or failure of the elders to reach a verdict, the parties could appeal their case to the temple priests and thus to God (see Exod. 22:7–8; Deut. 17:8–13; 1 Kings 8:31–32). The other party in this psalm seems to be referred to in verses 3–4. The parties in the case could express their confidence in the outcome by reciting such psalms as this one. Frequently, the priests may have been able to determine if one was guilty or innocent of the charge. If they could not, then the parties could swear their innocence in an oath or self-imprecation. The confidence in this psalm suggests that the worshiper, although having been charged, was certain of his or her relationship to the Deity and that the charge was a falsehood (see v. 4). The worshipers with such certainty in their innocence could throw themselves upon the Divine and claim the Deity as their place of refuge and the hope of their salvation. The psalmist also denounces confidence in human status and wealth, declaring low and high estates to be worthless when placed in the balances and weighed before God—"they are together lighter than a breath" (v. 9). Neither extortion nor robbery (do these reflect something of the charge brought against the psalmist?) is an object of hope, and riches should not be the object of one's ambitions. This suggests, in light of the preaching of repentance and the call to discipleship, that people must place everything humanly materialistic in its proper place in order to confront and answer the call to be a true follower.

The minister can use verse 11 in the context of the Christian year and the exposition of Jesus' call of the disciples. The proclamation of God's power to fulfill the promises involved in the call to service has been heard, the psalmist declares, more than once, and the message is always the same—"power belongs to God." Faithful hearing and following mean trusting in God's steadfast love and knowing that the task undertaken will be rewarded because God requites according to one's work (v. 12).

1 Corinthians 7:29–31

One of the first questions to be decided regarding this pericope is its limits. Strictly speaking, verses 29–31 are a self-contained unit, although the New Revised Standard Version combines them with the paragraph begun in verse 25. The Revised English Bible and the New Jerusalem Bible, however, conform to the latest edition of the Greek text and print them as a separate paragraph.

Verses 29–31 occur in the very heart of Paul's extended treatment of marriage in 1 Corinthians 7. They are crucial to Paul's remarks in the chapter as a whole for setting the eschatological framework in which his instructions are given. They make clear that the Corinthians' questions concerning marriage, about which they have written him (v. 1), were directly related to their eschatological expectations. Anxiety about the imminence of Christ's coming had widespread effects within the church. For those already married, it raised the question whether they should suspend or modify the normal demands of marriage (vv. 1–7). The unmarried wondered whether they should enter new relationships that, by their very nature, would divert their attention from spiritual matters and preparation for the Parousia (vv. 25–28, 32–35).

Broadly speaking, Paul's advice throughout the chapter is for the Corinthian Christians, whatever their marital status, to remain as they are. Each group addressed within the chapter is advised to remain as it is , if at all possible, primarily because of the unsettling conditions expected to precede the Eschaton. Such advice is eschatologically motivated: "the time we live in will not last long" (v. 29, REB); "this world as we know it is passing away" (v. 31, NJB). Here, of course, it is clear that Paul shares the early Christian expectation of the speedy return of the Lord (cf. 1 Cor. 16:22).

What is especially significant to notice about verses 29–31 is Paul's insistence that this overarching eschatological viewpoint relativizes the way we relate to ordinary human activities. Domestic priorities shift: "Those who have wives should live as though they had none" (v. 29, NJB). Personal human emotions are no longer absolute: "Those who mourn [should live] as though they were not mourning; those who enjoy life as though they did not enjoy it" (v. 30, NJB). Commercial and economic activity is likewise understood in a new way: "Those who have been buying property as though they had no possessions" (v. 30b, NJB). In short, one's stance toward "the world" is now redefined because God's purpose is much broader: "Those who are involved with the world [should live] as though they were people not engrossed in it" (v. 31, NJB).

What Paul is calling for here is the same type of sober reevaluation that instinctively occurs when we face a genuine crisis, particularly one that is sudden and unexpected. If our child is suddenly struck with some mystifying paralysis, our whole life routine suddenly halts. What

were previously pressing engagements immediately become postponable as we reorient ourselves to the truly life-demanding needs at hand. Nothing engages us in the same way until
the crisis is met, and once it is over, there is inevitably the residual effect of the reevaluation.
As we pick up where we left off, we usually do so resolving to live with a new set of priorities.

Viewed one way, Paul's remarks here are radically world-denying. They could easily be
taken to mean that Christians should suspend all normal activity as they prepare for Christ's
return. That he was so misunderstood is clear, as is the fact that this is not what he meant
(cf. 2 Thess. 3:6–13). They key phrase in verses 29–31 is "as though . . . not." Ordinary
activities continue as we await the Parousia: we continue to marry, weep, and rejoice, buy
and sell, and deal with the world; but we do none of these "as though" they were ultimate
ends in themselves. They are now seen as good and worthwhile activities of penultimate
value. They are properly viewed when set within the context of the transitoriness of this age
and properly valued when set over against a future that belongs ultimately to God. We can
live "now" seriously but not obsessively; we can look forward to the "not yet" confidently, but
not naively.

Mark 1:14–20

Before considering our text for today, three preliminary comments to the preacher might
be helpful. First, if last Sunday's sermon was based on the Gospel lesson, John 1:43–51,
the listeners may need some help in handling the shift to Mark 1:14–20. According to
Mark, Jesus began his ministry in Galilee, following John's imprisonment, and his first disciples
were fishermen of Galilee. This would be an appropriate time to make brief but clear remarks
about the integrity of each Gospel's purpose and perspective and the problems created by ho-
mogenizing them into one life of Jesus. Second, because today's lesson concerns the launching
of Jesus' ministry, one will be tempted to draw much supporting and clarifying material from
later chapters in Mark. However, Mark is the primary Gospel this year, and many more occasions for messages from Mark will be provided. Rather than stealing from the future, why not do
what Mark does? Invite the listeners to move with Jesus "on the way," asking and learning as
they go. And third, let the fact that this is an Epiphany text be the magnet that gathers the
several subthemes that entice us down sermonic side roads.

Mark 1:14–20 consists of two parts: verses 14–15 are pivotal, making transition from the
introduction (vv. 1–13) and providing a summary description of Jesus' public ministry; verses
16–20 give a concrete example of commitment to the word and work of Jesus. Having been
tested by Satan and empowered by the Spirit (vv. 12–13), Jesus begins his public ministry. By
stating without explanation that John had been arrested, Mark assumes that the reader knows
what he himself will relate later (6:17–29). The first image of Jesus is that of preacher, one of
Mark's three favorite portraits of him, teacher and exorcist being the other two. Jesus' message is that now is the fullness of time (Gal. 4:4); now is God's time, and the kingdom of God
has come near. (It is impossible from word study alone to know whether "has come near"
means "here" or "near." Both meanings are possible, for the kingdom is both present and future according to the Gospels.) The background for the idea of God's kingdom or God's rule
lies in Judaism. The reference is to the total reign of God (Isa. 52:7; Ps. 45:6; 103:19),
whether through the processes of historical events or as a divine interruption of history.
When history was so oppressive as to say no to the rule of God, hope remained tenacious and
said yes to God's sovereign rule as an act from above, breaking in upon history. Those who

heard Jesus' announcement of the presence of the kingdom were to repent of false assumptions and wrongdoing, turning toward God with full trust in the good news.

The second unit of our lesson, verses 16–20, is a concrete case of believing response. Jesus preaches the gospel and calls for disciples. The story is so brief as to be called "telescoped"; that is, an event that may have transpired over a longer period is presented as swift and complete. The fact is, Mark gives no details as to what might have been telescoped, and the absence of details makes the story even more vivid. The call of these four disciples is a call of crisp radicality. Discipleship means leaving property and family, says Mark. In the words of Martin Luther, followers of Jesus "let goods and kindred go."

In order to achieve focus on Mark 1:14–20, one must ask, In what sense is this an Epiphany text? Several answers are possible, all related to the appearance of Jesus in public as preacher and caller of disciples. But not to be overlooked is the expression "The time is fulfilled" (v. 15). In the New Testament are two words for time. One is *chronos*, from which we get chronology and which speaks of years and months and days, of calendars and clocks. The other word is *kairos*, which calls attention to a special time, an opportune time, a time in which the constellation of factors creates an unusually significant moment. In the Fourth Gospel, Jesus speaks often of his "hour": his hour has not come, his hour has come, now is the hour to be glorified. Such is the sense of Mark 1:15. Whatever the year or month or day; wherever the place; whoever may be in control or under control; suddenly or slowly, noisily or quietly, God acts, Jesus appears, and it is *kairos*. In today's reading from Jonah, Nineveh knew it; in the reading from First Corinthians, Paul knew it. In fact, everyone who hears and believes the good news experiences this kind of time.

Fourth Sunday After the Epiphany

Deuteronomy 18:15–20;
Psalm 111;
1 Corinthians 8:1–13;
Mark 1:21–28

Today's lections present us with an array of ways that God is among us, finally coming to expression in Jesus Christ. Psalm 111 recites the activities of God that Christians associate with the activities of Jesus. Deuteronomy 18 speaks of a prophet arising from among the people, a prophet Christians identified as Jesus. Paul writes to the Corinthians about the role of the living Christ in the church to create love, patience, unity, and humility. Finally, the Gospel of Mark presents Jesus in two roles not only prominent in Mark but also sometimes joined as two aspects of one ministry: the teacher and the exorcist.

Deuteronomy 18:15–20

The Book of Deuteronomy, composed of Moses' farewell address or addresses to the Hebrews just before they moved across the Jordan River, outlined for the people the ways of obedience and warned against disobedience in their new life in the Land of Promise. The book was thus concerned with the future and the shape that the future would take.

One element in that future is expressed in today's lection, namely, the coming of a prophet like Moses. The prophet noted in the text—"like me from among your own people"—it is generally assumed, refers to the line of prophets that appeared throughout the subsequent history of Israel and Judah. Thus it referred more to the office of prophet and the succession to that office than to a particular prophet per se. One, however, should not rule out that some specific prophet, like Hosea, may have been referred to. The prophetic task described in this text is multifold: (1) the prophet stands between God and the people, just as Moses stood between the assembly and God at the giving of the law at Horeb (probably another name for Mt. Sinai); the prophet is thus one "who stands between"; (2) the prophet is the one to whom the divine will is revealed, the one in whose mouth God's words are put; and (3) the prophet is also the proclaimer of the word of God to the people. The faithful prophet like Moses is thus the mediator between God and humankind, the recipient of divine revelation, and the proclaimer of that which has been revealed. As such a figure, the prophet can speak and act with divine authorization and authority. Verse 19 declares that when the prophet proclaims what God has revealed, then the prophet has fulfilled the major prophetic task. Once this proclamation has taken place, it becomes a matter between God and whoever would not heed the divine words. The text, finally, has Moses warn about the false prophet—whoever speaks a word not commanded by God or whoever speaks in the name of other gods. The false prophet, as noted elsewhere in Deuteronomy (see 13:1–5), is placed under the penalty of death.

In its original implication, the text on the prophet like unto Moses probably was intended to point to the succession of prophetic spokespersons who appeared throughout Israelite history. Deuteronomy 34:10–12, however, argues that as a prophet no one was Moses' equal, neither in terms of the relationship between God and the prophet nor in terms of the great signs and wonders that he performed. Perhaps Deuteronomy 34:10–12 represents a later interpretation of Moses' prophetic role than Deuteronomy 18:15–20.

At any rate, the text about a prophet like unto Moses came to be understood as the prediction of a single coming prophetic figure who would appear before the end of time, or the coming of the messiah. The Qumran community, which produced the Dead Sea Scrolls, for example, expected the figure mentioned in Deuteronomy 18:15–20 to be a herald of the coming eschatological kingdom of God.

The features associated with Moses throughout the Old Testament present a broad picture of his activities—much broader in fact than that of any normal prophet. Moses is pictured as the redemptive leader from Egyptian bondage, as a miracle worker, as a person of authority, as a lawgiver, and as the founder of Israelite religion. Thus to be a prophet like Moses involved an expanded number of roles and functions.

In the Gospel lesson for today, one sees Jesus not only acting as the spokesman who teaches with authority but also as one who carries out redemptive activity, that is, as a prophet like Moses of old.

Psalm 111

This psalm is a thanksgiving psalm, although its content is primarily a hymn of praise. In ancient Israelite worship, the individual or community offered thanksgiving after some calamity had passed or after a rescue from some state of distress. As a rule, thanksgiving psalms generally contain more material that is addressed to a human audience than is addressed directly to the Deity. Thanksgiving psalms were, therefore, a way of offering one's testimony. This, of course, is the exact opposite of the lament psalms, which fundamentally contain only address to the Deity. Thanksgiving psalms were thus primarily intended for the worshiping audience more than for the Deity. Psalm 111, although setting out to give thanks to the Lord, contains no direct address to God.

That this psalm was used in a context of thanksgiving is clear from the opening verse, as is the fact that the thanksgiving was offered in public worship—"in the company of the upright, in the congregation." The psalm, unlike most thanksgivings, contains no reference to the distress from which the one offering thanks may have been saved or to any special reason for offering thanks.

In fact, what we have in the psalm, following the opening verse, is a hymn of praise extolling the works of God and the divine fidelity to the covenant. That a thanksgiving takes the form of a hymn should not surprise us.

The works of God singled out in the psalm for praise are declared both worthy of study and of remembrance (vv. 2–4). The works or acts of God are seen as the deeds of Israel's sacred history. Three special acts are recalled. There is, first, the giving of food for those who fear the Divine (v. 5). This verse seems to allude, although not with absolute certainty, to the protection and care for Israel in the wilderness when the people were fed with quails and manna (see Exod. 16:13–35). Second, God displayed great power in giving the Israelites the land of Canaan as "the heritage of the nations" (v. 6). Finally, there is reference throughout the psalm to the covenant that was given at Sinai (see vv. 5, 7–9). The twofold stress of verse 9 emphasizes both the redemption of God and the commands of the covenant. Or we could say that the psalmist is declaring that in the redemptive acts of the past and in the commands of the covenant, one possesses the means to study and remember in obedience the works and ways of God (vv. 2, 4). Such study should lead to the fear of God, which is the beginning of wisdom (v. 10).

In the Christian tradition, the incarnation, celebrated in the birth of Jesus, is a mighty work of God, but it is also a work that demands our study and remembrance as well as obedient responsiveness. Acts of salvation must be responded to, and just as those acts in behalf of ancient Israel were viewed as obligating Israel to faithful obedience, so the act of God in Christ obligates the Christian to a life of fidelity.

1 Corinthians 8:1–13

The issues discussed in this single chapter are basically similar to those raised in Paul's earlier discussion in 1 Corinthians 6:12–20, treated earlier in the epistolary reading for the Second Sunday After the Epiphany. The immediate topic for discussion is "food sacrificed to idols" (8:1), another question about which the Corinthians had written Paul. His response actually encompasses chapters 8, 9, and 10, and our text for today is the first part of that response. He returns to these issues specifically in 10:23–30.

Again, one group within the Corinthian church, best understood as an intellectualist minority, was pushing Paul's view of "freedom in Christ" too far (cf. v. 9). Because of their insistence that they could conduct themselves in a radically individualistic fashion, the morale of the whole church was being affected adversely. Paul's ultimate concern is to see that the corporate strength of the church is built up and that the strong become more sensitive to the common good of the whole rather than pushing their individual rights too far.

Paul quotes slogans that were apparently being used and bandied about within the church: "all of us possess knowledge" (v. 1); "no idol in the world really exists" (v. 4a); "there is no God but one" (v. 4b). In each of these, "knowledge" (v. 1b) is the key word and the underlying attitude giving rise to the problematic position.

With respect to the question of food laws, it is clear that those "in the know" had no particular scruples about food laws. Even if meat bought in a butcher's shop had been previously used in a pagan sacrifice, because their theology was intact (they believed in only one God and knew that idols were not gods but lifeless objects) they could eat it with a clear conscience. And, if they could, why could not everyone else who had made the Christian confession in God, the Father, and Christ, the Lord (v. 6)?

This was precisely the problem, however. Knowledge does not automatically produce consideration; in fact, quite often it leads the one "in the know" to become impatient with the one "not in the know." The inevitable effect within a group is debilitating, with those "in the know" adopting a supercilious stance toward those less gifted and less privileged.

Paul thus opens his remarks by placing knowledge within the demands of love: "Knowledge puffs up, but love builds up" (v. 1b). What is more, knowledge is so often self-deceiving and illusory (note, in v. 2, "anyone who claims to know . . ."), and Paul thus reminds his readers that true knowledge consists in recognizing our ignorance. After all, one does not "know God" but is known by God, that is, if there is room at all in the heart for love (v. 3). Paul thus insists that the Corinthians must cease to think of knowledge as the only absolute good. In the church, it must coexist with love.

The latter part of Paul's remarks is directed toward reminding his readers that there are various levels of Christian maturity. The fact is, within every Christian group are those who understand, and perhaps even confess, the Christian creed theoretically, but practically they are far from having resolved all the implications this has for them. Pagans recently converted to Christianity required a socialization process through which the ways and means of their new life-style could be constructively assimilated, and this inevitably took time. Paul's advice, essentially, is that Christian knowledge must be tempered by Christian concern for one's brother and sister. Above all, this will require one to think less of one's own knowledge and individual freedom in Christ and think more of others' lack of knowledge and one's responsibility to behave so that genuine edification of the whole congregation occurs. Adopting such a stance will inevitably mean that the Christian imposes self-restraints, and does so willingly, but Paul saw this as a small price to pay for the sake of a weaker companion in Christ (v. 13).

Mark 1:21–28

Thus far during this Epiphany Season, Jesus has been revealed as King of the Jews, Son of God, Lamb of God, Messiah, a preacher, and one who calls disciples. In today's Gospel lesson, Jesus is presented as teacher and exorcist. The text does contain a new title, Holy One of God (v. 24), but it is spoken by a demon who is commanded to be silent. A demon speaking the truth is still a demon.

Mark 1:21–28 relates the second of six episodes (1:16–39) by which Mark presents the nature of Jesus' ministry. Although the six events are independent of one another, they have been arranged almost as "a day in the life of Jesus." The text before us is obviously a distinct unit, with verses 21 and 28 providing a typical opening and closing to a story. The account itself, however, is clearly a compound of two stories, one centering on Jesus teaching in the synagogue and the other on an exorcism. Notice that verses 21–22 present Jesus as teacher, and verse 27 resumes that focus, the crowds being amazed at the authority of his teaching. In between (vv. 23–26) is an account of an exorcism, but strikingly that which amazes the crowd is the power of Jesus' teaching. It is not uncommon in Mark to have split stories; that is, one story begins, another episode related but unrelated is told, and then the original story is concluded. Recall, for example, Jesus going to Jairus's house, healing the woman with the blood flow, then continuing on to Jairus's house where he raises the daughter (5:21–34); or the cursing of the fig tree, cleansing the temple, and then finding the fig tree withered (11:12–26). Obviously, verses 21–28 are similarly structured, for reasons we will explore below.

That Jesus was an exorcist all the Gospels except John testify. For Mark, it was a centrally important portrayal of Jesus. This was not because exorcizing demons made Jesus unique; other exorcists were at work (Matt. 12:27; Luke 11:19). Nor was Jesus' method of exorcism different from the usual pattern. Accounts of exorcisms usually began with the demon's recognition of the exorcist, the command to come out of the one possessed, the loud and demonstrative departure of the demon, and the amazement of the spectators. What is most striking in this text is Mark's setting the story of expelling an unclean spirit in the context of Jesus' teaching. Quite clearly, the exorcism is told to illustrate the power of Jesus' teaching (v. 27).

Given the brevity of Mark, the references to Jesus as teacher are more frequent than in Matthew or Luke. And what is most noticeable is the use of the term in connection with miracles: the teacher stills a storm (4:38), the teacher raises a dead girl (5:35), the teacher feeds the hungry crowd (6:34), the teacher cures an epileptic (9:17), the teacher curses a fig tree (11:21). It is not so much the content of Jesus' teaching that Mark wishes to stress. When Matthew says that Jesus taught with authority (7:28–29), the reader is given large blocks of that teaching (chapters 5–7), but in Mark 1:22, essentially the same expression occurs but with no indication of what Jesus said. This is not to say that teaching content is totally absent in Mark; chapter 4 is devoted to Jesus' parables. Rather, it is to say that for this Evangelist, the primary emphasis is on the power of Jesus' teaching.

John the Baptist called Jesus "the more powerful one" (v. 7), and Jesus himself referred to his mission as entering Satan's house and binding him (3:27). Jesus is the strong Son of God who has entered a world in which the forces of evil (Satan and demons) are crippling, alienating, distorting, and destroying life. According to Mark, the powers that seek to sabotage God's creating and caring work not only cause disease but also disturb the natural elements (4:37–39) and even insinuate themselves into the circle of Jesus' closest friends (8:33). But with Jesus comes the word of power to heal, to help, to give life, and to restore. In Mark, a battle is joined between good and evil, truth and falsehood, life and death, God and Satan. And sometimes, says Mark, the contest is waged in the synagogue! Even the structures of religion may house forces that oppose the gospel.

The preacher will, of course, need to locate and identify the forms and strategies of evil equivalent to the first-century demons. No service is rendered simply by announcing that we no longer believe in demons. Although that is true for most, not believing in demons has hardly eradicated evil in our world.

Fifth Sunday After the Epiphany

Isaiah 40:21–31;
Psalm 147:1–11, 20c;
1 Corinthians 9:16–23;
Mark 1:29–39

Even though the time of Epiphany, the time of divine revelation to the world, is not far behind us, the lessons today remind us of another dimension of life and of the Scriptures—divine concealment. Some experiences, even to the faithful, are difficult to understand. In the context of wonder at God's majesty, Isaiah 40 marvels that God's way is hidden, and the psalmist praises the God who made all things and cares for the nameless and forgotten of the earth. Paul engages the Corinthians in a discussion of servitude and freedom that is very difficult to follow, and Mark punctuates his account of Jesus' ministry with one of many statements about the secrecy of Jesus and the confusion of his disciples.

Isaiah 40:21–31

The controlling message of Second Isaiah (Isaiah 40–55) is the good news of the end of the Babylonian Exile. He proclaims over and over that the Judeans who live in the foreign nation are about to be released and allowed to return home. But that central proclamation rests on a strong theological foundation, the prophetic poet's confidence in both the power and the gracious will of Yahweh, who alone deserves to be called God. That theological foundation is articulated in today's lesson primarily in terms of the theme of God as creator of the world.

The section of which these verses are a part (40:12–31) follows the prophet's initial announcement of the end of the Exile and the return of God's people across the wilderness to their land (40:1–11). Graphic spatial images ("the nations are like a drop from a bucket . . . the isles like fine dust"; 40:15) and striking rhetorical figures communicate unbounded confidence in the ruler of creation. Frequently, the style is almost hymnic, praising God by describing him as the one who is over all the world (vv. 22–23).

The style and structure of our passage are dominated by questions, mainly rhetorical questions. As rhetorical questions, they both make assertions, for they assume answers, and lay the foundation for the responses that follow. Mainly, these questions are addressed directly to the audience, originally the dispirited Judean captives in Babylon, the "you" of verses 21, 25, 27, and 28. In the first section (vv. 21–24), the meaning of the questions (v. 21) is not clear until the answer is given. What is it that the audience has not known, that is, that they have or should have known from the beginning? Answer: that the one who sits above the circle of the earth—that is, the one over all space—is also the one who brings down princes and rulers—that is, is ruler over historical events (v. 23). Indeed, before the Lord, they—that is, the rulers—are like stubble before the wind (v. 24).

The second section (vv. 25–26) also begins with rhetorical questions. "To whom then will you compare me, or who is my equal?" means that the Lord is incomparable, without equal. But the question is answered, first with a command to look to the heavens, then with another rhetorical question ("Who created these?"), and then with an assertion of God's creation and control of the hosts of heaven. Given Second Isaiah's location in Babylon, there is an edge of polemic in these lines. Are the stars, identified in Babylon with divinities, comparable to Yahweh? By no means, for Yahweh created them and calls them out to their appointed places every night. Though they can hardly be counted, the Lord knows them all by name.

The third section (vv. 27–31) begins with an actual question addressed to Israel's sense of the absence of God. Why do the people say that Yahweh is unaware of their plight ("My way is hidden from the LORD") or that God ignores their just cause ("my right")? But this is also a rhetorical question asserting that the people are mistaken. Its response begins with the repetition of the questions of verse 21 ("Have you not known? Have you not heard?") followed by assertions and promises. The assertions move from the cosmic to the personal. Yahweh is the everlasting God, the creator of the whole earth who never tires and whose understanding is beyond human comprehension (v. 28). This same one "gives power to the faint, and strengthens the powerless." Then the promises draw the conclusion for the people of God, for those who now are saying that they have been abandoned by God:

> Those who wait for the LORD shall renew their strength,
>   they shall mount up with wings like eagles,
> they shall run and not be weary,
>   they shall walk and not faint. (v. 31)

To "wait for the Lord" is to have confidence, or faith, in the sense of committing oneself to God in hopeful expectation. (See Isa. 8:16–18 and cf. Exod. 14:14; Isa. 7:9.) The passage as a whole amounts to an argument that the dispirited and despondent exiles have good reason to be hopeful. The one who calls them to freedom is the God who created the earth, who calls out the stars, whose strength knows no limits, and who gives that strength to the faint and the powerless, giving those who wait for God the power to fly.

Psalm 147:1–11, 20c

This psalm is a hymn of praise about Yahweh and the great acts of the Divine. In many ways, the psalm's intention is to declare not only that God is concerned with and acts in great and universal ways but also that the fate of the weak and insignificant are of ultimate concern as well. The one who is ruler of the world is also the one who is redeemer of the weak. The one who puts the stars in their places and gives them their names is the one who stoops to care for the "nameless," those who are known only by the conditions that plague them. The Divine, whose concern with those issues transcends human hurts and heartaches, is also immanent to those in need.

The Lord who builds up Jerusalem and returns the exiles, and thus cares for and ensures the national life of the people, is also the one who heals the brokenhearted and binds up their wounds (vv. 2–3). The one numbering and naming and thus controlling the stars of the heavens is also the one who lifts the downtrodden and topples the wicked to the ground (vv. 4–6). The point this psalm is stressing is the mutuality that exists between God's power and God's concern. There is no clash between God's control of the universe and the divine compassion for the weak and the underprivileged.

The downtrodden and the brokenhearted in this psalm probably do not refer to people who were at the bottom of the economic and social totem pole in ancient Israel. There was nothing wrong with such a position in Israel's stratified social structure, for most people probably were content, during most periods, to retain the status that birth imposed on them. The downtrodden, brokenhearted, and others were probably those who had suffered some sudden calamity or catastrophe that upset the equilibrium of their lives. Thus the assurance that Yahweh aids these groups is an assurance of concern for those struck by disaster.

The same polarity of divine concern is illustrated in the fact that the same God who controls the weather and rain and makes vegetation grow—the major events in the agricultural year—is also the one who cares for the beasts and the young ravens (vv. 8–9).

Two emotions are most significant for the Deity and evoke the greatest divine pleasure—fear of the Divine (that is, obeying the will of the Deity) and hope in the Deity's steadfast love (v. 11). Fear and hope elicit more pleasure than the strength of horses or men (v. 10).

To stress fear and hope, like seeing the law as the greatest gift to Israel (vv. 12–20), is to stress characteristics that one might otherwise think insignificant. How important are the fear and hope of individuals over against the God whose very word of command regulates the universal order? The psalmist does not make explicit why Yahweh finds such pleasure in these qualities, though one might conclude that their intrinsic value lies in the fact that they are human responses that cannot be the product of divine coercion or the consequence of divine action in the world of nature. They are human responses, human gifts given to God.

The assurance that God aids the powerless and cares for those caught in the web of calamity and takes pleasure in those who fear and hope means that life and its worthwhileness are not postulated on possessing power, or strength, or wealth, but on inner disposition.

1 Corinthians 9:16–23

There is a sense in which Paul states in these verses the fundamental principle underlying the various instructions he gives throughout chapters 8–10. This should be stressed, because chapter 9 is often regarded as a digression within this larger discussion. It should rather be seen as fully integral to this discussion. Also worth noticing is the fact that all of chapter 9 is couched in an autobiographical mode. The first person is prominent throughout, and it becomes clear that Paul is adducing his own apostolic conduct as exemplary for the Corinthian church to follow. If there is any doubt that he is offering himself as a paradigm for their behavior, this is removed by looking at 10:31–11:1, the concluding section of the entire discussion with the final reminder, "Be imitators of me, as I am of Christ."

Immediately being discussed is Paul's own view of his apostolic charge to preach the gospel—his apostleship, in other words (cf. vv. 1–2). Through an elaborate set of arguments in verses 3–14, he shows that by all rights and privileges he was entitled to certain inalienable rights as an apostle, chief among these being the right to receive pay for his services. As incontestable as this right was, he had relinquished it for a higher principle: "we have not made use of this right" (to receive pay) to keep from putting an "obstacle in the way of the gospel of Christ" (v. 12).

More important than the particulars of Paul's financial situation—how he supported himself and why—is the underlying motivation for his action. This he spells out in verses 19–23, which are the heart of the pericope.

Paul's remarks are introduced with the freedom/slavery paradox so central to his thought: Christian freedom actually means becoming a slave. He then sketches what appear to be four different groups with whom he was involved during his apostolic ministry: the Jews, probably non-Christian Jews; those under the law, probably Christian Jews; those outside the law, probably non-Christian Gentiles; and the weak, probably Gentile Christians. By being willing to relinquish his human freedom, he had been able to accommodate to these various groups in order to relate the gospel to them. To the final group, however, he had especially accommodated himself. (Note that to each of the first three groups he became "as" each one of them; to the final group he actually became weak.)

But we must ask what fundamental point Paul is making in these remarks. Is it that he is versatile and accommodating, able to adjust his ministerial life-style to fit any set of circumstances? Or is it that relating to each group, because of its different demands and viewpoints, has inevitably cost him some of his freedom? It appears to be the latter. To be sure, such willingness to impose limits on his own freedom has caused him to be flexible, but this seems to be the secondary, not the primary, point.

This line of interpretation is further reinforced by the following paragraph, where Paul introduces the illustration of the athlete in training. The whole point here is that in order to achieve one's ends, one engages in self-discipline, quite often rigorous, and this inevitably entails "self-control" (v. 25).

It is Paul's own willingness to impose limits on his own freedom, to relinquish his own inalienable rights, to deny his own needs, that is in view here. Or, as he summarizes in 10:33, he conducts his apostolic ministry "not seeking my own advantage, but that of many, that they may be saved."

Paul's hope is that the Christian community at Corinth will find his conduct exemplary and will seek to translate his own personal ethic into a congregational life-style. To do so would inevitably mean that the strong would be willing to bear the burdens of the weak, that those "in the know" would be more tolerant of those "not in the know," and that those more practiced and experienced in religious matters would be more patient with those whose conversion to Christianity is their first real exposure to the regimen and ritual of a religion with high ethical demands.

Mark 1:29–39

The Gospel lessons for Epiphany have been thus far quite open and clear in their announcements of who Jesus was and what he was doing. After all, that is what Epiphany means: manifestation or revelation. But today's text, Mark 1:29–39, introduces what seems to be a countertheme—concealment. Actually, the idea of secrecy or silence about Jesus appeared in the Gospel lesson last week in Jesus' rebuke of a demon who identified Jesus as the Holy One of God. "Be silent," Jesus ordered, and expelled the spirit

(v. 25). Because insistence on concealment grows into a larger factor in the narrative, it produces curiosity and confusion in Jesus' followers, then and now. Jesus' call for secrecy and the disciples' inability to understand are two of the most striking characteristics of this Gospel.

The preacher may be inclined not to treat the Gospel reading in the sermon today for reasons quite apart from any internal difficulties. In the first place, the fact that Mark 1:29–39 is not a single unit creates homiletical problems. The text consists of four small units containing enough references to different times and places to indicate that Mark has joined four episodes with very little editorial cement. The first story is the healing of Simon's mother-in-law (vv. 29–31); the second concerns healings and exorcisms at sundown (vv. 32–34); the third deals with Jesus praying alone in the early morning (vv. 35–38); and the last is a summary comment about a Galilee-wide itinerary, preaching and expelling demons (v. 39). In the second place, these stories, although different from previous ones (vv. 14–28), actually reveal little that is new about Jesus' identity and ministry. However, after careful reading one finds in this text Mark's introduction of the two themes mentioned in the opening paragraph above. Because those themes will continue throughout this Gospel, no preacher can spend these many weeks in Mark and avoid them.

As Mark has arranged the episodes in our text, they move in this fashion: Jesus becomes extremely popular with the Galileans, Jesus responds to that popularity, and the disciples respond to Jesus. Time and time again Mark calls attention to the growing fame of Jesus: "At once his fame began to spread throughout the surrounding region of Galilee" (v. 28); "the whole city was gathered around the door" (v. 33); "Everyone is searching for you" (v. 37); "Jesus could no longer go into a town openly, but stayed out in the country; and people came to him from every quarter" (v. 45). Some once-popular "Life of Jesus" books called this period "Galilean Spring" in contrast to the later "Jerusalem Winter."

How did Jesus respond to this fame? How was he able to continue to minister to as many as possible and yet not be seduced by popularity? Mark gives four clues. First, according to Mark's arrangement of the stories, scenes of ministry to crowds are followed by scenes of Jesus in private. Notice: verses 21–28, public; verses 29–31, private; verses 32–34, public; verses 35–38, private; verses 39–45, public; 2:1, private. This public-private pattern may say something not only about Jesus' willingness to serve but also about his need for physical and spiritual recovery. Second, Jesus spends time alone in prayer (v. 35). His disciples see no reason to interrupt a popular tour with retreat and prayer, but to that matter we will return shortly. Third, Jesus moves on to minister to those who have not heard rather than to return to the applause of former ministries (v. 38). And fourth, Jesus sought to silence those who would publicize his name and deeds. This call for silence was given to demons (1:25, 34; 3:12), to those whom he healed (1:44; 5:43; 7:36; 8:26), and to his disciples (8:30; 9:9). To say Jesus was using "reverse psychology," knowing that a prohibition to speak would produce the opposite result, is a woefully inadequate explanation of Mark's portrayal of Jesus. Those who have traveled on the way with Jesus to Golgotha and the empty tomb know that for Mark, the confession of faith in Jesus that is complete and acceptable is at the cross (15:39). The confession of only one person who takes up the cross to follow Jesus means more than the compliments of one thousand pushing and shoving in Galilee.

But the disciples do not understand. The first clue to their lack of understanding, which will eventually lead to such confusion and fear as to cause them to abandon Jesus (14:50), is given in 1:35–38. Jesus was at prayer in a deserted place. This "deserted place" sends the reader's mind back to 1:12–13, where Jesus is described as being tested in the desert (wilderness). This sudden popularity could offer for him a new kind of test. Simon and others hunted for him (literally, "chased him down"), found him, and interrupted with what they thought was good news—we have a big crowd waiting. In Mark, "searching" for Jesus usually refers to the efforts of those who would distract him (3:32; 8:11) or oppose him (11:18; 12:12; 14:1, 11, 55). The disciples were correct; there was a crowd, and that is all they saw or wanted to see. They did not understand that there are seekers, and there are seekers.

Sixth Sunday After the Epiphany

2 Kings 5:1–14;
Psalm 30;
1 Corinthians 9:24–27;
Mark 1:40–45

The Gospel lection for today is Mark's account of Jesus healing a leper. Understandably, this story has attracted the account in Second Kings of the healing of Naaman, a leper. As an appropriate response, Psalm 30 praises God as one who heals and restores life. Paul's autobiographical statement in 1 Corinthians 9 is a bit distant from the other readings but joins them in referring to one's physical condition as an integral part of one's spiritual well-being.

2 Kings 5:1–14

This well-known story of Elisha and Naaman provides an Old Testament narrative parallel to the Gospel reading. Before examining the Naaman story more closely, two general factors should be noted.

First, the Elisha cycle of stories (2 Kings 2:1–8:6) and thus the career of this prophet seem to belong better with the events in Israelite history associated with King Jehu and his successors rather than with King Ahab. Presently, the stories are placed before Jehu becomes king. If we move these stories from the period of Ahab to the time of the rule of Jehu, then 2 Kings 2:1–8:6 would fit into the context of 2 Kings 10:32 and following, and Elijah would be the prophet in the stories of 2 Kings 8:7–15 and 9:1–10. There are several reasons for shifting these stories. Among the more important are the following: (1) the reign of Ahab was one when Israel was strong, whereas during Elisha's times, Israel was very weak (as the country was under Jehu and his son Jehoahaz); (2) the prophets were not cooperative with the Israelite monarch while Ahab was king, yet Elisha is shown in close cooperation with the Israelite king (see 2 Kings 3 and 8:1–6); and (3) Israelite-Syrian relations reflected in the Elisha stories are best understood against the historical background of about 843 BC following or, that is, after Jehu became king.

Second, the Hebrew term that denotes the illness of Naaman has been translated as "leprosy" but does not refer to the disease today called leprosy (see NRSV marginal note j). Leprosy (or Hansen's disease) was apparently not present in Palestine in Old Testament times and probably not in New Testament times either. The Hebrew term for the illness (*sarath*) referred to a broad range of skin and fungus infections but not Hansen's disease. That *sarath*, which is discussed in Leviticus 13–14, does not indicate leprosy is suggested by several factors.

1. Descriptions of *sarath* indicate that the sufferer was expected to recover. Leviticus 14 contains directions for purification of the healed sufferer. Hansen's disease, or leprosy, has of course been incurable.

2. Even clothes and houses could have *sarath* (see Lev. 13:47–59) or some type of fungus or mildew infection.

3. Human skeletons unearthed in archaeological excavations in Palestine do not indicate the presence of Hansen's disease. Hansen's disease was called elephantiasis in ancient times. In the Middle Ages, *lepra*, the Greek term used to translate *sarath*, also came to be used for elephantiasis, and this produced the confusion.

The story of Naaman's healing develops through the course of several scenes.

1. After verse 1 sets the stage by identifying the central character, the scene shifts to the Israelite maiden (vv. 2–3). The Israelite girl, a captive subjected to menial house duties in a foreign land, stands as a contrast to Naaman, the powerful general.

2. In scene two (vv. 4–5), the Syrian administration turns the proposed journey to Samaria (note that Elisha is "the" prophet of Samaria in v. 3) into a major production: royal commissioning of the trip, an advance letter to set the stage, and enough gifts to have financed a hospital.

3. In scene three (vv. 6–7), the letter arrives for the king of Israel, who thinks he is the one to heal Naaman. Of course, the Israelite king at the time was the weakest of monarchs and no doubt was the butt of many stories. As a vassal to Syria, he was a weakling who could exercise no power. Thus his response to the letter probably was intended to produce laughter when the story was told to Israelite audiences.

4. Again, it is the person at the periphery—this time, Elisha—who is the real representative of power in the story. In this scene (vv. 8–12), the Syrian general becomes the humiliated one. Expecting his cure to be a showcase extravaganza, he is treated instead to a visit from a subordinate messenger and the order to dip himself seven times in the Jordan. His response is that there are better rivers in Syria than the muddy old Jordan. The hearer of this story could realize the point: maybe Syria has better rivers than Israel, but Israel has something better—namely, its God.

5. In this last scene (vv. 13–14), it is again the lowly and the peripheral—the servants of the great one—who talk the master into obedience. Seven dunks in the river Jordan and Naaman emerged cleansed.

Psalm 30

This psalm of thanksgiving was originally composed for use in a worship service celebrating a worshiper's having been healed from some life-threatening illness. As a thanksgiving song, it calls upon the audience accompanying the worshiper (family, friends, fellow villagers) to join in the celebration (v. 4) and to listen to the testimony and preaching of the one healed (vv. 5–6).

Verses 1–3 spell out part of the experience undergone by the worshiper. As usual, the sickness/healing are described in very general categories because the psalm would have been employed on numerous occasions for different persons with different conditions of illness involved. Sheol and Pit in verse 3 refer to the realm of the dead. Here they do not mean that the individual died but are used metaphorically. To be subject to any form of sickness was already to be in the grip of Sheol, to be under the power of death. Weakness in life could be spoken of as being under the power of death. The verbs speaking of the rescue—"drawn me up," "healed," "brought up," "restored"—also use spatial images. These factors allowed such psalms as Psalm 30 to be used in the early church when talking about the resurrection (note the use of Ps. 16:8–11 in Acts 2:25–28).

The verses for this lection contain a call to fellow participants to join in the festivities of the thanksgiving celebration. Verse 6 seems to imply that the worshiper had gone through a phrase of life unconcerned with the Deity. This would have been in a period when things were prospering well and before the onset of trouble (see Deut. 8:11–20). If this is the case, one may assume that this attitude was one the worshiper was warning against. "Don't be as I was"—assuming that nothing could threaten life's prosperity. This may be said to be the anthropological lesson, what the case shows about human nature. The second lesson is theological, having to do with the character of God (v. 5). God's anger may be bitter and the reality of divine punishment strong, but these are transitory. It is divine favor and goodwill that are lasting. Tomorrow and the dawn can bring a new day. (This last description is probably based on the fact that worshipers spent the night in the temple and were given divine oracles in conjunction with the morning sacrifice.) This same imagery has impressed itself indelibly in the Christian vocabulary as a consequence of the Easter story.

Verses 7–12 of the psalm are direct address to the Deity—a thanksgiving prayer perhaps offered in conjunction with a thanksgiving sacrifice. As in most thanksgiving psalms, the speaker or psalm-user rehearses the "before" conditions and then what happened. That is, the psalm contains a statement of the distress from which one was saved and sometimes, as in verses 8–10, a summary of the prayer offered at the time of the sickness. The substance of these verses reflects something of a plea bargaining—the worshiper suggests that nothing was to be gained by his death; in fact, it would result in a loss to the Deity, namely, the loss of a faithful worshiper who could no longer offer praise to God in the dust of death.

The "after" vocabulary dominates in verses 11–12. Sackcloth and mourning have been replaced with dancing and gladness. The tears of nightfall have been replaced with the joy that comes in the morning.

1 Corinthians 9:24–27

In today's epistolary reading, two athletic images are prominent: the runner and the boxer. They form a fitting conclusion to chapter 9, in which Paul has spoken of his self-restraint as an apostle.

The question of eating sacrificial meats (1 Cor. 8:1) had exposed certain flaws in the corporate life of the Corinthian church. The "strong" were secure in their "knowledge" (1 Cor. 8:1), but were less practiced in "love" (1 Cor. 8:1–3). They were apparently more accustomed to answering to their own yearnings for individual expression than responding to the needs of weaker Christians. Consequently, in his earlier remarks Paul urges a corporate ethic in which members think less of their individual freedom and more of the common good

(1 Cor. 8:9). To reinforce this form of exhortation, Paul adduces his own apostolic behavior as an example for the Corinthians to follow. Specifically, he was entitled to receive pay for his work as an apostle (1 Cor. 9:3–12), but he had chosen consistently to relinquish this right (1 Cor. 9:12–18). It was a clear case of giving up an "inalienable right" for the sake of the gospel. His hope was that his own practice in this respect would serve as an example for the Corinthians.

It was typical practice among Greco-Roman moralists to provide both positive and negative examples to reinforce their ethical teachings. Thus, along with his own apostolic behavior as a positive example, Paul introduces Israel as a negative example (1 Cor. 10:1–13). Whereas he exemplified self-restraint, Israel exemplified self-indulgence.

But before discussing Israel, Paul concludes his discussion of his own apostolic self-restraint with an everyday illustration drawn from the world of athletics (1 Cor. 9:24–27). The images of the runner and the boxer are introduced as familiar images: "At the games, as you know . . ." (v. 24, REB). They are especially appropriate, given the prominence of the Isthmian games in the vicinity of Corinth. For centuries, Corinthians had witnessed these biennial games that had made runners and boxers, along with orators, dramatists, and poets, familiar figures participating in the festivals.

But one need not have been an inhabitant of Corinth to grasp the significance of these images. They were well publicized throughout the empire, both through artistic depictions and popular speech. Not surprisingly, they become common metaphors in the New Testament. Paul pursues the "not yet" of the resurrection faith as a runner "straining forward to what lies ahead . . . [pressing] on toward the goal for the prize" (Phil. 3:13–14; cf. 1 Tim. 1:18; cf. also Heb. 12:1). "Fight[ing] the good fight" (1 Tim. 1:18; 6:12; 2 Tim. 4:7) recalls the images of the boxer or wrestler. We are thus urged to "contend [earnestly] for the faith" (Jude 3).

In today's text, Paul is reminding us of the obvious: many compete, but one wins (v. 24). Rather than despairing of the competition, we are urged to "run to win" (v. 25, REB). The motivation is not a "fading garland" (v. 25, REB). This may recall the practice, apparently distinctive at the Isthmian games, of rewarding the winners with a wreath of withered celery, as opposed to the fresh, green wreaths that were used at other games, such as the Olympian games. An unfading wreath, by contrast, awaits the Christian athlete who hopes for the eschatological crown of life (cf. 2 Tim. 2:5; 4:8; 1 Pet. 5:4; James 1:12; Rev. 2:10; 3:11).

But the main point of today's text seems to lie elsewhere—the need for "strict training" (v. 25; *egkrateia*). The fundamental notion here is self-control, the capacity to impose limits on ourselves for the sake of a higher, nobler good. It is an attribute that is counted among the Christian virtues (Gal. 5:23; 2 Pet. 1:6), a worthy topic of preaching deemed attractive to pagans (Acts 24:25), and sufficiently important to be a qualification for an elder in the church (Titus 1:8). This point is elaborated toward the end of our passage as Paul insists that he is no shadow boxer. Rather, he bruises his own body, "bring[ing] it under strict control" (v. 27, REB). The athlete willingly inflicts pain for the sake of self-discipline, knowing that a life without any restraints will lead to softness and in the end to rejection.

The effect of this set of athletic images is to call us to a life of discipline in which we impose restraints on our behavior for the sake of a higher good. In this case, the higher good is the good of the congregation, the people of God. What is needed is the capacity to relinquish certain "freedoms," which by all rights are ours but which may not necessarily be edifying to the whole church.

Mark 1:40–45

Mark's story of Jesus healing a leper is shared by both Matthew (8:2–4) and Luke (5:12–16), both of whom have it in briefer form. Luke also has an account of Jesus healing ten lepers (17:11–19). Mark locates the event quite early; it is the last in a series of six vignettes (1:16–45) in which Mark shows the nature of Jesus' ministry, its location, its power, and its public impact. Jesus is a preacher, a teacher, an exorcist, and a healer. But the reader is not, like the crowds, to be caught in a spell of undifferentiated amazement. Rather, the reader is to ask, What is it really that Jesus is doing?

Last Sunday's lection ended with Jesus on a ministry tour of Galilee. Apparently, during that tour the healing of the leper occurred. Luke says he was in one of the cities (5:12). Lepers—although they were required to distance themselves (Luke 17:12) from others, crying, "Unclean, unclean!"—tended to gather near centers of population in order to collect alms. As outcasts, they were not permitted in places of employment. (For the Jewish regulations about leprosy and lepers, cf. Lev. 13–14.) Apparently, leprosy designated a number of skin diseases ranging from serious to nonserious. Even clothes and houses contracted leprosy, possibly a kind of mildew or rot. At any rate, for one to show signs of having this disease meant that one was ritually and religiously unclean, not allowed in places of worship. One was also socially ostracized—separated from family, friends, and all public life. The economic effects were, of course, devastating, because all business and employment ceased. The leper was a corpse haunting the edges of the community he could no longer enter.

So desperate is the leper in Mark's story that he crosses the distance that he should observe and approaches Jesus (v. 40). Directly or indirectly he has come to the belief that Jesus has the power to heal him. The only barrier is "If you *choose*" (v. 40). The preacher may want to note the difference between "if you choose" here and "if you are able" at Mark 9:23. Jesus responds quite differently to the two approaches. In the healing, Jesus touched the leper, putting him at risk of having to join the leper colony himself. This is important for understanding Jesus' ministry and that of those who would continue his work. Jesus did not minister long distance, safe from all that plagued the lives of those he would help. His work of forgiving brought him in contact with sinners; his work of lifting placed him among the fallen; his words of encouragement were given among the hopeless; his healing put him with the diseased; his giving new life took him to the tomb.

That Jesus healed the man meant more than a change in skin texture. The domestic, social, religious, and economic effects are immediately evident.

No preacher will want to treat this as an isolated miracle, as a private blessing, as another "Jesus and I" story. The fabric of healthy relationships is mended. Jesus has struck a blow at one of the forces that cripples, alienates, and destroys human life. To reduce the ministry of Jesus and the ministry of the church to some inner change in the soul is just that, a reduction.

Following the healing, the leper is given two instructions. First, be quiet about what happened. This is not a case of Jesus using reverse psychology in an effort to advertise his ministry. Jesus wants no publicity; he wants people to come to faith understanding who he is and what he is about. He is not seeking to be a star, known for relieving people of burdens and difficulties. All the way to the cross Jesus will be trying to get those who think "where the messiah is, there is no misery" to accept a new perspective—"where there is misery, there is the messiah."

The second instruction is to follow the requirements of the law and go through the ritual of restoration with the priest (v. 44; Lev. 14:2–32). Disregarding law and tradition does not in itself prove that one is a new person.

That the healed man could not contain the news of his restoration should not be viewed harshly. In retrospect, one wonders if the Christian cause might not be better served if only those who had something significant to report were allowed to speak, all others keeping quiet. But it must be said that the man's broadcasting had a negative effect on Jesus' ministry (v. 45). The publicity created audiences, not congregations, and Jesus had to avoid the towns, keeping himself in the countryside. But still they came to him from everywhere, and understandably so.

Seventh Sunday After the Epiphany

Isaiah 43:18–25;
Psalm 41;
2 Corinthians 1:18–22;
Mark 2:1–12

The texts for today affirm the gracious activity of God toward us in spite of our sin and weakness. This is especially affirmed, says Paul in 2 Corinthians 1, in Jesus Christ, who is God's yes to us. And Isaiah asserts that God says yes to a forgetful and stubborn people by once more forgiving their transgressions. Psalm 41 testifies to a healing, forgiving, and vindicating visit from the Lord; and Mark, in an unusual story, tells of Jesus granting forgiveness and healing in the life of a man who needed both.

Isaiah 43:18–25

That Isaiah 40–55 stems from an anonymous prophet who preached to Jewish exiles in Babylon just before the capture of the city by Cyrus in 539 BC is now almost universally conceded. Deutero- or Second Isaiah, as this unknown speaker is designated, had several goals in mind: (1) one objective was to convince the exiles that their stay in Babylon as punishment was sufficient penalty for their sins (see Isa. 40:1–2); (2) Deutero-Isaiah wanted to convince the exiles that God was still in control of history and that the budding conquest of the Persians was the work of Yahweh (see Isa. 45:1–7); and (3) the divinely guided events of history were soon to result in the release of the exiles and their return to the homeland. It is the last of these objectives that is the focus of today's lection.

All of 43:18–25 is presented as a divine speech addressed to the exiles. It is difficult to know where the unit of which verses 18–25 is a part really begins and ends. It at least includes verses 16 through 28.

Verses 18–19a form the linchpin in the speech: "Do not remember the former things, or consider the things of old. I am about to do a new thing." Interpreters have long discussed what the expression "former things" refers to. (1) Is this a reference back to the great salvation events of Israel's past—the exodus from Egypt? The imagery in verses 19b–21 might suggest this. (2) Or are the former things those events immediately preceding the destruction of Jerusalem and the beginning of the Exile? Verses 27–28 would suggest the latter, for verse 27 talks about the "former father (translated "first ancestor" in NRSV) who sinned" (probably an allusion to King Zedekiah), whose rebellion brought an end to the sanctuary (the destruction of the temple in 586 BC).

If the reference is to the Exodus, then Deutero-Isaiah is telling the exilic audience that the great events of the Exodus can be forgotten because something greater is on its way. One could doubt, however, if anyone in ancient Israel would have advised an audience to forget the Exodus, the central feature in Israel's symbolic world! If the reference is to the events associated with the beginning of the Exile, then Deutero-Isaiah is telling the hearers that they can forget the preaching of judgment that preceded the fall of Jerusalem. The words of judgment are over; God is now ready to do a new and totally different thing. The day of salvation is at hand.

The forthcoming salvation will be analogous to the Exodus: God will make a way through the wilderness between Babylonia and Palestine (v. 19b) just as God made a way through the sea when the Hebrews came out of Egypt (v. 16; see Isa. 11:16; Exod. 14). The inhospitable desert will be transformed, and the wilderness wildlife will acknowledge and honor Yahweh (see Isa. 11:6–9). The function of the redeemed community is to praise Yahweh (v. 21b). Redemptive and redeemed existence is here presented as an occasion of celebration.

Verses 22–24 appear to be highly condemnatory of the people. They are formulated in such a way as to highlight verse 25. Verses 22–24 declare that there is nothing in the people's actions and behavior that constitutes the basis and grounds for divine redemption. Instead, it is Yahweh who of his own free will and for his own sake wipes away the people's transgressions and remembers their sins no more. The gospel was the gospel, even in the Old Testament!

Psalm 41

This psalm concludes the first book of the Psalter. This is indicated by the doxology found in verse 13. (Most modern translations such as the NRSV actually insert a heading "Book II" following v. 13, although no such statement is found in the Hebrew text.) Other such doxologies are found in Psalms 72:18–20; 89:52; and 106:48. These doxologies divide the Book of Psalms into five books. These five books were probably put together to be read in conjunction with the five books of the Torah (the Pentateuch). A consecutive portion of the Torah and a psalm would have been read weekly in synagogue services so that Genesis would have been read along with the first book of Psalms (Pss. 1–41), Exodus with book two (Pss. 42–72), and so on. In a three-year lectionary, all of the Pentateuch and all of the psalms would have been read and the process begun again.

Psalm 41 is the prayer of one ailing, living surrounded by enemies, and awaiting healing and the opportunity to get back at the enemies. In a fashion, the plight of the worshiper in this psalm is analogous to that of the ill person in the Gospel lesson, although in the psalm even the person's closest associate offered no consolation but only further ridicule.

Verses 1–3 of the psalm appear to have been spoken by the priest or a cultic/worship leader in charge of the service of personal intercession. The content of these verses is primarily addressed to a human audience but is not confessional in nature (note that God is addressed in vv. 2b and 3b). The opening verses seem to promise that God will show mercy and concern for those who show mercy and concern: "Happy is he who is thoughtful of the wretched; in bad times may the Lord keep him from harm" (v. 1, NJPSV).

The supplication of the sick person begins in verse 4. In the opening plea, the request for grace and healing is connected with sin. It is not said that sin is the cause of the sickness; the two are simply connected, as in the Gospel reading.

In one of the Dead Sea Scrolls (the so-called Nabonidus text), a story is told of how the Babylonian king was healed by a Jewish exorcist after his sins had been announced forgiven.

The sickness may not have been considered so much the consequence or result of the sin as a warning to alert the person of something wrong in his or her life. The author of Ecclesiasticus (or Sirach) warned those who were sick to "give up your faults and direct your hands aright, and cleanse your heart from all sin" (38:10).

The psalm is as much concerned with the ill person's human relations as with the sickness. Enemies already anticipate the sufferer's death (v. 5). Visitors spread rumors about the victim's condition (v. 6). Others whisper about the person's condition, always imagining the worst (v. 7). People make their own prognosis of the disease (v. 8), and even close companions can no longer be relied upon (v. 9).

We might pause to ask why ancient clerics who wrote the psalms would have worshipers express their feelings and conditions in this form. First, when persons become ill, particularly terminally ill, the world does or at least may appear to take a different attitude toward them. Second, isolation from social life and withdrawal from the routines of life create a strong sense of alienation, a period when merely the passage of time lies heavy on the sufferer. The psalm writers probably felt that it was best to verbalize such feelings, even if the sick had to be compelled to speak them, rather than let the feelings exist unarticulated. Third, even the feeling that sin and sickness are somehow related is better expressed than merely left to brew. The natural human reaction to calamity is to ask, "What did I do to deserve this?" Finally, the statements about friends, enemies, and other associates force the sick person to focus on the divine-human relationship. People have to realize that when the worst comes there is nothing much others can do. The road to the cemetery is ultimately traveled alone. (Except in war, few people died very quickly in antiquity.)

The psalm closes with an upbeat attitude (vv. 10–12, NJPSV). At least God can be counted on.

> But, You, O Lord, have mercy on me;
> 　let me rise again and repay them.
> Then shall I know that You are pleased with me:
> 　when my enemy cannot shout in triumph over me.
> You will support me because of my integrity,
> 　and let me abide in Your presence forever.

2 Corinthians 1:18–22

Of the many ways Christ is presented in the New Testament, today's epistolary passage is one of the most distinctive and unusual—Christ as God's yes. One characteristic that makes this christological claim so striking is that it is not a personal metaphor, as is so often the case: Christ as Son of God, Son of Man, High Priest, Savior. Rather, the christological "title" in this case is an adverb!

What prompts this highly unusual way of speaking of Christ is a controversy involving Paul's own behavior. From the preceding verse, it becomes clear that some of Paul's opponents accused him of being "vacillating" and acting "according to ordinary human standards" (v. 17). Elsewhere, it appears that some objected to the two faces Paul presented: strong in print, weak in person (2 Cor. 10:10). What emerges is a perception of Paul as someone who is unreliable, who cannot be counted on to do what he promises, who makes plans and changes them, who says both yes and no, who speaks out of both sides of his mouth.

Naturally, these charges raise Paul's ire, so he speaks in his own defense. First, he grounds his defense in the character of God: "As surely as God is faithful" (v. 18). That God is faithful becomes something of an axiom in the New Testament, perhaps because of its strong Old Testament underpinnings (Deut. 7:9; Ps. 145:13). It can be a word of reassurance used to conclude a prayer (1 Cor. 1:9) or to reinforce a word of exhortation (1 Cor. 10:13; 2 Thess. 3:3). It is often used in an eschatological context to reassure us that God is capable of delivering us to our ultimate destiny (1 Thess. 5:24; also 1 Cor. 1:9). The fidelity of God is unaffected by the infidelity of humans: even "if we are faithless, [God] remains faithful" (2 Tim. 2:13). God's faithfulness can be linked with God's promises: what God promises, God delivers (Heb. 10:23; 11:11). Especially is this true of the promise of forgiveness (1 John 1:9).

The reason that Paul can so closely identify his own behavior with the faithfulness of God is that it is finally "God who establishes us . . . in Christ and has anointed us, by putting his seal on us and giving us his Spirit in our hearts" (vv. 21–22). As one commissioned by God, Paul sees himself as God's co-worker (2 Cor. 6:1), as the one through whom God appeals to humanity (2 Cor. 5:20). The assumption here is that Paul's message is an extension of God's voice: "in Christ we speak . . . as persons sent from God" (2 Cor. 2:17).

Given this close identification between God's message and Paul's voice, he can claim that his word and conduct are unambiguous: "what we tell you is not a mixture of Yes and No" (v. 18, REB). And why? Because "all the promises of God have their Yes in him" (v. 20, REB). Paul could insist that Jesus Christ was the essence of what he preached (2 Cor. 4:5). But more than this, Paul insisted that Christ was the one in whom God confirmed "the promises given to the patriarchs" (Rom. 15:8). All the promises that littered the history of God's people from the time of Abraham forward finally found their yes in Christ, the "end of the law" (Rom. 10:4; Gal. 3:29).

Because God has said yes to us through Christ, when we pray and "give glory to God" (v. 20, REB) we say "amen" to God through Christ. Our yes in prayer meets God's yes in Christ. God's unambiguous affirmation is met by our unambiguous prayer offered in faith. It is in keeping with this train of thought that the Johannine Apocalypse speaks of Christ himself as "the Amen" (Rev. 3:14).

God has done more than spoken. God has also acted, and acted decisively in confirming the yes of the divine promises. By giving the Spirit within our hearts "as a pledge" (v. 22, REB; cf. 5:5; Rom. 8:23; Eph. 1:14), God has imprinted us with the divine seal that marks us decisively as belonging to Christ (cf. Eph. 1:13). In this way, the yes of God's word, mediated through the preached Christ, becomes engraved in our hearts, and our lives become as unambiguous yesses in God's behalf as God has become in ours.

The homiletical possibilities of this text are many. For one thing, the preacher might consider the ways in which God has said yes to humanity through Christ. The many contexts in which yes is uttered, and the decisive difference it can make, provide numerous ways for us to reflect on Christ as God's yes. Our text suggests that through the sending of Christ, God finally tilted in our favor with an emphatic declaration in our behalf. We should not conclude that it was a begrudging yes, a qualified yes, a muffled yes. "In him it is always 'Yes'" (v. 19, REB).

Mark 2:1–12

Having given a dramatically brief sketch of Jesus' ministry and his sudden rise to great popularity in Galilee, Mark now presents the darker side of that ministry—conflict and controversy. In 2:1–3:6, Mark records five of these clashes, stating the issue, the opponents, and Jesus' way of dealing with it. Very likely the early church preserved these stories to provide guidance for its own handling of criticism and debate. Our lesson today, 2:1–12 (also in Matt. 9:1–8; Luke 5:17–26), is the first of these controversies.

The event occurred in Capernaum where Jesus was "at home" or "in a house" (2:1). Mark frequently remarks that some act or teaching of Jesus took place "in a house" (7:17, 24; 9:28, 33; 10:10). This expression not only serves Mark's overall emphasis on Jesus' desire for privacy and resistance to instant success but also enables Mark to distinguish between private and public teaching. Sometimes Jesus is in a house; sometimes he is pressed by the crowds. In 2:1, his being pressed by the crowds while in a house is a union of the two scenes into one, setting the stage for high drama.

The preacher will notice immediately some unusual features of this story. In it are joined two ministries of Jesus, healing the sick and forgiving sin, and the two are joined by the repetition of the phrase "he said to the paralytic" (vv. 5, 10). In fact, the issue of forgiveness occupies the central verses (6–10), and healing is the subject matter in verses 3–5, 11–12. More awkward is the joining of the two ministries in terms of which is easier and which is harder (v. 9). The category of relative difficulty hardly seems to fit. In addition, in verses 10–11, healing the cripple is offered as proof of authority to forgive sins. Neither in Judaism nor in Christianity did power to heal imply or infer power to forgive sins. Only God can forgive (v. 7). Forgiving sin was never associated with the work of the expected messiah. For Jesus, and by implication for the church, to announce forgiveness of sins was an act of a person or persons representing God and speaking God's word of grace. The discontinuity between the healing and the forgiving is also evident in the conclusion to the story. That which amazed the crowd was the healing, not the forgiving (v. 12), even though the forgiveness of sins was far more remarkable. Could it be that the crowd was aware only of the healing? And Mark says *all* were "amazed and glorified God" (v. 12). Does that include the questioning and accusing scribes of verses 6–7?

These features of Mark 1:1–12 have led many students of the passage to theorize that Mark has joined two stories by inserting into a healing (vv. 1–5, 11–12) an account of Jesus' forgiving sin (vv. 6–10). Inserting one story into another is a familiar literary pattern in this Gospel. Recall, for example, the account of raising Jairus's daughter (5:21–24, 35–43) into which Mark places the healing of the woman with the blood flow (vv. 25–34). Mark 11:12–25 is another example. This theory relieves the passage of many of its literary and logical difficulties.

However, whether it is treated as a unit describing a single event or a Markan construction joining two events, 2:1–12 offers to the preacher and the listeners several strong themes. The passage announces clearly the power of Jesus over sin and disease. That sin and suffering are joined in the human condition is the testimony of both Scripture (Gen. 3; John 5:14; 9:2; Rom. 8:18–26) and experience. This is not to say that the Scriptures subscribe to modern psychosomatic views or that every case of suffering signals the presence of a sinful act. Jesus shattered the notion that anyone suffering is guilty of some sin both by his word (John 9:3) and in his own crucifixion. Jesus did not suffer because he had sinned, but because others did. Rather, the Bible joins sin and suffering in a more cosmic sense, alienation from God being the root cause of all human woes. As a minor theme, the preacher may want to comment on the representation of faith in the story. It is not that of the paralytic but of those who brought him (v. 5). Here is the church in miniature: a person being sustained by the faith of others when his or her own condition—physical, spiritual, or mental—is at least temporarily far short of sufficient.

Eighth Sunday After the Epiphany

Hosea 2:14–20;
Psalm 103:1–13, 22;
2 Corinthians 3:1–6;
Mark 2:13–22

If the preacher would find a theme common to the lessons for today, surely it would be the affirmation that God is continually doing a new thing, creating anew and entering into new covenants. God's new activity cannot be confined in old wineskins nor can it be clothed by repairing the old garment (Mark 2). Both Paul (2 Cor. 3) and Hosea refer to God as the maker of new covenants. God has done wondrous things in the past, says the psalmist, but those are not to be recited as the sum of what God does. In fact, the past pales before the new creative and redeeming activity of God toward us.

Hosea 2:14–20

Running through all texts for this Sunday is the theme of newness, of a new covenant, or of a new relationship to God. For Hosea, the image is that of a new relationship with Yahweh reminiscent of that made at the beginning of their history together.

Hosea 2:14–20 is part of a larger unit that extends from 1:10 to 2:23. In the speech, the wife/mother figure symbolizes the city-state of Samaria. (In spite of centuries of interpretation to the contrary, the people of Israel in Hosea is always understood in masculine imagery, as in Hos. 11:1, and not in feminine imagery. In the Old Testament, tribes are masculine; cities are feminine.) In 734 BC, Pekah captured the city of Samaria and threw the people's lot behind a western coalition set on defeating the Assyrians (see 2 Kings 15:25–31; Isa. 7:1–9). King Ahaz of Judah refused to join, and so the coalition members attacked Jerusalem to kill Ahaz, wipe out the Davidic family, and put a foreigner on the throne of Judah (2 Kings 16:5; Isa. 7:1, 6). The Assyrian king, Tiglath-pileser III (744–727), put down the rebellion, rescued Jerusalem, but returned home leaving Pekah on the throne in Samaria to be defeated by troops headed by Hoshea (2 Kings 15:29–31) and the loyal Assyrian vassal Ahaz.

Hosea 1:10–11 is a call for Judeans and Israelites to unite as a mighty army under one commander, probably Hoshea, to "take possession of the land," that is, the territory held by Pekah and Samaria (v. 11). (The prophets often advocated positions and certain actions in the form of predictions about what would happen.) Because Pekah and Samaria had broken a treaty with Assyria, sworn in the name of Yahweh, they were guilty of acts constituting grounds for divorce

(Hos. 2:1–2). Verses 3–13 describe the actions God will take to punish his ex-wife and to reclaim the gifts bestowed upon her.

Verses 14–15 describe Yahweh's renewed courtship of Samaria. The place of the romantic undertaking will be back in the wilderness where Hosea claims Yahweh originally found Israel "like grapes in the wilderness" (9:10). Yahweh will allure her for a rendezvous in the desert and there court her again, speaking tenderly to her (literally, "upon the heart"). Like the husband, Yahweh will bestow gifts upon her ("her vineyards") and like a new bridegroom will lead her to a new start in the land. The Valley of Achor ("Trouble") refers to the locale where Israel, in the person of Achan, was disobedient in the account of the initial conquest (see Josh. 7). The old valley of trouble will become the doorway of hope, the path of a new life.

In the wilderness, Samaria/Israel will be a loyal and responsive bride responding as she did in the original journey from Egypt (v. 15b). Here Hosea draws upon the view that the time Israel initially spent in the wilderness between Egypt and the Promised Land was a good time marked by obedience and good relations. This portrayal is also found in Deuteronomy 8:1–4; 29:5; Jeremiah 2:1–3. (Most of the Old Testament, however, describes the stay in the wilderness as a time of murmuring and disobedience.)

The new relationship to Yahweh will mean that Samaria can address God as "my husband" (literally "my man") and no longer as "my Baal" ("my lord" or "my husband"). Presumably, the prophet is here emphasizing that the word "Baal" will no longer be used by the Israelites. The word "Baal" was used with a number of meanings in the Old Testament: as the name of the god Baal, as a term referring to the husband as the "owner or possessor" (the baal) of the woman, or as a term meaning "treaty partner." The latter usage occurs in ancient Assyrian texts and in such biblical texts as Genesis 14:13; "the allies [the baals of the covenant] of Abram." The references to baals in Hosea probably refer more to the allies/lovers of Samaria in their coalition against Assyria than to the gods (the Baals) worshiped by allies such as Syria and Phoenicia.

As part of the new arrangement, Yahweh promises to establish several new conditions. First, reference is made to Yahweh's establishment of a treaty or covenant between the woman and the various components of the animal kingdom: wild animals (beasts of the field), birds of the air, and creeping things on the ground. This would include all the animal kingdom except for the domesticated animals (for the various classes, see Gen. 1:20–25, although water creatures are omitted in Hosea's statement). The prophet apparently conceives of God redoing the orders of creation and bringing the human and animal kingdoms into close harmony and reconciliation (see Isa. 11:6–9). Note here that the covenant is not between Yahweh and the people but between the people and the animals. God is the mediator, not the subject of the covenant relationship.

Second, peace will prevail in the land (v. 18b). The bow and the sword (the military armaments) and warfare itself will be destroyed from the land, and people can rest in safety. Like Isaiah 2:4, this text gives expression to the universal longing for a world without war. The land of Palestine, so frequently drenched with the blood of battle, was also washed with tears shed from eyes longingly looking for peace.

Third, Yahweh promises to betroth her to himself forever and offers to her righteousness, justice, steadfast love, and mercy as the bridal gifts to the betrothed (v. 19). Possessing these, the future Israel will be faithful. In Israelite life, betrothal was a binding, legal obligation requiring the equivalent of a divorce to break its binding quality. Here God then is committing himself anew to a renewed marriage with his rebellious wife.

Finally, she "shall know the LORD" ("be devoted to the Lord," NJPSV) for she will be betrothed in faithfulness (v. 20).

Psalm 103:1–13, 22

This psalm may be understood as a meditation on theology and anthropology, or the divine-human relationship. It is essentially a psalm of thanksgiving, but thanksgiving expressed in hymnic form. The psalm contains no direct address to the Deity, nor does it describe any predicament from which the worshiper has been redeemed. The text has a homiletical flavor about it.

On the basis of content, the psalm may be seen as expounding on the activity of God (vv. 1–6), the nature of the divine-human relationship (vv. 7–14), and transitory human life in the embrace of divine mercy and fidelity (vv. 15–19).

The composition begins as a self addressing the self (v. 1). In the final stanza, the range of vision is greatly expanded, arching out to include the angels, the heavenly hosts, and all the works of creation.

The verses selected for the lection are fundamentally theological affirmations; their content is composed of descriptive statements about God. If we include verse 6 with verses 1–5, and this is a possible although not an obvious division, then the first six verses speak of seven deeds of the Deity:

A. forgives iniquity
B.   heals diseases
C.   redeems from the Pit
X.   crowns with steadfast love and mercy
C.'   satisfies with good as long as one lives
B.'   renews youthful vigor like that of an eagle
A.' works vindication and justice for all oppressed

The depiction of these actions—structured in an ABCXC'B'A' scheme—are expressed through participial forms of the verbs. One might take such formulations, like participles in English, as describing states of being. Thus the actions denoted are taken as descriptions characteristic of the Deity.

Verses 8–13 contain a second series, this time comprising six items that describe the character of Yahweh, particularly with regard to the divine reaction to human error, wrongdoing, and rebellion. Verse 14 should be considered in conjunction with these verses because it offers anthropological insight and rationale for divine behavior, offering reasons anchored in human existence for God's grace and mercy.

Throughout this section, descriptions of God's treatment of the sinner and explanations of divine behavior are interlaced. Each verse makes independent but interrelated points.

1. God's nature is oriented to mercy and grace; the Divine is not easily upset, and when God is, there is mercy abounding (v. 8).

2. God does not perpetually torment or nag incessantly, for divine anger does not abide forever. The text does not deny that God has anger and does react in wrath; however, the Divine is willing to let bygones be bygones (v. 9).

3. God does not operate on a tit-for-tat basis. The punishment is not made to fit the crime. God is free to reduce the penalty, to soften the shock of human actions (v. 10).

4. Divine mercy is compared to the greatness of the heights of the heaven above the earth (v. 11).

5. The vertical dimension used in verse 11 is replaced by a horizontal dimension in describing the removal of transgressions. East and west, or literally the rising and setting (of the sun), is a way of stressing the radical separation (v. 12).

6. The parent-child relationship and parental pity form an analogy by which to understand divine love. It should be noted that such pity is granted to those fearing (obeying the will of God, v. 13; note vv. 17–18). The human condition helps incline God to mercy: God knows the weakness of the human condition—people's dusty origin and their dusty destiny (v. 14).

2 Corinthians 3:1–6

As is the case with much of Second Corinthians, today's epistolary lesson is written in response to charges made against Paul by his rivals. One of their complaints was that Paul engaged in excessive self-commendation. At issue may have been the exceptional nature of Paul's apostolic call, and hence the legitimacy of his apostolic credentials.

Unlike the original apostolic circle, Paul could not claim to have been with Jesus or to have been directly commissioned by the historical Jesus. Instead, his apostleship was exceptional (1 Cor. 15:8–9). We can imagine that without this historical link with Jesus and the apostolic circle, Paul could be perceived as one whose credentials were self-generated. Given the strength of his personality, we can also imagine his detractors accusing him of preaching himself rather than the gospel. Thus he must insist that he does not preach himself (as Lord), but Christ Jesus as Lord (2 Cor. 4:5).

Another factor leading to this perception may have had to do with Paul's theology of preaching as reenactment of the cross. So closely did he identify his apostolic sufferings with the suffering of Christ that he often rehearsed what he had to endure as part of the message he preached (cf. 1 Cor. 4:9–13; also 2 Cor. 6:4–10; 11:23–29).

Whatever the reasons for this adverse perception of Paul, we find him explaining the nature of authentic apostolic existence. He contrasts himself with his opponents "who commend themselves" by engaging in games of one-upmanship (2 Cor. 10:12). What was especially painful to Paul is that they had gained an entrance within the Corinthian church and had begun to win the favor of those for whom he felt a divine jealousy (2 Cor. 11:2, 4). In the end, Paul insists, what matters is not whether we approve of our own actions but whether the Lord does (2 Cor. 10:18). Consequently, every effort to get a hearing for the gospel must be anchored in the proper understanding of ministry. If we commend ourselves, it must be as "servants of God," nothing more, nothing less (2 Cor. 6:4). Moreover, when we seek to gain favor for the sake of the gospel, it must be "by the open statement of the truth" (2 Cor. 4:2). It cannot be by the use of cunning, underhanded methods that can flourish only when hidden from view (2 Cor. 4:2). What we do, we do "in the sight of God" (2 Cor. 4:2). Paul is calling here for a form of ministerial authentication that operates in the public arena.

One way to be commended was through the well-established practice of using letters of recommendation. When the new convert Apollos sought to go to Achaia in order to preach, the brethren first wrote letters of recommendation on his behalf (Acts 18:27). Even Paul himself wrote letters of recommendation for "Phoebe, a deacon of the church at Cenchreae" (Rom. 16:1–2) and Mark, the cousin of Barnabas (Col. 4:10). Apparently, Paul's opponents had employed this same practice to gain an entrance within the church. But the last thing he needed in order to document his standing with the Corinthian church was letters of recommendation, either to them or from them (v. 2). This might have been acceptable had he been unknown to them, but he was their "father through the gospel" (1 Cor. 4:15).

Consequently, they themselves were Paul's letter of recommendation (v. 2). Whether he conceives of these letters as written on the Corinthians' hearts ("your hearts," RSV) or on the hearts of Paul himself and his co-workers ("our hearts," NRSV, REB, NJB, NIV) is a disputed textual point. It was probably the latter, because it makes more sense of the text to think of the church's own existence and reputation as what would have been "known and read by all" (v. 2). It was, after all, the church who remained in the apostle's heart (2 Cor. 7:2). They were the seal of his apostleship (1 Cor. 9:2). Whether he had anything to commend him depended upon whether the church had anything to commend it. The litmus paper test of the minister's work is the minister's church. The results of ministry either commend or condemn the minister.

But more is involved here than the notion that the church is a mirror image of the minister. They were to see themselves as "a letter of Christ, prepared by us, written not with ink but with the Spirit of the living God, not on tablets of stone but on tablets of human hearts" (v. 3). After all, the church was not self-generated, nor was it even generated as an act of apostolic prowess. It was a "church of God" (2 Cor. 1:1) established in Christ (2 Cor. 1:21). Nor had the work of God in Christ been inscribed on hearts of stone, as was the case with the tablets of testimony God gave Moses (Exod. 31:18; 32:15–16; Deut. 9:10). Rather, what had been promised by God through the prophets had now come to pass: the human heart was the place where the imprint of God's Spirit could be traced (Ezek. 11:19; 36:26; cf. Jer. 31:33; also Prov. 7:3). The work of God is now penciled in the heart of those to whom God's Spirit had been given as a guarantee (2 Cor. 1:22).

Seen this way, the minister is not the prime actor in God's work among churches. It is not the minister's sufficiency, or lack of it, that legitimates this process: "our sufficiency is of God" (v. 5, KJV). Consequently, the minister's confidence is not self-generated; it is derived. It occurs "through Christ toward God" (v. 4).

The mention of "tablets of stone" (v. 3) prompts Paul to introduce the notion of the "new covenant" (v. 6; cf. Jer. 31:31). Fundamental to his discussion is the distinction between "letter" and "Spirit" (v. 6). What is written in letters of the alphabet, whether with a pen on papyrus or with the finger of God on stone tablets, is said to "kill." This doubtless refers to Paul's conviction that the law written on stone produced despair and finally death (Rom. 3:9–20; 7:13). In the end, the law was incapable of giving life (Gal. 3:21–22). It is the Spirit, finally, who can give life (Rom. 8:6, 11; cf. 1 Cor. 15:45).

As homiletical possibilities, the preacher may want to explore the question of what constitutes authentic ministry. In doing so, one could examine the relationship between the minister and the church. But today's text would insist that this relationship is never merely a matter of human engineering; it must rather be construed primarily as an arena in which God is at work—through the minister to be sure, but not as the primary agent whose sufficiency and confidence are self-generated.

The distinction between letter and Spirit also holds germinal possibilities. Our inclination to "have it in writing," as noble as it is and as secure as it makes us feel, may serve as a reminder that a contract, however properly drawn up and however precise, is only as good as the human hearts within which it finally has to be negotiated.

Mark 2:13–22

Mark 2:13–22 (Matt. 9:9–17; Luke 5:27–39) is the record of the second and third of five controversy stories in the section 2:1–3:6. (For comments on this section, see the material in the Gospel section for the Seventh Sunday After the Epiphany.)

Both of the controversies before us today have to do with table fellowship, in the first instance, with whom, and in the second, when. It was and remains a matter of importance. This is not the time to chide the Jews about rigid food laws. Remember that much of the pleasant and unpleasant for both Jesus and the early church occurred at table. Simon Peter was called on the carpet for eating with Gentiles, and his criticism came from church members (Acts 11:2–3). Paul reports a crisis in the church at Antioch when several leaders formed separate tables at the fellowship dinner (Gal. 2:11–14). And not incidentally, it was at "lunch counters" that the battles for racial equality often began in our own recent history.

In verses 13–17, the dispute over one's table partners arose at a dinner attended by Jesus, his disciples, and many tax collectors and sinners. Jesus had recently called as a disciple a tax collector named Levi (v. 14; Luke 5:27; Matthew calls him Matthew, 9:9). Luke 5:29 clearly states that the dinner was in Levi's house, and the NRSV so translates Mark 2:15, although the text literally says "his house" (whose? Jesus'? Levi's?). Tax collectors were treated as outsiders because they gathered burdensome taxes for a foreign power, Rome. "Sinners" was a label for persons expelled from the synagogue for reasons moral or ritual. Because table fellowship meant full acceptance, the scribes' question addressed the very heart of Jesus' ministry. That the question was put to Jesus' disciples indicates that it remained in the church a very real question: Why accept such people? The question is still a vital and probing one, and if Jesus' response is not still sufficient, then his church is in grave difficulty.

It is quite clear that the controversy over fasting (vv. 18–20) has also been framed by Mark so as to address the church. The question put to Jesus was not "Why do you not fast?" but "Why do your disciples not fast?" In other words, Mark presents a church issue that was worked out in relation to two religious groups with whom the church shared a common heritage: the Pharisees and the followers of John the Baptist (v. 18). The Pharisees were required to fast on the Day of Atonement and in times of special need, but it was quite common to do voluntary fasting in the practice of piety. The followers of John were imitating their leader in their fasting, "for John came neither eating nor drinking" (Matt. 11:18). Jesus, even though he fasted in the desert of temptation (Matt. 4:2), "came eating and drinking" (Matt. 11:19), drawing the criticism that he was a glutton and a drunkard.

According to Mark, the issue is not whether or not to fast. After all, Jesus says, "The days will come when the bridegroom is taken away from them, and then they will fast on that day" (v. 20). If "that day" refers to Jesus' death, then the text instructs Jesus' followers that during Jesus' life fasting was not appropriate, but it would be appropriate upon Jesus' departure. Fasting, in other words, was to be joined to some occasions but not to all. During his trials alone in the desert, Jesus fasted, but not during his work of healing and preaching the good news of the kingdom of God. One does not fast at a party. There is a time to fast, and there is a time to kill the fatted calf. The coming of Jesus and the joyful news of the kingdom's arrival were radically new, demanding forms of expression appropriate to this new age.

Conversely, continuous banqueting would violate certain seasons of the soul and critical moments in the life of the church. As Jesus predicted, the days came for fasting. The church at Antioch fasted prior to the sending out of Barnabas and Saul (Acts 13:2–3). The appointing of elders for every church was done with prayer and fasting (Acts 14:23). According to Matthew, fasting along with prayer and alms were the staples in the practice of Christian piety (6:1–6, 16–18). In fact, Matthew's expression "when you fast" assumes that the practice is well in place, and the instruction needed is in the area of genuineness, without hypocrisy. As with all practices that become regularized, however sincere and prayerfully motivated at the outset, the dangers of empty routine and false display are never far away. One detects for example, a hollow ring in the instruction given in an early Christian document: fast on Wednesday and Friday and not on Monday and Thursday as the hypocrites do (*Didache* 8:1). It is the endless business of the church to keep its words and acts alive, appropriate, and toward God.

The closing part of our lesson, verses 21–22, consists of proverbs about garments and wineskins. These proverbs, as is true of most proverbs, give themselves to multiple applications. In their present location in Mark, they refer to the arrival of something so vital and new that it cannot be contained in the old rituals and forms of piety. It is important to notice that in these verses Mark is not attacking the old. There is concern expressed about the loss of the old garment and the old wineskin just as there is about the loss of the new. Each has its integrity, and it would be a violation of both to treat the Christian faith as a compromise of the old and the new, a synthesis of the two at the level of lowest common denominators. No one gains by pretending Hanukkah is Christmas or that Christmas is Hanukkah. To try fasting at a party is to make a display of fasting and to wreck the party. Like so much of life, the key is very often in the timing.

Ninth Sunday After the Epiphany

Deuteronomy 5:12–15;
Psalm 81:1–10;
2 Corinthians 4:5–12;
Mark 2:23–3:6

Today's Old Testament reading focuses our attention on keeping the sabbath, reminding us that pausing to rest may in itself constitute obedience. A note of celebration is sounded in Psalm 81, which served to stress the importance of obedience to the covenant law. The epistolary lection is one of the richest christological passages in Paul because of the way in which his ministerial self-understanding is anchored in his experience of dying with Christ. Conflict is a major theme of the Gospel text, as we see Jesus encountering stiff resistance as he pursues his ministry in Galilee.

Deuteronomy 5:12–15

The Old Testament reading for today is a single law from Deuteronomy's version of the Decalogue, the commandment concerning the observance of the sabbath. For a discussion of the Decalogue as a whole—to be sure, in the Exodus version—see the commentary on Exodus 20:1–17 for the Third Sunday in Lent in this volume.

It is important to be aware of the literary context in which the Decalogue is embedded. The broad context of the Decalogue in Exodus 20:1–17 is a narrative framework, the account of the exodus from Egypt and the wandering of the people of Israel in the wilderness. Its more immediate context is the establishment of the covenant between God and people. The most important conclusions from these observations are, first, that God's saving activity precedes and is the basis for the laws, and second, that the laws are given and reiterated in a religious service in which God and people establish their relationship with one another. The context of the Decalogue in Deuteronomy, on the other hand, is not a story of salvation but a series of long speeches by Moses. (In fact, the entire Book of Deuteronomy can be viewed as the account of the last words and deeds of Moses.) But the crucial dimension of the Exodus narrative is preserved in Deuteronomy in the opening words of the Decalogue. Moses speaks, but he then quotes the Lord: "I am the LORD your God, who brought you out of the land of Egypt, out of the house of slavery" (Deut. 5:6). Thus Deuteronomy makes the same point: The law was and continually is given to a people redeemed by their God.

118

Moreover, the establishment or renewal of the covenant defines all that Moses says and does in the Book of Deuteronomy.

The Decalogues contain more than the laws themselves. Each law is a short and absolute apodictic directive, either a command or a prohibition, but many of them are followed by additional expressions, either explanations of the meaning of the laws or exhortations to obey them. Thus Deuteronomy 5:12–15 has two distinct parts. Verse 12a contains the law itself: "Observe the sabbath day and keep it holy." Verses 12b–15 present the explanations and exhortations. This second part is, in effect, a little exegetical sermon on a text. Three moves are visible in the comments following the law. First, there is the appeal to divine authority: ". . . as the LORD your God commanded you." This reference in the third person to the Lord is striking if one remembers that according to verse 6 the Lord is the speaker. Second, in verses 13–14 there is an explanation of the meaning and purpose of observing the sabbath day. Third, in verse 15 an appeal is directed to the hearers as they are exhorted to obey this law.

In almost all respects, the Decalogues in Exodus and Deuteronomy are identical, but there are remarkably significant differences between the two versions of the sabbath law, and these differences provide insight into our text. First, the law itself is formulated differently. Where Exodus 20:8 says "Remember" (from the Hebrew *zkr*), Deuteronomy 5:12 says "Observe" (from the Hebrew *shmr*). This is doubtless because the deuteronomic writer uses "remember" in a distinctive way, as seen in the hortatory comments on this law (5:15). But the more dramatic differences are in the commentaries on the law. In Exodus, the sabbath is explained in terms of creation, with a direct allusion to Genesis 2:1–3. One should remember the sabbath, "for in six days the LORD made heaven and earth, the sea, and all that is in them, but rested the seventh day" (Exod. 20:11). Obedience is justified in terms of the origin of the day; the emphasis is upon sacred time. Those who refrain from work on the seventh day thus participate in a divine rhythm of work and rest. The whole creation rests because God rested.

In both texts the sabbath is a day of rest rather than a day set aside specifically for worship. But in our text, unlike Exodus 20, the deuteronomic writer justifies obedience not in terms of the origin but the purpose of the day. Moreover, that purpose is directed toward the needs of others. It is a moral and humanitarian rather than a specifically religious concern with the sacredness of time: Observe the sabbath "*so that* your male and female slave may rest as well as you" (v. 14, emphasis added). The explanation of the sabbath's meaning is explicitly inclusive. It is a day to refrain from all work, that is, economic endeavor (see Amos 8:5). But that day of rest is not just for the holy people of God, but for all over whom they have any control: "you, or your son or your daughter, or your male or female slave, or your ox or your donkey, or any of your livestock, or the resident alien in your towns . . ." (v. 14). The fact that domestic animals as well as human beings are included in the day of rest recalls and to some extent parallels the sabbath year, when the land is allowed to rest (cf. Deut. 15:1).

It is only when the law is laid on the hearts of the people that the deuteronomic writer uses that word "remember" (*zkr*): "Remember that you were a slave in the land of Egypt . . . therefore . . . keep the sabbath day" (v. 15). Recollection that they were slaves will evoke kindness toward slaves—and even toward themselves. The moral power of the past, of events that happened only once and long ago, is unleashed by memory. By actively bringing that story to mind and living out its implications, the people know both who their God is and who—and whose—they are. Obedience is response to God's historical activity. And, remarkably, obedience in this case is not in doing something, but in taking a rest from work.

Psalm 81:1–10

Psalm 81 was a frequently used psalm in worship during the Second Temple period. Seven psalms were selected for singing in the temple during the course of a week. These were Psalm 24 (Sunday), 48 (Monday), 82 (Tuesday), 94 (Wednesday), 81 (Thursday), 93 (Friday), and 92 (Saturday). Thus this psalm was used throughout the year. Its choice for such usage was probably based on the psalm's call for obedience.

Psalm 81 has frequently been interpreted as a prophetic liturgy used in worship to remind the people of the necessity to obey the law or even as part of a covenant renewal ceremony. In such an analysis, verses 1–3 call for the assembly to offer praise and worship to God; verses 4–5b provide the reasons for worship; and verses 5c–16 contain the prophetic sermon spoken as a direct address of the Deity to the people, as was common in prophetic speech.

Verse 3 connects the psalm's original usage with a festival or feast day. The new moon was the first day of the month in a lunar calendar. The full moon, or the fifteenth day of the month, is here stipulated as the feast day. The soundings of the trumpets to mark the first day of the seventh month is commanded by Leviticus 23:23–25. This is the day that was and still is celebrated as Rosh Hashanah, or New Year's day. (The term actually means "the head of the year.") The fifteenth day of the month marked the beginning of the Feast of Tabernacles, or Booths (Succoth), which lasted for seven days (Lev. 23:33–36).

One of the features associated with the Feast of Tabernacles, according to the legislation in Deuteronomy, was the reading of the Book of Deuteronomy. According to Deuteronomy 31:10–13 (RSV), Moses commanded, "At the end of every seven years, at the set time of the year of release, at the feast of booths, when all Israel comes to appear before the LORD your God at the place which he will choose, you shall read this law before all Israel in their hearing." Psalm 81 may be seen as part of the admonition to observe the law that formed a part of the great autumn feast.

The opening verses of this psalm call for various forms of praise: singing, shouting, and the playing of various musical instruments. (See 2 Sam. 6:12–19 for some of the celebration that went on at festival times.) The rabbis noted that verse 1 refers to the God of Jacob, and they questioned why none of the other patriarchs are mentioned. The answer they arrived at was in terms of Balaam's statement in Numbers 23:21. "Why did Balaam choose to mention Jacob—not Abraham and not Isaac—only Jacob? Because Balaam saw that out of Abraham had come base metal—Ishmael and all the children of Keturah; and he also saw that out of Isaac there had come Esau and his princes. But Jacob was all holiness (*Midrash on the Psalms*)."

The motivation for celebrating the festival is given in verses 4–5; namely, God commanded it and established it as a statute, ordinance, and decree.

The divine oracle consists of two types of material: reviews of the past (vv. 6–7, 10a, 11–12) and admonitions to obedience (vv. 8–9, 10b, 13–16). The reviews of the past, on the one hand, stress the redemptive action of Yahweh by emphasizing the deliverance from Egypt and the testing in the wilderness. On the other hand, the reviews highlight the people's unfaithfulness to which God responded by giving them over to their stubborn hearts and allowing them to follow their own counsels (v. 12: a good sermon topic!). The admonitions call upon Israel to hear, to listen, to have no other gods (see Exod. 20:3; Deut. 5:7), to be receptive to divine blessings—all with the promise that such responses will be rewarded abundantly.

2 Corinthians 4:5–12

In today's epistolary lection, Paul's opening remark "For we do not proclaim ourselves" (v. 5) doubtless responds to the charges of his detractors who accused him of self-commendation (2 Cor. 3:1). As the letter shows, at issue was what constituted authentic ministry, or, what form of ministry most adequately expressed the heart of the gospel. Was it ministry whose appeal and authority derived essentially from the minister's personal charisma, powerful presence, and strength as demonstrated in rhetorical ability or the ability to perform signs and wonders? Or was it ministry anchored in human weakness, human frailty, and actual experiences of human suffering, that derived its appeal and authority from its capacity not merely to endure these but to transcend and transform them—to experience strength through suffering, power through weakness, and living through dying?

For Paul, it is the latter. The former way of viewing ministry tends to make the minister a lord. In verse 5, Paul may in fact be saying, "For we do not proclaim ourselves (as Lord), but Christ Jesus as Lord." Consequently, that form of ministry will tend to be authoritarian and stress rank more than service (cf. 2 Cor. 1:24). By contrast, Paul's essential role is that of servant (1 Cor. 3:5). At the heart of his gospel is the basic Christian confession "Jesus Christ is Lord" (cf. Rom. 10:9; 1 Cor. 12:3; Phil. 2:11; also Col. 2:6). Paul is not insisting here that he preaches the gospel apart from his own person, or personality, for preaching inevitably occurs through a human personality. The important question, however, is, What message is mediated through the preacher's personality? As verse 6 shows, Paul insists that the ultimate source of revelation for his gospel is the Creator God who said, "Let light shine out of darkness" (cf. Gen. 1:3; Ps. 112:4; Job 37:15; Isa. 9:1–2). Just as God gave light to the universe through the spoken word at creation, so now has God brought light to all humanity through the new creation accomplished in the Christ-event. Just as the face of Moses radiated the brilliant splendor of God's revelation (cf. 2 Cor. 3:7–13), so now the "face of Christ" radiates the unveiled splendor of God's new revelation.

In verses 7–12, the metaphor shifts. No longer is the gospel seen as dazzling light shining through darkness (cf. 1 Pet. 2:9; Acts 26:18; Eph. 5:8; 1 Thess. 5:4–5; 2 Pet. 1:3), but as a "treasure in clay jars" (v. 7; cf. 2 Cor. 5:1; Lam. 4:2). The image of the clay pot serves to underscore the weakness and fragility of the minister as messenger. The message of the gospel mediated through the messenger is "treasure," to be sure (Matt. 13:44; Eph. 3:8), but it derives its value not from the case that contains it but from its intrinsic worth. Thus the transcendent power of the gospel is derived from God, not from the minister.

As evidence of this, Paul rehearses in schematic fashion the afflictions he has endured as an apostle (v. 8; also 1:4, 8; 7:5; cf. 1 Cor. 4:9–13; 2 Cor. 6:3–10; 11:21–29). In every case, however, he has overcome, for while in his afflictions he was "carrying in [his] body the death of Jesus," precisely through these afflictions the "life of Jesus" manifested itself (v. 10). He has not been forsaken (cf. Heb. 13:5). He has literally been given up to death in these experiences of human suffering and "dying," and through them he has reenacted the event of the cross itself (cf. 2 Cor. 1:5; 13:4; Gal. 6:17; 1 Cor. 15:38). Yet through them resurrection has also been at work (Rom. 6:8; 8:17; Phil. 3:10–11). He has experienced living through dying, and in doing so has proclaimed the essence of the gospel of the crucified Christ: through death comes life (cf. Phil. 1:20–21; 1 Cor. 6:20; 2 Cor. 6:9). As the message of the crucified Christ has been proclaimed through his own apostolic life-style, those who have heard him preach and seen him live have themselves come to experience life: "So death is at work in us, but life in you" (v. 12).

Mark 2:23–3:6

Today's Gospel lection contains the last two in the collection of five conflict stories recorded in Mark 2:1–3:6. This material is called a collection because the stories are joined topically rather than chronologically. This is evident from three characteristics of the section: (1) the stories have other locations in Matthew and Luke; (2) the stories have different settings (at home, 2:1–12; in Levi's house, 2:13–17; no setting given, 2:18–22; in a grain field, 2:23–28; in a synagogue, 3:1–6); and (3) each story has a Markan style introduction and is rounded off at the end. Hence, stories that probably circulated separately are here clustered, perhaps as a kind of arsenal for the early church members who looked to Jesus for both precedent and pronouncement to enable them to handle their own conflicts.

However, it is striking that Mark has placed this section at this point in his Gospel. At the same time that Jesus is drawing huge and favorable crowds in cities, villages, countrysides, and by the sea (1:28, 33, 37, 39, 45), Mark says Jesus is also drawing hostile attention from religious leaders. In fact, the opposition mounts to the point of a conspiracy against his life, according to 3:6, which apparently is intended as the conclusion to the entire section, instead of just 3:1–5. And thus as early as 3:6 Jesus' death enters the story, a subject that will dominate Mark's narrative after 8:31.

Our text, 2:23–3:6, records conflicts four and five. The first three concerned charges of blasphemy, eating with sinners, and not observing fasts, the latter two having to do with sabbath regulations. The fourth occurs in the grain fields (2:23–28). The disciples pluck heads of grain, an act for which the law made provision as long as none of the grain was put in containers and taken home (Deut. 23:25). According to the Pharisees, however, what they did constituted harvesting on the sabbath. Jesus' defense of his followers consisted of citing a precedent from David's career (1 Sam. 21:2–7) in which human need took precedence over the law. (Ahimelech and not Abiathar was high priest; some manuscripts of Mark have made the correction by omitting the name, as Matthew and Luke have done.) Verses 27–28 contain two pronouncements (Matt. 12:8 and Luke 6:5 use only the second) for which the story serves as introduction. The pronouncements are different, and it is unlikely that both would have been stated on one occasion. The first (v. 27) is a general principle that law is to serve human life, not vice versa. The second (v. 28) is a christological claim made by One far greater than either David or the law.

The fifth conflict (3:1–5) involves a healing in a synagogue on the sabbath. The pronouncement at the center of this brief account is in the form of a stabbing question that silenced those who lay in wait for Jesus. They were silent because their own law made provision in emergencies to care for both animal and human life on the sabbath (Matt. 12:11; Luke 14:5). Though the healing he did here might not be classified as an emergency, Jesus is announcing by his act and word that it is never the wrong day to do good, to heal, to save life. The hostility against Jesus produces one of those odd unions that overriding hatreds sometimes create: Pharisees in league with Herodians (8:15; 12:13), religion and politics clutching the same sword.

It requires no great act of imagination to observe how similar are the conflicts that lie in the path of discipleship today. Structures of religious custom and tradition, originally designed to praise God and serve humanity, can become corrupted and cruel. Hence, occasions arise in which both human life and tradition cannot be preserved unbroken.

Last Sunday After the Epiphany
(Transfiguration Sunday)

2 Kings 2:1–12;
Psalm 50:1–6;
2 Corinthians 4:3–6;
Mark 9:2–9

The Last Sunday After the Epiphany always centers on the Transfiguration, and the texts for today dramatically point to the pivotal event in the ministry of Jesus. The Gospel record is Mark's brief but forceful account, and it is the Gospel text that attracts to itself the other readings. Elijah appears with Jesus on the mountain; 2 Kings 2 tells of Elijah's glorious ascent to heaven. Psalm 50 speaks of the appearance of God attended by fire and storm. And Paul in 2 Corinthians 4 uses the imagery of Old Testament theophanies and of the Transfiguration to speak of God's presence in Christ and of Christ's presence in us, veiled in flesh to be sure, but glorious nonetheless.

2 Kings 2:1–12

The selection of this Old Testament text for Transfiguration Sunday is based on the fact that Elijah appears in the narrative of Jesus' transfiguration and that the story of Elijah's ascension to heaven forms an analogous parallel to the ultimate ascension and glorification of Jesus that are anticipated in the Transfiguration.

In this narrative, three features help structure the story and increase the tension of the plot. There is, first, the travel itinerary of Elijah and Elisha. The two begin their journey at Gilgal, where the Hebrews first made camp after crossing the Jordan River (Josh. 5:1–9). Then they progress to Bethel, one of the sacred temple sites of Israel, the place where the national shrine was constructed for the Northern Kingdom (1 Kings 12:26–29). From Bethel the two return to Jericho, the site of the Hebrews' first triumph on the western side of the Jordan (Josh. 6). They next go to the Jordan River, which the Hebrews earlier crossed in miraculous fashion (Josh. 3:14–17). Finally, the journey carries the men across the Jordan after Elijah parts the water with his mantle. Why the storyteller structured his story around these geographical points remains uncertain. Perhaps the ancient hearer would have thought that one of these great and famous sites would be the place of departure, but one by one they are bypassed. It is as if Elijah conducts a miniature tour of the Land of Promise before departing this world from a location "beyond the Jordan."

A second feature in the story is the persistent fidelity and loyalty of Elisha, who faithfully follows his master without leaving his presence. Elisha is the true disciple. The story of Elijah's first meeting with Elisha is a paradigm of the true follower (1 Kings 19:19–21). In his call, Elisha, initially hesitating to follow Elijah, begs first to bid farewell to his family. Elijah would have none of this. To show that he was forsaking the past and "burning his bridges behind him," Elisha slaughtered his yoke of twelve oxen, his means of livelihood, and offered them up as a feast for the people. In 2 Kings 2:1–12a, Elisha has the option of ceasing to follow Elijah wherever he goes, but still he follows loyally.

A third feature of the story is the unveiled mystery of Elijah's departure. It is an open secret, for all the "sons of the prophets" (members of the prophetic guilds) remind Elisha that the time of his master's departure is near. The departure is certain; only the circumstances and the place remain uncertain. (Note a similar emphasis on the uncertainty and questioning about Jesus' "departure" in Mark's account of the Transfiguration.) The narrative of Elijah's departure does not conclude before Elisha asks to be the true successor of his master; however, he wants to possess double the spirit of Elijah. One requirement is placed on Elisha: he must witness, actually see, the departure of his master. The text is careful to note that this occurred. At Elijah's departure, Elisha calls to him with two honorific titles: "father" out of respect for his position, age, and authority; and "the chariots of Israel and its horsemen!" to indicate the importance of Elijah in the earlier history of Israel—he was more powerful than the instruments of war.

This narrative, like the accounts of the Transfiguration, is filled with mystery, awe, miracle, and legend. All of these factors in their own way were used by the ancients to show that a person had unusual, superhuman qualities. Such persons are those in whose very existence dwell the quality and power of the other world.

Psalm 50:1–6

These opening verses of the psalm form part of a call to worship that constitutes an affirmation of the coming of Yahweh to judge the people. The remainder of the psalm is composed of speeches of Yahweh to the worshipers placing them under judgment and condemnation. This psalm thus appears clearly to have been part of a liturgy of judgment carried out in the context of worship, perhaps a service of covenant renewal or of national lamentation. Some officiating priest perhaps spoke verses 1–6, and a prophet proclaimed the judgment of God in the remainder of the psalm. This psalm, like the Transfiguration scene, speaks of the presence of awesome phenomena as attendant upon the coming of God—devouring fire and mighty tempest. Such descriptions were at home in speech about Yahweh's appearance in theophanies, especially about the theophany at Sinai (Exod. 19:16–19). Just as God appeared at Sinai when the law was given with the accompaniment of unusual phenomena, so in similar terminology Psalm 50 describes the appearance of the Deity to judge the people.

The psalm opens with a piling up of divine names—El ("Mighty One"), Elohim ("God"), Yahweh ("the LORD"). This threefold ascription of names, which stresses the honorific power of the Divine, is followed by a threefold summons to assemble for judgment. God summons the earth (v. 1), then the heavens and the earth (v. 4), and finally "my faithful ones," the members of the covenant community. The heavens and the earth are to appear as witnesses to the proclamation of judgment that follows, for they, as permanent features of the world, are also witnesses to the initial giving of the law and the demands for obedience.

The significant points of connection between this reading from the psalm and the Transfiguration of Jesus are the reference to God's shining forth (v. 2) and the statement that God is judge (v. 6). In Psalm 50, God calls and speaks from the heavens. In the Transfiguration, God speaks from the cloud. In addition, God's appearance and Jesus' transfiguration are presented with unusual features, features that call for a response of awe in the presence of the other world.

2 Corinthians 4:3–6

These words from Paul clearly echo themes found in Mark's account of the Transfiguration of Jesus. Perhaps most striking is the recurrent theme of "light," which is, of course, central to the transfiguration story itself. As the Gospel account stresses the dazzling radiance of Christ, flanked by Moses and Elijah, so does Paul focus attention on the "light of the gospel of the glory of Christ, who is the image of God" (v. 4). Rather than drawing his imagery from the Sinai theophany, as does the transfiguration story, Paul is informed by another part of the biblical witness—the Old Testament account of creation. Directly quoting Genesis 1:3, Paul says that the God who said, "Let light shine out of darkness," is also the God who brought light to the Christian's heart by giving "the light of the knowledge of the glory of God in the face of Jesus Christ" (v. 6).

The Sinai theophany has already figured centrally in Paul's remarks in chapter 3, where he insisted that the "glory" or "splendor" of Christ can now be viewed directly "with unveiled faces" (2 Cor. 3:18). Those whose confidence is "through Christ toward God" find themselves being gradually transformed into his likeness as they acquire this dazzling glory of the Lord. Paul fully recognizes that for some, his gospel is veiled (v. 3). Blinded by the "god of this world" (v. 4), unbelievers find themselves in a position analogous to the disciples in the transfiguration story who, at first, were unable to see the transfigured Christ. However, with the voice from heaven acclaiming him "the beloved son," and with the injunction that they are now to "listen to him," God's revelation in Christ is placed in the public domain.

The verses immediately preceding today's text indicate that Paul had been accused by his opponents in Corinth of obstructing the message of Christ in some way. Paul insists, however, that his methods of preaching were fully compatible with the nature of the gospel itself. He refrained from the use of rhetorical devices or underhanded methods and rather insisted that his gospel could in no way be understood as oriented toward himself. The content of his gospel is not himself (v. 5), but the crucified Christ. He made a considered effort to keep himself in a servant role as minister of the gospel of Christ (v. 5b).

Nevertheless, Paul acknowledges that the gospel cannot be preached apart from the human personality. As he states in the following remarks, the gospel must ultimately be mediated through "earthen vessels" (v. 7); and because of this intrinsic human dimension of the gospel, Paul makes sure that his own life is "cruciform" in order adequately to convey the central message of the crucified Christ (vv. 11–12).

Paul's use of the creation story, with its emphasis on God's power to give light to the world in the creative act of making light shine out of darkness, is carried through even further in 2 Corinthians 5, where he speaks of the "new creation." The Christ-event itself is viewed as a second creation in the sense that the whole cosmos is reordered, and the one who is "in Christ" comes to share in this newly created eschatological reality. Accordingly, through the Christ-event it may be said that God gave light to the world once again, in a much more spectacular sense. Now, however, as the new age has dawned, it is the "face of Jesus Christ" (v. 6) that serves as the source of this dazzling radiance.

It is worth noting that as Paul's remarks continue in verses 7–12, they resemble in many senses the nature of Jesus' instructions to his disciples after the Transfiguration in the Gospel account. There, he begins to speak of the necessity of his death and suffering, even as does Paul in verses 7–12. It might be said that the Epiphany of Christ (note "made visible" in v. 11) takes its most legitimate form within our mortal flesh as we reenact the suffering and death of Christ, as did Paul.

Mark 9:2–9

On this closing Sunday of Epiphany we will consider Mark's major contribution to this season, the story of the Transfiguration of Jesus (9:2–9). Here Mark gathers up in a single event what the Fourth Evangelist scatters throughout his Gospel—the glory of Christ. This is, in the dramatic sense, the scene of recognition, the moment in which the reader and a chosen few present are permitted to see the principal character in full glory. The Transfiguration recalls the baptism of Jesus, with the voice from heaven and the identity of Jesus as God's Son. Here, however, the voice speaks to the disciples, not to Jesus. Transfiguration also anticipates resurrection, although there is in Mark no actual resurrection appearance (16:1–8). But this story, located almost exactly at the midpoint of the Gospel, has its own structure and in Mark's purpose, its own message. Let us look at the text internally and then seek to understand the point of the story in Mark's theology.

Quite clearly, Mark 9:2–9 is patterned after the stories of Moses' experiences of God on Mt. Sinai. One would do well to read Exodus 24 and 34 in preparation for understanding the text. All the elements of Mark's account are there: the six days of waiting, the cloud, the glory, the voice, the descent from the mountain. Moses' face shone due to his experience in the presence of God. Exodus also describes the making of the tent of meeting. Peter, James, and John as the inner circle invited to share special experiences are frequently mentioned in Mark (5:37; 13:3; 14:33). As to the appearance of Elijah and Moses, these two had come to be associated with the Messianic Age in both Judaism and Christianity (Mal. 4:1–6; Deut. 18:15–18; Rev. 11:3ff.). That they appear with Jesus says that the anticipated messiah and the end times are fulfilled in Jesus. That they disappear, leaving only Jesus, says that the old is ended; the new has come. As at the baptism, Jesus does not act or speak; God acts and God speaks concerning Jesus. And the message of the occasion is for Jesus' followers. They do not understand the event, being afraid and confused. Peter's fumbling effort to honor and preserve the moment is met with silence. Therefore, they are enjoined to be silent about the experience until after the resurrection (v. 9). They are not ready to be witnesses to Jesus' messianic role, nor are their auditors ready to hear it. Apart from the cross, the full story cannot be told.

What, then, is Mark saying in this account? Gospel writers reveal their intent either in how a story is told or in when a story is told; that is, where it is located in the narrative. It is the latter clue that is most helpful here. The Transfiguration is located in the central section of Mark 8:22–10:52. This section opens with the healing of a blind man and ends with the healing of a blind man. In between, however, the disciples remain blind. Jesus three times predicts his death (8:31; 9:31; 10:33–34), but on each occasion the disciples amply demonstrate their inability to accept a cross and death as being anything but a contradiction of all that messiah and kingdom mean. Peter's confession has the right words but the wrong meaning (8:29–30). After all, how can persons who have lived with the motto "When the messiah comes, there will be no misery" understand suffering and death as kingdom experiences? And so, between the first announcement of his passion and the passion itself comes the Transfiguration. Disciples who had been hearing death talk are given a glimpse of who Jesus really is. A corner of the curtain is lifted, and they are permitted to see and hear for a moment. But they miss it, really. Simon Peter, who had interrupted Jesus at prayer to call him back on stage before an applauding crowd (1:35–38), now wants to perpetuate this marvelous moment. Here is the real glory, without suffering, without death. Jesus' silence before Peter's offer says to him and to all followers that glimpses of the glorious future are permitted, but not possession of that future. That future, like the past, is not the proper dwelling place for the church. For these disciples, and all who follow, there is one more mountain to climb—Golgotha.

Some readers of Mark position themselves over against the disciples, critical of them in their confusion, doubt, and cowardice. Others identify with the disciples and bow over this text—indicted, penitent, and forgiven. It is not easy to resist the offer of a gospel of success, an invitation into what Reinhold Niebuhr once described as a kingdom without judgment through a Christ without a cross.

Ash Wednesday

Joel 2:1–2, 12–17 or Isaiah 58:1–12;
Psalm 51:1–17;
2 Corinthians 5:20b–6:10;
Matthew 6:1–6, 16–21

The texts for Ash Wednesday initiate the Season of Lent with calls to confession and repentance, prayers for forgiveness, and admonitions to engage in fasting. They also caution people not to display their acts of contrition before others, but only before God. The Old Testament reading from Joel has a call to repentance at its center. In the alternate Old Testament reading from Isaiah, the people of Israel are confronted with their rebellion and their propensity to fast as a public display rather than as an expression of penitence. The responsorial psalm, one of the penitential psalms, is a confession of sin with the goal of restoration to the joy of salvation. The epistolary reading is likewise a call to be reconciled to God. The Gospel text sounds the warning about doing alms or fasting in order to impress others with one's righteousness.

Joel 2:1–2, 12–17

The Book of Joel is the most liturgically oriented of all the prophetic books. Concern with cultic affairs and the use of cultic language and formulations all point to the fact that Joel was probably a cultic prophet or that the book which bears his name was originally composed and used within ancient Israel's religious ceremonies.

A central feature in the book is the call for fasting and repentance in light of an approaching or present disaster. The calamity is depicted as the onslaught of a locust plague (1:4), an agricultural failure (1:17–18), or an invasion by foreign forces (2:20). All of these may be ways of speaking about a single phenomenon described under a variety of images. As in many cultures, calamities and disasters in ancient Israel could be portrayed in a range of metaphors. The use of such metaphorical and pictorial language, like modern cartoons, allowed for the exaggeration of features and characteristics that could highlight the traumatic character of the threat and at the same time verbalize the feelings of those threatened. The purpose of many laments was to allow the worshiper or worshipers to provide a depiction of the threat and in so doing at least to gain a certain control over it. Description and identification aid in taking steps to overcome. Sometimes, of course, such depictions were also intended to awaken the audience or reader to the seriousness of the threat and thus to convince them that a particular course of action was most appropriate.

The selection of this text from Joel for Ash Wednesday is based on two features: the text proclaims the coming of the day of the Lord and also summons the people to repentance and preparation for the day that includes fasting and services of public penitence.

The entire Book of Joel is rather complicated in form and structure, and this is the case even with the few verses of today's lesson. Verses 1–2 call for the sounding of an alarm (the blowing of the shofar) in light of the distress and disaster that have overtaken the land. Verses 12–13a contain God's call to return and repent, stipulating some of the personal features of the penitential ritual. Verses 13b–14 are the prophet's parallel call to return and to repent. Verses 15–17a are the prophetic directions for carrying out the communal aspects associated with the general assembly of the people as an embodiment of their return to God. The text, of course, continues with the plea of the people (v. 17b) followed by a favorable oracle of response from the Deity (vv. 18–27), but these lie outside today's lection.

Verses 1–2 describe the coming distress to which the fasting ritual should be a prelude or response. It is frequently difficult to know in some prophetic texts whether the event described is already taking place or is yet to come. Verses 1–2, for example, seem to imply the future coming of the calamity, whereas verse 3 suggests the opposite. Whatever the calamity, it was viewed as an act of God, a day of Yahweh's judgment.

The oracle of God (vv. 12–13a) presents some of the characteristic personal acts of penitence. Both external and internal acts are emphasized, thus indicating the necessity of involving the whole person. The external acts are fasting, weeping, and mourning; the internal acts focus on the heart, which should be torn like a garment. Rituals of penitence not only represent a break in the normal pattern of life but also partially simulate the conditions that penitence seeks to avoid. In such rituals, the normal course of life is given up so that the abnormal state will not become normal. One weeps, mourns, and goes without food not only to demonstrate the total contriteness of heart but also to help avoid making these features the characteristics of life by appealing to God for intervention. Both the external and internal features of penitence should be stressed and given expression in Ash Wednesday services.

The prophet's plea for the people to return (vv. 13b–14) is based on theological arguments. There is first the appeal to the character and nature of God. Because God is "gracious and merciful, slow to anger, and abounding in steadfast love, and relents from punishment" ("repents of evil," RSV), there is certainly the hope that God can be trusted to give a sympathetic and sensitive hearing. Second, the summons to penitence is based on the expected future, namely, that God would respond favorably, change what he is doing, and leave behind a blessing. (This seems the general sense of verse 14, although who is being talked about is somewhat unclear.)

The seriousness and the totality of the fast are demonstrated in the prophet's reiteration of the summons and description of some of the cultic activities associated with the public service of penitence in verses 15–16. The people are called on to fast and to assemble at the sanctuary, and the priests are commanded to weep and offer intercessory prayers. The assembly involves the total community, from the elders to the nursing infants, for all are threatened by God's judgment. The sanctification of the communal fast involved desisting from food, work, and sexual intercourse. Thus the joy of the bridal couple and the consummation of their marriage must be interrupted.

Ancient Israelite cultic practices creatively combined many features of external and internal religious matters. These texts from Joel demonstrate how both emphases were present, as they always should be in religious observations. Although the activities of Ash Wednesday are not performed to ward off a coming disaster, they nonetheless inaugurate a period that calls for both internal and external signs of penitence.

Isaiah 58:1–12

This text is assigned for reading on Ash Wednesday because of its definition of the true fast in terms of the moral life. As the prophets frequently stress, acts of worship cannot take the place of specific acts of social justice (Amos 5:21–24; Isa. 1:10–17). Moreover, it is a fundamental error of biblical interpretation to drive a wedge between concern for piety—individual or corporate prayer and worship—and concern for social justice. The psalms, as the fullest expression of piety, overflow with the same stress on justice and righteousness that one finds in the prophets.

Our passage is part of the so-called Third Isaiah (Isa. 56–66) and very likely stems from the years soon after the return of the exiles from Babylon. The reading reflects some of the religious practices that developed during the Exile and afterwards, and also indicates some of the divisions that were emerging in the newly reconstituted community of faith in Judah. The mood of disappointment and frustration with the new life in Jerusalem is similar to that reported in Haggai 2:1–9 and Zechariah 7.

The reading is part of a composite unit of literature (Isa. 58) concerned with the general topic of cultic activity. Verses 1–12 concern fasts; verses 13–15 turn to the issue of proper observance of the sabbath.

In some ways, the form of the passage is similar to the prophetic torah, or instruction, in Micah 6:6–8 (see also Amos 5:21–24 and Isa. 1:10–17), with a question from the laity answered by a religious specialist. But the dialogue here is more like a dispute than a request and an answer. It is clear that the addressees are the people in general, but the role of the speaker is not so obvious. Generally, he speaks with prophetic authority, on behalf of God. It is quite possible that the setting for such a discourse was the sort of community of worship and teaching that later became the synagogue.

In verses 1–2 Yahweh speaks to instruct the unidentified speaker in what he is to say to the people. He is told to be bold and direct, proclaiming to the people their "rebellion" and "sin." Those violations are not specifically identified, and it is presumed in verse 2 that those same people have regularly inquired of the Lord concerning his righteous will.

Next (v. 3ab), this speaker responds to the divine instructions by quoting the words of the people. They complain to God because their fasts have not been effective. The assumption is that fasts are a form of prayer, probably of penitence. Fasts in ancient Israel, along with the use of sack-cloth and ashes (v. 5), generally were associated with rituals of mourning, but they were also used as part of petition and intercession (2 Sam. 12:16, 22). Public fasts became important in the exilic and postexilic periods, and several such days were known (Zech. 7). The rituals for the Day of Atonement must have included fasts (Lev. 16:29–31; 23:27–32; Num. 29:7).

Then (vv. 3c–4) our speaker responds with an indictment of the people for their attitudes and their behavior on fast days. Business as usual, and oppressive business at that, continues on such days (v. 3c). People are contentious when, verse 4 implies, the public fast should be a reverent expression of solidarity before God.

To this point the author has said, in effect, that fasts are not effective because the participants do not take them seriously, do not devote themselves reverently to fasting. In verses 5–7, however, he begins to question the very idea of fasts (v. 5) and then to state what kind of "fast" would evoke the desired response from God (vv. 6–7). In a series of rhetorical questions, each expecting the response "yes," an answer is spelled out in four points: "loose the bonds of injustice," "undo the thongs of the yoke," "let the oppressed go free," "break every yoke" (v. 6).

It turns out that these four metaphors refer to one activity—to care for the poor, to set them free from oppression, from the bonds of their poverty. Verse 7 states the point in very practical terms. Those complaining should see that the ones in need have food ("share your bread"), housing ("bring the homeless poor into your house"), and clothing ("when you see the naked, to cover them"). The final line of the verse is best read "And not to ignore your own kin" (NJPSV), that is, your fellow Judeans. This catalogue of social responsibilities is similar to that in Zechariah 7:8–10 and is an echo of Isaiah 1:10–17, which advocates justice and righteousness, especially for widows and orphans, as the necessary prerequisite for genuine worship.

Verses 8–9a promise that when these conditions are fulfilled, the people will live in the light of God's presence, and God will hear their prayers. That point is extended in detail in verses 9b–12. If the people will abide by that "fast" described in verses 6–7, then God will indeed be their guide; they will be like "a spring of water, whose waters never fail," and the ruins—presumably of Jerusalem—will be rebuilt (vv. 11–12). It is possible to take this promise as a form of works righteousness, that good works will earn salvation. Good works would then only replace fasting as a means of earning God's favor. Doubtless, many heard—and many will continue to hear—these words in that way. However, the more fundamental meaning is that those who attend to justice and righteousness thereby live in the presence of the just and righteous God; they are part of God's people. Moreover, when the people attend to the needs of the hungry, the homeless, and the naked, they have their own reward: the solidarity of the community is strengthened, their "light" breaks forth, their "healing" springs up, and their "vindication" (v. 8, NRSV footnote) goes before them.

Reflection on this text at the beginning of Lent certainly would call attention to physical acts, including fasting, as a means of confessing sin (v. 2) and repenting. Such reflection will also recognize that "fasting" includes physical actions that are not so obviously "religious." The fast that the Lord chooses is not simply abstaining from eating, but sharing one's bread with the hungry, one's shelter with the homeless, and one's clothing with the naked (v. 7). In short, God's preferred fast is "to loose the bonds of injustice . . . to let the oppressed go free" (v. 6).

Psalm 51:1–17

Psalm 51 is probably the best known of the classical seven penitential psalms (6, 32, 38, 51, 102, 130, 143). The heading, perhaps supplied by the collectors of the Psalter, associated this psalm with David's contrition after being confronted by the prophet Nathan following the Bathsheba affair (see 2 Sam. 12:1–23). This association probably represents a late way of exegeting the psalm by defining a precise historical situation that might have given it birth. That is, the collectors of the psalms felt that this was the type of prayer for forgiveness that David might have or should have prayed after having been reproached by Nathan.

The psalm opens with a plea for God to have mercy, to forgive, and to cleanse the one praying (vv. 1–2). The worshiper does not claim any special status or any moral worth but can only cast himself or herself upon the love and mercy of God. Three terms are used for the person's wrongdoing—"transgressions" (rebellion against authority), "iniquity" (a perverse action or straying), and "sin" (missing the mark), and three terms are employed for removing the sin—"blot out," "wash," and "cleanse." The piling up of terms suggests a strong recognition of sin and a passionate need for its removal. It is possible to develop the picture suggested by these terms, although the author may not be consciously speaking of three different types of sin but only seeking to emphasize an extreme sense of wrongdoing and thus separation from God. "To blot out" suggests the idea of a book in which one's activities were recorded (see Neh. 13:13; Dan. 7:10). "To wash" suggests a stain that has become ingrained. "To cleanse" suggests that sin has contaminated and rendered one culticly impure and thus unfit for full participation in the worship of the temple.

The opening plea of the psalm is followed by a confession of sin (vv. 3–5). Three elements in this confession are noteworthy: (1) The matter of sin is depicted as primarily a matter between the worshiper and God. No particular sin is mentioned. Stress is laid instead on the disruption of the divine-human relationship. The same sentiment is found in 2 Samuel 12, where David acknowledges that he has sinned against God (v. 13), although his actions had led to Uriah's death. Because the ordering of the world and the giving of laws were acts of the Divine, infringement of these could be seen as sins against God as well as crimes against others. (2) The psalmist is quite contrite about the acknowledgment of sin. There is no attempt to escape the reality and consequences of sin or to leave the issue merely at the level of shame about sin. Thus the psalmist can affirm that "you [God] are justified in your sentence and blameless when you pass judgment" (v. 4b). (3) The psalmist acknowledges that his or her entire life—that is, the psalmist's very nature—is sinful in orientation. This is expressed in the affirmation "I was born guilty, a sinner when my mother conceived me" (v. 5). This assertion is about as close to a doctrine of original sin as there is to be found in the Old Testament.

After the confession of sin, the psalm reading continues with a plea or petition (vv. 6–12), which requests not only the forgiveness of sin but also the restoration of the worshiper's relationship to the Deity and the total transformation of the person. Both the positive and the negative aspects of penitence and forgiveness are emphasized. In verse 6, for example, there is the request for internal changes at the depth of being and willing, whereas verse 7 emphasizes the external purgation and ritual washing used in the cult to symbolize spiritual purification. A similar polarity or balance is found in verses 8 and 9, where verse 8 contains a prayer for positive restoration and verse 9 reflects the more negative aspects of sin's removal.

The pinnacle of the prayer occurs in verses 10–12, where the psalmist requests renewal and re-creation—that is, to become, in Pauline terms (see 2 Cor. 5:17), a new creation with a new inner life and spirit resting on the constant presence of and a close association with the Deity. The prayer that the divine Holy Spirit remain with the worshiper is perhaps equal here to the prayer that God's presence remain with the worshiper. (For the only other Old Testament occurrence of the phrase "Holy Spirit," see Isa. 63:10–11.) Such a presence restores the joy of divine salvation. Finally, the psalmist asks that God continue to uphold him or her, implying the recognition that forgiveness and restoration must be accompanied by the continuing support of the Deity, otherwise the future would be only a repetition of the past.

In verses 13–14, the worshiper vows to show thankfulness for forgiveness by teaching other transgressors and sinners the ways of God. "My tongue will shout aloud of your deliverance" means that the worshiper would offer public testimony, probably in the form of a thanksgiving ritual and a recital of the worshiper's case history.

Verses 15–17 have the worshiper acknowledging that what really matters when one is a guilty sinner is true repentance, a broken and contrite heart, and not merely a sacrifice alone. Although the actual sacrifice is here downplayed, nonetheless the service in which this psalm was used probably included a sacrifice as a specific sign of the person's sorrow for sin.

This psalm, more than any other, exposes the true nature and depth of penitence—a central theme of Lent—and at the same time recognizes what is required to become a radically changed person, a new creation.

2 Corinthians 5:20b–6:10

We entreat you on behalf of Christ, be reconciled to God" (v. 20b). It may seem odd that Paul urges the Christians at Corinth to accept God's reconciling act. Some commentators, in fact, have suggested that his remarks have a missionary flavor and were aimed primarily toward those who were not yet Christians. But this is to misunderstand Paul's theology of reconciliation. Far from being a once-for-all act fully experienced or achieved at the time of one's conversion, reconciliation should be seen as an ongoing process in which the Christian participates.

As part of the eschatological work of God, who is at work in the world to bring about righteousness, reconciliation involves not only the individual's relationship with God in a personal sense but also the individual's relationship with humanity as a whole, indeed with the whole cosmos. Paul elsewhere makes clear that the cosmos as a whole is undergoing transformation "in Christ" (Rom. 8), and the one who has been incorporated into Christ participates in this process. Through the work of Christ, God has initiated a process at work in the world in which death gives way to life. To be sure, the Christian who experiences baptism reenacts the death and resurrection of Christ in a single act, but not as if this becomes a single moment in the past that grows increasingly distant as one grows older. It is rather a reenactment that initiates a way of life that is itself typified by dying and rising. Even "in Christ" one continues to die to the world even as one experiences the power of the resurrected Christ. Thus, within each individual Christian in whom the Spirit of Christ works to bring about filial obedience there occurs the eschatological renewing, triggered by the Christ-event and continued by the ongoing work of God in the world—God's reconciling work.

It is only natural that Christians be charged to "be reconciled to God" (v. 20b), that is, to accept the reconciliation God offers. To do so requires penitence, which, of course, is the note on which the Lenten Season begins. Ash Wednesday, in particular, as an expression of public penitence on the part of the individual Christians and Christian communities, becomes an appropriate occasion to hear this injunction of Paul. A cross etched with ashes on the forehead provides a vivid symbol for all to see how the cross of Christ continues to serve as the means of bringing humanity into reconciliation with God and the world.

It should also be noted that Paul makes this appeal "on behalf of Christ." This phrase recalls his earlier statement in verse 20, where he says that "we are ambassadors for Christ," that is, "on behalf of Christ." The Christian is here viewed as the emissary, or the legate, of Christ through whom an official appeal is made. If these remarks are more directly applicable to the Christian minister, they suggest the sacramental dimension of the minister's work, both the work of preaching and pastoring. There is the clear sense that God's work and word through Christ is continued through the work and word of those who are "in Christ." This is stressed even more in the language of 6:1, where Paul quite audaciously suggests that we are actually God's co-workers in the work of reconciliation.

Another way of understanding reconciliation is to see it as accepting "the grace of God" (6:1), and this too is obviously ongoing for the Christian. The Old Testament quotation (Isa. 49:8) underscores the divine initiative: God has extended an open ear and has offered help "on a day of salvation." Paul insists, however, that the "acceptable time" and the "day of salvation" are now (6:2). Through the Christ-event, the future has invaded the present, so that the God who stands at the end of time summons hearers to receive the gift of salvation through the preached Word.

True penitence begins when we recognize that Christ became sin in our stead (5:21). Through the crucifixion, he became sinner (Gal. 3:13) even though he was sinless, that is, innocent. In a similar fashion, our salvation is paradoxical; in the crucifixion Christ took on a status that was not rightfully his. So too, through God's reconciling act we acquire a status that is not rightfully ours.

Matthew 6:1–6, 16–21

Today is Ash Wednesday, the beginning of Lent—a day of profound meaning for some, a day only casually marked by others, and a day viewed with suspicion among those Christians who feel the key to genuine spirituality is the minimizing of all rites and ceremonies. It is appropriate to look to Matthew for instruction at this time, for he knew as well as anyone in the New Testament both the depth and the emptiness of what he calls "practicing your piety" (6:1). He understood and felt keenly the difference between altars that served as stations on one's pilgrimage and cold stones that stood along the road to nowhere.

Our lesson today consists of an introductory warning about practicing piety (6:1) followed by instruction in the practice of true piety in these areas: alms (vv. 2–4), prayer (vv. 5–6), and fasting (vv. 16–21). The warning does not concern whether or not these acts are to be done but before whom—human spectators or God. The instructions in these acts of devotions are catechetical and formulaic, certain phrases being repeated in each case: "whenever you give alms" (pray, fast); "not be like the hypocrites"; "be seen by others"; "your Father who sees in secret"; "they have received their reward"; "your Father . . . will reward you." Matthew chose to insert here (vv. 7–15) the Lord's Prayer with attendant comments. One can easily see the balanced threefold nature of the passage without the insertion. Therefore, it is well to consider verses 7–15 separately, even though they do deal with the subject of prayer introduced at verse 5. The passage assumes that these three acts are well-established practices in Matthew's church and that they have been observed long enough to become, for some, empty and void of meaning except as displays of religion.

In three very clear ways the church reflected in Matthew 6 is in continuity with Judaism.

First, both communities (church and synagogue) held in high regard these three acts of devotion. Jewish writings speak of alms, prayer, and fasting as indications that one has grown beyond the minimal requirements of the law, as acts of special merit and of such favor in God's eyes as to atone for other breaches of the law.

Second, both communities contained practitioners who missed the point of the acts but did see benefit for themselves in public displays of religion. It was a practice in some synagogues to announce in the assembly the names of donors to the alms box and the amounts given. Some Christians will recognize parallels in their own churches. All the possibilities for competition, improper motivation, and the dehumanization of the recipients are too obvious to require comment.

And third, both communities had prophetic calls for reform. Jesus' voice here joins those of Isaiah 58:5ff., Jeremiah 14:12, Zechariah 7:5ff., and Joel 2:12 in seeking to keep alive in the community of faith the faculty and voice of self-criticism. Without it, hypocrisy and idolatry move in quickly. It is important to see these parallels in the two faith communities lest one be seduced into making false contrasts and false dichotomies. For example, one certainly wants to avoid giving the impression that Judaism as a whole was hypocritical, whereas Christianity was as a whole genuine, or that Judaism was an "outward" religion, whereas Christianity was "inward." On the contrary, the text presents Jesus instructing his church on precisely these same "outward" rites: alms, prayer, fasting.

Students of this text do not agree on the immediate background for these sayings of Jesus. Did the synagogue practices in Matthew's community involve trumpets, masked faces, and playing to the crowds, or has Matthew portrayed those and all such public displays of religion in the language and images of the Greco-Roman theater of that time? Because "hypocrite" means "actor," one can easily see how trumpets, masked or disfigured faces, and applauding audiences could have been drawn from the analogy of theatrics.

Whatever the source of Matthew's analogy, the point being made in these sayings of Jesus is clear: God is the proper audience for all our acts of devotion; and because God is in secret and sees in secret, no display is necessary. In the final analysis, it is God with whom we deal in all our work and worship. If the clear assurance that God sees is not in itself payment in full, then our piety will go in search of additional recognition, with occasional applause. Again, it should be understood that the call for correction of abuses is not a call for the cessation of these acts of devotion. Sometimes a sincere but simplistic call for reform would attempt to cure hypocrisy by passivity. But it is a flawed logic that says that if we do not attend worship service we are the true worshipers, if we do not pray our spirits are in tune with God, if we do not fast we honestly care, and if we do not give any money we have sincerely given our hearts. Is there not, after all, such a thing as reverse hypocrisy?

First Sunday in Lent

Genesis 9:8–17;
Psalm 25:1–10;
1 Peter 3:18–22;
Mark 1:9–15

The Old Testament readings for the Second through the Fifth Sundays in Lent provide a survey of much of the Old Testament story and might form the basis for a series of sermons. With one exception, the texts concern covenants, beginning this week with the covenant with Noah and next week the one with Abraham. Then follows Exodus 20:1–17, the Decalogue, which is at the heart of the covenant at Sinai. The reading from Numbers on the Fourth Sunday in Lent reports Israel's querulousness that prompted the Lord to send poisonous snakes as punishment, and the story of the curative bronze snake—a story about covenant breaking, in a roundabout way. The final reading is Jeremiah's promise of a new covenant, written on the heart.

In the other readings for today, Psalm 25, a psalm of lament, is both an expression of trust and a prayer for grace and mercy. The epistolary text from 1 Peter gives expression to the theme of suffering, as experienced by both Christ and Christians. The Gospel text gives the remarkably compact version of Jesus' baptism, temptation, and inaugural preaching in Galilee for which Mark is well known.

Genesis 9:8–17

The Old Testament readings for the five Sundays in Lent in Year B provide a survey of much of the Old Testament story and might form the basis for a series of sermons. With one exception, the texts concern covenants, beginning this week with the covenant with Noah and next week the one with Abraham. Then follows Exodus 20:1–17, the Decalogue, which is at the heart of the covenant at Sinai. The reading from Numbers 21 on the Fourth Sunday in Lent is the report of the rebellion of Israel and the serpent lifted up in the wilderness, taken as anticipation of the cross of Jesus. The reading for the Fifth Sunday in Lent contains Jeremiah's promise of a new covenant, written on the heart.

Genesis 9:8–17 presents the conclusion to the story of the Flood and spells out the results of the events that begin in Genesis 6:5. It will be remembered that the flood story is part of the primeval or prepatriarchal narrative in Genesis 1–11. The Flood is the next-to-last event in a history which—after the initial acts of creation—is an account of the origin and spread of human sin. The last event in this sequence is the story of the Tower of Babel in Genesis 11.

The present account of the Flood is the combination of two sources, the Yahwist (J) and the Priestly Writer (P). When the sources are separated, two virtually complete stories emerge, each with its distinctive emphasis. Our reading comes from the Priestly Writer and resumes some of the important themes in that document's account of creation in Genesis 1. In this version of the Flood, the "fountains of the great deep . . . and the windows of the heavens" (7:11) had been opened to allow the waters of chaos to return, the same waters that God had separated and pushed back in order to establish the world (Gen. 1).

The Priestly Writer, who was also interested in genealogy and chronology, viewed human history in terms of a series of covenants. Each era was marked by a covenant with particular stipulations; thus the passage before us spells out the covenant for the era following the Flood. The differences between the era before and the era after the Flood had been spelled out in the paragraph that immediately precedes our reading (Gen. 9:1–7). The command to be fruitful and multiply from Genesis 1:28 is reiterated, as is the stipulation that human beings are to be over other creatures. But there are significant changes. The rest of creation will fear the human beings, who now are allowed to eat not only plants but also animals, provided they do not eat flesh with the blood. Furthermore, murder is specifically prohibited. All this indicates that the new age acknowledges the existence of human violence and sinfulness.

Apart from the introductory formulas in verses 8 and 17, the entire passage is presented as a divine speech. Until the last verse, God addresses both Noah and his sons, thus emphasizing the validity of what is said for all future generations, and for Gentiles as well as Jews. Two things transpire in the speech: (1) in solemn, almost juridical language God establishes a covenant; and (2) God designates the rainbow as a sign of that covenant.

It seems clear that our writer was aware of the older Babylonian flood story, and that he depended upon ancient oral and perhaps even written traditions when he composed the account. Evidence for this is seen in several duplicates in the passage. Several matters are mentioned twice: the covenant promise (vv. 9 and 11), the sign of the covenant (vv. 12 and 17), and God's seeing the bow and remembering the covenant (vv. 14 and 16). In the present form of the story, such repetitions serve to emphasize the most important points.

Clearly, the most important message of this text concerns the covenant. In the Old Testament, covenants are sworn agreements, either among human beings or between God and people. Both in form and content they are different from contracts, which are legal agreements attested by witnesses and enforced by law. Covenants have two basic elements, the promissory oath or conditional self-curse, and the contents or stipulations. Parties solemnly promise something concerning their future relationships. Most covenants are between two unequal partners, both of whom swear to stipulations. The central and decisive Old Testament covenant is the one made between God and Israel at Mt. Sinai, which often was summarized in a short divine speech: "I will be your God and you will be my people."

The covenant in Genesis 9:8–17 is dramatically distinctive in several ways: (1) it is made between God and all future generations, and not just with Israel; (2) it is made not only with human beings but also with all creatures of the earth; its scope is thus cosmic and universal; and (3), most dramatic of all, only one party to the agreement—God—speaks at all. No response on the part of Noah and his sons is called for or given, not even their acknowledgement of acceptance. The covenant with Noah, then, is an act of a free and gracious God in behalf of a world that did not have to ask for it or earn it, or even respond to it.

The content of the covenant is underscored in the recurring refrain "never again" (twice in v. 11 and once in v. 15). God promises never again to destroy the earth and its creatures by water. The earth is the Lord's, and God has decided that it will remain. All creatures can count on the stability of nature. The sign of that covenant promise is the rainbow. Covenants often had signs, such as the pile of stones that Jacob and Laban erected to remind them of their agreement (Gen. 31:43–50). Most readers of Genesis 9 have assumed that the rainbow sign is a reminder to human beings of the divine promise. Certainly, that is one effect of the account. However, the text makes it clear more than once that the rainbow is for God, to keep him aware of the covenant made with Noah and all his descendants.

So the story, like both the Gospel and Epistle readings, has to do with God's response to the human condition understood realistically. The sinful nature of the human creature is taken for granted. God's response here is to take the initiative, to make a covenant, and to provide the stable conditions for all life on the earth. The alternative to chaos is God's covenant.

Psalm 25:1–10

This psalm, in keeping with the interests of the Lenten Season, gives expression to the sense of sinfulness, to waiting upon God, to trusting in the Divine, and to the expectation of a life lived according to God's way and truth.

Two factors should be noted about the psalm as a whole. There is, first of all, the movement back and forth between prayer and proclamation. Verses 1–7 are addressed directly to the Deity and thus clearly take the form of a prayer. Verses 16–22 are similar in form. Verses 8–10 and 12–14, however, are not addressed to the Deity but to some human audience. (Note that in these verses, the Deity is spoken of in the third person.) They are proclamation or preaching. How might we explain this alternation between prayer and proclamation in the psalm? One might imagine the worshiper moving from prayer to proclamation during the course of worship. Both the Deity and a human audience are addressed by the worshiper. If this were the case, verses 8–10 and 12–14 could be seen as the worshiper's statements of confidence. Or, and perhaps more likely, the praying worshiper recited verses 1–7 and 16–21 asking for forgiveness, deliverance, and guidance, whereas verses 8–10 and 12–14 were part of a homily or sermon addressed to the worshiper by the official or priest participating in the service. Verses 11 and 15 would then represent the worshiper's confessional responses to the priestly preaching or instruction. Thus one can see this psalm as originally part of a ritual in which a worshiper and a worship leader (priest) participated in a service of personal prayer and priestly proclamation. Exploring the psalm in light of such a ritual can greatly elucidate the content of the psalm as well as allow the members of the congregation to picture themselves as participants in such a ritual and to experience the sentiments of the psalm.

A second factor is the alphabetic character of the psalm. That is, the psalm was written so that the first line began with the first letter of the Hebrew alphabet, the second line with the second letter, and so on right through the entire alphabet. (One or two letters are now missing from the psalm, probably having been accidentally omitted when the psalm was copied in antiquity. In addition, verse 22 is not part of the alphabetic poem.) Three suggestions have been made to explain why this and other psalms (Pss. 9–10; 34; 37; 111; 112; 119; 145) were written in an alphabetic form: (1) the practice may reflect the great poetic skill of the author and thus be seen as an artistic device; (2) the use of the alphabetic structure may have been an aid to memory; in reciting the psalm a person would move through the alphabet; and (3) others see the alphabetic pattern as a means for expressing completeness. As we would say, the alphabetic poem is inclusive from "A to Z." In spite of all suggestions, the exact reason for such alphabetic or acrostic compositions, which one finds also in the Book of Lamentations, cannot be finally determined.

The ten verses of today's lesson from the Psalter fall naturally into two parts: verses 1–7, which are a lament prayed to God, and verses 8–10, which speak of God and the divine ways. The prayer reflects the attitudes of the worshiper—trust, waiting, a desire to learn—as well as a request that earlier sins might no longer be remembered. The worshiper speaks of enemies (v. 2), but these are not further defined. In versus 2–3 we encounter a common pattern found in the psalms, a pattern that may be called a "double wish." The worshiper asks not to be put to shame (the positive wish) and requests that the treacherous (the enemies?) be made to be ashamed (the negative wish). People in ancient Israel were quite willing to pray, "Save me [us]" and "Destroy my [our] enemy."

Many of the worshiper's petitions request knowledge of God's ways and guidance in the truth (vv. 4–5). Thus they are focused on the future and request not only enlightenment and knowledge but also divine leadership to keep one on the right path and ways. Knowledge of the way must be undergirded by continuous divine aid. The psalm also expresses a deep sense of sin. In verse 7, God is asked to remember not (that is, to forget) the past sins (of youth) and present transgressions (see v. 11). The word "remember" occurs three times in verses 6–7 (translated as "be mindful" in v. 6) and could provide the structure for preaching on this text. God is asked to remember his mercy and steadfast love, not to remember one's sins, but to remember me (the person). The one praying does not ask, "God remember me," but, "God remember me according to your steadfast love." Between the worshiper and the Divine lies the passion of God's love. The proclamation in verses 8–10 seeks to assure the worshiper that God can be relied on, that God does do what the petitions in verses 4–5 request. God instructs, leads, and teaches because the Lord is good and upright. Those who obey God's will, manifested in covenant and testimony, can rest assured that the paths of the Lord are love and faithfulness.

1 Peter 3:18–22

At the beginning of Lent, Christians begin to focus their attention on the suffering of Christ. Today's epistolary lection is especially fitting in shaping our reflections concerning the Lord's passion, for it opens with the statement "For Christ also suffered for sins once for all." It should be noted that the example of Christ is introduced at this point in the letter to reassure Christians who themselves were suffering for the sake of Christ (1:6; 3:14; 5:9–10). Earlier in the letter, the readers were introduced to the example of the suffering Christ (2:21–25).

Today's text reminds us (1) that Christ's death was sacrificial and atoning ("for sins," cf. Gal. 1–4; Heb. 9:28); (2) that this preeminent sacrifice had ultimate finality ("once for all," cf. Heb. 9:12, 26); (3) that his suffering and death were vicarious ("the righteous for the unrighteous"); (4) that Christ's death has a reconciling effect ("brings you to God," cf. Eph. 2:18; 3:12; Heb. 4:16; 7:25; 10:22; 12:22); (5) that his death was transcended by resurrection life ("he was put to death in the flesh, but made alive in the spirit," cf. John 6:63; 1 Cor. 15:44); and finally (6) that its effects were far-reaching: it had retroactive power in that Christ was able even to rescue the wicked who had suffered destruction in the Flood (vv. 19–20, cf. 4:6).

Much of the language in verses 18–19 is traditional. For this reason, it has been suggested that these verses should be regarded as a baptismal hymn, possibly extending through verse 22.

They are not printed strophically, however, in NRSV, REB, or NJB, and for this reason they should probably be read and treated homiletically as straight prose. Even so, the preacher does well to note that virtually every phrase, especially in verses 18–19 and 22, is rich in meaning and association. For example, the emphasis on Christ as "the Righteous One" who died as an innocent martyr is deeply embedded in the substructure of early Christian preaching (cf. Matt. 27:19; Luke 23:47; Acts 3:14; 7:52; 22:14; 1 John 2:1). We are dealing with a text, then, rich with possibilities for Christian reflection and devotion.

The presence of baptismal imagery within the passage should also be noted. Historically, Lent served as a time for preparing catechumens for baptism at Easter. Thus, as the church thought about the passion and death of Christ, it became natural during this period of meditation, prayer, and fasting to instruct potential converts in the meaning and significance of their ritual reenactment of Christ's death and resurrection. Used and understood in this catechetical setting, this text reminds soon-to-be Christians that baptism is no mere bath ("not as a removal of dirt from the body"), but "an appeal to God for a good conscience" (v. 21). Their formal entry to the Christian faith marks an inward renewal of the human spirit empowered by the resurrection of Christ. To be sure, the connection between Noah's household being "saved through water" (v. 20) and Christian baptism appears somewhat stretched. But both are acts of divine redemption. It is at this point that the Old Testament reading (Gen. 9:8–17), which speaks of God's covenant with humanity after the Flood, relates directly to the epistolary text.

Seeing these connections between today's epistolary lection and the church's practice of preparing catechumens for baptism during the time of Lent may provide a homiletical point of departure. If baptism is seen as the ritual and symbolic reenactment of Christ's own passion and death, the beginning of Lent becomes an appropriate point to reflect on one's point of formal entry into the Christian faith. This text at least reminds us that "suffering and death" are part and parcel of Christian life and thought, even as it already introduces Easter themes in verses 21b–22: "through the resurrection of Jesus Christ, who has gone into heaven and is at the right hand of God, with angels, authorities, and powers made subject to him." Although it may be premature to exploit this strong Easter affirmation this early in Lent, there is nonetheless a strong note of reassurance that should not be pushed to the periphery of Christian reflection.

Mark 1:9–15

Mark 1:9–15 records three episodes in the beginning of Jesus' public life; his baptism (vv. 9–11), his temptation (vv. 12–13), and his first preaching in Galilee (vv. 14–15). Because verses 9–11 were treated during Epiphany on the Sunday of the Baptism of the Lord and verses 14–15 were discussed for the Third Sunday After the Epiphany, we will here attend only to verses 12–13, the temptation in the wilderness. One can hardly think of a more appropriate consideration for the First Sunday in Lent.

Speaking of temptation, the preacher will need to be on guard against gravitating toward Matthew or Luke in preparing the message. Not only are the longer temptation narratives of Matthew and Luke more familiar, but Mark's brevity may seem at first inadequate as source and substance for a sermon. But full attention on Mark will yield more than enough for the day.

Mark ties Jesus' temptation directly to his baptism. Apparently, the theme of a new exodus, developed in the portrayal of John's ministry in 1:1–8, is being continued here. As Israel experienced God in passing through the waters of the Red Sea only to encounter trials and tests in the wilderness, so Jesus, still wet from the Jordan, is plunged into the wilderness. (In 1 Cor. 10:1–13 Paul compares Israel's baptism and temptation to the experience of Christians.) The forty days is also reminiscent of significant periods in Israel's relation to God. The intensity of the experience for Jesus is underscored in Mark both by the brevity of the account and by the vigor of the language: drove him out (literally, threw or cast him out); tempted (tested, put through trials); Satan (the adversary, the opposing one); wild beasts (wild animals and demons were in the wilderness, Isa. 34:8–14; some believed demons dwelt in wild beasts); angels waited on him (not after the temptation but during it, in a contest with Satan).

One has to be impressed and affected by the reality of Jesus' experience in the wilderness. Not even protests that we no longer subscribe to driving spirits, demon-possessed animals, Satan, and ministering angels can obscure the clear resonance of our own experiences with that which Mark describes. If there is any reticence to accept the temptation account, the reason probably lies not in the highly symbolic nature of the description but in the fact that it is happening to Jesus. Many Christians wish to protect Jesus from trials and temptations and other difficulties common to humankind for fear that convictions about his uniqueness will be eroded by such experiences. When faced with assertions such as, "For we do not have a high priest who is unable to sympathize with our weaknesses, but we have one who in every respect has been tested as we are, yet without sin" (Heb. 4:15), some would respond that Jesus was not really tempted but was setting examples for us. Such a view of Jesus seems blind to the fact that anyone who walks through experiences that are not personally engaging or demanding just to set an example is not setting an example. Such approaches, however sincere, rob Jesus, the Scriptures, the gospel, and life itself of reality.

Mark's record is straightforward and clear. Jesus fully identifies with the people of God who were, and are, tested in the wilderness. For Israel, the wilderness symbolized some extraordinary experiences of God (Exod. 19; Hos. 2:14); and the Israelites recalled those bittersweet days annually with the Feast of Tents. But there was a darker side to the wilderness, for there they had often failed the test (temptation), rebelled against God, and suffered God's wrath (Ps. 78; Ezek. 20:13–22). Jesus, then, has not withdrawn into pensive retreat, but Spirit-driven, he endures testing appropriate to his person, his powers, and his relation to God. In other words, the greater one's abilities, power, and influence, the greater one's temptations. Although Mark gives no details concerning the nature of Jesus' testing, we can be sure it was strong and ingeniously deceptive, given Jesus' relation to God, the many needs of the people about him, the several paths of ministry available, and the military, political, and religious forces ready to counter him. Jesus' temptation, then, is a preview of the many struggles that will test him during his ministry, sometimes involving demons, forces of nature, opposing clergy, and even his own close friends, and of the victory yet to come. It is natural, when reading this brief account, to look ahead to Gethsemane. Gethsemane was a garden, but for one night it, too, was a wilderness.

Second Sunday in Lent

Genesis 17:1–7, 15–16;
Psalm 22:23–31;
Romans 4:13–25;
Mark 8:31–38 or Mark 9:2–9

Today's Old Testament reading is closely linked with the epistolary reading from Romans; indeed, the account of God's covenant with Abraham in Genesis 17 is specifically cited by Paul and functions centrally in his overall argument for Abraham as the paradigm of faith for believers in every generation. A central element in the psalm is the promise that all the nations will eventually turn to the Lord and worship him, also a critical point in Paul's argument. The first Gospel reading is Mark's account of the first passion prediction followed by Jesus' instructions concerning discipleship, whereas the second reading is Mark's account of the Transfiguration.

Genesis 17:1–7, 15–16

As the Old Testament reading for the previous week concerned the covenant with Noah, this one concerns the covenant with Abraham. The biblical context is the stories of the patriarchs, which began with the call of Abraham in Genesis 12:1–3. Like Genesis 9:8–17, Genesis 17 comes from the hand of the Priestly Writer and carries forward his interpretation of human history as a series of covenants, each progressively narrower than the previous one and culminating with the covenant at Sinai (Exod. 19–Num. 10) between the Lord and the people of Israel under the leadership of Moses. Finally at Sinai the detailed laws for Israel were revealed, but before that there were covenants that included not only Israel but other peoples as well. Abraham, as this chapter explicitly points out, was "the ancestor of a multitude of nations," and therefore Muslims as well as Jews legitimately claim him as their ancestor.

Viewed as a whole, the patriarchal narratives have an overarching theme, that of God's promise concerning land and progeny. To be sure, not every individual story develops that theme, but it is central in Genesis 17. Moreover, the major sources in Genesis, J and P, treat the theme quite differently. It is the Yahwist who speaks quite directly of the promise, as in Genesis 12:1–3. When the Lord calls Abram to leave his country and go out, the Lord promises to make of the patriarch a great nation, to make his name great, so that he will be a blessing to all the families of the earth. At other points the Yahwist reports the promise that the descendants of the patriarchs will possess the land of Canaan, in which they themselves were only resident aliens. Similar words are uttered to Isaac and to Jacob. The Priestly Writer communicates the content of similar promises, as in our text, in the context of covenants with the ancestors.

All of the patriarchal stories in Genesis 12–50, with the exception of Genesis 14, are family stories. That is, they concern not public, historical events but matters that take place in the household between husbands and wives, parents and children, brothers and sisters. Public figures such as kings and pharaohs appear on the scene occasionally, but they are important only insofar as they have a bearing on the successive generations of this great family.

These accounts of how the promise came down through the families are recounted from the perspective of later generations. In the case of the Yahwist, the perspective is that of a people who have experienced the fulfillment of the promise. He wrote probably during the era of Solomon or soon thereafter, at the height of Israel's glory and power. The Priestly Writer, on the other hand, viewed the events from the perspective of a people who had experienced the loss of the land and nationhood through the Babylonian Exile. He insists, however, that the ancient covenant is still valid and that the people of God will once again see the promises fulfilled. Moreover, when he speaks in Genesis 17 of Abraham as the ancestor of nations and understands a covenant that extends beyond Israel, we should keep in mind that he and his contemporaries have experienced persecution and destruction at the hand of some of those very nations.

The setting for the events reported in Genesis 17 is given quite briefly in the first half of verse 1. The writer considers it relevant to report of Abraham's situation only that he was ninety-nine years old and that God appeared to him. The remainder of the passage except for verse 3a is a series of divine speeches. At the end we hear that "Abraham fell on his face and laughed" (v. 17). He was incredulous; how could such old people as he and Sarah have children? God responds by reaffirming the promise of progeny and makes it quite specific that Sarah will have a son whom they are to name Isaac. Moreover, God will establish a covenant with him as well (vv. 19–20).

The substance of the chapter is formed by the speeches of God to Abraham. First, there is a general statement of God's intention to make a covenant, multiplying Abraham "exceedingly" (vv. 1–2). Second, God spells out the contents of the covenant promise (vv. 4–8). It includes the promise of progeny so that "a multitude of nations" and even kings will come from the patriarch, the assurance that Abraham's descendants will possess the land of Canaan, and the vow of an everlasting covenant with those descendants. The granting of the covenant entails a change of names, from Abram to Abraham. Third, God calls for Abraham to "keep" the covenant by circumcising all male descendants (vv. 9–14). (The lectionary tactfully omits the detailed instructions for circumcision in verses 11–14). Fourth and finally, God addresses Abraham concerning his childless wife, changing her name from Sarai to Sarah, extending to her the promise that she would be the mother of nations and kings, and indicating that the first step in the fulfillment will be a son.

The central focus of this passage is the covenant with Abraham and—to be sure—Sarah. On the meaning of covenants as promissory oaths, see the discussion of last Sunday's Old Testament reading, Genesis 9:8–17. The initiative for the establishment of the covenant comes from God. Among the promises granted to Abraham and Sarah and their descendants, the divine affirmation, "I will be their God" (v. 8), stands out. That is not a stipulation along with the others, but states the essence of the covenant itself.

Unlike the covenant with Noah and the parallel to this text in Genesis 15:7–21, the recipient of the covenant is expected to respond with specific acts of obedience. The response is both general, "keep my covenant" (v. 9), and specific, "Every male among you shall be circumcised" (v. 10). To keep a covenant is to be faithful to its stipulations, and in this case there is only one, in perpetuity. The Priestly Writer understands that there were just a few ordinances that predated the law of Moses given at Sinai. These included observance of the sabbath, the prohibition of eating meat with the blood, and circumcision. These regulations had particular meaning for the people who had lost the temple and the land and were living in Babylon as exiles, for they were portable religious practices.

In ancient Israel circumcision was an explicitly religious observance; its meaning had nothing to do with hygiene. It was practiced also in Egypt but not in Assyria and Babylon; the Philistines are ridiculed with the epithet "the uncircumcised." The story of Moses and Zipporah (Exod. 4:24–27) seems to suggest that it had once been a puberty rite that only later became an act performed on the eighth day after birth. At its most fundamental level, it was a sign of membership in the covenant community. (See the story of Dinah and the people of Shechem in Gen. 34.) The ritual was genuinely sacramental, an outward and visible sign of the acceptance of God's election, and parallel in meaning to the baptism of infants.

Names are of great significance in this account, as they are throughout the Bible. The initiator of the covenant identifies himself as El Shaddai, read in most translations since the Septuagint as "God Almighty." But the precise meaning is uncertain; it is simply a divine proper name, given here because it is essential that the parties to the covenant be identified. The names of the other parties are changed with the establishment of the agreement. Both "Abraham" and "Sarah" are dialectical variants of their earlier names. "Abraham" does not literally mean "father of a multitude"; the explanation in verse 5 is a popular etymology, a pun. Critical here is the understanding that the new names, like the names of the other patriarchs Isaac and Jacob/Israel, are given by God. Moreover, the new names signal transformation to a new reality. Their names confirm their destiny under the covenant with God. In a genuine sense, they become what they are named, as God has promised to be their God. They—and their descendants after them—have now become God's people.

Psalm 22:23–31

This psalm, with its emphasis on suffering, humiliation, and passion, comprises one of the readings for Good Friday, and is discussed further at that point in the lectionary. The present lection emphasizes those passages in the psalm that speak of vindication and celebration. The break between the two main portions of the psalm comes after verse 22, which comprises the supplicant's vow. From verse 23 on, the psalm is concerned with celebration and praise, not humiliation and supplication. How can we account for this radically different content of the psalm and the radical break following verse 22?

One way of reading the psalm in its totality is to see verses 1–22 as a prayer for help that was followed by a priestly oracle assuring the worshiper that God had heard and answered the request. Note that the last line of verse 24 declares that God has heard. Verses 23–31 are thus the psalmist's celebration and fulfillment of the vow made in verse 22.

The material in verses 23–31 falls into the following categories: (1) appeal to a human audience calling upon the people to praise God (vv. 23–24), (2) worshiper's prayer of thanks to God (v. 25a), and (3) proclamation to the human audience of the consequences of the salvation that has been experienced (vv. 25b–31).

In verse 25a, the worshiper interprets the praise now offered as coming from God. Because this is addressed to the Deity, such a statement represents an indirect form of thanksgiving. The great congregation before whom praise and proclamation are offered would be the worshipers assembled in the temple for a festival or for some royal celebration of victory or recovery if the user of this psalm was the king. In the earlier vow (v. 22), the worshiper promised to "tell of your name to my brothers and sisters; in the midst of the congregation I will praise you." What is referred to here is the participation in a thanksgiving ritual that included sacrifice and thanksgiving as well as "offering testimony" concerning God's saving power and his redemption. The offering of testimony played a significant role in Israelite worship and to some extent parallels types of testimonials frequently heard in churches a generation or so ago.

Two characteristics about offering testimony in the psalms should be noted. First, testimony was given in rather stereotyped language that described in general rather than specific terms the distress from which a person had been saved. This style was used so that the same psalms, probably written by cultic officials or priests instead of individual worshipers, could be used repeatedly. The use of stereotypical and metaphorical language allowed the worshipers to plumb their misery in great depth and to describe it in more colorful and dramatic language than would have been the case if they merely recited the realistic details of their turmoil.

Second, the testimony offered moved into the realm of what might be called proclamation or preaching. That is, worshipers were allowed and encouraged, even required, to speak about the dire straits from which they had recovered and also to preach to the audience of friends and family at the thanksgiving ceremony.

The fulfillment of vows is spoken of in verses 25b–26, where persons are called upon not only to share in the praise but also to eat and be satisfied. The afflicted, or poor, in verse 26 may refer to persons of this class or perhaps to those persons who sought asylum in the sanctuary and thus lived off the services of the temple. The sharing of food in lavish form is, as every mother knows, a universal act expressive of well-being and contentment. Note that in the psalm "sharing follows receiving" and is a gesture of the blessed to incorporate others into the blessing. The Old Testament has special concern for the poor and afflicted so much so that orphans, widows, and others were allowed to share in the tithes and sacrifices of others (see Deut. 14:29; 16:10–14; 26:12).

The consequences of the worshiper's salvation and thanksgiving, given in verses 27–31, suggest that the person involved was the king, because the salvation of a single ordinary individual would not have had the universal implications noted in these verses. These royal features, of course, made it easy to apply this psalm to Christ or to use it for understanding him.

Although the text of verses 27–31 contains many problems and makes translation somewhat difficult, what it suggests is rather clear. First of all, there is reference to the universal impact of the situation. The "ends of the earth" is a way of saying everywhere. The text states that people throughout the world will worship Yahweh, the God of Israel. (This seems to have been a common expectation held in the cult and court of Jerusalem; see Isa. 2:1–4 and Mic. 4:1–4.) As king in Jerusalem, Yahweh was also king over the nations of the world.

Verse 29 seems to imply that perhaps even the dead or at least the dying will also bow down before him (God). This idea may sound farfetched, but the Apostles' Creed declares that Jesus descended into hell (see 1 Pet. 3:18–20).

Not only the present (vv. 27–28) and past generations (v. 29) but also generations yet to come will tell of the redemption of Yahweh and proclaim his deliverance to generations yet to be born. The missionary and universal tone of this psalm is one of its key characteristics.

Romans 4:13–25

Like the Old Testament reading from Genesis 17, today's epistolary lection focuses on God's covenant with Abraham. In fact, Genesis 17:5 is directly cited by Paul in Romans 4:17, and Genesis 17 and Genesis 15 provide the basis of much of Paul's argumentation in Romans 4 (cf. vv. 3, 10, 18–19). For Paul, no Old Testament character exemplified genuine faith better than did Abraham, "the father of all of us" (v. 16). In Romans 4, Paul insists that Abraham is the prototype of faith for all who believe, both Jews and Gentiles (v. 11–13). In Abraham, Paul saw established the principle of justification by faith.

For Paul, it was crucial that in the storyline of Genesis Abraham was said to have been justified by God prior to his receiving the covenant of circumcision, and Paul pushed this distinction to its logical limits. This could only mean that the basis on which God's promise to Abraham—and to his seed—was sustained was "through the righteousness of faith" and not through the law (v. 13). The capacity to believe in God's promises, as incredible as those promises might appear, was prior to, and, in a real sense, transcended the principle of obeying Torah.

Today's epistolary lection, then, focuses on the kind of faith Abraham displayed. Paul insists that, qualitatively speaking, the faith of Abraham is essentially the same as the faith of the Christian. For one thing, Christian faith, for all its stress on the person and work of Christ, is fundamentally faith in the God who "gives life to the dead" (v. 17). That this is the case is seen in Paul's concluding remarks, where he introduces Christ into the discussion (vv. 24–25). Notice: If we "believe in him [i.e., God] who raised from the dead Jesus our Lord, who was delivered to death for our sins and raised again to secure our justification" (Phillips). It is the God who brought death to life in the womb of Sarah (v. 19) who also brought Jesus to life from the dead. What Abraham was asked to believe was as incredible as what those who heard Paul's missionary preaching were asked to believe. Yet Abraham becomes exemplary for all those who have lived after him—Jews and Gentiles alike—precisely because he did not "waver concerning the promise of God" (v. 20). On the contrary, he was "fully convinced that God was able to do what he had promised" (v. 21).

If we ask how Abraham's faith might inform Christian life and thought during Lent, several suggestions occur. First, Abraham reminds the penitent that the God who promises forgiveness can be trusted implicitly. Genuine penitence often reopens the question of whether God does, or indeed can, forgive. To be truly meaningful and constructive, however, penitence must be predicated on the firm conviction that what God has promised, God is able to perform (v. 21). Second, today's text reminds us that justification by faith and salvation by grace go hand in hand (v. 16). To have implicit trust in a faithful God is to recognize that we are saved by a generous and uncalculated gift of divine grace. Seen this way, salvation is always gift, never reward. It is never even a reward for penitence! As the church discovered during the Reformation, even penitence can become a work looking for a reward, but salvation as Paul conceives it is no quid pro quo, extended as a reward for works of penitence. Third, our text speaks for the commonality of all who genuinely believe in God—both Jews and Gentiles. It might be worth noting that even Christians have no monopoly on the kind of faith Paul describes in Romans 4.

Mark 8:31–38

Mark is a Good Friday Gospel in the sense that the cross is central to understanding Jesus and the nature of discipleship. It is fitting then that the first prediction of the cross and crossbearing (8:31–38) be a Lenten lesson.

Our text for today introduces a new phase in the ministry of Jesus. "Then he began to teach them" (v. 31) is Mark's signal that the disciples are now to hear from Jesus a word unlike prior teaching, a word for which they are not prepared. The disciples had left boats, jobs, and families to follow Jesus. The pace of their work was hectic and exhausting, but in spite of occasions of opposition and suspicion, they had found it exciting. Sometimes they had not understood Jesus, but the fact that they were called to be disciples surely meant the work was to continue and to grow. They are not to be censured for failing to grasp the meaning of suffering, rejection, and death as the fate of their leader.

Mark 8:31–38 consists of two parts: instruction to the disciples (vv. 31–33) and instruction to the multitude together with the disciples (vv. 34–38). Both private and public instruction on matters difficult to understand (parables, divorce, wealth, and the kingdom) is a common pattern in Mark. Immediately preceding this passage is the account of Peter confessing and of Jesus rebuking his disciples, demanding silence on the matter (vv. 27–30). These preceding verses are important for sensing the pattern of the narrative: Peter confesses and Jesus rebukes; Jesus confesses that his real mission is suffering and death, and Peter rebukes. However, for Mark, and quite unlike Matthew, the confession of Peter is not central to this section. Rather, Mark's focus is upon the prediction of the passion and the fact that Jesus' passion is definitive for the life of a disciple (vv. 31–38). On these twin themes there is no charge to silence; there is no mystery concealed in a parable: "He said all this quite openly" (v. 32). The language is intense and strong. The rebukes and counter-rebukes (vv. 30, 32, 33) and the charges to silence are the same expressions used by Jesus when "shouting down" demons during an exorcism. Peter is rebuked because his rejection of Jesus' announced path of suffering represents as real a temptation as any experienced in the wilderness.

And so Jesus begins to teach his followers that the Son of Man must suffer, be rejected, be killed, and be raised again. Three brief comments need to be made on verses 31–33. First, the term "Son of Man" is complex with multiple uses, and, unless the preacher is careful, efforts to explain it can be an endless side trip. In verse 31, it can be taken as the equivalent of "I." Matthew so understood it at this point (Matt. 16:21–23). In verse 38, "Son of Man" refers clearly to an apocalyptic figure coming in judgment and salvation. Second, the rather elaborate reference to suffering, rejection, and death in contrast to the very brief mention of resurrection is significant. This same proportion holds at the end of this Gospel. Clearly, Mark does not want his church to use Easter to escape Lent and Good Friday. Third, at the heart of the passion prediction is rejection by the religious establishment, both lay and clergy. That may have been the sharpest pain of all. Whether the cross-bearing Christ still suffers such fate is a judgment each one has to make. One popular preacher recently explained his approach by saying, "You cannot succeed preaching the cross. People do not want to hear that; they already have enough problems." No wonder he is popular.

The second part of our text, verses 34–38, has been defined and interpreted by verses 31–33 and requires little comment. Verse 34 makes it clear that the way of the cross was not only for the Twelve but also for the multitudes. Of course, there is no way the multitudes (v. 34) could have known what Jesus said in private to the disciples (vv. 27–33), but that is not the issue in this literary arrangement, which joins private and public instruction. The point is, the reader has access to both and hence cannot escape the full force of the total passage. In other words, suffering and sacrifice for one's faith are not items of first-century history but are inherent in the Gospel. Verses 35–38 are a composite of four sayings, found in different contexts elsewhere (Matt. 10:33, 38–39; Luke 12:9; 14:27; 17:33). Being proverbial in nature, they are appropriate to many settings with many applications. The passage closes with an apocalyptic orientation, placing disciples in the presence of the Father, the Son, and the holy angels (1 Tim. 5:21; Rev. 1:45). Warning against apostasy in the face of terror and threat, Mark soberly reminds his readers that decisions about the Christ described in verses 31–37 have ultimate and eternal consequences.

Mark 9:2–9

This alternate Gospel reading may seem to offer the preacher a message radically different from Mark 8:31–38, for in that lection Jesus' prediction of his passion is the central theme, whereas here the focus is upon the Transfiguration. In fact, the Transfiguration appears at first to be an unlikely consideration for Lent. Closer examination will reveal, however, that the passage is more continuous than discontinuous with the preceding narrative. Even so, Lent, too, has its Sundays and its times of song and praise.

Mark 9:2–9 consists of two parts: 9:2–8 and verse 9. Usually 9:1 is treated as falling within the preceding unit, 8:31–9:1. The future coming of the Son of Man with the holy angels was announced in 8:38, and 9:1 continues the thought, extending it with the assurance that the end will occur soon, within the lifetime of some in the audience. The imminence of the coming of the kingdom is a common theme in Mark, even occurring at 13:30, a section otherwise instructing the reader not to be misled; the end is not yet. Our lection closes at verse 9 with Jesus instructing Peter, James, and John to be quiet about this experience until after the resurrection. The reasons probably are two: (1) it is obvious they had not understood what had occurred, so their witness would be both confused and confusing, and (2) the glory of the Son of Man waits on the crucifixion. This is vital in Mark; talk of glory prior to the cross is premature and theologically inadequate. The instruction in 9:9 is in keeping with the secrecy motif elsewhere in Mark.

At the center of today's lection and governing the literary and theological territory around it is the Transfiguration (vv. 2–8) of Jesus in the presence of the three who were privy to other critical moments in Jesus' life (5:37; 13:3; 14:33). The reader will recognize ways the scene is reminiscent of Moses' experience with God on the mountain. Exodus 24:15–18 contains the mountain, the clouds, the glory, and the six days; and according to Exodus 34:29–35, the experience gave to Moses a shining face because he had been talking with God. Clouds are a common feature of theophanies and Christophanies (Exod. 16:10; Mark 13:26; Acts 1:9). Elijah was widely understood to be the prophet of the end times (Mal. 4:1–6; Mark 9:11–13), but Moses, whom some believed also to have been translated (Deut. 34:6), joined Elijah as a figure of the end of the age. The two appear together as faithful witnesses in Revelation 11:3–13.

Mark often interprets an event as much by its location in the narrative as by comments offered. Such is the case here. The Transfiguration comes at the very center of the Gospel and is the only "mountaintop" story in Mark. Only here and at his baptism does Jesus receive divine confirmation visibly and audibly. It is significant that this confirmation occurs here and not at the cross or resurrection. The absence of a resurrection appearance in Mark (assuming the text ends at 16:8) and the glorious appearance of Jesus in this scene have combined to convince some scholars that the Transfiguration is a "misplaced resurrection story." For Mark it is not misplaced; in fact, the scene is deliberately located in the narrative. Bracketed on either side by Jesus' talk of his suffering and death (8:31–38; 9:12; 30–31), the event provides the moment of recognition. The glorious coming of the Son of Man, which had been predicted in 8:38 and said to be imminent in 9:1, is now previewed at a time when talk of Jesus' passion is the shocking new subject of Jesus' teaching. The Transfiguration is only a preview, however. The error of Peter and the others (vv. 5–6) is their wanting to seize the moment and make present the glory that cannot be fully consummated apart from the cross.

Peter is not alone among Jesus' followers in the desire to steal from the future and bypass Golgotha.

Third Sunday in Lent

Exodus 20:1–17;
Psalm 19;
1 Corinthians 1:18–25;
John 2:13–22

Specific connections between the Decalogue in Exodus 20 and the New Testament readings for the Third Sunday in Lent are difficult to discern. A portion of the psalm (vv. 7–14), however, is an expression of praise to God for the perfection of the law, which reveals itself in the entire creation. The Gospel lection may be taken at one level as Jesus' condemnation of the corruption of what the law had called for, and the Epistle on another level sets the Christian proclamation against what Jews and Greeks seek. In New Testament contexts in general, the Decalogue may be taken to stand for the Old Testament law as a whole.

Exodus 20:1–17

At least two aspects of the Old Testament context of the Decalogue are important for its interpretation in Christian worship and preaching.

First, one should keep in mind the place of this law code in its narrative framework. It is part of the story of the Exodus and Israel's wandering in the wilderness. The introductory sentence actually summarizes the story: "I am the LORD your God, who brought you out of the land of Egypt, out of the house of slavery" (v. 2). Theologically, this is of the greatest significance. The law is given to a people who have been, quite literally, saved, rescued from slavery. Consequently, their salvation and election are not earned by obedience to the law: God's action comes first. Obedience to the law is the appropriate response to what God has already done.

Second, the immediate context of the Decalogue is liturgical. Exodus 19–24 describes a religious ceremony, the establishment of the covenant between God and Israel. The ritual aspects of the event, including purification, processions, the recitation of solemn words, and even a meal, would not have taken place only once, but were celebrated in various ways over the centuries. That is to say, the report in Exodus reflects actual cultic practices. The ceremony establishes and reestablishes the relationship between God and people, in which the laws, including the Decalogue, provide the stipulations.

The question of the literary source or document to which this code belongs is not very important for its interpretation. It sits loosely in the older sources, J and E, and is distinct from the Priestly legislation that follows in Exodus 25:15ff. All the sources agree that the law and the laws were given through Moses at Mt. Sinai. But in any case, the laws in Exodus 20 are much more ancient than any of the written sources of the Pentateuch.

The individual laws in the Decalogue belong to one of the two types of Israelite law, the apodictic. The other is the casuistic, the statement of a case and its consequences in third person style, for example, "When someone steals an ox or a sheep, and slaughters it or sells it, the thief shall pay five oxen for an ox, and four sheep for a sheep" (Exod. 22:1). Such case law was typical of ancient Near Eastern codes, such as the laws of Hammurabi. Apodictic laws, on the other hand, are short, second person commands or prohibitions. They are not linked or restricted to any specific circumstances, but are unequivocal. They are a distinctly Israelite form of law and are presented as the expression of the will of Israel's God.

This insight into the form of the laws becomes useful when applied to our text. It is obvious that some of the laws in Exodus 20:1–17 are much longer than others. The difference, however, is not in the length of the laws themselves, but in the commentaries on some of them. In verses 3, 13, 14, 15, and 17 we have only the laws without comment, but in all the other cases there are supplementary remarks, mainly of two kinds. Some, as in verses 4b–5a, 9–11, and 17b, are explanatory; that is, they spell out the meaning of the law. Others, as in verses 5b–6, 7b, and 12b, are more homiletical; that is, they urge that the law be observed and give reasons for obeying it. Such elements in the text indicate that the Decalogue was used in ancient Israel in teaching and preaching. As we preach on the present text, then, we are only continuing a process that began long before the Bible was completed.

That process is particularly visible when one compares this text with its parallel in Deuteronomy 5:6–21. The laws in both instances are the same. The only significant difference is in the interpretation of the sabbath ordinance. Whereas Exodus 20:9–11 bases it on the divine order of creation, Deuteronomy 5:13–15 relates it to Israel's release from Egyptian slavery. The former relates to cosmic order, the second to historical and humanitarian concerns.

In terms of formulation, all but two of the laws are prohibitions, the exceptions being the Fourth and Fifth Commandments. In terms of contents, the first four concern obligations directly to the Deity and the last six to relations among the covenant people. It would be a mistake, however, to distinguish sharply between religious or ritual laws and ethical concerns, for such a division seems not to have been made in the Old Testament. In a genuine sense, all obligations are directly related to the God of the covenant; relationships within the family and the community are to be treated as sacred.

If there is any priority among the laws, it is clear that the first is the most fundamental. The prohibition against the worship of other gods is the basis for all other regulations. It is not, however, the same as monotheism; quite the contrary, it assumes that there are alternative gods to worship. But as far as the covenant people are concerned, there is to be only one God. The Second Commandment is a direct extension of the first, voicing polemic against those whose gods can be represented by images or likenesses. The Third Commandment continues the same line of thought, prohibiting magic, or the attempt to manipulate God through improper use of the divine name. The expectations expressed in these commandments should be taken with utter seriousness today, no less than in ancient Israel. But as preachers, perhaps the greatest challenge we face is to present these lines before our congregations and our world in a nonlegalistic, nonmoralistic fashion. One is enabled to avoid such pitfalls, first, by remembering the narrative context of the code, that God has already taken the initiative to save the people. To obey, then, is to act in grateful response, to live out one's role in a covenant. Second, the basic force of these, as well as other Old Testament laws, is to define the limits of what it means to be a covenant people. One who fails to live by these stipulations has placed himself or herself outside the covenant. Third, one would need to reflect upon some of the New Testament interpretations of the function of the law; for example, it serves to make one aware of human limitations, including sin.

Psalm 19

This lection forms an appropriate parallel to the reading of the Decalogue because much of it is concerned with the law. This psalm is generally divided into two parts and sometimes even seen as the secondary combination of two separate psalms. Verses 1–6 declare that nature and creation—especially sky and sun—proclaim the glory of God and testify to divine will. Verses 7–14 praise the law (Torah) of God, which has been made known in commandment, precept, and ordinance. The character of the psalm is further complicated, however, because the "law" section, verses 7–14, can be further subdivided. In verses 7–10, the law is praised and God spoken about in the third person, whereas verses 11–14 are a prayer addressed directly to God.

In spite of its complexity, the psalm can be seen as a unity. The nature portion, verses 1–6, declares that creation, without normal words, voice, or speech, points to divine will and control and thus prompts expressions of praise. The law portion, verses 7–10, focuses on the written law formulated in words that elicit attitudes of praise. Verses 11–14 are a prayer that one might be aware of sins, faults, and errors in order to live a life that is without great transgressions. The final plea, in verse 14, requests that not only the words but also the unspoken meditations of the heart be acceptable to God. Thus the psalm moves from describing the unarticulatable expressions of nature, which proclaim God's work and fill the whole expansive realm of creation, down to the inarticulated meditations of the heart. Thus the thought of the psalm moves from the outer reaches of the natural world to the inner recesses of the human personality, the human heart.

Verses 7–14 are primarily concerned with the praise and glory of the law and the worshiper's petition offered in light of the will of God manifest in both nature and law. The antiphonal praise of the law, verses 7–10, knows the Torah as an object of praise and not as a burden or a yoke to be borne in grumbling servitude.

Six synonymous terms are used to speak about the Torah: law, testimony, precepts, commandment, fear, ordinances. Perhaps these six terms were used to express the fullness and completeness of the known will of God. The adjectival descriptions of the Torah are extremely positive in their affirmations: perfect, sure, right, pure, clean, true, righteous. Four aspects or benefits from the Torah are noted. The Torah revives the soul; it is life-giving and sustaining. It makes wise the simple by providing them with understanding. It rejoices the heart, making one glad to know the will and way of the Lord. It enlightens the eyes by providing a perspective within which to view the world and one's own life. Thus the law of God is a nobler and finer possession than gold and is sweeter than honey. The law is to be more desired than the most precious of human treasures or the sweetest and most reviving of foods.

This praise of the law and its life-giving qualities was characteristic of much Israelite and Jewish thought about Torah. Christians, viewing matters from the Pauline perspective on the law as found in Galatians, frequently have difficulty affirming the value and goodness of law. Yet the positive aspects of the written Torah should be emphasized, for Torah provides persons with specific directions, allows us to locate ourselves with regard to the understood will of God, and thus provides a sense of security. The law provides not only a general map for human living but also specific directions along the highway of life. With verse 11, the focus of the psalm moves from the world of creation and the praise of the law to the sentiments and concerns of the individual worshiper. The law, which like the sun is perfect, sure, and faithful, touches all so that "nothing is hid" from its preview. In light of this judging and quickening aspect of the law, the worshiper recognizes that the law not only warns but also calls into question human adequacy and constancy. Thus the psalmist prays to be kept from hidden faults, that is, those things one might do without realizing they are faults (v. 12), as well as presumptuous sins, that is, grave sins of arrogance or pride (v. 13). If one can be kept from hidden faults and presumptuous sins, then surely one is blameless, for these represent the two extreme poles.

The praise of God's glory in creation and the meditation on the law, in this psalm, led naturally to critical self-examination and to a focus on the whole range of disobedience, from secret, hidden sins to overt, callous acts of open transgression. In the concluding petition, verse 14, the psalmist requests full acceptance from the words of the mouth, the external articulated word, to the meditation of the heart, the internal unarticulated thought.

1 Corinthians 1:18–25

Paul was painfully aware that the message of the crucified Christ scarcely commended itself to first-century hearers, Jews or Greeks. For Jews, the notion of a suffering messiah was a contradiction in terms (cf. Mark 8:31–33 and parallels). To be crucified, or "hanged from a tree," was a sure sign of criminality (Deut. 21:23; 27:26) and therefore offensive to readers of Old Testament Scripture. Greek notions of heroic ideals were many and varied, but a hero who died ignominiously had little lasting appeal to them. The philosopher was a much more popular ideal for most Greeks. To be sure, for Paul to say that "Jews demand signs and Greeks desire wisdom" (v. 22) was a caricature, but like most caricatures there was a core of truth.

Paul could, however, at least speak out of his own experience of preaching the gospel, and it was his experience that the crucified Christ was a "stumbling block to Jews and foolishness to Gentiles" (v. 23). Even though some Jews and Gentiles had become Christians, they had done so by confronting directly the scandal of the cross. In one sense, this scandal remains even for those who have already become Christians, and who have been Christians for a long time. As one reflects on the passion of Christ, it never becomes a sensible message. In fact, the longer one lives with the Christian message the more one becomes convinced of its essential paradox. The words of today's epistolary lection stress the paradoxical nature of the Christian gospel: "God's foolishness is wiser than human wisdom, and God's weakness is stronger than human strength" (v. 25).

It is only natural for us, as human beings, to assess and scrutinize the ways of God, to employ human wisdom in trying to make sense of divine realities. As laudable as this might seem to us, for Paul it represents a fundamentally wrong way of conceiving the relationship between us and God. In verse 19 Paul cites Isaiah 29:14 as a way of reminding his readers that God's ways are beyond the scope of human wisdom. In defense of God, Paul asks rhetorically, "Where is the one who is wise? Where is the scribe? Where is the debater of this age?" (v. 20). For human beings to place God in the dock is but another form of human presumption.

The proper stance from which one can view the work of God is confessional. Paul recognizes that accepting the gospel is a subjective act. The gospel is the power of God to "us who are being saved" (v. 18). It is out of our own experience of the saving work of God that we are able to recognize the crucified Christ as "the power of God and the wisdom of God" (v. 24). As Paul says, this perception is possible "to those who are called" (v. 24). One is first summoned, and in the summons one experiences the saving work of God. Then, and only then, does one possess the vantage point from which to view the work of God—from the inside.

In many respects, Paul's attitude toward human wisdom as expressed in 1 Corinthians 1:18–25 is difficult for many modern Christians to accept. We are, after all, children of the scientific age and have been taught to think for ourselves, and to think critically and rationally about the world around us. The phenomenal achievements of modern science are vivid testimony to scientific inquiry and the application of reason to life.

It is worth remembering, however, that Paul's remarks in First Corinthians have a specific focus and context. Some of his readers placed a high premium on wisdom and knowledge. Whether they were "Gnostics" in the technical sense is debated. Nevertheless, they seemed to have valued the intellect, and in doing so constricted their understanding of the gospel. Accordingly, Paul reminds them that "knowledge" should be balanced by "love" (1 Cor. 8:1–2). He also censures them for the way in which their stress on wisdom and knowledge had created elitism within the church.

Paul's words notwithstanding, inquiring Christians still find themselves searching to understand the ways of God. Given the essential paradox of the cross, the Christian message will remain a mystery to be probed. Even if it does not "make sense" to outsiders, and possibly not even to ourselves at times, the Christian gospel does nevertheless "make sense of us" in a way that is finally redemptive.

John 2:13–22

All the lections for today dramatically curb any tendency to allow Lent to degenerate into a period of self-flagellation or efforts at self-improvement. The listener to these texts is confronted by a God of wisdom, of power, and of ethical demand. It is before God and not before a mirror that the penitent stands. Our Gospel reading from John, companion to Mark in this year of the lectionary, is no less confrontive than the other lessons.

John 2:13–22 is the Fourth Evangelist's account of the cleansing of the temple. All four Gospels carry this story, but the Synoptics place it near the end of Jesus' ministry, where it provides the precipitating factor in the decision to kill Jesus. But it is not so here. John removes the story from logical and chronological sequences and places it here, almost at the beginning of the Gospel, so that it may be understood in and of itself as a theological event. After all, the Evangelist is not interested in *causes* of Jesus' death, for to him Jesus' life and death were not shaped by circumstances and historical contingencies. On the contrary, no one took his life; he himself laid it down and he took it up again (10:17–18). What, then, does Jesus' cleansing the temple mean for John?

First, it is a Passover story (v. 13). This means that it relates to the death and resurrection of Jesus. This is the case with other Passover stories such as feeding the multitudes, which is clearly eucharistic and focuses on the body and blood of Jesus (chap. 6). The actual account of Jesus' death (19:31–37) is told in this Gospel as a Passover story. The reader of 2:13–22 is therefore alerted at the outset to the fact that the real subject here is Jesus' passion.

Second, this is a story of a conflict of values, a conflict between what Jesus Christ really means and those values espoused by the structures of religion with which Jesus contended.

The writer knew that the issues at stake here were not clear to Jesus' followers at the time, but after the resurrection they remembered (vv. 17, 22). The form of the narrative is the one common to the many stories in this Gospel: Jesus speaks "from above" and his auditors hear "from the earth"; Jesus speaks what is true and they hear what is apparent. "Destroy this temple, and in three days I will raise it up" (v. 19) is met with, "This temple has been under construction for forty-six years" (v. 20). Such dialogues constitute dramatic irony, for the reader of the story knows what Jesus' audience does not; that is, that Jesus is speaking of his own passion. Jesus was asked for a sign, and he gave the ultimate and final sign, his death and resurrection. The contrast is painfully clear. A temple, built as a witness to God and as a means of drawing persons near to God, is now an object of adoration, an end in itself. It is, therefore, ripe for destruction. But in the throes of death and in a move toward self-preservation, the temple keepers will destroy the One in whom God and humankind meet.

And finally, this is a story directed to the church. John does not relate this event as a dance over the grave of a grand institution or as an attack upon all rites, customs, and special places, but upon their tendency to receive the devotion due to God and God alone. The ancient evil is tenacious, insidious, and slow to die. Who has not known persons who were apparently faithful in attention to all Christian duties but who, when there was a change in the building or minister or pattern of worship, suddenly ended all participation? It is a painful and costly lesson offered by our text; we want to be in charge of our own lives and manage all our relationships with God. Some will even kill if that control is threatened. Why is it so difficult to kneel first before God and listen and then proceed from that perspective to build our altars and frame our liturgies? Those who know that Christ is our sanctuary also know what the church building is, and is not.

Fourth Sunday in Lent

Numbers 21:4b–9;
Psalm 107:1–3, 17–22;
Ephesians 2:1–10;
John 3:14–21

Because Lent provides an occasion for us to come to terms with our stubborn wills, the account of Israel's resistance to God in today's Old Testament text is singularly appropriate for pointing up how God can both punish and cure disobedience. The psalm is a prayer of thanksgiving offered to the God who redeems and makes well. Echoing similar themes, the epistolary reading speaks of the transition from death to life that occurs in conversion, and the well-known Gospel reading introduces the Johannine view of everlasting life made possible in the Son.

Numbers 21:4b–9

This is the Old Testament text assigned for Holy Cross, September 14, in each year of the lectionary cycle. See the commentary for that special day in this volume.

Psalm 107:1–3, 17–22

Psalm 107 is a thanksgiving psalm but a thanksgiving psalm with unique features. Neither a communal nor an individual psalm, it was composed for use in a special thanksgiving ritual. Persons who had been involved in various dangers—lost on a caravan journey, imprisoned, sick, or endangered at sea—and had vowed and made promises to God in the midst of their life-threatening experiences were given the occasion to offer thanks and fulfill their vows.

The psalm calls upon these redeemed (v. 2) to celebrate their redemption—namely, to celebrate their being saved from death in the desert, in prison, from sickness, at sea—by offering thanksgiving to God and testimony before the congregation (see vv. 22 and 32). Thanksgiving services were times of merriment and indulgence (recall the celebration at the return of the prodigal son in Jesus' parable). Sacrifices made for thanksgiving were primarily eaten by the worshipers; in fact, they had to be consumed on the day of the sacrifice or the day following (see Lev. 7:11–18).

The psalm is composed of an introduction (vv. 1–3), four sections focusing on four different categories of celebrants (vv. 4–9, 10–16, 17–22, 23–32), and a hymnic epilogue (vv. 33–43). Within each of the four central sections, a double refrain occurs. The first (vv. 6, 13, 19, and 28) reports that those in peril cried out to Yahweh, and he delivered them from their distress. The second (vv. 8, 15, 21, and 31) calls upon the redeemed to give thanks to God for his love and redemption.

Verses 17–22 report on those who had been ill or through their foolishness (see NRSV marginal note) had endangered their health. This psalm associates the illness with sinful acts and sees the latter as the cause of the former. The conditions of illness (v. 18) were reversed when the supplicants cried out to God for help (v. 19) and were healed by divine intervention (v. 20). Offering sacrifice and bearing testimony in the community of worship are presented as the proper response of thanksgiving (vv. 21–22).

Ephesians 2:1–10

On the Fourth Sunday in Lent, penitential mourning gives way to joy. Its name, Laetare Sunday, derives from the opening words of the Mass text "Laetare Jerusalem" (Rejoice, O Jerusalem). This theme of joy came to be celebrated in the ancient church in various ways; for example, by the use of a rose in connection with the liturgical celebration. This practice is attested as early as the eleventh century and seems to have derived from the Roman custom of using flowers in celebration to mark the beginning of spring.

Today's epistolary text sounds this note of triumphant joy. Ephesians 2 opens by noting the contrast between death and life: "even when we were dead through our trespasses, [God] made us alive together with Christ" (v. 5). Death giving way to life is vividly attested through the blooming flowers of spring, and the rose symbolism of Laetare Sunday effectively conveys this. The stress on our former state of disobedience (vv. 2–3) recalls the earlier period of Lent, when penitence and mourning were in the forefront. But, as this passage unfolds, there is a marked shift to the new life. In this respect, today's text shifts the attention of the reader more directly toward Easter.

On the Wednesday following the Fourth Sunday in Lent, the apostolic creed was handed over to catechumens (*traditio symboli*). They were now moving closer to the full appropriation of the paschal mystery of Christ. The baptismal imagery of today's text would thus take on additional significance.

First, we should note that God is the subject of the action described in verses 4–7. The drama of reenactment thus unfolds as one in which God is the chief actor, for God is, after all, the true administrator of baptism. The initiative of salvation is God's love: "Out of the great love with which he loved us" (v. 4). It is God who "made us alive together with Christ" and "raised us up with him" (vv. 5–6).

Second, the repeated use of participatory language should be noticed, especially the preposition "with": "made us alive together *with* Christ . . . raised us up *with* him . . . made us sit *with* him in the heavenly places" (vv. 5–6). The one who reenacts the death and resurrection of Christ does so not as a symbolic ritual. Instead, God may be said to reenact the death and resurrection of Christ within the baptism of each believer. God, the chief actor in the paschal drama of Christ through which death gave way to life, takes the one baptized through the same sacred drama. The newly attained status of the believer is depicted quite phenomenally as sitting enthroned with the risen Christ in the heavenly places. This stands in sharp contrast with Paul's theology of baptism described in Romans 6, where the believer's full appropriation of resurrection remains unrealized in this life.

The concluding portion of this text is reminiscent of the epistolary reading for the Second Sunday in Lent. Here again stress is on salvation given through the grace of God and "not because of [human] works." The Pauline emphasis is still central here. To emphasize that salvation is "not your own doing [but] . . . the gift of God" (v. 8) is a natural extension of the thought in verses 4–7, where God is portrayed as the initiator and chief actor of the drama of salvation, both of Christ and Christians. Accordingly, the people of God are the handiwork of God—"we are what he has made us" (v. 10). We are who we are as a result of the activity of God.

The readers are also reminded that this drama had its origin in primeval history (v. 10). As stated in Ephesians 1:4, it was prior to the foundation of the world that God chose us. This is in keeping with the cosmic outlook of Ephesians, where the drama of salvation history is sketched from the beginning of time until the end of time as encompassing the whole universe. This provides a salient reminder to all believers, catechumens and converts alike, that the sacred drama into which we have been introduced, which we have appropriated, and in which we participate as joint participants with Christ, extends far beyond our life and time. In appropriating the Christian story for ourselves, we become part of a historical and cosmic process that has preceded us and will succeed us, but in which we ourselves are nevertheless actively engaged.

John 3:14–21

After a first reading of the four lessons for today, two words come to mind as a summary expression of what is being said: judgment and grace. It is not uncommon to think of judgment and grace as two separate actions of God. Some texts speak of God's repeated acts of grace, when rebuffed or denied, being followed by acts of judgment. Other texts speak of God's judgment upon the people and then of God's turning toward them in favor and grace. However, in our Gospel for this Sunday one act of God is spoken of as being both judgment and grace. That act is God's sending Christ into the world.

As readers of the Gospel of John know, it is extremely difficult to divide the text into discrete units. The words of Jesus and the words of the Evangelist are interwoven, and lengthy speeches close with theological summaries. In chapter 3, editors differ as to where to place the quotation marks in Jesus' conversation with Nicodemus: after verse 13, verse 15, verse 16, or verse 21? Fortunately, the meaning of verses 14–21 does not depend on the identity of the person who said it. Actually, verses 14–21 consist of two distinct units: verses 14–15 and verses 16–21, neither of which is dependent on verses 1–13. Our lection is one of many theological summaries in this Gospel, placed immediately after conversations or conflicts but not materially related to them (3:31–36; 5:14–24, 25–29, 30–47 are other examples).

The first unit, verses 14–15, is a self-contained statement based on the ways in which Christ's redemptive act is analogous to the event of the brazen serpent recorded in Numbers 21:4–9. In the Numbers story, the people were suffering God's punishment for sin, but the elevation of a bronze serpent upon a pole provided relief and life for all who looked upon it. Likewise, Christ is lifted up for the life of all who look to him in faith. The lifting up of Christ in this Gospel has a double meaning: it refers to the manner of his death (12:32–33) and also to his exaltation to the presence of God. Both John 3:14–15 and Numbers 21:4–9 are accounts of God's grace, God's initiative for the salvation of the people.

The second unit, verses 16–21, is a theological reflection upon the meaning of Christ coming into the world. The governing image in the passage is light, a favorite of this Gospel (1:1–9; 8:12; 11:9–10). The light metaphor is appropriate to the idea of revelation, of God being made known to us, which, according to John, is the purpose of the incarnation. No one has ever seen God, but the only Son has made God known (1:18), and to know God is life eternal (17:3). But light is also a most appropriate metaphor for expressing both the judgment and the grace implicit in Christ's coming. Christ did not come to judge, but his coming is a judgment in the same way that turning on a light can be the exposure and conviction of those who prefer darkness because their deeds are evil (v. 20). At the same time, the light is for others a gift and the occasion for joy (v. 21). The Scriptures reveal that an act of God's love has both positive and negative effects. A stepping-stone may be for some a stumbling block; a feast may be the occasion for illnesses that result from gluttony. A saving presence can also be a disturbing presence. It is only in the make-believe world of a child that one can turn on a light without creating shadows. All who preach and live the gospel know this painful truth. To speak the good news, to voice the love of Christ in some gatherings, is not to be unanimously received with applause and blessing. Other forces are aroused by that word of God's grace. All who would be centers of power and influence for good must live with this fact. This is what it means to make a difference in the world. This is what John means when he says Jesus Christ is the crisis, the difference, the judgment of the world (v. 19).

Fifth Sunday in Lent

Jeremiah 31:31–34;
Psalm 51:1–12 or Psalm 119:9–16;
Hebrews 5:5–10;
John 12:20–33

Today's Old Testament reading, an unqualified announcement of salvation, contains the only explicit reference to the New Testament, that is, the new covenant. As we approach the end of a season of penitence and preparation, Jeremiah 31:31–34 anticipates a particular aspect of the good news of Easter—that God will transform human hearts. Psalm 51, one of the most famous laments, poignantly links penitence, confession, and a plea for moral renewal. A slightly different emphasis is offered in the alternate psalm reading, where the law of the Lord is seen as the center of gravity for the faithful worshiper. Jesus' passion is highlighted in the epistolary reading, which places perfection on the other side of suffering. An ominous note is sounded in the Gospel reading, which speaks of Jesus' impending death.

Jeremiah 31:31–34

This reading, an unqualified announcement of salvation, contains the only explicit Old Testament reference to the New Testament, that is, the new covenant. As we approach the end of a season of penitence and preparation, Jeremiah 31:31–34 anticipates a particular aspect of the good news of Easter, that God will transform human hearts. But just as Easter comes only after the death of Jesus, so in Jeremiah's vision of the future the new covenant comes only through and beyond suffering, in this case that of the Babylonian Exile. Thus these hopeful words come from a time of crisis and transition, when many people would have been asking if God's covenant with the people has come to an end. Jeremiah insists that judgment is not God's final word.

The context of Jeremiah 31:31–34 is important. It is part of what has been called the little book of comfort (chaps. 30–31), a collection of announcements of restoration. What follows in chapter 32 is the report of something Jeremiah did during Nebuchadnezzar's siege of Jerusalem. The prophet had been imprisoned in the court of the guard for saying that the Babylonians would be victorious. While he was there, he bought a field in Anathoth from his cousin as an action symbolizing God's future for the people. Even before Jerusalem was destroyed, he announced: "Houses and fields and vineyards shall again be bought in this land"

(Jer. 32:15). So a powerful spiritual vision of changed lives and obedient hearts is followed by, of all things, a real estate transaction. The point seems clear: So long as they are on this earth, even the people of the new covenant still need a place to live, actual ground for growing food, and a marketplace where things are bought and sold.

Like so much of the Old Testament, this promise comes from a time of crisis and transition, the disaster of the Babylonian Exile. When the prophet hears the Lord promise to make a new covenant with the house of Israel and the house of Judah, he has in view the situation of the exiles in Babylon. These lines respond to the most serious question on the minds of those people. Has the covenant ended? Is this blow the Lord's final word to us?

The initial words "The days are surely coming" stress that this is a future hope. References elsewhere in the book make it clear that Jeremiah expected the Exile to last some seventy years. Consequently, he did not expect to live to see the promises completely fulfilled.

One who speaks of a new covenant must also have in mind an old one. Verse 32 spells that out directly by recalling the covenant at Mt. Sinai following the Exodus and reminding the people that this is the covenant they broke. But there were other old covenants as well, each of them new in its time. Before Mt. Sinai, there were the covenants with Noah, Abraham, Isaac, and Jacob. After Sinai, Moses led the people in a renewal of the covenant on the plains of Moab, as did Joshua at Shechem. Later Samuel led the tribes in a covenant when kingship was established. In Jeremiah's time there was the hope of reestablishing the covenant under young King Josiah.

All these covenants were viewed as occurring at critical moments in the life of the community. When transitions and changes brought life and faith into doubt, it was time for a covenant or for the renewal of the old covenant. All were taken as initiated by God and as responses to God's initiative. Moreover, all involved promise.

The language in Jeremiah 31:31–34 is particularly intimate. In recalling the old broken covenant, the prophet hears the Lord saying, "I took them by the hand," as a mother leads a child, and "I was their husband." He has no problem at all with mixing the metaphors, for the message is clear. Even in the past, the Lord was as close to the people as flesh and blood. The way has been prepared for the new level of intimacy of the covenant on the heart.

The word that stands at the center of the passage is "covenant." A covenant is a special kind of relationship in which parties pledge themselves to one another. Old Testament covenants generally had two parts: a promissory oath and the stipulations or contents of what was promised. The fact that the law here is written, even on the heart, suggests that the basic reference is to the stipulations. In that respect, the covenant is like the written law. Israel will not forget what they have sworn to do.

This promise of a new covenant contains one of the most ancient and persistent formulations of the covenant vows: "I will be their God, and they shall be my people" (v. 33). Though the stipulations could be spelled out in lists of laws and even books of laws that defined how a covenant people behaved, this simple sentence said it all. All the people had to do to make a covenant was to say, "We will be God's people."

It should be emphasized that the making of a covenant with God was not an individual, but a communal, act, the work of the community of faith. It was Israel's covenant with God at Mt. Sinai that made them a people, the people of God, binding them not only to God but also to one another.

What then is new about the new covenant? That God initiates the covenant, that God forgives sins, and that Israel will "know" the Lord intimately had been features of older covenants. What is without precedent is the law written on the heart, the covenant at the core of one's being. The newness is a special gift, the capacity to be faithful and obedient. In the Old Testament, the heart is the seat of the will (see Jer. 29:13; 32:39; Ezek. 11:19; 36:26); consequently, the special gift here is a will with the capacity to be faithful. God thus promises to change the people from the inside out, to give them a center. This covenant will overcome the conflict between knowing or wanting one thing and doing another. In the new covenant the people will act as if they are owned by God without even reflecting upon it.

Which laws, then, are written on the heart? All the laws of Moses? Just the Decalogue? The answer is all of these things, and none of them. Just these words will suffice: "I am yours, and you are mine," says the Lord. That is the language of love and faithfulness.

Psalm 51:1–12

This psalm has been previously discussed as one of the readings for Ash Wednesday.

Psalm 119:9–16

The 176 verses of this psalm divide into twenty-two stanzas of eight lines each. In each individual stanza, all eight lines begin with the same Hebrew letter, working through the alphabet in order. In each of the stanzas there is a play on a series of synonyms for the law or the will of the Deity. Generally, there are eight such synonyms per stanza, and generally the same eight are used throughout the entire psalm. In the second stanza, which comprises verses 9–16, the terms used are *word*, *commandments*, *statutes*, *ordinances*, *decrees*, *precepts*, and *ways*, with some of these repeated. All of these terms are to be understood as synonyms, and all refer to the will of God as understood and embodied in laws and teachings.

The author answered the question about how young people can keep their way pure (v. 9*a*) by declaring that one's way must be guarded by conforming life to God's word (v. 9*b*). Then in a confessional statement, the writer stresses how one should seek, understand, meditate, and act on the basis of the divine laws and teachings.

Hebrews 5:5–10

The Fifth Sunday in Lent, traditionally called "Passion Sunday," originally marked the beginning of Passiontide, the final two weeks prior to Easter. The suffering of Christ received even greater emphasis during this time. Whereas the first four weeks in Lent were a time for personal reexamination and penance, the last fourteen days became a time for thinking more exclusively about the Lord's passion. It was an early custom to drape crucifixes, statues, and pictures in the churches with a purple cloth to signify that this was a period of intense mourning.

In keeping with this emphasis, today's epistolary lection focuses on the suffering of Christ. In this respect, it is typical of the Christology of the Epistle to the Hebrews, with its repeated emphasis on the humanity of Christ. It is in this epistle that we find the most thoroughly and systematically developed Christology in the New Testament, and it is especially distinctive for the way it captures the human dimension of Christ. The choice of "high priest" as the overarching christological image is itself telling, because this provided Jewish readers a ready point of reference and identification. The high priests they knew were obviously human figures, and this enabled the unknown author of Hebrews a point of contact through which he could develop a systematic understanding of the work of Christ. Consequently, Hebrews especially emphasizes Christ's humanity and his ability to sympathize with human weakness (Heb. 2:17–18; 4:15; 5:2).

The passage opens by referring to Christ's refusal to glorify himself (v. 5) and moves to the "days of his flesh" (v. 7), that is, the days of his earthly life. The reference to Jesus' offering up "prayers and supplications, with loud cries and tears, to the one who was able to save him from death" (v. 7) may recall the Gethsemane episode (Matt. 26:38–46 and parallels; cf. also John 12:27). The Gospel accounts of Gethsemane, however, do not mention "loud cries and tears." Even so, the Gospel accounts do convey the intense distress that Jesus experienced in Gethsemane. This became even more intensified in the later tradition, as seen in the clearly later textual addition to Luke 22:44, which states, "His sweat became like great drops of blood falling down on the ground." Jesus is said to have cried out with "a loud voice" while hanging from the cross (Mark 15:34; Matt. 27:46), and this may in fact be the point of reference in Hebrews 5:7.

One puzzling feature of our passage is the statement that "he was heard because of his reverent submission" (v. 7). The phrasing is influenced by Psalm 22:24: "When he cried unto him, he heard" (KJV). God may have "heard" Jesus in the sense that the prayer in Gethsemane, "Abba, Father" (Mark 14:36), or the prayer on the cross, "My God, my God, why have you forsaken me?" (Ps. 22:1*a*), came before God, but certainly not in the sense that God answered Jesus' prayer for deliverance from death. Another way of understanding the phrase is to render it: "And being heard [was set free] from fear" (Montefiore).

For the author of Hebrews, Jesus' being the Son of God did not exempt him from suffering. Here, the true significance of verse 8 should be noted. It was not simply that Jesus was a son who learned obedience, for after all, it is the lot of sons to learn obedience. Rather, it was that *the* Son of God should have to learn obedience. The true import is seen if we render the phrase: "Even though he was the Son of God . . . " Suffering as the Son of God and learning obedience are conspicuously human experiences. Many Christians, though believing in some sense that Jesus was both human and divine, still find it difficult to believe that he shared our humanity. For them, it is difficult to see how Jesus could "learn" anything, much less obedience. Yet this is precisely the point that our text makes—and stresses. Submitting to death on the cross became the supreme test—and example—of Jesus' filial obedience to the Father (cf. Phil 2:8).

The text speaks of this as a perfecting process ("having been made perfect," v. 9). Earlier in Hebrews 2:10, we are told that God saw fit to make Jesus "the pioneer of . . . salvation perfect through sufferings" (cf. also 7:28). From our own experience, we know that suffering, rightly experienced and interpreted, has the capacity to refine our own character and make us more complete, or make us perfect in ways that we previously were not. But more is implied here. It is not simply a question of Jesus' character being refined or perfected, but that the death on the cross was the final act through which the work of Christ came to completion. Through it, the work of God in Christ was consummated. Jesus' suffering and death became the ultimate refinement of his character and also the consummate act through which his mission was completed.

In this respect, Jesus became the pioneer (cf. 2:10) for all believers and the "source of eternal salvation for all who obey him" (v. 9). Elsewhere in the epistle, this is linked directly with Jesus' role as high priest, the note on which this passage ends (v. 10). Jesus as a high priest "according to the order of Melchizedek" is developed more fully in Hebrews 7:1–28. This appropriation of an Old Testament character provides the author a way of articulating the uniqueness of Jesus' high priestly role.

John 12:20–33

The hour has come for the Son of Man to be glorified" (v. 23). The glorifying of the Son is this Gospel writer's way of referring to the death, resurrection, and exaltation to former glory of the one who became flesh and dwelt among us (11:4; 13:3; 17:1–5). By his announcement that the hour has come, Jesus is telling his disciples (and the readers) that the chain of events leading to his passion will now begin. Prior to this time, Jesus' actions and even threats against his life were "explained" with the expression "his hour had not yet come" (2:4; 7:6; 7:30; 8:20).

Jesus' comments about his impending death and what it would mean for the world were prompted by the coming of Greeks (perhaps to be understood as Greeks who had embraced Judaism) to see Jesus. The desire of non-Jews to benefit from Jesus' ministry represents the beginning of the fulfillment of two preceding passages: "He prophesied that Jesus was about to die for the nation, and not for the nation only, but to gather into one the dispersed children of God" (11:51b–52); and, "Look, the world has gone after him" (12:19). But how are the nations of the world to be blessed by Jesus Christ, whose ministry was so narrowly confined in time and place? Our text is an answer to that question.

The Greeks approach Jesus indirectly through Philip and Andrew. This could be explained logically by the fact that these two were from Galilee, which had a large Gentile population, and they had Greek names. It could also be the case that at the time of the writing of the Gospel, Philip and Andrew were associated with missions to the Gentiles. In our text, the Greeks are treated symbolically, representing the world seeking Jesus, for once they make their request they disappear from the story. Jesus' response, "The hour has come," means that he now must make himself available to the world. That cannot be in his present ministry in Judea, Samaria, and Galilee, but as the glorified Christ who abides through his word and through the Spirit with believers everywhere. That promised presence is a dominant theme in the farewell discourses and farewell prayer (chaps. 14–17). The Johannine church, separated by time and space from the initial events of Jesus' ministry, needed very much to hear this word of the presence and availability of Christ. They needed to be assured that living in another place in another time did not place them beyond the life-giving and saving work of Christ. And we, too, need to hear that. We are not second-class disciples at a distance, born at the wrong time in the wrong place, trying desperately to survive on the thin diet of recorded memories of what it was like when Jesus was here. Christ *is* here. "And I, when I am lifted up from the earth, will draw all people to myself" (v. 32).

But this is the point: Christ's availability to believers everywhere required his death. His reflections upon his death are here offered in a threefold commentary: (1) there is a law in nature that demands death if there is to be more life (v. 24); (2) there is a principle of discipleship that demands death to self-interest in order to have life eternal (vv. 25–26); and (3) is the agent of nature's creation and the master of the disciples to be exempt from this principle of death and life? Jesus responds in a word to God, "No, it is for this reason that I have come to this hour" (v. 27). This Gospel's Christ does not writhe in agony, does not struggle in Gethsemane, does not offer up a cry of dereliction. Rather, he embraces God's will and a voice from heaven confirms his decision (v. 28). Not all heard the voice, of course; not all of us ever do.

Whatever troubling of soul Jesus experienced (11:33–35, 38; 12:27) in approaching his own death, that troubling is now over. It is as though death were a past experience. The ruler of this world has been driven out (v. 31). From this point on, the passion story in John will be without anguish and tears. As Lent moves us in quiet preparation for Jesus' Good Friday and Easter, perhaps it might also move us to prepare for our own.

Sixth Sunday in Lent
(Passion/Palm Sunday)

Liturgy of the Palms:
Mark 11:1–11 *or* John 12:12–16;
Psalm 118:1–2, 19–29;

Liturgy of the Passion:
Isaiah 50:4–9*a*;
Psalm 31:9–16;
Philippians 2:5–11;
Mark 14:1–15:47 *or* Mark 15:1–39 (40–47)

For the Liturgy of the Palms, either the Markan or Johannine account of Palm Sunday is read along with a portion of Psalm 118 that depicts the victor's triumphal entry into the city or temple.

For the Liturgy of the Passion, a portion of the third Servant Song serves as the Old Testament reading. With its reassuring promise that God will vindicate the cause of the one who is unjustly treated, it sets an appropriate tone for this Sunday. A fitting complement is provided by the reading from Psalm 31, for it expresses the thoughts of the soul in distress, scorned by adversaries and broken by the conspiracies of one's enemies. The classic epistolary text from Philippians sketches the journey of the obedient Son from the heights of God's presence to the depths of human despair. For the Gospel reading, in either its longer or abbreviated form, the Markan passion narrative provides a starkly realistic account of the Lord's passion.

Mark 11:1–11

Mark 11:1–11 and Psalm 118:19–29 herald the opening of the gates of worship for this special day and the days that lead to Easter. These texts are, therefore, celebrative and joyous, announcing, "This is Palm Sunday!" whereas the lections for the day carry the other word, "This is Passion Sunday."

The celebration described in Mark 11:1–11 has about it the abandon appropriate to the full release of tenacious hopes and ancient trust in the God who will redeem the people. A new colt is pressed into service, the owner being told that the Lord needs it and will return it (v. 3). Branches cut from the fields after the manner of the celebration of the Feast of

Tabernacles (Lev. 23:40) are spread on the road. Some of the crowd removed garments and placed them in the path of Jesus (v. 8). Preceding and following Jesus were the throngs of people who are so often in Mark portrayed as positive and supportive of Jesus, even though they did not understand his mission. The shout "Hosanna," which originally meant "save us" (the term has the same root in Hebrew as the word *Jesus*), probably had become by this time an enthusiastic burst of praise.

The occasion Mark describes here is a Christophany, a manifestation of the Christ. But this needs to be said with the same caution that Mark has built into the account. The pilgrims sing of "the coming kingdom of our ancestor David!" (v. 10) but do not call Jesus the Son of David. In the preceding episode, Bartimaeus, who was blind, gave Jesus that title (10:46–52). Later, Jesus would clearly and firmly reject the Davidic image of the messiah (12:35–37). The kingdom of which the crowds spoke was not present but "coming" (v. 10), one bit of evidence supporting Albert Schweitzer's view that the people welcomed Jesus not as messiah but as Elijah, the forerunner of the messiah. A final word of caution, which subdues Mark's record of Jesus' arrival at Jerusalem, is that the celebration generated by Jesus' presence occurs near the city (v. 1) but not in the city. Mark makes it clear that verses 1–10 present the festival and that Jesus does not enter Jerusalem until verse 11 (the NRSV begins a new paragraph here). He is pictured entering the city and the temple alone and leaving the city with the Twelve. Jerusalem itself is not the scene of joyous reception; rather, it is the place of controversy, hostility, and death. Therefore, unlike Matthew 21:45, Mark does not quote Zechariah 9:9, even though it lies in the background, probably because the prophet was addressing Jerusalem with a call to shout and sing.

One final look at Mark 11:1–11 prepares the reader for what is to come. The larger unit, 11:1–13:37, has about it a clear symmetry. It opens with Jesus at the Mount of Olives (v. 1). The place had messianic associations (Zech. 14:4) and closes with Jesus' apocalyptic discourse delivered from the Mount of Olives (13:3). This section opens with Jesus going to the temple (v. 11), and although he says and does nothing, two phrases project dark prospects: "when he had looked around at everything" and "it was already late" (v. 11). When the section closes, Jesus is sitting "opposite the temple" (13:3) predicting its destruction. Within 11:1–13:37, the focus is on the cleansing of the temple and a series of controversies with religious leaders that take place in the temple. At his trial, witnesses report having heard Jesus say that he would destroy the temple and build another in three days (14:58). For Mark, the coming of Jesus means the end of the temple and the beginning of a new time and place for meeting God.

John 12:12–16

This alternate Gospel lection for the Liturgy of the Palms is John's account of Jesus' entry into Jerusalem. The Fourth Gospel has had a major influence in shaping traditional observances of this Christian festival. For example, it is this Evangelist who identifies the branches used as palm branches (v. 13), and this account has figured in calculating the day as the Sunday before Good Friday ("six days before the Passover," v. 1, and "the next day," v. 12).

However, this record of the event differs in significant ways from the Synoptic accounts. In the first place, John 12:12–16 is much briefer, even, than Mark. Second, Jesus is not coming from Galilee through Jericho to Jerusalem as in the other Gospels, but he has been ministering for some time in Jerusalem. In fact, these verses are within a larger unit, verses 12–50, which centers in the raising of Lazarus at Bethany near Jerusalem. Six days before the Passover, Jesus is in Bethany (12:1) and the next day goes into the city (v. 12). Third, the crowd present for Jesus' entry does not consist of pilgrims coming with him but rather of those who had come for the feast and went out to meet Jesus (v. 12). The crowd is large and excited because they had either witnessed or heard about the raising of Lazarus (vv. 17–18). Fourth, the event is initiated by the crowd in Jerusalem (v. 13), and Jesus responds by finding a colt and riding it (v. 14). By so doing, he fulfilled Zechariah 9:9, which is here more paraphrased than quoted (v. 15). It is obvious that what Jesus does is unknown to the crowd; in fact, his own disciples do not understand until after the resurrection (v. 16).

Briefly stated, then, John 12:12–16 tells of a large crowd, excited by a sign Jesus had performed (raising Lazarus), responding by proclaiming Jesus king of Israel. This sounds familiar. After the sign of feeding the five thousand, a large enthusiastic crowd sought to make Jesus king (6:15). On that occasion, the crowd misunderstood, and when Jesus explained that he was the true bread, available to them in his death, they forsook him. Here now in Jerusalem there is the enthusiasm spawned by a sign performed but misunderstood, for the raising of Lazarus was not only prophetic of Jesus' passion, but would, in fact, precipitate his arrest and crucifixion (11:45–50; 12:9–11). In a few days the crowd would get to see Jesus publicly heralded as king, but it would be on a placard placed by Pilate on the cross of Jesus (19:19).

Jesus is King, but not because the crowd elevated him or made him so. He is King by virtue of who he is. Not even faith makes Christ King; faith only recognizes that he is.

Psalm 118:1–2, 19–29

This portion of Psalm 118 was selected for this point in the lectionary because it describes a victor's triumphal entry into the city or temple and thus parallels in imagery Jesus' triumphal entry into Jerusalem on Palm Sunday.

As a whole, Psalm 118 is a very complicated psalm in which many different participants and speakers were involved. In addition, portions of the psalm, especially verses 26–27, present enormous difficulties for translators. The psalm is best understood as the spoken accompaniment of a great thanksgiving ritual involving the return of a victorious king to Jerusalem and his entry into the temple accompanied by a host of followers. Verses 1–4, with their references to Israel, Aaron, and those who fear the Lord, demonstrate that the psalm was used in a great public thanksgiving liturgy.

Verses 5–18 recount the distress of battle from which the principal character—the king, no doubt—was rescued and given victory over his opponents. The king describes the battle and his triumph to a human audience. Thus, like most thanksgiving psalms, this one contains a description of a former distress that has now passed and can be viewed from a position of triumph. With verse 19, the psalm becomes more complicated in terms of the speakers and addressees. The following represents one possible way of looking at the psalm in terms of an entry ritual:

verse 19—the victorious king requests entry to the temple

verse 20—priests or others respond to the request

verses 21–22—the king offers thanksgiving addressed directly to God verses 23–24—worshipers or a choir proclaim the celebration as a consequence of God's intervention

verse 25—people, choir, or priests offer a prayer to God

verses 26–27—the king is blessed as he enters the sacred precincts of the temple, and reference is made to part of the festal celebrations

verse 28—the king offers thanksgiving

verse 29—a general summons to offer thanks

Several aspects of Psalm 118:19–29 are worthy of special note: (1) the celebration that is reflected in the psalm is one of triumph, success, and victory; (2) the royal features of the ritual—that is, their connection with a ruler or king—seem clearly evident; (3) the celebration is one in which a key emphasis is God's action and intervention on behalf of the triumphal figure; and (4) the triumphal figure describes himself as one who has been rejected but who has now become victorious. In verse 22, we have what was apparently a common proverb: "The stone that the builders rejected has become the chief cornerstone." Such a saying implies that someone or something has moved from a state of rejection to a position of prominence, in fact, to a position that is irreplaceable. "The head of the corner," or "chief cornerstone," would suggest either a corner or foundation stone or perhaps the keystone in an arch. The first part of the psalm refers to how the figure was threatened, challenged, and nearly defeated on the field of battle before God granted him triumph.

The numerous parallels between this psalm and Jesus' career and triumphal entry into Jerusalem, the Holy City, should be obvious, although Psalm 118 should not be read as a prophetic prediction of Jesus. The analogy between the psalm and Jesus' activity is to be found in the fact that in both God worked to elevate and exalt the lowly and the threatened to a place of prominence. Though in each case the lowly had to move through oppression and opposition, they were not overtaken by death, literal or otherwise (see v. 18).

Isaiah 50:4–9a

I saiah 50:4–9a is the third of the Servant Songs in Deutero-Isaiah. The others are 42:1–4; 49:1–6; 52:13–53:12. The songs stand out in their literary context because of their highly personal style and content, their particular understandings of the role of the servant, and their view of suffering. Although some commentators have argued to the contrary, it seems most likely that the songs were composed by the author of the remainder of Isaiah 40–55, the Second Isaiah.

The original historical context, then, of this passage is the very end of the Babylonian Exile, 539 BC, and the words were first uttered in Babylon. The prophet, among the exiles, proclaims a consistent message of salvation. The Judeans who were taken captive some fifty or sixty years earlier—and their descendants—are to be set free to return to Jerusalem. This, he announces, is a "new thing" that the Lord is about to do, but it will be like the old Exodus from Egypt. God, who is Lord of the world and of history, is about to use the Persian king Cyrus to accomplish his purpose. All of this is good news, and its general relationship to the Christian Easter Season is obvious. But more immediately relevant for Passion Sunday and for the third Servant Song is the new understanding of suffering that seems to have arisen out of the painful experience of the Exile. Through the darkness of the Exile, Second Isaiah could see a light. He and other faithful ones also realized that the suffering of some, or even of one, could benefit others, perhaps even the whole world. Suffering, when in obedience to God, can be vicarious.

The song employs the first person singular throughout. It is as if the prophet himself is speaking, but it is not clear to whom. No addressee is identified. In terms of form and themes, the poem is similar to some of the psalms. Some parts (vv. 5–6) echo the language of individual laments; others (vv. 7–9) are like songs of confidence in the Lord's support. There are especially close parallels to Jeremiah's complaints (Jer. 11:19, 21; 18:18; 20:10).

The identification of the servant in Second Isaiah and in the Servant Songs is one of the more debated issues in biblical scholarship, primarily because it is difficult to make one figure, either corporate or individual, fit all the texts. In this case, the speaker is the servant himself, and, if he is not the prophet, his role is a prophetic one.

The song has two main parts, verses 4–6 and 7–9. The first section is confessional, almost autobiographical. Initially (vv. 4–5a), the speaker refers to his call. The vocation concerns words and the organs of communication, the tongue and the ears. God, he confesses, constantly gives him the ability to hear and to speak a word that sustains the weary. Next (v. 5b), the servant reports that he was faithful to his duty through personal suffering. It appears, then, that he has suffered because of his vocation. The second part of the song consists of expressions of confidence and trust in God, by virtue of which the servant has been sustained. In verses 8 and 9 the language of the ancient Israelite law court is employed, as it frequently is in Second Isaiah. The Lord is the one who "vindicates" or declares innocent. The speaker invites any "adversary" who wishes a trial ("contend") to appear formally in court ("stand up"). No one can declare him guilty, for the Lord God helps him.

The suffering, indignities, and shame that the servant experienced are the direct result of his divinely ordained role. Because he was faithful he was beaten and scorned. But because he trusts in God he can see through that experience to vindication. The song may have arisen out of the prophet's own experience—that his message, although it was good news, was rejected and he himself persecuted. But it is not surprising that in the earliest church these words took on a new and deeper meaning. They were heard as Jesus' self-expression. The words that he spoke to the weary were given to him by God. He suffered because of faithfulness to his role, and to the end and even beyond, he trusted completely in God's vindication.

Psalm 31:9–16

Psalm 31 is a prayer of lament that could have been prayed by one in trouble or distress. Verses 9–16 are part of the description of the distress (vv. 9–13), followed by a statement of the worshiper's confidence (vv. 14–15) and a plea for redemption (v. 16).

The description of the distressful situation in verses 9–13 presents the person as one decimated by physical suffering (vv. 9–10) and as a social outcast forced to endure life at the periphery of society without the benefit of friends or close acquaintances (vv. 11–13).

Few psalms use such graphic descriptions to depict human misery and affliction as does Psalm 31. The descriptions are very graphic although reasonably nonspecific. Thus, when persons used this psalm in worship to describe their state of being, they could vent true feelings yet do so in highly stylized terms.

Praying this psalm allowed persons to verbalize and express the deep-seated sense of alienation and hurt that they were feeling. The language appears to be highly metaphorical, probably using stereotypical and formulaic expressions that were highly graphic in content and emotional in nature. The labeling of one's troubles in such graphic fashion was probably therapeutic in and of itself, for it allowed one to express sorrow and grief in realistic fashion and with full psychic involvement. The expressions drawn from the arena of illness, in verses 9–10, if taken literally, suggest that the person was near death and had suffered for years in misery. The common words of suffering and affliction appear throughout these verses: distress, grief, sorrow, sighing, misery, wasting away.

In verses 11–13, the depiction of the distress uses the language of social ostracism. The descriptions here seek to present the worshiper's distress in the severest form possible. Adversaries, neighbors, acquaintances, and even the persons encountered in casual street meetings are all depicted as standing in terror and expressing disdain at the person's appearance (v. 11). Perhaps the supplicant was a person with some physical malady that rendered him or her unclean and required special isolation from general society (see Lev. 13:45–46). Job's description of his predicament, in Job 19:13–22, sounds very much like the cries of the outcast in verse 11.

The psalmist declares that he or she is like one already dead—passed out of life and even out of memory; cast aside like the shattered pieces of a broken pot; unwanted, useless, fit only for the garbage heap of the city dump (v. 12).

In fact, the psalmist describes the many out there who not only dislike him or her but who even scheme and plot to take his or her life (v. 13). Such language as this may sound like the ravings of a paranoid but should be seen as therapeutic language that allowed distressed persons to objectify their suffering to its most graphic, even exaggerated, level.

This psalm is not simply a recitation of a vale of sorrows. Throughout the text there are frequent statements of a calm confidence in the Deity. Such is to be found in verses 14–15, in which the worshiper confesses trust in God and affirms that come what may the times of one's life are in the hand of God, who can deliver one from the hand of enemies and persecutors.

Confidence in the Deity fades naturally into plea and petition for salvation (vv. 15b–16). In spite of the description of the supplicant's condition in such sorrow-drawn and affliction-etched contours, confidence and calm flow through the psalm like a soothing stream. In this way it may parallel the composure of Jesus as he rode into Jerusalem—the man of sorrows but one confident of being in the hands of God.

Philippians 2:5–11

This passage opens with an exhortation (v. 5) which, in turn, introduces what many scholars regard as an early Christian hymn (vv. 6–11). In spite of this emerging scholarly consensus, there is not a similar consensus among biblical translators. These verses are printed strophically in NRSV, NJB, and NIV, but not in REB.

How the opening exhortation and the hymn that follows are related to each other is disputed. The fundamental exegetical question here is whether the Christ-hymn is quoted in order to provide the readers an example of humility and self-abnegation, or whether it rehearses the Christ-story in order to lay out the basis of the moral exhortation in the preceding verses. The Greek wording of verse 5 is obscure and may be rendered in at least two ways: "Have this mind among yourselves which was also in Christ Jesus" and "Have this mind among yourselves, which is yours [or which has been made possible] in Christ Jesus." In the former interpretation, the Christ-hymn unfolds the example of Christ to be followed. In the latter interpretation, the story of Christ's incarnation and exaltation is told to establish the basis of the ethical instruction.

In this latter view, the Christ-hymn provides the "indicative" that underlies the Christian "imperative."

These two interpretive options are reflected in the various modern translations. The KJV reads: "Let this mind be in you, which was also in Christ Jesus." The NRSV reads: "Let the same mind be in you that was in Christ Jesus." The alternative rendering is acknowledged in a note: "Let the same mind be in you *that you have* in Christ Jesus." In the REB text we read: "Take to heart among yourselves what you find in Christ Jesus."

Although the difference of the wording in these various translations is slight, the preacher will need to be attentive to the wording of the text being used, because the various translations might point in different homiletical directions.

The chief theological difficulty is this. Although the Christ-hymn in verses 6–11 has traditionally been understood as an *imitatio Christi* passage, and in this regard has exercised great influence on Christian piety, the work of Christ unfolded in the hymn is, strictly speaking, inimitable. The descent of the Savior from heaven and his acceptance of human form in which he became obedient to death, although exemplary in its broadest sense, can only be regarded as uniquely possible for the Son of God. In what sense, realistically, could the Philippian church imitate this cosmic drama of descent and ascent?

And yet, to suggest that the drama of Christ's incarnation and exaltation is unfolded merely to show how and why the Christian exhortation in verses 1–5 is possible is not altogether convincing. The exhortation seems to call for an example, yet the example offered is not one Christians can easily identify with.

In any case, there is broad agreement that verses 6–11 contain an early Christian hymn and that it predated Paul. He appears to have quoted this early hymn at this juncture, even though he makes certain editorial changes. Precisely how the hymn should be arranged into strophes and stanzas is not clear. Generally, it is arranged in two strophes consisting respectively of verses 6–8 and verses 9–11 (so, NRSV). Each of these strophes can then be subdivided into three stanzas.

The hymn unfolds a "V-shaped" Christology, where the descent of Christ to earth is narrated first (vv. 6–8), followed by his ascent or exaltation (vv. 9–11).

The drama, of course, begins with the preexistent position of Christ (v. 6), and the language is reminiscent of wisdom traditions (cf. John 1:1–16). Christ voluntarily relinquishes his heavenly status, choosing to take the form of a slave. This language probably recalls the Suffering Servant imagery from Deutero-Isaiah (cf. Isa. 53:3, 11). His humanity is further stressed (v. 7; cf. Rom. 8:3), and the "descent" stage culminates in his obedience unto death. The phrase "even death on a cross" (v. 8) appears to be Paul's editorial addition to the hymn. The theme of obedience echoes that of texts treated earlier in the Lenten Season (cf. Heb. 5:7–10; 12:2).

With verse 9, there is an abrupt change ("therefore"). At this point, God becomes the subject of the action: "God also highly exalted him." This phrase includes both his resurrection and ascension. In other New Testament passages, these two stages of Christ's exaltation are kept separate (cf. Acts 2:33; 5:31). The name "above every name" (v. 9) anticipates the final acclamation in verse 11: "Jesus Christ is Lord." The submission of the whole universe to the exalted Lord is an expansion of Isaiah 45:23 (cf. also Rom. 14:11).

In one sense, the Christ-hymn might appear inappropriate as a reading for Palm Sunday, because Good Friday is so thoroughly overcome by Easter and Christ's exaltation to heavenly preeminence. Even Paul seems to sense the danger of an exclusively triumphalist reading of this hymn, for he inserts "even death on a cross" in verse 8 as a salutary reminder of the centrality of the crucifixion. Philippians 3 suggests that some readers might well have begun to think that "resurrection life" was the *summum bonum* of the Christian life.

There is ample time in the Christian year to celebrate the triumph of Christ in the resurrection and ascension, and the minister's task here may be to see that the passion of Christ is not passed over too quickly.

Mark 14:1–15:47 *or* Mark 15:1–39 (40–47)

On this and several other occasions, the lectionary offers a choice of readings. For this Sunday, the choice is not between different Gospel lections but between a lengthy passage and a briefer selection from within that passage. In all such cases, the principle followed in this commentary is to discuss the larger reading on the assumption that the more inclusive one will be of more value to a larger number. Each preacher, of course, must make the decision as to the particular focus for a message drawn from this body of Gospel material. That decision, although certainly sensitive to the practical question of how much text can profitably be read in a service, will take into account a number of factors. For example, what does one wish to achieve on Passion/Palm Sunday?

One may wish to give the listeners a sense of the sweep of events contained in the passion narrative (Mark 14:1–15:47), beginning with the conspiracy to arrest Jesus and concluding with his burial. Or a particularly critical moment in Jesus' final days or a Markan accent recurring in the narration may be deemed most appropriate for treatment in the sermon. Whatever the choice, the minister will want to think through the other services planned for Holy Week so that no subsequent message be robbed of its text by the choice for Passion Sunday. And in any case, reading through Mark 14:1–15:47 and listing the separate episodes will be immeasurably helpful, for Mark's message is not solely in the episodes but in the arrangement of events into a narrative. We will explore this characteristic of the Gospel shortly.

There are several features of Mark's passion narrative that impress themselves upon the reader.

First, there is restraint in the telling. The actual death of Jesus is quite briefly recorded (15:22–39), leading us to conclude that it was not the author's aim to use gory details to milk melancholy from the story, to create sympathetic sadness, and to draw tears from the readers. Feeling bad about it all is hardly faith, and manipulating emotions is hardly preaching. According to Jesus' own statement, he would suffer many things, be rejected and killed. The suffering and rejection are a major part of the story, not simply because of interest in historical reconstruction but because of the immediate need of Mark's church. What does it mean to the Christians to follow Jesus? Both internal and external evidence point to persecution; they are facing suffering, rejection, and, in some cases, death. As we know from other contexts (1 Pet. 2:20–23; 3:15–17), the church drew meaning and support not only from Jesus' death but also from what he endured.

A second feature of Mark's narrative is the primacy of what happened to Jesus rather than of what Jesus did. The first half of this Gospel attends to what Jesus does, to the power of his preaching, healing, and exorcising. Jesus binds Satan and plunders his house (3:27). But it is not so in 14:1–15:47. In Mark, not even the triumphal entry is within the passion narrative (11:1–10). There is here a reference to God's power (14:36) and to the future power of the Son (14:62), but the verbs controlling the story describe what is done to, not by, Jesus: conspired against, anointed for burial, denied, betrayed, captured, tried, sentenced, mocked, crucified, buried. If the incarnation means anything, it means that Jesus identified with the common human experience of not being in control. Mark's church, and ours, can find in this identification both mercy and "grace to help in time of need" (Heb. 4:16).

Third, Mark's account of the passion repeatedly recalls Jesus being abandoned by those who could have given him support and strength. Mark has in mind the Twelve. He alone among the Evangelists says that at the Last Supper they *all* drank the cup (14:23), and though all pledged loyalty till death (14:31), they *all* abandoned Jesus (14:50). The inner circle of three could not watch for an hour (14:32–42), and the betrayer of Jesus is identified three times not simply by name but as "one of the twelve" (14:10, 20, 43). And Simon's denial of Jesus is not related as an episode in itself; rather, it is interwoven with Jesus' confession before the Jewish council. Once in this Gospel Jesus identifies himself as the Christ, the Son of God (14:61–62), thereby incriminating himself and drawing the death penalty. In Mark's dramatic arrangement, that confession is preceded and followed by Peter's denials. Note 14:54 (Peter); 14:55–64 (Jesus); 14:66–72 (Peter). Neither the confession nor the denial could be more forcefully presented. But the Gospel is not preached if these texts release in the preacher a tirade against the Twelve. In some churches, it may be appropriate to ask if we, too, are among the Twelve. In others, the word might be found more clearly in the church's identification with Jesus the forsaken. Some messages, some decisions bring loss of public favor, members, and financial support. In fact, courage and faithfulness to the Gospel may mean experiencing at times a silent heaven. "My God, my God, why have you forsaken me?" (15:34).

Monday in Holy Week

Isaiah 42:1–9;
Psalm 36:5–11;
Hebrews 9:11–15;
John 12:1–11

Among the readings for Monday in Holy Week, specific links are evident between the Old Testament reading and the epistolary text. Both have in view a covenant that will bring salvation to all peoples. In Hebrews 9:11–15 it is through the shedding of blood that Christ has become the mediator of a new covenant. The psalm is a hymn of praise, especially for God's steadfast love and justice, paralleling some aspects of the Old Testament reading. The Gospel reports an event six days before the Passover, the day before Jesus' triumphal entry into Jerusalem.

Isaiah 42:1–9

Our Old Testament text consists of two distinct parts that probably were composed and possibly circulated separately before they were combined in the present context. Isaiah 42:1–4 is the first of the Servant Songs, and Isaiah 42:5–9 is a distinct prophetic address. There is no serious reason to doubt that both parts stem from Second Isaiah in the last year or two before the end of the Babylonian Exile (539 BC). As the Book of Isaiah has been handed down to us, the two sections of our reading are meant to interpret each other, but we may better understand the whole if we first look at the parts.

In this first Servant Song (vv. 1–4), the Lord, who is the speaker throughout, refers to the servant in the third person. The words appear as a public proclamation, though no audience or addressee is specified. This song appears first in the book, but it is also the first one logically, for it begins with the divine designation and election of the servant (v. 1a). No reasons for the selection are given except God's pleasure. In verses 1b–4 the Lord announces that the servant has been given the divine spirit, and then proclaims the servant's task. Although it is impossible for us to identify the servant in the original context, the poem leaves no doubt about his task; it is stated three times. He will bring "justice to the nations" (v. 1); he will faithfully "bring forth justice" (v. 3); he will establish "justice in the earth" (v. 4). The meaning of justice in the prophetic tradition is clear: fairness, equity, protection of the weak, the rule of law. The unmistakably distinctive note here is that such justice will be universal, to foreign nations, to all the earth.

The remainder of the unit states how the servant is to accomplish the establishment of justice and how he will behave. The means of accomplishing the goal is stated only negatively (vv. 2–3a), specifying only what he will not do. He will not operate by public proclamation and will not oppress those who are hurt. He will thus be gentle and sympathetic, especially to those in trouble. That he will not fail or be discouraged (v. 4a) suggests already that he will encounter opposition.

The understanding of the servant's role here is primarily royal, that is, messianic in the Old Testament sense. Kings were designated publicly, as in verse 1, and they were the ones responsible for seeing that justice was done. But there are also prophetic features ("my spirit upon him," v. 1b) and perhaps priestly ones as well, for priests were responsible for instruction in the law (v. 4b).

God is also the speaker in the second unit (vv. 5–9), but the divine speech is introduced by a prophetic messenger formula. Moreover, the speech, unlike verses 1–4, is a direct address that frequently employs the second person. The introductory messenger formula, "Thus says God, the LORD," is filled out with a series of three clauses defining God (v. 5). The remainder of the unit (vv. 6–9) is the divine speech proper.

These verses amount to an almost systematic theological summary of the message of Second Isaiah. Both first and last, there is the statement of the nature of God. God is creator of all that is (heaven and earth), and the one who gives life to all peoples (v. 5). His name is Yahweh, the Lord, and he gives his glory to no other, especially not to graven images (v. 8). Elsewhere in the book this point is even more explicit: there is no other God. Second, the God who created the world has chosen and saved Israel (v. 6). The central message of the prophet is that God is about to set the captives in Babylon free, just as he had acted in the past to save his people. Third, Israel is chosen and saved for a purpose consistent with the faith in a single God for the whole world. They are to be "a covenant to the people, a light to the nations" (v. 6). That is, they are to bring enlightenment and unity to all peoples. Moreover, they are to open blind eyes and set prisoners free. Election, as the prophets as early as Amos had insisted, entails responsibility.

In verses 5–9 it seems clear that the servant is the people of Israel as a whole. They are the ones who have been redeemed, and their proper response is to be a light to the nations. The present context then suggests that the servant of verses 1–4 is also Israel, though when verses 1–4 are read independently other possibilities appear, including a royal or a prophetic individual. But however the question of the identity of Second Isaiah's servant is resolved, there are several important contributions that these verses can make in the context of the remembrance of the passion of Jesus. In particular, they call to mind the role of God's chosen servant to establish justice, and systems that maintain justice, in all the world. Moreover, they serve to remind all those who have been redeemed by the Lord that they may be a light to the nations, and that light shines when and where justice prevails.

Psalm 36:5–11

In verses 1–4 this psalm opens with a description of the wicked that takes the form of a proclamation to a human audience. One would assume that this, using a pattern like that in Psalm 1, would be followed by its counterpart, namely, a description of the righteous. Instead, what we have in verses 5–9 is hymnic praise of attributes of the Deity, addressed directly to God as if in a prayer. Verse 10 forms a petition or request addressed to God.

Consciously, the psalmist seems to be contrasting the life of the wicked with life under the grace of God. That is, the psalm does not describe the life of a godly man but instead talks about God and the benefits that come from him. Over against the reality of sin and the sinner, the psalmist sets God and the divine benefits.

In verses 5–6, God's love and faithfulness are extolled in terms of their immeasurable quality. In height, they extend to the heavens and up to the clouds. In constancy, they are like the mountains and the great deep beneath the earth. In breadth, God's concern to save is not limited by the boundaries of human existence but extends even to the beasts of the earth.

In verses 7–9, the poet focuses attention on the human benefits that accrue from the Divine or on what might be called the delights of enjoying God and his love. In verse 7, the neutral inclusive term "all people" is used instead of the more customary "children of Israel." One could suppose that the psalmist here made a deliberate choice so as to universalize those included under divine favor. The image for protection in the verse—"in the shadow of your wings"—may draw upon the protective role of the parent fowl in caring for its young. Such imagery, however, could be based on the fact that the ark, the representative symbol of God, rested in the Holy of Holies beneath the outstretched wings of the cherubim (see 1 Kings 8:7).

Just as verse 7 emphasizes the nature of protection offered by the Divine, so verse 8 emphasizes the divine provision of food and drink. Some uncertainty exists about what "your house" refers to. Is it a reference to the earth or the world as a whole? (See Psalm 93:5, where this appears to be the case.) Or is it a reference to the temple as the house of God? In the former, "feast on the abundance of your house" would refer to eating the fruits and products of the earth. In the latter case, the expression would refer to the sacrificial meals consumed in the temple precincts, where eating and drinking were common (see 1 Sam. 1:3–8). In any case, the psalm emphasizes the value and worth of the more sensual aspects of life—eating and drinking—which should be viewed and enjoyed in relationship to the Divine.

Two images characterize the statement in verse 9—life and light. God is seen as the source of all life, and divine light as the source of human light. Lest the blessings of God prove to be temporary, the psalmist prays that God will continue divine love and salvation (v. 10). Here the bequest is hemmed in somewhat when compared with verse 7b. In verse 10, those who know God and the upright of heart are the expected recipients of God's favor. Verse 11 requests that the worshiper not be trampled under the foot nor smitten by the hand of the enemy.

The association of this psalm with Holy Week can be made through its emphases on God's lovingkindness and on the divine blessings bestowed upon humanity.

Hebrews 9:11–15

Today's lection occurs in a section of the epistle that shows how the sacrificial death of Christ exceeds the Mosaic sacrificial system administered by the Levitical priesthood (8:1–10:39). It opens by asserting that "Christ came as a high priest of the good things that have come" (v. 11). Early in the epistle, Christ is introduced as "a merciful and faithful high priest in the service of God" (2:17–18), and this christological image is repeated and elaborated as the epistle unfolds (cf. 3:1; 4:14–5:10). As high priest, Christ was able to identify with human needs and weaknesses (4:15), and he, like Aaron, was divinely appointed by God (5:1–6). As a priest "according to the order of Melchizedek" (6:20), Christ is infinitely superior to his Levitical counterparts. Unlike them, he exercises his priestly function perma-nently (7:24). In addition, his moral qualifications far exceeded theirs; he is "holy, blameless, undefiled, separated from sinners" (7:26). But, most decisively, unlike them, he was "exalted above the heavens" (7:26). Both the scope and the locus of his priesthood transcended the Levitical priesthood.

Today's lection introduces a section (9:11–10:18) that explores further the sacrifice of Christ. It should be noted that Christ is presented here not only as the high priest who officiates in the "heavenly sanctuary," but also as the sacrificial victim. He is both priest and sacrifice.

Several themes, already introduced in the epistle, converge in today's lection: (1) Christ as the high priest (v. 11); (2) heaven, or the heavenly sanctuary, as the place where he officiates (vv. 11–12; cf. 8:1–5); (3) the finality of Christ's sacrifice—"he entered once for all into the Holy Place" (v. 12; cf. 9:26; 10:11–12); (4) the superiority of the blood of Christ to the blood of animal sacrifices (vv. 12–13; cf. 10:4–10); and (5) Christ as the mediator of a new, and there-fore better, covenant (v. 15; cf. 8:6–13).

Although Christ as the high priest is developed extensively in Hebrews, Christ as the sacri-fice, or the paschal lamb, is developed elsewhere in the New Testament. In 1 Corinthians 5:7, Paul refers to Christ as "our paschal lamb" who has been sacrificed. In Revelation, Christ is frequently referred to as the "Lamb that was slaughtered" (Rev. 5:6, 12–13; 7:14; 12:11; 13:8). In the Fourth Gospel, Christ is understood as the paschal lamb, seen by the fact that the death of Christ is made to coincide chronologically with the slaying of the sacrificial animals on the eve of Passover.

Today's text has several problematic features with which the preacher will need to deal before moving on to proclamation.

First, there is the question, Did Christ appear as a high priest of "the good things *that have come*" or of "the good things *to come*"? Has Christ's high priesthood already achieved all the promised blessings, or does Christ preside as high priest over eschatological blessings that are still unrealized? There are strong textual grounds for adopting the latter reading (followed by NJB, but not by NRSV, NIV, and REB). Theologically, this offers hope for Christians and enables the celebration of Holy Week to direct their thoughts to the future, which belongs to God. This eschatological theme is further reinforced in verse 15, where Christ is said to be "the mediator of a new covenant, so that those who are called may receive the promised eter-nal inheritance."

A second difficulty occurs in verse 11b in the phrase "through the greater and perfect tent" (tabernacle), which, we are told, is "not made with hands, that is, not of this creation." Is this the "tent" of Christ's resurrected body, or does it refer to the heavenly tabernacle? If it is the former, it is an unusual way for the author to refer to Christ's risen body. If it is the latter, the following phrase in verse 12a ("he entered once for all into the Holy Place") ap-pears redundant. In spite of the apparent redundancy, it appears to be the latter. In his death and resurrection, Christ was "exalted above the heavens" (7:26), and there became seated "at the right hand of the throne of the Majesty in the heavens, a minister in the sanctuary and the true tent that the Lord, and not any mortal, has set up" (8:1–2). The heavenly tabernacle is envisioned here as the place through which Christ the high priest proceeds, ultimately en-tering the Holy Place. But he does so with a difference. He does not offer the blood of sacrifi-cial animals, but the blood shed in his own sacrificial death. The argumentation here becomes a fortiori: if the blood of sacrificial animals was effective in achieving purification, how much more effective is the blood of the ultimate sacrifice—Christ himself—in purifying our pol-luted consciences? In contrast to the animal sacrifices, the sacrifice of Christ was "without blemish" and occurred as "a spiritual and eternal sacrifice" (v. 14, NEB). His sacrifice is neither physical nor temporal, as were animal sacrifices; it transcended the physical and penetrated to the eternal.

From all this, it follows that Christ is the "mediator of a new covenant." His high priesthood operates in the heavenly realm where God dwells and where the Levitical priesthood was unable to penetrate. For that reason, the effects of Christ's sacrifice were retroactive, extending even to redeem those who died under the law (v. 15; cf. Heb. 11:39–40).

John 12:1–11

From Passion Sunday through Easter, the Gospel lections will be drawn from the passion narratives. Because these accounts have always been regarded as containing the heart of the gospel, it is likely that the narrative of Jesus' final days—his arrest, trial, and death—hardened quite early into a fixed tradition among the churches. Some scholars believe that this may account for the fact that all four Evangelists relate the story with basically the same outline and with strikingly similar details. However, each Evangelist has his own purpose in writing, and each church addressed has its own needs; therefore, episodes from a common tradition are related from different perspectives. The preacher will want to be alert to this fact in order to avoid preaching from a composite of four accounts rather than from the particular text for the day.

The Gospel for today is John 12:1–11 and not the general topic, "the anointing of Jesus." All four Gospels record the event (Matt. 26:6–13; Mark 14:3–9; Luke 7:36–39) but with important differences. Matthew and Mark place the story in Bethany in the home of Simon the leper, where "a woman" anoints Jesus' head. Anointing the head was in the biblical tradition the ceremony for the coronation of a king. Luke locates the act in Galilee in the home of Simon the Pharisee, where a sinful woman anoints Jesus' feet with tears and with ointment. Luke, like John, knows of Jesus' visits to the home of Martha and Mary, but Luke 10:38–42 and John 12:1–11 are otherwise quite different. For this message, we give our attention solely to the text before us. What would John have us hear?

First, in this Gospel the anointing at Bethany is a passion story; that is, it focuses on the death of Jesus. In this regard John is like Matthew and Mark but unlike Luke, whose anointing story is early, unrelated to Jesus' death, and is told to dramatize the nature of forgiveness. John not only locates the anointing within the passion narrative but weaves into the brief account all the dark forebodings of death. The scene is Bethany, where there waits an empty and available tomb (11:38–44); at the table is Lazarus to whom Jesus gave life, an act that will now cost Jesus his (11:4; 12:9–11); the time is Passover (12:1), which in this Gospel is death time; into this pleasant circle of friends comes Judas, the dark intruder, who, in the time and place of this Gospel, was viewed as betrayer and as thief (12:46); and finally there is Mary's act, an anointing for Jesus' burial. The approaching death of Jesus is clearly the governing theme of the story.

Second, this Evangelist repeats a conviction common to the entire Gospel: in relation to Jesus Christ, the words and acts of others have meanings and effects far beyond what may have been intended at the time. Caiaphas, the high priest, unwittingly prophesied that Jesus' death would save the world (11:49–52); the Pharisees unwittingly acknowledged that the whole world was going to Jesus (12:19). So here, Mary performs an act of hospitality, friendship, and gratitude for a brother restored, but in that act she unwittingly prepares Jesus for burial. However, this is a message not only in John, but in the entire Bible: God uses our acts beyond our intent or capacity. Abraham was hospitable to strangers and entertained angels unawares; two disciples from Emmaus invited a fellow traveler to rest and eat, and a supper became a sacrament; Paul wrote letters to the churches and a New Testament canon had its beginnings. We never know; our task is to speak and act in a way appropriate to faith's response to the occasion and to leave the conclusions to God.

Third, Mary's act will bless and plague every minister who has to counsel and evaluate similar acts of devotion and gratitude. Three hundred poinsettias announce Christmas; five hundred lilies embellish Easter; and then there are the memorial chimes, the memorial silver Communion ware and the memorial window. "A gift in gratitude," says the donor; "a sinful waste," says not only Judas but everyone who has looked into hollow eyes and heard the cries of a hungry child. Sound sense and Christian duty know the need is for potatoes not perfume, and yet checking the shopping list even of the poor reveals that among flour, beans, and pork there will be candy and cologne. The appropriate word is not easily found or easily spoken.

Tuesday in Holy Week

Isaiah 49:1–7;
Psalm 71:1–14;
1 Corinthians 1:18–31;
John 12:20–36

The readings for this day continue the preparation of the community of faith for the crucifixion and resurrection of Jesus. The psalm is an individual lament similar in some ways to Psalm 22; it combines cries for help with expressions of confidence in God. The epistolary text interprets the meaning of the cross, and the Gospel reading reports events in Jesus' last week, especially a number of his sayings that anticipate the crucifixion and resurrection. In this context, although the Old Testament reading expresses especially the feeling that the work of God's servant has been in vain, it also proclaims that his mission is to bring salvation to all the earth.

Isaiah 49:1–7

Isaiah 49:1–6 is the second of the Servant Songs in Deutero-Isaiah. The speaker in these verses is the servant, the one designated by God in the first Servant Song, Isaiah 42:1–4 (see the comments on the texts for Monday in Holy Week in this volume). The unit is introduced and structured as a prophetic address, beginning with a summons to attention (v. 1a) and presenting a message from God (v. 6). It is important to keep in mind that the addressees of the speech are the "coastlands," the "peoples from far away" (v. 1a); that is, the servant's message is not for Israel alone but for the world at large, the Gentiles in particular.

After the summons to attention, the servant reports how he was called and equipped for his task (vv. 1b–3). Like Jeremiah, he was designated before birth (Jer. 1:5) and identified by name (see also Isa. 43:1). He uses metaphorical language ("sword," "polished arrow") to describe the equipment for his duty, which entailed communication ("mouth"). God, he reports, formally declared him to be his servant (v. 3). At this point the poem clearly indicates that the servant is Israel.

The next movement in the poem is the servant's account of his response to his task (v. 4). He reports on the one hand that he thought his work had been in vain, and on the other hand that he is confident that he has God's approval. Frequently, in their reports of their vocations the prophets indicate a deep sense of unworthiness (Isa. 6:5; Jer. 1:6). But the account here does not seem to belong to the category of the call report as such. It expresses

181

not unworthiness when called but frustration with the results of the work. The servant was called and equipped for the mission, but felt that he had failed.

The next element in the poem is a very expansive messenger formula (v. 5), which introduces the divine speech in the next verse. The formula "And now the LORD says" is filled out by subordinate clauses that describe the Lord and his reason for calling the servant. The Lord is the one who formed the servant in order to bring Israel back from exile, the one who honors the servant, and the one who is the source of the servant's strength.

The last element of the song is the divine message (v. 6). From the first verse it was clear that this word is addressed to the foreign nations. Now it appears that the message the nations are to hear is something that God says to the servant. The servant is, as already indicated, to raise up and restore Israel. But more than that, he is given as a light to the nations in order that God's salvation "may reach to the end of the earth." That is a proclamation of the universal reign of the Lord of Israel, parallel to the purpose for the servant's designation in the first place, that is, to establish justice in all the earth (Isa. 42:1–4).

Verse 7 is distinct from the poem as a prophetic announcement of salvation concerning the Lord's chosen. In that verse the servant clearly is understood as Israel, once despised and abhorred by nations, but eventually vindicated.

In the Servant Song itself, as it now stands, it is also obvious that the servant is Israel. Some commentators, however, have argued that "Israel" in verse 3 is a secondary addition. More substantial objections to the easy identification of the servant as the people are the highly individualistic and personal language and the fact that the servant has a mission to and for Israel. This second point has led some to see the servant as ideal Israel or a group within Israel. The identity is so elusive that one is tempted to conclude that it is intentionally ambiguous.

Far more important than the identity of the servant in the original historical context at the end of the Babylonian Exile is the understanding of the mission of the servant of God. On this point the text is quite clear. There are two tasks. First, the servant has a role in the return and restoration of Israel. Second, and dominant in this passage, is the universal mission, all the more dramatic when seen in the era of the Babylonian Exile, when the first hearers of this text were subjects of foreign powers. The servant is to be a light to all nations in order that the Lord's salvation may reach to the ends of the earth. As the Gospel reading for today has it, Jesus is that light (John 12:35–36). When he is lifted up he will draw all people to himself (John 12:32).

Psalm 71:1–14

The fabric and texture of Psalm 71 are the products of heartfelt supplication and lament interwoven with statements of great trust and confidence in God and interspersed with petitions and appeals to the Deity.

All of the basic components of a lament are to be found in this psalm. The passage selected for this lection contains an opening address to the Deity (v. 1), an appeal pleading for help (vv. 2–4), a statement of the worshiper's confidence in God (vv. 5–8), a description of the distress (vv. 9–11), and a second appeal (vv. 12–14).

We can examine the salient features of this psalm in terms of (1) the nature of the distress, (2) the worshiper's statements of confidence, and (3) the nature of the help requested from God.

1. The troubles undergone by the worshiper are related primarily to enemies. The gallery of opponents are described as "the wicked," "the unjust and cruel," "enemies," and "accusers" who seek the worshiper's life.

The bitterest opponents appear to be those enemies who consider the person forsaken by God and thus without help and support (vv. 10–11). One might assume that the malady or problem the person had was taken as a sign that God had forsaken or was no longer supporting the one praying.

2. This psalm is permeated by a strong sense of trust and confidence. As the person looks back to the past, he or she affirms that God has been his or her trust from youth. God is even seen as the one who, like a midwife, took him or her from the mother's womb (v. 6). Looking to the future, the psalmist prays that the trust in and association with God, which was begun as a child, will continue into "old age and gray hairs" (vv. 9, 18). A common theme throughout the psalm is that God is a refuge. The worshiper confesses that God is a refuge and at the same time prays that God will be a refuge (cf. vv. 1 and 7 with v. 3). The concept of a refuge is further explicated with reference to God as a strong fortress and a rock—all expressive of both stability and protection.

An interesting feature of the psalm's statements of confidence is the reference to the special role the person has for making known or proclaiming God not only to the contemporaries of the day but also to generations yet to come (vv. 7–8, 18). This would suggest that the psalm was not originally composed for an ordinary Israelite but was probably written for the king, who had a special responsibility for proclaiming the nation's God.

3. The petitions and appeals made to God for help focus primarily on the requests that God not forsake the worshiper (vv. 9–10) or let the person be put to shame (v. 1). Shame plays both a positive and a negative function in the psalm. The worshiper asks to be preserved from shame (v. 1) and at the same time prays that the accusers will be put to shame and consumed (v. 13). Shame, of course, meant being put in a humiliating situation, and at the same time having to accept the identity that the situation imposed.

This psalm can be exegeted and preached in the context of Holy Week because it expresses many of the factors that we think of in terms of Jesus' suffering: the opposition of enemies who do not believe that God is his supporter, the trust and confidence of the worshiper, and a message to be proclaimed and made known to generations yet to come.

1 Corinthians 1:18–31

Paul's exposition of the "message about the cross," that is, preaching "Jesus Christ, and him crucified" (1 Cor. 2:2), begins in 1:18 and extends through 2:5. For this reason, the limits of this passage should be extended to include the next paragraph (1 Cor. 2:1–5). In this passage, we get close to the center of Paul's gospel, and in doing so, find ourselves more fully drawn into the passion of Christ as we move through Holy Week.

The overall structure of this passage should be noted. First, the essential paradox of the cross is stated: God has chosen weakness through which to display power. What humans regard as inexplicably foolish is, in fact, a display of divine wisdom. In this standoff between human wisdom and divine wisdom, the ways of God transcend human ways. When judged by human standards, God comes up short. This turns out to be an indictment, not of God, but of humanity itself. For human beings to presume to subject God to human standards of judgment is to misconceive both who we are and who God is. Sitting in judgment on God stems from human presumption, or "boasting" (1:31).

To counter this attitude of human presumption, Paul develops two lines of argument.

First, he appeals to the example of the Corinthians themselves (1:26–31). On any showing, they were an unimpressive lot, relatively speaking: few of them were wise, powerful, or well-bred (1:26). In their own right they had nothing to commend themselves before God. Yet they existed as a community of God's people, a position, incidentally, from which they presumed to sit in judgment on God. With three emphatic declarations, Paul reminds them that they are who they are because of God's initiative and action: (1) God chose what is foolish in the world (the Corinthians) to shame the wise; (2) God chose what is weak in the world (the Corinthians) to shame the strong; and (3) God chose "what is low and despised in the world [the Corinthians] . . . to reduce to nothing things that are" (1:28), that is, to shatter all pretensions. The Corinthians are vivid testimony of the paradoxical work of God. How can they "boast in the presence of God" (1:29)? If their existence as a people of God can be explained only as an act of God, as an act of divine creation and power, how can they be presumptuous before God? They are not the source of their own existence. They are reminded, therefore, that God is the "source" of their life in Christ Jesus (1:30a). They are not self-generated. They are instead generated by a miracle of divine power in which they were transformed from "nothing" into "something." Their own conversion and continued existence as a community of God's people serve as the most vivid testimony of God's strength, power, and wisdom.

Second, Paul adduces the example of his own preaching (2:1–5). Here he insists that what he preached and how he preached ("my speech and my proclamation," 2:4) did not derive its strength and power from human eloquence or wisdom (2:1). His preaching occurred instead in "demonstration of the Spirit and of power" (2:4). The preaching through which God called them into existence was no pure and simple human effort. Its content was "Jesus Christ, and him crucified" (2:2). The heart of his message was foolish and senseless, and ran against the grain of human wisdom. In no way, then, could their response to the gospel be a "rational response," one that met the approval of human judgment. Consequently, their faith could in no way "rest . . . on human wisdom" (2:5). The source of their faith was the power of God.

In summary, neither the preaching that they originally heard nor their form of existence as a community of God's people could have been humanly conceived or humanly executed. In both cases, God was at work in and through them to display divine strength and wisdom. If it appears to them that God's ways are weak and foolish, this is their own self-indictment.

John 12:20–36

For a discussion of this Gospel lection, the reader is referred to the commentary on John 12:20–33 for the Fifth Sunday in Lent. Even if this text provided the message for that Sunday, the emphasis on God's love and grace toward all nations will be no less appropriate here. All the readings for today carry that theme, which, in a time of international suspicion, fear, and violence, must not be neglected. The importance of the issue overrides the preacher's fear of repetition.

It should be noticed that today's lection extends beyond that of the Fifth Sunday in Lent (12:20–33) to verse 36. These additional verses do not, however, alter the central thrust of the passage. The Evangelist is simply following a pattern familiar in this Gospel, that of concluding with a brief theological summary, not just of the preceding speech but of the whole Gospel. Here in verses 34–36 that summary is framed on the favorite metaphor of light and darkness.

Wednesday in Holy Week

Isaiah 50:4–9*a*;
Psalm 70;
Hebrews 12:1–3;
John 13:21–32

L inked as it is on this day with the report that one of the disciples will betray Jesus (John 13:21), the Old Testament reading emphasizes the obedience of God's servant through suffering and humiliation. Both the psalm and the Epistle lesson likewise carry the theme of response to persecution and suffering.

Isaiah 50:4–9*a*

The Old Testament reading for Wednesday in Holy Week is the same one assigned for Passion/Palm Sunday, and has been commented on at that point in this volume.

Psalm 70

T his entire psalm is practically identical in form to Psalm 40:13–17. In Psalm 40, this material comprises part of a ritual text that was probably used by the king in worship before battle. What now appears as Psalm 70 is the lament or supplication portion that requests God's help in a coming crisis.

Psalm 70:1–3 provides a good example of what has been called the double wish of the lament psalms, because the request/wish to be saved is balanced by a request for the destruction of one's enemies or opponents. Frequently, the calamity that is requested to befall one's enemy is very similar to the condition that the one praying faced. Thus numerous psalms reflect something of that attitude, so widely felt, namely, that those who plan evil should have a corresponding evil beset them. Christians often shy away in horror from the prayers in the psalms that request a destruction or a calamity to fall on one's enemies. Such sentiments seem contrary to the teaching and life of Jesus. We must, however, understand that the psalms sought to give full and appropriate outlets for people to express their true feelings and sentiments. It may be that only by verbalizing such sentiments and expressions can they be overcome or transcended. Expressions of one's truest and deepest feelings may be necessary before one can release them and replace them with better feelings. In many ways, some of the psalms probably allowed persons to vent their anger and hostility to such a degree of animosity and with such a degree of revenge that the mere recital of such cursing wishes relieved the anxiety and pent-up emotions of the worshiper (e.g., Ps. 109).

The opening verse of Psalm 70, with its plea for God to hasten and to deliver, is followed by two verses asking that the enemies be put to shame and turned back; that is, that their plans go awry, so they will end up being shamed. If the prayer was originally offered by the king, then the adversaries could be foreign powers or nations who were threatening hostile military action.

Verse 4 is an intercessory prayer, although the worshiper is included in the group being prayed for. The intercessor requests that all those who seek God and love his salvation rejoice and proclaim forever that God is great. This is obviously a prayer asking that the king and his subjects be victorious over the enemy or that they be spared a possible impending conflict. In the final verse, the worshiper reverts to an appeal on his or her own behalf. The fact that the one praying is described as poor and needy does not mean that the person was destitute and in poverty. Such expressions are metaphorical statements characterizing the person in the most sharply drawn and the humblest terms in order to evoke God's aid.

The association of this psalm with Holy Week can be made in two ways: (1) like Jesus, the psalmist was challenged by enemies who sought his death and destruction; and (2) like Jesus, the psalmist prayed and made intercessory requests on behalf of others.

Hebrews 12:1–3

These verses form a fitting conclusion to the well-known eleventh chapter of Hebrews in which various Old Testament figures are presented as exemplifying the life of faith (*pistis*). They should be read as words of exhortation addressed to fainthearted Christians and designed to bolster their faith and confidence (cf. 5:11–12; 10:25, 35; 12:12–13; 13:17). It should be remembered that the entire epistle is a "word of exhortation" (13:22) written with the same general purpose.

Today's passage resembles many other passages in the epistle that are hortatory in nature. Especially frequent are exhortations introduced with the words "let us . . ." (cf. 4:1, 11, 14, 16; 6:1; 10:22, 24; 12:28; 13:13). These hortatory subjunctives function as gentle words of encouragement. They are less direct than outright imperatives and derive from the author's sensitive pastoral concern. Clearly, the author senses that some of his readers are in danger of falling "away from the living God" (3:12).

In this exhortation, the author employs an athletic metaphor (cf. 1 Cor. 9:24–27; Phil. 1:27–28; 3:14; 1 Tim. 6:12; 2 Tim. 2:5; 4:7–8; Jude 3). The image is that of the footrace in a stadium full of spectators. The Old Testament heroes of faith are envisioned as "so great a cloud of witnesses" (v. 1), the host of spectators assembled to watch the race. The participants are surrounded by a crowd who are not merely spectators, but who themselves have already run the race and presumably have won. It is as if those who are surrounding the track have finished their race, passed on the baton, and have gathered to shout for their teammates running the final leg of the race. This is indicated by the use of the word "witnesses" (*martyres*), which no longer connotes merely "those who watch or testify" but has already begun to move in the direction of its later sense, "martyrs" (cf. 11:39–40; also Acts 22:20; Rev. 2:13; 17:6).

The readers are urged to "lay aside every weight" and "run with perseverance the race that is set before us" (v. 1). The former phrase doubtless refers to the final disrobing that precedes the start of the race. The "sin that clings so closely" suggests the image of a robe or garment that would obviously hinder running. Given the prominence of "faith" in the previous chapter, it is likely that the "sin" referred to here is the sin of unbelief, or the inability to persevere in the life of faith. The image of removing clothing to symbolize the removal of sin became a frequent metaphor in early Christian teaching (cf. Rom. 13:12; Eph. 4:22, 25; Col. 3:8; 1 Pet. 2:1; also James 1:21).

Athletic contests involve "perseverance" (*hypomone*), or endurance. In the teaching of Jesus, endurance was seen as a prerequisite to the life of faith (Luke 8:15; 21:19). Paul also stressed that "suffering produces endurance, and endurance produces character" (Rom. 5:3–4) and several times indicated the need for Christians to have endurance, or steadfastness (cf. Rom. 8:25; 15:4–5; 2 Cor. 6:4; 12:12). Quite obviously, in contexts of suffering, Christians are called upon to "endure" (1 Thess. 1:3; James 1:3–4; 5:11; Rev. 2:2–3, 19; 13:10; 14:12). As the following verse (v. 3) shows, the readers are encouraged not to "grow weary or lose heart," the temptation of every athlete, particularly in the final moments of the contest.

To this point, it is those who have preceded us in the life of faith that serve as the models of steadfastness and endurance. Now, however, another model of endurance is introduced: "Jesus the pioneer and perfecter of our faith" (v. 2). He too is envisioned as having previously run the race and won. But he is not merely one of the many spectators in the gallery of Old Testament witnesses. He is instead singled out for his unique capacity for faithful endurance (5:8–9). In this respect, he was also regarded as the patriarchs' motivation for endurance (11:25–26). The connecting link between the previously employed athletic metaphor and the example of Jesus is "endurance," for it was he who "endured the cross" (v. 2). It was precisely in this sense that he "paved the way," becoming the "pioneer" (*archegos*) and "perfecter" (*teleiotes*) of our faith. Not merely endurance, however, commended the example of Christ, for the cross carried with it shame (cf. Gal. 3:13). Yet he was motivated by the "joy that was set before him." This may refer either to the "joy that lay ahead of him" (NJB, also REB), that is, his final joyous exaltation with the Father, or the "joy that was open to him" in his preexistent state (cf. REB, note). If the latter, it should be rendered "who, in place of the joy that was open to him, endured the cross" (cf. Phil. 2:6–11; 2 Cor. 8:9).

Christ serves as the model of endurance: "Consider him who endured such hostility against himself from sinners" (v. 3). This final verse brings into focus even more sharply the example of Christ's endurance in the face of enmity and hostility.

It should not be difficult to see how this passage can be used during Holy Week. After all, it brings Christian readers, particularly those who are fainthearted and lack confidence, face-to-face with the host of our ancestors in the faith, and especially with Christ himself. To believe is often to despair, especially in the face of hostility and suffering. Believers are confronted with many reasons and experiences that tempt them to "fall away from the living God." The challenge to persevere is constant, even for believers; perhaps especially for believers.

John 13:21–32

Because the Gospel lections for today and tomorrow are from John 13, let us take a moment to familiarize ourselves with this portion of the Gospel.

In John's Gospel the ministry of Jesus as the revealer of God on earth is presented in chapters 1–12. That ministry is one of signs and speeches in the presence of the disciples, the crowds, and the opponents. Although the writer is quite aware of the reader and the reader's situation, as evidenced by the way the story is told, still these twelve chapters are *about* Jesus in *his* historical context. The reader overhears and observes. However, beginning in chapter 13, the reader (that is, the church) is more directly addressed. The crowds, the opponents, and the public scenes are gone, and Jesus turns to prepare the church for betrayal, death, departure, and the coming of the Spirit as "another Advocate" (14:16); chapters 13–20 could well be entitled "Farewell." These chapters contain the account of the farewell of Jesus (chaps. 18–20) and a rather lengthy preparation for that farewell (chaps. 13–17). By prediction, promise, warning, charge, encouragement, and exemplary act Jesus prepares his followers for the first major crisis of the church, his departure and absence. It is vital that, following his return to God, Jesus' disciples remain in continuity with the historical Jesus. That continuity will be maintained by remembrance of Jesus' words, apostolic tradition, and the Holy Spirit. These chapters (chaps. 13–17) make that abundantly clear.

Chapter 13 begins this section with an account of Jesus' farewell meal with his disciples. During that meal Jesus indicates his betrayer, and Judas leaves the table to attend to his dark business. The writer closes the scene (vv. 21–30) with a statement more symbolic and dramatic than informative: "And it was night" (v. 30). However, it is interesting that "night" is preserved in the earliest of our traditions about the Last Supper: "The Lord Jesus on the night when he was betrayed took a loaf of bread" (1 Cor. 11:23).

The scene and drama presented in John 13:21–32 center on the roles of three persons: Jesus, the disciple Jesus loved, and Judas. Jesus, in the characteristic Johannine portrait, knows what is to happen (v. 21) and who will do it (v. 26). He also is totally in charge, commanding Judas to do quickly what he has to do (v. 27). After all, no one takes the life of the Johannine Christ; he lays it down and he takes it up again (10:18). However, the description of Jesus as "troubled in spirit" (v. 21) seems to portray a Christ more like ourselves. What does it mean? It could be in the same vein as 11:33; that is, Jesus is emotionally disturbed by the events before him, in this case betrayal by a friend. But "troubled in spirit, and *declared*" (v. 21, italics added) can also be a description of the prophetic state immediately preceding a prophecy. The preacher will have to make an exegetical decision here, setting this paragraph within the portrayal of Jesus throughout this Gospel.

The second significant figure in this text is the disciple whom Jesus loved (v. 23). The commentaries will aid in attempts to guess the name of this disciple traditionally identified as John the son of Zebedee. This unnamed disciple appears in six scenes in John 13–21 (13:21–30; 18:15–18; 19:25–27; 20:1–9; 21:47; 21:20–24); and except for the scene at the cross with Jesus' mother (19:25–27), he is in the company of Simon Peter. This person, obviously very close to Jesus, provides the Johannine church with continuity with Jesus and gives it apostolic authority. This disciple also precedes Simon Peter in knowledge, in faith, and in relation to Jesus. If there were Johannine and Petrine circles of Christianity, then this writer is certain who lies closest to the heart and truth of the tradition about Jesus.

The third important character in 13:21–30 is Judas Iscariot (vv. 26–30). Other than Jesus, Judas receives more attention in 13:1–30 than any other person. Why? Perhaps because the treason by a close associate put the heaviest burden upon those who interpreted the story for the church. Perhaps it was to assure Christians that even in betrayal and death Jesus was not a victim but the one who orchestrated the redemptive drama. Or perhaps it was a warning to that church or to any church of the real possibilities of loss of affection, of unbelief, of self-serving departures from Jesus. After all, the writer says that none of the disciples knew themselves or one another well enough to be sure. "The disciples looked at one another, uncertain of whom he was speaking" (v. 22). Rather than speculating on what social, political, economic, or psychological forces created a Judas, perhaps it would be better for the church to respond as Mark says the original disciples did: "They began to be distressed and to say to him one after another, 'Surely, not I?'" (Mark 14:19).

In verses 31–32, Jesus is again speaking, but not to say to the remaining eleven, "It is all over." On the contrary, Jesus sets the painful events lying before them in the larger context of God's purpose. In what is about to happen, God will be glorified, and the Son will be glorified. The disciples could not at that time understand what the reader understands: God is glorified in the death and resurrection of Jesus in that God's gracious purpose for the world is fulfilled; Jesus is glorified in that his being lifted on the cross means, in this Gospel, his being exalted again to the presence of God.

Holy Thursday

Exodus 12:1–4 (5–10) 11–14;
Psalm 116:1–2, 12–19;
1 Corinthians 11:23–26;
John 13:1–17, 31b–35

Nothing was more influential on early Christian thinking about the death of Christ than Israel's observance of Passover, whose origin is described in today's Old Testament lection. The accompanying epistolary text, Paul's account of the institution of the Eucharist, underscores the importance of community solidarity as the church observes this sacred meal. The Gospel text, the Johannine account of the Last Supper, includes the distinctive Johannine tradition of Jesus' washing the disciples' feet, which visibly enacts his command for the disciples to love each other. The verses from Psalm 116 portray the psalmist's utter dependence on God, who heals human affliction, and its expressions of thanksgiving echo eucharistic themes.

Exodus 12:1–4 (5–10) 11–14

The account of the institution of the Passover, a highly appropriate Old Testament lesson for Holy Thursday, stands very close to the heart of the Old Testament story and ancient Israel's faith. Nothing was more central to that faith than the confession that Yahweh brought Israel out of Egypt. The Passover, believed to have been instituted on the very night that Israel was set free from Egypt, takes its meaning from the connection with the Exodus. Thus each time the Passover was celebrated, including in the time of Jesus, the people of God remembered that they were slaves set free by their God.

Although the section before us is relatively straightforward, it is part of a very complex section in the Book of Exodus. Because it is the climax of the Exodus traditions, it has attracted a great many diverse elements. The unit, which reports the events immediately surrounding the departure from Egypt, begins in Exodus 11:1 and does not end until Exodus 13:16. One can identify four distinct motifs within this section. The most important is, of course, the departure from Egypt itself. Although this is noted quite briefly (12:37–39), it is the focal point of all other motifs. Second is the report of the final plague, the killing of the firstborn children of the Egyptians. This disaster is quite distinct from those that preceded it, both in the fact that it was effective and in the extensive preparations for it. The third and fourth motifs are the religious ceremonies connected with the Exodus, the celebration of Passover and the Feast of Unleavened Bread. Passover is linked to the final plague because it entailed a procedure for ensuring that the Israelite firstborn would not be killed, and it is connected in very direct ways with the immediate departure from Egypt. The final plague is what motivated the pharaoh to release Israel, and the Passover was the ritual of departure.

Within this section of the Book of Exodus there are duplicates, repetitions, and inconsistencies that reveal the presence of at least two sources, the Priestly Writer and the Yahwist. The style and technical terminology of Exodus 12:1–13 reveal that it comes from the Priestly Writer and thus would date from the postexilic period, approximately 500 BC. Exodus 12:14 begins a section that probably comes from the J source, perhaps as early as 900 BC.

It is important to keep in mind that this passage is part of a narrative, a story more of divine actions than human events. Its literary context is the history of salvation, the account of Yahweh's intervention to set his people free. In that framework Exodus 12:1–14 is a report of divine instructions to Moses and Aaron concerning the celebration of the Passover. Thus everything except verse 1 is in the form of a speech of Yahweh, a direct address to Moses and Aaron. These instructions have the tone and contents of rules established for perpetuity and thus reflect the perspective of Israelites centuries after the events.

The instructions are precise and detailed with regard to both time and actions. The month in which the Exodus takes place is to become the first month of the year, and the preparations for the Passover begin on the tenth day of that month (vv. 2–3a). It is a family ceremony, with a lamb chosen for each household—that is, unless the household is too small for a lamb, in which case neighboring families are to join together to make up the right number to consume the lamb (vv. 3b–4). A lamb without blemish is to be selected and then killed on the fourteenth day of the month (vv. 5–6). The people are to smear blood on the lintels and doorposts of their houses; they are to roast the meat and eat it with unleavened bread and bitter herbs (vv. 7–9). The meal is to be eaten in haste, and anything not consumed by morning is to be burned (vv. 10–11).

After the instructions follows an explanation of the meaning of the meal and of the practices associated with it. The Lord will pass through the land of Egypt to destroy the firstborn, but will see the blood and "pass over" the Israelites (vv. 12–13). Verse 14, which comes from another writer, stresses that the day is a "day of remembrance," and forever. In celebrating this day, later generations will remember the Exodus.

In both the present text and later practice, Passover was combined with the Feast of Unleavened Bread. The former was a one-night communal meal, and the latter was a seven-day festival. The combination was quite ancient, but the two originally were distinct. It seems likely that the Feast of Unleavened Bread was a pre-Israelite festival related to the agricultural year in Canaan. Passover, on the other hand, probably originated among seminomadic groups, such as the Israelites, as a festival related to the movement of their flocks from winter to summer pasture. The feast certainly was a family ceremony during the early history of Israel. In later generations, Passover was one of the three major annual pilgrimage festivals for which the people were to come to Jerusalem (Deut. 16:2–7).

The word "passover" (Hebrew *pesach*) is explained in this passage by connecting it with a verb for "to skip" or "hop over," but the actual etymology of the word is uncertain. Throughout the Old Testament it refers either to the festival described here or to the animal that is killed and eaten. Many passages use the word in both senses (e.g., 2 Chron. 35:1–19). The ceremony had both sacrificial and communal dimensions in that the animal was ceremonially slaughtered but then consumed as a family meal.

No ceremony was more important in ancient Israel or early Judaism than Passover. It was the festival in which the people acknowledged and celebrated who they were and who their

God was. In remembering the day as the memorial day for the Exodus (Exod. 12:14), they acknowledged that God is the one who sets people free and makes them his own. They knew thereby that they were God's people. Moreover, in the gathering of family and friends for a communal meal in which the story of release from slavery was told, they bound themselves together and to that God who acted to make them who they were.

Psalm 116:1–2, 12–19

These verses of Psalm 116 are the opening and closing portions of a thanksgiving psalm and are concerned with the fulfillment of vows made earlier, probably at the time when the worshiper petitioned God for deliverance from trouble, most likely suffering from a debilitating illness. In the Judaism of Jesus' day, Psalms 113–118 were sung as part of the observance of Passover. These psalms were sung in the temple by the Levites as the Passover lambs were being slaughtered and then again in the homes as the Passover meal was being eaten. Psalm 116 was most likely selected for use in the Passover ritual or Seder meal because of the reference to the cup in verse 13. Four cups of wine were ritually drunk in the Passover ritual, and Psalm 116 seems to have been used at the point in the meal when the fourth and final cup was consumed.

The selection of this psalm for use in the Holy Thursday service is, of course, based on its use in the Passover ritual that Jesus is said to have observed with his disciples on Thursday in Holy Week. Because many churches celebrate Holy Communion on Holy Thursday, this psalm can be reused in a context comparable to its early usage in Judaism.

Psalm 116 would have been used originally in the context of a thanksgiving service at the sanctuary. Verses 1–2 are a public confession of love for Yahweh based on God's having heard the worshiper's prayer. Verses 3–4 describe the distress and anguish that the person had undergone during a sickness when death seemed near. After offering general thanksgiving to and praise of God for deliverance, the worshiper moves to the fulfillment of vows made earlier (see v. 18).

In rendering the vows, which would certainly have included the offering of sacrifice, the worshiper addresses a human audience (vv. 12–15, 18–19) as well as the Deity (vv. 16–17). We should think of such thanksgiving rituals as times of great happiness and jubilant celebration. A person whose life had been threatened, disoriented, and removed from the normal course of activity had been restored to wholeness. The life that had fallen into the grip of hell itself and had been invaded by the power of death was now free of both the illness and the anguished turmoil that the sickness brought. Now the worshiper can look back and speak of the sorrowful plight of the past, which now is only a life-transforming memory. There certainly must be "scars" from such a past, but they are signs of past triumphs and the residues of God's grace, to be cherished and celebrated, not embarrassingly hidden. At such a celebration, friends and family of the formerly ill person would have attended worship with the redeemed. Such worship would have included thanksgiving not only in word but also in feasting, drinking, and dancing. These festive symbols marked the end of a former state and the beginning of a new state of living. They were enjoyed as the sacramental signs of God's concern and care.

In verses 12–15, the worshiper addresses a human audience of friends and family. The elements of the thanksgiving spoken of included the offering of a cup of salvation, the worship of God, and the fulfillment of vows. The cup mentioned is best understood as the drink offering made as part of the thanksgiving sacrificial ritual (see Num. 28:7) or perhaps the cup of wine drunk in the thanksgiving meal (Ps. 23:5). Such a cup symbolized God's deliverance, the opposite of the cup of God's wrath (see Isa. 51:17; Jer. 25:15). The worshiper reminds the listeners that God does not wish the death of one of his faithful worshipers, because for God such a death is a serious, weighty matter (v. 15; not "precious in the sight of the LORD," as in the NRSV). The place of the thanksgiving celebration was the temple in Jerusalem where sacrifices could be made (vv. 18–19). In such thanksgiving services, most of the animals sacrificed would have reverted to the worshiper to be cooked and eaten in the temple precincts before the next day had passed (see Lev. 6:11–18). Thus the sacrifice of thanksgiving imposed lavish and extravagant eating and communal sharing.

Verses 16–17 would have been prayed directly to God in conjunction with offering the thanksgiving sacrifice. The worshiper thus declared his or her status before God, "I am your servant," a status dependent upon the redemptive work of God, "You have loosed my bonds."

1 Corinthians 11:23–26

Here we have one of the earliest versions of the tradition pertaining to the institution of the Lord's Supper. As the opening language suggests ("received," "handed on"), it was a sacred tradition that even preceded Paul, in fact could be traced to the Lord himself. Paul had received it "from the Lord" (v. 23) in the sense that the tradition originated with Jesus.

Paul introduces this sacred tradition as a way of correcting abuses within the congregational worship of the Corinthians. As the context makes clear (1 Cor. 11:17–22; 27–34), some of the Corinthians failed to see the full import of this sacred event, and even less, the significance it had for their life together. From Paul's description of the situation at Corinth, it appears that the congregation was stratified along socioeconomic lines. Rather than serving as a means of binding the "haves" and "have nots" into a community linked to a common purpose, the Lord's Supper was becoming an occasion for accentuating social differences within the church.

The Corinthian Christians are reminded that the sacred meal inaugurated by Jesus, which had deep roots in the Jewish observance of Passover, consists of two elements, both of which symbolize the way in which Jesus' life and death occurred in behalf of others. The words of remembrance over the bread are: "This is my body that is *for you*" (v. 24, italics added). The cup of the new covenant (v. 25) was intended not only to bind believers to the Lord, but to each other, as the covenant between God and Israel had done.

Noting Paul's use of this sacred tradition here serves to remind us that our participation in Holy Week not only deepens our individual faith, but also binds us to the community of faith—both the congregation where we worship and the larger Christian community. We are reminded that as we re-live this sacred story, we do so along with hosts of others whose lives have been radically shaped by the Christ-story. Just as the Exodus has been decisively formative in Jewish self-understanding, so has the Last Supper been for Christians in every age.

Like every significant ritual, the Lord's Supper connects us with what we understand to be sacred time. It takes us back to events that remain for us definitive for the way they establish the beginning of our own sense of history. Yet it also establishes a future reference point by which we chart our pilgrimage. And in reflecting on this event, we come to a better understanding of our own place in the larger story and the difference this makes in how we relate to the various communities of which we are members.

Doing something often need not make it trivial. What matters is whether our repeated celebration of certain events firmly anchors our self-understanding in God's larger story and enriches that understanding in ways that make us appreciate even more the significance of certain events of the past, now long gone.

John 13:1–17, 31b–35

Now before the festival of the Passover" (13:1), says this Evangelist, alerting the reader that the account that follows will be different from the Synoptic records of the last meal. In the Synoptics, Jesus eats the Passover meal with the Twelve (Matt. 26:17–19; Mark 14:12–16; Luke 22:7–13, and especially Luke 22:15) and, following the meal, institutes the Lord's Supper (Matt. 26:26–29; Mark 14:22–25; Luke 22:15–20). In John, the last meal is before Passover, and there is no account here of the institution of the Eucharist. For this Evangelist, Jesus does not *eat* the Passover; he *is* the Passover, bleeding and dying as the Passover lamb (19:31–37). In chapter 6, John presents the feeding of the five thousand as a Passover meal with a eucharistic interpretation. The commentaries will discuss whether John is to be taken as a correction of the Synoptics, as exhibiting evidence of a different source, or as the writer's willingness to sacrifice chronology for theology.

For this Evangelist, therefore, the last meal is the occasion, the setting, for particular words and acts of Jesus. The central act of Jesus in this text is the washing of the disciples' feet (vv. 2–5). The act is not understood (v. 7), even though it is followed by two interpretations (vv. 6–11, 12–20). It is very important, however, for the reader to understand that Jesus knows exactly what he is doing and what it means. Notice: "Jesus, knowing that the Father had given all things into his hands" (v. 3); "for he knew who was to betray him" (v. 11); and, "I know whom I have chosen" (v. 18). This portrayal of Jesus is consistent with the way John presents him from the prologue through the entire Gospel. Whatever clashes with other portraits of Jesus this may create for the reader, it should be appreciated that John is giving confidence and engendering faith (v. 19) in Christians who might otherwise look upon the events of betrayal, arrest, and death as defeat. After all, John's readers were experiencing betrayal, arrest, and death (15:20–16:3), and to understand these events in Jesus' life as part of a divine plan of redemption would help them interpret their own experiences as having purpose. In other words, Jesus was not really a victim, and, even in death, neither are they victims.

The scene, then, is a powerful and moving one. Jesus is fully aware of his origin in glory; he is fully aware that he is soon to return to that glory; he is further aware that while on earth, all authority from God is his (vv. 1–3). The stage is set by verses 1–3 for Jesus to act in a dazzling way. Will he be transfigured before their eyes? Will he command the disciples to bow in adoration? No; instead, he rose from the table, replaced his robe with a towel, poured water in a basin, washed the disciples' feet, and dried them with the towel (vv. 4–5).

Following the foot washing, two interpretations of the act are offered. Whether the fact that there are two represents two traditions about the meaning of Jesus' act or whether both were from the beginning associated with the event is a matter debated in the commentaries. As we will see, the two interpretations are not unrelated. The first (vv. 6–11) insists that the church is in the posture of recipient, having its identity and character in the self-giving act of the servant Jesus. The church exists by the cleansing act of Jesus. (Some ecclesiastical traditions therefore associate the washing with baptism.) It is this understanding that Simon Peter resists (vv. 6–9). The church in the person of Simon Peter does not want its Lord and Savior to wash its feet.

The second interpretation (vv. 12–17, but it actually extends through v. 20) understands Jesus' act as a model of humility and service that the church is to emulate. The servant is not greater than the master; and the posture of washing feet, whether understood literally or figuratively, vividly holds that truth before the church's eyes. This has been the more widely embraced interpretation, both by the few churches that have accorded foot washing sacramental status and the many that have not. The lesson is not lost even among those who do not continue the practice of foot washing. Perhaps one reason this second interpretation is more widely embraced than the first is that giving service is easier for the ego than receiving it. However, the two interpretations are not necessarily independent of each other. In fact, the church in a state of spiritual health and with a clear sense of its own nature and calling would practice the second because it had embraced the first.

In verses 31b–35 the writer turns up the lights to their brightest, and the dark of Judas' betrayal is scattered by the declaration of God's purpose. (See comments at the end of the previous lesson.) Jesus' prediction of his passion is almost gentle: "Little children, I am with you only a little longer" (v. 33). But whether soft or harsh (as in Mark), the disciples must deal with the absence of Jesus, and they will be able to do so if their relationship with each other is informed and determined by his relationship to them. "As I have loved you" (v. 34) is the key. In fact, this is probably the sense in which the command to love is new. If referring to love as a command is a problem, it most likely is due to thinking of love as a feeling. However, if love is the way God acts toward the world and the way Jesus acts toward his disciples, then love means telling the truth, being faithful in one's witness, and caring for others, even to the point of death.

This commandment, joined to the instructions about foot washing (in this Gospel) and to the Eucharist (in the others and in 1 Cor. 11), gives to Holy Thursday the ancient designation "Maundy," a form of the word *mandate*.

Good Friday

Isaiah 52:13–53:12;
Psalm 22;
Hebrews 10:16–25 *or* Hebrews 4:14–16; 5:7–9;
John 18:1–19:42

The fourth Servant Song in Second Isaiah has long been the traditional Old Testament reading for Good Friday, and with good reason. No other Old Testament text more clearly describes the messiah as a Suffering Servant of God, one who was obedient to death, and one whose suffering and death were vicarious. This text, above all others in the Hebrew Bible, enabled the earliest Christians to understand and communicate to one another and to the world at large the meaning of the death of Jesus (see Acts 8:34; Rom. 5:21; 1 Cor. 15:4).

Psalm 22 belongs in the liturgy for Good Friday not only because its initial words were spoken by Jesus on the cross but also because its description of suffering corresponds to that of the servant in Isaiah 52:13–53:12 (see esp. Ps. 22:6–8, 12–15). Moreover, Psalm 22:18 is cited in the Gospel lection (John 19:24) as part of the report of the death of Jesus.

The epistolary texts, like the Old Testament reading, stress the obedience of the Messiah through suffering and his ability to sympathize with our weaknesses.

Isaiah 52:13–53:12

The fourth Servant Song in Second Isaiah continues to be a powerful text not only because of what it says—especially when heard in the context of the Christian community on Good Friday—but also because of the way that content is expressed. Some attention to its structure and poetic characteristics will thus be of value to the interpreter. Its structure is relatively easy to recognize if one is attentive to the shifts in the speakers. The poem has three parts, and in none of them does the servant speak. At the beginning (52:13–15), God speaks to proclaim the exaltation of the servant and the astonished response of nations and kings. In the central section (53:1–11*a*), some unnamed group speaks to report on the life and death of the servant as well as their response to it. Finally (53:11*b*–12), God speaks again to confirm the meaning and effect of the servant's suffering; he will be exalted because he "bore the sin of many."

The passage is a genuinely distinctive poem, but it does have affinities with other Old Testament traditions. The account of the servant's suffering is indebted to the cultic tradition of individual complaints such as Psalm 22 and individual thanksgiving songs. However, in such psalms it is the person in trouble who gives an account of that suffering and salvation, whereas here the suffering of a third party is described and interpreted. The body of the song includes words of confession by the unnamed speakers (esp. vv. 4–6), suggesting a service of penitence. Moreover, the citation of the words of God at the beginning and the end is like that in prophetic speeches. Although it echoes these and other biblical themes, the poem is a highly artistic creation, using a wide range of images to hammer home its message. Although it stands out dramatically in its context, it probably was composed by the same prophet who wrote Isaiah 40–55.

It seems unlikely that the question of the identity of the servant in the original historical context can be resolved decisively. Analysis of the form, however, suggests an answer to part of the eunuch's question in Acts 8:34: "About whom, may I ask you, does the prophet say this, about himself or about someone else?" The prophet is speaking about another. It is also clear from the introduction that he is speaking of the same one introduced in the first Servant Song, Isaiah 42:1–4. But whereas the context of the first song takes the servant to be Israel as a whole, this one clearly speaks of an individual. Those commentators who interpret the servant as Israel take the personal language of Isaiah 52:13–53:12 metaphorically. Israel's suffering and humiliation through the Exile are seen as highly personal; they were on behalf of the world, and Israel will be vindicated. However, far more important than the historical identity of the servant is the meaning of his life and death.

This text is so rich in meaning that it would be a serious mistake to reduce it to a single point. Nevertheless, its major themes are unmistakable. First, and in the broadest sense, the message is stated at the outset: God will vindicate and exalt his suffering servant. That point, not only in its original context but in all others—including the report of an execution—is a reversal of expectations. God's power and authority are manifested in weakness; God acts through one whose suffering is so great that it makes him repulsive to all who see him. Second, there is the poignant account of a life of innocent suffering, from youth (53:2) through a trial and death (53:7–8). Third, the servant's life of suffering and humiliation is both vicarious and efficacious. That is, it is on behalf of others, and it effectively removes their sin (53:6, 8, 12). Others do not have to pay the price because he has already paid it. Some of the language seems to allude to ritual sacrifice ("poured out," 53:12), but the song as a whole goes far beyond what one finds elsewhere in the Old Testament concerning sacrifice for sins. Finally, the servant will be vindicated before the whole world, for his suffering is on behalf of the transgressions of all ("many," 53:12).

This text, above all others in the Hebrew Bible, enabled the earliest Christians to understand and communicate to one another and to the world at large the meaning of the death of Jesus (see Acts 8:34; Rom. 5:21; 1 Cor. 15:4). The Christian community at worship on Good Friday, as it seeks the words to respond to the crucifixion of Jesus, could hardly find more appropriate language than the central portion of this song (53:1–11a). The speakers of those words, while reporting on the suffering of the servant, confessed their own sins. But at the same time, in acknowledging that his suffering is vicarious and efficacious they profess that God's servant has removed those sins.

Psalm 22

Probably no other psalm is more appropriate for use on Good Friday than Psalm 22. It expresses, in the most powerfully drawn imagery, a sense of suffering and a feeling of being abandoned by God. In addition, this psalm greatly influenced the early church's interpretation of Jesus' death as well as the way in which early Christians shaped and told the story of the passion and death of Jesus, using even the words of the psalm (see Matt. 27:39, 46; Mark 15:24, 34; Luke 23:34).

Within the psalm are interwoven descriptions of distress (vv. 1–2, 6–8, 12–18), statements of confidence (vv. 3–5, 9–10), and general appeals for help (vv. 11, 19–21) to form a tapestry of a soul in torment. The worshiper describes the distressful situation in terms of both sickness and oppression by enemies. As frequently in the psalms, such language may be highly metaphorical and formulated to solicit the concern of God. The language is that of personal chaos, of life in complete disarray, of troubles that torment one to the breaking point.

Two themes run through the statements about the person's distress: a sense of alienation from the Deity and hostile opposition from opponents.

The theme of God's distance and, correspondingly, the person's sense of alienation are sounded in the opening lines. A sense of divine forsakenness pervades the words. God is so far away that he cannot hear the sufferer's groanings; day and night move through their ceaseless revolutions, but for the worshiper there is neither answer nor rest from God but only dismay at the divine silence and the loneliness of feeling forsaken.

The theme of human opposition parallels that of divine alienation. If God is too far distant, humans are too near. Human opposition and enmity are described in various ways. People mock, wagging their heads and making faces, ridiculing the person's dependence and seemingly futile reliance on God (vv. 7–8). Powers described as bulls, lions, and dogs, a company of evildoers, assail the worshiper (vv. 12–13, 16). The depiction might suggest that the speaker was a king and the enemies were foreign powers. In any case, the opponents are portrayed as menacing, life threatening, and life destroying. They seize the person's abandonment by God as the occasion for attack.

The consequences of the worshiper's status are described in terms suggesting low self-esteem, complete despair and disorganization, and overall desperation. The image of a person's self-designation as a worm implies a feeling of utter hopelessness and helplessness, a state of feeling horribly subhuman (v. 6). Fright and incapacitation run through the imagery of verses 14–15 and 17–18, which is extremely graphic. Life seems no longer to have legitimate boundaries and normal structures ("poured out like water"); things do not function as they should ("bones are out of joint"); fear pervades everything ("heart is like wax . . . melted"); strength has ebbed away ("dried up like a potsherd"); speech fails ("tongue sticks to my jaws"); death seems to be the only foreseeable certainty; and emaciation exposes the body's boney structure ("count all my bones"). The enemies are pictured as already going through the postmortem ritual of dividing up the belongings of the deceased as if death had already occurred. The psalmist speaks of his or her own demise and the distribution of his or her goods in a game of fortune and luck. Although not greatly emphasized in the psalm, God appears as the real enemy of the worshiper. The last line of verse 15 declares that it is God who has already laid the supplicant in the dust of death. Behind the opposition and oppression of the enemy lies the activity of God, and God becomes the real opponent.

In spite of the dismal picture that the descriptions of distress paint, the psalm is shot through with statements and confessions of great confidence in the Deity. Verses 3–5 affirm that God is holy and that in the past the faith and trust of the fathers were rewarded with divine favor. Such confidence in the worshiper was based on both the nature of God and the experience of the past; that is, the paradigm of the past functions as a source of hope for the future. The confidence in God, expressed in verses 9–10, stresses the prior intimacy that existed between the one praying and God. The psalmist seems to be implying that previously God had been his or her "father," his or her caretaker from the days of birth and youth.

The confidence in God displayed throughout the psalm moves in verses 22–31 to pride of place and suggests that the worshiper received from God some oracle or sign affirming that a reversal of fate was in store, that tears and pains would be replaced by songs and celebration. Perhaps the lection for Good Friday, however, should end with the pain and tribulation, not with victory and triumph.

In relating Psalm 22 to the passion of Jesus, one should not expound it as a prophetic prediction of his suffering and death in spite of the fact that the early Christians used this psalm as one of the primary Old Testament texts for understanding the passion and suffering of the Messiah. Its lines and view of the suffering righteous raised to triumph and praise helped Christians overcome the scandalous execution and suffering of Christ the deliverer.

Hebrews 10:16–25

This first epistolary reading, which begins with a citation of Jeremiah 31:33–34, constitutes one of the strongest exhortations in the Epistle to the Hebrews. In the latter part of the passage, the phrase "let us . . ." abounds (vv. 22, 23, 24). As such, it is a litany of appeals to the Christian community, calling for "assurance of faith," holding steadfast "to the confession of our hope without wavering," and provoking "one another to love and good deeds."

It is a passage intended to build confidence in the readers and hearers. As is well known, the Epistle to the Hebrews is addressed to readers who are dispirited and who have grown tired in their faith. The lofty reflections on Christ's high priesthood that are developed in the letter are intended to raise the sights of believers whose vision has grown dim.

Part of the author's strategy is to delineate the true significance of Christ's sacrificial death. And one way to see this is to realize that it gives us access to God in unprecedently immediate form—boldness to enter private quarters heretofore off-limits, except to the high priest. Access to God's presence means the ability to stand before God in true confidence, not only certain that our sins are forgiven but also encouraged that the life of faith is worth continuing.

The connection between the promise of a new covenant—which envisions a community of God's people where God is present among them in heart and mind, and where our sins and lawless acts are not held against us—and the sacrificial work of Christ is not artificial. For today's text presents Christ as the one through whom such a community is made possible, and the one who enables this intimate relationship between God and sinner.

Hebrews 4:14–16; 5:7–9

Because Hebrews 5:7–9 was treated earlier in our remarks on Hebrews 5:5–10, the epistolary reading for the Fifth Sunday in Lent, here we will limit our remarks to Hebrews 4:14–16.

Again, the text focuses on the high priesthood of Jesus, a theme already introduced in the epistle (2:17; 3:1) and one that continues to be central to the Christology of the epistle (5:5, 10; 6:20; 7:26; 8:1; 9:11; 10:21). Unlike the Levitical high priest, however, Jesus has been "exalted above the heavens" (7:26; Eph. 4:10), and in this exalted status officiates in our behalf as the Son of God (6:6; 7:3; 10:29).

But it is not so much the exalted status of Christ that is in the forefront here. Rather, it is his complete identification with our human condition that is stressed. It is his ability to "sympathize with our weaknesses" (v. 15; also cf. 2:17–18; 5:2) that enables him to identify with us. He is "one who in every respect has been tested as we are" (v. 15). This crucial phrase is effectively rendered in NJB: "[he] has been put to the test in exactly the same way as ourselves, apart from sin." Earlier in the epistle we are told that Christ "had to become like his brothers and sisters in every respect [kata panta]" (2:17, italics added). The author's insistence on Christ's likeness to us is unqualified (cf. also Rom. 8:3; Phil. 2:7). The reference to his being "tested" may recall the Synoptic account of Jesus' temptation by Satan (Matt. 4:1–11 and parallels; also Luke 22:28). These three temptations, or "tests," that occurred at the beginning of his ministry struck at the heart of his messianic vocation. They have long been regarded as representative of the ways in which filial obedience to God can be tested. As such, all children of God are able to identify with the Son of God.

But if our text asserts without qualification that Christ was tested "in every respect . . . as we are," it is also unequivocal in asserting that he remained "without sin" (v. 15). This conviction was widely shared among early Christians and is attested in various strata of the New Testament (cf. John 7:18; 8:46; 2 Cor. 5:21; Heb. 7:26; 1 Pet. 2:22; 3:18; 1 John 3:5). In this respect, of course, Christ differed from his Levitical counterparts (Heb. 7:27–28). His complete humanity enables him to identify and sympathize with our weaknesses, but his unsullied life enables him to mediate in our behalf.

We should note that our text is not merely christological reflection, but exhortation: "Let us hold fast to our confession" (v. 14); "let us therefore approach the throne of grace with boldness, so that we may receive mercy and find grace to help in time of need" (v. 16). It is significant that such exhortations are grounded in the Christ-event. Because of the finality of Jesus' sacrifice, the quality and degree of his humanity, the perfection of his life, we can be justifiably confident in our confession of faith. Also, we can pray to God boldly in order to "receive mercy and find grace to give us timely help" (v. 16, REB). Similar assurances are given elsewhere in the New Testament (cf. 3:6; 10:19, 22, 35; 1 John 3:21; Rom. 5:1–2).

We can now see why this text is joined with Hebrews 5:7–9 as the epistolary lection for Good Friday. It opens with a triumphant statement of Christ's exaltation, and then it turns to his humanity. The companion lection, however, focuses more strongly on Jesus in "the days of his flesh" (5:7), his anguish ("loud cries and tears"), probably in Gethsemane but possibly on the cross itself, his prayer for deliverance, the obedience learned through suffering, and the perfection or completion of his messianic work through his death on the cross. The theme of "weakness" in 4:15 certainly carries over into 5:7–9 and provides one direction for homiletical development. In fact, 5:7–8 serves to elaborate on 4:15, for it makes more precise the ways in which the crucified Christ identifies with our own "cries and tears."

Several themes, thus, emerge from these two texts: (1) Christ's complete identification with human weakness; (2) his sinlessness; (3) his anguish that was experienced in the "days of his flesh"; (4) his prayer to God offered in godly fear; (5) his unqualified obedience through suffering; (6) the completion or perfection of his filial vocation as the Son of God; (7) his deserved status as the quintessential high priest, who serves as "the source of eternal salvation" to those who render similar obedience to God; and (8) his exalted and unique status as a high priest after the order of Melchizedek.

John 18:1–19:42

On those days when the lectionary offers a longer reading, choices within the passage may be made by the preacher. For Good Friday, the choice may be determined largely by the kind of services provided. If there is but one service of usual length, one may well choose to deal only with the crucifixion (19:17–30). However, if the three-hour afternoon services are scheduled, then the entirety of John 18:1–19:42 could be used.

A text of this size and significance can hardly be treated in one sermon, but it can be approached, even if not too closely. One way of approaching this body of materials is to see it as a narrative in five episodes: arrest (18:1–12); interrogation by religious leaders (18:13–27); interrogation by Pilate (18:28–19:16); crucifixion (19:17–30); and burial (19:31–42). Telling the story as John tells it has its own appropriateness and power. Another approach would be to draw from the narrative the accents, the emphases that the Evangelist makes. In other words, be especially sensitive to overhear what this Gospel writer understands as the meaning of Jesus' passion. Here we will try to combine the two approaches in a necessarily brief sketch.

The arrest of Jesus (18:1–12) is related with drama, with more details than in the Synoptics, but without the emotion of the other accounts. There is no crying or beating the breast here, for John's Jesus does not agonize, neither here nor on the cross. Gethsemane is "a garden" (v. 1). This Evangelist alone says that Roman soldiers (vv. 3, 12) were involved in the arrest. A "detachment of soldiers" (vv. 3, 12) was a "cohort," about six hundred men, and an "officer" was a "chiliarch" (v. 12), an officer over a thousand soldiers. By mentioning their presence, along with officers of Judaism (v. 3), John says the whole unbelieving world, political and religious, joined in opposition to the Word of God. Through it all Jesus is in charge. Judas, Peter, the soldiers—all receive their directions from Jesus. Because his hour has come, he allows those who could not arrest him earlier (7:30, 44; 8:20, 59; 10:39; 12:36) to do so now. The interrogation by religious leaders (18:13–24) is minimally related by John, the only official action being the questioning before Annas (vv. 13, 19), who does not appear at all in the Synoptics. Caiaphas is mentioned four times, but with sarcasm ("the high priest *that year*," v. 13, italics added), and was disregarded as a factor in the story. Jesus' hour had come; what power did they have in the case? Significantly, more attention is given to Peter than to Jesus' trial. After all, the trial of Jesus has been settled since 12:18, but the trial of Peter, of the disciples, and of the church continues. The writer again shows himself more preacher than historian.

The interrogation by Pontius Pilate (18:28–19:16) is, compared with the Synoptics, quite lengthy. There are seven episodes, alternating between Pilate questioning Jesus inside the praetorium and dealing with the Jews outside. The account is full of irony: Jesus the prisoner is in charge; Pilate the governor shuttles back and forth indecisively like a frightened lieutenant; the Jews, in this Gospel the epitome of "the world," have death in their hearts but refuse to enter a Gentile building lest they be ceremonially defiled (v. 28). Pilate's only success is in getting the religious leaders to make what is their real confession of faith, "Caesar is king." At Passover, on the anniversary of freedom from the pharaoh, the pharaoh is embraced. Contemporary parallels flood the mind of every preacher.

The crucifixion (19:17–30) is briefly recorded. Even Mark is more extended here. Jesus is still in control, carrying his own cross (there is no Simon of Cyrene), acting and speaking so as to fulfill Scriptures and bring the intention of Judaism to completion (vv. 24, 28), making arrangements for his mother's care (vv. 26–27), and giving up his spirit (v. 30). He dies as Good Shepherd and as King. As Good Shepherd he cared for his own to the end and gave his life for the sheep (10:11–18); as King, he was unwittingly enthroned by those who mocked, who unwittingly called him King of the Jews. "And I, when I am lifted up from the earth, will draw all people to myself" (12:32). Even human wrath serves to praise God.

The burial (19:31–42) receives as much attention as the crucifixion itself even though the story of Jesus and his disciples is now the record of a corpse and its caretakers. This passage contains two stories about the body of Jesus, verses 31–37 and 38–42. The second provides closure to the preceding events, prepares for the resurrection story, and tells how two hesitant and uncertain believers, Joseph and Nicodemus, found courage in Jesus' death that they could not find during his lifetime. The first, verses 31–37, interweaves two interpretations of Jesus' death. Jesus died as the Passover Lamb, and his body was so treated (Exod. 12:2, 46; Num. 9:12). The Evangelist describes the Passover to end all Passovers, thereby proclaiming a new exodus, not from the slavery of Egypt but from bondage to sin and death (chap. 8). Related to the Passover theme is the sacramental interpretation. The church has understood the water and blood to which John calls special attention (vv. 34–35) as symbolic of baptism and the Eucharist. See also 1 John 5:6: "This is the one who came by water and blood." The writer is thereby telling the reader that the subject is not really the corpse of Jesus but the body of Christ.

Holy Saturday

Job 14:1–14 *or* Lamentations 3:1–9, 19–24;
Psalm 31:1–4, 15–16;
1 Peter 4:1–8;
Matthew 27:57–66 *or* John 19:38–42

A wistful note is sounded in the Old Testament reading from Job, a passage about the transiency and unpredictability of life that raises the possibility of life after death only to reject it. In the alternate Old Testament reading, the psalmist's candid cry of distress gives way to affirming hope and as a result is slightly more upbeat than the Job passage. Images of security dominate the selections from Psalm 31, and, appropriately enough, the psalmist places complete trust in God and asks to be delivered from enemies and persecutors. The epistolary reading is a retrospective reflection on the suffering and death of Christ and the implications it has for the life of faith. The Gospel reading from Matthew reports Pilate's transfer of the body of Jesus to Joseph of Arimathea, and the subsequent effort to secure the tomb. The alternate Gospel reading is the Johannine version of Joseph's actions, with some intriguing elements.

Job 14:1–14

Both the mood and the contents of this reading from the Book of Job provide important—one could argue, essential—preparation for Easter morning. Those who look forward to the proclamation of the resurrection of Jesus may dwell just one more day with the dark background for the light of the good news.

The passionate arguments of Job can be understood in part as challenges to a popular ideology in Israel, prominent in the wisdom literature and among the sages, an ideology that equated suffering and trouble with sin and guilt. The author of the book, through Job's speeches, has no patience with simple answers to real problems. He rejects the arguments of his friends—who express the views of the sages—that all suffering is the result of sin because God is just. To be sure, often it could and still can be observed that evil or unwise actions lead to baleful consequences. But not always. Consequently, Job even throws down the gauntlet to God, whom he accuses of being unfair.

In the text before us, Job goes beyond the problem of the suffering of the righteous to complain about the human condition as a whole. Our reading is part of the second cycle of speeches in the book, in which Job responds in sequence to his interlocutors, speaking both to them and directly to God. In 14:1–14 he continues the address to God begun in chapter 13. The section, like other material in Job, has some of the features of a legal argument: "I have indeed prepared my case; I know that I shall be vindicated" (13:18). Job's goal is to prove to God that he is innocent and thus suffers unjustly (13:23–27). He pleads that God withdraw his hand and no longer terrify him (13:21).

In 14:1–14 the poet has Job argue his case in four movements. First, Job makes a general statement about the human condition (vv. 1–3). His complaint encompasses every human being. Every mortal is "few of days and full of trouble" (v. 1). Life is not only short, as ephemeral as a flower or a shadow, but it is filled with pain. Thus the argument concerns both life and death, life because it is full of trouble and death because it comes too soon. He uses these observations—to him "facts"—as a basis for his argument with God, whom he addresses directly with rhetorical questions: Why would you bother to pay any attention to such a creature, or "bring him into court before you!" (v. 3, REB).

The second movement in the argument (vv. 4–6) leads to a plea that God simply leave human beings alone to count their days like laborers count their hours. The plea is driven by Job's protest that human days are determined, God knows the length of those days, and God has "appointed the bounds that they cannot pass" (v. 5). This probably does not refer to a specific length set by God in advance for every individual, but to death, that final boundary for all mortals.

The third movement (vv. 7–12) continues the train of the argument concerning human mortality, vigorously but unhappily affirming that "mortals die . . . humans expire" (v. 10). Job emphasizes the unfairness of that sad fact by comparing humanity with the tree. Even a tree has "hope," for if it is cut down it will live again; all it needs is water. The poet explicitly denies that mortals can rise again when they lie down; when they die they cannot "live again" (v. 12, REB). When he says that the dead remain so "until the very sky splits open" (REB) or "until the heavens are no more" (NRSV), he is not speaking of an apocalyptic transformation of the world but is using hyperbole: There is as much chance of the dead living again as there is that the sky will split open.

In the final movement (vv. 13–14), Job almost wistfully expresses the hope for the impossible. He wonders if God could hide him away in the underworld (sheol) until God's wrath is past and then release him. The same Job who vehemently asserted that death is the end has his doubts, or possibly moments of denial. In the verse that follows our reading, Job expresses the wish that God would then long for the work of his hands, that is, his servant Job. Throughout the passage, Job alternatively wishes that God would let him alone in his miserable human condition, and hopes to be with God, a God who will accept him. Thus he bemoans both the presence and the absence of God.

An argument that begins with the sadness of life is driven by the acknowledgment of death. The rejection of immortality or resurrection is so vehement that it might be polemic against such beliefs, for example, as found in Egyptian religion from the earliest times. But Job's view is typical of ancient Israel and widely assumed in the Old Testament. With the exception of two texts that speak of resurrection (Dan. 12:1–3; Isa. 26:19), the Old Testament takes it for granted that death is the final boundary. Although that view can lead to Job's frustration with God or Qohelet's disillusionment, it is remarkable that the people of Israel—and individual Israelites—could throughout the centuries live the life of faith within the boundaries set by birth and death. Above all, on the day before Easter, the day before Jesus was raised from the dead, Christians could well ponder the fact that the resurrection of Jesus and the Easter faith mean little without death as a reality.

Lamentations 3:1–9, 19–24

Framed in the Book of Lamentations by four complaints of the community, chapter 3 is the complaint of an individual, the unnamed "one" (NRSV; "man," REB) of verse 1. The identity of the community in the other poems in the book is clear: it is the people of Israel. But for whom does the complainant of chapter 3 stand? In the liturgical context of the Christian church on Holy Saturday, the words of the sufferer will be heard as the voice of Jesus, very much in the sense of the words of Psalm 22 (another individual complaint) uttered from the cross: "My God, my God, why have you forsaken me?" But because Jesus in his suffering and death stands with all who suffer and die, these words may express their feelings as well.

The background and the theme of the Book of Lamentations is the destruction of the city of Jerusalem by the Babylonians in 587 BC. During and after the Exile, these poems functioned in liturgical settings—quite possibly on fast days—to help the survivors and their descendants come to terms with that national disaster and the crisis of faith it produced. The laments are similar in mood, tone, and function to dirges or funeral songs. By recounting and bewailing the destruction, and even acknowledging that God had become the enemy, the people expressed and hoped to come to terms with their sense of loss, their grief, and their anger. Moreover, by understanding the destruction as punishment for sin, those people confessed their corporate sins.

Like the four other poems in the book, chapter 3 is an alphabetic acrostic; that is, successive lines begin with successive letters of the Hebrew alphabet. But chapter 3 stands out from the others as the voice of an individual. It would not have been surprising if this individual were a woman, for the other complaints often personify the destroyed city of Jerusalem as a woman. But the individual clearly is male, and that fact has led to many attempts to identify the speaker. Because the prophet Jeremiah often uttered similar complaints, he has been proposed as this individual. Others have argued that the complainant is the servant in Isaiah 40–55, at times an individual but also identified as Israel. But within the literary and liturgical context of the book, chapter 3 most likely views the national disaster and disgrace from the perspective of an individual who experienced it.

Our reading encompasses two parts of the fuller lament. In the first section (vv. 1–9, 19–20), the unidentified individual utters his complaints against God. The leading image is darkness (vv. 2, 6), contrasting with living in the light of God's presence. The tone of the complaint is similar to that of the Book of Job, seen in the other Old Testament reading for Holy Saturday. But although Job objected to unfair or unmerited suffering, in this prayer the sufferer is struggling for a way to live with suffering that is justified, that is punishment for sins. God has turned his hand against this person, and even refuses to answer his prayers (v. 8); God has put him in chains and boxed him in (vv. 7, 9). The particulars of the suffering are not detailed and could fit any number of circumstances, including physical illness. But the petitioner makes it abundantly clear just how much he has suffered. This account of suffering continues through verse 20.

The second part of our reading (vv. 21–24) begins a longer unit in which the mood, tone, and contents are dramatically different. Now the petitioner expresses his hope (vv. 21, 24) and confesses his confidence in the Lord. He knows that the "steadfast love" and the "mercies" of the Lord never cease, that God is faithful, and therefore the one in trouble can turn to him.

This poem, including the shift of mood and contents, is parallel in many ways to the individual complaint songs of the Book of Psalms. The central element of these songs is a petition, a request that God help the one in trouble. They also contain complaints about the suffering and God's failure to help, or complaints about God's absence, as well as confessions of sin or of innocence. There will be expressions of confidence in God's capacity and willingness to help. Parallel to Lamentations 3:21–24 are the affirmations that God has heard and will act (e.g., Ps. 6:8–10). It is very likely that in the liturgical use of such songs another voice, that of a priest, would have been heard just before these affirmations. The priest would have pronounced a salvation oracle, a message from God to the petitioner, for example, "Fear not, the Lord has heard your prayer."

Songs such as this one, and the liturgical patterns they reflect, may provide guidance for our meditations, our words, and our actions. This poem moves toward the affirmation of faith in the gracious and merciful God who hears prayers, but it begins with vigorous complaints against God. Ancient Israel clearly believed that all feelings could be brought before God. Can prayers—even those that confess the experience of divine punishment or the absence of God—be answered unless they are expressed?

Psalm 31:1–4, 15–16

Few psalms use such graphic descriptions to depict human misery and affliction as does Psalm 31. The descriptions are very graphic although reasonably nonspecific. Thus, when persons used this psalm in worship to describe their state of being, they could vent true feelings yet do so in highly stylized terms.

Praying this psalm allowed persons to verbalize and express the deep-seated sense of alienation and hurt that they were feeling. The language appears to be highly metaphorical, probably using stereotypical and formulaic expressions that were highly graphic in content and emotional in nature. The labeling of one's troubles in such graphic fashion was probably therapeutic in and of itself because it allowed one to express sorrow and grief.

The overall structure of the psalm is as follows: (1) a general opening address to God, which already contains an initial plea for help (vv. 1–2); (2) a statement of confidence and trust in God (vv. 3–6); (3) a future-oriented statement of confidence (vv. 7–8); (4) a description of the trouble and distress (vv. 9–13); (5) a third statement of confidence (vv. 14–15a); (6) a second plea for help (vv. 15b–18); (7) a fourth assertion of confidence (vv. 19–20); (8) proclamation (v. 21); (9) thanksgiving (v. 22); and (10) admonition (vv. 23–24).

The relevance of this psalm for Holy Saturday lies in its use of the imagery of death to describe a human situation. The psalmist declares that he or she is like one already dead—passed out of life and even out of memory; cast aside like the shattered pieces of a broken pot; unwanted, useless, fit only for the garbage heap of the city dump (v. 12).

In fact, the psalmist describes the many out there who not only dislike him or her but who even scheme and plot to take his or her life (v. 13). Such language as this may sound like the ravings of a paranoid but should be seen as therapeutic language that allowed distressed persons to objectify their suffering to its most graphic, even exaggerated, level.

This psalm is not simply a recitation of a vale of sorrows. Throughout the text there are frequent statements of a calm confidence in the Deity. Such is to be found in verses 14–15, in which the worshiper confesses trust in God and affirms that come what may the times of one's life are in the hand of God, who can deliver one from the hand of enemies and persecutors.

Confidence in the Deity fades naturally into plea and petition for salvation (vv. 15b–16). In spite of the description of the supplicant's condition in such sorrow-drawn and affliction-etched contours, confidence and calm flow through the psalm like a soothing stream. The crucified, dead, and buried awaits the resurrection, life in the morning.

1 Peter 4:1–8

There are many ways to reflect on the suffering and death of Christ, and today's epistolary text represents one possibility—its moral implications for the life of the believer. This is worth noting, because thinking about Christ's passion may easily turn into a kind of sentimentalism that turns in on itself.

Here the main question is, So what? What difference does the death of Christ make in the life of the believer? To what practical effect did Jesus die?

Our text answers these questions by calling us to "arm [our]selves also with the same intention" (v. 1). Rather than living by "human desires," we are called to live "by the will of God" (v. 2). From these remarks, it seems clear that Christ's death is being viewed as a negation of the human will, the refusal to give in to human desire, most especially the desire to survive at any price. It apparently recognizes that some things are more important than survival; and in this case, yielding to the divine will came into conflict with the impulse toward self-preservation.

This same conflict between self-preservation and self-transcendence, which was exposed in the death of Jesus, is now seen as recurring within the life of believers. Even though the consequences of our acts may not be death in every case, or even in most cases, the dynamics of choice that we experience are not unlike what Jesus experienced. Thus the life of self-indulgence that is profiled in verse 3 (licentiousness, passions, drunkenness, revels, carousing, and lawless idolatry) represents a life left behind, and former associates are surprised by the sudden change in life-style. Because they have one less companion in dissipation, they hurl verbal abuse at the life that is seeking redirection and reconstruction. Yet they are warned that they too must ultimately confront the consequences of their dissolute life.

All of this culminates in a call for sober reflection. We are reminded that "the end of all things is near" (v. 7). Looking into the future unblinkingly often leads us to be serious, disciplined, and prayerful, for as we eye the future we become all too aware of the fragility of life and the finality of death. Inevitably, such reflection causes us to look for company—friends and companions whom we can love and with whom we can be absolutely candid about our sins. Our friends usually know them anyway, especially how numerous they are and how debilitating they can be. Yet it is precisely within these bonds of friendship that the disciplined life of steadfast witness is best sustained.

Matthew 27:57–66 *or* John 19:38–42

For those churches providing Holy Saturday services, alternate readings are available. Both are accounts of the burial of Jesus.

Three observations may be in order here. First, these are alternate readings and are not to be conflated or harmonized. Matthew and John do have a number of common elements (Joseph of Arimathea, request for the body from Pilate, Friday evening, new tomb, etc.), but one needs to respect the different purposes and audiences of the Evangelists. Second, the burial of Jesus is not an insignificant item in Christian theology. Perhaps proof of the resurrection of the body is involved here. Or the writers may be addressing those Christians found in some early churches who had no place for the physical in their views of Jesus Christ. Persons who denied that Jesus Christ had come in the flesh were certainly known in the Johannine community (1 John 4:2–3). But whatever the reasons, the burial of Jesus came to be stated explicitly in Christian confessions as early as 1 Corinthians 15:4 and as officially as the Apostles' Creed. And finally, restraint on the part of both preacher and liturgist is essential for the worship to be truly a Holy Saturday service. It is, of course, tempting and easy to steal from tomorrow, to break the seal on the tomb, and to have a pre-Easter Easter service. Admittedly, it is difficult for the church to say, even for two days, "Jesus is dead."

Matthew devotes two paragraphs to the burial of Jesus (vv. 57–61, 62–66). There needs to be a conclusion to the crucifixion story. After all, closure demands answers to basic questions: What happened to the body? Who prepared it? Where was it entombed? But Matthew has more in mind; he is concerned to argue for, to provide proofs for, the resurrection of Jesus. Therefore, he tells the reader that the body was released to Joseph by Pilate's order; Joseph placed the body in a new tomb hewn out of the rock; a huge stone was placed over the opening to the tomb; two women witnessed all this; religious authorities secured the support of Pilate to prevent a theft of the body and a claim of resurrection; the tomb was governmentally sealed (a stronger safeguard than a police cordon today); Roman guards kept sentinel watch. Matthew is not simply witnessing to the resurrection, as was the case with early Christian preaching (Acts 2:32; 3:15; 4:33), but he is already involved in what later became quite common, attempts to *prove* that Jesus was raised from the dead. Such an approach to the resurrection, and to other doctrines, assumes that faith is the response of the mind to the evidence presented. Such faith is not without merit, but it is *belief that*, not *trust in*.

John also devotes two paragraphs to the corpse of Jesus (vv. 31–37, 38–42), but only the second is our concern here. The former is an extraordinary theological treatise relating the body of Jesus to fulfilled prophecy, the Jewish Passover, the Eucharist, and baptism. In verses 38–42 it seems important to this Evangelist to point out that two disciples who had been private, secretive, and fearful in their relation to Jesus now act openly, with courage and at great expense. Some readers of this account are quite critical of Joseph and Nicodemus, observing that the two come out of hiding now that the battle is over. Jesus needed disciples, they say, not caretakers. Other readers are more positive, finding in this burial scene the consistency of John's theology. Even in his death, they say, Jesus continues to draw the hesitant and unbelieving. Jesus had said as much: in death I will draw all people to myself (12:32).

Easter Vigil

Genesis 1:1–2:4a
   Psalm 136:1–9, 23–26
Genesis 7:1–5, 11–18
   8:6–18; 9:8–13
   Psalm 46
Genesis 22:1–18
   Psalm 16
Exodus 14:10–31; 15:20–21
   Exodus 15:1b–13, 17–18
Isaiah 55:1–11
   Isaiah 12:2–6
Baruch 3:9–15, 32–4:4 or

Proverbs 8:1–8, 19–21; 9:4b–6
   Psalm 19
Ezekiel 36:24–28
   Psalm 42 and 43
Ezekiel 37:1–14
   Psalm 143
Zephaniah 3:14–20
   Psalm 98
Romans 6:3–11
   Psalm 114
Mark 16:1–8

Easter Vigil is traditionally a service of readings with little or no homily. The selection of readings span the Old Testament, rehearsing representative themes from the grand, overall drama that were seen to foreshadow events in the Christian story. The epistolary text links the believer's baptism with the death and resurrection of Christ, highlighting some of the ethical implications of co-participation in Christ's dying and rising. The Gospel reading is Mark's curiously brief, enigmatic account of Easter morning.

Genesis 1:1–2:4a

Ordinarily, the Old Testament lessons for the Easter Vigil are simply read, not preached, taking the worshiping community through a summary of ancient Israel's history. Read in this order and on this occasion, these texts present a history of salvation in preparation for the death and resurrection of Jesus. The story begins with the first chapter of the Bible.

This reading contains the Priestly Writer's account of creation. The mood of the story is solemn and measured; the repetition of phrases lends a liturgical dignity to the recital. If the account was not actually put into this form for worship, it certainly was shaped by persons with a deep interest in liturgy.

In terms of structure, the report consists of two uneven parts, Genesis 1:1–31 and Genesis 2:1–3; that is, the six days of creation and the seventh day of rest. One of the purposes of the story in its present form is to account for the sabbath rest. It was divinely ordained from the very first and thus is taken by our writer as the most universal of laws.

Creation is not *ex nihilo*, out of nothing, but out of chaos. Before creation there were the primeval waters, within which God established the world, and—as the NRSV translation indicates—those waters were troubled by a mighty wind ("wind from God," or "mighty wind"). Moreover, as the Priestly account of the Flood indicates (Gen. 7:11), the waters of chaos stand as the alternative to creation. If God withdraws his hand, the waters can return. In that sense, then, this chapter actually understands God as both creator and sustainer of the world.

In sharp contrast to the other account of creation, which begins in Genesis 2:4*b*, God is transcendent and distant. The only actor or speaker in this chapter is God, by whose word or act all things that are come into being. Human beings certainly occupy an important place. They are created last of all and then given stewardship over the creation. If this moving and majestic account can be said to have a major point, it is in the divine pronouncement that recurs throughout: "And God saw that it was good." The natural order is good not only because God created it, but also because God determined that it was so.

Psalm 136:1–9, 23–26

Psalm 136 is a communal psalm of thanksgiving recalling the great activities of God in the past. In its structure it parallels much of the first six books of the Bible—the Hexateuch, Genesis to Joshua. The following is the structure of the psalm: (1) the community is called to offer thanksgiving (vv. 1–3); (2) God is praised as creator (vv. 4–9); (3) as the one who brought Israel out of Egypt (vv. 10–15); (4) as the one who led the people in the wilderness (v. 16); (5) as the one who granted the people the land of promise (vv. 17–22); and (6) as the one who continues the divine action of providing for the people (vv. 23–26). The constantly repeated refrain "for his steadfast love [or mercy] endures forever" indicates that this psalm was sung or chanted antiphonally.

The verses selected for the Easter Vigil are those concerned with God's acts in creation (vv. 4–9), the personal affirmation of divine care (vv. 23–25), and the call upon all to give thanks (vv. 1–3, 26). The account of creation given in the psalm is far more poetic than the creation account in Gen. 1:1–2:4*a*.

Genesis 7:1–5, 11–18; 8:6–18; 9:8–13

Like Genesis 1:1–2:4*a*, the account of the Flood is part of the primeval history. That is, this is the story of the ancestors of the entire human race and not just of Israel. Between that initial chapter and Genesis 7 a great deal transpired. There was the second account of creation coupled with the story of the Fall, ending with the expulsion of the original pair from the garden. Next came the story of Cain and Abel, when a brother kills a brother. Then follow genealogies, along with short reports of events in the lives of the earliest generations. The immediate background of the flood story is the short account in Genesis 6:1–4 of how the "sons of God" took the "daughters of humans" and gave birth to a race of giants. From the accounts of creation to the time of Noah, the story is basically one of human sin and disorder, culminating in God's decision to put an end to the race, with the exception of Noah and his family.

The Flood marks an important turning point in biblical history; but as the Book of Genesis is organized, it is not the most decisive division of time. Following the Flood, the history of human sinfulness continues, with the story of the Tower of Babel. The critical event is reported in Genesis 12:1ff., the call of Abraham. To be sure, sin continues, but now, with the promise to Abraham, the direction of history is known. It becomes a history of salvation.

The verses chosen for this reading comprise a rather full account of the Flood, with the exception of the report of God's decision to set the disaster into motion and his instructions to Noah. The assigned text comes mainly from the hand of the Priestly Writer, but some of it is from the Yahwist, whose name for God in most translations is LORD. It is also the Yahwist who reports that seven pairs of clean and one pair of unclean animals went into the ark; the Priestly Writer reports one pair of every kind. Moreover, according to the Priestly Writer, the water comes when the floodgates of heaven are opened; the Yahwist speaks of rain. But according to both writers, God put an end to all human beings except that one family, and afterward vowed not to do it again. The reading appropriately ends with the good news that the natural order will abide and the rainbow will be a sign of God's promise.

For further comment on the conclusion of the flood story, see the notes on the Old Testament reading for the First Sunday in Lent in this volume.

Psalm 46

Psalm 46 belongs to a group of psalms that extol the greatness of Jerusalem (Zion) and thus may be classified as one of the songs of Zion (see Ps. 137:3). Behind these songs of Zion are two fundamental assumptions that were widespread in the ancient Near East. First of all, a sacred city and a deity were closely associated with each other. Although a god might be worshiped anywhere, it was taken for granted that a particular locale was more sacred and special to the deity than any other. For Yahweh, the God of Israel, Jerusalem, or Zion, was the divinely chosen and especially elected place. Second, sacred sites and cities were frequently associated with the belief in sacred mountains as the dwelling places of the gods—like Mt. Olympus in Greek mythology. Such mountains were often seen as the location of the original paradise, that is, as the site of the Garden of Eden (see Ezek. 28:11–19). Streams that watered the earth were believed to have their origin in this sacred mountain (see Ezek. 47:1; Gen. 2:10–14).

We should imagine Psalm 46 and the other Zion hymns as being sung in the context of a great festival that celebrated Yahweh's choice of Jerusalem and the construction of God's temple (God's house) on Mt. Zion.

Psalm 46 consists of three stanzas or strophes: verses 1–3, 4–7, and 8–11. The last two strophes have a common refrain: "The LORD of hosts is with us; the God of Jacob is our refuge." The fact that stanza 1 is a line shorter than the other stanzas would suggest that the same refrain once followed verse 3. The content of these three stanzas may be designated the lord of creation, the lord of history, and the lord of peace.

The first stanza declares God to be a source of strength and refuge and a help in time of trouble. This theme is then expounded in terms of a total disruption in the world of nature or in terms of cosmic conflagration. Verses 2–3 declare that the faithful or the inhabitants of God's city have no reason to fear even if chaos should invade the cosmos—the earth should change, mountains fall into the sea, and the flood waters of the deep roar and foam, causing the mountains to tremble. Behind this idea of the threat of chaos and the disarray of creation lies the biblical belief that the world was founded over the water of chaos. In the flood story, when the world was again returned to its watery state, it was because the foundations of the deep broke forth to inundate the earth (Gen. 7:11). Because of God's special protection, Zion has no need to fear even the powers of chaos itself.

Just as verses 2–3 of this psalm affirm God's protection of Zion against the cosmic threat of chaos, verses 4–6 affirm the stability and security of the city against historical enemies. This section opens with a reference to a river whose streams make glad the city of God. There, of course, was no actual river that flowed in Jerusalem. Here we are dealing with mythological imagery and the idea of the sacred mountain as the source of the waters of the earth. Verses 5–6 declare that the city of God is impregnable. Because God is in her midst and will help her right early (or "at the turn of the morning"), the city need not fear. Nations may rage and kingdoms come and go, but God who is in Zion can utter his voice and the earth will melt.

Verses 8–10 call upon the worshipers to behold the works of Yahweh and thus to find peace and calm. God works desolation in the earth, makes wars cease, breaks the bow, shatters the spear, and consumes the chariots with fire. Although the psalm proclaims these as acts of God already accomplished and thus something one can behold, nonetheless there is a touch of the unachieved, the eschatological, about these verses that points forward to the future. In worship, the people celebrated God's salvation as a reality experienced but not yet fully realized.

Verse 10 contains an oracle of God that calls the people to an acceptance of divine rule—an acceptance that can be realized in "stillness." This oracle, spoken by some official in worship, expresses the same call as that of the prophet Isaiah: "In returning and rest you shall be saved; in quietness and in trust shall be your strength" (Isa. 30:15). God proclaims his rule over the affairs of nations (the historical process) and over the earth (the world of nature).

Genesis 22:1–18

If one does not keep in mind the framework in which this reading appears—both in the Book of Genesis and in the Old Testament—important aspects of it will be missed. The context is the narrative of the patriarchs, Abraham, Isaac, Jacob, and the sons of Jacob, the leading theme of which is the promise that their descendants will become a great nation, will own their land, and will be a blessing to all the peoples of the earth (Gen. 12:1–3). The fulfillment of those promises comes beyond the Book of Genesis, first with the Exodus and then with the occupation of the land of Canaan as reported in the Book of Joshua.

The immediate prelude to this story is the report in Genesis 21:1–7 of the birth of Isaac. The promise of descendants had been repeated to Abraham and Sarah over and over. Just when it appeared that all hope was lost, they are given a son in their old age. Isaac is not merely symbolic testimony that the divine promise is trustworthy; he is also quite literally the first step in the fulfillment of that promise.

And then comes the account in Genesis 22:1–18 of God testing Abraham by means of a command that threatened to take away the child of the promise. It is certainly one of the most poignant and moving stories in the Bible, and all the more so because of its restraint. Emotions are not described or analyzed, but the reader or hearer will sense with horror the patriarch's dread and grief. Even though we know how the story comes out, each time we read it we can experience the rising tension, feeling that the results may still be in doubt. Will Abraham go through with the sacrifice of Isaac? Will the angel speak up before it is too late?

The story is so meaningful and fruitful and has been told in so many ways over the centuries that it would be a serious mistake to reduce it to a single point. At one level, in the old oral tradition it probably dealt with the question of child sacrifice. Living among cultures where child sacrifice was a genuine possibility, some early Israelites could well have asked, "Does our God require that we sacrifice our children?" The answer, through this account, is a resounding no. Our ancestor was willing, but God did not require it. The sacrifice of a ram was sufficient. In the framework of the Easter Vigil, one is reminded that God gave his Son.

The leading theme of the story, as recognized through centuries of interpretation, is faith. It is, as the initial verse says, the test of Abraham's faith. What is faith? The biblical tradition answers not with a theological statement, nor with a set of propositions, nor with admonitions to be faithful, but with a story. It is the story of Abraham, who trusted in God even when God appeared to be acting against his promise. Faith is like that. Faith in this sense is commitment, the directing of one's trust toward God. And it entails great risk, not in the sense of accepting a set of beliefs, but by acting in trust. Did Abraham know that the God he worshiped would not require the life of Isaac? We cannot know, for the story leaves this question unanswered. We are told only how the patriarch acted, and how God acted.

Psalm 16

The ancient rabbis understood this psalm as David writing about himself. In addition, they understood the text as speaking about actual death, at least in verse 3a. This text, that the rabbis read as "the holy that are in the earth" (and therefore dead), was said to speak about the deceased because "the Holy One (God) does not call the righteous man holy until he is laid away in the earth. Why not? Because the Inclination-to-evil [the evil yet-zer of the human personality] keeps pressing him. And so God does not put His trust in him in this world till the day of his death. . . . That the Lord will not call a righteous man holy until he is laid away in the earth is what is meant." (*Midrash on Psalms.*)

In spite of the translation difficulties found in verses 2–4, where the worshiper appears to refer to the worship of other gods ("the holy ones" and "the noble" may denote the holy and mighty god mentioned in v. 4), the remainder of the text makes reasonably good sense. (In addition to the NRSV, one should consult the NJPSV.)

Verses 5–11 open with a short confessional statement addressed to a human audience (v. 5a) and is immediately followed by a confessional statement of trust addressed to God (v. 5b). The terminology of this verse, as well as verse 6, speaks of what one has inherited or been given in life—portion, cup, lot, lines, and heritage. The NJPSV translates:

> The Lord is my allotted share and portion;
>> You control my fate.
> Delightful country has fallen to my lot;
>> lovely indeed is my estate.

Instead of being guilty of worshiping false gods, the psalmist is depicted as one who constantly thinks of God (vv. 7–8). The counsel God gives (v. 7a) is matched by that of the person's own conscience (NRSV: "heart," although literally "the kidneys," denoting the inner self). The term translated "night" in verse 7b is actually the Hebrew plural "nights" ("watches of the night," "every night," or "the dark night"). The human activity and consistency (v. 8a) are matched by God's consistent preservation, with the consequence that the psalmist can confess, "I shall not be moved," that is, threatened or overcome.

The last section (vv. 9–11) returns to direct address to God, confessing assurance that the request made in verse 1 will be granted; that is, the person will live and not die. It was this section that led to the psalm's usage in early Christian preaching and confession. Again, the NJPSV conveys the meaning better than the NRSV:

> So my heart rejoices,
>   my whole being exults,
>   and my body rests secure.
> For You will not abandon me to Sheol,
>   or let Your faithful one see the Pit.

Sheol and Pit refer to the realm of the dead. Probably the psalm was used originally by persons near death as a result of some sickness. Of course, they do not want to die but want to remain alive to enjoy their heritage (vv. 5–6, 11b).

Exodus 14:10–31; 15:20–21

With this reading we come close to the heart of the Old Testament story and the Old Testament faith. In ancient Israel's faith no affirmation is more central than the confession that the Lord is the one who brought them out of Egypt. Traditions concerning the Exodus provide the fundamental language by which Israel understood both herself and her God. The basic focus of most of those traditions is upon the saving activity of the Lord; the history is a story of salvation.

The account in Exodus 14 actually follows the Exodus itself. The departure from Egypt had been reported in chapters 12 and 13; the rescue of the people at the sea happens when they are already in the wilderness. The two themes that mark the stories of the wandering in the wilderness are already present in this chapter, namely, Israel's complaints against Moses and the Lord (14:10–12), and the Lord's miraculous care (14:13–18, 30–31). The report does mark, however, Israel's final escape from the Egyptian danger, and this relates directly to the theme of the Exodus itself.

This reading, like the flood story, is the combination of at least two of the sources of the Pentateuch, those of the Priestly Writer and of the Yahwist. In the full story of the rescue at the sea, two virtually complete accounts have been combined. The writers tell the story differently, with P reporting a dramatic crossing of the sea between walls of water (v. 22), and J speaking of a "strong east wind" (v. 21), and the chariots clogged in the mud as the water returns (v. 25). But a more important implication of the source division for our use of the text in the context of worship is the recognition that the sources place very different theological interpretations upon what happened. For the Priestly Writer, the emphasis is on revelation. The Lord "hardened the heart of Pharaoh" (vv. 8, 17) to pursue the Israelites in order to "gain glory for myself over Pharaoh and all his army" (v. 17). That is, the Lord's purpose is for the Egyptians to "know that I am the LORD" (v. 18). For the Yahwist, the purpose is the salvation of the people (v. 13) and their consequent faith, not only in the Lord, but also in Moses (vv. 30–31). In the combined report, both themes are important. God acts in order to reveal who he is and also to save the people.

The reading appropriately concludes with 15:20–21, the account of the Song of Miriam, identified as a prophet and the sister of Aaron. The two-line couplet in verse 21 is the typical beginning of a hymn or song of praise, calling upon the people to sing and giving the reasons why the Lord is praiseworthy. These lines, generally taken to be among the most ancient material in the Hebrew Scriptures, parallel the opening of the Song of Moses in 15:1–17. The difference is that Miriam's song is a call to sing ("Sing"), and Moses' is a first person expression of the song ("I will sing"). Thus there are few occasions in the lectionary when the responsorial psalm follows more directly and naturally from the Old Testament reading than here.

Exodus 15:1b–13, 17–18

The psalm text overlaps with the Old Testament reading and continues where it left off. Moses, having led the Israelites in their escape from the Egyptians at the sea, now leads them in worship. This psalm of praise is generally identified as the Song of Moses, and much of it is in the first person singular, "I will sing to the LORD." But the introduction points out that it was sung by Moses and the people, and its communal, congregational character is evident throughout. Although the song is not in the Psalter, it is a psalm nonetheless and probably was used in worship by faithful Israelites through the centuries. The initial lines are placed in the mouth of Miriam in Exodus 15:21, except that there they are in the second person instead of the first; she calls for the people to sing to the Lord.

The song is a hymn of praise, specifically praise of the Lord for saving the people at the sea. The hymn is for the most part narrative in form; that is, it praises God by recounting the story of the divine mighty deeds. In one sense, what emerges is another interpretation of the rescue at the sea, different in some respects from the accounts in Exodus 14. But the language is at points highly metaphorical and rich in imagery that goes beyond the immediate events.

Recollection of the Lord's saving activity at the sea evokes two leading themes in the hymn. The first concerns God's awesome power over events and nature. The specific form of that theme here stresses the image of Yahweh as a warrior who triumphs over God's enemies. But it also emphasizes that the God praised here is incomparable; there is none like this one (vv. 11, 18). The second theme of the hymn concerns God's love and care for the people whom God has redeemed. God is strength, song, salvation (v. 2), the one who cares for the people out of steadfast love (v. 13). Moreover, God's past care for the people gives rise to the hope that God will continue to act in their behalf in the future (v. 17) and will reign forever (v. 18).

Isaiah 55:1–11

Again, as is so often the case in the lectionary as a whole, and especially during Easter, the words of Second Isaiah come before us. This text from the end of the Babylonian Exile was a call for hope and trust and a promise of salvation to the hearers; it reiterates that same call and promise during the Easter Vigil.

The passage has two distinct parts, verses 1–5 and 6–11, which are similar in both form and content. In the first section God is the speaker throughout, addressing the people of Israel as a whole. It begins with a series of imperatives (vv. 1–3a) that resemble on the one hand Lady Wisdom's invitation to a banquet (Prov. 9:5) and on the other hand the calls of street vendors. The invitations to come for what the Lord has to offer are both literal and metaphorical: God offers actual food, and "food" that enables one to live the abundant life ("that your soul may live," v. 3a, RSV). What the people are invited to "come, buy, and eat" is the proclamation of salvation that follows in verses 3b–5. God announces that the ancient covenant with David (2 Sam. 7) now applies to the people as a whole. Again, Israel has in no sense earned this new covenant; it is a free act of God's grace. Moreover, just as the Lord made David a witness to the nations, now all nations will come to the people of Israel. The proclamation of salvation, then, is ultimately directed toward all peoples.

The second section (vv. 6–11) also begins with imperatives, calls to "seek the LORD" and to "call upon him." The "wicked" and "unrighteous" are invited to change their ways and "return to the LORD." These invitations, although addressed to the human heart, are quite concrete. To "seek" and "call upon" the Lord refer to acts of prayer and worship. For the wicked to "forsake their way" is to change behavior. The foundation for the imperatives is stated at the end of verse 7, "for he will abundantly pardon." The remainder of the section (vv. 8–11) gives the basis for responding to God's call. God's plan for the world ("ways," "thoughts") is in sharp contrast to human designs. That plan is the announcement of salvation that the prophet has presented throughout the book, the redemption and renewal of the people. The will of God is effected by the word of God, another theme found throughout Isaiah 40–55. That divine word is the one uttered at creation (Gen. 1:3ff.), and it is the divine announcement of the future through the prophets. In its emphasis on the word of God and its contrast between human and divine wisdom, this concluding section of Second Isaiah alludes to the beginning of the work (Isa. 40:1–11).

Isaiah 12:2–6

Not all Old Testament psalms are found in the Psalter. Isaiah 12 actually includes two, along with traces of the liturgical instructions (vv. 1a, 4a). The songs conclude the first section of the Book of Isaiah and suggest that the prophetic book was used in worship even before an official canon of Scripture was established. Both psalms are songs of thanksgiving. The first (vv. 1–3) celebrates and gives thanks for deliverance from trouble. In verse 2 is echoed the vocabulary of the Song of Moses (Exod. 15:2), moving from thanks for a specific divine act to generalizations about the nature of God as the one who saves and who is the strength, song, and salvation of the worshiper. The second psalm (vv. 4–6) consists almost entirely of calls to give thanks and praise (v. 4). God is praised especially for God's mighty deeds. Because God, the Holy One of Israel, is great, all the earth should know, and those who live in the shadow of the temple in Zion should sing for joy.

Baruch 3:9–15, 32–4:4

This passage, often characterized as a hymn to wisdom, is not actually a song of praise such as those in the Book of Psalms. Although it does characterize and praise wisdom, it is basically an admonition to the people of Israel that they listen to and learn from wisdom.

The Book of Baruch is attributed to Jeremiah's scribe and placed in the Babylonian Exile, but it actually stems from a later time. The section from which this reading comes is like other late wisdom literature such as the Wisdom of Solomon and Ecclesiasticus. It identifies wisdom with the law of Moses, "the commandments of life" (3:9), and "the way of God" (3:13; see also 4:1). Behind that answer stands a question that became prominent in the so-called intertestamental period: Is there a conflict between the truth that can be discerned by human reflection or wisdom and that which is revealed in the law?

Our text alludes to the Babylonian Exile (3:10–13), but it is characterized as a spiritual situation of separation from God rather than the actual Babylonian captivity. The verses not included in the reading (3:16–31) also contain somewhat spiritualized allusions to the history of Israel. The lection finds its place in the Easter Vigil, first because of the references to death and its alternative. Israel, growing old in a foreign land, is as good as dead (3:10–11), because the people have forsaken "the fountain of wisdom" (3:12). If they will attend to wisdom, they will gain strength, understanding, life, and peace (3:14). All who hold fast to wisdom will live, and those who forsake her will die (4:1). The second reason for the use of this passage in the Easter Vigil is its theme of wisdom as the gift of God that reveals the divine will to human beings. This is quite explicit in 3:37, which is echoed in John 1:14, and has been taken as a reference to the coming of Jesus.

Proverbs 8:1–8, 19–21; 9:4b–6

The reading from Proverbs 8 is part of a unit that is among a series of twelve extended addresses or speeches in Proverbs 1–9. All of them are instructions concerning wisdom or speeches by Wisdom herself. Each one is comprised of reflections upon the nature of wisdom as well as admonitions and exhortations to follow wisdom. Each is a carefully crafted composition that probably arose among Israel's sages for the purpose of teaching their students.

Chapter 8 is the eleventh address. Following an introduction of the speaker in verses 1–3, the remainder is an address by Wisdom herself. Beginning with rhetorical questions (v. 1), the writer sets the stage for the speech by Wisdom, personified as a female figure. As in the NJPSV, one can appropriately capitalize her names: Wisdom and Understanding. Her speech will be in all kinds of public places: "On the heights," "beside the way," "at the crossroads," "the gates," "the entrance of the portals." These lines indicate that wisdom is easy to find, and eager to be heard by all.

In verses 4–8 Wisdom speaks in the first person, urging all to pay attention, but she particularly urges the "simple ones" to listen to her. Then she gives the reasons why people should attend to her words: She speaks only "noble things," "what is right," "truth," and straight words that are "righteous."

Verses 19–21 continue to present reasons for following the words of Wisdom. First, the fruit of wisdom is better than gold and silver (8:19). Second, Wisdom walks in and therefore leads her followers in the paths of justice and righteousness (8:20). Here we see that the sages were concerned with the same values as were the prophets. Third, it is prudent to follow Wisdom because the one who does so prospers (8:21).

Wisdom, understood as present in the world, describes herself as the first of God's creations, the principle that guided God's formation of all that is (8:22–31). Certainly, those who wrote and those who read wisdom literature were concerned about the relationship between wisdom and the revealed law, between knowledge gained by experience on the one hand and piety on the other. They concluded that, in the final analysis, there was no conflict between the two: "The fear of the LORD [genuine piety] is the beginning of wisdom, and the knowledge of the Holy One is insight" (9:10).

The verses from chapter 9 come from the twelfth and final address in this initial section of the Book of Proverbs. They may serve as a fitting conclusion to the reading for the day, for Wisdom urges "those without sense" (9:4b) to set out on a path of growth by eating and drinking what she has to offer.

Psalm 19

This psalm of hymnic praise of God declares that God has communicated the divine will and knowledge of the Divine through nature—verses 1–6—and through the law, or Torah—verses 7–13. Without speech, God's voice is heard in the world of nature, and divine communication, like the light of the sun, falls everywhere and nothing can hide from it. In the Torah, God's will is embodied in commandment and precept, and offers its blessings to those whose ways it directs and guards. For a fuller discussion, see the Third Sunday in Lent.

Ezekiel 36:24–28

This reading is the central section of a passage in which Ezekiel presents the divine announcement of a new Israel. God, through the prophet (see vv. 22, 32), is the speaker. This dramatic announcement of good news presupposes that the people of God are in trouble. The description of that trouble is given in the context (vv. 16–21) and alluded to in our reading. Israel is in exile, away from the sacred land, but the trouble is even deeper. Separation from the land corresponds to separation from their God. They are in exile because of their sin, their disobedience that led to uncleanness. Now God is about to act, not because Israel deserves it, but for the sake of his "holy name" (v. 22).

There are two aspects to God's expected work of salvation, one external and one internal, corresponding to Israel's present plight. First, the Lord will gather up the people and return them to their land (v. 24). But if they are to remain there (v. 26), a major transformation must occur. That is the second aspect of the good news, the establishment of a new covenant (see Isa. 54:10; 55:3) with a new Israel. This transformation is spelled out in terms of three distinct steps: (1) the Lord will sprinkle (cf. Exod. 24:6) the people with water, purifying them from their uncleanness; (2) the Lord will give them a new heart and a new spirit, replacing their heart of stone with one of flesh (cf. Jer. 31:31); and (3) God will put his own "spirit" within them. "Spirit" here represents both the willingness and the ability to act in obedience. The promise is summarized by the reiteration of the ancient covenant formula "You shall be my people, and I will be your God" (v. 28). The radical difference between this new covenant and the old one is that the Lord himself will enable the people to be faithful.

Psalm 42 and 43

Although divided into two psalms in the course of transmission, Psalms 42 and 43 were probably originally one psalm. This is indicated by the repeated refrain in 42:5, 11 and 43:5.

It is possible that we overpersonalize such a psalm as this and try too hard to discover some individual's face beneath the poetic mask. It is entirely possible that this psalm was written to be used by worshipers and sung antiphonally as pilgrims set out on their way to some pilgrimage in Jerusalem. The portrayal of the present discontent with life thus forms the backdrop for the expectations of coming worship (see Pss. 84 and 120).

This psalm can be closely associated with the sentiments of Ezekiel 36:24–28, the Old Testament lesson to which it is a response. Ezekiel predicts the coming rescue of God's people from exile and the transformation of the human personality and will. The psalm, originally used as an individual lament, early became associated with the Easter Vigil because it expressed the people's longing for redemption and their lamenting over being absent from the sanctuary. The psalm presupposes that the speaker is living away from the Sacred City. The psalmist's thought about former days when the worshiper went on a pilgrimage to Jerusalem only intensifies the depression and despair that accompany living in a foreign and hostile land and heightens the desire to be at home again in the temple.

Ezekiel 37:1–14

Ezekiel's vision of the valley of dry bones, like so many other Old Testament readings for this season, stems from the era of the Babylonian Exile. That it is a vision report is indicated by the introductory formula "The hand of the LORD was upon me," which the prophet uses elsewhere to begin reports of ecstatic experiences (Ezek. 3:22). The narration is in the first person and, like most prophetic vision reports, consists of two parts: the description of what was revealed (vv. 1–10) and the interpretation (vv. 11–14). Throughout there is dialogue between Yahweh and the prophet.

The message from the Lord communicated through the report is the response to the problem stated in verse 11. The people of Israel are saying, "Our bones are dried up, and our hope is lost; we are cut off completely." In the vision Ezekiel sees himself carried by the spirit of Yahweh to a valley full of bones, like the scene of an ancient battle. When the Lord asks if the bones can live again, Ezekiel gives the only possible answer, "O Lord GOD, you know" (v. 3). Although the meaning of this response is not immediately plain, it becomes clear in the context: the God of Israel can indeed bring life in the midst of death. When the prophet obeys the command to prophesy to the bones, a distinct sequence of events transpires: bones to bones, sinews to bones, flesh on the bones, and then skin covering them. The importance of the next step is emphasized by the interjection of a further divine instruction. The prophet calls for breath to come into the corpses, and they live. The view of human life as physical matter animated by the breath that comes from God is found throughout the Old Testament (cf. Gen. 2:7).

The interpretation of what has transpired (vv. 11–14) emphasizes that the vision is a promise of national resurrection addressed to the hopeless exiles. In no sense is the seriousness of their plight denied. They are indeed as good as dead, and death in all possible forms is acknowledged as a reality. But the word of God in the face of and in the midst of death brings to the people of God a new reality, life. It is a free, unconditional, and unmerited gift. When read on the eve of Easter, this text is a strong reminder that God is the Lord of all realms, including that of death. Moreover, the promise of life is addressed to the people of God, and resurrection is a symbol not only for a life beyond the grave but also for the abundant life of the community of faith this side of physical death.

Psalm 143

Another of the classical seven penitential psalms, Psalm 143 was composed to be prayed by individuals during times of crisis. The psalm is a true prayer, with its entire contents addressed to the Deity.

A special characteristic of the entire psalm is the supplicant's recurring appeal to divine qualities or characteristics as the motivation or basis for redemption. There is no assertion that redemption should come as a consequence or result of the worshiper's righteousness or sinlessness. Note the appeals in the following phrases: "in your faithfulness," "in your righteousness," "for your name's sake," and "in your steadfast love." The psalmist is willing to leave his or her welfare up to the Divine. "You are my God" (v. 10) and "I am your servant" (v. 12) are the essence of the psalm's confession.

The nature of the distress being described in the psalm remains a bit uncertain. The most likely suggestion is that the psalm was composed for use by persons who felt themselves falsely accused of some act. In such circumstances, persons could appeal their case to God and undergo a ritual process in the sanctuary during which the priests, acting on behalf of the Deity, reached a decision and handed down a verdict or placed the litigants under a self-imprecation or curse (see Deut. 17:8–13; 19:15–21; 1 Kings 8:31–32 for references to such rituals).

In the opening address to the Deity (vv. 1–2), the worshiper throws himself or herself on the mercy of God, appealing for God to act on the basis of God's own character rather than on the basis of the worshiper's status. A sense of unworthiness or the fear of the judgment of God in the temple court is allowed to overwhelm the worshiper, who can only plead not to be judged. This fear is then undergirded by a sweeping theological truism: "No one living is righteous before you." Thus the universality of human sinfulness and the incompleteness of every human are affirmed as reflective of the status and condition of the worshiper.

The description of the distress (vv. 3–4) mentions the enemy who has made life miserable for the worshiper. Nothing explicit is said about the enemy; perhaps it was the accuser in a court case. At any rate, the psalm describes the state of distress as a state of psychological exhaustion. One might be tempted to see the person as paranoid except for the fact that little interest is shown in the enemy. In preaching and counseling, the minister can learn much from the psalm writers. Note the vivid terminology expressive of a distraught state: "pursued," "crushed," "darkness," "dead," "faints," and "appalled." The cult in ancient Israel did not try to stifle genuine sentiments (as we moderns are so prone to do when we try to convince people that nothing is wrong or that they should not feel the way they do). In fact, the psalms and religious worship frequently provided the occasion and even forced the worshipers to express their feelings, to intensify their emotions, to exaggerate the states of distress and depression, and to give vent to the sense of total fear and fright. Theologically, one can say that such exaggeration was intent on eliciting a divine hearing. Psychologically, one could say that it was the means for therapeutic catharsis. In preaching, the minister should seek ways to imitate the psalmists and thus to legitimate and encourage a temporary abandonment to the emotions, or what pop psychology calls "getting in touch with one's feelings."

In spite of all the circumstances depicted in verses 1–4, the psalmist moves in verses 5–6 to a statement of faith and confidence. Thus there is a movement in the psalm from the low, depicted in the description of the distress, to the high, found in the statement of confidence.

The source of confidence is located neither in the status or achievements of the worshiper, as is so often the case in modern culture, nor in some view about the future (which is always supposed to be getting better!). Instead, confidence is based on a backward look to lessons from the past. It is "the days of old," "all your deeds," and "the works of your hands" that allow the worshiper not to surrender to the tyranny and terror of the present but to expect and pray for divine aid on the analogy of the past.

The petitions in verses 7–8 request divine aid for the worshiper. The Lord's help and presence are depicted as standing between the worshiper and death. (The pit is a euphemism for the realm of the dead.) The reference to hearing in the morning (v. 8) suggests that the priests proclaimed their verdicts as the decisions of the Deity in conjunction with the dawn of a new day and the rising of the sun. Worshipers involved in such rituals may have spent the night in the temple in a nocturnal vigil (known technically as incubation) awaiting an early morning resolution or word from God. The morning, with its normal connotations of newness and hope, took on special meaning and content in such circumstances.

Zephaniah 3:14–20

The last of the Old Testament readings for the Easter Vigil is a shout of joy and an announcement of salvation to Jerusalem. The passage begins with a series of imperatives addressed to the Holy City, calling for celebration (v. 14). The remainder of the unit in effect gives the reasons for celebration. These reasons include (1) the announcement that the Lord has acted in behalf of the city and is now in its midst as king (v. 15) and (2) a series of promises concerning the renewal of the city and the return of its people (vv. 16–20). Both the mood and contents of the text anticipate the Easter celebration.

Our unit is the fourth and last section in the Book of Zephaniah and stands in sharp contrast to the remainder of the book. The section that immediately precedes this one (Zeph. 3:1–13) had announced a purging punishment upon the city and its people. But now darkness has become light; fear and terror have become hope and celebration.

The prophet Zephaniah was active in the seventh century, not long before 621 BC. He was concerned with the coming judgment upon his people, particularly because of their pagan religious practices. It is possible that this concluding section of the book was added in a later age, perhaps during the Babylonian Exile (cf. 3:19–20), by those who had actually been through the fires of destruction and who looked forward to celebrating God's forgiveness, which the return from exile represented. But in any case, the theological interpretation presented by the structure of the book in its final form is quite clear: The celebration of God's salvation follows the dark night of judgment and suffering.

Psalm 98

Like Zephaniah 3:14–20, this psalm is an exuberant affirmation of divine triumph and success. This affirmation is noted by the word "victory" in each of the first three verses. The psalm proclaims the victory of God and calls upon the whole world to break forth into song and the sound of musical instruments. As part of the Easter Vigil, this psalm contributes its call for a celebration of salvation and for the recognition of God as king. For a fuller discussion of Psalm 98, see the Third Proper for Christmas and the Sixth Sunday of Easter.

Romans 6:3–11

The liturgy of the Easter Vigil consists of four parts: (1) the service of light, (2) the liturgy of the Word, (3) the liturgy of baptism, and (4) the celebration of the Eucharist. The time for the celebration of this service has fluctuated through the ages. Originally, it lasted through the night, but gradually through the centuries this Roman liturgy was moved to Saturday. Eventually, it was restored as a night celebration, beginning after nightfall and ending at dawn.

When celebrated as a night service, the Easter Vigil provided the occasion for the baptism of those who had been properly prepared through teaching and fasting. This was done at midnight, when the celebrants gathered at the baptismal font and the candidates were presented to the community. Several features accompanied the liturgy of baptism: (1) the consecration of the baptismal water, (2) a homily by the priest addressed to the catechumens, (3) the candidates' divesting themselves of ornaments and jewelry before entering the water, (4) the candidates' renunciation of Satan and their profession of faith, (5) the anointing of the newly baptized, and (6) the clothing of the newly baptized in the white garments to be worn through the duration of Easter Week.

The use of Romans 6:3–11 in the Easter Vigil service provides a direct link with the liturgy of baptism. It is obviously an excellent text for a homily addressed to catechumens. In this text, Paul unfolds his own theology of baptism, showing how in baptism the believer dies and rises with Christ. Equally important is his insistence on the ethical implications that follow (v. 11, also vv. 12–14). But we would miss the point were we to regard the text as only for catechumens on the verge of being initiated into the Christian faith. After all, Paul addresses these words to mature Christians. He couches his remarks in the first person plural, thus including himself with those whom he addresses. This is worth noting, because some Christians apparently misunderstood his teachings concerning salvation by grace. They seem to have concluded that being saved by grace meant that they could sin even more abundantly, for this would simply provide a greater occasion for the grace of God to work (cf. v. 1). Paul's remarks on baptism in Romans 6 are designed to show that salvation by grace, far from encouraging sin, actually signals the death of sin and its hold on the one who is in Christ.

The symbolism of this text read at this time should not be missed. This is, after all, the night in which Jesus lies in the tomb, enclosed as it were in the bonds of death. Those who have been baptized into Christ have been baptized into his death (v. 3); that is, those who have been incorporated into Christ through baptism have actually been plunged into "death." Being immersed in the baptismal waters, as the early Christians were, became their symbolic entry into the tomb. They were thereby "walled in by death." Paul thus can speak of their baptism as being "buried with him" (v. 4). Even though we already know how the story ends, we still do well to relive Jesus' entombment on this night prior to the resurrection.

For all its emphasis on the believer's co-participation in the death of Christ, this text brims with anticipation: it speaks not only of death, but also of resurrection. During the Easter Vigil, as night approaches dawn, there is a noticeable shift in mood from despair to hope, from grief to joy. Already in the service of light, there is the celebration of the transition from darkness to light, from death to life. In today's passage, Paul also stresses that the one who is baptized shares in Christ's resurrection. There is a difference, however, in the way Paul conceives both sides of the antithesis. Consistently, when he discusses the believer's death, he understands it as something already achieved. By contrast, the believer's union with Christ in the resurrection (v. 5) is consistently kept in the future tense: it is still to be realized. As Paul says in verse 8, "We believe that we *will* also live with him" (italics added). This is not to say that the believers' resurrection life is postponed entirely until the Eschaton, for in this life, through our death and resurrection with Christ, we can consider ourselves "alive to God in Christ Jesus" (v. 11). Resurrection life begins here, but does not end here. The Easter Vigil, then, directs our attention toward Easter morning and the resurrection hope; it also directs us ultimately toward Christ's second coming, when our life with him is experienced fully.

Psalm 114

This psalm, read as a response to Paul's discussion of the association of Christian baptism with the death of Jesus, is a celebration of the Exodus from Egyptian bondage and of the entry into the promised land. Typologically, one might say that the Exodus, like Christ's death, symbolizes the end of an old state of life and the dawning of a new state. The entry into the promised land, like Christian baptism, was a time when the benefits of redemption became real. In this psalm, exodus from Egypt and entrance into the promised land are closely joined, so that parallel events are seen as characteristic of the two episodes. At the Exodus, the sea fled and the "mountains skipped like rams"; at the Jordan, the river rolled back and the hills skipped like lambs (vv. 3–4). The address to the sea and river, the mountains and hills in verses 5–6, which is continued in the address to the earth in verses 7–8, serves as the means for making contemporary the exodus and entrance events. Thus the users of the psalm, which was always read at the celebration of Passover, "became" participants in the past events of salvation just as the Christian in baptism becomes contemporary with the death of Jesus. For further discussion of this psalm, see Easter Evening.

Mark 16:1–8

If there was a Saturday service, then worshipers were led to place themselves between Good Friday and Easter on that cold, silent, and empty day when the darkest sentence imaginable is pronounced: Jesus is dead. If Jesus lives again, it will be by an act of God. We do not vaguely believe in immortality; we believe in resurrection from the dead. In the meantime, there is a death in the family; people want to help, but there is nothing for them to do. No one goes to work; no one goes to school. There is too much food, and no one is hungry. Time drags itself along. But now this is an early Easter service; all are excited as they run from the empty tomb!

Mark 16:1–8 is the proper text because it lies on the border between Saturday and Sunday; that is, if verse 8 is accepted as the conclusion of Mark, as the most ancient and respected manuscripts indicate. Of course, "and they said nothing to any one, for they were afraid" is an unusual way to end a Gospel. There is no shout of victory, only astonished silence; no leap for joy, only running in fear. It is understandable that both Matthew and Luke end their accounts with resurrection appearances, reunion with the eleven, and a commission to preach. It is understandable that some scholars have theorized that the scroll of Mark had become worn and the end frayed and the last lines lost. It is understandable that in the second century, longer and "more appropriate" endings were added, the more familiar being what we now have as verses 9–20. And it is also understandable that editors of English language New Testaments have difficulty deciding what to do: close at verse 8 and put verses 9–20 in a footnote (RSV, 1946), put verses 9–20 in the text and explain in a footnote (RSV, 1971), or add both the shorter and longer additions to 16:1–8 in the text with explanations in footnotes (NRSV, with shorter and longer additions in brackets). Whatever conclusion is reached by the reader, our lection for today is 16:1–8. In this writer's opinion, this is Mark's conclusion. Mark's accent, central focus, and climax is the cross. Mark, of course, believed in the resurrection (9:9; 14:28), but he did not include any dramatic resurrection appearances that would transcend and, in a sense, reduce the centrality of the cross as the definition of messiahship and of discipleship. For Mark, the resurrection served the cross; Easter did not eradicate but vindicated Good Friday. And if worshipers do not experience Jesus as dead, they can hardly experience him as resurrected.

Mark 16:1–8 completes the strange conclusion of this Gospel in which insiders become outsiders and outsiders do the work of insiders. A Roman centurion, not a disciple, confessed faith at the cross (15:39). The disciples fled (14:50), and their places are taken by the women who saw the crucifixion from afar (15:40), observed the burial (15:47), and then anointed the body (16:1). The burial was handled not by the disciples but by Joseph of Arimathea, a member of the council that had condemned Jesus to death (15:43–46).

What the women find early on the first day of the week is the stone rolled away, the tomb empty, and a young man in a white robe (an angel with the appearance of lightning, Matt. 28:2–3; two men in "dazzling clothes," Luke 24:4). As evidence of the resurrection, the young man points to the empty tomb and tells the women that Jesus has risen. He sends them out to tell the disciples to meet Jesus in Galilee, where Jesus said he would be after he was raised (14:28). The women ran, amazed, afraid, and silent.

Whether the meeting in Galilee was to be for a resurrection appearance, as Matthew understood it (Matt. 28:16–20), or was an intimation of Galilee as the site of the return of Christ, as some scholars hold, the reader has to decide first of all whether Mark 16:1–8 ends or begins a story. It certainly contains that word of grace, that offer of renewal necessary for a new beginning. To the fearful disciples who abandoned Jesus and to Peter who denied him, the word from the risen Christ is, "I will meet you again in Galilee." And even the reader is drawn into the story by its open-endedness. Perhaps the women's fear and flight place them in the same unfavorable light as the disciples (14:50). Even so, astonishment, trembling, fear, and silence do not seem inappropriate for Easter morning. They will find their tongues and they will witness, but early in the morning is no time to be glib and chatty about an empty tomb and a risen Lord.

Easter Day

Acts 10:34–43 or Isaiah 25:6–9;
Psalm 118:1–2, 14–24;
1 Corinthians 15:1–11 or Acts 10:34–43;
John 20:1–18 or Mark 16:1–8

*(If the first lesson is from the Old Testament, the
reading from Acts should be the second lesson.)*

The passage from Isaiah, one of the very rare Old Testament texts containing an explicit promise of the abolition of death (v. 8), is placed on Easter Day among the classical New Testament resurrection texts. Both the epistolary reading and the speech of Peter in Acts 10 contain creedal summaries of the meaning of the life, death, and resurrection of Jesus; the Gospel texts give accounts of the discovery of the empty tomb.

Acts 10:34–43

The Cornelius episode is decisive in the Acts narrative, as seen by its location in the second stage of mission to the region of Samaria. The amount of space devoted to it is also significant (chaps. 10–11). It represents the moment of revelation for Peter as well as for the Jerusalem church as a whole, both of whom recognize that it was God's will for the Gentiles to receive full admission to the messianic community. In one sense, these two chapters record two conversions—that of Cornelius and that of Peter himself as he comes to know that Christian salvation is devoid of ethnic barriers.

The abbreviated summary of Peter's sermon to the Roman centurion is remarkable in several respects. Though similar to other statements of the early Christian kerygma, it shows distinctive Lukan formulations and should be interpreted in the light of Luke's overall theological and literary purpose. The opening declaration of God's impartiality relates the sermon directly to the preceding narrative, which has vividly depicted Peter's own "conversion" from religious and ethnic exclusivism. God as an impartial judge who does not discriminate between nations in dealing with them is also an important Pauline theme (Rom. 2:11; Gal. 2:6; Eph. 6:9; Col. 3:25; cf. 1 Pet. 1:17), with Old Testament roots (Deut. 10:17). Placed here on the lips of Peter, it reflects his own changed outlook that resulted from the heavenly vision. Having been censured by God for his narrow vision of humanity, he now more fully recognizes that he should not "call anyone profane or unclean" (Acts 10:28). The terms of God's acceptance turned out to be more broadly defined than he imagined: fearing

God and doing what is right are the terms for acceptance by God. What is more, these two admission requirements—one attitudinal, the other behavioral—know no racial boundaries; those "in every nation" who fear God and do what is right find acceptance with God.

As Paul insists elsewhere, the impartiality of God is a corollary of belief in the one God (Rom. 3:30). The one God does not have separate means of justifying humanity: both Jews and Gentiles are justified before God in the same way—by faith. This theological claim is also reinforced by the christological claim that Jesus Christ is "Lord of all"—not of some. One group, no matter how keenly they feel elected, cannot lay exclusive claim to God or to Christ. Even though God first sent the "word"—the Christian message of salvation—to Israel, the good news of "peace by Jesus Christ" extends to all humanity. Obviously, Luke tackles the serious theological question with which he and the early church struggled—how and why salvation first came to Israel. Because of the universality of Christ's Lordship, "everyone who believes in him receives forgiveness of sins through his name" (Acts 10:43). Logically extended, this would preclude the existence of separate Jewish and Gentile churches, each relating to God through Christ in different ways and on different terms. Luke's inclusion of the Jerusalem Conference (Acts 15) finally resolves this difficulty.

The similarity of Peter's sermon with the broad outline of the Gospel of Mark has often been noted: the Gospel story begins with John the Baptist—no infancy stories—the baptism of Jesus, and Jesus' works of benevolence and healing. The geographical transition from Galilee to Judaea is also similar, as is the passion the climax of the kerygma. The references to appearances, however, are Lukan (cf. Luke 24).

Typical of the Gospels, the sermon climaxes in the declaration of Christ's death and resurrection. The Easter faith is boldly and simply proclaimed. The risen Lord was not revealed to all but to those "chosen by God as witnesses, . . . who ate and drank with him after he rose from the dead" (10:41). This recalls Luke 24 as well, with its eucharistic overtones. There the Easter faith dawns in the context of the sacral meal where genuine enlightenment and communion with the risen Lord are most intimately experienced. The elevation of Jesus to the status of eschatological Lord is a role uniquely his, because he alone has died and lived. Elsewhere, his eschatological Lordship receives its underpinnings from his resurrection (Acts 17:31).

Isaiah 25:6–9

This passage from Isaiah, one of the very rare Old Testament texts containing an explicit promise of the abolition of death (v. 8), is placed on Easter Day among the classical New Testament resurrection texts.

But Isaiah 25:6–9 should also be viewed in its own literary and historical context. It appears in the collection of mainly eschatologically oriented materials generally called the Isaiah Apocalypse (Isa. 24–27), generally and reliably considered to be much later than the time of the prophet Isaiah. Although this section is not apocalyptic in the narrow sense of the term, it contains numerous motifs and ideas that appear in apocalyptic literature. Above all, these chapters express the confident view that, beyond a day of judgment, the reign of God will be established.

In terms of form, Isaiah 25:6–9 is an announcement of salvation with strong eschatological overtones. That is, unlike earlier prophetic announcements that saw the intervention of God in terms of historical events such as military defeat or return from exile, this one sees a radical transformation of the human situation. Its main focus is a banquet that the Lord will prepare on Mt. Zion ("this mountain," v. 6). The meal will include the richest possible food, and "all peoples" will participate. In the background of this promise stand cultic meals (Exod. 19; 24:9–11) that symbolize the intimate relationship between Yahweh and Israel, and perhaps also the sharing of sacrifices. One day, the visionary says, all peoples will come to the holy place for communion with one another and with the one God.

But there is more. With the eschatological banquet, God will inaugurate a new age of joy and peace. The "shroud that is cast over all peoples, the sheet that is spread over all nations" (v. 7) must refer to the attire for mourning, for God "will wipe away the tears from all faces" (v. 8). Mourning cannot be ended as long as there is death; consequently, "He will swallow up death forever" (v. 7). This language seems to be indebted to Canaanite mythology, which tells of the defeat of the god Mot (Death), but it has a very different construction here. Death is not another deity, but a human reality; and its defeat does not recur each year in the Spring, but is a single act of God when the new age begins. The apostle Paul cites the verse in his account of the nature of the resurrection (1 Cor. 15:54).

One of the most important features of this passage should not be overlooked on Easter Day. The announcement of the new age of joy and peace extends to all peoples.

Psalm 118:1–2, 14–24

Portions of Psalm 118 formed one of the lections of Passion/Palm Sunday, and at that point in the lectionary commentary we sought to show how the ancient psalm, used on the occasion of a king's triumphal reentry into Jerusalem for a service of thanksgiving, parallels the experience of Jesus' entry into the Holy City. As part of the Scripture readings for Easter Day, the verses selected for today's reading focus on victory and triumph, God's redemption of the one threatened.

Verses 1–2 form part of the call to offer thanksgiving to God; verses 14–18 are hymnic praise of God for the victory given the ruler in battle (see vv. 10–13), and verses 19–24 are part of the litany of entry into the temple.

Psalm 118 is a community psalm of thanksgiving, and the call to offer thanks in verses 1–4 includes all of ancient Israel—the lay and the clergy. Thanksgiving is to be offered by declaring that God's steadfast love endures forever. Thus the opening words of the psalm clearly proclaim and anticipate the note of victory that follows, a victory already anticipated in the reference to the character and love of God.

In verses 14–18, the triumphant leader returning from victorious battle affirms and proclaims the deliverance worked by God, even deliverance from death itself. The description of the struggle and battle in the field has given way to praise and thanksgiving. Like Moses of old, the ruler and the victorious proclaim a triumph wrought by the right hand of God (see Exod. 15).

In verses 17–18 the experience of battle and the triumph of victory are described in terms of a life and death struggle. The distress and trouble of battle are declared to be the chastening of God, yet God does not surrender the king to the power of death. These verses are thus very similar or analogous to what Christians proclaimed about Jesus: both his suffering and his triumph over death were the work of God. In both, misfortune and humiliation as well as victory and triumph are seen as components in divine activity.

With verse 19, we move to the entry litany itself, which was discussed in conjunction with the lesson for Passion/Palm Sunday. Insofar as Easter Sunday is concerned, the choral response in verses 23–24 (following the royal thanksgiving in vv. 21–22) is the text to be highlighted. The choir proclaims that what has taken place and is now celebrated has been the work of God, and thus it is marvelous (beyond belief, transcending the normal). It is the day in which God has acted and made the rejected stone the cornerstone (v. 22). The response to such activity should be rejoicing and celebration, because the sound of battle and the presence of death have been replaced with songs of victory and the gift of life.

In early Judaism, at the time of the origin of the church, Psalm 118 formed the concluding psalm sung in the Passover celebration. It was used both in the temple and in home observances. As such, it marked and celebrated the triumph of God that had brought the Hebrews out of slavery and bondage in Egypt and toward freedom and service of God in the promised land. Thus it is fitting that such a psalm play a role in the Christian celebration of Easter, which affirms the triumph of God in Christ as the triumph of life over death.

1 Corinthians 15:1–11

This is the earliest tradition of the resurrection of Christ preserved in the New Testament. As it stands, the text is set in First Corinthians, which was written in the early fifties, and thus precedes by several decades Mark, the earliest Gospel written. The wording used by Paul makes it even clearer that his gospel of Christ's death and resurrection preceded him. He says, "I handed on to you . . . what I in turn had received" (v. 3). The terms "delivered" (*paredoka*) and "received" (*parelabon*) are technical terms used by both Jewish and Graeco-Roman authors to describe the transmission of ancient sacred traditions. Paul, thus, "received" this tradition of Christ's death and resurrection from those Christian witnesses who preceded him, and he passes it along as a faithful witness with impeccable credentials (cf. 2 Tim. 2:1–2). When we celebrate the Easter faith, we may be assured that it represents one of the very earliest strata of Christian preaching and that it is a sacred message traceable to the very dawn of the Christian church.

The heart of this tradition of early Christian preaching occurs in verses 3–4. The language is traditional, suggesting that this formulation of the message is pre-Pauline. In its present form, the gospel is summarized in a four-part scheme, but this is likely already an expansion of an earlier two-part scheme. Quite likely, early summaries of the gospel message were two-pronged: the Christ who (1) died has also been (2) raised (cf. Rom. 10:9). Here, however, we see an expansion of this two-part kerygma:

(1)   Christ died

        for our sins

        in accordance with the scriptures

(1a) he was buried

(2)   he was raised

        on the third day

        in accordance with the scriptures

(2a) he appeared

        to Cephas

        then to the twelve

> then . . . to more than five hundred brothers and sisters
>
> then . . . to James
>
> then to all the apostles
>
> also to me.

Here we see that (1) and (2) represent the original points of early Christian proclamation. In each case, the element of proclamation is buttressed by a formulaic expression. "For our sins" gives the purpose of his otherwise inexplicable death, suggesting that it was vicarious. The language is reminiscent of Isaiah 53:5–6: "he was wounded for our transgressions, crushed for our iniquities." (Cf. also Isa. 53:8–9, 12.) By interpreting his death in light of this and other Old Testament passages, early Christians were able to proclaim that his death had occurred "in accordance with the scriptures."

With regard to the second main element of proclamation, Christ's resurrection, we also find two formulaic expressions to buttress this claim. The first is "on the third day," which again recalls Old Testament language (cf. Hos. 6:2; Jon. 2:1). That Jesus arose on the third day became part and parcel of early Christian preaching (cf. John 2:19; Matt. 16:21). As was the case with the first element, so here, the Old Testament enabled Christians to interpret Christ's resurrection. They thus proclaimed the Easter faith as having occurred "in accordance with the scriptures."

Although we cannot be certain, (1a) and (2a) appear to have entered the tradition at a later point and served to anchor the primary elements of proclamation. If Christ died, it should have been self-evident that he was buried. But, early on, rumors circulated that his body had been stolen (cf. Matt. 27:62–66). At a later period, some Gnostic teachers claimed that Christ had not in fact literally died, but only appeared to have done so. In either case, the tradition of his burial served to anchor the preaching in history.

Similarly, the appeal to appearances by the risen Lord served to buttress the proclamation of his resurrection. What is interesting about the list of appearances in this text is that, unlike the Gospel accounts, women are omitted. It is also obviously longer. We can see not only that the tradition of appearances is quite early, with Peter and the Twelve occupying conspicuous places of importance, but also that Paul places himself in the company of those to whom the Lord appeared. To be sure, his was an exceptional case (v. 8), but valid nonetheless.

We should notice that this "elementary" Christian tradition is introduced for the benefit of those who are already Christians. They are being "reminded" of that with which they are already familiar (cf. v. 1). As the remainder of chapter 15 shows, there was misunderstanding concerning the final resurrection. Because the latter was predicated on the truth of Christ's resurrection, Paul begins the discussion with this elemental statement of the Christian gospel. The gospel he preached, which they received, provided them with a place to "stand" (v. 1; cf. also 1 Cor. 10:12; 16:13; 2 Cor. 1:24; 1 Thess. 3:8). This suggests that "death and resurrection" provide the existential basis for Christian life, in the sense that it both forms the center of gravity for Christian existence and creates the perspective from which Christians view life. As Paul's life showed, "dying and rising" became more than a message that he preached; it was a life-style through which the gospel itself became heralded (cf. 2 Cor. 4:7–12).

Also important to notice is Paul's insistence that by this gospel Christians were "saved" (v. 2). The REB correctly renders this phrase, capturing its continuing dimension: "which is now bringing you salvation." The message of Christ's death and resurrection must be appropriated by Christians continually, for in doing so the saving work of God continues to transform their lives. The annual celebration of Easter is but one way in which the Easter faith exerts its ongoing power to shape and transform our existence through our own experience of the risen Lord.

John 20:1–18 *or* Mark 16:1–8

We will devote our attention here to John 20:1–18, because Mark 16:1–8 was the Gospel lesson for Easter Vigil. Before looking at John 20:1–18 in particular, two observations need to be made about resurrection materials in general and one about the Johannine shape of those materials.

1. We need to remind ourselves that the New Testament offers no account of the act of the resurrection of Jesus. What we have are reports of an empty tomb and appearances of the risen Christ. The various accounts in the Gospels and in 1 Corinthians 15:3–8 reflect different sources and different purposes.

2. We should appreciate how restrained are the uses of resurrection stories in the New Testament. Unlike some noncanonical accounts that have the risen Christ appear to passersby—the disinterested and unbelieving—in order to overwhelm and coerce faith, in the canonical Gospels Jesus appears to believers to vindicate and confirm the faith of his followers.

3. And more directly to our present consideration, in the Fourth Gospel the resurrection materials are shaped into a carefully constructed piece of literature consisting of two stories (20:1–18; 20:19–29). Chapter 21 has a resurrection appearance, but it is clearly an epilogue to the body of the Gospel itself. Each of the two stories contains two parts, and all four episodes are said to have occurred on Sunday (20:1, 19, 26); perhaps they existed once as separate stories for use in Christian worship. As they now stand in the Gospel, the two principal stories center on the responses of some of the original disciples to the resurrection, each focusing on the experience of a particular person. In the first narrative (20:1–18), that person is Mary Magdalene; in the second (20:19–29), it is Thomas.

In John 20:1–18, the response of Mary Magdalene is interwoven with that of Simon Peter and "the beloved disciple." In these two related episodes the writer is able to show how faith in Christ's resurrection was generated in different ways. In the case of Peter and the disciple whom Jesus loved, as we have now come to expect (13:22–25; 18:15–16), the disciple Jesus loved is first, first to the tomb and first to believe. Peter arrived second but entered the tomb first, looked around, saw everything and yet nothing, and left. The beloved disciple entered and "he saw and believed" (v. 8). Even though they did not yet understand the Scriptures concerning the resurrection (v. 9), this disciple believed. With no evidence but an empty tomb and grave cloths, this disciple was so close to Jesus that his faith did not need the scaffolding of vision and voice.

Mary Magdalene, on the other hand, represents faith formed another way. The empty tomb, rather than even hinting resurrection, saddened Mary with the thought of Jesus' body being stolen. So far from faith is she that even the appearance of two angels (v. 12) does not break her sorrow. In fact, the voice and the appearance of Jesus do not at first stir her to belief (v. 14). Only when he speaks her name (he knows his own, calls them by name, and they know his voice, 10:3–4) does she believe (v. 16). Unlike the beloved disciple, Mary comes to faith through the word of Christ, and by that word she must be sustained. Mary Magdalene cannot resume her old relationship with her Lord. This is Jesus to be sure; the risen Christ is none other than the crucified Jesus, but the ministry of the historical Jesus is over. Now begins the ministry of the glorified Christ, who relates to his followers by giving them the Spirit who will abide with them forever (14:16). Therefore Jesus says to Mary, "Do not hold on to me" (v. 17). She and the disciples and the church are not to long for the way it was or wish to return to some past relationship with Jesus Christ. Rather they, and we, are to believe his word: it is best for you that I go away (16:7); "if I do not go away, the Advocate [Spirit] will not come to you" (16:7); the Spirit will not leave as I am leaving but will live with you forever (14:16); because I go away to the Father, greater works than I have done you will do (14:12).

Not everyone takes the same path to faith in the risen Christ, and the preacher will not want to give the impression that one way is normative. Some respond to a word, others to evidence, and others to a relationship. But whatever the path, and whether sudden or slow, faith removes the distance between the first Easter and our own.

Easter Evening

Isaiah 25:6–9;
Psalm 114;
1 Corinthians 5:6b–8;
Luke 24:13–49

These readings are for occasions when the main (eucharistic) Easter service must be late in the day. They are not intended for Vespers (Evening Prayer) on Easter Evening. The Old Testament reading is an eschatological vision of Zion, the site of a messianic feast prepared for all peoples, that holds out hope that death will be swallowed up forever. Psalm 114 recalls Israel's flight from Egypt, poetically depicted as an upheaval of the natural order, and thus provides a useful precedent for Christian reflection of the significance of the resurrection. The epistolary reading shows Paul interpreting the death of Christ by using Passover imagery. Quite appropriately, the Gospel text records the Emmaus road encounter that carries the resurrection story into the evening (Luke 24:29).

Isaiah 25:6–9

For a discussion of this text, see the commentary on the texts assigned for Easter Day.

Psalm 114

In Jewish worship, Psalms 113–118 came to be associated closely with the festival of Passover. This collection of six psalms came to be called the "Egyptian Hallel" because they were seen as praise for the redemption from Egypt. How early this use of these psalms developed cannot be determined, but it was certainly already a custom at the time of Jesus.

The lambs designated for Passover were slaughtered and dressed in the temple in the afternoon to be cooked for the Passover dinner eaten in the evening. (Additional lambs were often cooked if the size of the Passover party required it. But at least one lamb, from which all observers ate a portion, had to be so designated and slaughtered and cleaned in the temple.) The people with their lambs were admitted to the temple in three different shifts. As the lambs were slaughtered on each of the shifts, the Levites sang Psalms 113–118 in the main courtyard of the temple. These psalms were again sung as part of the Passover meal. Psalms 113–114 were sung at the beginning of the meal and Psalms 115–118 at the conclusion.

Psalm 114 was clearly written for the celebration of Passover. Some of these psalms were originally composed for other celebrations and secondarily adopted for Passover usage.

The psalm opens with general summarizing statements about the Exodus from Egypt and the occupation of the land of Canaan (vv. 1–2). Egypt is described as the land of a people of strange language. The Egyptian language belongs to a completely different language family (Hamitic) from Hebrew (Semitic) and was written, of course, in a strange, nonalphabetic hieroglyphic form. In verse 1, "Israel" and "house of Jacob" refer to the larger inclusive Hebrew people (both Israel and Judah). In verse 2, "Israel" and "Judah" denote the Northern and Southern Kingdoms after the death of Solomon. That Judah is claimed to be God's sanctuary suggests that Judah is considered more special than Israel, which is spoken of as God's dominion. It also suggests that this psalm originated in Judah. The reference to sanctuary is no doubt an allusion to Jerusalem and the temple.

In verses 3–6, four entities are noted—the sea, the Jordan River, the mountains, and the hills. The references to the (Red) sea and the Jordan River hark back to the stories of the crossing of the sea in the Exodus from Egypt (see Exod. 14) and the crossing of the Jordan River to move into the promised land (see Josh. 3, especially vv. 14–17). In both cases, the water parted, fled, or turned back to allow the Hebrews to cross. It is interesting to note, and certainly appropriate for the setting of this psalm in the Passover observance, that the Passover preceded the Exodus from Egypt (see Exod. 12) and was the first celebration of the Hebrews in the land of Canaan (see Josh. 5:10–12). The Passover was thus celebrated as the last taste of Egypt and as the first taste of the promised land. The Passover recalls not only the scars of Egypt but also the first fruits of the land of promise.

The mountains and hills that skipped like rams and lambs (vv. 4 and 6) are not mentioned in the Exodus and Joshua stories. That they are mentioned as skipping around suggests that the language is metaphorical. The same might be said for the action of the sea and the Jordan River, although the final editors of the Hexateuch took both crossings as miraculous but actual events. Verses 5–6 are a taunt so formulated to heighten the action described. The one responsible for such actions does not get mentioned until verse 7, which refers to the presence of Yahweh.

The psalm concludes (vv. 7–8) with a call to the earth to "dance" (probably a better translation than the NRSV's "tremble"). Whether one should read "earth" (=the world) or "land" (=the promised land) remains unknown, although the latter seems more likely. The land is called on to break out in celebration at the presence of God, who worked wonders in the wilderness.

1 Corinthians 5:6b–8

In this text, Paul asserts that "our paschal lamb, Christ, has been sacrificed" (v. 7). It is quite a remarkable assertion, for it is the only time in all of his writings that he refers to Christ in this manner. In this respect, his understanding of the sacrificial death of Christ is close to that of the Fourth Gospel, in which the death of Christ occurs at the time of the slaying of the paschal lamb prior to the Passover meal (cf. John 19:14; also John 1:29, 36).

This christological claim occurs within the context of moral instruction. As the previous verses show, not only did the Corinthians tolerate gross immorality within their midst; they actually boasted about it (cf. 5:2, 6). Paul's concern is to bring them to their senses and to remind them of the moral character required of a community of Christians. He seizes on the metaphor "leaven" because of its close association with what is impure and corrupt. Its use as a fermenting agent meant that it was a contaminating substance and was regarded as ritually unclean (cf. Lev. 2:11). Thus, in preparation for the Passover, Israelites were instructed to remove all leaven from the house (Exod. 12:15; 13:7). Only unleavened bread was to be used during the Passover meal (Exod. 12:8). The order here should be noted: first, all leaven was to be removed from the house; then the paschal lamb was to be slain. Those wishing to participate in the Passover feast had to eliminate all leaven from their midst.

By adopting this metaphor and engaging in allegorical exegesis, Paul reminds the Corinthian church that their corporate conduct, which not only allows but fosters gross immorality, does not conform properly to the sacrifice of Christ, the paschal lamb. As a community of faith for whom Christ was sacrificed, they should eliminate all corruption and impurity from their midst. Only when they have so prepared themselves and have made themselves "unleavened" can they "celebrate the festival" (v. 8). He thus charges them to "clean out the old yeast" so that they can become what they actually are—"unleavened" (v. 7).

What is worth noting about this passage is that our celebration of the death and resurrection of Christ has moral implications not only for the community as a whole, but for individuals as well. The ethical instruction is grounded in the Christ-event itself. The church is expected to behave in a manner appropriate to the sacrifice of Christ. Corporate responsibility is also in view here. As Paul insists, "a little yeast leavens the whole batch of dough" (v. 6). The presence of "yeast" within the community of faith has a contaminating effect, and each celebration of Easter should serve as an occasion to remove "the old yeast, the yeast of malice and evil," and to celebrate with the "unleavened bread of sincerity and truth" (v. 8). So understood, Easter becomes more than celebration. It also becomes an occasion for moral renewal.

Luke 24:13–49

Sometimes the lectionary offerings are too rich; neither preacher nor congregation can dine without surfeiting. Such is the case for this service. Easter Evening worship should not ask too much of us; it is a time for reflection. For that reason and two others we will here confine ourselves to Luke 24:13–35. Because Luke 24:36b–48 will be our Gospel for the Third Sunday of Easter and Luke 24:44–53 for Ascension Day, the decision to conclude at verse 35 is not one of deletion but of delay. In addition, verses 13–35 constitute a unit, a conscious work of the storyteller's art, literarily and theologically complete. For a preacher to deal with this story along with something else seems not only impractical but also insensitive.

The story is set on resurrection day (v. 13) and is placed between the account of the disciples' unbelief ("these words seemed to them an idle tale," v. 11) and that of their cautious belief ("in their joy they were disbelieving and still wondering," v. 41). This narrative has no parallel in the other Gospels, and the appearance of the risen Christ to Cleopas and his companion (man or woman?) is not listed among the appearances recorded in 1 Corinthians 15:3–8. However, the list mentions an appearance to Peter (1 Cor. 15:5), which has its only Gospel reference in this passage (Luke 24:34). A few ancient manuscripts add after 24:11 a line about Peter coming to the tomb, but this is obviously borrowed from John 20:1–10. Whatever may have been the source of this story, it is available to us as clearly Lukan, not only in its aesthetic qualities but in its theological thrust. As a story, it reminds the reader of certain Old Testament accounts of God's appearances incognito (Gen. 18:1–15). As a Lukan story, it recalls for the reader two themes vital to this Evangelist: the centrality of the Hebrew Scriptures for Christian faith and the experience of breaking bread together as an experience with Christ. In other words, the twin themes are Word and Table. At the risk of inflicting the harm that analysis can do to a story, let us isolate these two themes for special attention.

The risen Christ joins two dejected disciples, and "then beginning with Moses and all the prophets, he interpreted to them the things about himself in all the scriptures" (v. 27). At this point Christ is to them a stranger. Just as at the Transfiguration and the Ascension, "clouds" and "sleep" preserve the revealed/concealed quality of God's revelation (Luke 9:28–36; Acts 1:6–11), so here Luke says, "But their eyes were kept from recognizing him" (v. 16). Why? Because faith is not generated by the experience of being overwhelmed but by gaining clarity about the true meaning of Scripture. Later, as the two reflected on the experience they said, "Were not our hearts burning within us while he was talking to us on the road, *while he was opening the scriptures to us?*" (v. 32, italics added). Nothing is more repeatedly clear in Luke: "If they do not listen to Moses and the prophets, neither will they be convinced even if someone rises from the dead" (16:31). This proper understanding of Scripture is the substance of the church's preaching in Acts. The hold of ignorance is broken, and now it can be seen that God's purpose with Israel and with the church is one and the same—to offer repentance and forgiveness to all people (24:47).

The second theme in the story has to do with the meal and how Jesus "had been made known to them in the breaking of the bread" (v. 35). The meal was nothing unusual at the outset; the two disciples shared their bread with a tired and hungry traveler. They prepared supper, and his presence made it a sacrament. Luke clearly has the Eucharist in mind: "When he was at the table with them, he took bread, blessed and broke it, and gave it to them" (v. 30). This text may provide the occasion for recalling for the listeners the theological significance of the table for this Evangelist, or at least to sense the cumulative effect of the variety and number of table stories: in the home of Martha and Mary; as guest of Simon the Pharisee; observing the behavior of hosts and guests at a banquet; responding to attacks that he ate with sinners; in a parable about a rich man who refused to share bread with Lazarus. In these and many other stories, Luke makes table fellowship the evidence of full acceptance of sinners by Jesus and of one another by us. So also in Acts, story after story points to the conclusion that eating together is the mark of full accord in the church. For Luke, the question to the church is not so much, Would you baptize them? but, Would you eat with them? (Acts 11:3).

But even if this enlargement of the theme of breaking bread is not pursued, the Emmaus story alone is enough for today. What could be a more appropriate act for Easter Evening than to sit at table with one another, and with Him?

Second Sunday of Easter

Acts 4:32–35;
Psalm 133;
1 John 1:1–2:2;
John 20:19–31

On the Sundays following Easter, the first lessons are supplied by the Book of Acts, which unfolds the story of the Spirit-filled church empowered by the Easter faith. The various readings represent a range of episodes from these early, formative days of the church, yet they all have in common the deep-seated conviction that the Lord, though risen, was present among the disciples.

The second lesson during the Easter Season is taken from First Peter, First John, and Revelation for Years A, B, and C respectively. For all their variety, the selected texts illustrate the bracing confidence that stems from the Easter faith, even though the circumstances in which this confidence emerges are quite different.

The Gospel readings include various accounts of post-Easter appearances by the risen Lord, and from the Fourth through the Seventh Sundays the farewell discourses and prayers of Jesus from the Fourth Gospel.

In today's first lesson, the church is described as a community that showed its solidarity by sharing its possessions. Unity and harmony are also praised graphically in Psalm 133. In the epistolary lesson, fellowship within the Christian community is seen as deriving from having fellowship with God through Christ. The Gospel lection relates the post-Easter appearance of the risen Lord to the disciples, where he bestows the Spirit on them, and the subsequent interchange with Thomas.

Acts 4:32–35

This is one of several summaries placed at crucial points in the narrative of Acts (cf. also 2:42–47; 5:12–16; also summaries of the church's growth, 2:47; 6:7; 9:31; 11:21; 12:24; 16:5; 19:20; 28:31). With these vignettes, in which certain motifs are repeated, Luke highlights significant aspects of the early Christian community.

This summary occurs after a major triumph. Peter and John have been arrested for healing a lame man and preaching the Gospel (3:1–26). They were brought before the authorities, but were released (4:1–31). As confirmation that God had been at work in these events, there was an outpouring of the Spirit, which gave new vitality to the apostolic ministry of the Word (4:31).

Before recording the second major crisis faced by the Christian movement, the second arrest of the apostles (5:12–42), Luke pauses to summarize the state of affairs within the community of faith, calling attention to several features of its life.

1. *It was a unified movement.* "Now the whole group of those who believed were of one heart and soul" (v. 32). "Heart and soul," a phrase reminiscent of the Old Testament (Deut. 6:5; 10:12; 11:13; 13:3; 26:16; 30:2, 6, 10; also 1 Chron. 12:38), suggests that the level of unity among believers was deep and genuine, penetrating to their innermost being. Not every church in the first century exhibited this degree of unity, although it remained an ideal (cf. 1 Cor. 1:10–17).

2. *The community shared its possessions.* "No one claimed private ownership of any possessions, but everything they owned was held in common" (v. 32b). Here we see Christian unity being translated into Christian charity. Their willingness to dispossess themselves of what they owned became a concrete expression of the solidarity of their fellowship. Of the Gospel writers, Luke in particular lays heavy stress on the sharing of possessions as an earmark of Christian discipleship (cf. Luke 8:3; 12:33; Acts 2:45). In this instance, Christian charity took the form of community of goods (cf. 2:44), but this is not the only way in which responsible use of possessions is presented in the New Testament, particularly Luke-Acts. At least two other possibilities are presented: (1) the complete renunciation of possessions as a prerequisite of discipleship (Luke 5:11, 28; 14:25–33; 18:18–23) and (2) the giving of alms (Luke 11:41; 21:1–4).

If we realize that Luke's portrait of the early church at this point is but one of several mandates that he gives for the responsible use of possessions, then "Christian communism" cannot be presented as the single ideal toward which the church should strive. It may be an appropriate response, given the right time and place, but should not be seen as the only, or even the most laudable, form of Christian charity.

The important thing to notice is that "there was not a needy person among them" (v. 34). By seeing to it that the needy are cared for, the early church came to embody the Old Testament ideal (cf. Deut. 15:4). Yet by sharing their goods in common, they also came to embody the Greek ideal, which held that "for friends all things are common." Clearly, Luke is presenting the early church as the embodiment of both the Jewish and Greek ideal community in which unity and charity thrive.

3. *It continued its proclamation of the resurrection of Christ.* "With great power the apostles gave their testimony to the resurrection of the Lord Jesus" (v. 33). The phrase "great power" doubtless implies the continued demonstration of power through signs and wonders (cf. 4:30; also 2:22; 3:12; 4:7; 6:8; 8:13; 10:38; 1 Thess. 1:5; 1 Cor. 2:4–5). Bearing witness to the resurrection lay at the heart of early Christian proclamation (Acts 1:22; 2:32; 3:15; 5:32; 10:41; 13:31; 1 Cor. 15:1–11, 15; also Luke 24:46–47). It is worth noting that the ministry of the Word was carried on along with the ministry of goods. In this respect, Luke's portrait is exemplary, for it suggests a worthwhile paradigm for the modern church. The concern to proclaim must be balanced with concern for the needy.

One should also be cautious in trying to replicate this image of the ideal church in a modern setting. For one thing, it is the needy among the church who are cared for here. At this juncture, Christianity was not of sufficient strength to reach out beyond its own circle and administer assistance, although this need was soon recognized (cf. Gal. 6:10).

In using this text on the Second Sunday of Easter, the preacher should notice, first, that it sketches the image of a church empowered and emboldened by the Easter faith. Central to its life was the proclamation of the risen Lord, and this message was accompanied with powerful signs and wonders. Luke wants to leave no doubt that it was a Spirit-filled community and that its capacity to preach boldly arose from the power of the Spirit. Second, the text shows that the Easter faith came to expression in the community of faith. Concretely, this was seen in the unity that existed among believers and the love and concern they had for one another. It is Luke's conviction that the messianic community embodies both the Jewish and Greek ideal of life together.

Psalm 133

This psalm has been selected for this Sunday because it stresses fraternal harmony and brotherhood, themes found especially in the reading from Acts.

Psalm 133 belongs to a group of psalms (Pss. 120–134) that bear the heading "Psalms of Ascent," or perhaps better, "Pilgrim Psalms." These psalms were probably sung as pilgrims made their way to Jerusalem to worship. The emphasis in Psalm 133, in such a context, would be in praise of the fellowship enjoyed in the city of Jerusalem during festival occasions. Such an interpretation fits harmoniously with the description of the early church in the opening chapters of the Book of Acts.

Kindred living (or worshiping, as NEB footnote indicates) together is praised in verse 1. Although the psalmist probably did not have this in mind in composing the psalm, it is interesting to note how frequently trouble between brothers and among kindred is used as a theme in the Old Testament (Cain and Abel, Jacob and Esau, Joseph and his brothers, Absalom and Amnon, Solomon and Adonijah). The lack of brotherly unity and peace so often tears at the fabric of a family that one can sense the reason the psalmist might focus on this universal motif. When Jerusalem was overrun by pilgrim-worshipers during the great festivals of Passover and Tabernacles, it was necessary for the people to coexist in peace in order to enjoy and benefit from the occasion.

Brotherhood and fraternal unity are described metaphorically in verses 2–3. One image speaks of the precious oil poured on the head of Aaron, which runs down the beard and onto his clothes. This picture is probably derived from the ordination ritual of the high priests in which anointing oil was used (see Exod. 29:7; Lev. 8:10–13). For us, the imagery seems slightly less than stupendous, but what is probably emphasized are the extravagance of the act and the joy that characterized the occasion. The ordination of a new high priest in Israel would have been something like the inauguration of a president, especially in postexilic days when there was no king and the high priest was the chief official in the community.

Brotherhood is also compared to the "dew of Hermon." Mount Hermon, standing over nine thousand feet in elevation, was the tallest mountain in Syria-Palestine and the source of much of the headwaters of the Jordan River. Towering over the region, the mountain may have given its name to the dew that falls in late summer to nourish late crops toward maturity.

A secondary theme of this psalm is the greatness of Zion—the goal of pilgrims. The centrality of Zion for the life of the people is found in numerous psalms (Pss. 46, 48, 76, and so forth). Zion is described in verse 3 as the place that God has blessed and where the blessing is bestowed for abundant life.

1 John 1:1–2:2

Many of the themes celebrated in the Easter Season come to expression in this passage: life (1:1–2), light (1:5, 7), and joy (1:4). The themes are played out in the distinctive Johannine key and naturally recall similar themes in the Fourth Gospel. Let us look first at the overall structure. The first section (1:1–4) constitutes the preface of the epistle and introduces themes and motifs that are more fully exploited elsewhere in the epistle. These verses look quite different when compared with other opening sections of the New Testament in that they contain no personal greetings (cf. 2 John 1–3; 3 John 1–4). They look much more like the opening words of a homily and may suggest that the epistle as a whole should be read more as a sermon than as a letter. The address is couched in terms of endearment, seen by the way in which the readers are addressed (2:1, 7, 12, 18, 28; 3:13; 4:1, 4, 7; 5:21).

The second section (1:5–10) begins the sermon proper, with its emphasis on light, fellowship, and the life of faith as walking in the light.

The third section (2:1–2) is a self-contained unit and is so rendered in NRSV, NJB, and REB. In this section, the author urges his readers to break with the life of sin.

The opening words are reminiscent of the Gospel accounts of the Easter appearances, with their emphasis on "seeing and touching" the risen Lord (John 20:20, 25; Luke 24:39). This directly links the epistolary lection with today's Gospel lesson. The apostles' proclamation was based on what they had seen and heard (Acts 4:20; cf. also John 1:14). We should note the extent to which the senses are being activated here. This is doubtless prompted by the Gnostic threat, which denied the humanity of Christ (cf. 1 John 4:1–3). The author thus emphasizes that the testimony being proclaimed has been experienced at multiple levels: audible, visual, and tactile. All of these have informed the verbal or oral proclamation. Here we see how the entry of the Logos into the world had palpable effects on those encountered by it; hence the claim that "this life was revealed" (v. 2; also cf. 1 John 4:9; John 1:14; Rom. 3:21).

But our text does more than anchor the Christian message in Easter faith and experience, for the opening words push back to "the beginning." We think immediately of the opening words of the Fourth Gospel, "In the beginning was the Word" (John 1:1), and the author of this epistle shares this conviction that the Christian story actually begins with Christ, who was "from the beginning" (1 John 2:13). This interpretation of the opening verses assumes that "the word of life" (v. 1) refers to Christ, the Logos of life, and that it is Christ who is the antecedent of verse 1. It is Christ, the Logos, who "was from the beginning, what we have heard, . . . seen, . . . and touched." Another way of construing it, however, is to understand "word of life" as the "message of life," or the gospel itself. If this is the case, then "beginning" may not refer to the primordial beginning of time, but to the beginning of the Christian witness (cf. 2 John 6).

Also central to today's text is the fellowship (*koinonia*) created among those who have accepted the Christian testimony of faith. The word "fellowship" actually does injustice to the dynamic content of *koinonia* and is better rendered participially, for example, "sharing." The life shared together has two dimensions: it is with each other as well as with "the Father [and] his Son Jesus Christ" (1:3). The later verses show, however, that such mutual fellowship can only be sustained through moral renewal (1 John 1:7; cf. also 1 Cor. 1:9; Phil. 1:5). It is also nurtured by love for one another (1 John 2:10; 4:7–12) and is typified by joy (cf. John 3:29; 15:11; 16:24; 17:13; 2 John 12; 2 Cor. 1:24).

The fellowship envisioned here is understood in strongly dualistic terms, characteristic of the Johannine outlook, but not uncommon in first-century Judaism, for example, within the

Qumran community. There is a strong polarity between light and darkness, predicated on the conviction that "God is light and in him there is no darkness at all" (1:5; cf. James 1:17). Similarly, Christ is understood as the bringer and embodiment of light (John 1:4–5; 9:5; 11:10; 12:35, 46). This way of understanding may itself have been informed by Old Testament passages (cf. Isa. 9:2; 42:7; 49:6; 60:1, 3). It was not, however, a uniquely Johannine outlook (cf. Matt. 5:14; 1 Thess. 5:5; Phil. 2:15). To define moral conduct in terms of conformity to light and darkness represents a continuation of the Johannine understanding of the mission of Christ (John 8:12). Even though the author of the epistle strongly enjoins his readers not to have truck with the ways of darkness, he nevertheless fully recognizes that Christians can and do sin (1 John 2:8, 10). What is called for is the willingness to confess (1:9) and to recognize that the blood of Christ continues to have the power to cleanse us from sin (1:7; cf. Heb. 9:14; Rev. 1:5; 7:14). Also called for is the willingness to recognize our human shortcomings and the refusal to practice deception, either of others or of ourselves (cf. Prov. 28:12–13; 29:5). We can live in the assurance that God is both "faithful and just" (1 Cor. 1:9; 10:13; 2 Cor. 1:18; 1 Thess. 5:24; 2 Thess. 3:3; 2 Tim. 2:13; Heb. 10:23; 11:11; Rev. 1:5; Deut. 32:4).

Besides a faithful God, members of the Christian fellowship possess an "advocate" (*parakletos*, 1 John 2:1) who in this case is Christ himself, although in the Fourth Gospel it is the Holy Spirit (cf. John 14:16, 26; 15:26; 16:7; Luke 24:49). In addition, Christ is the "expiation" for our sins, a very controversial term (cf. 1 John 4:10; Rom. 3:25; Heb. 2:17). The issue is whether the sacrifice of Christ should be understood as that which placates an angry God or that which removes defilement (REB). In either case, the effects of his atoning death are universal—for the sins of the whole world (John 11:51–52; 2 Cor. 5:19).

This text is obviously rich with possibilities for the preacher, with its many themes that continue the joyous celebration of Easter. One might choose to focus exclusively on the christological aspects of the passage, such as Christ the Logos of life (1:1), our advocate with the Father (2:1), or the expiation for our sins (2:2). Or another direction worth exploring might be the nature of Christian "fellowship" and what this entails in the Johannine understanding, and whether this still serves as a viable way for modern Christian churches to define themselves. Still another possibility might be moral renewal and the Christian's need for open confession and reliance on a faithful God.

John 20:19–31

The Easter Season provides opportunities for the church to reflect on the biblical witness concerning the disciples' experiences of the risen Christ and to appropriate anew the blessing upon those who have not seen and yet who believe (v. 29). As stated in comments on the Gospel for Easter Day (John 20:1–18), the Fourth Evangelist provides testimony to the resurrection in the form of parallel "double-stories": two disciples and Mary Magdalene (vv. 1–18) and ten disciples and Thomas (vv. 19–29). Each double-story speaks of faith (the beloved disciple, v. 8; the ten disciples, v. 20) and of doubt overcome by a special appearance of Christ (Mary Magdalene, vv. 11–18; Thomas, vv. 24–29). These four experiences of the risen Christ are certainly not random examples by the writer; they are recounted as further testimony to a central conviction in this Gospel: there are different types and levels of faith. Throughout the book, the Evangelist has shown that there is faith based on signs and there is faith that needs none; there is faith weak and faith strong; faith shallow and faith deep; faith growing and faith faltering. In this Gospel faith is not a decision made once but a decision made anew in every situation. As a case in point, notice that the last "convert" in this Gospel is Thomas, already a disciple, even one of the Twelve. This understanding of faith should encourage as well as instruct members of the church who are made to feel guilty that their faith was not born full grown in one dramatic experience.

We focus now on John 20:19–31 with four observations that grow out of the text. The first concerns Thomas. Even though this Gospel elsewhere portrays him as courageously devoted to Jesus (11:16) and theologically alert (14:5); even though a noncanonical Gospel bears his name; even though tradition associates him with a mission to India, Thomas has been, because of this text, tagged "Doubting Thomas." But see him in the Johannine context. The beloved disciple believed with no evidence but an empty tomb, Mary Magdalene believed because of a word, and the ten disciples believed because they saw the Lord (v. 20). But for the absent Thomas, faith could come only with difficulty; too much was at stake. He could be sure only after physical contact (v. 25), but whether he actually touched Jesus is not clear (vv. 27–29). For some, faith is as gentle as a child on grandmother's lap, but for others, it is continual wrestling with doubt.

Our second observation concerns Jesus' response to Thomas (v. 29): "Blessed are those who have not seen and yet have come to believe." This statement is most important, for the Evangelist has been concerned throughout the Gospel to assure his readers that faith is no less a possibility for them than for the original disciples. Faith is available to all persons in all places and times with no loss of efficacy due to distance from Jesus of Nazareth. Therefore, having recited different ways faith was generated in the earliest Christian community, the writer pronounces upon the readers the blessing of Jesus Christ. This blessing complements the prayer of Jesus in 17:20: "I ask not only on behalf of these, but also on behalf of those who will believe in me through their word."

The third observation has to do with the gift of the Holy Spirit. The promise of the Spirit, so repeatedly given by Jesus in the farewell discourses (chaps. 14–16), is here fulfilled: "He breathed on them and said to them, 'Receive the Holy Spirit'" (v. 22). Brief as it is, this is the Johannine Pentecost. Whereas many functions and benefits of the Spirit are stated in chapters 14–16, only here are the apostles given authority to grant or refuse to grant forgiveness of sin (v. 23; Matt. 16:19; 18:18). Through the apostles the church is joined in continuity of mission, authority, and benefit to Jesus Christ.

Finally, verses 30–31 obviously are a conclusion, not to the preceding narrative alone but to the entire Gospel. There may have been a time when the Gospel closed here, before chapter 21 was added as an epilogue. If so, the Evangelist's last word was to state as the purpose of the Gospel the generation of faith. Because the book assumes that the readers already have some faith in Jesus Christ, this purpose is clearly to clarify, inform, and deepen faith to the end that it be full and life-giving. The last word to the world that crucified Jesus is not a judging but a gracious word: "That through believing you may have life in his name" (v. 31). The assurance of 3:16 has not been forgotten: "For God so loved the world."

Third Sunday of Easter

Acts 3:12–19;
Psalm 4;
1 John 3:1–7;
Luke 24:36b–48

In today's first lesson, a man is healed because the name of Jesus exercises power in the post-Easter church as if Jesus himself were still present—a testimony to the living presence of Jesus within the early Christian community. And among other things, Psalm 4 offers the reassuring message that the Lord hears us when we call. The epistolary lesson explores what it means to be children of God, but not in sentimental, soft terms; rather, it issues a call for children of God to be open-eyed with respect to sin and lawlessness. In the Gospel lesson, the disciples are confronted by the reality of the risen Lord and subsequently charged to be his witnesses to all nations.

Acts 3:12–19

The words of today's text come from Peter's sermon delivered in the precincts of the temple in response to the healing of the lame man at the Gate Beautiful (3:1–10). This was the first of the "wonders and signs" done through the apostles that Luke chose to record (cf. 2:43). The response of "all the people" (v. 11), that is, the Jews gathered for worship at the hour of prayer, was one of utter astonishment (v. 11). It was this response that gave rise to Peter's sermon.

The sermon, or more correctly, Luke's summary of Peter's sermon, is given in verses 12–26. Thus today's first reading actually consists of only the first part of the sermon, and in fact stops in the middle of the sentence in verse 19! If one wants to abbreviate the text at all, a more appropriate cutoff point would be either at the end of verse 16 or at the end of verse 21. Preferably, the text should include verses 12–26.

The sermon does not stand alone but is directly related to the preceding narrative, which reports the healing of the lame man. This is typical of the way in which the rest of Acts is constructed. At various points in the narrative, speeches occur, but they are invariably connected closely with a narrative episode, usually preceding the speech. In this instance, certain parts of the sermon are linked directly with the healing story (cf. vv. 12, 16). Perhaps as important is the prominence given in the sermon to the prophets (vv. 21–25). This may suggest that Luke understands the work of Peter and John as standing in the prophetic tradition. If this is Luke's intended connection, then the healing of the lame man (vv. 1–10) and the sermon that follows (vv. 12–26) should be construed as a single episode depicting a prophetic deed and word.

243

The connection between the sermon and the preceding miracle is made in the opening verse when Peter disclaims personal responsibility for the miracle. "Why do you stare at us, as though by our own power or piety we had made him walk?" (v. 12). It was only natural, when a divine miracle occurred, that onlookers would regard the human agent as the source of divine power rather than its conduit. Peter insists that neither their power nor their piety accounted for the miracle. Rather, it was God who had been at work in what had happened. Even more to the point, it was the God whom the Jewish audience had come to the temple to worship who had been at work here: "The God of Abraham, the God of Isaac, and the God of Jacob, the God of our ancestors" (v. 13; cf. Exod. 3:6, 15–16; also Luke 20:37; Acts 7:32; 4 Macc. 7:19; 16:25). Because Peter is trying to clarify the true source of divine power, the phrase "God . . . glorified his servant Jesus" (v. 13) should probably be understood as referring to the miracle. To paraphrase, "It was the God of your own ancestors Abraham, Isaac, and Jacob who was responsible for this miracle, and in doing so God manifested the glory of his servant Jesus." Luke wants his readers to see that the church is the divinely appointed messianic community through which the God of Israel is now at work in new and decisive ways. What the prophets had spoken of earlier (cf. vv. 22–25) has now become a reality. The people are called on to see the work of Peter and John, God's new prophets, as the continuation of the salvation history that they already knew.

The locus of divine activity has now shifted, however. Formerly, the presence of God, the Shekinah, dwelt in the temple. Now it is focused in the name of Jesus (v. 16). The healing of the lame man has shown that God no longer exercises divine power exclusively in the precincts of the temple, but does so where prophetic deeds are performed in the name of Jesus. Already, then, in the narrative of Acts, Luke begins to show how the temple is being displaced as the locus of God's presence and action. This becomes progressively more apparent as the narrative unfolds and is explicitly stated by Stephen (7:47–51).

The sermon also points up the fundamental paradox of the death of Christ. This is seen especially in the Lukan antitheses: "Jesus, whom you handed over . . . rejected . . . killed . . . God raised from the dead" (vv. 13–15). "You . . . asked to have a murderer given to you, and you killed the Author of life" (vv. 14–15). In the Lukan passion narrative, the death of Christ is presented as a gross miscarriage of justice. The death of Christ is seen as the death of an innocent martyr (Luke 23:4, 14–15, 20, 23) who is finally vindicated through the resurrection. Luke underscores the irony of the situation: given a choice between one who took life (Barabbas, the murderer, Luke 23:18–25) and one who is the very Author of life, the Jews opted for death over life. Now that Easter has righted this injustice, such a horrible choice is seen to have been done "in ignorance" (v. 17; Acts 13:27; 17:20; also Lev. 22:14; Num. 15:22–31). Now the appropriate action is repentance and reformation of life (v. 19) through which forgiveness is possible. "Times of refreshing" (v. 20) are also promised, that their repentance will enable them to enjoy the Parousia when God's appointed Messiah, Jesus, comes again (vv. 20–21).

Some of the themes that might be explored homiletically include the following: (1) the risen Lord as the locus of God's activity as opposed to supposedly sacred places, in this case the temple; (2) God's messengers as the conduits rather than the source of divine power; (3) the misplacement of emphasis on human "power and piety" in accounting for the work of God in the world; (4) the Easter faith as that which illuminates and overcomes human ignorance as well as offering repentance and the forgiveness of sins; and (5) the messianic community as the continuation of Israel and the place where the prophetic succession continues.

Psalm 4

This psalm was in all probability originally used in worship when a person felt that he or she had been wrongly accused of some deed. Ancient Israelite society recognized the right of persons in this predicament to appeal for a hearing in the temple before God (see Exod. 22:7–8; Deut. 17:8–13; 19:15–21; 1 Kings 8:31–32). In such religious adjudication at the temple, both parties in a case might appear and present their arguments, and the priests would render a verdict regarding guilt and innocence or else make both parties swear an oath of self-imprecation.

Something of the legal proceedings can be seen in the structure of the psalm, which switches back and forth between different addressees. The following is a plausible outline of the psalm: address and plea to God (v. 1), worshiper's address to the opponents (vv. 2–3), priest's address to parties in the dispute (vv. 4–5), and the worshiper's address to God manifesting confidence and trust (vv. 6–8).

One factor of interest about this psalm is the possibility it raises that people, in this case litigants in a case, spent the night in the precincts of the sanctuary. Verses 4–5, if these can be related to the ritual in the temple, bring together sleeping and the offering of sacrifice. Verse 8 has the worshiper speak about lying down to sleep in peace. Sleeping in the sanctuary in order to receive dreams, revelations, or priestly interpretations about one's condition—called incubation—was widely known in antiquity. The priests may have observed the worshipers during this period and drawn conclusions about guilt and innocence on the basis of the person's activity and sleeping patterns. Reference to sleeping has been the basis for considering this text to be an evening psalm.

Two features of this psalm are worthy of special note and can be related at least indirectly to the reading from Acts, which has the disciples defend themselves against false charges.

First, it is clear that the supplicant lamenting a case before God considers himself or herself to be falsely accused. The person's honor has been challenged, and vain words and lies have produced shame (see v. 2). Thus the worshiper has undergone the turmoil and pain of accusation and felt the psychic blows of opposition.

At the same time, a second emphasis in the psalm is the person's sense of innocence and firm reliance on God to act for the worshiper's vindication. Such assurance can be seen in verse 1, which appeals to past relations ("you gave me room when I was in distress"), in verse 3, where the worshiper expresses confidence ("the LORD hears when I call to him"), and in verse 7, where God is seen as the cause for rejoicing ("you have put gladness in my heart"). The apex of confidence is expressed, however, in verse 8, where the worshiper speaks of the ability to lie down and sleep peacefully, confessing that God alone is the source of peace and tranquillity. The guilty soul may frequently find sleep to be lacking, but an innocent conscience is a blessing when one seeks rest in sleep.

1 John 3:1–7

To conclude today's epistolary reading with verse 7 seems slightly arbitrary, because the sentence begun in verse 7 appears not to end until verse 8 (so, Nestle, 26th ed.; REB). Still, it is not at all clear where the thought-unit ends (cf. NRSV, NJB, NIV). The preacher would do well to consult several translations before deciding on the limits of the pericope.

Taking verses 1–7 as the lection, we may analyze the text thematically: (1) being children of God (vv. 1–3), and (2) living as children of God (vv. 4–7).

First, the text treats *our status as children of God,* which is introduced with an air of incredulity: "Think of the love that the Father has lavished on us, by letting us be called God's children" (JB). To be sure, enabling us to become children of God is understood in the Johannine writings as part of the mission of the incarnate Logos (John 1:12; 11:52). The Gospel tradition represents Jesus speaking of this as a possibility (Matt. 5:9, 45; cf. Luke 20:36), as does Paul (Rom. 8:16; Gal. 3:26–27; Eph. 1:5). But today's text emphasizes especially that we are God's children not by nature, but by gift ("what love the Father has given us," v. 1). In one sense, of course, all humans are God's children in that we have been created by God (Acts 17:28–29), but the relationship spoken of in First John is more specific than this. It is childhood brought about by divine regeneration (2:29; 3:9; 5:1, 4, 18; cf. John 1:13; 3:1–15) and explainable only in terms of divine love (John 3:16).

Being children of God is an existential reality for us ("and that is what we are," v. 1), but not necessarily a visible reality, especially to those who do not share our experience and understanding of God—the "world" in Johannine terms (John 1:9–11). Our true identity and self-understanding may be veiled to the world (cf. 2 Cor. 4:3–4), but so did Christ's true identity and mission elude the world (John 7:28–29; 8:19, 55; 14:7; 15:21; 16:3; Matt. 11:27). The obscurity we experience living our lives within the gospel is but an extension of Christ's own experience. His inscrutability becomes our own.

But our text also points to another ambiguity about being children of God: it is both actual and potential, realized and unrealized. "We are God's children now," yet what this means fully will not be realized until later (v. 2). At the human level we understand this. Children, in one sense, know that they have parents and experience the benefits of parental love, but full understanding does not occur until much later, when they are no longer children. In a limited way, this enables us to see the eschatological dimension of our text: at the Parousia, our vision of God will be transparent, and only then will we realize our true identity. Children of God live in the knowledge that there is more to come (Col. 3:1–4; Rom. 8:9) and that before they can "see God" they must be transformed (1 Cor. 15:43, 49, 53; Rom. 8:29; 12:2; 2 Cor. 3:18; Eph. 1:19–22). So then, children live in "hope" (v. 3), but this hope produces the desire for moral purity, always a prerequisite for seeing God (Matt. 5:8; Heb. 12:14; John 1:18). Notice that we purify ourselves (it is a volitional act; cf. 2 Cor. 7:1) and that Christ is our example ("as he is pure," v. 3).

On this note, the text shifts to the second major theme—*living as children of God* (vv. 4–7). The tone of these remarks is one of hard practicality. The text speaks quite bluntly about "doing righteousness" and does so in black-and-white terms. Committing sin is not a form of lawlessness; it is lawlessness (3:4; cf. 3:8*a*; 5:17; Matt. 7:23; 2 Thess. 2:3, 8). The ethical outlook is definitely Johannine, with no shades of gray allowed.

Such ethical dualism is directly related to the Johannine understanding of Christ, who was not only sinless (John 7:18; 8:46; 18:37; also cf. 2 Cor. 5:21; Heb. 4:15; 1 Pet. 2:22; 3:18; also Isa. 53:9), but whose work was to "take away sins" (John 1:29; cf. 1 Pet. 2:24; Isa. 53:4–5, 11–12). Presupposed here is the Johannine understanding of Christ as the Paschal Lamb sacrificed for the sins of the world (cf. John 1:29; also 1 Pet. 1:19; Rev. 5:6, 12; Isa. 53:7; Jer. 11:19; also Matt. 8:17).

So strongly stated is the moral position here that it stands in tension with remarks made earlier in the epistle. Earlier we are told that no Christian should ever feign sinlessness (1:8–10), and full allowance is made for Christian sinfulness (2:1–2). Here, however, we are told, "No one who abides in him sins" (v. 6); and later, "Those who have been born of God do not sin" (v. 9). The tension here is real and should not be resolved too easily. One possibility is that in 3:6, 9 the author is speaking of habitual sinfulness on the part of the child of God. Thus no one who genuinely abides in Christ is habitually inclined toward the life of sin. Rather, being born of God means that one's life inclines toward doing what is right (v. 7). A similar outlook is expressed by Paul (Rom. 6:14), although not in terms as unqualified as this. For the author, (habitual) sinning precludes true vision and knowledge of God (cf. 2:4; 3 John 11).

As before, Christ himself is the moral imperative. We do what is right because Christ is righteous (vv. 7, 10; 2:29).

Today's text might profitably be explored as illustrating the relationship between the Christian indicative ("being children of God") and the Christian imperative ("living as children of God"). As we have seen, neither of these is as straightforward as it appears. The sermon may address the ambiguity of our status as God's children—by gift not by nature, actual but veiled, realized but not fully. Or the preacher may wish to pursue the moral implication of the text, asking whether the theology of sin and righteousness expressed in this text is still viable and, if so, how.

Luke 24:36b–48

In preparing to explore the meaning of today's Gospel, the reader is urged to review Luke 24:13–35 and the comments made about those verses for the Easter Evening service.

Those earlier verses bear upon these for today because the narrative pattern of verses 13–35 is repeated in verses 36–48. That pattern consists of the appearance of the risen Christ, the failure to recognize him, the reprimand for the disciples' doubt, the sharing of food, the opening of the meaning of the Scriptures, and the response of wonder and joy. Because these resurrection narratives and those in other Gospels bear clear resemblances to one another, it is quite understandable that in the process of transmission details of one account would bleed into another. For example, the close of verse 36 and verse 40 clearly carry borrowings from John 20:21–27. However, none of these variations in the text materially affects the story.

In Luke's telling of the resurrection narratives, several themes are recurrent and vital to the whole message of the early Christian writer. One of them, the centrality of the Jewish Scriptures for the ministry of Jesus and the message of the church (vv. 14–17), was discussed in the comments about Luke 24:13–35 for Easter Evening and need not be repeated here. A second theme considered at that time was the importance of eating together for Jesus' work (Gospel) and the mission of the church (Acts). However, in verses 39–43, another dimension of eating is added. Here Jesus' act of eating fish, joined with his offering of his hands and feet for examination, says something about the resurrection. By insisting on the corporeality of the risen Christ, Luke is saying no to those forms of Christology that said Jesus only "seemed" (docetism) to be human. Even the resurrected Jesus says, "Touch me and see; for a ghost does not have flesh and bones as you see that I have" (v. 39). Luke is also saying no to those doctrines of resurrection that were really pagan notions of the immortality of the spirit. Christians believe in the resurrection of the dead, not escape into a spirit world. And Luke is saying no to those notions of spirituality that view the body and all things physical as inherently inferior or evil. Those who view themselves as just passing through this evil world tend to neglect the physical, economic, and political needs of other human beings. Luke reminds us that the risen Christ said, "Look at my wounds," and, "Do you have anything to eat?" No one can follow this Christ and say that discipleship means being only concerned with "souls."

A third theme in this resurrection account, only implicit in the Emmaus story (vv. 13–35), here takes the form of an injunction of Scripture and a command of the risen Lord. This is Luke's version of the commission to preach the gospel to the nations (vv. 46–49). However, because verses 46–53 will be our Gospel lesson for Ascension Day, we will reserve comment for that time. As we are now leaving the Easter narratives to move to other Gospel texts, a final word about the resurrection stories might be appropriate. In comments on Easter Day we reflected upon the restraint of New Testament writers in the use of this material. Let us add a second word to that description—realism. This may not seem accurate at first, given the appearance of dazzling angels and of Jesus suddenly present and just as suddenly gone. But focus upon the believers to whom Jesus appeared; how realistically they are portrayed! They took resurrection stories as idle tales; they were startled, frightened, and confused; they "disbelieved for joy." Minds and hearts raced. What does this mean? Do we continue where we left off? Do we begin anew? Will Jesus now go to God and leave us here alone? What will happen to us? Will anybody believe this? Will we be resurrected as Jesus was? These are realistic Easter thoughts, and the preacher who lives among these questions and treats them with respect is more the pastor than the one who misses the pathos and solemnity of resurrection joy.

Fourth Sunday of Easter

Acts 4:5–12;
Psalm 23;
1 John 3:16–24;
John 10:11–18

In today's first lesson, we see how proclaiming the Easter faith in public places inevitably meant that early Christian evangelists were called before formal groups, such as the Sanhedrin, to defend their actions. If being called to account requires reassurance, no psalm exudes the spirit of confident faith better than the Twenty-third. Another kind of boldness is introduced in the epistolary reading—that which comes from a clear conscience. With the Gospel lesson, we move away from post-Easter appearances to Jesus' discourse about his being the Good Shepherd, which, of course, resonates with today's psalm.

Acts 4:5–12

Here we have a capsule summary of the first recorded defense speech given by a Christian before religious authorities. Peter and John had healed a lame beggar at the gate of the temple (3:1–10), and Peter had subsequently proclaimed to the astonished crowd that it was the work of their own God, the God who had raised Jesus from the dead (3:11–26). The temple authorities, most notably the Sadducees, took umbrage at their theology of resurrection and arrested them (4:1–4). The next day Peter and John were brought before the Sanhedrin for a hearing. This provides the setting for Peter's defense.

The inquiry centered not on Peter and John's theology of resurrection, but on their ministry of healing. They were asked, "By what power or by what name did you do this [miracle of healing]?" (v. 7). There was no question about the validity of the miracle itself, for the man who had been healed stood beside them as living testimony (vv. 10, 14). This could not be denied. Rather, the question was, In whose name was the deed done?

According to the Gospels, Jesus had warned his disciples that they would be brought before Jewish religious authorities and interrogated. But he had also promised them that they should not be anxious about how they would react or what they would say, for the Holy Spirit would give them the words (Luke 12:11–12; also Matt. 10:19–20). In this, they could have the same reassurance Yahweh had given Moses (Exod. 4:12). Thus we are told that Peter was "filled with the Holy Spirit" (v. 8), thereby fulfilling the promise of Jesus in the narrative of Acts itself. This is but one of numerous instances in Acts where the Holy Spirit inspires the fledgling church, offering divine confirmation of its work and mission (cf. Acts 2:4; 4:31;

5:32; 9:17; 13:9, 52; cf. 16:7; 19:6). So empowered were Peter and John that their boldness was visible to the Sanhedrin (v. 13). This may also have been the dead giveaway that they had been with Jesus (v. 13).

In response, Peter (typically presented as spokesman) provides the proper context in which to understand the miracle of healing—the power derived from the name of Jesus Christ of Nazareth, whom God had raised from the dead (v. 10). Here he continues the theme he introduced in his public proclamation (3:12, 16). In similar fashion, he introduces the antithesis: the man whom you crucified, God raised from the dead (v. 10). Indirectly, then, the Jewish authorities were responsible for the miracle, but they had been unwitting accessories in the plan of God. To underscore the dramatic turn of events, Peter cites Psalm 118:22: "The stone that the builders rejected has become the chief cornerstone." But he does so with a crucial difference; he personalizes it: "The stone that was rejected *by you, the builders*" (v. 11, italics added). This passage, which so pointedly expressed the divine reversal that had taken place at Easter, became deeply embedded in early Christian preaching (cf. Matt. 21:42; 1 Pet. 2:4, 6–8; cf. also Isa. 8:14; 28:16; Rom. 9:33; Eph. 2:20). To their rejection, God had responded with exaltation.

To climax his defense, Peter unambiguously locates salvation in Christ: "There is salvation in no one else, for there is no other name under heaven given among mortals by which we must be saved" (v. 12). With this exclusive claim, there is an interesting play on words. Earlier, Peter had asked, "If we are questioned today . . . how this man has been healed" (v. 9). The word for "heal" is *sozo*, also translated "saved" in verse 12. The speech operates on two levels: it deals with the "healing," or "making whole," of the lame man, but moves beyond this to the "healing," or "making whole," of everyone under heaven (cf. 2:21). We begin to see that Peter is not merely addressing the Sanhedrin, but the reader of the narrative for whom the lame man is serving as a mirror.

Out of this simple miracle story there arises proclamation of the Easter faith. "A good deed done to someone who was sick" (v. 9) has become the occasion for universal proclamation of salvation. Irony pervades the narrative: it is "uneducated and ordinary men" (v. 13) who point out to the religious authorities the connection between "a good deed done to someone who was sick" and the work of God in which they themselves had unwittingly participated. The literary artistry with which Luke has told the story should itself be instructive for the one who preaches from this text.

One theological question presented by the text, and which may provide the theme for the homily, concerns the absoluteness of the claim made in verse 12. Especially in the modern world have we become more fully aware of religious pluralism. The study of the history of religions, both Western and Eastern, has pointed up many similarities that cannot easily be ignored. It has certainly become more difficult for proponents of any religion to make absolutist claims as they once did. Perhaps it would be worthwhile to explore this text in the light of the modern dilemma and in the context of history, with attention given to such historical episodes as the Crusades or the Holocaust.

Psalm 23

Psalm 23, with its expressions of confidence in God and its portrayal of overcoming turmoil, has been selected as a text suitable to accompany the healing episode read from Acts as well as the text from John concerning sheep and shepherding. Although Psalm 23 probably is the best known and best loved of all the psalms, it provides the interpreter with numerous problems, especially with regard to how it was understood and used in ancient Israelite worship.

With an economy of words, but with expressive and descriptive metaphors, Psalm 23 describes the relationship between God and worshiper and the sense of serenity that prevails when troubles have been overcome and resolution and repose prevail.

If we analyze Psalm 23 in terms of speaker and addressee, we find the following pattern: the worshiper, confessing confidence in God, apparently speaks to some human audience (vv. 1–3); the worshiper, addressing the Deity, stresses what God has done (vv. 4–5); and finally, the worshiper, again addressing the audience, summarizes the person's assurance of divine favor (v. 5).

It is possible to understand the images of God in this psalm in two different ways. In one, God is the skillful and compassionate shepherd who leads the worshiper like a good shepherd who cares for his sheep, a widespread view of both gods and kings in the Near East (vv. 1–3). If the shepherd imagery in verses 2–4 is applied to verse 5, it can be said that the shepherd looks after the feeding and care of the sheep. Shepherds in the Middle East (Lebanon and Syria) are said to have used the expression "to set the table" when referring to preparing fields for grazing. Such activities included uprooting poisonous weeds and thorns and clearing the area of the sheep's enemies such as snakes and scorpions' nests. In the evening, as the sheep were corralled, the injured or sickly ones were separated from the others and treated with oil and a curative drink made of fermented material and herbs sweetened with honey. If one follows this line of interpretation, then the imagery of the shepherd runs throughout the psalm.

It is also possible to look at the psalm as presenting a double image of God, that of shepherd for the sheep (vv. 1–3) and that of a human host for a guest (vv. 4–5). (Note that this breaks the text between the section spoken to a human audience, vv. 1–3, and that spoken to God directly, vv. 4–5.) The image of God as host emphasizes not only the sufficiency of the Divine to feed but also the care that God takes to meet the other needs of the guest—anointing oil for the head and soothing cup for the psyche.

To decide between these two alternative interpretations is almost a matter of taste, although the latter is certainly found more widely in literature on the psalms.

If the psalm compares the experience of God and his care to that of a shepherd and/or a human host, then to what does the imagery of the person's distresses refer? That is, what happened to the worshiper? From what straits has he or she been saved? Some possibilities are these: (1) one could see the imagery to be that of sheep changing or entering new pastures; thus the psalmist could be describing one of life's points of transition; (2) another view is to see the prayer as one offered by a wandering traveler who has safely returned to Jerusalem; (3) the entire imagery may be simply that of a worshiper who eats a sacrificial meal in the sanctuary; (4) a further alternative is to see all the imagery as merely verbal images without any exact frames of reference; and (5) a final interpretation suggests that this psalm may have been used by a fugitive guilty of manslaughter or accidental killing who took refuge and sought asylum in the temple and who thus lives beyond the reach of the family of the deceased. (See Exod. 21:12–14; Deut. 19:1–13; 1 Kings 1:49–53; 2:28–35 for this practice.) Dwelling in the temple or house of God would thus be taken literally. There the fugitive could eat in the temple in the presence of his or her enemies.

Regardless of how one interprets the psalm, the general picture of what is stressed is quite clear. One who has known trouble or experienced life-threatening situations has also experienced the protection of the Divine. The psalm exudes confidence that God protects, so that whatever life brings to the people, they will not be overwhelmed.

Preaching on this text, one could focus on the diverse expressions of human experience found in the psalm. One set emphasizes the troubles that threaten to overwhelm human life: valley of the shadow of death (or darkness or total darkness), evil, and enemies. Another set stresses the positive instruments and acts of God's care: green pastures, still waters, reviving of the soul, reliable paths, rod and staff, table, oil, and cup. Human life, of course, experiences both the negative and the positive. At times, even the shepherd must use the rod and staff against his own sheep for their best interests.

This psalm presents the human predicament without any illusion about persons' being superhumans and above pain, loneliness, and lostness; yet the symbol of God as protector and even corrector affirms the potential of a tranquil life lived amid adversaries and the harsh realities that are the ingredients of every life.

The closing verse affirms that goodness and mercy, not tribulation or ravenous enemies, will be a constant companion. To dwell (or to return) to the house of Yahweh in this verse did not refer to immortality but to either residence in the temple (by a priest or a fugitive) or, if read as return, to a visit to the temple.

1 John 3:16–24

Even though verse 16 occurs in the middle of a paragraph (so, Nestle, 26th ed.; NRSV, REB, NJB), it is a natural point to begin the pericope.

Several distinct yet interlocking themes emerge from today's epistolary lection:

1. *We cannot love God and ignore those in need* (vv. 16–17). Christ's capacity to transcend his own self-interest is expected to be replicated in the Christian.

2. *True love is love acted rather than love spoken* (v. 18). It is one thing for love to be "a matter of theory or talk," quite another for it to "show itself in action" (REB). The supreme paradigm of active as opposed to spoken love is Christ, who "laid down his life for us" (v. 16; cf. John 10:15). Somewhat related is the distinction made elsewhere in the New Testament between "hearing" and "doing" (cf. Matt. 7:21; Luke 12:47; Rom. 2:13; James 1:22; 4:11).

3. *Active love is the sole basis of Christian assurance* (v. 19). By loving "in deed" we come to know that we are "from the truth" (v. 19), or "that we belong to the realm of truth" (REB), which, of course, is the realm embodied by Christ himself (cf. John 5:33; 8:40, 45; 16:7; 18:37; 1 John 2:21; 2 John 4).

4. *The life of faith is not without dilemmas of conscience* (vv. 19–20). There is the recognition that even the Christian heart needs reassurance (v. 19b) and that there are times when our own hearts condemn us (v. 20a; cf. also 1:8–10; 2:1–2). To speak openly of the tensions of the inner life is merely to recognize what every sincere Christian knows: inward conflict is part and parcel of Christian experience. What sustains us, however, is the knowledge that "God is greater than our hearts, and . . . knows everything" (v. 20b; John 21:17; 1 John 4:4; Ps. 103:14; cf. also 1 Cor. 4:4–5; 8:2–3; 13:12). If our love for God is genuine and expresses itself in our love for one another, even with our lapses of faith and their attendant pains of conscience, the omniscient God is able to see that these represent us at our atypical worst.

Before adopting this more positive interpretation of verses 19–20, the preacher should recognize that these verses are very difficult to understand. Closer exegesis will be required before one moves too quickly to proclamation. In a word, these verses may be read in at least two ways: (1) as words of hopeful reassurance or (2) as a cautious warning against complacence.

5. *Along with the conflict, there is also confidence* (vv. 21–22). These verses speak of the other dimension of Christian existence where the norm is confidence toward God (cf. 2:28; 4:17; 5:14; also Heb. 3:6; 4:16; 10:19, 35; also Rom. 5:1–2) and where such confidence enables us to engage in natural conversation with the God who has begotten us. We ask and God gives (cf. John 11:22; 14:13–14; 15:7, 16; 16:23–24, 26; 1 John 5:14–15; also cf. Matt. 7:7–11; 18:19; 21:22; Mark 11:24; James 1:5–6; Jer. 29:13–14; Prov. 8:17). Here again, Jesus' relationship with his own Father becomes the paradigm (cf. John 11:41–42).

6. *Reduced to its barest minimum, the Christian life consists of two things: faith and love* (v. 23; cf. 1 Cor. 13:13). Neither of these is conceived as Christian virtues in the broad ethical sense. They are rather understood with specific reference to Jesus Christ. The faith called for here is faith in the name of God's Son, Jesus Christ (cf. John 1:12; 6:29; 20:31; 1 John 5:13). The love called for is the "new commandment" required by the Son who embodied self-giving love (cf. John 13:34; 15:12–13, 17; 1 John 2:7–11; 3:11; 4:7, 11–12; 2 John 5; also Gal. 6:2; 1 Pet. 1:22).

7. *The prerequisite to sustained mystical union with God is filial obedience* (v. 24; John 6:56; 14:20; 15:4–7; 17:23; 1 John 1:3; 2:24; 4:13–16), the express sign of which is the indwelling of God's own Spirit (John 16:7–15; 1 John 3:6; 4:13; 5:6–8; also Rom. 8:9; Acts 2:11, 32–33).

Today's epistolary lection, with its emphasis on confidence, directly echoes themes expressed in the reading from Acts. Similarly, its note of reassurance is also sounded in Psalm 23. The Gospel reading focuses on the active love of Christ, who voluntarily lays down his "life for the sheep" (John 10:15). Today's readings blend well with one another and suggest various homiletical possibilities.

John 10:11–18

The preacher learns quickly that when dealing with the Fourth Gospel one must be careful not to assume that beautiful imagery means simplicity of thought. The fact is, the converse is more likely true. When Jesus speaks in images or figures (analogies, parables), the message is not obvious at all. "I have said these things to you in figures of speech. The hour is coming when I will no longer speak to you in figures, but will tell you plainly of the Father" (16:25). In John 10:11–18, Jesus refers to himself as the shepherd, which was, says the writer, a figure Jesus used with his listeners (v. 6).

We are, therefore, engaged today with a beautiful, familiar, and yet complex passage. The commentaries will provide a discussion of the complexities. One difficulty is chronological. Does 10:1–21 belong with 10:22ff. and therefore should be located in Jesus' ministry during the Feast of Dedication (10:22), or does 10:22 begin an entirely different episode? Another problem is literary. Does 10:1–21 belong with chapter 9, so that we may assume the same audience? With such uncertainties, it seems wisest not to tie 10:1–21 too closely to what precedes or follows. The passage has its own integrity and probably is best interpreted without drawing upon the larger context.

Our Gospel lesson, John 10:11–18, is the third of four subunits in 10:1–21. The first, verses 1–6, is replete with images of the shepherd, the door, thieves, and robbers. The second, verses 7–10, seems to be a commentary on verses 1–6. The fourth subunit, verses 19–21, is the familiar summary of mixed responses to Jesus' speech. Our text, verses 11–18, is less complex than the first two subunits, leaving behind the images of thief, robber, shepherd, door, and gatekeeper, and focusing on the single contrast between a shepherd and a hired hand.

In verses 11–18, Jesus is presented as the model shepherd who gives his life as the ultimate act of caring. This act of love stands out impressively against the dark backdrop of hired workers who, at the slightest threat of danger, abandon the sheep. This passage may recall the story of David risking his life against bear and lion in behalf of the sheep (1 Sam. 17:34–35). In the early church, this model of Christ as shepherd was held up before pastors, urging them to care for the flock in spite of the dangers of false teachers (Acts 20:28–30) or violent persecution (1 Pet. 5:1–2). The Johannine church, facing social and religious ostracism and even death at the hands of fanatics claiming to be God's servants (15:18–25; 16:1–4), was surely challenged and encouraged by this image of Jesus, just as it was warned about pastors-for-pay who resign quickly when difficulties arise. In fact, there has never been a time in the history of the church when there were not faithful shepherds who, like Jesus, gave their lives for the flock. Before Roman sword or Nazi boot, burning cross or constant harassment, economic pressure or political reprisal, they remained with the sheep. And then there are the hired hands.

Regarding verse 16, scholars are not of one mind in identifying the "other sheep that do not belong to this fold." Most interpreters take one of three views. First, this is a reference to the Gentile mission, a concern certainly underscored elsewhere in this Gospel (11:52; 12:19–24). Second, this is an expression of Jesus' desire to have all his followers united as one flock under one shepherd. This view assumes that already at the time of this Gospel there were many circles of Christianity moving apart from one another. Such groups probably formed around various leaders: Peter, Paul, James, Apollos, and others. Unquestionably, this passion for the unity of believers is found in this Gospel; in fact, it is a major theme in Jesus' prayer in chapter 17. Third, the "other sheep" may be understood as subsequent generations of believers who were to regard themselves as members of the original body of disciples. These, too, receive this Evangelist's attention elsewhere (17:20; 20:29). The preacher whose sermon moves in any one of these three directions will not violate the love and care of the Good Shepherd.

Fifth Sunday of Easter

Acts 8:26–40;
Psalm 22:25–31;
1 John 4:7–21;
John 15:1–8

In today's first reading, the impact of the Easter faith reaches remote Ethiopia, represented by the God-fearing minister of Queen Candace. In many ways, this incident illustrates the expectation of the responsorial psalm that all nations would eventually turn to God and worship him. The Epistle lesson is dominated by the theme of mutual love among Christians, a prominent Johannine theme. The organic relationship between God, Christ, and believers is metaphorically represented in the Gospel reading, Jesus' discourse about the vine and branches.

Acts 8:26–40

This story of the conversion of the Ethiopian eunuch is a superb illustration of Luke's storytelling ability. It is a tightly crafted literary piece, with fine attention to detail. We are given the crucial essentials: time (noon), place (deserted road, chariot), character (the Ethiopian, a eunuch, minister of the queen, God-fearer who had traveled to Jerusalem to worship), and plot (an inquiring searcher has his questions answered and his life changed).

We also see in the story some of the major themes of Luke's theology:

1. *The Holy Spirit as the primary catalyst in the extension of the gospel into the world* (Acts 2:4; 4:8, 31; 9:17; 13:9, 52). Here it is the Spirit who, in the form of an angel of the Lord, speaks directly to Philip, instructing him concerning his mission (cf. 10:19; 11:12; 13:2; 21:11). Throughout Acts we see evidence of the Spirit's direction (11:28; 15:28; 20:23; 21:4). As the story begins with the Spirit, so does it end with the Spirit snatching up Philip for mission work in other parts (cf. Ezek. 11:24; 1 Kings 18:12; 2 Kings 2:16; 2 Cor. 12:2, 4; 1 Thess. 4:17). The picture painted here is consistent with that seen throughout Acts: even after the Lord ascended, he remained at work through his Spirit, motivating his messengers and extending the frontiers of the kingdom.

2. *The universal impact of the gospel as it breaks through geographical and ethnic barriers, reaching beyond Jerusalem to Samaria, even to Ethiopia* (cf. Luke 1:29–32; 24:27; Acts 1:8). This too represents a fulfillment of the Old Testament hope that envisioned a time when

foreigners would come to the house of God to worship (1 Kings 8:41–43; also cf. Ps. 68:31; Zeph. 3:10). The story is inclusive in another sense. The primary character is a eunuch who, according to Deuteronomy 23:1, should be excluded from the assembly of the Lord (cf. also Isa. 56:3–7). Here he has not only joined other God-fearers who were attracted to the worship of the one God of Israel (Acts 10:2, 35; 13:16, 26), but is baptized and incorporated into the people of God and returns home rejoicing (v. 39). This incident becomes one scene in the large tapestry woven by Luke to depict the inclusion of the Gentiles into the people of God (Acts 2:39; 11:18; 13:46–48; 28:26–29).

3. *The theme of promise-fulfillment with Jesus as the interpretive key unlocking the meaning of the Old Testament Scriptures* (Luke 24:27, 44–45). The interpretation of Isaiah 53:7–8 is a central element of the story (vv. 32–33), a story that shows both how Jesus serves to make sense of the Old Testament and how the Old Testament serves to make sense of Jesus as well as the disciples' experience of the Easter faith (cf. Acts 17:2, 11; 18:24, 28; 1 Cor. 15:3). In Luke-Acts, the promise-fulfillment theme is worked out on several levels. On the one hand, Jesus is presented as the fulfillment of the Old Testament promises, as the one of whom Isaiah spoke. On the other hand, at various points in the narrative (e.g., in the Gospel), promises are made and fulfilled at a later point (e.g., in Acts). The preaching of the gospel to the Ethiopian eunuch, taking place as it does in Samaria, fulfills the promise made earlier by the risen Lord (Acts 1:8).

One way of appropriating the story homiletically might be to focus on the two central characters, the eunuch and Philip, treating them respectively as paradigms for the earnest inquirer and the faithful messenger of God.

A character sketch of the eunuch might include the following observations: (1) his initial inclination toward faith in God, seen in his status as a God-fearer willing to journey to Jerusalem to worship; (2) his searching in the Scriptures and the commendable trait of his questioning spirit, which included not only his willingness to ask searching questions but the ability to ask the right ones; (3) his eagerness for divine guidance (cf. John 16:13; Rom. 10:14); and (4) his initiative in following through his quest by requesting baptism.

A complementary sketch of Philip might include the following elements: (1) his responsiveness to the Spirit (vv. 26, 29, 39); (2) his forthrightness in asking penetrating questions (v. 30); and (3) his knowledge of the Scriptures and skill in interpretation (v. 35).

These are naturally only suggestions, but perhaps they will point to ways in which the modern reader can relive this episode on a deserted road and identify with these ancient figures in whom the Easter faith lived.

Psalm 22:25–31

This psalm, with its passages on suffering, humiliation, and passion, comprised one of the readings for Good Friday. The present lection emphasizes those passages in the psalm that speak of vindication and celebration. The break between the two main portions of the psalm comes after verse 22, which comprises the supplicant's vow. From verse 23 on, the psalm is concerned with celebration and praise, not humiliation and supplication. How can we account for this radically different content of the psalm and the radical break following verse 22?

One way of reading the psalm in its totality is to see verses 1–22 as a prayer for help that was followed by a priestly oracle assuring the worshiper that God had heard and answered the request. Note that the last line of verse 24 declares that God has heard. Verses 23–31 are thus the psalmist's celebration and fulfillment of the vow made in verse 22.

The material in verses 23–31 falls into the following categories: (1) appeal to a human audience calling upon the people to praise God (vv. 23–24), (2) worshiper's prayer of thanks to God (v. 25a), and (3) proclamation to the human audience of the consequences of the salvation that has been experienced (vv. 25b–31).

In verse 25a, the worshiper interprets the praise now offered as coming from God. Because this is addressed to the Deity, such a statement represents an indirect form of thanksgiving. The great congregation before whom praise and proclamation are offered would be the worshipers assembled in the temple for a festival or for some royal celebration of victory or recovery if the user of this psalm was the king. In the earlier vow (v. 22), the worshiper promised to "tell of your name to my brothers and sisters; in the midst of the congregation I will praise you." What is referred to here is the participation in a thanksgiving ritual that included sacrifice and thanksgiving as well as "offering testimony" concerning God's saving power and divine redemption. The offering of testimony plays a significant role in Israelite worship and to some extent parallels types of testimonials frequently heard in churches a generation or so ago.

Two characteristics of offering testimony in the psalms should be noted. First, testimony was given in rather stereotyped language that described, in general rather than specific terms, the distress from which a person had been saved. This style was used so that the same psalms, probably written by cultic officials or priests instead of individual worshipers, could be used over and over again, like our hymns. The use of stereotypical and metaphorical language allowed the worshipers to plumb their misery in great depth and to describe it in more colorful and dramatic language than would have been the case if they merely recited the realistic details of their turmoil.

Second, the testimony offered moved into the realm of what might be called proclamation or preaching. That is, worshipers were allowed and encouraged, even required, to speak about the dire straits from which they had recovered and also to preach to the audience of friends and family at the thanksgiving ceremony.

The fulfillment of vows are spoken of in verses 25b–26, where persons are called upon not only to share in the praise but also to eat and be satisfied. The afflicted or poor in verse 26 may refer to persons of this class or perhaps to those persons who sought asylum in the sanctuary and thus lived off the services of the temple. The sharing of food in lavish form is, as every mother knows, a universal act expressive of well-being and contentment. Note that in the psalm "sharing follows receiving" and is a gesture of the blessed to incorporate others into the blessing. The Old Testament has a special concern for the poor and afflicted so much so that orphans, widows, and others were allowed to share in the tithes and sacrifices of others (see Deut. 14:29; 16:10–14; 26:12).

The consequences of the worshiper's salvation and thanksgiving, given in verses 27–31, suggest that the person involved was the king, because the salvation of a single ordinary individual would not have had the universal implications noted in these verses. These royal features, of course, made it easy to apply this psalm to Christ or to use it for understanding him.

Although the text of verses 27–31 contains many problems and makes translation somewhat difficult, what it suggests is rather clear. First, there is reference to the universal impact of the situation. The "ends of the earth" is a way of saying everywhere. The text states that people throughout the world will worship Yahweh, the God of Israel. (This seems to have been a common expectation held in the cult and court of Jerusalem; see Isa. 2:1–4 and Mic. 4:1–4.) As king in Jerusalem, Yahweh was also king over the nations of the world.

Verse 29 seems to imply that perhaps even the dead or at least the dying will also bow down before God. This idea may sound farfetched, but the Apostles' Creed declares that Jesus descended into hell (see 1 Pet. 3:18–20).

Not only the present (vv. 27–28) and past generations (v. 29), but also generations yet to come will tell of the redemption of Yahweh and proclaim his deliverance to generations yet to be born. The missionary and universal tone of this psalm is one of its key characteristics.

1 John 4:7–21

Endearing terms are used to introduce this poignant exhortation to love, which NRSV divides into three parts: verses 7–12, the exhortation itself (note the hortatory subjunctive "let us love"), which may be an early Christian hymn (it is printed strophically in Nestle, 26th ed.); verses 13–16a, which speak of the Holy Spirit as the proof of abiding love; and verses 16b–21, which continue themes from the first two sections but introduce the new theme that perfect love eliminates fear. The section addresses the "Beloved," the form of address frequently used in the epistle; the word itself is expressive of the theme of love.

These verses reflect the utter realism of the author, who knows too well that Christian communities need to be encouraged to love one another. As the author's later remarks indicate, he understands that the Christian fellowship can be permeated with hate; and what's more, Christians can make the dubious claim of living in the love of God while at the same time exercising active ill will toward one another (vv. 20–21).

Such an impassioned plea for mutual love within the Christian fellowship may be directly related to the author's previous remarks, which actually form a digression (vv. 1–6). He has just spoken of the need to be discriminating in listening to prophetic utterances. Earlier, he warned against the Gnostic threat, noting that false teachers had originally been part of the Johannine community, but they had now left (2:18–25, esp. 19). The debilitating effects of doctrinal disputes are well known, and doubtless the Johannine community had been seared by such disputes. If modern examples of such disputes are any indication of the dynamics at work within the community, we can surmise that members had taken sides, positions had become polarized, and heated debates had characteristically degenerated into ad hominem verbal assaults. That we have not exaggerated the situation is suggested by the other two Johannine epistles (cf. esp. 3 John 10).

The exhortation to love is straightforward and recalls similar teaching by the Johannine Jesus (John 13:34; 15:9, 12–13, 17; also 1 John 2:7–8; 2 John 5; cf. also Gal. 6:2; 1 Pet. 1:22; 1 Thess. 4:9). Of interest here is the basis given for the exhortation.

1. God is the source of love: "Love is from God" (v. 7; also v. 16). Love as it is presented here does not, and cannot, derive from our own human capacities. Rather, it stems from God's own initiative. It is not "that we loved God but that he loved us" (vv. 10, 19). Fundamental to the Johannine outlook is the notion that love is properly understood, not as a universal human emotion inherent within the evolutionary process, but as something that transcends us and originates beyond us. God must be understood as prior to ourselves, especially in love (4:19; also cf. Deut. 7:8; Wis. of Sol. 6:16; Matt. 18:33; Rom. 8:31–32; 2 Thess. 2:16).

2. God is the essence of love: "God is love" (v. 8; also v. 16). We should not understand this to mean that God is an abstract principle, as the Greeks understood it. The proper background here is the Hebrew understanding of Deity as a dynamic personal force who acts

rather than is. To say that God is love is equivalent to saying that God loves, in the sense that all the acts of God through and in history have been directed toward our ultimate well-being. Nor has the love of God been hidden and inscrutable, but has been "revealed among us" in the giving of God's Son (v. 9; also 1 John 1:2; John 1:4; Rom. 3:21). Here we hear a direct echo of John 3:16 and perhaps an indirect echo of the sacrifice of Isaac (Gen. 22:12; cf. also John 1:14, 18; Matt. 21:37; Rom. 8:32; Heb. 11:17).

3. Our human capacity to love is derivative, not original: "Everyone who loves is born of God" (v. 7). To be able to love as God loved when he sent his Son is possible only through divine regeneration (cf. 1 John 2:29; 3:9; 5:1, 4, 18; also John 1:13). When we love, it is only proof that a divine seed has been sown in us.

4. Knowledge of God is properly defined only in terms of love (v. 8). The tendency among Gnostics was to elevate knowledge to an unqualified virtue, so much so that it became essentially an act of the head, not of the heart. Paul, for example, reminds gnostically inclined Christians that knowledge should be combined with love (1 Cor. 8:1–3), observing that "knowledge puffs up," whereas "love builds up." Thus, whatever one might claim, this text insists that "whoever does not love does not know God" (v. 8). Loving God and hating fellow Christians are mutually incompatible (vv. 20–21).

Closely linked with the knowledge of God is the vision of God, which, in certain mystical traditions, can be achieved largely through human powers of concentration and religious devotion. We are thus reminded that "no one has ever seen God" (cf. Exod. 33:20; John 1:18; 5:37; 6:46; 14:9; 17:24; also 1 Tim. 1:17). This may be seen as another way of saying that whatever knowledge we have is partial (cf. 1 Cor. 13:9–13). The way in which true and sustained union with God occurs is through our love for one another (v. 12). In this way, God's love comes to complete expression (cf. 1:7; 2:5; 4:17–18; 5:3). This too may be an indirect slap at the Gnostics, for whom perfection was essentially a mental act.

There are obvious affinities between today's epistolary reading and the Gospel reading from John, especially if the latter is extended through verse 11. The vine and branches metaphor may be fruitfully explored as the means for achieving union with the Father through love.

John 15:1–8

On this and the remaining two Sundays of the Easter Season the Gospel lessons will be drawn from the farewell discourses and prayer of Jesus in the Gospel of John (chaps. 14–17). This may be the point at which to comment briefly about the nature of that material and the approach the preacher may take.

Chapters 14–17 address the question, What does the risen and departing Christ have to say to his church? We can expect, therefore, that this section will be rich in assurances, warnings, instructions, and promises. However, the form of the material presents difficulties for the preacher. There are frequent and lengthy repetitions that may best be handled by gathering the subject matter under themes such as promises, the work of the Spirit, warnings of dangers to come, and so forth. In addition, the task of subdividing the material into clear and meaningful units is difficult because of the absence of the usual transitional signals (shifts of time, place, activity, or audience). Commentaries will differ, but the preacher can usually discover controlling images or governing themes that will enable divisions of the text without violation of its sense.

Creators of the lectionary surely experienced these difficulties in deciding upon 15:1–8 as our reading for today. One could argue for verses 1–6 as a unit, because the vine and branches imagery shifts at verse 7 to the categories of love and obedience. The NRSV makes paragraphs of verses 1–11 and verses 12–17; the REB makes units of verses 1–4, 5–6, 7–10, and 11–17. Verse 18 clearly is a transition point. Our lection, verses 1–8, has the double advantage of a controlling image and a central verb. The image is that of the vineyard, which, like that of the shepherd in chapter 10, evoked rich associations with the Hebrew Scriptures and with everyday life. The vine image is, in Johannine terms, a "figure" (in contrast to direct speech), a form of speaking that we discussed last Sunday in considering John 10:11–18. The central verb is "abide," one of the most significant words in this Gospel. A concordance will lead the reader to meaningful expressions such as "Teacher, where do you abide?"; "they abode with him that day"; "Jesus abode with them for two days"; "in my Father's house are many abiding places"; "my Father and I will come and abide with you." But here in 15:1–8 the word reaches its peak in frequency of use.

Two messages in this text are inescapable. One has to do with the relationship of Christ to the church. That the relationship is possible, whatever the terms used to characterize it, is a gift of grace and the occasion for gratitude and joy. That the relationship is necessary is evident both in Scripture and in experience. Without it, the church is powerless (vv. 4–5), wordless (vv. 3, 7), prayerless (v. 7), fruitless (vv. 2–8), and hopeless (vv. 2, 6). The purpose of the relationship is primarily to bear fruit. What is meant by fruit is not specified. However, the search for a definition would best be pursued not in Paul ("the fruit of the Spirit," Gal. 5:22–23) but within this Gospel. For example, in 12:20–27 fruit-bearing refers to preaching and witnessing to the gospel among all nations. That understanding could hardly be inappropriate here.

The second clear message in this text centers on the often neglected statement "My Father is the vinegrower" (v. 1). The vinegrower comes into the vineyard with a knife, and every plant is severely cut. Some are cut away ("removes," v. 2) because they are fruitless, and some are pruned (v. 2; the Greek words for "remove" and "prune" are variations on the same root word) in order to be more fruitful. But how is the church to know the difference? Both experiences are painful. Is it not the case that pruning (severing of debilitating relationships, loss of burdensome things, cessation of meaningless pursuits) is often understood by those suffering the pain as being cut away from God, leaving believers hurt, confused, and angry? Perhaps the Johannine church, experiencing such extreme difficulties (16:1–4), needed to be reminded that they could be undergoing pruning for greater fruitfulness. Churches that move through hardships to increased commitment to the mission have, indeed, been pruned. Those that pull back in concern for their own comfort and security have, indeed, been removed.

Sixth Sunday of Easter

Acts 10:44–48;
Psalm 98;
1 John 5:1–6;
John 15:9–17

As is evident from today's first lesson, for Gentiles to receive the Holy Spirit meant their full inclusion within the messianic community. The joyous mood of celebration in Psalm 98 is closely related to God's vindication before the nations. Christological confession, with strong insistence that Jesus actually did come in the flesh, figures centrally in today's epistolary lesson. The Gospel reading is a continuation of last week's lesson, Jesus' discourse on the vine and branches, with an explicit call for the disciples to love each other as Jesus had loved them.

Acts 10:44–48

Today's text focuses our attention more directly on the work of the Holy Spirit in the life of the church, as we approach the end of the Easter Season and move toward Pentecost. For Luke, the breakthrough event in the life of the early church was the conversion of Cornelius (10:1–11:18). This is seen not only by the amount of space he devotes to the episode, but also by its placement in the overall narrative. It is genuinely transitional and pivotal in the story line, coming immediately after the conversion of Saul (9:1–30) and setting the stage for his mission work among the Gentiles (cf. 11:25–26; 12:25). It also represents a "double narrative," for the story told in chapter 10 is repeated, in summary form, in chapter 11. It figures prominently in Luke's overall depiction of the incorporation of the Gentiles into the people of God (11:1, 18; 13:48; 14:27; 15:7, 11; 28:23–29). In fact, the episode ends on this triumphant note: "And they [the Jewish Christians in Jerusalem] praised God, saying, 'Then God has given even to the Gentiles the repentance that leads to life'" (11:18).

Our passage today occurs at the end of Peter's sermon preached before the house of Cornelius in Caesarea. We are told that during the very course of Peter's sermon (10:34–43), "the Holy Spirit fell upon all who heard the word" (v. 44; 11:15). This has puzzled many commentators because it breaks the pattern. Normally, in Acts believers receive the Holy Spirit after they have heard the Word proclaimed and in conjunction with their baptism (cf. 2:38; 5:32). But surely the important question is not when the Holy Spirit engulfed them, but why. This is at least the question that the text makes central.

As the text suggests, what was significant was that the six Jewish Christians, "the circumcised believers" (v. 45; cf. 11:2; Gal. 2:11), who had accompanied Peter to Caesarea, witnessed this spiritual outpouring. Clearly, its effects were audible: "For they heard them speaking in tongues and extolling God" (v. 46; cf. 2:4, 11; 19:6; Mark 16:17; 1 Cor. 14). No doubt, we are to understand this as ecstatic utterances and not foreign languages. As the text unfolds, we hear echoes of the account of Pentecost in Acts 2: the coming of the Spirit and the speaking in tongues. For this reason it is often referred to as "the Pentecost of the Gentiles." And it is clear that Luke wants the reader to understand it this way.

From Peter's remarks in chapter 11, it was also a moment of illumination for him. He noticed, too, that the Holy Spirit fell on the Gentiles assembled (11:15), but this triggered his memory. He recalled "the word of the Lord, how he had said, 'John baptized with water, but you will be baptized with the Holy Spirit'" (v. 16). He could only conclude that what he and the other apostles had experienced at Pentecost, the Gentiles were now experiencing. They were now both witnessing and experiencing the breaking in of the messianic kingdom of God, whose earmark, as expected and predicted, was the coming of the Holy Spirit (Joel 2:28–32). To have excluded them from formal initiation into the kingdom of God by preventing their baptism with water would have been tantamount to "withstanding God" (cf. Mark 3:28–30 and parallels).

Worth noting at this point are the ingredients of Peter's own "conversion": (1) he witnessed again the coming of the Holy Spirit, which reminded him of Pentecost; (2) he recalled "the word of the Lord" and interpreted this experience in light of it; (3) he drew the inevitable conclusion: God has been at work among the Gentiles; and (4) he conformed his practice to his newly informed perspective; he instructed the Gentiles to be baptized with water (10:48; cf. 8:36; 11:16; Matt. 3:14; Mark 1:4 and parallels).

We should also note that the believers were baptized in a manner conforming to the new realities of the messianic kingdom that they had experienced; they were "baptized . . . in the name of Jesus Christ" (cf. 2:38; 8:16; 19:5).

This incident is illuminating in several respects, most notably in the way it depicts a shift in perspective, not only for Peter but for the resistant Jewish Christians—a shift from exclusiveness to inclusiveness. At first they were truculent (11:3), but finally they rejoice (11:18). Not surprisingly, Luke stresses the role of the Holy Spirit in enabling these Jewish Christians to transcend their own narrow vision of the kingdom. The sermon based on this text might well address the narrowness of modern conceptions of the church that are more keen to find ways to exclude than to include.

Psalm 98

Psalm 98 is one of a group of psalms (Pss. 47, 93, 96–99) that proclaim the enthronement and kingship of God. Various motifs are found in these psalms: Yahweh as king, the judgment of the world, the stabilization of the created world, and the universal rule of God. The selection of Psalm 98 to be read in conjunction with Acts 10:44–48 was made on the basis of the concern of both texts with the universal aspects of God's salvation.

Verses 1–3 call upon the people to sing to Yahweh a new song to celebrate God's victory. What victory is the text concerned with? Different answers have been given to this question: (1) the redemption from Egypt, (2) the return of the Jews from exile, (3) some victory in warfare, (4) the creation of the world, or (5) the annual celebration of God's creation of the world. The latter seems the most likely possibility. Such an interpretation assumes that every year at the fall Feast of Tabernacles, the people led by the king celebrated Yahweh's rule as king over history, the nations, and creation. Because this was the time of the new year, the festival celebrated the creation of the world, and it was assumed that Yahweh re-created the world and reestablished the orders of creation at this time. (If the idea that God annually created the world sounds unusual, we should compare it with the fact that we sing every Christmas that Christ is born today!) As creator, Yahweh thus ruled as king and judge over the whole of creation. The victory would thus be God's triumph over chaos or disorder and God's establishment of cosmos or order in the universe. In many ancient cultures, it was assumed that the creation of order involved the victory of the Creator God over the powers of disorder and chaos (see Ps. 89:9–10). Every year, order had to be reestablished, the hostile powers subdued, and a new beginning made. What God did in his victory is related both to Israel and the nations (the Gentiles) and thus has a universal quality about it.

Verses 4–6 call for the whole earth to praise and sing to Yahweh, with various musical instruments, because Yahweh is the universal king. Interpreters of the Bible used to assume that the idea that God ruled over the world developed rather late in Israel. One can argue, however, that this was a very old idea and that God's kingship was celebrated in the Jerusalem temple from the time of David. It is true that Yahweh did not actually rule over the whole world; that is, Yahweh worshipers were not found universally nor did God's special people rule the whole world. This did not prevent the cult from proclaiming this fact. In a sense, one might say that such proclamations were "predictions" or facts to be realized.

The final verses of the psalm (vv. 7–9) talk about the roaring of the sea and the world, floods clapping their hands and hills singing for joy before Yahweh. Here we are obviously in the realm of metaphorical speech. But it is speech that is right at home when talking about the creation of the world. Thus it is a call for the natural and human world to accept the fact that Yahweh is judge, that is, that Yahweh establishes and upholds order in the world of the universe.

The problem of the particular (the elect, the chosen, the people of God, the Jews) versus the universal (the outsiders, the nonelect, the Gentiles) in religion has always plagued believers. The early church had to struggle with universalization of its faith and the inclusion of Gentiles. Such psalms as Psalm 98 demonstrate that the Old Testament itself already had strong universal interests and inclinations incorporated within its pages—a universalism that dares to challenge any totally exclusivistic reading of the work of God in the world.

1 John 5:1–6

Favorite Johannine themes are interwoven into this passage, any one of which could be connected with other passages in both the Fourth Gospel and the Epistles, and developed in its own right: believing, knowing, loving, obeying, begetting, and overcoming. They are all listed here in their participial form as a way of emphasizing their dynamic quality. John, for example, prefers the verb "believe" (*pisteuo*) to the noun "faith" (*pistis*), for the former captures the active and dynamic force of the concept in a way the latter does not.

This text opens with the favorite Johannine couplet: "believing and knowing" (vv. 1–2; cf. 3:23–24). The object of believing, in this case, is the confession "that Jesus is the Christ" (cf. 2:2; Acts 5:42; 9:22; 17:3; 18:5, 28). A variation of this confession is repeated in verse 5, the one "who believes that Jesus is the Son of God." So much emphasis is placed on this confession here that we are probably still hearing echoes of the Gnostic denial of the humanity of Christ (cf. 2:18–25; 4:1–6). This likely explains, in part at least, the emphasis on the "water and blood" in verse 6: "This is the one who came by water and blood, Jesus Christ, not with the water only but with the water and the blood" (cf. Matt. 3:16 and parallels; John 1:31, 33; 19:34). Once again, the author is insisting on the undeniable humanity of Jesus.

Not merely the content of the confession, but its creative power should be noticed. The one who believes in this confession "has been born of God" (v. 1). The notion of divine begetting is, of course, a central Johannine concept (John 3:3; 8:42; 1 John 2:29; 3:9; 5:4, 18; also John 1:13). For John, coming to believe in Christ can only be understood properly as an act of God (John 6:44). It is that which God initiates rather than that which we come to intuitively.

Closely connected with "believing" is "loving": "every one who loves the parent loves the child," or literally, "every one who loves the begetter also loves the begotten (v. 1b). This recalls the exhortation to love given earlier in the letter (4:7; cf. comments on epistolary lection for the Fifth Sunday of Easter), as well as the comments immediately preceding concerning the impossibility of loving an invisible God while hating a visible neighbor.

How, then, can we know that we actually love God's children? (v. 2). By loving God and keeping his commandments, which appear to be one and the same thing. Again, the author's instructions are hard and practical: they lay great stress on commandment keeping (cf. 1:6; 2:3, 9; 4:20; John 14:15; 15:16; 21:23; 2 John 6; also cf. Titus 1:16; Wis. of Sol. 6:18). As he goes ahead to say, "For the love of God is this" (v. 3); that is, "This is the [way we show the] love we have for God" (objective genitive)—by keeping God's commandments. Realizing, perhaps, that this may sound too heavy-handed, he pauses to note that God's commandments are not "burdensome" (cf. Deut. 30:11; Matt. 11:25–30).

At this point, the text moves to another theme—overcoming the world (vv. 4–6). The Johannine world is sharply dualistic with the "world" seen as the major adversary of believers. Similarly, our struggle is with the chief adversary of the world, the Devil himself, and in this respect represents an extension of Jesus' own struggle (cf. John 16:33; 1 John 2:13; 4:4; also 1 Cor. 15:57). The believer is promised victory in this cosmic struggle (1 John 4:4; also Rom. 8:37; Eph. 6:16), but it is predicated on proper understanding of the identity of Christ, that is, the confession of his humanity (v. 5).

In the final verse, we are introduced to the work of the Spirit: "And the Spirit is the one that testifies, for the Spirit is the truth" (v. 7), and this links directly with the reading from Acts 10:44–47. The Spirit as the one who leads into all truth is traceable to the Johannine Jesus (cf. John 4:23; 14:17; 16:13), and we should note the important distinction in the Fourth Gospel between the promise made by the historical Jesus and the bestowal of the Spirit made by the risen Lord (John 20:22). The Spirit is promised before Easter but is not bestowed until after Easter; this is the Johannine way of showing the distinctive difference the resurrection made for the life of faith.

By linking the work of the Spirit with the Johannine understanding of victorious faith, the preacher can expound this text both by looking back to Easter and by looking forward to Pentecost.

John 15:9–17

It may be helpful to the preacher to review the introductory comments on John 15:1–8 for last Sunday before moving to verses 9–17. Again, the difficulty of identifying units without violating the integrity of a passage or wresting it wrongfully from its context is with us. However, it seems safe to say that today's lection consists of two parts: verses 9–11 center on the expression "abide in my love"; verses 12–17 are a distinct unit in that they form an inclusion, a literary form in which the beginning and the ending are the same. In both verse 12 and verse 17 the disciples are commanded to "love one another." A case can be made, however, for treating these two subunits together in that the same key words occur throughout and verses 12–17 seem to be an elaboration on the theme of verses 9–11. We will approach the passage by attending to the key terms within it: abide, love, joy, commandment, friends.

The departing Christ, who has promised not to leave his disciples orphaned (14:18), bridges the distance between himself glorified in God's presence and the church on earth. The key word is "abide," which we explored in last Sunday's lection. The word characterizes a relationship of trust, knowledge, love, and unity that exists between Christ and God. While on earth Christ was able to remain or to abide in God from whom he came. In the same way, the disciples will be able to abide in Christ even after he has returned to God. Abiding in Christ and in Christ's love (vv. 9–10) is similar to Paul's characterization of life "in Christ Jesus" (Phil. 2:5). The love of Christ is the arena, the sphere, the location of Christian living.

To be understood here, "love" (*agapē*) has to overcome the many popular overuses and misuses of the word. The word here does not primarily represent a feeling, nor is it a synonym for "like." To love is to be *for* another and to act *for* another, even at cost to oneself. The supreme act of love is the giving of one's life for the other (v. 13). The primary canon by which love for one another is measured is God's love for the world (3:16) and Christ's love, which carried out in full and final obedience that love of God.

To live in the world and yet within the constancy of this love is to know the joy (v. 11) of which Christ speaks. This joy has its source in God, whose presence is sometimes described as joy. ("Enter into the joy of your [Lord]," Matt. 25:21, 23; "the joy . . . set before him," Heb. 12:2.) Given the hatred and hostility of the world (vv. 18–25), this word of assurance enables the church not simply to survive but to flourish in fullness of life.

The word "commandment," frequent in these farewell discourses and also in today's Epistle (1 John 5:1–6), needs special attention for two reasons.

First, this Gospel actually contains surprisingly little moral or ethical instruction such as we find in Matthew. What are the commandments to which Jesus refers (v. 10)? He kept God's commandments, and we are to keep Christ's. It is best not to rush to another Gospel to find a few commandments to put to the people. For this Evangelist, it is enough to say that we have the model of Jesus, who came to do God's will, which he obeyed even to death (v. 10), and that the one clearly stated commandment in the discourse is to love one another. The writer apparently understands that this command includes and fulfills all others. What that means in each given situation can be known by those who abide in God's love and who are taught by the Spirit (14:26).

The second reason the word "commandment" needs attention is that it is repeatedly associated with love, not only as the motivation for keeping the commandment, but as the very content of the commandment. We do not easily associate love or friendship with command (v. 14). For many of us, love and friendship lie in the feelings, and no one can command feeling; we do not even command our own. But it is helpful to recall that love in this Gospel is not a feeling; rather, it is being for the other person and acting accordingly. Emotions are not absent, of course, but neither are they central.

And what about friends? Do friends obey (v. 14)? It is servants who obey. In what sense are disciples no longer servants (v. 15)? Certainly not in the sense that they have graduated from doing for others what love dictates. There is no upward mobility in the kingdom; otherwise, the footwashing by Jesus and the frequent reminder that a servant is not greater than the master (12:26; 13:16; 15:20) would be meaningless. Followers of Jesus are the friends of Jesus in that they know what he is doing (v. 15). Jesus has made God known to them. From this context, Jesus' followers make their prayers, asking what they will because what they will is bathed in the knowledge and love of God (vv. 7, 16). But let the church beware: wherever a strong sense of community ("our church is like a family") prevails, elitism and exclusivism can creep in and make outsiders of everyone else.

Finally, notice how all these significant terms—love, abiding, obedience, friendship, and joy—are set within an order of continuity. The sequence—from God, through Christ, to the church—is clear and vital. In case anyone missed the point, Jesus consolidates it in a statement that both assures and warns the church: "You did not choose me but I chose you. And I appointed you" (v. 16).

Ascension of the Lord

Acts 1:1–11;
Psalm 47 or Psalm 93;
Ephesians 1:15–23;
Luke 24:44–53

All of the readings, in one way or another, relate to ascension or heavenly exaltation. The first lesson is the Lukan account of the Lord's ascension, a narrative way of theologizing about the Lord's departure. In Psalm 47, an enthronement psalm, reference is made to God's ascension (v. 5) and exaltation (v. 9), which makes it a natural psalm to read on the occasion of celebrating Christ's ascension. Similarly exalted tones are also present in the alternate psalm, Psalm 93. The magisterial tone of the epistolary reading underscores Christ's ascension from a different perspective, with repeated emphasis on his exaltation "in the heavenly places" (Eph. 1:20). The Gospel reading is the final section of Luke's Gospel, with its cryptic reference to Christ's ascension (v. 51).

Acts 1:1–11

Of the many New Testament passages that speak of Christ's ascension, this narrative account by Luke is the most descriptive. Among the Gospels, Matthew contains no tradition relating to the Ascension, nor does Mark in its first edition. A later supplement to Mark notes, "So then the Lord Jesus, after he had spoken to them, was taken up [*anelemphthe*] into heaven and sat down at the right hand of God" (Mark 16:19). The Fourth Gospel anticipates the Lord's ascension, but makes no attempt to record it (John 3:13; 6:62; 20:17). The fact that the risen Lord instructs Thomas to touch him seems to imply that he had already ascended (20:27; cf. 20:17). Luke alone of the Gospel writers provides a narrative account of the Lord's ascension, in fact records it twice, once at the end of the Gospel (Luke 24:50–53; cf. also 9:51) and here at the beginning of Acts (1:2, 6–11, 22).

Oddly, the two Lukan accounts are discrepant. In the Gospel account, the Ascension occurs on Easter Sunday, as do all the events recorded in Luke 24, whereas in Acts 1 it appears to occur at the end of a forty-day period of appearances by the risen Lord (1:3). To be sure, the account in Acts is not clear on this point. It may very well imply that Christ, having ascended on Easter Sunday, at various times appeared from heaven to the disciples, though the narrative seems to suggest that the Ascension took place at the end of the forty-day period. The early church recognized these difficulties, as seen by the complicated textual tradition relating to Luke 24:50–53 and Acts 1:6–11.

Within other strata of the New Testament, the tradition of Christ's ascension is known, though variously conceived. Quite often, the resurrection of Christ and his ascension are conceived as a single "exaltation," with no clear attempt made to differentiate them as separate events (cf. Rom. 1:4; 10:6; Phil. 2:9; Eph. 4:8–10; 1 Pet. 3:22; Heb. 4:14; 7:26; esp. 1 Tim. 3:16).

In Lukan theology, however, resurrection and ascension begin to be regarded as separate stages of Christ's exaltation (cf. Acts 2:32–33). Psalm 110 becomes crucial in early Christian interpretations of Christ's exaltation, as do other enthronement psalms (cf. the Psalter reading for today). This theological separation thus is expressed in narrative form in Luke 24 and Acts 1. The historical development of the celebration of Ascension Day as a separate feast day may be regarded as a legitimate liturgical expression of the tendency we already detect within the New Testament itself.

Even though the ascension of Christ is given separate treatment in Luke-Acts, it is striking how restrained Luke's narrative description is. Compared with later apocryphal accounts, such as that found in the apocryphal Gospel of Peter, Luke's account is "unsentimental, almost uncannily austere" (Haenchen).

Today's text falls into two parts: (1) the preface (vv. 1–5), which recalls the earlier preface in the Gospel of Luke (Luke 1:1–4) and (2) the account of the Ascension (vv. 6–11).

The Preface. Several features should be noted here: (1) the reference to the beginning of the ministry of Jesus (cf. Luke 3:23; Acts 1:22; 10:37); (2) the risen Lord's commandment through the Holy Spirit to the apostles whom he had chosen (cf. Matt. 28:20); (3) the emphasis on the risen Lord as "living" (*zonta*, v. 3) after his passion; (4) his appearances during forty days (cf. Acts 13:31), during which he preached the kingdom of God (cf. Acts 28:31); (5) his table fellowship with the disciples (taking verse 4 as "while at table with them," NJB, as opposed to "staying," NRSV and REB; cf. Luke 24:30); (6) his charge not to depart from Jerusalem, which was to be the center of the messianic ingathering (cf. Isa. 2:2–4); and (7) his promise of the coming Holy Spirit (cf. Luke 3:16 and parallels; also Acts 11:16), the sign of the dawn of the messianic era (cf. Joel 2:28–32).

The Ascension. The account of the Ascension actually includes the previous conversation in verses 6–8, and in a sense the sequel in verses 12–14, where we are told, incidentally, that the Ascension occurred on the Mount of Olives (cf. Luke 19:29; 21:37; also Zech. 14:4). Especially noteworthy here are the following: (1) the disciples' question concerning the restoration of the kingdom of Israel (v. 6; cf. Matt. 17:11; Mal. 4:5; also Acts 3:21), indicating their persistent concern with apocalyptic timetables (cf. Luke 9:27; 17:20; 19:11; 21:31; 24:21); (2) the risen Lord's disallowance of eschatological speculation (v. 7; cf. Matt. 24:36 and parallels); (3) the promise of power (cf. 1 Thess. 1:5; Rom. 15:19) and the outpouring of the Holy Spirit (cf. Acts 2; also Isa. 32:15); (4) the disciples' future role as witnesses (cf. Luke 24:48; Acts 1:22; 5:32; John 15:26–27; 1 Pet. 5:1); (5) the prediction of the universal spread of the kingdom, which provides the geographical outline of the Book of Acts: Judea (Acts 8:1; 9:31; 11:29; 26:20; 28:21); Samaria (Acts 8:5, 9, 14; 15:3; also Luke 9:52); the ends of the earth (Acts 28; also cf. Isa. 49:6).

The Ascension is described in an unadorned fashion, though with some Old Testament reminiscences (cf. 2 Kings 2:11; also Prov. 30:4; Deut. 30:12; Bar. 3:29; 4 Esdras 4:8; Wis. of Sol. 18:15–19; 1 Enoch 39:3). We are simply told that "a cloud took him out of their sight" (v. 9; cf. 1 Thess. 4:17; Rev. 11:12). Two men (cf. Luke 24:4; also 2 Macc. 3:26) clad in white (cf. Mark 9:3; 16:5; John 20:12; 2 Macc. 11:8) calmly provide the proper interpretation: the ascended Lord will return in similar fashion (v. 11; cf. Luke 21:27).

The way in which Luke describes the Lord's ascension is in itself instructive—and suggestive. He is less interested in the event as a personal event the disciples experienced than as an event they witnessed as the church's representatives. It sets the stage for the birth and growth of the church. We should also note the almost matter-of-fact way in which the event is depicted, with special attention to the disallowance of eschatological speculation. The risen Lord says no to the disciples' eagerness to talk about the restoration of the kingdom and to establish a calendar date for the ways of God. They are instructed instead to wait—then to be empowered by the Holy Spirit and go about their appointed business as witnesses to the Easter faith. The business of eager disciples may be to wait patiently, hope realistically, and learn to live with the long duration begun with the Lord's ascension, knowing that eventually he will return.

Psalm 47

In the church's life, Psalm 47 has traditionally been associated with Christ's ascension primarily because of the psalm's emphasis on God's ascension in verse 5 and the reference to exaltation in verse 9. As one of the enthronement psalms, Psalm 47 speaks of Yahweh's enthronement and his rule over the nations of the world. Thus it forms an appropriate lection to be used in conjunction with the opening section of Acts, which reports the ascension of Jesus.

This psalm probably had its original usage in the Jerusalem cult, when once a year God was reenthroned and proclaimed as king. In this ceremony, the ark, representing the Deity, was carried out of the temple and then returned to symbolize God's reentry. While the ark was away from the sanctuary, the temple underwent ritual cleansing (see Lev. 16).

This psalm, a hymn sung about God, may be divided into three sections based on the content of the passages. Verses 1–4 are a call to praise God and give reasons for such praise. Emphasis is placed on Yahweh as a great king who rules over the world but who in a special way looks after Israel, the chosen people, by giving them dominion over others. Verse 4 stresses the special character of Israel; but this emphasis on Israel's particularity and election, however, is clearly set within a context proclaiming Yahweh king of the whole created order and thus places it within a universal perspective. The call for the people to clap and shout refers to the noise and jubilation that accompanied the acclamation of a new king (see 2 Kings 11:12), in this case, Yahweh as the reenthroned monarch.

The second section, verses 5–7, stresses the actual enthronement of Yahweh. Verse 5 clearly refers to the going up of Yahweh to assume his position as king. The divine ascension to the Holy of Holies, where God was enthroned, was accompanied by human shouts and the blowing of trumpets, as was the case at royal coronations. Five times the call goes out: "praise him," the king, the king of the earth. Pilgrims and participants in the festival must have celebrated with joy the reestablishment of Yahweh as king and judge over the world.

The third section, verses 8–9, speaks of Yahweh's reign as king. The "princes of the peoples" probably denotes foreign representatives who may have been present in Jerusalem to participate in the official ceremony. Even so, the psalm seems to have an eschatological flavor to it in that it talks about conditions that have not yet been fully attained, such as the universal rule of Yahweh and the participation of leaders from other nations in his worship.

In like manner, the ascension of Jesus is depicted as his exaltation to universal rule, but a rule that has not yet been fully realized.

Psalm 93

Psalm 93 was probably used originally as part of the fall festival (the Feast of Tabernacles). During the festival, there was a declaration and celebration of God's reenthronement as king. Thus the opening line of the psalm can be translated, "The LORD [Yahweh] has become king"; that is, Yahweh has resumed and reasserted God's role as king of the world and, like an earthly king, is dressed in regal robes.

The content of the psalm moves from the kingship of God to the theme of creation. The kingship of God is manifest in the establishment of the world. In establishing the world, God's throne and divine rule are simultaneously secured (vv. 1–2). This idea of the divine establishment and permanence of the world seems to modern persons a rather insignificant concept. For the ancients it certainly was not, for to them the world was far more uncertain, unknown, and threatening than it is now. In the rhythm of the seasons, people experienced the regularity of nature; but in disease, drought, distress, and death, the ancients experienced life and the world in enigmatic terms. To confess and believe that God had founded the world meant that God's will was seen as the basis of the natural order and that life and the world were under divine control and thus possessed an order and rationality. People could therefore live with a certain sense of "at-homeness" in the world and with confidence in the world's operations.

Psalm 93:3–4 proclaims God's rule over chaos and anarchy. Yahweh is mightier than the floods, mightier than the thunders of many waters, and mightier than the waves of the sea. The imagery of waters, waves, floods, and the sea has its roots in general Near Eastern thought. In Mesopotamia, where the lands were subject to periodic floods, it was believed that cosmic order and structures ruled over and were created out of turbulent waters. These waters and the depths they represented embodied the constant threat of chaos, just as they had at the beginning of creation. In Canaanite religion, the god Baal had to fight and defeat the chaotic waters personified in the god Sea. (Note that it is the sea which God splits to allow the Hebrews to leave Egypt; Exod. 14.) After his defeat of Sea, Baal was acclaimed king of the gods, and a house or palace was constructed for him. Much of this Near Eastern imagery has been applied to Yahweh in Psalm 93. It is Yahweh who establishes the earth and against whom chaotic powers may struggle but over whom they cannot triumph.

The last verse of the psalm is short and terse and has often stumped interpreters. The decrees referred to are probably best understood as the laws established by God to regulate creation. These decrees find reflection in the opening chapter of Genesis, where God is depicted as regulating the orders of creation (see also Gen. 8:22). The idea that God has set bounds and limits to creation occurs in Jeremiah 5:22–24, where the prophet compares the regularity and obedience of the "natural world" with the disobedience of Israel. Elsewhere the prophet compares the permanence of the fixed orders of creation to the eternal character of God's love (see Jer. 31:35–36).

Just as God created laws to regulate human life and institutions, so also God ordained decrees and laws by which the created order operates. The reference to the house of God in verse 5 probably does not refer to the earthly temple but instead refers to God's heavenly abode or to the world of creation itself. Just as on earth, cosmic order and holiness befit the house of God. What establishes divine order in the cosmos (vv. 1–2) and subdues the powers of chaos (vv. 3–4) are God and the divine decrees (v. 5).

Ephesians 1:15–23

I f Luke's narrative description of the Lord's ascension in today's first reading is restrained, this magnificent prayer from the opening chapter of Ephesians bursts through all restraint in its depiction of the exalted status of the risen Lord. Like the first part of the prayer (vv. 3–5), this section has participles piled on top of one another and abounds in superlatives. It is a richly textured passage and should be read magisterially, for this is the tone and mood intended by the author. In keeping with the mood of triumph and glory of Ascension Day, this passage sketches the triumph of Christ's exaltation on a truly cosmic scale, in keeping with the rest of the outlook in the Epistle.

The text opens with a reference by the author to the readers' "faith in the Lord Jesus and . . . love toward all the saints" (v. 15). This couplet is reminiscent of earlier epistolary lections from First John that similarly single out these two fundamental realities of Christian faith (cf. 1 John 3:23; 5:1 and comments on the epistolary lections for the Fourth and Sixth Sundays of Easter).

The remarks are part of the author's thanksgiving: "I do not cease to give thanks for you" (v. 16). One should compare other epistolary thanksgivings (cf. Col. 1:3–4, 9; also Rom. 1:8–9; Philem. 4–5). What follows in verses 17–23, however, constitutes the author's prayer in behalf of the readers.

The prayer resists neat outlining, but does exhibit distinct emphases in its two halves. In the first part (vv. 17–19), the focus is on the ways God can illuminate and enrich the hearts and minds of the readers. In the second part (vv. 20–23), which in one sense is merely a continuation of the first request, the emphasis shifts to the figure of Christ, so that it becomes a majestic statement of his exalted status.

The Prayer for the Readers (vv. 17–19). Appropriately, the prayer opens by referring to "the God of our Lord Jesus Christ, the Father of glory" (cf. 1:3; also Acts 7:2; Rom. 6:4). The prayer is that God may give the readers a spirit of wisdom (cf. Isa. 11:2; Wis. of Sol. 7:7) and a spirit of revelation (cf. 1 Cor. 14:6), or as the REB says, "spiritual gifts of wisdom and vision." With these spiritually bestowed gifts, there would come true and full knowledge of Christ (cf. Col. 1:9–10). It is also hoped that this illumination would be genuinely "eye-opening," as in the words of the REB, "that your inward eyes may be enlightened" (cf. Matt. 6:22 and parallels). With such inward illumination will come true knowledge of the Christian hope to which they are called (cf. 4:4, Col. 1:5, 27). This includes realizing the "riches of his glorious inheritance" (cf. 3:16; also Rom. 9:23; 10:12; 11:33; Col. 1:27; Phil. 4:19) and the nature and extent of their legacy (cf. Col. 1:12; 3:24; also Acts 20:32; 26:18; Heb. 9:15; 1 Pet. 1:4; Deut. 33:3–4; Wis. of Sol. 5:5). In addition, they are called on to recognize the vast resources of power at work within them (cf. 3:20; Col. 1:11; 2:12; also 2 Cor. 13:4; Isa. 40:26; Dan. 4:30). The source of this power at work within believers is, of course, God, who has already unleashed this force in raising Jesus from the dead. It is at this point that the focus of the prayer shifts to Christ himself.

The Position of the Exalted Christ (vv. 20–23). The supreme demonstration of divine power occurred in Christ's resurrection (cf. Rom. 4:24; 10:9; 1 Pet. 1:21). As already noted in the comments on today's first reading, we detect the first signs of a two-stage distinction between Christ's resurrection and ascension: (1) God raised him from the dead and (2) made him sit at his right hand (v. 20). The latter stage is being interpreted in the light of the enthronement of Yahweh (Ps. 110:1). Distinctive is the description of the location of his reign: "in the heavenly realms (REB; cf. 2:6), which is reminiscent of the fourfold occurrence of "into heaven" in

Acts 1:6–11. But Christ's universal dominion is phenomenally extensive here: "far above all government and authority, all power and dominion" (REB; cf. 2:2; 3:10; 6:12; also Col. 1:13, 16; 2:10, 15; cf. Rom. 8:38; 1 Cor. 15:24; 1 Pet. 3:22; Heb. 2:5; 2 Pet. 2:11). Moreover, it exceeds the authority of every other name before which one might conceivably do homage (cf. Phil. 2:9–10). Not only is the reign cosmic; it is eschatological, extending from this age to the coming age (cf. Rom. 8:38, "nor things present, nor things to come"). Employing the language of Psalm 8:6, the author attributes to God the subjection of all things to the dominion of Christ (cf. Matt. 28:18–20; also Dan. 7:14; Rev. 12:10). In this position, Christ is "head" over all things (4:15; 5:23; Col. 1:18; 2:10, 19; also 1 Cor. 11:3), most notably the church, his body (cf. 4:12; Rom. 12:5; Col. 1:18, 24; 2:19), in which position he embodies the very fullness of God (v. 23; 3:19; 4:10, 13; Col. 1:19; 2:9–10; 3:11; also John 1:16; Jer. 23:24).

This epistolary lection and the reading from Acts give two angles of vision on Christ's ascension: one in narrative form; the other in highly theologized form, though no poorer in its imagery. Although this epistolary lection grants the believers unique privileges in understanding the mystery of the faith, it does not extend the language of exaltation to the believers themselves, as is the case in the later verses (2:6–7). Because some traditions of the celebration of Ascension Day emphasize not only Christ's ascension but that of believers as well, it may be that the preacher will want to juxtapose 1:15–23 and 2:1–10 in order to include this dimension. As Chrysostom said, "Through the mystery of the Ascension we, who seemed unworthy of God's earth, are taken up into heaven. . . . Our very nature, against which Cherubim guarded the gates of Paradise, is enthroned today high above all Cherubim" (*Hom. in Ascens.*, PG, 50, 444).

Luke 24:44–53

That Jesus Christ is Lord, seated at the right hand of God, is an affirmation found frequently in the New Testament, often framed on the declaration of Psalm 110:1: "The LORD says to my lord: 'Sit at my right hand until I make your enemies your footstool.'" Less frequent, however, is the expression of the lordship of Christ in the form of an ascension story. The narrative in Acts 1:1–11 is the most complete, but in the Gospel lection for today reference to Christ's ascension is made.

Luke 24:44–53 continues the Lukan resurrection narrative (24:1–53). A review of the comments on Luke 24:13–49 for Easter Evening will set our verses for today in context. The two parts to verses 44–53 are instruction, commission, and promise (vv. 44–49), and blessing, departure, and waiting (vv. 50–53). In verses 44–49, several Lukan themes are stated and are central to the entire Luke-Acts presentation of Christ and the church. One such theme is the continuity of Jesus' mission with that of Israel. What the risen Jesus is saying is what the pre-resurrection Jesus said, and these teachings are totally congruous with the Old Testament (v. 44). Luke has repeatedly stressed this point (2:21–40; 4:16–30; 24:25–27; 24:44–45). The death and resurrection of Jesus and the proclamation of the gospel to all peoples were in the plan of God revealed in the Hebrew Scriptures and do not constitute a new departure following the failure of previous efforts. However, it is the risen Christ who enables this understanding of Scripture (v. 45; see also at vv. 25–27). Given this perspective, Luke insists that the Scriptures are sufficient to generate and to sustain faith (16:27–31). A second theme is the universality of God's offer of repentance and forgiveness of sins (v. 47). Luke made this point as early as the presentation of the infant Jesus in the temple (2:29–32), and Jesus placed it on his agenda at the opening of his ministry in Nazareth (4:16–30). Of course, both the commission (Acts 1:8) and its fulfillment in the proclamation to the nations (Acts 2:1–36) are central to Luke's second volume. And just as justification by grace through faith is the gospel for Paul, for Luke it is repentance and forgiveness of sins, another theme.

An additional theme in verses 44–49 lies in the command to the disciples to stay in Jerusalem until they receive "power from on high" (v. 49). Jerusalem is the center from which the word of the Lord is to go to the nations (Isa. 2:3), whereas Mark 16:1–18 and Matthew 28:10, 16–20 focus upon Galilee as the place of the risen Christ's reunion with the disciples. For Luke here and throughout Acts, Jerusalem is the center of Christian mission. However, that activity has to wait on the outpouring of the Holy Spirit (v. 49; Acts 1:8). Without the Holy Spirit, they would not be able to take the gospel beyond the comfort zone of Israel to all the nations of the world.

The second portion of our lection, verses 50–53, relates very briefly the departure of Jesus from the disciples on whom he has pronounced his blessing. The manuscript evidence for the phrase "and was carried up into heaven" (v. 51) is mixed and debated, but if it is absent here, the account appears quite fully in Acts 1:9–11. The disciples return to Jerusalem and to the temple in particular. For Luke's story both of Jesus and of the church, the temple in Jerusalem is important (Luke 2:22–38, 41–51; Acts 2:46–3:1; 22:17). The disciples' waiting for the Holy Spirit was in joy, praise (vv. 52–53), and constant prayer (Acts 1:14). The reader of Luke is now ready for volume two, Acts.

Seventh Sunday of Easter

Acts 1:15–17, 21–26;
Psalm 1;
1 John 5:9–13;
John 17:6–19

As the season of Easter draws to a close and we move toward Pentecost, the lectionary readings become concerned with transitions. In the first lesson, we have Luke's account of the replacement of Judas by Matthias, hence the reconstitution of the Twelve as preparation for the events of Pentecost. The Gospel reading, part of Jesus' farewell discourse, anticipates his departure and the effects it will have on the disciples left behind; consequently, it expresses explicit concern for their care and protection in his absence. The epistolary reading is not as directly concerned with passing the torch, but does locate eternal life in the ever-present Son of God. The psalm, which serves to introduce the entire Psalter, draws contrasting profiles between the righteous and the wicked.

Acts 1:15–17, 21–26

The omission of verses 18–20 in today's reading from Acts serves to bracket the place of Judas in the larger text; it is unfortunate, for this is one of the more intriguing features of the passage. This definition of the pericope serves to direct our attention to the selection of Matthias and the reconstitution of the Apostolate.

Even so, we should note that the tradition of Judas' death preserved by Luke has its own character, differing substantially from Matthew, who reports that Judas died by hanging (Matt. 27:3–10; influenced by Zech. 11:12; Jer. 18:2–3; 19:1–2; 32:6–15). According to the tradition preserved in Luke, Judas died ignominiously: "falling headlong, he burst open in the middle and all his bowels gushed out" (v. 18). This version has also been influenced by the Old Testament (cf. Num. 5:21–22, 27; Ps. 109:18; 69:23–24). In this respect, Judas' bitter end is typical of those in Luke's story who vainly sought to obstruct the ways of God (e.g., Herod, Acts 12:2–23; Ananias and Sapphira, Acts 5:1–11).

The behavior of Judas obviously created a major problem for the earliest Christians. The betrayal is a firmly entrenched part of the passion narrative in all the Gospels (cf. Mark 14:43–50; Matt. 26:47–56; 27:3–10; Luke 22:47–53; John 18:2–12), even though the motives for his actions are variously treated. Matthew and Luke connect him with the "potter's field," a cemetery for strangers (cf. Matt. 27:9–10; Acts 1:19). Of all the Gospel writers, Matthew is the kindest to Judas; he confesses his sin ("I have sinned by betraying innocent blood," Matt. 27:4), returns the money, and hangs himself—the quintessential expression of remorse (Matt. 27:5). For Luke, Judas' actions were a divine necessity (Acts 1:16), and he was thus an unwitting instrument in bringing God's purposes to fulfillment.

But it is less the fate of Judas than the choice of his successor that accounts for the placement of this episode here, immediately prior to Pentecost. The beginning of the messianic community cannot be told until the nucleus of that community, the Twelve, is reconstituted. Theirs is, after all, an eschatological role (cf. Luke 22:30), and the Apostolate occupies a special place in Luke's theology. He does, of course, use the term "apostle" in a nontechnical sense (Acts 14:4, 14), but except for this he mostly confines the role of apostle to the Twelve (cf. Luke 6:12–16). As today's text shows, the Twelve serve as the vital link between the risen Lord and the church; they guarantee the tradition of the earthly ministry of Jesus "from the baptism of John until the day when he was taken up from us" (Acts 1:22). As such, they become the witnesses to the resurrection (Acts 2:32; 3:15; 4:33; 5:32; 10:41; 13:31).

Because of the theological importance Luke attaches to the reconstitution of the Twelve, he tells the story to make two points especially: (1) Scripture was fulfilled, both with respect to the fate of Judas (vv. 16, 20) and the choice of his successor (v. 20); and (2) the choice was God's doing (vv. 24–25). Luke thus succeeds in preparing the way for the breaking in of the eschatological age. Events have worked out according to divine necessity, and the omniscient God (v. 24; cf. 15:8; Luke 16:15) has taken the last necessary step in bringing about the divine will. Today's first reading serves as the natural prelude to Pentecost. As such, it continues to illustrate the Lukan outlook, with its emphasis on promise-fulfillment and the importance attached to the Twelve as the witnesses to the faith and the guarantors of the apostolic tradition. As the narrative of Acts unfolds, the Israel of the Jerusalem temple is gradually supplanted by the eschatological Israel, which includes both Jews and Gentiles. As Acts shows, such a new reality can only be understood as the work of the Spirit.

Psalm 1

The opening psalm of the Psalter contrasts two types of persons, two ways of life, and two sets of consequences for human behavior. The contrast is between the blessed (v. 1), or the righteous (v. 5), and the wicked. The idea of humans being confronted with two ways or types of life between which one must choose is a very common motif in the literature and wisdom of many cultures.

The blessed person is defined first negatively and then positively (vv. 1–2). Negatively, the person does not walk, stand, or sit (note the graduations of action from the less impersonal to the more personal) in the advice (counsel) of the wicked, in the way of sinners, or in the seat of scoffers (again note the movement from the more general to the more specific). Perhaps the writer also expressed gradations in the terms used for the unrighteous: the wicked (guilty of a particular charge), the sinners (those constantly missing the mark and deviating from the acceptable), and the scoffers (the self-sufficient and haughty who ridicule). Positively, the blessed person is one who delights in and meditates on the law of God. That is, the one blessed in life is the one who knows the Torah, the way, the instruction of the Lord, and delights in what is found there.

The righteous person becomes like a tree transplanted by ever-flowing streams so that its yield and growth are predictable (v. 3). A similar image is found in Jeremiah 17:5–8. As a tree located by the waters naturally grows and yields its fruit, so does the person who contemplates and lives by the law, which is considered here to be good and beneficial.

The description of the wicked suggests a picture opposite to that of the righteous. Unlike the firmly anchored tree, the wicked are described as chaff that is driven whichever way the wind blows. The imagery is a familiar one used elsewhere in the Bible. The chaff of wheat and other grains is lighter than the grain heads and is blown farther away than the grain when both are tossed into the wind together at the threshing floor. The wicked, like the chaff, are persons without much presence or substance. Because of the behavior of the wicked, they will have no weight, influence, or respect in the place of judgment. When persons meet to decide a course of action or to determine guilt or innocence, the wicked will have no place there (v. 5). The way of the righteous is said to be known or protected by God, whereas the wicked are simply left to perish.

1 John 5:9–13

Standing at the end of Easter, we look back at a period of extended celebration centered in the heart of the Christian faith: the conviction that after Jesus died he came to experience life in an unprecedented and unique manner. This form of renewed, transformed life the New Testament calls "resurrection." This is to be distinguished from the various ways first-century people understood revivification, and certainly it meant far more than that Jesus "lived on" in his deeds and words in the memory of his disciples.

The Johannine way of expressing this utterly new and different reality is "eternal life" (*zoe aionios*). Already in the Fourth Gospel, we are introduced to this understanding of life (3:15–16, 36; 6:40, 47; 10:10, 28; 11:25–26; 20:31). It is that which God, the Father, embodies (5:26*a*), and by extension comes to be embodied in the Son (5:26*b*), who was begotten of the Father. Receiving it, or coming to share in this extraordinary life, is predicated on believing and trusting in the Son (3:15). In no way should this life, so conceived, be understood merely as an extension of biological existence as we know it here; rather, it transcends our ordinary experience of life in that it is qualitatively different from human existence as we know it.

Accordingly, experiencing it is not postponed until after we die; by believing fully in the Son we are thrust into this "eternal life" here and now. We may be said to "have" eternal life—now (3:36; 6:47; esp. 5:24). There is, nevertheless, a future aspect. Through faith, we experience "eternal life" now, yet it is our human fate to die. But believing in the Son of God means that we are able to transcend even this form of death: "Those who believe in me, even though they die, will live" (11:25).

This is what is presupposed in our text today when it says: "And this is the testimony: that God gave us eternal life, and this life is in his Son. Whoever has the Son has life; whoever does not have the Son of God does not have life" (5:11–12). Earlier in the passage the phrase "the testimony of God" is to be understood as "the testimony that comes from God, or which God has given" (subjective genitive).

As the Fourth Gospel shows, the form of this witness has been channeled through the incarnate Logos, God's Son, whose own words and deeds are themselves God's own revelation to us (cf. John 5:19–47). Were this revelation merely an oracle from heaven, it could little be heeded. But it is more than that, because it is substantiated by the incarnate Logos, whose historical existence was seen, heard, and experienced—by John the Baptist, the "testimony of men" (v. 9: cf. John 5:36), by the apostolic witness that became embodied in the confession of faith (cf. 5:5; also 2:22–23; 4:2), and, perhaps as important, by the community of faith: "Those who believe in the Son of God have the testimony in their hearts" (v. 10a). In addition to these, or rather through all of these, the Spirit has born witness, and through this witness truth has been revealed (5:7).

This, then, is what the author is asking his readers to believe and continue to accept: extraordinary, transcendent life given by God in and through the Son to those who believe. The passage ends on a note of reassurance: "I write these things . . . that you may know that you have eternal life" (v. 13).

This is the faith of Easter.

John 17:6–19

Today is the last Sunday of Easter prior to Pentecost. Easter is fulfilled in Pentecost. A church without Pentecost cannot shout "He is risen" loudly enough to sustain Easter week after week. Inevitably, there comes the post-Easter slump, the special efforts to keep attendance up, and the growing cynicism of ministers complaining about those who worship only at Christmas and Easter. Luke says that Easter is not only shouting but waiting in prayer for the coming Spirit. John says that Easter is also listening to Jesus pray for us (chap. 17).

As stated in previous lessons, John 14–17 is farewell material. Jesus is returning to God, leaving behind disciples who are confused, afraid, and forlorn. Chapter 17, although in the form of a prayer, really belongs to the discourses. Prayers of Jesus in this Gospel are sermonic (11:42; 12:30), and therefore the readers of 17:1–26 are as a congregation overhearing a pastoral prayer. We are not directly addressed, but we are very much in the mind of the One who is praying. The prayer is of the Christ who is already ascending (vv. 11–13). In this sense, it is uttered between earth and heaven, a prayer both of the historical Jesus and the glorified Christ.

The prayer comes to us in a noticeably stylized form with poetic qualities. Although scholars differ as to the transitional points within the prayer, a case can be made for a threefold division: Jesus asks to return to God (vv. 1–5); Jesus intercedes for his disciples (vv. 6–19); Jesus intercedes for the readers of the Gospel who are believers at least once removed (vv. 20–26). Our lection is Jesus' prayer for his disciples.

At first it may not seem all that important to listen to Jesus pray for the Twelve, for probably by the time this Gospel was written they were all dead. Why not concentrate on prayer for the early church and for our church? The fact is, Jesus' prayer for his disciples *is* in behalf of the church through succeeding generations, for it is vital to the life of the church to know that the revelation, the truth, from Jesus has been faithfully transmitted. In other words, can we trust the tradition we have received? Verses 6–19 say yes. The apostles were given by God to Jesus (v. 6); Jesus gave to them the word of God (vv. 6–8); they received that word, believed it, and kept it (vv. 6–8); they had not been corrupted by the world, for they were not of the world, which, in fact, hated them (vv. 9–16); even though one of them had gone astray, even that was within God's knowledge and according to Scripture (v. 12); just as Jesus had sanctified himself in total dedication to God, so were the apostles set apart (consecrated) for the truth (vv. 17–19); and the apostles had as their sole purpose the continuation of the mission that Jesus had from God (v. 18). The Evangelist has left no doubt to plague subsequent generations of believers: the church is not an orphan in the world, the creation of a religious imagination, the frightened child of huddled rumors and popular superstitions. For those who need to examine the credentials of the church's life and message, here is truth's pedigree: from God, to Christ, to the apostles, to the church.

For some of us, this line of thinking has not been a formalized part of our faith. We have done most of our singing, praying, and witnessing within a circle of believers who agreed with us before we spoke. But the church that takes seriously Christ's mission, that moves out into a world that is hostile and yet the object of God's gracious love, will be asked, and will ask itself, about the reliability of its tradition. John 17:6–19 is one response to one church that, under heavy pressure (15:18–25; 16:1–4), needed to hear this word. Next Sunday is Pentecost, a time for celebrating the charismatic dimension of the church's life. Spending this time reflecting on the tradition that has come to us from Christ himself is an excellent way to affirm and appropriate Pentecost without being caught up in its excesses and manufactured imitations.

Pentecost

Acts 2:1–21 or Ezekiel 37:1–14;
Psalm 104:24–34, 35*b*;
Romans 8:22–27 or Acts 2:1–21;
John 15:26–27; 16:4*b*–15

The central reading for this day is, of course, the one that fixes the day as Pentecost, Acts 2:1–21. The other New Testament readings concern the Spirit of God, promised as the Counselor and the Spirit of truth (John 15 and 16), and as the Spirit who helps us in our weakness (Romans 8:22–27). The special note in this regard in Psalm 104:24–34, 35*b*, a hymn of praise, concerns the power of God's Spirit to create and renew. Ezekiel 37:1–14 is also one of the texts for the Easter Vigil (see earlier commentary), and in that context its message is one of life out of death. When the passage is read on the Day of Pentecost, the emphasis will fall upon the power of the Spirit of God as a gift that enlivens the people of God.

Acts 2:1–21

With the circle of the Twelve reconstituted through the selection of Matthias (Acts 1:12–26), the nucleus of the newly constituted messianic community is in place. The time is now right for it to be legitimated, and this is done through a divine sign (of which there are many in Luke-Acts), doubly forceful because it is both audible and visible. The prophetic words cited from Joel and attributed to Peter are programmatic not only for the structuring of the Pentecost story as Luke narrates it, but for what follows in the rest of Acts. The opening words of Joel's prophecy have been altered to appropriate fully the prophetic message for Christian readers who were living "in the last days," the final period of salvation history. As God's Spirit had been poured out previously in times of rebirth and renewal, so now the birth of the newly constituted messianic community receives divine in-breathing and legitimation in similar fashion.

The prophetic message is programmatic. Major themes, which are unfolded and developed on a grand literary scale in Luke-Acts, are articulated here.

1. *The New Age as the era in which God's Spirit generates new life and expectations, but especially as it launches the rebirth of the prophetic witness.* It was widely held that the voice of the prophets had been silenced (1 Macc. 4:46). With the coming of Messiah Jesus, however, God had raised a new prophet (Acts 3:22; 7:37). Not only does Luke, throughout the Gospel,

especially portray Jesus as God's prophet (Luke 4:18–19, 24–30), but he also portrays the main characters of the formative years of the church as prophetic figures, most notably Peter (Acts 2–12) and Paul (Acts 13–28). Both are prompted and directed by the Spirit in their words and actions (e.g., 4:8; 9:17; 22:17–21).The gradual spread of the messianic movement, accordingly, is attested by "wonders and signs" (Acts 2:43; 4:30; 5:12; 6:8; 7:36; 8:13; 14:3; 15:12), Luke's way of indicating its divine legitimation.

2. *The universality of God's spiritual outpouring in the messianic kingdom.* The Spirit is promised to "all flesh" (v. 17). No longer will the messianic community be defined along ethnic lines or national boundaries. That all nations, first the Jews, then the Gentiles, are to become incorporated into the messianic community is a recurrent theme of Luke-Acts, and one that receives special treatment (cf. Acts 2:39). The vivid language of the prophecy signifies that the level of participation will be broad: young and old, men and women will participate in the excitement of the prophetic outpouring.

Quite possibly, the apocalyptic signs of verses 19–20—blood, fire, cosmic eclipses—refer to events accompanying the crucifixion (cf. Luke 22:44–45). If so, the "Lord's great and glorious day" (v. 20) most likely refers to the crucifixion itself, not to the final judgment. Consequently, this prominent theme of the eschatological day of the Lord here undergoes a major reinterpretation in light of the Christian conviction that the final, eschatological age was ushered in by the Christ-event. Consequently, with the inauguration of God's New Age through Christ's death and resurrection, the call to salvation becomes truly universal; henceforth, from the dawn of the church onward, whoever cries out to the Lord from the depths of despair will receive salvation—both Jew and Gentile.

How thoroughly the prophetic message has influenced the structure of the Lukan narrative should be noted. The detailed list of "the nations" who were present on Pentecost naturally serves to underscore the universality of the Gospel message. Accordingly, the event of Pentecost is seen to "fulfill" the words of the prophecy, and the way the narrative is structured reinforces this even more. Similarly, the opening words of the narrative, which mention the "rush of a violent wind" and the "divided tongues, as of fire," may be seen as descriptive features that also serve to fulfill the Joel prophecy. The scene as described attests the occurrence of "portents in the heaven above" and "signs on the earth below" (v. 19). The way the narrative is constructed here is typical of how Luke tells the story throughout. His narrative technique becomes an extension of his theological program of prophecy-fulfillment. By the end of the story, the attentive reader can hardly remain unconvinced that the account of God's prophet Jesus and God's people, the church, is the inexorable fulfillment of God's promise, beginning in the Old Testament and continuing in the unfolding drama.

Ezekiel 37:1–14

Ezekiel 37:1–14 is also one of the texts for the Easter Vigil, Year B (see the commentary earlier in this volume), and in that context its message is one of life out of death. When the passage is read on the Day of Pentecost, the emphasis will fall upon the power of the Spirit of God as a gift that enlivens the people of God.

Although the central point of the text is the renewal of the people of Israel, an important aspect of that message concerns the "Spirit of the Lord." The understanding of that Spirit in Ezekiel is by no means the same as the Christian doctrine of the Holy Spirit, or even the New

Testament beliefs in the Counselor, or the Spirit. However, the Hebraic view is important background for the later ones, and the prophetic text has contributions of its own to make to our reflections on the Day of Pentecost.

The same Hebrew word is used throughout the passage in several different senses. It is appropriately translated both "spirit" (vv. 1, 14) and "breath" (vv. 5, 6, 8, 9, 10). In the English translation we miss the deliberate plays on the word. These different uses in Ezekiel only touch the surface of the many ways the word (*ruach*) is used throughout the Old Testament. The spirit is associated both with the created world and with God. It is wind or breath (Job 9:18) that gives life to both human beings and animals (Gen. 6:17), or it is the "spirit" of a person in the sense of one's emotions or will (Gen. 41:8). It also refers to God's power, both as a creative force (Gen. 1:2) and as inspiring prophecy (Isa. 61:1 and often in Ezekiel).

Certainly, not all these senses are visible in Ezekiel 37, but some are. It is the Spirit of Yahweh that makes the vision possible; the breath comes like the four winds and brings— under the authority of the prophet's divinely directed words—life to the dead bones. The point of the vision report is that God can and will—through the Spirit—bring to life a community that considers itself dead.

Psalm 104:24–34, 35*b*

Psalm 104 is a hymn that praises God as the Creator of the universe and everything that is in it. In primitive encyclopedia fashion, the orders and elements of creation in the psalm are paraded forth as the works of God.

The selection of this lection for Pentecost Sunday is based on its emphasis on the role of God's Spirit in creation (see v. 30) and the psalm's universal perspectives. Verses 24–34, however, should be seen within the overall structure of the psalm.

Six realms of creation, somewhat similar to the six days of creation in Genesis 1, are described in poetic style: sky (vv. 2–4), earth (vv. 5–9), water (vv. 10–13), vegetation (vv. 14–18), moon and sun (vv. 19–23), and sea (vv. 24–26). Each of these realms and their component parts are seen as integral elements in the created order with an existence brought into being by divine power and sustained by the Creator's loving care.

Today's lection contains the descriptive praise of the sea (vv. 24–26), a hymnic statement about the dependence of all life upon God (vv. 27–30), and a final reflection on God's glory (vv. 31–34). (The omission of verse 35*a* by those producing the lectionary is probably a concession to modern tastes and sensitivities!) Except for the opening line in verse 1 and verses 31–35, all of the psalm is addressed directly to the Deity; this is unusual for hymns that generally are a genre in which the human audience addresses itself.

The section on the sea (vv. 24–26) begins with an emphasis on the diversity within the creation, yet confesses that God in divine wisdom made all and that all are creatures of the Divine—a point and a perspective we have come to learn anew in light of the modern ecological crisis. (Should one wish to do so, comparison could be made between the great diversity of the world's creatures—both small and great—and the diversity of languages and backgrounds reflected in the audience present in Jerusalem at Pentecost.)

The sea is presented as a boundless expanse of water teeming with things too numerous to count, with ships moving on its surface, and with giant monsters frolicking in its midst. Leviathan (in v. 26) appears to have been one of the names assigned to the great dragon whose slaughter, in the ancient myth, preceded the formation of the earth (see Job 7:12;

26:12; Pss. 74:13; 89:10; Isa. 51:9). Here the monster is depicted as a mere playful "critter" sporting in the water. In fact, the line mentioning Leviathan could be translated "Leviathan, which you have made to play with him." Such an interpretation of the text makes the dragon a toy of play for the Deity. In Israelite faith, the demon of old mythology has been domesticated to live at home in a world of God's creation! This psalm, like Genesis 1, certainly knows of no realm or creature beyond the reach and touch of the Creator or a realm hostile to God and the divine purposes. The psalm, in other words, presents a world in which all things—both small and great—are at home. Here is a monotheism that delights in the whole of the created order.

In verses 27–30, the psalmist offers praise to God for the gift of life itself. Life presented here is not simply existence in itself or some possession of beast and humankind, but is the consequence of the continuing and constant action of God. All living things look to God for the source of their sustenance. The continuity and character of life are seen as the consequence of God's actions: God gives, they gather; God opens his hand, they receive and are filled.

The psalmist is aware of the fragility and precariousness of life. Life is always at the will of the Divine and always in the shadow of death. Without the presence of God's face (that is, God's concern), humans are dismayed, overwhelmed; when God withdraws their breath, they return to the dust from which they were shaped. But in like fashion, the presence of God's Spirit brings creatures into being and changes the face of the ground. Thus both the good and the bad in life and in death are related to the action of the Deity.

In the doxology at the end of the psalm, verses 31–35, the psalmist expresses the wish that God may rejoice in his works; that is, that God may delight in and not destroy what his hands have made. Two thoughts, like dark portents, raise their heads and produce some doubt in the psalmist's mind. Earthquakes and volcanoes—the earth trembling and the mountains smoking—appear as the dark side of God's action. But worst of all is human sin and wickedness, which the psalmist prays will be consumed from the earth and be no more (v. 35a).

Verses 33–34 contain a vow and a request. The vow is to sing praise to God as long as life is present. Such a vow comes in the context of the mention of the dark side of creation and thus is an affirmation of faith "in spite of." In spite of the disharmonies that intrude into the created order, the psalmist affirms, "I will sing to the LORD as long as I live. . . . I rejoice." The request is that even the inner being, the meditation, of the poet be pleasing to God.

Romans 8:22–27

Today's epistolary text is one of the most profound New Testament passages dealing with the work of the Spirit within Christians. One might say that in this text Paul personalizes the outpouring of the Spirit that is presented in narrative form in Acts 2:1–21. Certainly, in celebrating the feast of Pentecost, we are able to probe Paul's words here to discern how we might appropriate the Spirit within our own lives; or, to put it more felicitously, how we might understand the way in which the Spirit works within us, even if unconsciously.

The text must be understood in the light of Paul's apocalyptic outlook. As seen in verses 18–21 and as noted in verse 22, Paul envisions that the "whole creation" (*pasa hē ktisis*) has been experiencing cosmic birth pains ("groaning in labor pains") as it metamorphoses under the impact of the Christ-event. This text is further illuminated by his remarks in 2 Corinthians 5:17: "If anyone is in Christ, there is a new creation; everything old has passed away; see, everything has become new!" Seen against the background of Paul's theology of the new creation (2 Cor.

4:1–6), in which the Christ-event was understood as an even more dramatic enactment of the creation in Genesis 1–2, this passage from Romans indicates that Paul regarded the whole cosmos as being transformed as part of the eschatological process.

That which is happening on the cosmic scale also goes on within those "in Christ": "we ourselves . . . groan inwardly while we wait for adoption" (v. 23). We do so because we have experienced the "first fruits of the Spirit" (cf. 2 Cor. 1:22; 5:5; Eph. 1:14). By being incorporated into Christ, we have already received the Spirit (8:9–11) and therefore have already tasted of the eschatological era, the dawning of the reign of God. Through the Spirit, God has reached out to us from the future, the "age to come," and allowed us to share, partially at least, in the resurrection life that Christ already experiences fully. We thus wait for our adoption as children of God, that is, as heirs of God (cf. 8:15; Gal. 4:5–6; Eph. 1:5), and for the full redemption, or transformation, of our bodies (cf. Rom. 3:24; 1 Cor. 1:30; Col. 1:14; Eph. 1:7, 14; 4:30; also Ps. 130:7; cf. also 2 Cor. 5:6–7; 4:18).

Hope is an intrinsic part of existence *en Christō*. We already experience salvation in one sense, but not fully. Hope, after all, has a built-in element of unrealization: "hope that is seen is not hope" (v. 24; cf. Heb. 11:1). As Paul says elsewhere, "For through the Spirit, by faith, we eagerly wait for the hope of righteousness" (Gal. 5:5; also Rom. 8:19; 1 Cor. 7:19). We nevertheless do so "with patience" (v. 25; also Rom. 5:1–5).

Here Paul exposes the anxiety felt by every Christian who lives in the tension between the "already" and the "not yet." Though we have begun to experience transformation, we continue to experience the agony of human existence (cf. 2 Cor. 5:2–5). It is in such weakness that our own inability to know ourselves and our own needs becomes most fully exposed: "we do not know how to pray as we ought" (v. 26). At this juncture, the Spirit steps in and "intercedes with sighs too deep for words" (v. 26).

Too sharp a distinction between the intercessory work of Christ himself and the Spirit should not be drawn (cf. Rom. 8:34; also Heb. 7:25). The lines are blurred even in Paul's own language, for earlier he spoke of the "Spirit of God" in one breath, and the "Spirit of Christ" in another (8:9). However the presence of the Spirit is conceived, what is significant here is that the very Spirit who knows us even better than we know ourselves (cf. Rev. 2:23; 1 Cor. 4:5; Ps. 139:1) intercedes for us in our weakness, and on our behalf, conforming our wills to the will of God. As Paul says earlier in this chapter, "When we cry, 'Abba! Father!' it is that very Spirit bearing witness with our spirit that we are children of God" (8:16). By recalling the very words of Jesus in Gethsemane (Mark 14:36; also Gal. 4:6), Paul suggests that the Spirit who brought about filial obedience in the will of Jesus also works within us to achieve the same quality of filial obedience, enabling us to say, in our own lives, "Abba! Father!"

Here, then, we have a profound interpretation of the work of the Spirit within the life of the Christian—the level perhaps at which the true significance of Pentecost should be experienced and understood. True, the text speaks of the cosmic work of the Spirit in bringing about the transformation of the universe as we know it, but it also speaks of the anxieties we all feel and the work of the Spirit in bringing us to genuine filial obedience.

John 15:26–27; 16:4*b*–15

Today is Pentecost—for Jews an early harvest festival that came to be also a commemoration of the giving of the law at Sinai; for Christians a celebration of the outpouring of the Holy Spirit upon the church. Luke is alone among the Gospel writers in presenting in chronological order the events of Easter, Ascension, and Pentecost, placing them on a calendar covering a fifty-day period (Acts 1–2). But Luke is not alone in witnessing to Jesus' promise of the Holy Spirit and in linking the coming of the Spirit to Jesus' departure to God's presence. The Gospel of John speaks clearly and repeatedly on this subject.

According to the Fourth Gospel, the Holy Spirit is associated with Jesus. The Spirit descended upon Jesus at his baptism (1:33), and it is Jesus who baptizes with the Holy Spirit (1:33). But according to this Evangelist, the gift of the Spirit to Jesus' followers had to wait upon Jesus' death and ascension to God (7:39). Even the word to Nicodemus about being born of the Spirit assumes the ascension of Jesus as precondition for this work of the Spirit (3:13). In other words, the resurrected, glorified Jesus would send the Spirit upon his church. This promise occupies a central place in the farewell discourses of Jesus (13:31–16:33), discourses that address the pressing question, What does the departing Christ have to say to the church he is leaving behind?

As Luke says that Easter is completed at Pentecost, so John says that the departure of Christ is relieved in its pain and fulfilled in its joy by the coming of the Holy Spirit. This is the theme of our Gospel lections for today. John 15:26–27 and 16:4b–15 contain the last three of the five Holy Spirit sayings in the farewell speeches. In the first saying, Jesus promised that the Spirit as Advocate, Comforter, or Helper would come to his followers and would dwell with them, never leaving them alone (14:16–17). In the second, Jesus promised that the Spirit would be a teacher as he had been and would bring to their remembrance all that Jesus had said to them (14:26). This theme of remembering is important here and elsewhere in the Gospels, for although there is value in rehearsals prior to events, there is also value in reflecting upon what has happened. We should not make fun of hindsight; the Christian life is to a large extent an act of memory.

To these descriptions of the work of the Spirit, today's reading adds three important statements.

1. The Spirit will bear witness to Jesus just as the apostles who shared his earthly life bear witness (15:26–27). Notice the double attestation to the truth about Jesus: the Spirit and the apostles concur. The importance of this cannot be overstated. The church is not left with only the promptings of the Spirit, opening wide the door to ecstasies, visions, mystic trances, and all sorts of nonverifiable claims by inspired speakers. Neither is it the case that the church is left with just the reports of men of antiquity. Rather, the church has both the Spirit and the tradition, and the gospel is located where these two intersect.

2. The Spirit will prove the world wrong about sin, righteousness (justice), and judgment (16:7–11). "Convict" is probably a better translation than "prove the world wrong" (v. 8), because the image is of a courtroom trial. Here the function of the Spirit is to provide the church with a true interpretation of the life, death, and significance of Jesus. In the eyes of the world, Jesus was tried, sentenced, and executed as an enemy of the state. But the Spirit, as interpreter of Jesus, enables the church to testify to what "really" was going on: in unbelief the world acted unjustly against the Christ whom God has vindicated as the judge of his judges. As Jesus interprets God, so the Spirit interprets Jesus and provides faith's reading of the story.

3. The Spirit will guide the church into all the truth and declare the things that are to come (16:12–15). This text has been used to bless every fad and notion, but the fear of the new and different must not cause the church to abandon this promise. When the church

becomes protective and defensive, the present ceases to be God's time, and preachers become curators. The Spirit continually presses the question, What is the meaning of Jesus Christ today? and leads to answers. This is not to say that the church is left prey to all who proclaim in the name of the Spirit, "Lo, here," and "Lo, there." The apostolic and biblical witness remains as a canon for testing the spirits, for the Holy Spirit does not speak apart from or contrary to the historical Jesus (vv. 12–15). Rather, the Spirit keeps the voice of Jesus a living voice in the church.

Trinity Sunday

Isaiah 6:1–8;
Psalm 29;
Romans 8:12–17;
John 3:1–17

The New Testament readings for Trinity Sunday continue from the Pentecost emphasis on the Spirit of God and at the same time call attention to the threefold nature of God. Psalm 29, a hymn of praise, celebrates the awesome power of the voice of God in the world; its final verses describing the Lord on his throne are linked directly to Isaiah's vision. Isaiah 6, because of the threefold Sanctus and the fact that God speaks in the first person plural ("Whom shall I send, and who will go for us?" v.8) has long been a classical Christian Trinitarian text.

Isaiah 6:1–8

Our reading, Isaiah's report of his call to be a prophet, is one of the most familiar in the Old Testament. For that very reason it bears careful reading and study, lest our familiarity lead us and our congregations to miss important aspects of the account. It is a strange, startling, and dramatic sequence of events that unfolds, and is stranger still if the remainder of the chapter (vv. 9–13) is added to the lection.

The location of the vocation report in the Book of Isaiah is unusual. Those of Jeremiah and Ezekiel are found more logically at the very beginning of the books. Isaiah 6 is preserved with a series of other reports and accounts, mainly concerning the prophet's activities (Isa. 6:1–9:7). Moreover, the reports appear to interrupt a previously established collection of the prophet's speeches, each concluding with the expression "For all this his anger has not turned away, and his hand is stretched out still" (see 5:25; 9:12, 17; 10:4). This collection began in 5:8 and, following the reports, is resumed in 10:1. These features of the book suggest that the material in Isaiah 6:1–9:7 probably once circulated independently among the prophet's followers before it was combined with the surrounding speeches. Thus the text before us bears the marks of various communities of faith for whom it communicated the word of God.

The calls of prophets and of other servants of God are very private and individual matters. It is all the more remarkable, therefore, to discover that Isaiah's report of his call has a great many features in common with other Old Testament vocation reports. These include the vocation accounts of Moses (Exod. 3:1–4:17), Gideon (Judg. 6:11–24), Jeremiah (Jer.

1:4–10), and Ezekiel (Ezek. 1–3). In all cases there is a report of an encounter with God, either directly or through a messenger, a commission to do the Lord's will or speak the Lord's word, and a ritual act or sign symbolizing the designated role. In all cases except Ezekiel, the one who is called objects to the vocation and then is given reassurance. The persistence of this particular feature in vocation reports indicates that the resistance to the call is not linked so much to individual personalities as it is to the experience of standing in the presence of God. It is part of the office, even verifying that one is called by God, to feel unworthy in one way or another.

In its more specific features, Isaiah 6 closely parallels Ezekiel 1–3. Both are reports of visions of the Lord's heavenly throne. Similar also is the scene described by Micaiah ben Imlah in 1 Kings 22:19–22: "I saw the Lord sitting on his throne, with all the host of heaven standing beside him. . . ." Neither Isaiah nor Ezekiel sees God directly, but both have the sense of being on the outskirts of the heavenly throne room and hearing the deliberations going on there. This Old Testament imagery is indebted to ancient Near Eastern traditions concerning the heavenly court. In those polytheistic traditions, the court includes the chief god and other deities; in the Old Testament, God holds court with his messengers (see also Job 1:6–12).

Isaiah's vocation report begins with a date formula that also sets the mood. "The year that King Uzziah died" would have been about 742 BC, but that king's death signaled the end of an era of relative independence for Judah. During most of Isaiah's lifetime, the nation lived under the threat of Assyrian domination. The prophet was active for some forty years, from the date indicated here until at least 701 BC.

But the date formula is mainly a preface to the description of the vision of Yahweh as king on a throne (vv. 1–4). The fact that "the hem of his robe" filled the temple indicates that the prophet stands at the entrance to the sacred precincts and that probably the ark was thought of as the symbolic throne of Yahweh. Other aspects of temple worship are the antiphonal hymn of praise sung by the seraphim, and the smoke, probably from offerings, which filled the "house"—that is, the temple. The seraphim who attend the Lord must cover both their "feet" (a euphemism for their nakedness) and their faces because no one can see God directly and live.

Isaiah's response to the scene is a cry of woe (v. 5) similar to a confession of sin and an expression of mourning for both himself and his people. In the presence of the Lord he knows that he is unclean, though by the priestly criteria he would have been judged ritually clean before he approached the temple. In reaction to his confession, one of the seraphim performs a ritual of purification combining word and deed. He touches Isaiah's mouth with a coal from the altar and pronounces that his guilt is removed and his sin is forgiven. This ritual parallels those in the vocation reports of both Jeremiah and Ezekiel in that all of them concern the mouth of the prophetic spokesman for God.

The vision report reaches a climax when the prophet overhears the Lord asking the heavenly court whom he shall send, and the prophet steps forward (v. 8). The remainder of the chapter, which consists of the Lord's terrible commission to the prophet to bring a word of judgment, is interrupted only by the prophet's prayer of intercession.

Viewed in the context of other vocation reports, the purpose of this account becomes clear. Frequently, the authority of prophets to speak was challenged (see Amos 7:10–17), especially if their message was one of judgment. Because prophets in Israel had no "official" standing comparable to that of, for example, priests, their right to speak in the name of the Lord was open to question. The vocation reports were their responses to such challenges. They were not only entitled but also compelled to speak because of their calls. In the case of Isaiah 6, the prophet specifically justifies his harsh message by reporting his vocation.

A great many features of this passage cry out for proclamation. There is first the emphasis on the sacred, including its cultic dimensions. In the temple Isaiah experiences the awe-inspiring presence of the Lord, is aware of his uncleanness, and is purified. The holiness of God—the radical difference between divine and human—is a persistent theme in the words of Isaiah. Second, there is the call itself and the prophet's response. God does not address Isaiah directly, but the one purified by the divine messenger is able to hear the call and accept the commission. Third, there are the specific elements of this passage related to Trinity Sunday, the threefold Sanctus and the fact that the Lord speaks in the first person plural. Neither of these is a direct allusion to the Trinity, and there is no doctrine of the Trinity as such in the Bible. Still, there are indications of the experiences that gave rise to the doctrine. God is encountered in different ways, and human language must find means to express the reality of those encounters.

Psalm 29

The themes of the lections for this Sunday are the various forms of the manifestation of God and the human responses to that manifestation. Psalm 29 focuses on the revelation of God in the awesome power of the thunderstorm.

Modern scholarship is generally agreed that this psalm probably had an origin outside Israel and was adapted for use in the Israelite cult. The psalm seems to presuppose a polytheistic background (note the reference to the sons of gods in verse 1; see NRSV note). Perhaps the text was once at home in some Phoenician setting, as is suggested by the geographical references.

The unifying phrase in the psalm is "the voice of the LORD," that is, the thunder that accompanies a severe Mediterranean rainstorm. Seven times this voice is referred to.

No doubt this psalm praises the coming and appearance of God in the first thunderstorm of the autumn rainy season. In Palestine, the summer from late May to early October is completely dry with no rainfall whatever. This summer drought is broken when clouds move in from the Mediterranean (see 1 Kings 18:41–46). The first rains moisten and soften the ground so that sowing and plowing can take place.

This psalm may be outlined as follows: the glory of God—*Gloria in Excelsis* (vv. 1–2); the gathering of the storm (vv. 3–4); the shattering onslaught of the storm (vv. 5–7); the passing and subsiding of the storm (vv. 8–9); and the peace—the *pax in terris*—that follows the storm's passage (vv. 10–11).

In the opening prelude, there is a threefold repetition of the phrase "Ascribe to the LORD." Although it is the heavenly beings that are called on to praise God, no doubt this psalm was sung in the temple worship of Jerusalem by cultic choirs. Thus the earthly worship of humans was joined to the heavenly worship of the angelic beings.

The gathering of the storm depicted in the first strophe (vv. 3–4) can be understood in the pattern of a typical Palestinian thunderstorm. The voice of God rumbles over the sea and gradually comes closer, becoming more powerful the nearer it approaches.

The second strophe (vv. 5–7) depicts the violence of the storm as it moves from the west onto the coastal mountain region, ripping at the great cedars of Lebanon. These great trees, symbolic of strength and solidity, are shattered and broken in the manifestation of God's voice. Sirion, or Mt. Hermon, whose snowcapped peaks at over nine thousand feet in height towered over and were visible throughout the region, is treated by the storm as if it were a calf or some young wild ox. Before the majesty and might of the Divine, they skip in awe and fear. Lightning that flashes forth like flames of fire accompanies the thunderous voice of God.

The third strophe (vv. 8–9) describes the dying away of the storm as it moves into the desert shaking the wilderness, whirling trees, and stripping bare the forest. The ominous presence and power of the Deity in the storm leaves nature battered, bruised, and wounded. Yet in the Lord's temple all say, "Glory!" The response to the presence of God is here described as a response of pure adoration extolled in worship.

The postlude (vv. 10–11) concludes the psalm, first, with a confession that Yahweh sits enthroned upon the flood—that is, God reigns over the chaotic waters—and rules as king forever. The violence of the thunderstorm is not seen as the unleashing of the destructive powers of the deep but as the life-giving and hope-restoring rainfall that nurtures the earth and begins a new agricultural year with all its promises and expectations of abundance. Finally, the benediction (in v. 11) asks that God give strength and peace to his people.

This psalm—which praises the presence and revelation of God not just in nature but also in one of nature's most dramatic expressions, the storm—delights in the God who displays his rule and his blessing in such momentous fashion.

Romans 8:12–17

In this passage Paul speaks of God, whom we address in prayer as "Abba! Father!" (v. 15); of Christ as God's own Son (v. 3), with whom we as children of God are fellow heirs (v. 17); and of the Spirit of God (v. 14), or alternatively, the "Spirit of Christ" (v. 9). Paul appears not to draw a sharp distinction between the Spirit of God and the Spirit of Christ, and this reminds us that Paul's language here is triadic rather than Trinitarian. He does not operate with a clearly differentiated view of the Trinity, as was the case in later Christian centuries, when elaborate efforts were made to distinguish the three members of the Godhead and to define their respective roles. Even so, we should not conclude that his understanding of the Spirit and its role in the life of the Christian was vague and undefined. Quite the contrary! Our epistolary text today attests the vitality of Paul's understanding of the Spirit. It has served as one of the most illuminating passages in Paul's writings for the way in which it clarifies the role of the Spirit in the moral life.

We should notice the sharp antithesis between "flesh" and "spirit"—a distinction Paul typically makes, indeed insists on (Gal. 5:16–25; 6:8). Earlier, he distinguishes between two opposing outlooks: the outlook of the unspiritual nature and the spiritual outlook (vv. 5–8, REB). Clearly, these are not only philosophical worldviews, but moral options, for he speaks in verse 5 of living "according to the flesh" ("on the level of the old nature," REB) and living "according to the Spirit" ("on the level of the spirit," REB).

For Paul, "flesh" is not synonymous with skin and bone. Neither is it the same as "body." Rather, it stands for that which is "human," "physical," "earthly," or that which has to do with "this world." It stands over against God: in fact, it may be said to exclude God. Its relationship with God is one of hostility and enmity (v. 7). It tends to be self-serving rather than self-giving. Excluding the transcendent, "flesh" is unable to transcend itself.

"Spirit," by contrast, points in a different direction. It emanates from God as an eschatological reality mediated to "this age" through Christ. The Spirit is the agent, or source of power, through which God raised Christ from the dead and as such becomes the empowering source for Christians (v. 11). There is a direct connection between the Spirit and resurrection: the power unleashed by God in Christ's resurrection has been unleashed in this age. This power is essentially life-giving, for as God gave life to Christ in raising him from the dead, so does God give life to the Christian through the indwelling Spirit (v. 11).

The Spirit is the supreme eschatological reality ushered into "this age" by the resurrection of Christ. With it comes life and peace; without it, death is inevitable (v. 13). Through it, we can "put to death the deeds of the body" (v. 13), and thereby experience genuine life (cf. Gal. 5:24; Rom. 6:6). Accordingly, it is a force within us, but also external to us, for we can live either "by it" or "against it." As such, it serves as a moral norm by which one can walk and to which one can conform one's behavior. It provides a clear option to walking "according to the flesh" (v. 12). More than this, however, the Spirit is said to exercise dynamic force over the Christian. Not only are we "in the Spirit" in the sense of living within its world, or sphere of influence, but also it is said that the Spirit dwells in us (v. 9). We may be said, then, to be "led by the Spirit" or "guided by the Spirit" (NJB; cf. also Gal. 5:18). As a living force indwelling us, the Spirit becomes an active force shaping who we are and what we do.

Specifically, the Spirit enables us to understand our identity as God's children. The metaphor is actually more specific here. The contrast is between Christ as God's own Son (v. 3), who cried, "Abba! Father!" (cf. Mark 14:36), and us as "children of God" (v. 14), who experience resurrected life through the Spirit and thereby truly become the heirs of life, even as Christ did. Hence, we are fellow heirs with Christ (v. 17). By recalling the Aramaic language of prayer that Jesus used in Gethsemane, Paul draws an analogy between Christ's experience of suffering and our own. The thrust of his remarks suggests that he saw the Spirit as the empowering agent of Jesus in the garden: to the degree that Jesus himself was "led by the Spirit of God" he became the Son of God through his complete obedience. Similarly, he did not recoil in fear as a slave, but rather prayed in confidence as a true and obedient Son. Similarly, when we confront moments of severe testing that call our very existence as children of God into question, it is God's, and perhaps even Christ's, own Spirit who jointly confirms what our own inward spirit knows—that we are children of God. The Spirit becomes the very catalyst for genuine and complete filial obedience that it wrought in Christ himself in the garden.

Paul's remarks recall, in many respects, the language of the Gospel reading for today, with its sharp distinction between flesh and Spirit and its emphasis on "birth from above." What the Spirit accomplishes is a change in our status—from being slaves to the flesh and thus debtors to the flesh (cf. 2 Tim. 1:7) to becoming children of God (cf. 8:23, Gal. 4:6–7; Eph. 1:5; also Deut. 14:1). As such, we share in Christ's own exalted status as an "heir" (cf. Mark 12:7; Heb. 1:2; Rev. 21:7). There is also the sobering reminder, however, that this relationship inevitably entails suffering (v. 17; also 2 Tim. 2:3, 12; 1 Pet. 4:3; 5:1), even though such suffering will eventually give way to glorification with him (cf. 2 Cor. 4:10).

John 3:1–17

Our Gospel for today continues the subject central to this season—the Holy Spirit. However, as the text will make clear to us, the subject is also Jesus Christ. But more careful listening to the text reveals that the primary subject is God, from whom came both Christ and the Spirit. John 3:1–17 opens and closes with statements about God, reminding us that talk of the Spirit or of Jesus Christ must take place as part of our talk about God.

Because the lection extends to verse 17, the first task of the preacher is to decide how to handle a passage with two textures. It is not simply a matter of ascertaining where the quotation marks go (after v. 15 or after v. 21?) but determining what to do with verses 16–17, which belong to the theological summary (vv. 16–21), which the writer often places after conversations and sign stories (e.g., 3:31–36; 5:19–29). One way to look at the text without interfering with its integrity is to regard the conversation with Nicodemus (vv. 1–15) as cradled between an introduction (2:23–25) and a summary (3:16–17). The introduction provides a setting not only of time and place (Passover, Jerusalem) but also of general response to Jesus (many believed because of the signs). Nicodemus becomes, then, a particular case of faith based on signs. Following the conversation, the central truth about God, which seems to have escaped Nicodemus, is declared openly: "For God so loved . . . not to condemn . . . might be saved" (vv. 16–17).

The conversation unfolds beautifully. Two men, both teachers, meet in private to discuss a subject vital to both, the kingdom of God. They meet "by night" (the Greek word designates *kind* of time, not a point in time or duration of time), alerting the reader to ambiguity and mystery. Through the common Johannine device of double meanings, two quite different views of life in the kingdom are unfolded. By use of a word that may be understood two ways, Jesus calls for birth "from above," which Nicodemus hears as being physically born "again." At verse 7 the conversation is enlarged into a sermon, as is evident by the shift from singular to plural "you." Now the readers are being addressed in what is clearly a post-Easter Christian sermon. Note: Christian baptism and its association with the Holy Spirit (vv. 5–8); the plurals "you" (vv. 7, 11, 12) and "we" (v. 11); the reference to Christ's ascension as a past event (v. 13); and in John, the giving of the Spirit as a post-ascension event (7:39). And so a private conversation opens into a presentation of two widely divergent perspectives on life before God. The one seeks sufficient proofs, historical and logical, in order to arrive at a faith that is safe, solid, and clearly the conclusion that one has reached on the basis of the evidence admitted into the case. The other insists that life in the kingdom is given by God and is unachieved. Being from above, this life is uncontrolled and uncalculated, like the whence and whither of the wind. The shift from succeeding in religion to having eternal life is as radical as being born anew.

Were we to use the language of Paul, we would say that the subject here is the grace of God. Jesus Christ is the subject in the sense of his being the revealer of this truth about God. The Holy Spirit is the subject in the sense of its being the active presence of God effecting the radical change of perspective. But the overall affirmation of the text is that God is a life-giving God. This is no new word, as though God had ceased to be a wrathful judge and had now mellowed into forgiving love. The Hebrew Scriptures had declared God's grace in the story of the brazen serpent in Numbers 21:4–9 (vv. 14–15). Our text proclaims, then, what has always been true of God, and what is comforting to hear again: God loves the world; God desires that none perish; God gives the Son that all may live; God has acted in Christ not to condemn but to save. To trust in this is to have life anew, life eternal.

Proper 4 [9]
(Sunday between May 29 and June 4 inclusive (if after Trinity Sunday))

1 Samuel 3:1–10 (11–20);
Psalm 139:1–6, 13–18; or
Deuteronomy 5:12–15;
Psalm 81:1–10;
2 Corinthians 4:5–12;
Mark 2:23–3:6

The season after Pentecost, or Ordinary Time, which begins with Trinity Sunday and continues for the next twenty-six weeks, provides an extended period of time uninterrupted by special events and observances. As a result, it provides an opportunity for continuity in the reading and study of Scripture, and the *Common Lectionary* capitalizes on this.

In Year B, the Old Testament readings in the *Common Lectionary* during this period derive from 1 and 2 Samuel (Propers 4–14, 28–29), 1 Kings (Propers 15–16), the Wisdom writings (Propers 17–25), and Ruth (Propers 26–27). The readings from 1 and 2 Samuel and 1 Kings focus primarily on David, while the selections from Song of Solomon, Proverbs, Esther, Job, and Ruth represent the diversity of perspectives that characterize wisdom traditions.

In other lectionary traditions, Old Testament readings are not selected in order to provide continuous exposure to various portions of Scripture, but rather because of some thematic or analogical connection with the Gospel reading for a particular Sunday. Consequently, they are drawn from all over the Old Testament.

As usual, regardless of the principle of selection for the Old Testament reading, the psalm is chosen in connection with the Old Testament text and serves as a form of meditation or reflection on the first reading.

In all the lectionary traditions, the Gospel for Year B is Mark, and the Gospel readings for the period after Pentecost take us rather systematically through Mark's Gospel. Because of the relative brevity of Mark's Gospel, however, supplementary readings from John's Gospel serve as the Gospel reading for Propers 12–16.

The epistolary readings for this period are taken from 2 Corinthians (Propers 4–9), Ephesians (Propers 10–16), James (Propers 17–21), and Hebrews (Propers 22–28).

Whether one follows the *Common Lectionary* during this period and chooses the Old Testament semicontinuous readings, with their accompanying psalm, or opts for the Old Testament readings (and their accompanying psalms) that are more closely related to the Gospel text for the day, in either case the choice should be consistent for the entire period after Pentecost.

Depending on which tradition one chooses, unifying themes or connections between a set of texts for a given day may or may not be present.

In today's set of texts, the Old Testament reading in the *Common Lectionary* begins the series of texts on the Davidic covenant with the account of God's revelation to the boy Samuel. The responsorial reading, portions of Psalm 139, reveals the God who knows us intimately.

In other lectionary traditions, the Old Testament reading is Deuteronomy 5:12–15, the portion of the Decalogue enjoining sabbath observance. The connection with the Gospel text is clear: in both sections of the Markan text, Jesus' conduct on the sabbath is the critical issue.

The second reading, which begins the semicontinuous reading from 2 Corinthians, shows how Paul's ministerial self-understanding of ministry is anchored in his experience of the cross.

1 Samuel 3:1–10 (11–20)

In the *Common Lectionary*, this reading begins a series of fourteen semicontinuous lessons from the Books of Samuel and Kings. In the center of those texts stands the account of the life and times of King David, but David is seen in the broader context of Israel's history. The first texts concern those leaders who preceded David, especially the towering figure of Samuel, but also Saul. The concluding readings in the sequence take up Solomon.

These verses from 1 Samuel 3 are assigned for reading on the Second Sunday After the Epiphany in Year B and have been commented on at that point in this volume. The text emphasizes Samuel's vocation and authority as a prophet. In the readings for this season, Samuel's role in the establishment of the monarchy—including the designation of the first two kings—will come to the fore.

Psalm 139:1–6, 13–18

This lection was discussed earlier for the Second Sunday After the Epiphany.

Deuteronomy 5:12–15

This text is also assigned for reading on the Ninth Sunday After the Epiphany in Year B and has been discussed with the other texts for that day in this volume.

Psalm 81:1–10

This reading was discussed earlier in the lections for the Ninth Sunday After the Epiphany.

2 Corinthians 4:5–12

This epistolary lection begins a cycle of readings from Second Corinthians that extends over the next five weeks. Hence, a few preliminary remarks about this letter are in order.

It should be recalled that Second Corinthians probably comprises at least two, perhaps more, of Paul's letters to the church at Corinth. Chapters 10–13 seem to constitute a separate letter in its own right. With its severely polemical tone, it is best read as Paul's own defense of his apostolic ministry directed against his opponents. Chapters 1–9 form a separate letter and appear to have been written after chapters 10–13; in fact, chapters 8 and 9, which treat the collection of funds for the Jerusalem poor, originally may have been a separate letter, or letters. In any case, the mood and tone of chapters 1–9 are far less stormy, even though we still hear echoes of the controversy concerning Paul's ministry and his apostolic life-style. What unfolds in chapters 1–7, especially in 2:14–6:10, is an elaborate statement of Paul's theology of ministry. The epistolary lections for the first four weeks (2 Cor. 4:5–12; 4:13–5:1; 5:6–10 (11–13) 14–17; 6:1–13) derive from this section; the next lection (2 Cor. 8:7–15) derives from the section treating the collection; and the final lection (2 Cor. 12:2–10) derives from Paul's own defense (*apologia*) of his ministry.

In today's lection, Paul's opening remark, "For we do not proclaim ourselves" (v. 5), doubtless responds to the charges of his detractors who accused him of self-commendation (2 Cor. 3:1). As the letter shows, at issue was what constituted authentic ministry, or what form of ministry most adequately expressed the heart of the gospel. Was it ministry whose appeal and authority derived essentially from the minister's personal charisma, powerful presence, and strength as demonstrated in rhetorical ability or the ability to perform signs and wonders? Or was it ministry anchored in human weakness, human frailty, and actual experiences of human suffering that derived its appeal and authority from its capacity not merely to endure these but to transcend and transform them—to experience strength through suffering, power through weakness, and living through dying?

For Paul, it is the latter. The former way of viewing ministry tends to make the minister a "lord." In verse 5, he may in fact be saying, "For we do not proclaim ourselves [as Lord]; we proclaim Jesus Christ as Lord." Consequently, that form of ministry will tend to be authoritarian and stress rank more than service (cf. 2 Cor. 1:24). By contrast, Paul's essential role is that of servant (1 Cor. 3:5). At the heart of his gospel is the basic Christian confession "Jesus is Lord" (cf. Rom. 10:9; 1 Cor. 12:3; Phil. 2:11; also Col. 2:6). Paul is not insisting here that he preaches the gospel apart from his own person, or personality, for preaching inevitably occurs through a human personality. The important question, however, is what message is mediated through the preacher's personality. As verse 6 shows, Paul insists that the ultimate source of revelation for his gospel is the Creator God who said, "Let light shine out of darkness" (cf. Gen. 1:3; Ps. 112:4; Job 37:15; Isa. 9:1–2). Just as God gave light to the universe through the spoken word at creation, so now has God brought light to all humanity through the new creation accomplished in the Christ-event. Just as the face of Moses radiated the brilliant splendor of God's revelation (cf. 2 Cor. 3:7–13), so now the "face of Christ" radiates the unveiled splendor of God's new revelation.

In verses 7–12, the metaphor shifts. No longer is the gospel seen as dazzling light shining through darkness (cf. 1 Pet. 2:9; Acts 26:18; Eph. 5:8; 1 Thess. 5:4–5; 2 Pet. 1:3), but as a "treasure in clay jars" (v. 7; cf. 2 Cor. 5:1; Lam. 4:2). The image of the clay pot serves to underscore the weakness and fragility of the minister as messenger. The message of the gospel mediated through the messenger is "treasure," to be sure (Matt. 13:44; Eph. 3:8), but it derives its value not from the case that contains it but from its intrinsic worth. Thus the transcendent power of the gospel is derived from God, not from the minister. As evidence of this, Paul rehearses in schematic fashion the afflictions he has endured as an apostle (v. 8; also 1:4, 8; 7:5; cf. 1 Cor. 4:9–13; 2 Cor. 6:3–10; 11:21–29). In every case, however, he has overcome, for although in his afflictions he was "carrying in [his] body the death of Jesus," precisely through these afflictions the "life of Jesus" manifested itself (v. 10). He has not been forsaken (cf. Heb. 13:5). He has literally been given up to death in these experiences of human suffering and "dying," and through them he has reenacted the event of the cross itself (cf. 2 Cor. 1:5; 13:4; Gal. 6:17; 1 Cor. 15:38). Yet through them resurrection has also been at work (Rom. 6:8; 8:17; Phil. 3:10–11). He has experienced living through dying, and in doing so has proclaimed the essence of the gospel of the crucified Christ: through death comes life (cf. Phil. 1:20–21; 1 Cor. 6:20; 2 Cor. 6:9). As the message of the crucified Christ has been proclaimed through his own apostolic life-style, those who have heard him preach and seen him live have themselves come to experience life: "So death is at work in us, but life in you" (v. 12).

Mark 2:23–3:6

Today's Gospel lection is a portion of the collection of five conflict stories recorded in Mark 2:1–3:6. This material is called a collection because the stories are joined topically rather than chronologically. This is evident from three characteristics of the section: (1) the stories have other locations in Matthew and Luke; (2) the stories have different settings (at home, 2:1–12; in Levi's house, 2:13–17; no setting given, 2:18–22; in a grain field, 2:23–28; in a synagogue, 3:1–6); and (3) each story has a Markan style introduction and is rounded off at the end. Hence, stories that probably circulated separately are here clustered, perhaps as a kind of arsenal for the early church members who looked to Jesus for both precedent and pronouncement to enable them to handle their own conflicts.

However, it is striking that Mark has placed this section at this point in his Gospel. At the same time that Jesus is drawing huge and favorable crowds in cities, villages, countrysides, and by the sea (1:28, 33, 37, 39, 45), Mark says Jesus is also drawing hostile attention from religious leaders. In fact, the opposition mounts to the point of a conspiracy against his life, according to 3:6, which apparently is intended as the conclusion to the entire section instead of just 3:1–5. And thus as early as 3:6, Jesus' death enters the story, a subject that will dominate Mark's narrative after 8:31.

Our text, 2:23–3:6, records the last two conflicts. The first three concerned charges of blasphemy, eating with sinners, and not observing fasts, whereas both of these concern sabbath regulations. The first occurs in the grain fields (2:23–28). The disciples pluck heads of grain, an act for which the law made provision as long as none of the grain was put in containers and taken home (Deut. 23:25). According to the Pharisees, however, what they did constituted harvesting on the sabbath. Jesus' defense of his followers consisted of citing a precedent from David's career (1 Sam. 21:2–7) in which human need took precedence over the law. (Ahimelech and not Abiathar was high priest; some manuscripts of Mark have made the correction by omitting the name, as Matthew and Luke have done.) Verses 27–28 contain two pronouncements (Matt. 12:8 and Luke 6:5 use only the second) for which the story serves as introduction. The pronouncements are different, and it is unlikely that both would have been stated on one occasion. The first (v. 27) is a general principle that law is to serve human life, not vice versa. The second (v. 28) is a christological claim made by One far greater than either David or the law.

The second conflict (3:1–5) involves a healing in a synagogue on the sabbath. The pronouncement at the center of this brief account is in the form of a penetrating question that silenced those who lay in wait for Jesus. They were silent because their own law made provision in emergencies to care for both animal and human life (Matt. 12:11; Luke 14:5) on the sabbath. Though the healing he did here might not be classified as an emergency, Jesus is announcing by his act and word that it is never the wrong day to do good, to heal, to save life. The hostility against Jesus produces one of those odd unions that overriding hatreds sometime create: Pharisees in league with Herodians (8:15; 12:13), religion and politics clutching the same sword.

It requires no great act of imagination to observe how similar are the conflicts that lie in the path of discipleship today. Structures of religious custom and tradition, originally designed to praise God and serve humanity, can become corrupted and cruel. Hence, occasions arise in which both human life and tradition cannot be preserved unbroken.

Proper 5 [10]
(Sunday between June 5 and 11 inclusive
(if after Trinity Sunday))

1 Samuel 8:4–11 (12–15) 16–20 (11:14–15);
Psalm 138; or
Genesis 3:8–15;
Psalm 130;
2 Corinthians 4:13–5:1;
Mark 3:20–35

The Old Testament selection for the *Common Lectionary* is the account of Israel's request for a king; and Psalm 138, the responsorial psalm, is a prayer of thanksgiving attributed to David, which acknowledges that kings everywhere praise Yahweh.

In the alternate Old Testament reading from Genesis 3, God confronts Adam and Eve in the garden and condemns the serpent to a crawling existence. The accompanying psalm, Psalm 130, is a personal lament that acknowledges the pervasiveness of human iniquity.

The Gospel reading for today has Jesus' opponents accusing him of being in league with Beelzebul and the demonic order. Paired with Genesis 3, this text serves as a useful reminder that personified evil is always present to resist God's purposes.

In the epistolary reading from 2 Corinthians, Paul affirms faith in the God who raises the dead, and expresses confidence that life as we know it here, with all its afflictions and limitations, will eventually give way to an eternal form of existence.

1 Samuel 8:4–11 (12–15) 16–20 (11:14–15)

In the semicontinuous readings for this season, we have moved in one week from the beginning to the end of the life of Samuel, from his vocation as a youth to his old age. There he stands, responding to the elders of Israel who have come to present him with a request. Confronting him with the facts that he is old and his sons are unworthy to follow in his footsteps, they ask that he appoint a king over all Israel, "a king to govern us, like other nations" (v. 5). The reading for the day gives the substance of the old prophet's response, which is clear enough—Samuel does not mince words here. But Samuel's speech takes on deeper significance in both its ancient import and its contemporary implications when one considers its literary and historical contexts.

297

This scene comes at a key turning point in the story of the people of God—the transition between the form of leadership that had prevailed through the period of the judges and the monarchy, which will last until the Assyrian conquest of Israel (722/721 BC) and the Babylonian conquest of Judah (597 BC). In fact, a great deal of the book of 1 Samuel is preoccupied with this transition, for Samuel himself is the last of a line of leaders of a certain kind. He is a prophetic and a priestly figure, but he is also the last of the judges. First Samuel 7–15 records the traditions about the transition, in which Saul eventually becomes the first king. But Samuel is still around long enough even to preside over the designation of David as Saul's successor.

The literature and the traditions about the rise of kingship in Israel are diverse and complex. The chapters surrounding our reading preserve at least two quite distinct theological and political perspectives on the new form of government. On the one hand, there are materials (1 Sam. 9:1–10:16; 11:1–15; parts of 1 Sam. 13 and 14) that see the emergence of kingship more positively. The designation of Saul comes in response to a crisis between the Israelite tribes and the Philistines. Samuel, who is viewed mainly as a seer, supports Saul, a charismatic figure like the judges before him. The establishment of kingship is an act of God's grace. The Lord instructs Samuel to anoint Saul: "He shall save my people from the hand of the Philistines; for I have seen the suffering of my people, because their outcry has come to me" (1 Sam. 9:16). This is the viewpoint of what seem to be the more ancient traditions. On the other hand, the later perspective is much more negative about the new institution. In these traditions (1 Sam. 7; 8; 10:17ff.; 12; 15), Samuel is a judge who is said to have subdued the Philistines, but the people were dissatisfied with the old ways and asked Samuel to give them a king. As the reading for the day makes plain, Samuel resisted; but upon the somewhat reluctant and begrudging instructions of the Lord, he acquiesced and anointed Saul. The issue is posed in theological terms: If the Lord is king, then it is rebellious to ask for a human king.

It seems clear that this second set of traditions—including today's reading—interprets the origin of kingship from the perspective of people who have borne its burden, who have seen the price to be paid for it. Thus the institution is interpreted as the cause of most of Israel's later troubles. This point of view is close to that of the final deuteronomistic editors of the Books of Samuel and Kings.

To be sure, the different traditions are agreed on some fundamental points. Neither denies that God is king, the lord and ruler of Israel, and that the institution comes with God's approval. In both cases, Samuel is the Lord's servant who anoints Saul. But behind the different perspectives probably lies a genuine controversy in Israel, both when kingship arose and throughout its history. The controversy was over the proper form of government for the people of God.

In our reading, the desire to have a king "like all the other nations" is seen as the rejection of Yahweh. Then Samuel spells out the price to be paid for establishing a monarchy. Men will be conscripted as servants of the king, and not just to serve in his army. They will take care of his land—and presumably he will acquire a great deal of land—and work in his military industries. But women will not be exempt from service, being taken into household service in the palace. Moreover, the king will confiscate "the best of your fields and vineyards and olive orchards and give them to his courtiers" (v. 14). He will impose taxes in money and in kind to pay his officers and courtiers. In short, "you shall be his slaves" (v. 17). Moreover, when the people eventually cry out against the king's oppression, the Lord will not answer, for they brought it upon themselves. After all these warnings, the people still insist upon having a king, and Samuel—upon God's instructions—acquiesces.

This text, especially in its broader context, poses but gives no easy answer to the question of the appropriate form of government for the people of God. It is brutally realistic about the price of a centralized government. But in the literary and historical context, without such a central organization it would have been impossible to resist the Philistine threat—so the history of those people could have ended almost before it began. Unlike the understanding of the rise of kingship in, for example, Mesopotamia, where it is said that "kingship came down from heaven," the Old Testament tells the tales of human struggles, limitations, sins, and conflicts. The institution is seen to have emerged in the full light of history. So to the question, Will Israel have a king—a human institution—like the other nations? the answer is, Yes, so long as Israel is in the world, she will have human institutions.

Psalm 138

This psalm may be subdivided into three parts. Verses 1–3 thank and praise God; verses 4–6 extol the grace and glory of God and their impact on the rulers of the world; and verses 7–8 express trust in God.

The general tone of the psalm clearly identifies it as a thanksgiving. It differs, however, from most thanksgiving psalms in two ways: (1) there is no description of the trouble or the distress from which the person was rescued (see v. 3, which refers to an appeal to God at an earlier time of distress), and (2) the psalm is addressed directly to the Deity throughout (v. 8a is possibly an exception), whereas most thanksgivings are addressed to a human audience.

The person offering thanks in the original usage of this psalm was probably the king. This is suggested by the references in verse 4 to the kings of the earth who hear the words of Yahweh's mouth, perhaps words spoken by the Judean king. Also, the king was especially the man of God's right hand (v. 7; see Ps. 110:1).

Several elements in the psalm call for elucidation:

1. The reference to "before the gods" (v. 1) could mean one of several things. Ancient translations read "before the angels," "before kings," or "before judges." If the reference is to pagan gods, then the worshiper could be saying no more than, "I sing your praise in an alien culture." If the reference is to heavenly beings (see Pss. 29:1; 82:1), then the phrase could denote worship before the heavenly council of God.

2. To bow down toward the temple does not imply that the worshiper is in some foreign land or away from Jerusalem. This could be a reference to worship or activity at the temple gate, near the main altar, or in the temple courtyard.

3. The lowly may not refer to a class—the poor, the downtrodden, or others in similar conditions—but could be a self-designation, even of a king—the lowly over against the Divine.

4. The verb translated "to perceive" in verse 6b may mean, on the basis of an Arabic parallel, "to humble." Thus "the haughty he humbles from afar."

The statement of trust in verses 7–8 gives expression to a serene confidence—almost. Verse 8c still resorts to petition even after the statement of assurance. Note that the psalm does not assume that life will be free of distress and problems but only that God will preserve one through them all. Trouble and enemies are the givens in life; grace and preservation to endure and overcome them are the sustaining gifts.

Genesis 3:8–15

The results of the first sin [handwritten margin note]

The Old Testament reading comes from the story of the results of the first sin of the first human beings, and it needs to be read in the light of the first seven verses of chapter 3, the account of the act of rebellion itself, remarkably filled with insight into human psychology. Especially in view of a long and frequently misleading history of the interpretation of this story, several matters in those verses require comment. The serpent here is not the devil. In fact, the narrator carefully circumscribes his place and role. The translation "serpent" is too elegant; "snake" is more appropriate. He is part of creation, a "wild animal," made by the Lord God (3:1). He created neither sin nor suffering, but his role is to pose the questions in a subtle way, making possible and even encouraging the act of disobedience. He symbolizes and represents the experience of evil as external, coming from outside the person. Nor is the woman a temptress, as her husband will later suggest (v. 12). She simply offered the forbidden fruit to the man, and he accepted (v. 6).

The Yahwist's story is not so much one of the origin of sin as the origin of its painful effects in human life. In combination with the account of creation (Gen. 2:4b–25), its intent is to give an explanation of the way human beings have experienced their existence—and especially its brokenness—from the time of the writer down to the present day. It deals with the most profound theological questions in a typically biblical mode, by telling a story. Brokenness, pain, ambiguity, and suffering are given a moral explanation: they are the result of sin.

By no means are all of the effects of the sin presented as curses or punishments imposed by Yahweh. Some of them are seen simply to have been set into motion by the act itself. The first of these is noted in the verse that precedes our lection. The snake promised that eating the fruit—the text does not say what kind—would bring knowledge, and it does. When the eyes of the man and woman were opened, they knew they were naked (3:7); that is, they experienced shame (Gen. 2:25). The next effects were guilt and estrangement from Yahweh, to the point that they hid from him (vv. 8–10), but Yahweh immediately knows what they have done (v. 11). The next result, estrangement from each other and from their environment, is presented with an incredibly sensitive combination of the comic and the sad (vv. 12–13). Each in turn blames the other, and the man even blames Yahweh: "The woman whom you gave to be with me . . ." The sin that they had committed in common did not bind them together, but separated them from each other and from God.

Then follow the curses upon each in turn. Here the theological interpretation of facets of present existence becomes quite explicit. Behind the curse upon the snake (vv. 14–15) is probably an old explanation of why snakes crawl on the ground and why people—not just women, all the "offspring" of the first woman are included—dislike snakes so much.

In the verses that follow the assigned reading, the man and woman are not cursed directly, but pain, dissonance, and contradictions come into their lives. The address to the woman (v. 16) concerns her role as mother and wife in Israelite patriarchal society. Her excessive pain in childbirth and the anguish of her subordination to the husband, says the author, were not part of the plan of creation, but the effects of human sin. She will desire her husband, but instead of giving her fulfillment and rest, he will dominate and humiliate her.

The man's curse (vv. 17–19) is neither work nor death. Before the violation of Yahweh's prohibition, he had to till the garden (Gen. 2:15), and he had the intellectual work of naming the animals (Gen. 2:19–20). To be a full human being one must have work to do. The dissonance is that now his work is full of failures, time wasted, fruitless efforts. To punish the man, Yahweh curses the ground. Moreover, the final word does not introduce death as a new factor.

This creature had always been dust. But the difference is a monumental one: the man's death is placed before his eyes. Now the awareness of it will cripple life. It is true, however, that as the man and woman are driven from the garden they are prohibited from ever attaining immortality (Gen. 3:23). In ancient Israel, that was a divine prerogative.

The aim of the story as a whole is to explain the broken state of human existence. Life is filled with ambiguity. On the one hand, there is in all of us a deep awareness of the way things should be or could be. That is characterized here as life before the first sin. On the other hand, although those facets can always be recognized, life is not like that. The Yahwist raises the question of the origin of some forms of suffering and explains them in moral terms, as the results of sin.

The value of the story for us—and its place in Christian preaching and teaching—does not lie in the completeness of its answers. The meaning of human suffering is, finally, a mystery that is beyond us. Its contribution lies rather in the profound way that it mirrors our lives. It interprets us to ourselves. As with all tragic literature, we enter into and identify with the lives of all the characters and comprehend some of the forces that have led to tragic results. We thus achieve a deeper understanding of our own lives and of those around us.

Psalm 130

An initial word about the structure and content of the psalm is in order. Although the psalm may be read as rather straightforward and continuous in content, it is actually rather complex. This can be seen from the different addresses in the psalm. In verses 1–4, God is addressed in a petitioning, supplicating tone by an individual worshiper. In verses 5–6, some human audience is addressed in very confessional tones. Finally, in verses 7–8 the community (Israel) is addressed in an admonishing and directive tone.

The address to the Deity (vv. 1–4) is fundamentally a description of the human condition, although verse 2 appeals to and makes requests for help from God. The human condition is described as "the depths," or at least this is the condition from which prayer is offered. The term "depths" is frequently used to refer to the depths of the seas (see Isa. 51:10; Ezek. 27:34). As such, the expression could be used to symbolize remoteness from God and to characterize the distress of the human predicament (see Jon. 2:2–3). The "depths" may be another way of speaking about Sheol, the world of the dead, the world isolated and estranged from God. At any rate, the "depths" give expression to that experience of life when everything seems askew and out of harmony. It is that point that lies at the outer edge of human control.

A second description of the human condition is found in verse 3. Humans experience life and know themselves as sinners. If God kept a full record, a complete tab on human sin, then no one would warrant being spared (see 1 Kings 8:46; Ps. 143:2; Prov. 20:9). Other texts, for example Psalms 15 and 24, assume that human beings can measure up to divinely set standards. Here, however, we have a very pessimistic, or realistic, reading of the human situation.

Over against the human experience of being overwhelmed by life (the depths of v. 1) and the realization of the complete misalignment of our existence (the iniquities of v. 3), there stands a theological affirmation about God, an affirmation that relativizes the human predicament—with God there is forgiveness (v. 4). Such an affirmation of forgiveness in spite of the human condition led Martin Luther to speak of the Pauline quality of this psalm.

The second section of the psalm, verses 5–6, is a confessional statement to a human audience. In addressing God, the worshiper in verses 1–4 assumed a position of subordination, perhaps to elicit a favorable response from the Divine. In addressing the human audience, the worshiper is allowed to exude confidence and to affirm a hopeful expectation. The speaker describes the waiting as being as intense as that of a watchman—a military sentry—watching for the dawn, when he would be relieved of duty and allowed to relax without the strain and responsibility of staying constantly alert. Perhaps the worshiper has been charged with some crime or has been accused of some wrong. If so, then "to wait for God" was to wait for a verdict on the worshiper's case.

The final stanza, a call for the nation to trust in Yahweh (vv. 7–8), sounds a bit odd in the context. Does some individual worshiper suddenly address the nation? Or the community assembled in the temple? Or is this perhaps the king speaking? Or maybe a priest addressing worshipers assembled in the sanctuary? Under whatever circumstances, the psalm affirms that with God there is constancy of love and a plenitude of redemption. Ultimately, the power behind all life is benevolent and beneficent.

2 Corinthians 4:13–5:1

If being "afflicted," "perplexed," "persecuted," and "struck down" (vv. 8–9) are the inescapable lot of Paul's existence as an apostle, why continue? In today's lection Paul explains the basis of his confidence as an apostle.

First, he mentions the "same spirit of faith" as that of the psalmist who wrote "I believed, and so I spoke" (cf. Ps. 115:1, LXX; 116:10, NRSV). Although the Greek version of the psalm differs from that of the Hebrew Bible, it clearly speaks of one who has recovered from severe affliction. As the context of the psalm shows, the psalmist continued to trust in God even though "the snares of death encompassed [him]" and he "suffered distress and anguish" (Ps. 116:3, NRSV). In deep trust, he had cried to the Lord, "O Lord, I pray, save my life!" (Ps. 116:4, NRSV). His trust had been met with deliverance, and the psalm ends on a note of praise and thanksgiving.

In the same spirit of faith, or trust, Paul is able to "speak," both in the sense of proclaiming the gospel and edifying his churches through his teaching. Worth noting here is the strong connection between faith and proclamation: what one speaks, especially what one speaks with conviction, stems directly from the convictions of the heart, what one believes.

At the center of Paul's faith was the conviction that the God who raised the Lord Jesus from the dead would also raise those who shared the Easter faith (cf. 1 Cor. 6:14; 15:15, 20; Rom. 8:11; 2 Cor. 13:4). This, for Paul, was a matter of existential knowledge. (Note: "we know that," v. 14.) The resurrected life that the Lord Jesus had already experienced would eventually be that which all those "in Christ" would experience. Paul thus stresses his own solidarity with his readers: "will bring us with you into his presence" (v. 14). The work of God through Christ, as well as Paul's own apostolic work, was for their sake. Through the spread of the gospel, God's grace would be extended to more people, and as this happened, prayers of thanksgiving to God would also increase to the glory of God (v. 15).

A second basis for confidence is also given in verses 16–18: the eschatological hope and gradual transformation of the one who is in Christ. This obviously derives from his earlier mention of the God who raises the dead (vv. 13–15), which leads him to affirm, "So we do not lose heart" (cf. 4:1; also Gal. 6:9; 2 Thess. 3:13; 1 Tim. 6:14). Here Paul distinguishes between the "outer nature" that is wasting away and the "inner nature" that is being renewed daily (v. 16). It is not clear whether this is a psychological dualism that distinguishes the "inmost self" from the "(outer) members" (cf. Rom. 7:22; Eph. 3:16), or an eschatological dualism that distinguishes the part of us that conforms to "this age" from the part of us that conforms to "the age to come." It may be that both dimensions are in view here. As verses 17–18 show, the contrast is eschatological: this "slight momentary affliction" that we experience now is set over against the incomparable "eternal weight of glory" that we will experience then. Yet through the Christ-event God has already begun the process of transformation that will culminate in the Parousia, and in this sense the "present form of this world is passing away" (1 Cor. 7:31). Therefore, it is possible to distinguish between "what can be seen" and "what cannot be seen," the former being the world as we know it in its transient state, the latter being the world as it has begun to be transformed by the power of the resurrection.

Certainly, this changed perspective on the world order also alters the way we view our own existence. Our earthly existence is now comparable to that of a tent, the very symbol of transience; for like a tent, our human existence finally folds. In contrast to the earthly tent of our existence, however, God gives us a "house not made with hands" (cf. Mark 14:58; Heb. 8:2; 9:11, 24), "eternal in the heavens."

Mark 3:20–35

Mark will be our Gospel today and for the next six weeks, and then we will return to John. Given the broad differences between these two Gospels, the preacher will want to make the transition carefully and help the listeners do the same. In common, however, with the two preceding lessons from John is the subject of the Holy Spirit in today's reading, testifying again not only to its appropriateness for the Pentecost Season but also for any season. The Holy Spirit was the hallmark of early Christianity as portrayed in the major New Testament witnesses. Mark 3:20–35 registers how vital was the activity of the Holy Spirit in the early church and issues a frightening warning to those who attribute that activity to Satan.

In Mark, the geographical context is Jesus' home (3:19b). The phrase can also mean "in a house," probably a better rendering, for the text says that Jesus' family came to the place where he was to get him. Of course, Jesus could have had a home away from his family. The literary context places the event immediately after the appointment of the twelve disciples (3:13–19a). Our lection itself is a combination of two stories: Jesus' relation to his family and the scribes' charge that Jesus works in the name of Satan. In Matthew and Luke, the charge follows an exorcism (Matt. 12:12; Luke 11:14), and quite naturally so, for the accusation has to do with casting out demons. But in Mark the charge by the scribes not only follows the arrival of Jesus' family to seize him (3:21) but is inextricably tied to the family's attempt to take Jesus away. In a pattern typical of Mark, one story (3:22–30) is inserted between two parts of another story (3:20–21, 31–35). Mark divides the account about Jesus' family and sets the accusation about Satanic exorcisms within it. Why?

Mark may have joined the stories because the family's and the scribes' views of Jesus are similar, though differing in seriousness. The family apparently believed the public report that Jesus was insane, beside himself. Jesus was in a pressing crowd in the house, and it was impossible even to eat (vv. 20–21). The scribes from Jerusalem interpreted Jesus' behavior theologically: he is possessed by Beelzebul, the prince of demons. Beelzebul ("lord of the house") was a Syrian god whose name was mockingly corrupted by some Jews to Beelzebub ("lord of the flies"). Back of the charge was the common assumption that miracles could be performed not only by God but also by evil forces (Exod. 7:11; 8:7; 2 Thess. 2:9; Rev. 13:13). In Matthew 7:21–23, Jesus attributes the prophesying, exorcisms, and miracles of some persons to the power of evil. In other words, although we ask of the extraordinary, Did it really happen? The Scriptures ask, Who did it?

Jesus' response is not only to the scribes but to everyone, as is evident by Mark's familiar "And he called them to him" (v. 23). In a series of brief parabolic statements, Jesus provides a twofold answer: (1) to cast out demons in Satan's name is nonsensical; Satan against Satan would mean the self-destruction of evil, and (2) the real truth is not that evil is self-destructing but that Jesus has entered Satan's house and is overcoming the power of evil. Then comes the pronouncement (vv. 28–29) to the effect that forgiveness of sin and blasphemy is broad and embracing, but to attribute the work of the Holy Spirit to Satan, to charge the Spirit of God with evil, to call a blessing a curse is to thwart totally the dynamics of forgiveness. This pronouncement, says Mark, was prompted by the charge that Jesus had an unclean spirit (v. 30). Out of fear of confusing the works of God and Satan, the church has generally been cautious if not totally quiet about what are and what are not the words and deeds of the Holy Spirit. After all, no one wants to be guilty of blasphemy by claiming certainty about when, where, and how God works. But criteria had to be developed, as the document called *The Didache* testifies, to protect the church against self-appointed, money-hungry evangelists, prophets, and healers.

In verse 31 the account returns to the story of Jesus' family and Jesus' declaration that his true family consists of those who do God's will (v. 35). This dramatic but not isolated scene gives the allegiance of discipleship precedence over family ties (Mark 10:29–30; Luke 9:59–62; 12:51–53; 14:25–26). Some have had to make painful decisions in this matter.

Take one final look at Mark's picture. Outside are the two groups that one would assume should be inside: the family (Mark 6:3), perhaps blinded by familiarity, who do not understand and who believe rumors about Jesus; the scribes from headquarters, experts in Scripture who give theological put-downs to what they do not understand. And inside? A crowd sitting about Jesus, listening for God's will, apparently unaware that they missed lunch.

Proper 6 [11]
(Sunday between June 12 and 18 inclusive (if after Trinity Sunday))

1 Samuel 15:34–16:13;
Psalm 20; or
Ezekiel 17:22–24;
Psalm 92:1–4, 12–15;
2 Corinthians 5:6–10 (11–13) 14–17;
Mark 4:26–34

The suspenseful account of Samuel's anointing David to be king of Israel serves as to-day's Old Testament reading in the *Common Lectionary*. Psalm 20 provides assurance that the Lord will help the anointed king be victorious over enemies.

For those using other lectionaries, the messianic allegory of the cedar in Ezekiel 17 serves as the Old Testament reading, with the beginning and concluding portions of Psalm 92, which praises God's fidelity and likens the righteous to a flourishing tree, serving as the psalm meditation.

There are clear thematic connections between Ezekiel 17 and the Gospel reading, which consists of a pair of parables of growth: the seed growing secretly and the mustard seed.

A note of confidence is sounded in the Epistle lesson from 2 Corinthians, as Paul opens the veil of his apostolic self-understanding.

1 Samuel 15:34–16:13

This account of David's anointing as king continues the series of selections that survey or recapitulate the era of the rise of kingship, the life of David, and the times of his son Solomon. This initial reading reports how the Lord selected David and had Samuel anoint him to be king. The continuity of readings suggests the possibility of a series of sermons on David's life. Finally, the theme of kingship will be taken to its eschatological implications on the last day of this season and of the liturgical year (Proper 29 [34], Christ the King).

This passage gives an account of Samuel's final public act and of David's initial appearance in the biblical narrative. The old prophet designated and anointed the youngest son of Jesse to be king. In premonarchical times, and even subsequently on occasion in the Northern Kingdom, kings or other leaders were designated and anointed by prophets. The essential conclusion of this report is that David later became king in accordance with the will of Yahweh and received the

305

power and authority of Yahweh's Spirit: "And the spirit of the LORD came mightily upon David from that day forward" (16:13). The biblical tradition means to place that sentence as the heading for the entire life of David.

The setting for the story's plot is stated in 16:1, which recapitulates the events in the previous chapter, and especially in 15:34–35. Although he will continue to reign until his death, Saul has been rejected by Yahweh and is estranged from Samuel. What then is to become of the monarchy? The answer comes when Yahweh announces to Samuel that he is to go to Bethlehem and anoint one of Jesse's sons as king.

As Samuel responds to the word of the Lord and goes to Bethlehem, narrative tension develops (vv. 2–5). First, Samuel fears for his life. Saul will kill him if he learns that the prophet has gone to anoint another. Yahweh instructs him to take a heifer along with him and—if anyone asks—say that he is doing his duty, offering a sacrifice. Anointing in the context of a service of sacrifice is not unexpected, but we cannot miss the note of concealment and even deceit. The action is not to be known publicly. Second, when Samuel arrives in Bethlehem leading the heifer, he has to reassure the fearful elders of the city. We can only suppose that they—like Samuel—are afraid of Saul. Then this direction of the narrative—the possible threat from Saul—is quickly forgotten as the sacrifice is arranged.

The account is drawn out to its resolution. Like Samuel, we were told only that Yahweh has provided one of the sons of Jesse as a king. Neither he nor the readers have been informed which one it will be. First one and then another is brought forth and rejected in turn. Yahweh instructs Samuel, who is obviously impressed with the appearance of Eliab: "the LORD does not see as mortals see; they look on the outward appearance, but the LORD looks on the heart" (v. 7). When it seems that all the sons have been considered, Jesse acknowledges that there is one more, keeping the sheep (v. 11). Probably we are to understand that he was absent in the first place because he was too young to participate in the sacrifice. The description of this youngest son's attractive appearance (v. 12a) is surprising considering what is stated in verse 7.

Then comes the climax of the story with Yahweh's revelation that this is the one (v. 12b), and with Samuel's anointing (v. 13a). The final lines (v. 13b) give the denouement, the explanation of the meaning and implications of the events. Only now do we finally hear the name of the anointed one, David.

The point of the story is that David came to the throne, not because of ambition or anything he did, but through divine designation. Like Saul before him (1 Sam. 9:1–10:16), he was anointed by Samuel, not just in the moment of the nation's need but in advance. It is not a story of David at all—he says not a word and does only what he is told to do—but of the word of the Lord through the prophetic figure of Samuel. The process by which that word is made known is a combination of the prophetic—Yahweh speaks to him—and the priestly—the sacrifice and the pattern of events like election by lot.

Closely connected to the main theme is another—that the Lord makes the least expected choice. Expectations are reversed. The last is indeed made the first, and God's power is to be manifested in weakness.

Psalm 20

This psalm is a fitting reading to accompany the reading from 1 Samuel 16:1–13. The psalm was composed to be used in a liturgy in which the king was the central figure. The liturgy and the ritual were probably carried out prior to the departure of the monarch and his army for battle.

The psalm is comprised of three component parts: an address to the king (vv. 1–5), a confession of confidence spoken by the monarch (vv. 6–8), and a prayer of intercession on behalf of the king (v. 9).

The appearance of many terms associated with worship make it possible to sense many of the actions as well as the orientation of the ritual in which this psalm was used. The reference to offerings and burnt sacrifices (v. 3) suggests that the king offered these to gain the favor of God. The mention of "your heart's desire," "your plans" (v. 4), and "your petitions" (v. 5) indicate that the king, hoping to acquire divine blessing, offered prayers to God requesting plans and strategy for the future.

The address to the king, in verses 1–5, is the community's response to the king, offering him encouragement and well-wishing. It has the quality of indirect intercession. One can imagine the statements formulated as a prayer to God: "O Lord, answer the king in the day of trouble" (see v. 9, which has this prayer form), and so on. One can compare these to the form of certain of our well-wishes that are themselves forms of indirect prayer. "God bless you" when someone sneezes has this characteristic.

The community wishes a number of things for the monarch: an answer and protection from the Divine in the day of trouble, help and support from the temple, God's remembrance and favorable regard of the king's offering of worship, and the fruition of the king's plans and desires. Such texts as these clearly indicate that ancient Israel could closely associate human needs and desires with worship and see these as legitimate interests in worship. Prayers and worship focusing on success were common features of worship. Self-interest was certainly not ruled out of Israelite worship. In verse 5, the self-interest of the community becomes the focus, and the congregation expresses its hope that it might share in the king's victory and mark off its own territory.

In preaching on such texts, with their clear self-interest, the minister should not be apologetic about such a position. Instead, it can be emphasized that it may be best to express our wishes and self-interests in a religious context where that context and its theology can perform a moderating, enlightening role. In worship, the self-interest of the participants can be judged by other perspectives than merely the slide rule of success.

The king's responses, in verses 6–8, are expressions of confidence that God will answer and make the king victorious. ("His anointed" refers to the reigning king and could be translated "his [God's] Messiah.") The declaration "now" implies that something had happened in worship that gave the king assurance. It could have been the community's expression of its concerns (vv. 1–5) or some sign of the Divine's favor, such as a prophetic oracle or a special word from the priest.

The plural first person pronouns ("we") in verses 7–8 suggest that the king spoke on behalf of the entire community or that the community joined in the statements of assurance. These verses emphasize two things.

1. Hope of success in war is not to be found in chariots and horses but in God. (This, of course, doesn't mean that the ancient Hebrew army marched out to battle unarmed!) Here there is the acknowledgment that divine concerns lie behind human issues.

2. Those who boast of their armaments—horses and chariots—but do not worship God are doomed to failure, whereas those trusting God will be granted success.

The psalm concludes with an intercessory prayer in behalf of the king requesting that he be granted victory in the forthcoming battle (v. 9).

Ezekiel 17:22–24

It is likely that this reading has been selected for this day because Ezekiel's announcement about the tree is seen to serve as background for the Gospel reading, the parables of the seed growing secretly and of the mustard seed. And in the context of Christian worship, where these readings are juxtaposed, common themes appear, even beyond the imagery of growing things. Like Mark, Ezekiel has an enigmatic tone, and both see the coming of God's reign in terms of reversals in which the small becomes the great.

In the Book of Ezekiel, these verses stand as the conclusion to the long prophetic address of chapter 17. The first part of the chapter (vv. 1–21) contains a highly metaphorical presentation of the prophet's announcement of judgment. This section has features of the fable—animals and plants are characters that stand for human figures—and of the riddle, both making clear and concealing the point so that the hearer or reader has to ask about it. In almost allegorical fashion, the prophet tells the story of the eagle, the cedar, and the vine (vv. 3–10), and then gives its interpretation (vv. 11–21). It is not difficult to correlate the figures in the fable to actual historical characters, and thus to date the prophet's address. Ezekiel, taken with the first of the captives to Babylon in 597 BC, views with alarm the events transpiring in his homeland. The Babylonian king Nebuchadnezzar (the eagle in the tale), who had uprooted and humiliated the Davidic dynasty (the cedar), is moving to crush the rebellion of Zedekiah, the puppet ruler in Jerusalem (the seed from the land in the story). The interpretation makes it clear that Zedekiah and his rebels are doomed, and so they were, for Nebuchadnezzar destroyed Jerusalem in 586 BC.

Our reading for the day continues the language and some of the metaphors of 17:1–21, but its message stands in strong contrast to the first part of the chapter. In fact, the message of judgment is reversed to an announcement of salvation. Although this section probably comes from Ezekiel, it would have been composed later than the preceding verses.

Although in verses 1–21 the initiative seems to lie with the Babylonian king, here it is Yahweh who sets events into motion. Some of the same figures appear in verses 22–24, but the eagle has disappeared.

The unit begins with the prophetic messenger formula ("Thus says the Lord GOD") and ends with an expanded concluding formula for divine speech, the expansion affirming that the Lord will do what he says ("I will accomplish it"). Everything between these formulas is divine speech. In verses 22–23 the Lord sets out a series of actions that he will perform. As in 17:1–21, the language is indirect, metaphorical. The Lord promises to take "a sprig from the lofty top of a cedar" and plant it on a high and lofty mountain, a height in Israel. The sprig will grow to produce boughs and fruit, where all kinds of birds will live. The purpose of these actions is stated in verse 24: It is so that "all the trees of the field shall know that I am the LORD."

When read in its context, the meaning of the symbolic language is plain. It is a messianic prophecy. The sprig of cedar, like the cedar in verses 1–21, is the Davidic dynasty, which Yahweh promises to reestablish once again on Mt. Zion in Jerusalem, the "mountain height of Israel." Although the city and the temple now lie in ruins, Ezekiel is confident that Yahweh remains faithful to the old promise of a continuing king in the line of David and will reestablish that dynasty so that it flourishes. Thus there are strong thematic parallels with 2 Samuel 7 and Isaiah 11.

Why will the Lord do such a thing? Not for the sake of the Davidic dynasty itself, nor even for the people of Israel—certainly not because they have done anything to deserve the renewal of the kingdom. There is only one reason given for this free action of God—so that all the world "shall know that I am the LORD" (v. 24). God's coming acts of salvation are for the purpose of revealing that the God of Israel is God of the world.

Psalm 92:1–4, 12–15

This psalm, as the superscription suggests, was used in early Jewish worship services as the sabbath psalm. Seven psalms, which actually offer a summary of the basic tenets of Judaism, were sung by the Levites at the main temple services during the week: Psalms 24 (Sunday), 48 (Monday), 82 (Tuesday), 94 (Wednesday), 81 (Thursday), 93 (Friday), and 92 (Saturday). In Psalm 92, the Israelite name for God, Yahweh, occurs seven times (given as "the LORD" in the NRSV; vv. 1, 4, 5, 8, 9, 13, and 15). This can hardly be coincidental in a psalm intended for use on the seventh day of the week! The ancient rabbis even suggested that Adam was the author of this psalm and that he sang it on the first sabbath in the Garden of Eden.

This psalm is a thanksgiving, offering thanks for redemption from enemies (vv. 10–11). The first eleven verses are addressed directly to the Deity, whereas verses 12–15, proclamation or preaching, are addressed by the worshiper to a human audience.

Verses 1–4 declare that it is good to offer praise to God morning and evening. This may be a way of saying that it is good to offer praise "all the time." Or it may reflect the fact that daily sacrifices were offered in the temple in the morning and evening—when music would have accompanied the ritual (v. 3).

Verses 12–15 declare that the righteous, the faithful, are securely planted, firmly anchored, and will flourish and bear fruit even into old age. God is a rock upon whom life's house may be built with secure confidence, and the passing of time does not diminish the care and the products of life. Note the verbs that describe the faithful in verses 12–15: flourish, grow, produce fruit, are always full. In the imagery of the psalm, the faithful do not plant their house. They are planted in God's house; that is, they are a constant feature in temple worship.

2 Corinthians 5:6–10 (11–13) 14–17

Today's epistolary reading opens with a word of confident reassurance: "So we are always confident" (v. 6). Earlier Paul has insisted that he does not "lose heart," in spite of his apostolic afflictions (2 Cor. 4:1, 16). The clear hope of an "eternal weight of glory beyond all measure" (2 Cor. 4:17) does not eliminate the hard realities of earthly existence: "while we are still in this tent, we groan under our burden" (2 Cor. 5:4). Eventually, our mortal existence will be clothed with a new form of existence, or "be swallowed up by life" (2 Cor. 5:4). Even now, we have begun to taste this immortal life through the Spirit whom God has given us as a pledge (2 Cor. 5:5; cf. 2 Cor. 1:22; also Rom. 8:23; Gal. 3:14; Eph. 1:14). Mention of the Spirit prompts Paul to reaffirm that his courage is constant.

Christian existence is a dual existence. Those who have already experienced the "age to come," even partially through the earnest of the Spirit, can sharply distinguish between life in the earthly body and life with the risen Lord (cf. Phil. 1:22–26). Actually, "home" is existence in the earthly body, but preferably the Christian's home is "with the Lord" (cf. Phil. 3:20). Regardless of one's mode of existence, the ultimate aim is to "please him" (cf. Rom. 14:18; Eph. 5:10; Heb. 13:21). What makes it possible to remain confident in spite of this felt distance between earthly existence "in the body" and heavenly existence "with the Lord" is living by faith: "for we walk by faith, not by sight" (v. 7). The life of faith enables Christians to deal with life's optical illusions: things that are visible are transient, whereas things that are invisible are eternal (2 Cor. 4:18). One who walks by sight will obviously focus on the visible and thereby will see only what is temporary, whereas the one who walks by faith will see beyond the visible to what is permanent and eternal. The life of faith, then, by definition transcends bodily existence as it draws its sustaining power from the risen Lord whom we know but cannot see, except with the eyes of faith.

However much we might wish to be "away from the body and at home with the Lord" (v. 8), we nevertheless become responsible for life in the body. Ultimately, one must account for the "deeds done in the body" at the heavenly tribunal of Christ (cf. 2 Cor. 5:10; Rom. 14:10; Acts 10:42; also Rom. 2:16; 2 Tim. 4:1; 1 Pet. 4:5; also Eccles. 12:14).

The second part of today's epistolary lection is prompted by an apologetic concern. Paul remains sensitive to criticisms that he commends himself to his readers and he sometimes behaves as if he is beside himself (vv. 11–14). He reassures the Corinthians, however, that it is the "love of Christ," that is, the love that Christ has for him, that controls, or obsesses, him (v. 14). This prompts him to reflect on the work of Christ.

Paul's conviction was that "one has died for all" (v. 14). This doubtless means that Christ has died in behalf of all humanity rather than in humanity's stead (cf. 1 Tim. 2:6; also Gal. 1:4; 2:20; Eph. 5:2, 25; Titus 2:14; also Matt. 20:28 and parallels). The corollary is that "all (Christians) have died." The death of Christ was prototypical in that his self-emptying was complete, and in this sense he died the ultimate death. Similarly, those in Christ have experienced death both to sin and the law (Rom. 6:11; 7:4). Because Christ died for all, those who have gained life through his death may be said to have died to themselves in order to live for the One who died and was raised in their behalf (v. 15).

The effect of Christ's redeeming love on Paul was to alter his perspective completely. Once he had regarded Christ "from a human point of view," or "according to the flesh" (*kata sarka*). Most likely, this means that prior to his conversion and apostolic call, he had understood Christ in essentially human terms. He had failed to see in the Christ-event the eschatological turning of the ages, and thus for him it was merely an event of "this age." This point of view he held no longer, for he now saw the Christ-event as the triggering event of the New Age. In the Christ-event, God had reordered the universe. The God who brought light out of darkness in the first creation (cf. 2 Cor. 4:6) had effected a new creation, bringing even more dazzling light to the world through Christ. In the Christ-event, the old age had given way to the New Age.

To be "in Christ" means that one actually becomes a participant in this eschatological process in which the old age gives way to the new. Individually, this means that the one "in Christ" becomes a "new creature" (cf. Gal. 6:15; also Eph. 2:15; Col. 2:10). By experiencing death and resurrection with Christ, one is able to walk "in newness of life" (Rom. 6:4). Corporately, this means that one becomes a participant with God in bringing about reconciliation and peace (vv. 18–20).

Mark 4:26–34

All the lections for today register transitions of one type or another: historical, political, theological, or personal. The old comes to an end; something new is beginning. Our Gospel is no exception; Mark presents that something new as the kingdom, and he does so in parables about seed.

Mark 4 is devoted entirely to parables, an interpretation of one of them, and Mark's understanding of the role of parables in the ministry of Jesus. The parables found here are obviously a collection and do not represent a single teaching session by Jesus. In fact, it is not only a collection but a selection, a few samples, as verses 2, 33–34 make clear. The audiences for this material are two: a large crowd by the sea to whom Jesus speaks in parables (vv. 1, 34) and a smaller group of the Twelve and others with them to whom Jesus speaks about the parables (vv. 10, 34). Of the many things Jesus taught in parables (v. 2), Mark offers here only three, and they have the common theme of a seed that is sown: the sower (vv. 3–8), the seed growing secretly (vv. 26–29), and the mustard seed (vv. 30–32). Our lection consists of parables two and three and the closing comment about Jesus' use of parables (vv. 33–34). We will attend to this closing comment and then look at the two parables.

Mark's statement in verses 33–34 provides his understanding of the parables in Jesus' ministry, making as he does a general principle out of what he described in verses 10–12 as Jesus' method. On the basis of what is said in this chapter, several comments on Mark's view of parables can be made.

First, parables are not simple little stories used by Jesus so that everyone within the sound of his voice could understand his teaching. On the contrary, not everyone did understand, even though Jesus' offer was to anyone who had ears to hear (vv. 9, 23).

Second, parables are a form of literature that, like poetry, demand a great deal from the listener. They are not obvious to all and sundry, to every casual passerby who may or may not make any personal investment in Jesus or the kingdom. Parables, then, have a revealing/concealing quality, creating their own hearers and nonhearers.

Third, those who do hear are an inner circle, not of superior intelligence but of personal attachment to Jesus. They are "with Jesus." But even for these, understanding is not easy, even with Jesus' further instruction. As the interpretation of the parable of the sower illustrates (vv. 14–20), the explanation can be as difficult to grasp as the parable itself. But the point is, understanding is linked to one's relation to Jesus.

Fourth, the use of parables by Jesus is not surprising because Jesus was himself a parable of God. Jesus as the presence of God, as the Son of God, was not obviously so to everyone. He spoke of himself as the lamp; he spoke of light and shadow, of the revealed and the hidden (vv. 21–25). Only intentional, intense giving of oneself to him and his message is fruitful.

And finally, because the subject matter is the mystery of the kingdom, the listener should expect snatches of insight and partial discoveries rather than mastery of the subject matter.

And what do the two parables say of the kingdom? The parable of the seed growing secretly (vv. 26–29), which has no parallel in Matthew or Luke, has been interpreted from two perspectives. If verse 29 is the key, then the parable says that now is the time to reap the harvest; this is the end time; all that has gone before was but the growing season. More likely, however, is the interpretation that focuses more upon the growth that takes place totally apart from human effort (the sower sleeps and rises) and from human understanding ("he does not know how"). The seed carries its own future in its bosom, and efforts to coerce and force growth are futile. The kingdom of God is exactly that—the kingdom *of* God. The thought both chastens and encourages followers of Jesus.

The parable of the mustard seed (vv. 30–32) is clearly a word of encouragement. Let those concerned, frustrated, or even depressed by small beginnings, by the apparent insignificance of the enterprise to which life and resources are committed, take heart. Let the vision of the end ("the greatest of all shrubs") inspire and inform today's effort, knowing all the while that the end as well as the beginning are God's doing and not our own.

Proper 7 [12]
(Sunday between June 19 and 25 inclusive (if after Trinity Sunday))

1 Samuel 17: (1a, 4–11, 19–23) 32–49;
Psalm 9:9–20; or
1 Samuel 17:57–18:5, 10–16;
Psalm 133; or
Job 38:1–11;
Psalm 107:1–3, 23–32;
2 Corinthians 6:1–13;
Mark 4:35–41

Two options are provided in the *Common Lectionary* for Old Testament readings and the psalms of response. The story of David's slaying Goliath serves as the first option, with selected parenthetical verses serving to set up the story. The accompanying psalm selection heralds God's strength and willingness to side with those living against the odds.

The *Common Lectionary*'s second option relates events following the slaying of Goliath: David and Jonathan's deep friendship and Saul's jealousy of David. Psalm 133 offers a brief but moving paean on the pleasure of harmonious relationships.

For those not following the semicontinuous readings from 1 Samuel, the Old Testament reading is the first part of the Lord's speech to Job—a series of penetrating rhetorical questions inviting Job to probe the mystery of creation. The Lord's dominion over creation in all its fullness is praised in the selections from Psalm 107.

Yahweh's power to rule over chaotic creation is transferred to Jesus in the Gospel text, Mark's account of the stilling of the storm.

The epistolary selection presents Paul as God's co-worker, proclaiming the acceptable day of salvation and ministering through various forms of human chaos and tribulation.

1 Samuel 17: (1a, 4–11, 19–23) 32–49

In the previous reading in this sequence (1 Sam. 15:34–16:13), Samuel had designated and anointed David to be king over Israel; but he was still a boy, and the account made it clear that David would actually become king only in due course. The reading for today is one of the accounts of how David came to prominence and to the court of King Saul, necessary steps in his rise to the throne.

This is one of the best known and most charming stories in the Old Testament. It can stand on its own as a saga of the triumph of the weak over the strong, and doubtless it did as it was told orally in circles devoted to King David. But when viewed in its context in 1 Samuel, it is clear that the story of David's arrival in Saul's court had a complex and diverse history of composition. When in 1 Samuel 16 David appears in the Israelite camp bringing provisions for his older brothers, no one but his brothers had heard of him. He is introduced as young, beardless, and inexperienced as a soldier—although he reminds Saul that as a shepherd he had killed bears and lions, if not bare-handed, with only a club (vv. 34–36). But in the episode that immediately precedes this one (1 Sam. 16:14–23), we were informed that David had been called into Saul's court already, primarily because his musical skills were recommended as treatment for Saul's illness. But music was only one of his talents: David is said in addition to be "a man of valor, a warrior, prudent in speech, and a man of good presence; and the LORD is with him" (1 Sam. 16:18). Thus, as in the accounts of the rise of the first king, there were at least two distinct traditions that now are preserved side by side.

Moreover, this is not the only story of the defeat of the foreign giant named Goliath. According to 2 Samuel 21:19, it was not David but a certain Elhanan, one of David's heroes, who killed the giant. These parallels and contradictions reinforce what the contents and tone of the story of David's victory suggest, that this heroic account is not to be taken as historically reliable. Rather, it has its specific moral and religious points to make.

The story of David and Goliath is a beautifully told narrative. The scene is set in the lower hill country of Judah, in territory disputed by the Philistines. The two armies have gathered across a valley; but before the battle can be joined, the Philistine champion Goliath strides out and—in mocking tones—challenges Israel to send out someone to duel him. Both he and his armament are described in terrifying detail. His words and appearance have the desired effect, and no Israelite accepts the challenge.

Then David is introduced (v. 12). The scene shifts away from the battle to Bethlehem, to the home of a man named Jesse, who has several sons fighting in Saul's army; but one who is too young for battle has been taking care of his father's flocks. Jesse sends this son, David, to the camp with food for his brothers.

David arrived just as the armies were setting up the battle lines and, leaving the provisions with the "keeper of the baggage" (v. 22), he ran after his brothers just in time to hear Goliath issue his apparently daily challenge and to see the Israelites flee in fear (v. 24). As the soldiers talk about what has happened, David becomes more and more incensed, both at the Philistine, for defying "the armies of the living God" (v. 26), and at the Israelites for their timidity. When his brothers hear of his reactions, they chide him in a predictable way, pointing out that his duties lie back at home with the sheep (v. 28).

But David's talk has reached the ears of the king, who calls him in. David volunteers to fight Goliath and—when Saul objects—argues that he is indeed capable. David's reasons for fighting and his confidence are the same: this Philistine has defied the armies of the living God, and "The LORD, who saved me from the paw of the lion and the paw of the bear, will save me from the hand of this Philistine" (v. 37).

Still, the action does not yet move quickly. Saul has David clothed in his own armor and weapons. Again, as in the case of Goliath, the armament is described in detail. But the scene is almost comical. The tools of war are too large and too heavy for the young shepherd. Taking only his shepherd's staff and his sling with five stones, he approaches the giant.

Even now the pace of the narration is slow as the narrator describes the scene. We are shown the Philistine champion with his shield-bearer and are reminded that David is a ruddy youth, but to be sure a "handsome" one (v. 42). Goliath is insulted by the appearance of such an unworthy opponent, cursing David and vowing to feed his flesh to the birds and the wild animals. But David too must make his speech, and it is one of the most memorable in the Old Testament: "You come to me with sword and spear and javelin; but I come to you in the name of the LORD of hosts, the God of the armies of Israel, whom you have defied" (v. 45).

Now the climax comes quickly: as the enraged Philistine charges, David rushes forth, takes a stone, slings it and hits the giant in the forehead. Whether Goliath died from the missile or was only stunned and died when David cut off his head with the sword does not matter. The Philistine army quickly fled with the Israelites in pursuit. The aftermath of the story is that Saul took David into his court.

Certainly, one point of the story in ancient Israel was to glorify David and to legitimize his introduction into Saul's court. Moreover, the tale is not without its nationalistic pride, for the Israelites have the last word over the Philistines.

One of its central themes is the triumph of the weak over the strong, especially the righteous weak over the unrighteous powerful. And that is doubtless one of the most common homiletical readings of this story in the Christian church. To be sure, this is one of the most persistent and important themes of the Bible as a whole, that the last shall be first. But by no means should the account of David's triumph be turned into a heroic saga, although with all the concern with weapons as well as David's skill with the sling shot, that is tempting. It is by no means a lesson in the triumph of skill and bravery over brute strength. On the contrary, if David is presented as a model, it is as a model of faith. Increasingly throughout the story, the issue is posed in terms of the challenge to the God of Israel, and it has its climax more in David's sermon to Goliath than in the sling of the stone: "The LORD does not save by sword and spear; for the battle is the LORD's" (v. 47).

Psalm 9:9–20

Psalms 9 and 10 apparently were once a single, unified composition. The following are the components of verses 9–20; (1) a confession of faith in God's fidelity in times of trouble given as a statement about God (v. 9) and to God (v. 10); (2) a call to the people to praise God (vv. 11–12); (3) a plea addressed to God for help, combined with a description of an individual's trouble (v. 13); (4) a statement of a promise or vow formulated as a consequence clause (v. 14); (5) proclamation or an oracle (spoken by a priest?) addressed to the congregation (vv. 15–18); and (6) a final appeal for God to act (vv. 19–20).

Let us now highlight some of these elements. In the call to praise, four things are noted about God.

1. The Deity is described as the one who dwells or sits enthroned in Zion. Because the main Judean temple was in Jerusalem (Zion), then the Deity was associated in a special way with the city. As God's dwelling place, Zion was divinely protected (see Pss. 46; 48; 76). In later Judaism, Zion was considered the center, "the navel," of the world, the original point of creation, and the spot joining the earthly world with the upper and lower worlds.

2. Yahweh's reputation among the nations, the foreigners, is based on God's deeds; or conversely, God's deeds, manifest in the status and welfare of his people, are the means of establishing the divine reputation.

3. Yahweh is the one who holds people accountable for the shedding of blood. Throughout the Old Testament, God is the defender of life and holds humans accountable for killing (see Gen. 9:2; 2 Sam. 12:9–14). Even the taking of animal life was considered murder if the slaughterer did not give the blood (the life) back to God (see Lev. 17:1–4).

4. Finally, God is declared to be the helper of the afflicted, those oppressed, or the victims of misfortune. (The NJPSV translates verse 13 as "For He does not ignore the cry of the afflicted; He who requites bloodshed is mindful of them," reversing the two lines.)

The short pleas "Be gracious . . . See . . ." are followed by the nature of the trouble (suffering from enemies or haters) and an epithet of God; God is the one who lifts up from the gates of death (saves from sickness or from being killed). Perhaps the "I" here speaking was originally the king, and the enemies would have been foreign powers.

The promise/vow in verse 14 stipulates what the worshiper will do if redeemed: (1) recount God's praises (offer testimony) and (2) rejoice in thanksgiving/celebration. (See Ps. 118, a thanksgiving psalm in which the king offers thanksgiving for victory in battle; note the reference to opening the gates in 118:19, which suggests that the preceding thanksgiving took place outside the gates.)

The oracular proclamation in verses 15–18 functions as a priestly response to the appeal of the worshiper. The plans of the nations are declared as rebounding against themselves: they are caught in their own machination. The point made in the text stresses the close connection of deed/consequence, act/result. The nations are caught in their own devices, consumed by their own appetites, caught in their own traps. Here we have expressed the idea that the world and human actions operate in a sphere of moral equilibrium in which disruptions in life rebound against the offenders. In the four lines of verses 15–16, three have the process operate on its own. Only in 16a is God related to the judgment of the enemy/wrongdoer. In other words, in the action/reaction, deed/consequence relationship, God tends to function as the overseer of the process rather than as the avenging judge. Verses 17–18 are parallel to verses 15–16, although they express matters in different terms: the nations/the wicked shall end in Sheol, whereas the needy/the poor/the Israelites shall be remembered and saved. The NJPSV translates verse 19 as: "Not always shall the needy be ignored, nor the hope of the afflicted forever lost."

The appeal in verses 19–20 is a plea that God will act so that nations/humans would realize that they are but flesh and blood; that in the last analysis God rules. Although knowledge of the Divine is not stressed in these verses—there is no plea that God would act so that the nations would know he is God—one might say that self-knowledge is equivalent to divine knowledge. God's actions are to reveal humanity's true humanness; where there is true self-knowledge, there is God at work.

1 Samuel 17:57–18:5, 10–16

This reading in the semicontinuous Old Testament lessons for the season presumes the use of the alternative text in the same series, the account of David's triumph over the Philistine champion Goliath (1 Sam. 17 [1a, 4–11, 19–23] 32–49; see the commentary above). So it is another series of events in the story of David's rise to power. But it is also a story of Israel's first king, an episode in the tragic decline of Saul, especially if one includes the verses omitted from the assigned reading (18:6–9). No sooner has David entered Saul's service than Saul turns against him.

Although the narrative moves methodically to depict the rise of David and the decline of Saul, the text is filled with inconsistencies and even contradictions that reflect a complex history of traditions. First Samuel 17:57–58 presumes that David came to Saul's attention through his victory over "the Philistine" (Goliath's name is not mentioned here), and 18:10–11 presumes that David had already been brought into the king's court as a musician (1 Sam. 16:14–23). In 18:13 Saul makes David "a commander of a thousand," but in 18:5 Saul had already "set him over the army."

More important, Saul's growing hostility toward David is explained in three different ways, which in the narrative as a whole all serve to elevate the tension and sharpen the contrasts between these two characters. First, Saul's hostility is interpreted as jealousy. As the troops return from the battle, the women sing the praises of the king and the new hero:

> "Saul has killed his thousands,
>   and David his ten thousands." (18:7)

We hardly need to be told about Saul's anger, "for this saying displeased him" (18:8). Throughout the traditions about these two, David is shown to attract both men and women, whereas Saul becomes increasingly difficult to admire. "But all Israel and Judah loved David; for it was he who marched out and came in leading them" (18:16).

Second, Saul's hostility is interpreted in what we would call psychological terms. When the "evil spirit" comes upon him, "he raved within his house" (18:10), even trying to kill David with a spear. Saul's design is reported with the particularly vivid expression "I will pin David to the wall" (18:11). Saul's susceptibility to dark moods is well known. At no point does the narrator blame Saul, for he is out of control.

Third, both the rise of David and the decline of Saul are interpreted theologically. Even that evil spirit is "from God" (18:10). More fundamentally, David's success and his eventual ascension to the throne are divinely determined: "David had success in all his undertakings; for the LORD was with him" (18:14). This is the leading theme of the story as a whole. David is, to be sure, described as attractive and skillful as a soldier and a leader, but all those characteristics are gifts. On the other hand, the spirit of the Lord had departed from Saul. God is shown to be watching over events to ensure that his anointed comes to lead and govern the people of God.

Still, the human personalities play their parts. Saul is not portrayed as the villain in the piece. He is in every way a tragic figure and not blamed for his feelings of jealousy of David or even for his violent outbursts. We are led to understand and therefore to identify with him. Who has not experienced jealousy, moodiness, or possibly even felt tormented by evil spirits from the Lord? When we so easily identify with David's innocence, skill, and heroism, it is wise to remember that these are characterized as the presence of the Lord with him.

And there is that other character in this story, Saul's son Jonathan, noted only briefly but very important in the life of David. Jonathan's immediate and deep affection for David is noted without embarrassment. As soon as he sees him, Jonathan "loved him as his own soul" (better, "as himself," NJPSV, 18:1) and took the initiative in the friendship. We assume from the establishment of the "covenant" between the two that the affection was reciprocal, calling us to reflect on the importance of human friendship.

Psalm 133

This psalm has been discussed as one of the readings for the Second Sunday of Easter.

Job 38:1–11

This lesson, one of the best-known passages from the Book of Job—and justly so—is the beginning of the Lord's initial response to Job. Taken by itself, it may be heard as a rich and powerful statement about God, the created order, and human existence; it may be heard as an affirmation and praise of God's creation—just as "the morning stars sang together and all the heavenly beings shouted for joy" as the Lord laid the foundations for the earth (v. 7).

Read in the context of the book as a whole, however, the meaning of these lines is both deeper and more enigmatic. The broad structure of the book and its main themes are well known. It begins with a narrative account of the conversation between Yahweh—the divine name used also in this reading, but seldom in the body of the book—and Satan. The point at issue, the question that sets the book into motion, concerns human faithfulness or piety. Is that righteous man Job faithful because of his good fortune? Yahweh agrees to let Satan strike Job and his family in order to resolve the wager. And so it happens.

The poetic heart of the book seems to focus on a different question: Why do the righteous suffer? Job's three friends represent conventional wisdom and theology, with Job increasingly questioning God and challenging him to debate. Another and younger person, Elihu, offers less conventional answers to the point at issue. Then, in chapters 38–41, Yahweh responds to Job. That is followed by Job's confession (42:1–6) and a concluding narrative that reports Job's restoration to his previous circumstances and even more.

Given both what has transpired and what will come, the reader has every right to expect the divine speeches to be the resolution of the conflicts. Many readers over the centuries have seen that to be the case, and in rather straightforward ways: Yahweh asserts that he is God and Job is but a man whose knowledge is quite limited; therefore, Job should acknowledge God's wisdom, power, and justice. That reading may lead either to an agreement with the views of Job's friends—conventional wisdom and piety—or to the conclusion that the God who could agree to Satan's offer here merely rebukes Job and is a tyrant. Both these perspectives miss the complexity and depth of this passage and of the book as a whole.

Job 38:1–11 has two distinct parts. Verses 1–3 give the introduction to the entire divine discourse in chapters 38–41. That Yahweh "answered Job from the whirlwind" (better, "replied to Job out of the tempest," NJPSV) recalls Old Testament accounts of God's appearance attended by the disruption of nature (Exod. 19:16; Nah. 1:3). Moreover, this is just the way that Job said God would appear (Job 9:16–17), overpowering him. Yahweh's initial words directly refute what Job had said in 12:13. Most important, this introduction makes it clear that Yahweh has no intention of replying to Job's challenges. Instead of answers, Job himself will be questioned (v. 3).

The second part of our reading, verses 4–11, is the first move in Yahweh's lengthy address. And with his questions, Yahweh begins at the beginning: "Where were you when I laid the foundation of the earth?" (v. 4). Verses 4–7 concern God's creation of the earth, following the questions with images of the creator as architect ("determined its measurements"), engineer ("stretched the line upon it") and builder ("laid its cornerstone"). Verses 8–11 concern God's creative activity with regard to the primeval waters. The metaphors are mixed, involving both building boundaries and birth. The sea came out of the womb, and Yahweh shut it in with doors, "prescribed bounds for it, and set bars and doors" (v. 10). But above all, as in the account of creation in Genesis 1, it was God's word, God's command, that established the limits of the chaotic waters: "Thus far shall you come, and no farther" (v. 11).

One cannot miss the majestic affirmation of the Lord as creator, as well as the allusions to both biblical and nonbiblical creation traditions. But what is the force of this poetry in the context? The answer depends to a great extent on how one reads Yahweh's questions. They are rhetorical questions, to be sure, and as such make statements about Job and all humankind: You were not there at creation; I determined the measurements of the earth and established it; I am the one who brought light into darkness and set the limits for chaos. But they are also real questions that call for Job's response, and for ours. Do you know who you are? Do you know who God is? Those are the questions that lay the foundation for Job's confession in 42:1–6.

The Lord is presented as the one who established all that is—darkness as well as light, chaos as well as order. But that chaos has its divinely established limits. Job—and all who encounter darkness and chaos—is, finally, the one addressed by God. Having both suffered and struggled with God, he can face God as a different and full human being. And in the end, when God says that Job is the one who has "spoken of me what is right" (42:7), he includes not only the final affirmation of faith but the entire struggle that has brought him to that affirmation.

Psalm 107:1–3, 23–32

Psalm 107 is an all-purpose thanksgiving psalm for communal usage. Thanksgiving psalms were used after a period of trouble or distress had passed and thanks was given for redemption. The plight and redemption of various groups are reflected in this psalm: trouble in travel (vv. 4–9), imprisonment (vv. 10–16), illness (vv. 17–22), and danger at sea (vv. 23–32).

The opening verses of this psalm (vv. 1–3) are a general call to offer thanksgiving addressed to those who have experienced calamity but survived the ordeal.

Verses 23–32 describe those who were storm-tossed at sea and who experienced the negative mighty deeds of God in the surging waters of a storm that threatened to deposit their ship on the bottom of the sea. When courage failed and death threatened, an appeal to Yahweh led to the storm's calming and to a safe haven. One, of course, is here reminded of the story of Jonah. Simultaneously, the description of God's control of the watery unknown parallels the description of the sea in Job 38:1–11.

2 Corinthians 6:1–13

All this is from God" (2 Cor. 5:18). With these words, Paul prepares the way for our passage. Just before this, he has spoken primarily of the work of Christ (vv. 14-17), but now he emphasizes God's role in the work of salvation. Earlier he has stressed the initiative God has taken (2 Cor. 2:14, 17; 3:5; 4:1, 6, 14; 5:5), but now he elaborates on this more fully.

God's initiative may be seen in three areas: (1) the work of salvation, (2) the work of Christ, and (3) the work of ministry. First, God is the primary agent in the work of salvation.

The primary initiative in the work of reconciliation was taken by God. A similar point is made in 1 Corinthians 1:30: "He [God] is the source of your life in Christ Jesus." The Corinthians are what they are solely as the result of an act of God. Being made "the righteousness of God" (5:21) can be seen as nothing else than an expression of the "grace of God" (6:1). Paul quotes Isaiah 49:8 to reinforce this point: "At an acceptable time I have listened to you, and on a day of salvation I have helped you." The subject, of course, is God who lent an open ear to the prayers of fallen humanity and responded to the call for help.

God's saving work of reconciliation is first said to encompass "us" (5:18), that is, Paul, his colleagues, and doubtless all Christians. But the true scope is cosmic, for it is the world as a whole that is the object of God's reconciling love (5:19). Specifically, God's reconciliation means that God did not count the world's trespasses against them (5:19; cf. also Rom. 4:3–8). Reconciliation means, of course, that a relationship of enmity and hostility has been brought to an end, and in its place stands a relationship of peace and goodwill. Yet the initiative for bringing an end to the hostility existing between humanity and God lay with God: "all this is from God" (cf. Rom. 11:36; 1 Cor. 8:6).

Second, God is the chief actor in the work of Christ. The work of Christ is, of course, central, but Paul here stresses that Christ was the agent through whom God achieved reconciliation (5:18–19). This appears to be the sense of verse 19: "God was in Christ reconciling the world to himself" (REB). The well-known exegetical problem here is whether this is primarily a christological statement about the incarnation or whether it is primarily a soteriological statement emphasizing the reconciling work of God. If the former, the emphasis will lie on the first part of the verse, "God was in Christ," that is, incarnate, and reconciliation will be seen as that which was accomplished through the incarnation. If the latter, the emphasis will lie on the statement about reconciliation, and "in Christ" will be taken as parallel to "through Christ" in verse 18. In this case, Christ will be seen as the agent through whom the reconciling work of God was done. Given the way in which Paul's remarks in this passage stress the primacy of God in the work of salvation, the latter interpretation is to be preferred. This same emphasis is seen in 5:21: "For our sake he [God] made him to be sin who knew no sin." It was God after all, who took the initiative in sending the sinless One "in the likeness of sinful flesh, and to deal with sin" (Rom 8:3). The sinlessness of the Messiah became a cardinal belief in early Christian thought (cf. John 8:46; Heb. 4:15; 7:26; 1 Pet. 2:22) and was also a well-documented notion in Jewish thought of the time (cf. Psalms of Solomon 17:40–41; Testament of Judah 24:1; Testament of Levi 18:9).

Third, the work of ministry is ultimately initiated and accomplished by God. The ministry of reconciliation was given by God not only to "us"—that is, to Paul and his colleagues—but also to all Christians by extension. It should be regarded as a gift of God given by the mercy of God (2 Cor. 4:1), as a trust (5:19; also 1 Cor. 4:1); consequently, ministers are seen here as "ambassadors for Christ" (5:20), those speaking in Christ's stead (Philem. 9; Eph 6:20). Called to this ministry of service, ministers quite naturally see themselves as "servants of God" (2 Cor. 6:3). The language is quite clear: "God is making his appeal through us" (5:20). The person of the messenger simply becomes a vehicle, or conduit, through which the divine message is relayed, so that the appeal the messenger makes is God's own appeal: "Be reconciled to God" (5:20). It is in this sense that we can understand the quite audacious claim that ministers of reconciliation are God's co-workers (6:1; cf. 1 Cor. 3:9). As those who share in the "new creation" in Christ (5:17), they are participants in the eschatological work of God and thus are able to proclaim, "See, now is the acceptable time; see, now is the day of salvation!" (6:2; cf. Luke 4:19, 21).

The profile of ministry that results from God's divine activity within the apostle is sketched in verses 4–10. Remarkably prominent, of course, are the hardships Paul has endured in behalf of the gospel, yet he emerges as the irrepressible apostle whose cause is vindicated by the God he serves. It is worth noting that the theology of ministry that emerges here is consonant with his understanding and experience of the Christ-event. The arena where apostolic existence is finally proved is human hardship and pain, for it is here that the paradox of Christian living is experienced: living by dying, becoming rich by being impoverished, "having nothing, and yet possessing everything" (6:10).

Mark 4:35–41

Today's Gospel lesson records the first of several miracles joined by at least four crossings of the Sea of Galilee (4:35; 5:21; 6:45; 8:13) in the boat that had earlier been prepared for Jesus (3:1) and from which he had taught the crowds in parables (4:1). By means of the sea crossings, Mark is able to present the ministry of Jesus as extending to both Jews and Gentiles, with equal power to heal and to exorcise demons among both groups. This entire section, 4:35–8:21, highlights the power of Jesus and the failure of the disciples to understand who Jesus is.

Jesus' stilling the storm at sea (4:35–41) is clearly an exorcism story. That Jesus is exorcising a storm-demon is evident in the exorcism formula (the rebuke and command to silence) that Jesus used elsewhere in addressing demons (1:25). The story assumes the sea to be the abode of forces hostile to God (Pss. 74:13–14; 89:9–13; 104:5–9; Job 38:8–11) and portrays Jesus as possessing the power of God over those forces (Pss. 65:7; 89:9; Jon. 1:15–16). Our text, then, is a portion of that large portrait of Jesus in Mark 1–8 as the powerful Son of God, able to overcome disease, sin, demons, and death, a sharp contrast to the Jesus of Mark 9–15, who is in prospect and in fact the suffering and crucified Son.

Our text offers us one of those rare stories of Jesus' power being exercised in the presence of and for the benefit of his disciples alone. The boat scene is removed from Jewish crowds on one shore and Gentile crowds on the other (the story in 5:1–20 is an example of a ministry among Gentiles). What we have here is an occasion of Jesus alone with his followers, or in terms of Mark's situation, Jesus directly ministering to and addressing the church. What is being said?

The disciples are on a trip, not of their own choosing but at Jesus' command (v. 35). They are not alone, but they act as though they were. The world around them is one enormous storm of wind, wave, and rising water. Jesus is asleep, the picture of quiet confidence in the power of the God who made both land and sea (images and themes here recall Jonah 1: a ship, a storm, and the one person on board who trusts the Creator God is asleep). The activity that changes the situation is framed upon a double reproach. The disciples reproach Jesus (do you not care?), and Jesus reproaches them (why are you afraid?). This double reproach will appear again as the structure for the exchange between Peter and Jesus at Caesarea Philippi (8:27–33). What must not be overlooked here is that the power Jesus exercises over the storm is that of the "Teacher" (v. 38). In Mark this is the title for Jesus not only when he is teaching but when he is casting out demons. Read again 1:21–28 to recall how it is Jesus the teacher who exorcises and Jesus the exorcist who teaches. Undoubtedly, Mark is locating Jesus' power in his words, a matter of great importance for a church suffering in a persecuting world. Jesus' word is still present, and it is a word of power.

In this as in many stories to follow, the disciples do not understand. Their ignorance is not of the kind that results in poor grades in class; they do not know who Jesus is. So profound and destructive is this ignorance that they eventually will abandon Jesus (14:50). This not knowing Jesus lies at the root of their cowardice and fear. The story is not, as some sermons would have us believe, a simple one with the sequence of storm, fear, and then calm. The fear of the disciples is described as following Jesus' stilling the storm, following Jesus' reproach, "Why are you afraid? Have you still no faith?" (v. 40). It is then that Mark says, quite literally, "They feared a great fear" (v. 41). The NRSV's "They were filled with great awe" is hardly strong enough. The storm is frightening, to be sure, but they are in the presence of a power greater than the storm. They can only turn to one another and ask, "Who then is this, that even the wind and the sea obey him?" (v. 41). Mark ended the story with this question, confident that even if those first disciples did not know, the church to whom he wrote did. The church knew, but in the storm sometimes it forgot.

Proper 8 [13]
(Sunday between June 26 and July 2 inclusive)

2 Samuel 1:1, 17–27;
Psalm 130; or
Wisdom of Solomon 1:13–15; 2:23–24;
Lamentations 3:23–33 or Psalm 30;
2 Corinthians 8:7–15
Mark 5:21–43

The death of Saul and David's poetic tribute to his nemesis serves as the Old Testament reading for the *Common Lectionary*. A plaintive cry for deliverance is heard in Psalm 130, which concludes by acknowledging the Lord's steadfast love.

In the alternate set of readings, the Old Testament lection consists of two brief selections from The Wisdom of Solomon, both affirming God as the ally of life. Two responses are offered: the selection from Lamentations affirms the steadfast love of the Lord, while Psalm 30 also praises God as healer and giver of life.

God's capacity to give life and healing becomes exemplified in Jesus, who raises the daughter of Jairus and heals the hemorrhaging woman in the Markan text.

The epistolary lection comprises one portion of 2 Corinthians 8–9, the section of the letter dealing with the relief fund for the Jerusalem church.

2 Samuel 1:1, 17–27

It is important to remind ourselves of the narrative context of the death of Saul and Jonathan and of David's dirge. Between the appearance of David in the court of Saul—the preceding readings in this series—and the death of Israel's first king, a great deal has transpired. David has become one of Saul's leading warriors and has developed a very close friendship with Jonathan. Subsequently, however, Saul's illness has caused him to drive David away. Throughout Saul's life, Israel has struggled with the Philistines, and it was in a major battle with them that the king and his son lost their lives. But where was David? Remarkably, he and his band of men allied themselves with one of the Philistine kings, Achish of Gath, and engaged in a campaign against the Amalekites.

The report of the battle and of the death of Saul and Jonathan is given in 1 Samuel 31. The part of 2 Samuel 1 not included in the reading for the day (vv. 2–16) reports from the perspective of David's camp how he heard and responded to the news of the deaths. When the man from Saul's camp reported on Israel's defeat and the death of the king and his son, David's first response included the denial so familiar to us in similar circumstances. "How do you know that Saul and his son Jonathan died?" (v. 5). The man reports that he had actually been there, and, at the king's insistence, he had killed the mortally wounded Saul and then brought the crown and armlet to David. David's next response is mourning, including tearing his clothes, fasting, and weeping. Then, after asking the messenger almost rhetorically how it was that he was not afraid to destroy "the Lord's anointed," David has him killed. So much for the messenger.

David's lamentation is introduced with the equivalent of a modern footnote, "it is written in the Book of Jashar" (v. 18). Because the only other reference to this book (Josh. 10:13) also introduces poetry, it seems safe to conclude that the Book of Jashar was an ancient collection of songs and poems. Some of these songs and poems were quoted when the history of Israel was written, but most of them have been lost. The Books of Kings contain a great many "footnotes" such as this, citing "the Book of the Acts of Solomon" (1 Kings 11:41), "the Book of the Annals of the Kings of Israel" (1 Kings 15:31), and "the Book of the Annals of the Kings of Judah" (1 Kings 22:45).

Modern scholarship has identified the literary type or genre of a great deal of biblical literature, but this kind of song is one of the few identified by an ancient classification. It is a "lamentation," or dirge (see also Amos 5:1). The situation in which the dirge was used was, of course, the funeral. As a rule, such songs were composed according to a standard meter, with alternating lines of three and two accents. The mood, as befits the situation, is somber but dignified.

This lamentation contains no specifically religious expressions at all. There is no prayer or reference to God. This is consistent with the fact that the funeral in ancient Israel was not a religious occasion; in fact, contact with a corpse could render one ritually unclean. Through most of its religious history, ancient Israel considered death the end, a boundary that removed one even from the presence of God.

Perhaps the most valuable contribution such texts as this can render is to interpret us to ourselves. The situation to which it responds is all too common—death and the accompanying grief of those who remain. This dirge, like others in the Old Testament, contains many of the expressions that still are necessary at such times.

The elements include:

1. Wailing, moaning, and expressions of the pain of loss. Such notes recur throughout the song: "How the mighty have fallen!" (vv. 19, 25, 27); "I am distressed for you, my brother Jonathan" (v. 26).

2. A description of the catastrophe (v. 21).

3. Expressions of anger. In this case, they are directed both at the Philistines (v. 20) and even at the mountains where Saul and Jonathan died (v. 21).

4. A description of the situation before death, the life with those who died. The song speaks of the great contributions of those who died (vv. 22–24) and of the special relationship between the dead one and the bereaved (v. 26).

5. A call for others to mourn or grieve (v. 24).

Mourning and grief will include even more elements, but most of those are always present. What minister visiting a family who has just experienced death has not heard all of those expressions? The strength and value of the Old Testament lamentations, like many of ancient Israel's prayers as well, lie in their realism. One's anguish and grief deserve to be expressed fully and openly.

Psalm 130

This psalm was discussed as one of the readings for Proper 5 [10].

Wisdom of Solomon 1:13–15; 2:23–24

There is considerable uncertainty about the specific date and circumstances of the composition of The Wisdom of Solomon. The book definitely was not written by Solomon, to whom it is attributed on the grounds of the tradition of his great wisdom. The book was composed in the Hellenistic period by a pious and learned Jew living outside Palestine. It almost certainly was originally written in Greek, most likely in Alexandria, and probably in the first century before Jesus. The book as a whole, addressed to Jews in a pagan world, is a remarkable argument for faithfulness to the ancient covenant. The author both polemicizes against and is influenced by various aspects of the dominant Hellenistic culture.

Although the verses assigned for this day are taken out of context, they epitomize the main themes of the first section of the book, chapters 1–5. Those chapters contain a series of exhortations to live the life that is immortal. They are part of the book's larger argument for faithfulness. The main concern of this initial series of exhortations are immortality and death. The views articulated on those issues go far beyond those in the Hebrew Scriptures, but at the same time the writer makes explicit connections with ancient biblical traditions.

The reading for the day actually begins in the middle of a sentence. Verses 13–15 of chapter 1 depend directly upon verse 12. Verse 12 is an exhortation to avoid death and destruction by avoiding error and wrongful deeds, and verses 13–15 give the reasons or argument for the exhortation. Death is linked directly with error or unrighteousness (see also 1:8, 16), and righteousness with immortality. The fundamental point is that those who are unrighteous die and those who are righteous will have eternal life. Our verses argue that God is the creator of life but not of death: "He does not delight in the death of the living. / For he created all things that they might exist" (vv. 13–14).

The writer alludes here to the story of the creation and the so-called Fall in Genesis 2–3, and particularly to the words addressed to the man in 3:19: "you are dust and to dust you shall return." The argument is that because the righteous God created life, "righteousness is immortal" (v. 15), and therefore those who are righteous are immortal. It is important to emphasize that the writer is passionately concerned with morality, justice, and righteousness, and that he sees a continuum of the present and the eternal life of the righteous. Death, like injustice and unrighteousness, is an aberration. On the one hand, the words and deeds of "the ungodly" (1:16) are the cause of death, but on the other hand, death was brought into the world by "the devil's envy" (2:24).

The second part of the reading, 2:23–24, presents a summary and interpretation of the creation accounts in Genesis 1–3. The "image of God" (Gen. 1:26–27) is taken as immortality. The snake of Genesis 3:1 is viewed as the devil, and his motives are judged to be envy. The snake thus brought death into the world, and the first human beings perpetuated it by their disobedience of the divine command.

These views, which clearly stand in the background of such New Testament books as the Gospel of John and the Book of Hebrews, go far beyond those of the Book of Genesis, or the remainder of the Hebrew Scriptures for that matter. Although the meaning of "the image of God" in Genesis 1 is debated and debatable, it certainly did not refer to immortality. There is no expression of such an understanding of human life in the Hebrew Scriptures. When the afterlife becomes an issue, late in the development of the Hebrew Scriptures, it is fundamentally in terms of the resurrection of the dead in the framework of apocalyptic expectations of the end (Dan. 12:1–4). This interpretation of the snake in Genesis 3 moves to a dualism that is incompatible with the ancient Israelite affirmation of God's authority. In fact, Genesis 3:1 almost polemically emphasizes that the snake, although crafty, was one of the "wild animals that the LORD God had made." So we see how, in a new culture with its different understandings of the world and of human nature, the Scriptures are appropriated in new ways.

For all the text's preoccupation with eternal life, it is important to stress the moral context in which that issue is considered and argued. Righteousness is life. Those who are righteous live. Because God's righteousness is eternal, those who live out of that image of God will live eternally.

Lamentations 3:23–33

A portion of Lamentations 3 is one of the readings for Holy Saturday, and at that point in the commentary on the lectionary one can find a general discussion of the chapter and its context.

This particular reading was selected to parallel the reading from The Wisdom of Solomon because both address the problem of God and human suffering. Just as the reading from Wisdom denies that death ultimately derives from divine will, so the reading from Lamentations denies that God willingly afflicts or grieves anyone merely for the sake of imposing suffering.

The nub of this section culminates in verse 33, which has been variously translated. The NJB paraphrases a bit to read the sense: "For it is not for his own pleasure / that he torments and grieves the human race." The NJPSV translates:"For He does not willfully bring grief / Or affliction to man."

After reciting a litany of great suffering viewed as divine actions and punishments (3:1–19), the author changes the focus with verse 19. (The reading, to coincide with the sense, should begin with verse 19.) In the midst of unbelievably troubled times, the text states a thesis: "The kindness of the Lord has not ended, / His mercies are not spent" (v. 19; NJPSV). In spite of life so full of suffering that one forgets what happiness is (v. 17), the writer affirms that suffering is only the prologue, the backhand of God. Over against and underneath the negative actions of God, there remains the mercy of God.

In addition to affirming God's ultimate goodness and God's benevolent nature, the text also affirms the value and educational benefits that derive from divinely sent human suffering. Patience and waiting for life's fate to change are therapeutic (v. 26: "It is good to wait patiently / Till rescue comes from the Lord," NJPSV). The writer does not mention what steps one might have taken in lieu of waiting on God, but all of us can supply those: impatience, surrender to inevitability, pessimism, depression, despair, and so on.

This text comes the nearest to any Old Testament passage in arguing for the educational benefits that come from divine judgment.

> It is good for a man, when young,
>   To bear a yoke;
> Let him sit alone and be patient,
>   When He has laid it upon him.
> Let him put his mouth to the dust—
>   There may yet be hope.
> Let him offer his cheek to the smiter;
>   Let him be surfeited with mockery.
> For the Lord does not
>   Reject forever,
> But first afflicts, then pardons
>   In His abundant kindness. (vv. 27–33, NJPSV)

Psalm 30

This psalm was discussed previously as one of the readings for the Sixth Sunday After the Epiphany.

2 Corinthians 8:7–15

Today's epistolary lection should be read in light of chapters 8 and 9, which are devoted to the topic of the collection for the Jerusalem poor. Earlier, Paul gave directions to the Corinthians concerning this relief fund (1 Cor. 16:1–2), a project to which he had committed himself early on (Gal. 2:10). His former instructions were primarily matters of protocol on how the funds should be collected within the church. By the time he writes these two chapters, the Corinthians appear to have lost enthusiasm for the project, and Paul's task now is to convince them to make good their earlier intentions (v. 10). As it turns out, these two chapters constitute the most extensive set of remarks in any of his epistles concerning the question of financial stewardship. For this reason, they provide an abundant resource for modern Christians who often need to be challenged to contribute financially to worthwhile projects.

First, consider a few words about the collection. As we know from various references in the Pauline letters, this project had vast importance for Paul. It occupied much of his time and attention during his ministry in the Aegean area in the 50s. It was first, and foremost, a charitable gesture toward the poor in Jerusalem, and for this reason alone had merit (cf. Gal. 2:10; Rom. 15:26). But it was more than a relief fund. It also had great symbolic significance in that it served as a concrete expression of solidarity between the Gentile Christians and Jewish Christians. As Paul stresses elsewhere, because the Gentiles had shared in the spiritual legacy of the Jewish Christians, they should express their debt by alleviating the financial needs of the Jerusalem poor (cf. Rom. 15:27; also 2 Cor. 9:11–14). If successful, this collection could serve as a vivid symbol of the unity of the Jewish and Gentile churches.

In addition, there may also have been eschatological significance to this project. As Paul states in Romans 9–11, his hope was that the conversion of the Gentiles would eventually bring about the conversion of all Israel. Once this occurred, the Eschaton could be ushered in. The collection appears to have been a central element in his mission strategy and to this degree would have played an important role in his ultimate mission.

In today's epistolary lection, Paul appeals to the Corinthians in several ways to participate in the collection. First, he adduces the example of the Macedonian churches who had given generously even though they were in no financial position to do so (2 Cor. 8:1–5). They had given even beyond their capacity, and in this respect surprised Paul. Yet the clue to their generosity lay in their prior commitment of their very selves: "they gave themselves first to the Lord" (2 Cor. 8:5). He admits quite openly that he tells them about the keenness of the Macedonians in order to put their own love to the test (v. 8).

In appealing to the Corinthians, Paul begins by underscoring their abundance. They "excel in everything—in faith, in speech, in knowledge, in utmost eagerness, and in our love for you" (v. 7). He now hopes that their zeal to excel will translate into enthusiastic commitment to "this generous undertaking." Earlier, Paul had emphasized how abundantly they had been blessed (1 Cor. 1:5). What is striking is the way in which he inventories their pool of resources. All of these things that he mentions are spiritual gifts rather than monetary assets, yet Paul insists that they represent a store of abundance out of which the Corinthians can give. As he says later, they have become rich (v. 9; cf. 1 Cor. 1:5; 2 Cor. 9:11; also Eph 3:8). This becomes a salutary reminder that our possessions are not merely monetary, but that what we have come to enjoy in Christ must be accounted as genuine wealth.

Second, Paul adduces the example of Christ: "Though he was rich, yet for your sakes he became poor, so that by his poverty you might become rich" (v. 9). Here, of course, he is referring to Christ's exalted status prior to his incarnation (Phil. 2:5–11), which, on any showing, can only be regarded as a position of privilege, indeed wealth. In his self-emptying, however, he relinquished the supreme possession—life with God. As the Gospels make clear, the lot of the historical Jesus was one of modest possessions, if not poverty (Matt. 8:20; Luke 9:58).

The form of this verse is chiastic: Christ, who was rich, became poor, so that we, who are poor, might become rich. Some have suggested that this is a fragment from an early Christian hymn, and it may well be, although it is difficult to prove. By its chiastic pattern, however, the verse does serve to illustrate the paradox of the incarnation (cf. 2 Cor. 5:21; Rom. 15:3).

Though he does not do so here, Paul might well have appealed to his own example in this respect, for his own apostolic behavior also exemplified a willingness to pauperize himself in order that others might enjoy the riches of the gospel (cf. 1 Cor. 4:11; 13:3; 2 Cor. 6:10).

Third, Paul mentions their earlier commitment (vv. 10–14). For whatever reason, the Corinthians had earlier committed to the project but had not followed through. Perhaps the controversy with the opponents in the church had preoccupied their attention. Or they may simply have lost enthusiasm for the project. In any event, Paul stresses that they should give out of what they have and not try to give what they do not have (v. 12). He also stresses that the operative norm should be "fair balance" (vv. 13–14). In this instance, the Jerusalem poor are in need, and the Corinthians should give out of their abundance to meet the need. In the future, if it turns out that the Corinthians are in need, then from the abundance of the Jerusalem church the needs of the Corinthians will be supplied. He adduces the example of the people of Israel in the wilderness who, when fed with manna, were equitably served (Exod. 16:18).

Mark 5:21–43

As stated in the comments last week on Mark 4:35–41, two double crossings of the Sea of Galilee join the stories in 4:35–8:21. Mark says that Jesus ministered on both the Jewish shore and the Gentile shore of the sea. By this arrangement of the material, Mark is declaring that Christ blesses without partiality Jew and Gentile, near and far, clean and unclean. In the immediate context of our lesson, Jesus had crossed the sea (4:35; 5:1) and performed a most extraordinary exorcism in Gentile territory, among swine keepers, no less (5:1–20)! He has now returned to the western shore (v. 21) to Jewish territory, and the two stories that follow are Jewish in context and implication. One has to do with a synagogue ruler (vv. 22–24, 35–43) and the other with a woman who was, according to Jewish law (Lev. 15:25–30), unclean by reason of her flow of blood. Both stories also carry symbolically the tradition of Judaism in the number twelve: the woman was ill twelve years (v. 25); the ruler's daughter was twelve years old (v. 42).

We have spent enough time in Mark to recognize in the structure of our text a prominent feature of this Gospel: one story is split (vv. 21–24, 35–43) and another is inserted (vv. 25–34). We have noticed this trait earlier (1:21–28; 3:20–35) and will have other examples of it later. The question is, What does Mark intend by this? One could see here no more than the style of a good storyteller: the inserted story builds anticipation for the conclusion of the first. Or one could say that the inserted story is logically necessary to allow time for the condition of the child to worsen and for her to die. But because Mark has elsewhere used this structure to allow stories to interpret one another (as in 1:21–28 and 3:20–35), we may assume this to be the case here.

The stories are alike in their telling. Both involve cases of extreme need: the woman has exhausted all options and all resources and is now desperate; the girl is gravely ill and dies before Jesus arrives. In both, large crowds are on the scene but are not privy to what is really happening. As for the disciples, they are blind to the one healing and, except for the select three, are absent from the other. In the case of the woman, the disciples are so excited about the big crowd that they cannot distinguish between a push and a touch (vv. 30–31), and the responses to Jesus' ministry are similar: "fear and trembling" (v. 33) in one, "overcome with amazement" (v. 42) in the other. But the two stories are joined at a deeper level.

Perhaps it would be sufficient to say that Mark, concerned to show the power of the "stronger one" (chaps. 1–8), here offers examples of Jesus' overcoming sickness and death. That Jesus brought the helping, healing, life-giving presence of God to the human scenes of disease, fear, alienation, and death is good news for a lifetime of witnessing. But the issues are not solely medical, nor are the blessings solely private. Social factors are prominent. A girl is dead, and because a corpse defiles, certain taboos are now in place (Lev. 21). A woman has a discharge of blood and therefore is to her family, her friends, her neighbors, and her synagogue, an outcast (Lev. 15:25–30). But the Jesus who ministered among foreigners (vv. 1–20) is here among his own people moving across religious and social barriers to offer God's healing and restoring grace. This, says Mark, is not simply the church's belief about Jesus, but the warrant, in fact, the mandate, for its own behavior toward all persons.

Proper 9 [14]
(Sunday between July 3 and 9 inclusive)

2 Samuel 5:1–5, 9–10;
Psalm 48; or
Ezekiel 2:1–5;
Psalm 123
2 Corinthians 12:2–10;
Mark 6:1–13

David's anointing as king serves as the Old Testament reading in the *Common Lectionary*, while Psalm 48 responds by praising the God who dwells in Zion.

In other lectionaries, the Old Testament reading is the Lord's first commission to Ezekiel, commanding him to preach to a rebellious people. The plea of Psalm 123 is for the Lord to assist those who are scorned and held in contempt.

In the Gospel reading, Mark's account of Jesus' rejection at Nazareth and the subsequent call of the Twelve, Jesus' proclamation to his unreceptive hometown parallels the context in which Ezekiel's prophetic preaching occurs.

Paul's mystical experience of being caught up into the third heaven serves as the epistolary reading for today, a reminder that prophetic experience may involve both agony and ecstasy.

2 Samuel 5:1–5, 9–10

The account of how David became king over all Israel and then took the city of Jerusalem notes that seven and one half years have passed since the death of Saul and Jonathan. In those years David has become king over Judah in the South (2 Sam. 2:11), and Ishbosheth, a son of Saul, has been set up as king in the North by Abner, one of Saul's generals. But Abner has a falling out with Ishbosheth and decides to transfer his loyalty to David, even proposing to the elders of Israel that David should be king of all the tribes (2 Sam. 3:17–19). Abner's appearance in the South to make an alliance with David revives the old family feud between Joab, David's general, and Abner. The immediate background of our reading for the day is Joab's murder of Abner and the murder of Ishbosheth by several of his captains. When the murderers carry Ishbosheth's head to David in Hebron, thinking that he will be pleased, David has them executed. As 2 Samuel 5 begins, then, David is well established in the South, and the North is without a leader, either king or general.

Second Samuel 5:1–12, the broader context for the assigned verses, contains four distinct paragraphs. The first (vv. 1–3) reports how the representatives of the northern tribes took the initiative, came to Hebron, and anointed David. Two steps are described: first the designation by "all the tribes" and then the covenant ceremony with anointing by "all the elders of Israel." The tribes cite the divine promise that is hereby fulfilled: "The LORD said to you, 'It is you who shall be shepherd of my people Israel, you who shall be ruler over Israel'"(v. 2). David's authority thus derives from his election by Yahweh and also from the people who acknowledge him and that election. Moreover, David is the one who "made a covenant with them" (v. 3); that is, he submitted himself to the stipulations of the covenant. In ancient Israel, as we will see later in the life of David, the king does not stand over the law but is subject to the divine law and his obligations to the people. That fact is further underscored here by the note that the covenant was made "before the LORD," that is, in the sanctuary.

The second unit (vv. 4–5) is a historical note concerning David's age and the length of his reign. There is no serious reason to doubt the historical reliability of the information. The forty years of his kingship would have been ca. 1000–961 BC.

The third unit (vv. 6–10) reports how David took the city of Jerusalem and made it the capital of the now-united kingdom. The sequence of events is difficult to reconstruct, primarily because the anecdote unfolds as the explanation of a proverbial saying, "The blind and the lame shall not come into the house" (v. 8), that is, into the sanctuary. The original inhabitants of Jerusalem are said to have taunted David, asserting that even the blind and lame could defend the city against him. They could not, and he took the stronghold apparently by superior tactics. There was no pitched battle, siege, or destruction of the defenses. The action had two far-reaching consequences: (1) the earlier inhabitants were not killed but were incorporated into David's state, and (2) Jerusalem had not previously belonged to any of the tribes, and it was near the border of Judah and Israel. Consequently, it was an ideal neutral site to serve as the capital of the new kingdom.

The final paragraph (vv. 11–12) notes that David quickly attracted international attention and arranged for Hiram of Tyre to build him "a house," a palace of some kind. It concludes with the observation that not only had the Lord made David king and exalted the kingdom for the sake of his people Israel, but also that David recognized the activity of God in those events.

When these stories are viewed in their wider biblical context, a number of important theological issues and themes for proclamation emerge.

1. The Davidic king, the anointed one or "messiah" of God, and the Holy City, "the city of David," are perpetually linked. With these accounts of David's anointing and the taking of Jerusalem, we are reminded on the one hand that God's activity with human beings occurs in particular and concrete places, and on the other hand that some places are holy, set apart, because they are experienced as special meeting places of human beings with the divine presence.

2. David's kingship evokes reflection on several matters concerning faith and politics. He comes to the throne, we are told, in accordance with the will of the Lord. But the process by which that occurs is recounted with stark realism; it happened in the full light of history. Political intrigue, personal conflicts, murders, and wars all played their parts. The ancient Mesopotamian view of the origin of government is radically different. The Sumerian king list begins, "When kingship first came down from heaven . . ." Behind these Old Testament accounts of first Saul's and then David's acceptance as king stands a theological controversy: Should the people of God be ruled by a king? Some said, "Yes, it is the will of God." Others

said no, and for the reason expressed in Psalm 48: "Yahweh is our king." The prevailing Old Testament answer was that the people of God in the world would have a king—a human government—but one whose actions would be subject to God.

Psalm 48

One of the Old Testament lections for today tells the story of David's capture of Jerusalem. Psalm 48, one of the Zion psalms, provides us with some insight into what the Israelites came to believe about Zion. Thus it represents what one might call biblical Zionism. Like Psalm 46, it proclaims the impregnability of Zion—her protection by God from all her enemies.

Psalm 48, and the other hymns of Zion, were probably used during major festivals and were sung to express the people's faith in Jerusalem and in the God whose temple was there. The last part of this psalm, verses 12–14, seems to presuppose a pilgrim procession circling the city perhaps before entering it for the main festival celebrations.

The following is the structure of the psalm: (1) hymnic praise of Yahweh, the God who cares for Mt. Zion (vv. 1–3), (2) the divine protection of the sacred mount and the destruction of its enemies (vv. 4–8), (3) thanks offered to God for divine concern (vv. 9–11), and (4) the call to the people to circumambulate the city (vv. 12–14).

This psalm has drawn heavily on the mythological thought of the ancient Near East. Mount Zion is described in terms that greatly exceed any normal description; that is, the sacred mountain is depicted in terms of the ancient concept of a cosmic mountain conceived as the abode and specially defended preserve of the Deity. We will note some of these features throughout the psalm.

Verses 1–3 are a hymn that speaks of God in the third person. In these verses, Zion is described as God's holy mountain, beautiful in elevation, the joy of all the world. Mount Zion is also spoken of as in the "far north" or in the "recesses of Zaphon." Geographically, of course, Jerusalem was not located in the north of Palestine. This description probably has to be understood in light of Canaanite mythology. In the pre-Israelite religion of Canaan, the god Baal was enthroned and ruled as king on Mount Zaphon. The word *zaphon* in Hebrew came to mean "north" because Mount Zaphon was located north of Palestine in Phoenicia. The imagery of the Divine ruling on the mountain of the north has here been applied to the Israelite God and the city of Jerusalem.

The significance and beauty that are assigned to Zion are understood as the consequence of God's presence in the city where God's temple or home is. Enthroned in the temple, God rules over the world from Jerusalem, the center of the universe, as the great king. Within the city, God's defenses are sure. Such language about Zion is clearly intended to solicit and express feelings of confidence, contentment, and at-home-ness from the worshiper. Zion symbolizes a place of security, a place in which one encounters a special religious dimension, and, as such, Zion is a taste of the world as it was meant to be and someday will be.

Verses 4–8 speak of the enemy kings who assembled to attack Jerusalem only to be seized by panic, terror, and fright. The kings, once they see the sacred mount, become astounded and tremble as if they were women in the throes of childbirth. The reader of this psalm should not seek to find some historical event that gave birth to the psalm. No specific historical event lies behind the description of the assault on Zion; instead, the depiction is dependent on cultic, symbolic imagery. When the community celebrated and proclaimed

God's divine protection of the city, the enemies were any and all opponents against God and the Holy City. The reference to the ships of Tarshish in verse 7 clearly does not belong in any realistic presentation of an attack on Jerusalem, for the city was miles inland from the sea. Yet such imagery could be used as poetic license to illustrate that Zion is protected from all forms of attack.

Over against the rulers of the world and the enemies of God's people stands the sacred city, which God has established to stand forever. Note that each of the first two stanzas has this type of affirmation (in vv. 3, 8) to round off the content of each of these sections.

Verses 9–11, which take the form of direct address to the Deity, affirm that it was in worship, "in the midst of your temple," that the people gave thought to the love of God expressed in his care for Zion. The people confess that the true response to such love was praise, rejoicing, and gladness. One should note that verse 9 focuses on a particular locale—the midst of the temple—whereas verse 10 affirms that the praise of God has no locale; it extends to the end of the world.

The call in verses 12–14 to view Zion and march round its fortifications can be seen as the call for the people to be a link in the chain of tradition that passes on, from one generation to the next, the truth of God and the divine care for Zion. Thus the worshiper is invited to become a custodian of the lessons of the present for generations yet to come.

Ezekiel 2:1–5

These verses stand at the heart of Ezekiel's report of his vocation in Ezekiel 1:1–3:15. They contain his commission from the Lord—reiterated and further specified in 3:4–10—and as such directly address the questions of the role of the prophet and the content of his message to the people of God.

These verses present the first words of God to Ezekiel in the context of a vision. The book begins with an introductory specification of the date and location of the experience (1:1–3). The prophet was in Babylon, taken there with the first wave of Judean exiles in 597 BC. The date ("the fifth year of the exile of King Jehoiachin," 1:2) would have been 593 BC. What follows in 1:4–28 is the great vision of the divine throne room. Although more dramatic and detailed, this vision report parallels that of Isaiah 6 and 1 Kings 22:19–22. Thus Ezekiel's report and the experience itself stand in a long tradition. Even with all the awesome sights, Ezekiel did not actually see God: "This was the appearance of the likeness of the glory of the Lord" (1:28).

The narrative as a whole has most of the typical features of Old Testament vocation reports. (In addition to Isaiah 6 and 1 Kings 22, see Jer. 1:4–10; Exod. 3:1–4:17; Judg. 6:11–40.) There is the epiphany, or appearance, of God; the address to the one called with a commission to a particular task; the expression of reluctance or unworthiness; words of reassurance from God; and a sign or symbolic act of ordination. In the cases of the prophets, this sign relates to the mouth. Although in this account God reassures the prophet ("Do not be afraid of them, and do not be afraid of their words," 2:6), Ezekiel is never heard to express his fears or inadequacy. On the contrary, the Lord commands him to eat the scroll on which are written "words of lamentation and mourning and woe" (2:10); he eats it and reports that "it was as sweet as honey" (3:3).

In 2:1 the report turns from descriptions of what the prophet saw to the account of what he heard. To be sure, in the vision itself there had been noise (1:24–25), but now there are words. The first part of the divine address (vv. 1–2) put Ezekiel in the proper posture and position to hear the commission (vv. 3ff.). The prophet, who had obviously fallen on his face, is first commanded and then enabled to stand on his feet. The address begins with the designation used almost a hundred times in the Book of Ezekiel, *ben adam*, "mortal" (NRSV), more typically translated "son of man." This is not at all a messianic title in Ezekiel but a means of contrasting the human messenger with the God who has sent him.

The commission tells Ezekiel what to do and what to say. Like other prophets (see Amos 7:14–15), he is sent to a particular people. Although all that remains of the people are the Judeans, both in Babylon and in Judah, the broader theological designation "people of Israel" is used. At the very outset, the substance of the prophetic message is suggested, for they are "a nation of rebels who have rebelled against me" (v. 3). Thus Ezekiel's message will begin with the indictment of Israel for its rebellion against its God, stretching over the centuries and "to this very day." The heading for all of Ezekiel's words to Israel—what he is to say to them—will be "Thus says the Lord GOD" (v. 4). Like all the prophets before him, Ezekiel is to communicate the word of God. His words will interpret history and the present circumstances of the people in terms of God's will and ways with them, and theirs with their God. The final line of our reading, "they shall know that there has been a prophet among them" (v. 5), do not refer to the powerful presence of the prophet but to the presence of the word of God through that prophet.

The substance of the message will be specified further as indictment of sin, warnings and admonitions, and announcements of judgment. In short, they are in exile because of their unfaithfulness, and further trouble will come unless they change their ways.

The commission also includes the preparation of the prophet for difficult times ahead. He is to fear not and to be resolute in fulfilling his commission, although "briers and thorns" will surround him and he will "live among scorpions" (2:6; see also 3:8–9). He is to speak the words that the Lord God gives him, "whether they hear or refuse to hear" (v. 5). As 3:16–21 explains further, the word of God is a matter of life and death for the people of Israel, but the prophet's role is limited. Finally, it is up to the people to respond or refuse to respond. So the prophet's role, important as it is, is limited.

Psalm 123

This is one of the pilgrim psalms. The psalm begins with a first person singular speaker ("I" in v. 1) but shifts to the plural in verse 2 following. This perhaps suggests that the psalm was sung antiphonally by the pilgrims as they made their way to a festival. Verse 1 and verses 3–4 are expressed as a prayer to God, but verse 2 is a confessional statement in human-to-human address.

In verse 2, the hope is expressed that one's concentration will be so focused on God that one can obey the Deity like a servant who obeys the commands of another merely by receiving hand signals, without verbal communication having to take place.

The pleas for divine mercy in verses 3–4 speak of a situation of distress caused by being held in contempt by others. The lack of anything specific in the description makes it impossible to sense anything about the trouble other than its creation of a feeling of alienation.

The psalm provides an appropriate response for the reading from Ezekiel and like that text stresses the necessity of obedience as well as the hostility and scorn experienced when one's stance is not popular.

2 Corinthians 12:2–10

In the cycle of readings from Second Corinthians that began several weeks ago, only this passage stems from the larger section comprising chapters 10–13, Paul's apologia of his own apostolic ministry. The tone throughout this section is polemical, as Paul responds directly to the charges made against him by outside opponents who have entered the Corinthian church only to threaten his influence and leadership within the church. From his remarks in this section, it appears that he has been charged with being vacillating and undependable, saying one thing and doing another, behaving one way in their presence and another way when absent (cf. 2 Cor. 10:1, 10). What emerges from his polemical defense is a rather thorough treatment of his apostolic ministry. From what we can gather, it looks as if his opponents, who were themselves Christian apostles, or missionaries (2 Cor. 11:13), were authenticating their form of ministry by appealing to such things as signs and wonders, visions and revelations, or other such demonstrations of power. In Paul's view, they were "boasting according to human standards," or literally, "according to the flesh" (*kata sarka*, 2 Cor. 11:18). Even though he violently disagrees with this way of authenticating ministry, because of the seriousness of the situation he concedes to play their game on their turf. He constantly insists that such a line of argument is "foolishness" (2 Cor. 11:1, 16–21; 12:11), but he pursues it nevertheless.

In today's epistolary lection, Paul concedes that he is playing the game on their terms: "It is necessary to boast," he writes (v. 1), even though it is inappropriate. Given the criteria used by his opponents, he agrees to mention the "visions and revelations of the Lord" that he experienced. From other sources, we know of visions he had experienced (Acts 26:19), as well as revelations he had received from the Lord (Gal. 1:12; 2:2; cf. also 1 Cor. 14:6, 26; Rom. 2:5; 8:19; 1 Cor. 1:7; 2 Thess. 1:7).

He recalls a specific experience of a man in Christ he had known who had been caught up into the third heaven, or Paradise (vv. 2–4), fourteen years earlier. Even though he speaks in the third person, there can be little doubt that he is speaking of his own experience. Otherwise, why introduce it here? He does, however, seem to distinguish between the experience of "such a one" and that of himself (v. 5), but likely he is merely drawing a distinction between himself as a visionary and himself as a suffering apostle (v. 5). Descriptions of similar experiences are found in literature of the period (cf. 1 Enoch 39:3–4; 2 Enoch 7:1; 3 Baruch 2:2). In this ecstatic state, Paul tells us that he heard unspeakable things: "things that are not to be told, that no mortal is permitted to repeat" (v. 4). This is reminiscent of other instances in which a prophetic seer or visionary received sealed revelations (cf. Isa. 8:16; Dan. 12:4; 2 Enoch 17; Rev. 14:3).

In spite of the many puzzling features of this description, one thing is clear: Paul places little stock in it as an occasion for genuine boasting or for authenticating his ministry. He is aware, for one thing, that more is often made of such matters than they deserve (v. 6). They also lend themselves to exaggeration.

But Paul does not look to such experiences to authenticate his ministry. Rather, he finds that experiences "from below" rather than experiences "from above" provide the arena in which he has most keenly experienced the power of God. Thus, in spite of "the exceptional character of the revelations" (v. 7), he has had to contend with "a thorn [that] was given me in the flesh, a messenger of Satan" (v. 7), sent by God to harass him and curb his arrogant spirit. This, of course, is a much contested verse, and explanations for Paul's "thorn in the flesh" have ranged from psychological disorders to physical maladies such as bad eyesight, stomach problems, and epilepsy. We can never know, nor need we know. We do know that Paul earnestly appealed to the Lord for its removal, only to be told, "My grace is sufficient for you, for power is made perfect in weakness" (v. 9).

This revelation from the Lord, more than all his other visions and revelations, provided him with the hermeneutical key for interpreting his own experience. What he knew only too well was that "weaknesses, insults, hardships, persecutions, and calamities" (v. 10) were far more frequent and typical of his apostolic life than were visions and revelations. What is more, they placed him in more direct touch with the experience of Christ (Gal. 2:20; 6:17; 2 Cor. 4:10–11). In this respect, his life was analogous to that of Christ. Indeed, the crucifixion of Christ came to symbolize human suffering experienced in response to a divine calling. It was the cross, after all, that epitomized weakness and impotence; yet it was precisely through the cross, the symbol of weakness, that God had chosen to exhibit redemptive power. This was the paradox of the cross that formed the center of Paul's preaching (1 Cor. 1:18–31). Through the cross, weakness had become the means through which he experienced genuine strength.

Mark 6:1–13

The Gospel for today contains two units, verses 1–6 and 7–13. The first unit is a vivid reminder that the Christian confession of faith is not "I believe in Christ" but "I believe Jesus is the Christ." After all, to believe in a Christ or messiah, someone who will deliver, bring relief, set a people free, is not necessarily a Christian belief. Looking for messiahs is widespread in political as well as religious communities. But the early Christians said, "The Messiah has come, and it is Jesus of Nazareth." Mark 6:1–6 is about Jesus of Nazareth. Jesus is in his hometown (1:9), in his home synagogue, where he is identified in a number of ways. The citizens know him as a carpenter, as Mary's son, as sibling to four brothers and several sisters. As sharply as the New Testament states it anywhere, this text presents Jesus in what theologians sometimes call "the scandal of particularity."

Mark's account of Jesus' return to Nazareth and of his break with family, kin, and acquaintances has already been prefigured in 3:21–35, which tells about his unbelieving family who had come to take him away because they heard that he was beside himself. The Nazareth story is not pro-Gentile, anti-Jew in its perspective. The literary setting is the large unit 4:35–8:21, in which Jesus ministers to both Jews and Gentiles. He goes to the synagogue on the sabbath (6:2), as he had on other occasions (1:21, 39). In fact, Mark says that following the rejection at Nazareth, Jesus continued his ministry of teaching in other villages (6:6b), even sending his disciples in teams of two to multiply his work of exorcising, preaching, and healing (6:7–13). Rather than being either Jewish or Gentile in orientation, the story is about a response to Jesus in a community where one might expect acceptance, trust, and discipleship. As Mark reports it, the response to Jesus is captured in three words: astonished (v. 2), offended, (v. 3), and disbelieved (v. 6).

But of central importance is the question, To what do the people respond with astonishment, offense, and unbelief? It was not to miracles. In fact, with minor exceptions, Jesus could do no mighty work there (v. 5). This "could not" is softened to "did not" by Matthew (13:58) and omitted altogether by Luke (4:16–30). What astonishes Jesus' auditors and causes them to speak of his wisdom and power is his teaching (v. 2). In this regard, the scene parallels that of 1:21–28, in which Jesus teaches with authority in the synagogue at Capernaum; the people are astonished, and even after Jesus performs an exorcism, the point of amazement is the teaching. Mark is silent here about the content of that teaching, as he is in most references to Jesus' teaching. Mark's attention is upon the power and authority of the word of Jesus, the word that exorcizes, heals, and proclaims the good news of the kingdom. That word was still present and powerful in the church. Our text offers, however, a sober reminder: at the speaking of the word of Christ there is sometimes offense and unbelief. Even good news may be received and treated as bad news, and perhaps by those who would be expected to be most receptive.

Mark 6:7–13, the sending out of the Twelve, is the first portion of an account continued in verses 30ff. This unit has a Matthean parallel in 10:1–42, where it is but a part of a larger unit on instructions and warnings to Christian missionaries. Luke has two parallels, the sending of the Twelve (9:1–6) and the sending of the seventy (10:1–16).

In Mark, the mission of the Twelve follows immediately the rejection at Nazareth. This should not be taken, however, as implying a turning away from Israel toward Gentiles. The itinerary of the Twelve, like that of Jesus (6:6b), is clearly among villages of Israel, a fact made most explicit by Matthew (10:5–6). "The twelve" in verse 7 serves almost as a title, referring to those persons named in 3:13–19 and appointed to be with Jesus and to be sent out to preach. Mark usually refers to them as "disciples," only once calling them "apostles" (6:30). "The twelve apostles" is in the New Testament primarily a Lukan designation.

The account of the mission of the Twelve unfolds clearly: Jesus calls them to him, gives them authority over demons, and, judging by their activity, sends them to do exactly what he himself has been doing: preaching repentance, casting out demons, and healing (1:14–15; 1:32–39; 3:7–12). They are instructed not to take extra provisions but to depend on the hospitality of those who receive them. Neither are they to move around looking for the most comfortable lodgings, but rather they are to stay where they are first received. They are not told to pronounce judgment on the inhospitable and unbelieving, but simply to follow the custom of shaking off the dust from the places where they are rejected. Apparently, such a witness against the nonreceptive will be considered by God in the judgment. In other words, leave them to heaven and move on. The Twelve perform according to their instructions and the authority given them. Although frequently presented unfavorably by Mark, the Twelve here are "successful," undoubtedly because they are obedient and because they carry the word and the power of Jesus himself.

Our text is obviously not simply a bit of history about Jesus and the Twelve, but a word to Mark's church and subsequently to the church wherever this passage is received as Scripture. The work of Jesus is to continue, and for that purpose the church is called and sent. For that work Jesus grants the word and the power that characterized his own ministry. The church is to go trusting this to be true, never contradicting that trust with the excess baggage of security and wealth that offers the world the image of unbelief. There will be rejection and refusal to listen, to be sure, but there will also be those who will welcome both the ministry and the minister.

Proper 10 [15]
(Sunday between July 10 and 16 inclusive)

2 Samuel 6:1–5, 12b–19;
Psalm 24; or
Amos 7:7–15;
Psalm 85:8–13;
Ephesians 1:3–14
Mark 6:14–29

The Old Testament reading for the *Common Lectionary* today relates the impressively told transfer of the ark to Jerusalem and the festive jubilation that followed. Psalm 24, a processional psalm used by worshipers carrying the ark into the sanctuary, celebrates God as the King of glory.

For other lectionary traditions, the Old Testament reading is Amos's vision of the plumb line, followed by his interchange with Amaziah in which he rehearses his humble origins. The selection from Psalm 85 appears to be a prophetic or priestly oracle offering the prospect of hope to Israel.

The Gospel reading, Mark's unusually vivid account of the death of John the Baptist, sketches the fate of the prophetic figure contemporary with Jesus whom the church came to regard as an essential part of their story.

Today's epistolary reading, the magnificent opening prayer of blessing from the Epistle to the Ephesians, is the first of seven semicontinuous readings to occur over the next several weeks.

2 Samuel 6:1–5, 12b–19

Between David's anointing as king over all the tribes and his capture of Jerusalem—considered last week in the semicontinuous readings for the season—and today's reading, only two matters are reported: (1) he took more wives and concubines, who bore to him a number of children (2 Sam. 5:13–16), and (2) David had to deal with a threat from the Philistines, who understandably were disturbed to learn that all Israel had united behind him. Historically, this was of the greatest importance. It was the external threat from the militarily superior Philistines that had moved the tribes to establish a monarchy in the first place. Certainly, one of the most significant feats of David's rule is that he succeeded where Saul had failed, finally putting an end to the Philistine threat. Without that accomplishment, Israel never could have developed as an independent state.

Second Samuel 6 is the account of how David brought the ark to Jerusalem, thus making it the center of worship as well as the capital. The central figure in the story is the ark itself, not the king. This narrative picks up the account of the movements of the ark where it left off in 1 Samuel 6:21–7:2, which explains the presence of the ark in Kiriath-jearim. Our chapter is the last of a series of stories about the ark, one of which is the account of its capture by the Philistines, who finally let it go because of its awesome and dangerous power.

Our reading is a continuous though not quite complete report of the transportation of the ark to its home in Jerusalem. The account concludes in 6:19, but in the meantime the story of David's wife Michal, the daughter of Saul, has begun. She ridiculed David for his public display of exuberance during the procession into Jerusalem, and he put her aside.

The narrative has three distinct parts: it reports (1) how David and his men went to get the ark and began the procession to Jerusalem (vv. 1–5), (2) an incident on the way when Uzzah was killed because he touched the ark (vv. 6–10), and (3) how the procession to Jerusalem was resumed some three months later (vv. 12–19).

From beginning to end, the story is replete with liturgical language and ritual activities. Some of these allusions doubtless refer to ancient, premonarchical practices, but others must reflect later activities in the temple, such as those reflected in Psalm 24. The mood and rhetorical fullness of the language that characterizes the ark in verse 2b reveals it to be a liturgical formula. The processions (vv. 5, 12–15), like those on high occasions at the temple, were loud and joyous affairs, and the completion of the transfer is marked by sacrifices, offerings, and a feast (vv. 17–19). Moreover, David clearly performs priestly functions. He offers the sacrifice (v. 13) and wears a priestly garment (v. 14).

For all the descriptions of the ark and the accounts of its exploits, its precise nature and function remain elusive. This much is clear: it was a portable religious shrine, the symbol of the presence of Yahweh. Moreover, its origins almost certainly go back to the time before the Israelite tribes entered Canaan. It is identified variously as "the ark of Yahweh," "the ark of God," "the ark of the covenant," and "the ark of the testimony." The only detailed description of it (Exod. 25:10–22) comes from the Priestly Document, written long after the ark had disappeared. It would have been a box that contained other sacred objects and would have been large enough to require several persons—or an ox cart—to move it. Most likely it symbolized the throne of Yahweh. That certainly is the view of this tradition that speaks of "the ark of God, which is called by the name of the LORD of hosts who sits enthroned on the cherubim" (v. 2).

Although this is an easy story to tell, it is not an easy one to preach, primarily because of what transpires in its central scene. When the oxen pulling the cart stumbled and the ark was in danger of falling, Uzzah touched it. At this point, the Old Testament does not mince words: "God struck him there because he reached out his hand to the ark; and he died there beside the ark of God" (v. 7). How could those who told and heard this story believe such a thing? The answer lies in the understanding of holiness as terrifying and dangerous. No one could see God and live. In later times, even the name of God was considered so sacred that it could not be uttered out loud.

Obviously, it was possible and necessary for persons to approach the ark and even touch it. How else could it be loaded onto the cart? But it must have been believed that one could safely approach it only in certain ritually proper ways. What jars our modern consciousness is that correct movements, postures, and words were more important than one's motives, for clearly Uzzah reached out his hand with the best of intentions.

If we respond in anger at the injustice of Uzzah's death, we are not the first to do so. David himself was both angry and afraid (vv. 8–9). This strange story leaves us to ponder the fact that anger and fear are such close cousins. Furthermore, it may stimulate us to pause and reflect on sacredness as distance, on the God who is the radically other.

Psalm 24

The Old Testament reading for this Sunday from 2 Samuel 6 tells the story of how David and his supporters brought the ark of the covenant to Jerusalem from its resting place near Kiriath-jearim (see 1 Sam. 7:2). Psalm 24 was the litany for a cultic ritual in which the ark was carried into the temple during festival celebrations. It celebrates the reentrance of God into the holy place.

Of all the psalms, Psalm 24 probably illustrates most clearly the fact that the psalms were used as the spoken part of cultic rituals. Throughout verses 3–10, the material is comprised of a series of questions and answers probably recited by pilgrims and priests.

The psalm opens (vv. 1–2) with a hymnic praise of Yahweh that identifies the God of Israel as the possessor of the world and all that is in it. The ownership of the terrestrial kingdom is God's by right of creation. Yahweh is the one who anchored the earth in the midst of the seas and established it firmly upon the rivers (or streams) of the deep that ancients believed lay underneath the dry land. (Such a belief is partially based on the presence of springs and wells, which suggests that water lies beneath the earth.)

The questions in verse 3 were addressed by the pilgrims to the priests inside the temple as the pilgrims arrived at the gates of the temple. The questions concern the qualifications demanded of those allowed to enter the sacred precincts: "Who shall ascend the hill of the LORD [who can enter the temple precincts]? Who shall stand in his holy place [in the temple in the presence of God]?" The priestly answer in this catechism of admission (vv. 4–5) brings together two pairs of ethical qualifications: purity of outward deeds (clean hands) and purity of thought or inward truthfulness (pure heart), followed by purity of religious practice or unadulterated faith (not lifting up the soul to what is vain) and purity in speaking (does not swear deceitfully). These four principles in themselves provide a rather comprehensive perspective of ethical demands and requirements. If such demands as these were made as part of the worship, then one surely cannot accuse ancient worship services of being free from ethical interests and demands.

Verse 6 provides the worshipers' response to the requirements for entrance: "Those are the kind of people we are." Thus they claim the promises of verse 5—blessing and vindication from God.

With verse 7, the focus shifts from humankind and the moral values of living to God. The pilgrims or choir outside the sanctuary address the temple gates, demanding that they be lifted up so that the King of glory can come in. But how could God enter the sanctuary? No doubt the ark, the symbol of God's presence, had been carried out of the temple to reenter with the pilgrims on a high holy festival day. The choir or priests within offer a response in the form of a question, "Who is the King of glory?" God is then described as the one strong and mighty, mighty in battle. Perhaps part of the festival involved the proclamation of God's triumph over the forces of evil.

Early in the life of the church, Psalm 24 became one of the texts associated with Jesus' descent into Hades (hell) and his triumph over the forces of darkness. The influence of this psalm in the gate liturgy of Christ's descent into hell can be seen in the noncanonical Gospel according to the Hebrews, the Gospel of Nicodemus, and the Acts of Pilate. Thus Psalm 24 became a classic text used in expressing the idea of the harrowing of hell. The gates became those standing against Christ and the church, and the Christ became the King of glory.

Amos 7:7–15

This reading contains two distinct units of material from the Book of Amos. The first, 7:7–9, is the third in a series of five vision reports (7:1–3, 4–6, 7–9; 8:1–3; 9:1–4). The second, 7:10–15, is the first part of the report of the confrontation between Amos and Amaziah, the priest of Bethel. It seems most likely that, in an earlier stage in the transmission of the Amos traditions, the series of visions would have circulated as a unit. The story of prophetic conflict in 7:10–17 interrupts the series and probably was inserted at this point in the book on the basis of the common catchwords (Jeroboam) in 7:9 and 7:10.

In the first pair of visions, Amos sees threatening things—locusts (7:1) and fire (7:4); he intercedes on behalf of the people, and Yahweh relents (better, repents). In the second pair, the vision is not in itself threatening but is the occasion for an announcement of judgment; Amos does not intercede, and the judgment stands. In the third vision report (7:7–9), Amos sees Yahweh standing by a wall with a plumb line in his hand, and a dialogue transpires. Although there is great uncertainty about the translation of the rare Hebrew word generally understood as "plumb line," the point of the vision is unmistakable. It is the occasion for an uncompromising announcement of judgment on the Northern Kingdom ("my people Israel"). The blast of Yahweh's anger focuses on cultic and political institutions: "the high places of Isaac," "the sanctuaries of Israel," and "the house of Jeroboam." This announcement of the total destruction of the Northern Kingdom is the persistent and leading theme of the Book of Amos.

The account of the confrontation between Amos and Amaziah has two distinct parts. The first (7:10–11) provides the setting and the background for the second (7:12–17), which reports the direct encounter between the priest and the prophet. The first scene takes place offstage, reporting that Amaziah sent a message to the king accusing Amos, an outside agitator, of conspiracy against the royal house. The evidence for the charge is a quotation of Amos's announcement of death to the king and the exile of Israel. Behind the accusation stands the assumption—common to the prophets as well as their audiences—that the word of God through the prophet has the power to set into motion what it announces.

Then the curtain rises on the encounter between the priest and Amos. It is reported from the perspective of a third party who identifies with Amos, and it proceeds as a dialogue. Amaziah does not directly challenge the right of Amos to speak, although he does imply that Amos has economic reasons for acting as a prophet ("earn your bread," v. 12). The dispute concerns jurisdiction. Amaziah commands Amos to return to his homeland, Judah, and speak there, appealing to royal authority. The king—and he as the king's spokesman—has the authority to determine who speaks in Israel.

Amos first responds directly to Amaziah's speech and its assumptions about his office (vv. 14–15) and then announces judgment on Amaziah for his attempt to stifle the word of God (vv. 16–17). The initial words of this response are among the most debated in scholarship on the Book of Amos. Does the prophet say, "I am no prophet, nor a prophet's son" or "I was no prophet, nor a prophet's son"? The Hebrew has two noun clauses with no verb. To render them into English—and to determine their sense—requires some form of the verb "to be," but the tense is uncertain. If it is present tense, then he is denying that he is a prophet or a member of a prophetic guild, or possibly the understanding of prophet assumed by his opponent. If it is past tense, then the following lines do not contradict these words: "The LORD said to me, 'Go, prophecy to my people Israel'" (v. 15). The matter cannot be resolved on grammatical grounds but only in the immediate and larger context.

The key to the account is not in verse 14 but in verse 15. Amos makes it clear that he has the authority to act as a prophet, and in the land of Israel, because Yahweh called him and sent him. He does not give a full-blown report of his call but alludes to the central point that he was commissioned by Yahweh. Thus, whether he is not or was not a prophet, he is compelled ("the LORD took me") to act and speak as a prophet, and those who stand in his way stand in the way of the word of God.

It is misleading to interpret this text as an account of the conflict between institution and charisma, between organized cultic religion and the inspired individual. It is rather the struggle between institution and institution, both of them religious. The priest has the authority of established worship tied to the political institutions. The prophet has the authority of his vocation and the words given to him by Yahweh. But this vocation and these words also have institutional foundations, for all Israel's prophets claim the same authority. Amos, like Amaziah, stands in a long tradition concerning his office and role.

Psalm 85:8–13

This reading was discussed as one of the lections for the Second Sunday of Advent.

Ephesians 1:3–14

This text also serves as the epistolary text for the Second Sunday After Christmas in all three years. The reader may want to consult our remarks in that liturgical setting in each of the volumes. Related portions of the passage serve as epistolary lessons at other points in the liturgical year: Ephesians 1:11–23 for All Saints' Day in Year C, and Ephesians 1:15–23 for Ascension in all three years.

Today's text is the first of seven readings from the Letter to the Ephesians. The preceding two verses are similar in form and content to the introductory salutations in the Pauline letters. They are remarkable in several respects. First, even though the letter is attributed to the apostle Paul, its authenticity is widely disputed. Many of the themes treated in the letter echo themes found in the undisputed Pauline Letters, but there is a distinct shift in outlook.

Second, the letter is addressed to "the saints who are in Ephesus and are faithful in Christ Jesus" (v. 1). In some of the earliest manuscripts, the phrase "in Ephesus" is omitted, and this suggests that this letter originally was intended to have a much wider audience. It has been suggested that it served as a cover letter for the Pauline corpus. Certainly, the scope of the letter is general and widely applicable to Christians everywhere.

Verses 3–14 constitute the first part of a magnificent eulogy, which, in the original Greek, comprises a single sentence stretching to verse 23. In form, it is a prayer of "blessing" similar to those found in 2 Corinthians 1:3–7 and 1 Peter 1:3–9. This prayer sets a lofty tone that is to characterize the letter as a whole. Its mention of "heavenly places" (v. 3) signals the cosmic scope of the letter. As verse 10 states, it was God's purpose to "gather up all things in [Christ], things in heaven and things on earth." Equally broad is the time frame in which the work of God is set. God's redemptive work is said to have begun even "before the foundation of the world" (v. 4) and was achieved in "the fullness of time" (v. 10). One should also note the way in which superlatives are piled on top of one another throughout the prayer. We have here the excess of the language of worship, and the words are intended to elevate the reader to the very heights from which the work of God is seen to have emanated.

The object of blessing is "the God and Father of our Lord Jesus Christ" (v. 3). God deserves to be blessed inasmuch as those in Christ have been blessed with every spiritual blessing in the heavenly places. This stress on believers' having access to the "heavenly places" is typical of the letter. Those who have been raised with Christ are envisioned as actually sitting with God in the heavenly places in Christ Jesus (Eph. 2:6). The church becomes the means by which God's manifold wisdom is displayed "to the rulers and authorities in the heavenly places" (Eph. 3:10). The Christian struggle is envisioned as a cosmic struggle with principalities and powers "in the heavenly places" (Eph. 6:12). The mighty acts of God are unfolded.

1. *God's work of election is mentioned* (v. 4; cf. 2 Thess. 2:13). Even though Christians may experience God's call in the time and space of their earthly existence, they are reminded here that their salvation actually has primordial origins (cf. John 17:24; 1 Pet. 1:20). Even then, it was located "in Christ," who quite early on in Christian thinking was seen as a figure who preceded creation (Col. 1:15; Heb. 1:3). The purpose of God's election was to make those chosen "holy and blameless before him" (v. 4; cf. Eph. 5:27; Col. 1:22).

2. *God's work of predestination: "he destined us for adoption as his children through Jesus Christ"* (v. 5). This recalls a well-established Pauline theme (Rom. 8:29), that occurs elsewhere in the New Testament (1 Pet. 1:2). Unfortunately, what should have been taken as a statement of loving reassurance has often been interpreted too narrowly, with far too much emphasis on the individual's fate having been predetermined. As a helpful corrective, the corporate dimension of the passage should be noted. What is being affirmed is not that a certain number of saints have been chosen in advance, but that those who are "children through Jesus Christ" enjoy a status that was theirs long before they realized it or actualized it.

3. *God's grace lavishly bestowed and displayed through Christ.* The "glorious grace" of God is praised because it was freely bestowed in Christ, the Beloved (v. 6; cf. Mark 1:11; also Sir. 45:1; 46:13; Isa. 44:2). Through Christ we have redemption (cf. Rom. 3:24; 8:23; 1 Cor. 1:30; Col. 1:14; Eph. 4:30), and this was achieved through the shedding of his blood (Eph. 2:13; Rom. 3:25; Col. 1:20; Heb. 9:22; Rev. 1:5).

4. *God's work of revelation* (vv. 9–10). God's saving work here, as elsewhere, is conceived as a mystery concealed from the beginning of time, but now revealed in its fullness (cf. Rom. 16:25; Eph. 3:3–4, 9; Col. 1:26–27; 2:2; 1 Pet. 1:20). It is unfolded "with all wisdom and insight" (v. 9; cf. Col. 1:9) and thereby illuminates our own understanding, both of ourselves and God (Eph. 3:18–20). To be sure, the opening up of the mystery did not occur until the "fullness of time" (Gal. 4:4; also Mark 1:15; Col. 1:19; Tob. 14:5). Now, however, in Christ God's intention is manifest: the divine purpose is to bring about the unity of "all things in him" (v. 10), by which is doubtless meant the bringing together of Jews and Gentiles into a "new humanity" (Eph. 2:11–22). In doing so, heaven and earth are seen to become one.

5. *God's bestowal of the divine inheritance* (vv. 11–12). Even though God set salvation history in motion before the beginning of time, those in later generations became heirs to this promise. Here salvation is viewed as being incorporated into God's family. We are assured that

we were destined from the beginning of time to be children of God (v. 5; cf. John 1:12; Gal. 3:26; 1 John 3:1).

6. *God's promise of the Holy Spirit* (vv. 13–14). Part of hearing the gospel, the word of truth, is receiving the Holy Spirit, here spoken of as seal and pledge. Both metaphors express important aspects of this promise—the one its surety, the other its partiality. For what is implied here is not only that the Spirit has been given as a genuine, present experience, but also that an even fuller experience of God's presence is still to come. The locus of the Spirit's activity, however, is "God's own people."

Mark 6:14–29

There are several features of today's text that will interest both preacher and listener and that will have a direct bearing on the message heard in this remarkable story. First, notice the unusual location of this account, coming as it does between the sending out of the Twelve (vv. 7–13) and their return (v. 30). We have already noticed "split stories" in Mark (1:21–28; 3:21–35; 5:21–43), but what bearing does this arrangement have on one's understanding of Mark's message? Second, this is the only account in Mark's Gospel that does not have as its subject Jesus or his disciples. Why a John the Baptist story in a Gospel about Jesus Christ? Third, this is the lengthiest record of John's arrest, imprisonment, and death in the New Testament. Matthew and Luke are much longer Gospels, but their reports of John's death are noticeably briefer (Matt. 14:1–12; Luke 3:19–20; 9:7–9). Why does the shortest Gospel have the longest account of this event? Let us look first at the story itself and then return to these questions.

Both John and Jesus ministered during the time Herod Antipas was ruler (tetrarch) of Galilee (4 BC–AD 39). The Herod family left bloody footprints across the New Testament: Herod the Great tried to kill the infant Jesus (Matt. 2:1–20); his son Archelaus posed a threat to the holy family (Matt. 2:22); another son, Antipas, killed John the Baptist; a grandson, Herod Agrippa I, killed the apostle James and arrested Simon Peter (Acts 12:1–4); and a great-grandson, Herod Agrippa II, heard Paul's defense of himself at Caesarea (Acts 25:13–26:32). The Jewish historian Josephus said that while on his way to Rome and when a guest of his half-brother Philip, Antipas began the affair with Herodias, Philip's wife (*Antiquities of the Jews* 18.109–10). Antipas divorced his wife and married Herodias, who became to him what Jezebel was to King Ahab. Josephus differs slightly with Mark, however, in stating that Antipas killed John because he feared John as a popular leader.

Mark's account in 6:14–29 is moving and dramatic, having the characteristics of a story worn smooth by frequent telling in the circles of John and of Jesus. One small uncertainty lies in verse 22. The RSV followed the ancient manuscripts, which say that it was Herodias's daughter (the name Salome is not in the text) who danced at Herod's birthday party. The REB agrees, but the NRSV goes with the more difficult but well-attested reading, "When his daughter Herodias came in and danced."

There is no question but that this story, interesting in its own right, is very important to Mark. All the Gospel writers testify to the major importance of John, who had disciples, who baptized Jesus, who preached much the same message as Jesus, who died a martyr's death, and whose movement continued after his death, as far away as Alexandria and Ephesus (Acts 18:24–19:3). John's ministry, says Mark, was "the beginning of the good news of Jesus Christ"

(1:1–8). Each year, the Gospel lections for the Second and Third Sundays of Advent deal with the message and ministry of John.

Is the preacher, then, to preach on John the Baptist? No, not centrally, for in Mark this story serves the gospel of Jesus Christ. Located in the context of accounts of Jesus' immense popularity (6:7–13, 31–44, 53–56), the story moves the narrative of opposition to Jesus beyond the rejection at Nazareth by his own people (6:1–6) to the foreboding of death at the hands of a secular ruler. The sword of political power, whether in the hand of a waffling, vacillating Herod (vv. 20, 26) or a waffling, vacillating Pilate (15:6–15), will strike down God's prophets. Speculations about who Jesus really is (vv. 14–16) anticipate Caesarea Philippi (8:27–30). The burial of John anticipates the burial of Jesus (v. 29; 15:46). But Herod unwittingly testifies to the greater and the final truth: power has been released among us by a resurrection from the dead (vv. 14–16).

The story is about the passion and death of John, but Mark wants the reader to be thinking about Jesus.

Proper 11 [16]
(Sunday between July 17 and 23 inclusive)

2 Samuel 7:1–14*a*;
Psalm 89:20–37; or
Jeremiah 23:1–6;
Psalm 23;
Ephesians 2:11–22;
Mark 6:30–34, 53–56

The Old Testament lesson in the *Common Lectionary* contains Nathan's prophecy that the Lord has chosen David and his dynasty to rule over the people of God, and Psalm 89:20–37 is a direct response to it, containing not a prayer but the word of God confirming and affirming that dynasty.

For other lectionaries, the Old Testament reading is the prophetic oracle in Jeremiah 23 that God would restore Israel and raise up a righteous king in the line of David. If Judah's rulers are reproached as delinquent shepherds in Jeremiah 23, God is praised as the ideal shepherd in the Twenty-third Psalm.

The shepherd/sheep motif is continued in the Markan text, where the crowds following Jesus are "like sheep without a shepherd" who elicit compassion from him and receive his healing power.

Breaking down the divided wall of ethnic hostility and the union of Gentiles and Jews into a new humanity serves as the overarching theme in today's selection from Ephesians.

2 Samuel 7:1–14*a*

Second Samuel 7 is the pivotal chapter in the story of David. It records what for later generations was the most important event in his life, the Lord's covenant with David and with his descendants that they would occupy the throne in Jerusalem "forever" (vv. 13, 16). Its central location is stressed by the first verse, which emphasizes that David was settled into his own "house" in Jerusalem and the Lord had given him "rest" from his enemies. The promise then comes at the high point of David's life, after he has united the nation, moved the ark to Jerusalem, put an end to external threats (but note 2 Sam. 8), and before his serious troubles began.

The reading for the day consists of two major parts:

1. Verses 1–3 introduce the event and report David's dialogue with Nathan, who appears here for the first time. The king tells the prophet of his concern for the ark, indicating his intention to build a house for it. Although David's words are not phrased as a question, Nathan's response suggests that behind the dialogue lies the practice of consulting prophets or priests for the will of God before a major undertaking, such as going to war or constructing a temple.

2. Verses 4–17 contain, with narrative introduction and conclusion, Nathan's prophecy concerning David and his dynasty. The divine revelation is reported as it came to the prophet in the form of a message for the king.

Nathan's prophecy contains both ancient and later traditions, and is told here from the perspective of later generations who experienced and remembered the monarchy as the incarnation of the grace of God for the people of God. It is a thoroughly positive view, contrasting, for example, with Samuel's warning as reported in 1 Samuel 8:10–18. But it is not naive. Kings, even those elected by God, stray and need divine correction and punishment (v. 14).

Several features of the narrative in particular require comment:

1. Yahweh's initial response to David's plan (vv. 5–7) rejects the idea of a "house" and recalls the history of salvation from the time of the Exodus. Although these lines do not go as far as later prophetic critique of the temple cult, they do assume that the God of Israel cannot be bound to a single place.

2. The first part of the promise (vv. 8–11a) concerns only David and the people of Israel. Nothing is said of a dynasty. The Lord has chosen David and made him what he is in order to give the people peace. Whether this has already happened or will come in the future is an open question because it is not certain how the Hebrew tenses of verses 9b–11a should be read. Most modern translations read them as future, but they could just as well be past or present.

3. What now stands as the heart of the chapter is the prophecy extended to later generations (vv. 11b–16). It is a play on words. David wanted to build Yahweh a "house" for the ark, that is, a temple, but instead Yahweh promises to make a "house" for David, that is, a dynasty, and one that will stand forever.

4. Verse 13 stands out as a special note, one that is in contrast with the view of the temple stated at the outset. Without mentioning his name, it indicates that Solomon will be the one to build the temple. That was a historical fact that the tradition could not avoid. First Chronicles 22:7–10 gives a later explanation of the reason Solomon and not David was the one to build the temple.

This passage brings us close to the roots of important aspects of the biblical understanding of a messiah. The word *messiah* comes from the Hebrew word for "anointed one," applied to David and other kings. Its Greek equivalent is "Christ." More particularly, we have here an account of the roots of the New Testament understanding that the messiah will be a descendant of David. Between the time of David and the time of Jesus, however, a great many transformations took place. The covenant with David (see 2 Sam. 23:5) was understood early to be a continuation of God's saving history with Israel: the promise to the patriarchs, the Exodus, the leading in the wilderness, the covenant on Mt. Sinai, the granting of the land of Canaan—and now David and his dynasty. That faith grew in the southern state of Judah after the division following the death of Solomon, and more and more came to be idealized by both prophets (see Isa. 9, 11) and cultic song. After the end of the state and the monarchy at the hands of the Babylonians, hope for a king in the line of David became more and more an eschatological expectation.

Psalm 89:20–37

In 2 Samuel 7, we find Nathan telling David that God has promised to establish the house of David as the divinely elected dynasty to rule over Israel for all time. This promise of God, or covenant between David and God, became the basis for the Old Testament understanding of the king. It was also the seedbed from which grew the expectation of a future messiah who would bring salvation to God's people and God's rule on earth.

Psalm 89 is a royal lament in which we find many of the divine promises to the Davidic ruler. This psalm was used when the promises of God and the reality of the eternal covenant were called into question. As such, it is a prayer that God will restore the conditions of the covenant and manifest divine fidelity to the promises. The contents of the psalm may be outlined as follows: introduction (vv. 1–4), hymn of praise (vv. 5–18), recitation of the divine-Davidic covenant (vv. 19–37), description of the monarch's condition of distress (vv. 38–45), and an appeal for help (vv. 46–51).

In today's lection, the text focuses on the conditions and promises of the divine covenant with David. As such, the Scripture reading may be viewed as a commentary or exposition of the promises delivered to David by the prophet Nathan in 2 Samuel 7.

Verse 19, not included in the psalm reading, is the introduction to the section on the promises to David. It suggests that the promises to David were spoken in a vision to God's "faithful one" but does not make clear whether the "faithful one" was David himself or Nathan the prophet. The promises, however, are all presented in the first person as spoken by Yahweh. The opening divine statement, in verse 19b, emphasizes three aspects about David: (1) he is a mighty person (and certainly the Old Testament narratives about David present him as a successful and powerful person), (2) he is one whom God exalted (again the Old Testament text emphasizes that David was Yahweh's favorite, whose status depended on divine blessing), and (3) David was a person with common roots whose exalted position was based on divine choice and election (a point emphasized in the story of David's anointing in 1 Sam. 16:1–13).

Verses 20–29 in today's reading present the promises that relate initially to David; verses 30–37 concern David's posterity, the descendants and successors of David and their relationship to the law, and God's punishment for their transgressions of the law.

Verses 20–21 describe the process of David's selection as his "being found" by God. Unlike the situation in other Near Eastern cultures, where the king was regarded as a superhuman if not a god, such texts as this point to the commonness of David before his exaltation by God. A characteristic description of the ruler is that he is God's servant, and his role is to be an instrument of the Deity. The anointment, referred to in verse 20b, was the act by which the new monarch became the messiah ("the anointed one") in ancient Israel. If verse 21 is a continuation of verse 20, which seems most likely, then anointment could be interpreted as divine assurance of God's continuing presence and support.

The basic promises of God to David, or the consequences of the divine covenant, are given in verses 22–29. These texts present, in staccato fashion and with a brevity of words, the basic threads interwoven into the royal tapestry that rested so majestically upon the shoulders of every Davidic heir. Among these were the assurance that David would not suffer humiliation at the hand of his enemies (v. 22); that he would prevail over his foes and despisers (v. 23); that God would be true to the divine commitments and through God's name the king would be victorious and acclaimed (v. 24); that the Davidic dominion and rule would be universal, extending to the sea and rivers that encircle the habitable world (v. 25); that the king would possess the privilege of addressing God as "Father" and of being the son of the Divine (v. 26); that David's reputation would be unexcelled among the kings of the world, where he would be treated as firstborn and thus heir of twice the portion of any other (v. 27); that God's covenant would be forever established (v. 28); and that the Davidic line would rule forever or as long as the heavens endured (v. 29).

With verse 30, the focus of the psalm shifts to consider how God will respond when the descendants of David do not live according to the laws and commandments of God. This section thus introduces the qualifying conditional aspects related to the Davidic house. Verses 22–29 provide the positive aspects of the relationship ("this is how it is"), whereas verses 30–37, but especially verses 30–33, present the conditions that temper the absolutes of the promises ("however, one must also recognize that . . ."). The "however" of the relationship has God stipulating that when David's children, the members of the dynasty who rule after him, do not remain faithful to the revealed and understood will of God (see the emphasis on the king's relationship to the law in Deut. 17:18–20), then God offers assurance that their transgressions and iniquities will be severely dealt with—by punishment with rod and scourge. The rebellious son, according to Deuteronomy 21:18–21, could not be disinherited as a consequence of one disobedience but had to be disciplined (referred to in Ps. 89:32) and given a further chance to fulfill the parental will.

The concerns of Yahwism for social justice, moral passion, and governmental integrity placed the monarch under ethical scrutiny. Political wrongdoing, personal immorality, and religious irresponsibility, even or perhaps especially of the monarch, could not be allowed free reign. Royal status was not conceived as guaranteeing royal immunity. The king was to stand beside, not above, the law.

Nevertheless, in spite of the disciplinary action and punishment that might befall the monarch, God promises that divine fidelity to the covenant will never be withdrawn or altered, nor will God lie to David. Instead, the covenant is presented as lasting forever with a permanence comparable to that of the sun and the moon.

When preaching from this text, the minister must take into consideration that verses 19–37 present the Davidic covenant in all its exaggerated claims; therefore, the lament and distress, actually a complaint against God, in verses 38–45, will stand out in stark profile. The Deity is accused of lack of fidelity and a failure to keep God's promises.

Jeremiah 23:1–6

Jeremiah 23:1–6 consists of two distinct paragraphs, as all modern translations indicate. Verses 1–4 are an announcement of judgment against the "shepherds who destroy and scatter the sheep" and an announcement of salvation to the "flock": the Lord will remove their reasons for fear by giving "shepherds . . . who will shepherd them." The second paragraph (vv. 5–6) is an announcement of salvation: Yahweh will raise up a just and righteous king in the line of David. As they stand in the final form of the Book of Jeremiah, the second unit is both a contrast with and an extension of the first. But there are disjunctions between the units that suggest that they originated independently, and perhaps even come from different authors. The first paragraph speaks of "shepherds" (plural), whereas the second has a single king; the first is prose, and the second is poetic (although not all translations set these verses in poetic lines).

Commentators on this passage have disagreed about its authorship and historical provenance. Certainly verse 3, if not all of the first unit, assumes a situation after the time of Jeremiah, namely, the Babylonian Exile. On the other hand, the evil shepherds could very well be the last kings of Judah during the time of Jeremiah. Authorship of verses 5–6 is likewise an open question, although most recent commentators tend to attribute it to Jeremiah. The problem with that conclusion is that this would be the only point where Jeremiah, unlike Isaiah, expresses his hope for restoration in terms of the Davidic dynasty. However one resolves that question, the entire unit comes either from the era just before or during the Babylonian Exile.

The "shepherds," both good and bad, certainly represent political and religious leaders. Concluding a section of the Book of Jeremiah concerning the last kings of Judah, the reference definitely is to the series of rulers, but it could just as well apply to the officials as a whole. The "shepherds who will shepherd them" (v. 4) could be either the succession of righteous kings or, more broadly, political and religious leaders.

The juxtaposition of the unit about shepherds with the promise of a king in the line of David calls attention to the importance of pastoral imagery in the biblical messianic expectations. Surely, that imagery is indebted to some extent to the tradition that David himself was a shepherd. (See 1 Sam. 16:19.) When applied to David, the image is a rich combination of power and gentle care: the pastoral king, the royal shepherd.

Verses 5–6 provide a concise summary of the major features in the Old Testament of the messianic hope. The one who is to come will be a king in the line of David (2 Sam. 7; see the commentary on the other Old Testament reading for this day in this volume) and will be raised up by the Lord to prosper in all that he does. Justice and righteousness will characterize his reign (Isa. 9:6–7), bringing salvation to the people of God—in this case, the people of Israel and Judah. That he will reign as king means that he will be a monarch with real power and autonomy, neither a vassal of a foreign power nor controlled by officials of the royal court. The throne name given to him, "the LORD is our righteousness" (v. 6), suggests that through him the Lord vindicates the people as righteous.

Although the king is an ideal one, the promise is rooted in flesh and blood and history. This is the promise that the earliest followers of Jesus saw fulfilled in him, the divine will incarnate. Theologically, the Old Testament text enables us to keep our eyes fixed on two points also fundamental to the New Testament witness, the humanity of the Anointed One and the faith that through him God is at work.

Psalm 23

This psalm was previously discussed as one of the readings for the Fourth Sunday of Easter.

Ephesians 2:11–22

By the time this passage was written, Gentiles had won their right to be full-fledged members of the people of God. But it had been a titanic struggle, as the letters of Paul attest. In fact, this was clearly the most significant controversy faced by the early church in the first few decades of its existence. As the Book of Acts shows, it was not a fore-gone conclusion that Gentiles would be admitted to the church and enjoy equal status with Jews. Even some of the most prominent Jewish Christians, such as Peter, found it difficult to admit them as equals (cf. Gal. 2:11–21). Eventually the matter was resolved, largely through the efforts of Paul; and in today's epistolary lection, the author of Ephesians views this strug-gle in retrospect and interprets it theologically. For him, it is the "mystery of Christ," and he still marvels that "the Gentiles have become fellow heirs, members of the same body, and shar-ers in the promise in Christ Jesus through the gospel" (Eph. 3:6).

First, our passage depicts the changed status of the Gentiles. Their former condition is described in starkly hopeless terms. By the circumcised, they were pejoratively stereotyped as "the uncircumcision" (v. 11). This reminds us of how racial and ethnic struggles often degen-erate to the level of hurling clichés designed to exclude and belittle. The metaphors chosen are coldly distant: "without Christ, being aliens from the commonwealth of Israel, and strangers to the covenants of promise, having no hope and without God in the world" (v. 12). They, of course, reflect the perspective of those inside, but Jews knew only too well what it meant to be "strangers and sojourners" (Gen. 23:4; 1 Chron. 29:15; Ps. 39:12; also Heb. 11:13; 1 Pet. 1:1; 2:11). What we have here is an apt summary of pagan life as viewed through the eyes of Jews who saw themselves as the elect of God (cf. Rom. 1:18–32; 1 Thess. 4:5). It is the life of the disenfranchised and desolate.

In sharp contrast, the Gentiles' new life in Christ is depicted. In fact, the passage is built on two contrasting phrases: "at one time you were . . . , but now you are" (vv. 11, 13, and 19). It has been suggested that this may have been one way in which early Christian sermons were developed. What the Gentiles formerly lacked, they now have come to enjoy: they are now "citizens with the saints and also members of the household of God" (v. 19). Here, two metaphors are used: the city and the family. Both of these form the two fundamental social units, and now Gentiles are seen to be full participants in both. In addition, a third metaphor is introduced—the building, or temple, of God (vv. 20–22). Actually, the building metaphor is fused with the metaphor of the body, for it is said to "grow" (v. 21). Here, the church is envi-sioned as the Jewish temple reconstituted, with the apostles and prophets as the foundation (cf. Matt. 16:18; 1 Cor. 3:9–11; Eph. 3:5; Rev. 21:14) and Christ as the cornerstone (cf. Ps. 118:22–23; Matt. 21:42 and parallels; Acts 4:11; 1 Pet. 2:4, 6–8). In Christ, the whole build-ing coheres. It is now comprised of both Jews and Gentiles; and the Shekinah, the presence of God, that formerly dwelt in the Most Holy Place of the Jerusalem temple, is now replaced by the Spirit. This new temple is now the "dwelling place for God" (v. 22; cf. 1 Pet 2:5).

A second feature of the passage is the way in which the work of Christ is depicted. The unity of Gentiles and Jews is said to have been achieved "in Christ Jesus" (v. 13); that is, Christ has become the meeting place for divided humanity. The shedding of the blood of Christ is seen as the occasion through which those who were "far off" were "brought near" (v. 13; cf. Col. 1:20; also Acts 2:39). Christ is quite literally said to be "our peace" (v. 14; cf. Isa. 9:6), because through his reconciling work he "made peace" (vv. 14 and 15). In this re-spect, the fondest prophetic hopes are fulfilled (cf. Isa. 57:19; also 52:7). As the psalmist urged, "Seek peace, and pursue it" (Ps. 34:14), so had Christ blessed the peacemakers (Matt. 5:9). The reconciling work of Christ (2 Cor. 5:18–19) placed peace searching and peace making on the agenda of every Christian (Mark 9:50; Rom. 12:18; 14:19; 2 Cor. 13:11; 1 Thess. 5:13; 2 Tim. 2:22; Heb. 12:14; James 3:18; 1 Pet. 3:11).

Our passage states that the unifying work of Christ had been achieved through the aboli-tion of "the dividing wall, that is, the hostility between us," or "the law with its commandments and ordinances" (vv. 14–15). Regrettably, the Mosaic law became a symbol of exclusiveness, an "iron curtain," as it were, separating Jews and Gentiles (cf. Rom. 3:29–30). Here, the death of Christ is seen as an end to this dividing wall. In a similar vein, Colossians 2:14 asserts that Christ erased "the record that stood against us with its legal demands" and "nailed it to the cross" (also 2 Cor. 3:14). The image of the "dividing wall" is particularly graphic and offers numerous homiletical possibilities, because wall symbolism is universal and because modern people have firmly etched in their minds such images as the Berlin Wall, the Iron Curtain, to say nothing of the many other "no man's land" boundaries separating peoples and nations from one another. With the end of the cold war, we also now know the liberating and challenging effects of fallen walls.

The work of Christ is further defined as creating a "new humanity." In verse 15 we are told that Christ created in himself "one new humanity." Here, the Body of Christ is seen as a single corporate entity into which both Jews and Gentiles have been fused. They are both "reconciled in one body through the cross" (v. 16), with the result that hostility between them is brought to an end. Here, Jews and Gentiles are viewed as separate humanities who are now fused into a single humanity through the reconciling work of Christ. Christ becomes the sphere in which ethnic and racial distinctions become obliterated, and by extension, sexual and social distinctions as well (Gal. 3:26–27). No longer do Jews and Gentiles seek separate ways of access to God: the one through the temple and Torah, the other beyond temple and Torah. Now, both Jews and Gentiles "have access in one Spirit to the Father" (v. 18; cf. 3:12; also Heb. 4:16).

What is depicted in today's epistolary lection remains a grand ideal! Although the first-century church resolved the so-called "Jew-Gentile question" in one sense, in another sense it has never been resolved. Issues of inclusiveness and exclusiveness, whether based on race, nation, social status, or gender, still remain unresolved within the people of God. The ideal of a "new humanity" in Christ calls for proclamation, as does the work of peace and reconciliation. Both should be carried out in the hope that eventually hostility will be brought to an end (v. 16).

Mark 6:30–34, 53–56

The Gospel lection for today is the third and concluding reading from Mark 6. This passage joins the Old Testament reading in the portrait of Jesus as shepherd, recalling David, and joins the Epistle reading in presenting Jesus as the one who brings together the scattered and alienated into one flock, one family.

In his customary fashion, Mark inserts a story within a story in chapter 6. Verses 7–13 record Jesus' instructing and sending out the Twelve. Verses 30–34 tell of their return, their report to Jesus, and his response. In between is the account of the imprisonment and death of John the Baptist (vv. 14–29). This insertion is unusual, but it is difficult to believe Mark is here behaving like a distracted preacher who gets carried away from the point by a very dramatic and interesting story. A more reasonable assumption is that Mark is, by his literary device, instructing the reader about Jesus and his disciples. We will return to this point momentarily.

Mark 6:30–34 is an editorial transition, completing verses 7–13 and introducing verses 35–44, the account of feeding the five thousand. Withdrawing from the crowds for privacy is fairly common in Mark (1:35; 4:34; 9:2, 28; 13:3), but here it is associated not with a need for prayer or instruction but for rest after the mission. Matthew (14:13) relates this retreat to Jesus' hearing of John's death, whereas Luke, with no explanation for the action, says that Jesus and the disciples withdrew to the city of Bethsaida (9:10). Mark's "deserted place" is unspecified geographically but serves to get the Twelve out of the public traffic that has prevented their having time even to eat (note also 3:20), and sets up the scene for feeding the multitudes who come to the deserted place and are without food (vv. 35–36). It is difficult to reconstruct the precise movements of Jesus in Mark 4–8 that speak of ministries on both the eastern (Gentile) and western (Jewish) shores of Galilee with many crossings between, but in 6:32 the boat trip seems to be along the western shore and not across to the other side. The feeding on the eastern shore is recorded in 8:1–10.

In this brief lection, Mark tells us about the Twelve, the crowds, and Jesus. As for the Twelve, the portrait here is favorable, somewhat rare for Mark. According to verse 30, they did what they were sent to do, and their work was according to the model of Jesus, who was, in addition to preacher and exorcist, a teacher. Teaching is specified when their work is described, just as it frequently is when Jesus' ministry is presented. Most noticeably, the Twelve are here called apostles (v. 30). They went on a mission as the Twelve, as the disciples, but when they completed their assignment, they were called apostles, a new title signifying a new relationship with Jesus. Nowhere else in the Gospel does Mark refer to them by that term. For all the unfavorable attention Mark gives them, he knows that when the shepherd is smitten, the work will fall heavily on the apostles.

The crowds that gather about Jesus are, in Mark's accounts, very large and usually positive about Jesus (vv. 31–34; also 1:27–28; 2:2; 3:7–9; 4:1; 5:21; 8:1; 10:1). There is no indication that Mark suspects large crowds of having shallow faith, wrong motives, and herd mentality. Their presence and enthusiasm leave Jesus and the Twelve no time to eat (v. 31); they anticipate Jesus' destination and run on foot from all the towns (v. 33); they arrive ahead of Jesus and wait for him (v. 33); they stay with him until a late hour (v. 35). They are not only drawn to Jesus, but they are driven by their own desperation, being "like sheep without a shepherd" (v. 34; Num. 27:17).

To this wandering and leaderless flock, Jesus is the compassionate shepherd (v. 34). The image was a familiar one for describing the work of priest and prophet and the relation of God to Israel (1 Kings 22:17; Jer. 23:1–5; Ezek. 34:1–16). According to Mark's account, the first work of the shepherd was teaching the people (v. 34), and only later did his ministry include feeding them. Transcending both teaching and feeding, however, is the ministry of Jesus' death. The preceding account of John's death (vv. 14–29) hangs over this scene as a dark prophecy anticipating 14:27: the shepherd will be smitten and the sheep scattered (Zech. 13:7). But then came the resurrection, and there still continues the gathering of the scattered sheep (14:28; John 10:14–16; 12:32).

The preacher need not feel the necessity of dwelling on the concluding verses 53–56. The geographical location changes, but the scene is really the same—a huge throng pressing upon an immensely popular Jesus. The Jesus who taught them (v. 34), who fed them (vv. 39–44), now heals them (vv. 55–56). The rhythm of popularity and opposition, by now familiar to the reader of Mark, triggers the expectation that verses 53–56 will be followed by an account of hostility and resistance to Jesus. And so they are (7:1–23).

Proper 12 [17]
(Sunday between July 24 and 30 inclusive)

2 Samuel 11:1–15;
Psalm 14; or
2 Kings 4:42–44;
Psalm 145:10–18;
Ephesians 3:14–21;
John 6:1–21

David's theft of Bathsheba and subsequent murder of her husband Uriah are reported in unvarnished terms in the *Common Lectionary*'s Old Testament lesson for today. In Psalm 14, we hear the voice of one who cynically laments a society that has gone to hell, and one who vainly searches for a single soul who does good.

The first reading in other lectionaries is more upbeat—the story of Elisha's multiplication of loaves. The selection from Psalm 145 praises God, who graciously provides food in due season.

With the Gospel reading, we shift from Mark to John, where Jesus not only feeds the five thousand but also walks on the sea.

The epistolary lesson continues selections from Ephesians, this time a prayer to God for inner strengthening and deeper understanding of the surpassing love of Christ.

2 Samuel 11:1–15

The account of David's sin is part of what has been called the "Throne Succession Narrative," or the "Court History of David," an ancient source for the latter years of David's reign. Because the remaining texts for this season concerning David also come from that source, some general comments are called for. The Throne Succession Narrative includes at least 2 Samuel 9–20 and 1 Kings 1–2, and probably also some of the material in 2 Samuel 8. It is one of the finest examples of classical Hebrew prose handed down to us. On the basis of the writer's detailed and precise knowledge of the events and the characters in his story, as well as his point of view, scholars have dated the composition to the generation following David, that is, to the time of Solomon. The later Deuteronomic editors of the books of Samuel and Kings included the document with little or no modification.

What was the writer's purpose and point of view? Two themes run through the entire work and unify it. On the one hand, there is the question of the succession to the throne. Who will follow David? All of the most logical possibilities are considered and eliminated in one way or another. These include the surviving members of Saul's family, a possible union of the families of Saul and David—that is one point of the story of Michal's rejection in 2 Samuel 6:16–23—and the successive sons of David, including Amnon, the eldest, and Absalom, apparently next in line. Even the possibility of the dissolution of the kingdom arises. But finally, on his deathbed, David gives his blessing to Solomon. Our narrator had already prepared us for that result by telling us when Solomon was born that "the LORD loved him" (2 Sam. 12:24).

On the other hand, there is the theme of King David himself, and particularly his decline. The history begins when he is at the peak of his power, having completed his major accomplishments, settled down in Jerusalem, and received the divine promise of an everlasting dynasty. His last years are filled with so much trouble and anguish, both from within his own household and from without, that he is finally only a pale reflection of his former self. Why did the blessing turn to curse? The turning point is reported in our text for the day, the account of his sin with Bathsheba against Uriah the Hittite. Because of this, the sword does not depart from his house (2 Sam. 12:10).

The author was a historian, though not in the critical modern sense. He did not simply record events but tried to make sense of them, to explain causes and effects, balancing description with interpretation. He has a sensitivity for the characters in the drama and deals in a subtle way with their motivations and feelings. His theology of history is different from that of many of his predecessors and successors. God acts in history, he knows, but more through what we would call secondary causes and in and through human hearts. Direct divine intervention is rarely mentioned and thus is all the more important when he does report it. The decline of David is Yahweh's punishment, to be sure, but even a reader who did not believe in Yahweh could understand what happened in terms of David's guilt and his character. Solomon came to the throne by divine decree, but the path was a tortuous one through complicated family and political struggles.

The story of David's sin is told with the power of understatement. Even in the introduction, which sets the scene (vv. 1–2a), the reader is invited to draw some conclusions about David's emotional state. At the time "when kings go out to battle, David sent Joab. . . ." And one day when the king arose from his afternoon nap, he saw a beautiful woman bathing.

We are informed at the outset—and so is David—that Bathsheba is married, so that when she conceives and reports the fact to the king the stage is set for tragedy. We quickly recognize that the major characters in the story are Uriah, David, and—especially in the remainder of chapter 11—Joab, the faithful general. Bathsheba does not play a major role in the court history until its final scenes (1 Kings 1).

The court historian considers it unnecessary to explain David's motives in sending for Uriah. He simply tells the story, and it is a tale filled with irony. David brings Uriah back to Jerusalem, expecting him to spend the night with his wife and thus conceal the adultery. But Uriah's loyalty to the king and his faithfulness to his soldier's vow of sexual abstinence during the battle are his undoing. Even when, on the second night, David gets him drunk (v. 13), he still spends the night on the steps of the palace with the servants. So no alternatives appear to David but to have him killed in battle. The final stroke of irony is that Uriah carries his own death sentence back to Joab (vv. 14–15).

It is a story of David's sins against Uriah and consequently against the Lord. The writer attaches no blame to Bathsheba; David was, after all, the king. Given Israel's patriarchal perspective, adultery was a violation against her husband. But the story is not moralistic; we can all recognize how wrong the actions were, and how one violation, as bad as it was, led to another, even worse. Remarkably, in this stark account of human frailty we are able to identify in turn with all the characters. We can recognize how a tired and perhaps middle-aged king succumbs to temptation and goes from adultery to murder, how Bathsheba is a victim, and how Uriah's very loyalties contribute to his death. In this way the Old Testament narrative interprets us to ourselves and helps us understand the human predicament better. Consequently, even if we are not adulterers, murderers, victims, or soldiers trapped by our loyalty, our prayers of confession can be deeper and more realistic.

Psalm 14

A few psalms or portions of psalms appear more than once in the Old Testament. For example, Psalm 18 also appears as 2 Samuel 22. Psalm 14 recurs as Psalm 53, although with a few minor alterations, the most obvious being the use of the divine name Yahweh in Psalm 14 and the use of Elohim in Psalm 53. We really have no explanation as to why some material was repeated in such similar form other than the fact that, for some reason, it fitted well in two places. So far as the psalms are concerned, however, we have little more than conjecture to go on in explaining why any of them appear in the order they do.

Psalm 14 is clearly a lamenting or complaining psalm that protests about the widespread prevalence of evil in the world. Most of the lament psalms in the Psalter are true prayers; that is, they are addressed to the Deity about some particular trouble or general condition, and they request the Deity to rectify matters. Psalm 14, however, has no verses addressed directly to God; the Deity is spoken of throughout in the third person. Thus the psalm is not a prayer. It would be interesting to know how this psalm was used in worship. Who is speaking? the king? the high priest? an ordinary worshiper? someone who has been mistreated by the wicked?

The psalm has something of a didactic or teaching flavor about it. There is a descriptive, reflective quality about it, with its pessimistic depiction of the human situation. This descriptive character is further expanded in some copies of the ancient Greek version of the Old Testament, which adds the following between verses 3 and 4:

> Their throat is an open sepulcher:
>   with their tongues they have used deceit;
> the poison of asps is under their lips,
>   whose mouth is full of cursing and bitterness;
> their feet are swift to shed blood:
>   destruction and misery are in their ways;
> and the way of peace they have not known:
>   there is no fear of God before their eyes.

This insertion is paralleled by Romans 3:10–18. Perhaps Paul copied this from the Greek, or the Greek translator of the psalms, or a later copyist incorporated the material from Paul's letter.

If we take this psalm as a "homily" on the wicked, what does it say? (1) Verses 2–3 imply that all humans are corrupt, all are bad, all are perverse. No one does what is right. The two expressions "are wise" and "seek after God" are to be understood as synonymous. Thus the psalmist places everyone under a blanket condemnation. (2) The basic human problem as seen by the psalmist seems to be practical atheism, the assumption in the heart that "there is no God" or that God does not care or take human actions into account (v. 1). Such a position makes the person into the sole authority of what is acceptable or permissible. For the author, such behavior was corrupt, resulting in abominable deeds, in failure to do the good. (3) Real knowledge of the way things are should lead one to do the good and worship God (v. 4). Because of this lack of knowledge, people live without respect for one another, consuming one another with the casualness with which one would eat bread. There is wrongdoing; but even worse, there is no guilt or remorse. (4) In spite of all appearances to the contrary, God is still in control and is a refuge to the poor and the oppressed (vv. 5–6). The "poor" and the "righteous" are those opposed by the powerful. (Here the writer denies the absoluteness of the claim that all humans are bad that was expounded in v. 2.) (5) The final two verses are an expression of hopeful eschatology: someday the human condition will be as it should be.

2 Kings 4:42–44

This little tale of the miraculous feeding of the one hundred doubtless found its way into Christian lectionaries because of its thematic parallels—if not its tradition/historical connections—with the stories of Jesus' feeding the five thousand, one version of which is found in the Gospel reading for the day (see also Matt. 14:13–21; Mark 6:32–44; Luke 9:10–17).

The short and self-contained story is the last in a series of four prophetic miracle stories in 2 Kings 4. The others are Elisha's rescue of the children of a widow of one of the prophets from debt slavery by means of the miraculous jar of oil (vv. 1–7), the prophet's revival of a woman's dead son (vv. 8–37), and Elisha's transformation of the deadly stew into good food (vv. 38–41). Although there are significant differences—some are short anecdotes and others are complicated stories—all involve miraculous deeds by the prophet, and all mark the movement from death to life.

The context of the story is the travels of Elisha and his band of prophets, and the famine mentioned in 4:38. The tale is recounted simply and directly. A man arrives with some of the "first fruits" of the harvest, so the famine is ending. In order to emphasize that the feeding to come is miraculous, the narrator specifies the amount of food: "twenty loaves of barley and fresh ears of grain in his sack" (v. 42). Elisha instructs him to give it to the people to eat. The man's rhetorical question is an objection that the food is insufficient: "How can I set this before a hundred people?" (v. 43). Elisha repeats his instructions but adds the prophetic word "For thus says the LORD, 'They shall eat and have some left'" (v. 43). And thus it happens. They eat and have some left, "according to the word of the LORD" (v. 44).

In the ancient Israelite tradition, one of the main purposes of such legends was to evoke and strengthen faith in the prophetic figure and—more important—in the Lord whose word he spoke. Like most of the stories of the miraculous deeds of Elisha and, to a lesser extent, of Elijah, there is a strong air of folklore, including belief in magical causation of various kinds. In this case, the narrator emphasizes that the wondrous deed is effected by means of the word of the Lord through the prophet. Thus a major step has been taken to bring magical beliefs under the domain of faith in Yahweh and his word.

Although this and similar biblical stories of miraculous deeds may appear strange or even quaint to modern ears, they convey fundamental features of the biblical faith. There is, first, the concern for the poor and the needy. Elisha's band of prophets and most of the people whom they encountered daily were poor and often hungry. Two of the stories in this chapter concern women: one is a widow about to lose her sons to debt slavery, and the other has lost her only son. Three of the miracle stories concern food (the widow's oil, the bad stew, and the feeding of the one hundred). One cannot escape the biblical tradition's concern for the needy. Second, there is the importance of food itself. With all the concern for spiritual power, we must remember that such power provides for material needs. That is a persistent Old Testament theme. Physical needs—food, shelter, a place to live, freedom from violence—these are blessings from God. So if one cannot provide food for the hungry by performing dramatic miracles—or if one does not believe in such miracles at all—then one must find some other way to feed the hungry. One may not be able literally to multiply food through magical words, but the right words can set actions into motion. A soup kitchen or a food bank or an airlift of food to a starving people may not be the kingdom of God, but these certainly are signs of the reign of God. Third, the prophetic words in this text recall the word of God in Genesis 1 through which the created order—with its capacity to feed people—was brought into existence. The abundance of the earth for the people of the earth—that is an even greater miracle than the feeding of the one hundred.

Psalm 145:10–18

An alphabetic psalm, Psalm 145 consists of a series of short affirmations that extol the reign and kingship of God. The text oscillates between words addressed to the Deity (vv. 1–2, 4–7, 10–13a) and words spoken about the Deity but addressed to a human audience (vv. 3, 8–9, 13b–14). The lection for this Sunday consists of both types of material—speech about God (vv. 13b–14, 17–18) and speech to God (vv. 10–13a, 15–16).

Verses 8–9, which speak about God and constitute the central thesis of the psalm, offer a formulaic definition or description of God or what classical theology calls the attributes of God. The same description, in almost exact terminology, appears in Exodus 34:6; Joel 2:13; Jonah 4:2; and Psalms 86:15 and 103:8. Six characteristics of the Deity are emphasized, all of which stress the benevolent aspects of the Divine: gracious (or perhaps "dutiful," as in the appropriate relationship between master and servant), merciful (or "compassionate"), slow to anger (or "patient, long-suffering"), abounding in steadfast love (or "extremely loyal"), good to all (or "universally concerned"), and compassionate to all that God has made (or "tenderly caring for all God's creatures"). Such a text as this is the nearest one finds in the Old Testament to a descriptive definition of the Divine. Although the emphasis is placed on the benevolence of God, verse 20 indicates that moral considerations—the issue of justice and injustice—which receive so much emphasis elsewhere in the Hebrew Scriptures, are not ignored in the theology of this psalm.

The central topic in the praise of God in verses 10–13 is the kingdom of God. The kingdom of God is here understood, as in most places in the Bible, as the dominion, or rule, of God. In verse 13a, "kingdom" and "dominion" are parallel to each other and may be viewed as synonyms. Thus the focus of this text is concerned with the present manifestation of God's kingdom—God's rule as king at the moment—rather than an eschatological emphasis that comes to dominate in the New Testament. Nonetheless, the futuristic elements do appear in verses 10–11, where the verbs can be translated, as in the NRSV, in a future tense.

Both the deeds and the devotees of God—that is, the world of creation at large and the world of God's special people—offer their testimony regarding the rule of God (vv. 10–11). Both offer witness to humanity at large ("all people", v. 12; the NEB translates "their fellows"). Thus the creation and the covenant community point to the reign of God, a reign that is eternal and forever enduring (verse 13a). Verse 13b reiterates the emphasis on the eternal and continuing reign of God. God keeps faith with all the promises ("is faithful in all his words") and is unchanging in all that God does ("gracious in all his deeds"). Thus one can trust God and rely on his word.

The preaching on this text should stress the eternal, consistent, abiding character of God's reign. As creator, God is king, and the world and all that is in it are God's subjects. The remainder of the psalm (vv. 14–21), like verses 8–9, focuses on the benevolent character of the God who reigns as king (see Ps. 146 and Proper 27 [32]). The narrative reading from 2 Kings provides a legendary account of how the benevolence of God manifests itself.

Ephesians 3:14–21

Today's epistolary lection is a prayer consisting of an opening acclamation of the sovereignty of God (vv. 14–15), a set of petitions (vv. 16–19), and a doxology (vv. 20–21). The prayer actually begins in 3:1 but is interrupted by an extended excursus on the apostle's apostolic ministry to the Gentiles (vv. 2–13). In one sense, this prayer is a continuation of the prayer begun earlier in 1:15.

The prayer opens with an acknowledgment of God as Father, before whom the apostle bows his knees in prayer (cf. Luke 11:2; also Phil. 2:10). Just as Yahweh has numbered all the stars of heaven and named them all (Ps. 147:4), so has the Father named every family in heaven and on earth. The English translation obscures the play on words between "Father" (*pater*) and "family" (*patria*). Here is the acknowledgment that every "family unit," earthly or heavenly, owes its existence to the paternity of God (cf. Acts 17:28–29; 1 Cor. 8:6).

The second section of the prayer contains a set of petitions. First, there are two petitions made to the Father on behalf of the readers (vv. 16–17a). There is first the recognition that all the petitions that follow will be made out of the abundant "riches of his glory" (cf. 1:7; 2:7; 3:8; also Rom. 9:23; 10:12; 11:33; Col. 1:27; Phil. 4:19). Specifically, the Father is asked to grant the readers inner strengthening through his Spirit. Quite often, the Spirit is associated with power (*dynamis*), in fact, is seen as the source of divine power (Rom. 8:11; 15:13; 1 Cor. 2:4). Through Christ, one has access to sources of power that strengthen inner reserves (Eph. 6:10; Col. 1:11). We should also note that this strengthening takes place in the "inner being" (v. 16), that dimension of ourselves where genuine renewal occurs (2 Cor. 4:16; also Rom. 7:22; 1 Pet. 3:4).

In addition to inner strengthening, the Father is asked to bestow the presence of Christ in the hearts of the readers. This, of course, can occur only "through faith" (v. 17). In the Fourth Gospel, the Father and the Son are said to make their home in the hearts of those who love Christ and keep his word (John 14:23). That God would come to dwell within the midst of the people of God was a long-standing hope (Ezek. 37:27) and one that early Christians realized (2 Cor. 6:16; Rev. 3:20). The presence of God within them was quite naturally experienced in terms of the presence of Christ.

Following these two petitions for the Father to bestow the gifts of inner power and the presence of Christ on the readers, there occur petitions on behalf of the readers themselves. These, however, are predicated on their "being rooted and grounded in love" (v. 17; cf. Col. 1:23; 2:7). With this proviso, three petitions are made.

First, the apostle prays for them to have the capacity of comprehension (v. 18). This does not occur in isolation, however, for it is a capacity they have in common with "all the saints."

It is only as part of the whole people of God that the readers can probe the multiple dimensions of the Christian mystery—its breadth and length and height and depth.

Second, he prays for their capacity to know (v. 19). The object of their knowledge is the "love of Christ that surpasses knowledge." Here, no doubt, he has in mind the love that Christ has for us (2 Cor. 8:9).

Third, he prays that through their experience of the surpassing love of Christ they will be filled with all the fullness of God (v. 19*b*).

The prayer concludes with a doxology (vv. 20–21). The object of these words of praise is God, whose power to transform our inner natures exceeds human expectations (cf. Rom. 16:25; Jude 24; Eph. 1:19). God is often seen to be the source of energy motivating Christian action (Eph. 3:7; Col. 1:29; 2:1; 4:12; 1 Thess. 2:2). Accordingly, glory, both in the church and in Christ Jesus, is given to God (cf. Rom. 11:36; 16:27; Gal. 1:5; Phil. 4:20; 1 Tim. 1:17; 2 Tim. 4:18; Heb. 13:21; 1 Pet. 4:11; 2 Pet. 3:18; Jude 25; Rev. 1:6; 4:11; also 4 Macc. 18:24).

John 6:1–21

For five consecutive Sundays our Gospel lections will be drawn from John 6. It seems wise, therefore, to take a few minutes to make the shift from Mark to refresh ourselves on the Johannine perspective and to introduce chapter 6 in particular.

Many commentaries will debate the question of the location of chapter 6 in the overall scheme of the Fourth Gospel. Because chapter 4 concludes with Jesus in Galilee, chapter 5 is set in Jerusalem, chapter 6 has Jesus again in Galilee, and chapter 7 again in Jerusalem, some argue that chapter 6 is mislocated in the Gospel as we now have it. Geography alone would prefer chapters 4, 6, 5, and 7 in that order, having Jesus minister in Galilee and then return to Jerusalem. This is reasonable, but it pays more attention to itinerary and chronology than the Gospel does. But of more importance, the Fourth Evangelist apparently wants to highlight the fact that Jesus keeps the Passover as far as possible from Jerusalem, the scene of his rejection at another Passover time. Jesus will die as the Passover lamb in Jerusalem (19:31–37), but now he will observe a Passover meal with the more receptive people in the hill country on the other side of the Sea of Galilee (6:1). For this Evangelist, theology takes precedence over reasonable itineraries. Because this Gospel has no eucharistic last meal in an upper room, as do the Synoptics, this narrative is John's theological equivalent of "the last supper."

A second matter important to understanding John 6 is the linking of the feeding, the walking on water, and Peter's confession of faith. Matthew and Mark join the feeding and the walking on water with Peter's confession shortly thereafter (Matt. 14–16; Mark 6–8). Luke omits the walking on water but joins directly the feeding and Peter's confession (9:10–22). Whatever may be the relation of John's Gospel to the Synoptics, at least at this point we have a tradition that had already forged three stories into one narrative prior to the work of the Four Evangelists. Preaching on any one of the three stories should call attention to the whole unit as a witness to Christ.

That the feeding occurs at Passover is important for the writer. At passover, Jesus cleansed the temple and spoke of his death (chap. 2). At Passover, Jesus had a meal with his disciples in Jerusalem and spoke of his approaching death (chap. 13). In the account before us, the feeding will not only be told in eucharistic language (vv. 11, 23), but it will be followed by a discourse on the life-giving flesh and blood of Jesus (vv. 51–59). We have, then, a story that has significance beyond that of Jesus' compassion on hungry crowds. In fact, verses 5–6 make it abundantly clear that Jesus knew what he was going to do, that he would perform a sign providing something qualitatively better than what was expected. The preacher would do well not to reach back into the Synoptics to pick up the "compassion on the hungry" theme. Jesus feeds the people, to be sure, but the reader has already been alerted to look beyond the bread to the Bread. This is no isolated format in John; many of the stories are so developed. Jesus' mother wanted him to provide wine for wedding guests, and Jesus performed a revelatory sign beyond the expectation of Mary (chap. 2). Martha and Mary wanted a deceased brother restored, and Jesus responded in a way beyond resuscitating a corpse to offering resurrection and life to the world (chap. 11). To preach on John 6:1–21 is to open the door to a ministry of Jesus beyond the immediate wants and expectations of those who seek what he can give.

The crowd, after a good meal, is ready to proclaim Jesus as the successor to Moses, who also provided manna in the wilderness (Deut. 18:18). In fact, they want to control and assure their own future by enthroning Jesus as king (v. 15). They do not understand that Jesus' person and place is of God and has nothing to do with their approval or disapproval. There is a big difference between confessing faith in Jesus as Lord and sponsoring Jesus or setting him up as provider. However, we should not be too harsh with these Galileans; it is still easy to praise one who gives much and asks nothing. But Jesus' sermon is yet to come, and one suspects that the enthronement committee will soon be dissolved.

As stated above, the story in verses 16–21 is a companion to the feeding account and should not be isolated from it. In the exodus tradition, mastery over the sea and feeding the people in the wilderness had long been joined. Recall the recitation of God's caring in Psalm 78. Paul expected the Corinthian church to be instructed by Israel's experiences at the sea and in the wilderness feedings, experiences he saw as types of baptism and eucharist (1 Cor. 10:1–5). In John 6:1–21, therefore, Jesus is associated with Moses, and the achievement of Jesus is a new exodus for the people. In addition, because Jesus speaks to his disciples using the name of God ("I am," v. 20, note) to identify himself, the writer joins Mark and Matthew in treating this event as a theophany.

Proper 13 [18]
(Sunday between July 31 and August 6 inclusive)

2 Samuel 11:26–12:13*a*;
Psalm 51:1–12; or
Exodus 16:2–4, 9–15;
Psalm 78:23–29
Ephesians 4:1–16;
John 6:24–35

In the Old Testament lesson for today from the *Common Lectionary*, David is confronted by the prophet Nathan, using the parable of the ewe lamb. David's final confession at the end of the Old Testament reading, "I have sinned against the Lord," becomes a full-fledged prayer of lament in the form of Psalm 51.

In the reading from Exodus, we hear Israel complaining to Moses and Aaron about wilderness food and God answering their complaint by promising meat and bread. The selection from Psalm 78 is a reminiscence on God's sending Israel "the bread of angels," or manna from heaven.

In the Gospel text, we have a Johannine reminiscence of the Exodus story in the form of a discourse by Jesus on the bread from heaven, culminating in the christological claim "I am the bread of life."

The Epistle lesson, which continues the readings from Ephesians, calls for a form of life that honors common beliefs and commitments pursued through a variety of gifts.

2 Samuel 11:26–12:13*a*

Nathan's encounter with David is the direct consequence of the king's adultery with Bathsheba and murder of her husband Uriah. The section of the narrative between the readings for this week and last week (2 Sam. 11:16–25) reports how David's orders for the death of Uriah were carried out. Today's lesson begins with the note that David made Bathsheba his wife after her period of mourning was over, and that she bore him a son. In one of his significant interpretive asides, the court historian points out that "the thing that David had done displeased the LORD" (2 Sam. 11:27). The reading for the day will show just how displeased the Lord was and how David responded to that displeasure.

The body of the lesson consists of a dialogue between the prophet and the king, introduced by the briefest narrative framework: "And the LORD sent Nathan to David" (v. 1).

Short as it is, the note is not simply incidental; it makes clear at the outset what is confirmed later (vv. 7, 11, 13), namely, that Nathan does not speak for himself but for Yahweh. The prophets understood themselves to be messengers of the Lord.

Nathan tells the king a story (vv. 1b–4) of crass injustice, apparently asking for a royal judgment and possibly intervention. The contrasts are so sharp between the poor man, with his single ewe lamb that was almost a part of the family, and the greedy rich man that David readily pronounces the death sentence (vv. 5–6).

The prophet's reaction (vv. 7–12) reveals that the story was not the report of an actual event but a parable. Specifically, it is a juridical parable in which the addressee—in this case, David—is moved to pronounce judgment upon himself. Isaiah's parable of the vineyard (Isa. 5:1–7) is a close parallel. Such parables consist of a story and its interpretation or application. The interpretation of the parable begins with one of the most memorable Old Testament lines, "You are the man!" (v. 7a). Although Nathan's speech is not in poetic meter or parallelism, its basic structure is the same as that of the announcements of the prophets of the eighth and following centuries. It includes the messenger formula "thus says the Lord" at the beginning and as a key transition. The major parts are the indictment, or statement of reasons, for punishment (vv. 7–9) and the announcement of judgment or punishment (vv. 10–12).

The statement of reasons for punishment or indictment has two movements. First, Yahweh, through Nathan, reminds David of his gracious care (vv. 7–8). Yahweh had anointed him king, delivered him from Saul, given him Saul's house and wives—noteworthy in view of the sin with Bathsheba—and made him king over both Israel and Judah. Furthermore, the Lord was willing to do even more. The recital concerns God's grace toward David himself; there is no mention of the promise of a dynasty (2 Sam. 7). Second, the Lord states the indictment itself (v. 9). David has "despised the word of the LORD" by taking the wife of Uriah as a wife and killing him "with the sword of the Ammonites." At this point there is no mention of the act of adultery.

The announcement of punishment includes the judgments that the sword will never depart from David's house, that the Lord will raise up evil from his own house, and that David's wives will be given to another who will lie with them openly. All these things, we will see as the story unfolds, come to pass.

David's response is a short but full confession of sin (v. 13a), whereupon the prophet announces that the sin has been "put away" and the death sentence—which David had pronounced upon himself—set aside. Still, there will be punishment; the child of the adulterous union will die (v. 14).

Encounter with this story generates a wealth of issues for theological and homiletical reflection: (1) in the biblical faith, no one, not even the king anointed by God, stands above the law; (2) to act irresponsibly in society, especially against those who have less power, is to "despise the word of the LORD" (v. 9); (3) that election—in this case, as king—is a reason for punishment indicates that it entails accountability (see also Amos 3:1–2); and (4) what is the relationship between divine wrath and mercy? The punishment may appear harsh to us, and it is, but to the writer and the original hearers or readers, this was also a story of God's mercy. As far as David was concerned, the death penalty, which applied not only to murder but also to adultery (see Deut. 22:22), had been reduced.

Psalm 51:1–12

This psalm was previously discussed as one of the readings for Ash Wednesday.

Exodus 16:2–4, 9–15

According to all levels of Old Testament tradition, between the exodus from Egypt and the settlement of the land of Canaan, Israel wandered in the wilderness. The scene that is played out in chapter 16 is one that will recur over and over along the way from Egypt to Sinai and from Sinai to the edge of the promised land. The people of Israel complain because of some real or imagined need, Moses remonstrates with them and intercedes with the Lord, and the Lord responds graciously, but not always without anger. The most persistent themes concerning the wilderness wandering thus are expressed: the dramatic contrast between the people's persistent complaints and the Lord's gracious care and preservation.

Although the basic profile of the story as a whole is clear enough, Jewish and Christian commentators from the earliest times have recognized a large number of difficulties in the chapter. The rabbis in particular noticed that in verse 8 Moses gives divine instructions that he did not receive until verses 11–12, that the sabbath is observed but the commandment was not given until later at Sinai, and that there is an allusion in verse 34 to the tent of the meeting that was not built until later. Moreover, there are gaps, repetitions, and different descriptions of the manna. Only some of these difficulties are resolved by the recognition of different sources. Most of the chapter comes from the Priestly Writer, but some (mainly vv. 4–5, 27–31) comes from the Yahwist. The latter stresses the gift of the manna as a test, whereas the former emphasizes that the purpose was to demonstrate that it was the Lord who brought the people out of Egypt.

It would be difficult indeed for the modern preacher to develop a line of thought concerning the story of the manna and quails that has not already appeared in the history of the interpretation of this tradition, either elsewhere in the Old Testament, in the New Testament (see esp. John 6; 1 Cor. 10:1–13; 2 Cor. 8:15; Rev. 2:17), or in the history of the church and synagogue. The manna story has been used as the basis for moralistic homilies; it has been spiritualized; and there have been attempts even in the early Christian centuries to find a rational explanation for the miracle. Among the possibilities for homiletical reflection are the following:

1. Consider the murmuring or complaining of the people. The specific issue in Exodus 16 is food. Was the complaint legitimate or not, or—better—does the narrator of the story consider it a legitimate complaint? By his choice of words ("complained," or "grumbled," NJPSV) and by the way he phrases the complaint, our reporter disapproves of a whining people: "If only we had died by the hand of the LORD in the land of Egypt, when we sat by the fleshpots and ate our fill of bread . . ." (v. 3). That is the dominant view in the tradition, that Israel's complaints were unfair. (There is an alternative tradition that seems to think of the time in the wilderness as the period of Israel's full obedience to and dependence upon the Lord. (Cf. Hos. 2:14; 11:1; 13:4ff.; Jer. 2:1ff.) On the surface the complaint concerns food, but it is actually far more serious. In effect, the Israelites are objecting to their election, to the fact that Yahweh brought them out of slavery into freedom! Small wonder that preachers have used the Israelites in the wilderness as bad examples.

The Old Testament view about complaining to God, however, is not so unambiguous. Although one may not see God and live, one could certainly complain to God in the strongest possible terms and not only survive but hope for relief. Such complaints are found not only in the Book of Job but in more than fifty psalms of individual or corporate lament. There the individual or the community petitioned God for help in time of trouble, confessing either sin or innocence (cf. Pss. 6; 17; 22). The context for such prayers was worship, from which no human emotion or feeling was prohibited.

2. In Exodus 16 the gift is a test. When the Lord responds to the complaint with a promise to "rain bread from heaven," the Lord says it is in order to "test them, whether they will follow my instruction or not" (v. 4). What is the point, and what is the penalty for failure to pass the test? The instructions conceal a promise: "each day the people shall go out and gather enough for that day" (v. 4). The test is whether they will do just as they are told, no more and no less. Some of the people, however, fail the test, for they do not trust the promise that tomorrow there will be enough for that day. Contrary to the further instructions (v. 19), they tried to save some of the manna. What happens when one fails to trust in the promise of daily bread? How is punishment handed out to those who do not pass the test? Not without a sense of humor, the narrator reports that the hoarded manna "bred worms and became foul" (v. 20).

3. Then there is the giving of the manna itself. At one level, the chapter is a popular etymology of the name of the wilderness food, a play on the sound of the question "What is it?" (Hebrew *man hu*). But above all, the manna, like all good things to eat, is a gift. Deuteronomy views the gift as didactic, God's means of teaching the people one of the most fundamental points about life: "He humbled you by letting you hunger, then by feeding you with manna . . . in order to make you understand that one does not live by bread alone, but by every word that comes from the mouth of the LORD" (Deut. 8:3). Here "every word that comes from the mouth of the Lord" has a double meaning. On the one hand, it is spiritual, calling attention to the divine law and teachings. On the other hand, it alludes to the creative power of the word of God, by which all good things are brought into being. Thus the manna is a test and it is a lesson, but above all it is God's graceful response to an ungrateful and even rebellious people.

Psalm 78:23–29

Psalm 78 is one of the few psalms concerned with the history of Israel and Judah. Other examples are Psalms 105 and 106. The intentions of Psalm 78 are (1) to show that the people's—especially the northern tribes'—history was one of disobedience and lack of faith (v. 9–66) and (2) to claim that God had forsaken the Northern Kingdom and chosen the (southern) tribe of Judah, the city of Jerusalem (Zion), and the family of David (vv. 67–72). As with Psalms 105 and 106, this psalm illustrates how the people's historical traditions could be used for particular purposes in the people's later history.

The opening of the psalm is rather unique in that it begins with someone calling the people to listen to the recital of a historical presentation. (Ps. 49 is somewhat similar, but there it is an autobiographical rather than a national history that is the concern.) The sense of verses 1–3 and the use of the psalm are better represented in the NJPSV than in the NRSV:

> Give ear, my people, to my teaching,
>   turn your ear to what I say.
> I will expound a theme,
>   hold forth lessons of the past,
>   things that we have heard and known,
>   that our fathers have told us.

Verses 23–29 parallel the Exodus text and in a poetic form describe the sending of quail and the giving of manna. The manna is here depicted as the food of the angelic-heavenly beings, that is, as the grain of heaven and the bread of angels.

Ephesians 4:1–16

This passage marks the transition in the Letter to the Ephesians from doctrinal instruction to ethical exhortation. The author "begs" or "beseeches" his readers in the form of an appeal (*parakaleo*, cf. 1 Cor. 1:10, 16). Specifically, he urges them to follow a particular mode of life appropriate to their calling (cf. 1 Thess. 2:12; Col. 1:10; Phil. 1:27). "To lead a life" renders the Greek word for "walk," a typical expression of one's form of conduct (cf. Eph. 2:2, 10; 4:17; 5:2, 8, 15). Earlier, the readers were reminded of "the hope to which he has called you" (1:18). Within the New Testament, Christians are commonly spoken of as those who have been called, or elected, by God (1 Cor. 1:2; Rom. 1:7; 1 Thess. 1:4; 2 Thess. 2:13). Here the expectation is that the form of one's life should correspond to the elevated calling one has received from God. The appeal has special force, given the author's status as a "prisoner in the Lord" (cf. 3:1; Phil 1:7, 12–13; Col. 4:18; 2 Tim. 1:8; 2:9; Philem. 1).

He enjoins the readers to adopt a mode of life characterized by four qualities: humility, gentleness, patience, and loving forbearance. Paul's own behavior is elsewhere described in these terms (Acts 20:19; 1 Cor. 13:4–7). Even though they describe the expected behavior of Christians (Phil. 2:1–11; Col. 3:12–13), these qualities of life were also taught in the Old Testament (Isa. 57:15; 66:2; Mic. 6:8). Here they are seen to be the essential prerequisites to any form of unity and harmony within the church. In Galatians 5:17–23, such qualities are classified as the "fruit of the Spirit," whereas their opposites are said to be "works of the flesh." In a similar vein, the unity that is being sought here is seen as that which derives from the Spirit; the "unity of the Spirit" is the unity that the Spirit gives. Even so, the readers must "make every effort to maintain" such unity (cf. Phil. 1:27; Col. 3:14–15). The language suggests that unity is already a given that is to be actualized and "kept," rather than something that they themselves are to bring about. Hence, Christians are urged to "be of the same mind" (Phil. 2:2; 1 Cor. 1:10).

The appeal for unity is buttressed by the statement that there is "one body and one Spirit, just as you were called to the one hope of your calling" (v. 4). There follows what appears to be a primitive confession of faith: "one Lord, one faith, one baptism, one God and Father of all, who is above all and through all and in all" (vv. 5–6).

One body. The Body of Christ is, by definition, unitary, and those who are incorporated into it share a common existence. Earlier, Paul wrote to the Corinthians, "You are the body of Christ" (1 Cor. 12:27), insisting that although it has a plurality and diversity of members, it is nevertheless one (1 Cor. 12:12, 14–26). In Ephesians, this metaphor is carried further, and the universal church is identified as the Body of Christ (1:23; cf. Rom. 12:5; Col. 3:15). In this "one body" Gentiles and Jews become one (2:16).

One Spirit. To the Corinthians, Paul stressed that the multiplicity of gifts present among them all derived from the same Spirit (1 Cor. 12:4, 11). In fact, he insisted that the Spirit was the common administrator of our baptism, and consequently Christians "drink of one Spirit" (1 Cor. 12:13). Through a single Spirit we have access to the Father (Eph. 2:18). The "unity of the Spirit" mentioned in verse 3 is predicated on the existence of a single Spirit.

One hope. In God's call, one hope is held out to Christians, and this can be none other than the hope of the resurrection (1:18; cf. 1 Pet. 1:3; also Col. 1:5, 27).

One Lord. Although unspecified, this can be none other than the Lord Jesus Christ. As the primitive Christian confession preserved in 1 Corinthians 8:6 states, he is the one "through whom are all things and through whom we exist." It is interesting to notice that, in contrast to this form of the confession, the christological component is listed first here. This article of faith came to be tested severely in the early centuries of the church, when Christians were forced to choose between Christ, the one Lord, and the emperor, who in the imperial cult was worshiped as lord. Echoes of this are seen especially in Revelation.

One faith. Here "faith" is used in the sense of the repository of belief shared by all Christians; and more than likely, its essence was the christological confession that Christ had come in the flesh (cf. 1 John 4:2–3; Jude 3).

One baptism. As noted earlier, through baptism Christians came to drink of the "one Spirit" (1 Cor. 12:13), and this initiatory rite enabled them to become clothed with Christ (Gal. 3:26; also Rom. 6:3). It is worth noting that when the Corinthian fellowship began to dissolve, Paul grounded his appeal for unity in their baptismal experience (1 Cor. 1:10–17).

One God. Christians inherited from Judaism the cardinal belief in the one God, who was Father of all (cf. Mal. 2:10) and who brooked no rivals (Exod. 20:3; Deut. 6:4; Isa. 44:6–8). Belief in one supreme God—radical monotheism—became an article of their confession (cf. 1 Tim. 2:5). In the confession preserved in 1 Corinthians 8:6, Paul says, "For us there is one God, the Father, from whom are all things and for whom we exist." The oneness of God became axiomatic in Paul's thought as he argued for one mode of justification for all humanity, both Jews and Gentiles (Rom. 3:30). Here God is said to be "above all, through all, and in all." This is an affirmation of God's supremacy over all things as well as an expression of the conviction that God is present in all the affairs of the world, working through them and in them. One textual variant reads that God is "within all of us," in which case the text would be affirming the full presence of God within the church (3:19).

If the first part of today's passage delineates the beliefs we have in common, the second half (vv. 7–16) recognizes the variety of gifts within the church that enable a thriving fellowship. Those listed in verse 11 are functional gifts—apostles, prophets, teachers, and so forth—an indication of the diverse roles people played in the church. In spite of their functional diversity, however, they are deployed toward the common task of equipping the saints for ministry. What is hoped for is to attain a level of maturity that gives stability and order to the church. Our text recognizes full well that faddish doctrines come and go, that they are often promoted by tricksters and schemers, and it calls for us to be discriminating in what we accept as gospel. Above all, what is sought is a community of persons who are organically connected, whose common purpose is advanced, not hindered, by their diverse gifts, where growth and vitality are the norm, not the exception.

John 6:24–35

Today is the second of five Sundays on which the Gospel lessons are drawn from John 6. In addition to reviewing the introduction to this material in the commentary on last Sunday's Gospel, one might do well to pause here and reflect upon the achievement of the entirety of John 6. Otherwise the preacher could jump in, exhaust in the first sermon the homiletical value of "Jesus as the Bread of Life," and then be left with three Sundays of Gospel readings without further comment. If it is one's intention to have the sermons on these five Sundays focus primarily upon the Gospel readings, then the best counsel for developing those messages is to be found in the way John 6 itself unfolds. The lectionary is very helpful here, although the lections from the chapter show how stubbornly the Gospel resists division into smaller units. The preacher will notice that the lections only overlap at points in order to sustain the theme from week to week.

We return now to the principal story—feeding the multitudes, with the feeding being understood in more than one sense. What follows will remind the preacher of earlier texts in this Gospel: Jesus spoke of the temple of God, and his audience thought of a building (2:19–21); Jesus spoke of being born anew, and Nicodemus thought of a mother's womb (3:3–4); Jesus spoke of living water, and a woman thought of Jacob's well (4:7–15). So here Jesus will speak of true bread, and the crowd will think of their next meal. Phase one or level one of the narrative is the provision of bread and fish for a hungry crowd in the wilderness. At this level, the people are not only satisfied but excited about Jesus. They hail him as the new Moses and, in fact, want to enthrone him as king (vv. 14–15). We have observed, however, that Jesus has more in mind than a meal, evidenced by the usual Johannine preface to a sign (vv. 5–6) and by the eucharistic language (vv. 11, 23). The attention given to the bread with the fish disappearing from the story (vv. 13, 23) is not only out of eucharistic interest but in anticipation of the discourse on the bread from heaven.

Verses 22–24 set the scene for the second encounter between Jesus and the crowd, this time in Capernaum at the synagogue (v. 59). It is immediately clear that the people are stuck at level one of the event, the free meal. Their question "When did you come here?" (v. 25) is purely chronological and geographical, but the reader is thinking of the coming of the Son from God for the life of the world. And Jesus charges them with their blind willfulness. They are blind in that they see only food, not a sign of anything more satisfying, more life giving (vv. 26–28) than the next meal. They are willful in that they want to "perform the works of God" (v. 28); that is, they want to be in charge of their own lives and futures. Their attempt earlier to enthrone Jesus has made this abundantly clear. When told that the work of God is faith in the one God sent (v. 29), they still want to be in charge, even of faith itself. Show *us* a sign, *we* will see, *we* will weigh the evidence, *we* will draw conclusions, and *we* might even decide to believe (v. 30). It is not likely that this, or any audience, can insist upon being in control of their receiving and of their believing and still be open to a message on the bread that is God's gift from heaven.

Even though our lection continues through verse 35 and thus includes the first part of that message, we will wait until next Sunday to give full attention to the discourse on the bread from heaven. In the move to that message, however, the preacher will not want to disregard or to treat lightly the fact that Jesus did provide food for hungry stomachs before moving on to the sermon on the bread that lasts forever. John cannot be charged with spiritualizing the gospel to the point of abandoning basic creature needs, and neither should the preacher who presents John 6, nor the church that hears it.

Proper 14 [19]
(Sunday between August 7 and 13 inclusive)

2 Samuel 18:5–9, 15, 31–33;
Psalm 130; or
1 Kings 19:4–8;
Psalm 34:1–8;
Ephesians 4:25–5:2;
John 6:35, 41–51

The climactic event in Absalom's war of rebellion against David and David's grief over his son Absalom provide today's Old Testament reading for the *Common Lectionary*. The despairing cry that opens Psalm 130 might well be imagined as David's cry, although despair gives way to hope by the psalm's end.

In the other Old Testament lesson, a dejected Elijah sitting under a solitary broom tree receives nourishment from an angel and proceeds to Mt. Horeb. In the selection from Psalm 34, a prayer of thanksgiving, the psalmist speaks of the angel of the Lord, who encompasses the righteous and delivers them.

The Gospel reading continues from John's Gospel with Jesus' discourse claiming that he is the living bread come down from heaven.

A series of moral exhortations, concluding with a call to imitate God, constitute today's Epistle lesson from Ephesians.

2 Samuel 18:5–9, 15, 31–33

A great deal has transpired in the life of King David since last week's lesson in this series, and almost all of it bad. Nathan said that "the sword shall never depart" from David's house (2 Sam. 12:10), and indeed it does not. Following David's successful campaign against Rabbah (2 Sam. 12:26–31), we hear of a series of troubles among his children: rape, murder, sibling strife, and the rebellion of one of his sons against the throne. Second Samuel 13 reports the rape of Tamar by her half brother Amnon, David's firstborn, and then Absalom's calculated murder of Amnon. Absalom, who was acting to revenge his sister Tamar, then fled from David's wrath and subsequently was allowed to return to Jerusalem (2 Sam. 14). Though he was next in line for the throne, Absalom could not wait, so be began to plot a rebellion against his father, forcing David to flee with his faithful followers (2 Sam.

15). The report of the final episode begins in 2 Samuel 17:24. Absalom pursued David across the Jordan, and the battle is about to begin.

The story of Absalom's death is without a doubt one of the most dramatic and vivid scenes in the Old Testament. As the events unfold before our eyes, contrasts of character are revealed in such a way that moral issues are posed. The opening verse about David's organization of his troops reminds us of one side of David, the shrewd military tactician. The part of the story omitted from the lection (vv. 2–4) extends that point and adds to it David's bravery. He intended to lead the troops, but was dissuaded on the grounds that his loss would mean total defeat. On the other hand, the king's instructions to the commanders to spare Absalom reveal his weakness for his children. It was that very factor that had set into motion the events that led up to Absalom's rebellion; for when David would not deal with Amnon for the rape of Tamar (2 Sam. 15:21), Absalom began to take matters into his own hands.

The court historian (see the commentary on 2 Sam. 11:1–15 for Proper 12 [17] in this volume) tells us nothing new about Absalom. The fatal irony is that he was trapped, one might say, by his vanity. Second Samuel 14:25–26, in describing his great beauty, emphasizes that his hair was unusually heavy.

Then there is the unnamed man (vv. 10–13), doubtless a soldier, who discovered Absalom and reported to Joab. When the general rebukes him for not killing the rebel, his response shows prudence and insight. First he reminds Joab of David's instructions, vowing that he would not disobey the king for a thousand pieces of silver. Second, he boldly points out what Joab does not deny: if he had killed Absalom, the general would have left him to take the consequences alone (v. 13).

The central character in this episode, however, is Joab. Without visible hesitation or regret, he strikes down the son of the king. It was not an act of anger or revenge, but a calculated military and political decision, taken at no small personal risk. He acted not for himself but for David and the nation. And lest we dwell simply on his ruthlessness, consider the consequences. Immediately after the death of Absalom, Joab recalls the army (v. 16). The killing was over. As his own troops had reminded David (v. 3), once the head is removed the body dies.

It is a horrible scene, Joab and his bodyguard killing the now helpless pretender to the throne. Behind it stand human love and weakness (David), ambition and rebellion (Absalom), and loyalty (Joab). Was Joab right or wrong? The narrator, who clearly identifies with Joab, offers no simple answers but leaves us to struggle with the ambiguities of moral decisions, and tries to make us aware of the complex causes and motives that put Joab in such a situation.

If we understand the characters, we are left with no room for simple self-righteous condemnation of Joab. Nations and peoples have always asked such things of their young men and old soldiers, to kill for the sake of the community.

Psalm 130

This psalm was discussed previously as one of the readings for Proper 5 [10].

1 Kings 19:4–8

Today's text is part of the first episode in Elijah's wilderness travels in 1 Kings 19:1–18. It stands in sharp contrast with the preceding story, the account of Elijah's contest with the prophets of Baal on Mt. Carmel (1 Kings 18). It is a story of fire and rain, of life and death. Its backdrop is the royal couple, Ahab and Jezebel, their support of the Canaanite deity Baal, and their persecution of the followers of Yahweh. Elijah wins the contest dramatically, for in response to his prayers Yahweh ignites the fire of the sacrifice and then—in the midst of the drought—brings the life-giving rain. The people acknowledge that Yahweh is God, and the prophet of Yahweh has the prophets of Baal seized and killed (1 Kings 19:39–40). In that case, Elijah was the majestic, powerful, and successful advocate of Yahweh against Baal. In our text, however, he is a persecuted fugitive, full of self-doubt at the point of despair.

Verses 1–3 provide the transition from the Mt. Carmel episode and set the scene for all that follows in the chapter. Ahab, who is said to have been present when Elijah brought the rain and had the prophets of Baal killed, reports all this to Jezebel. She sends a "messenger" to Elijah with her vow—with the typical oath formulas—that she will see the prophet dead before the next day is ended (v. 2). The same Elijah who had commanded fire and rain, and had the enemies of Yahweh killed, flees to the south for his life (v. 3). The reference to Beersheba indicates that he will soon pass the boundary from the arable, inhabited land into the wilderness, and alone.

The next scene transpires under a "solitary broom tree" at some unspecified place in the wilderness. But, like the places where Jacob stopped when leaving and reentering the promised land (Gen. 28:10–22; 32:22–32), it is a place of divine encounter and revelation. Asking "to die," he goes to sleep. What follows are two dream theophanies; but as is often the case in such reports, the line between the dream and waking reality is obscure. The "angel," or "messenger," of Yahweh appears to the prophet (v. 5). The contrast between this messenger and the one sent by Jezebel (v. 2) is, quite literally, the difference between life and death. The first brings a death sentence, and the second brings food. The message is a simple one: "Get up and eat." Seeing bread and water, the prophet does as commanded and then sleeps again.

When the angel appears a second time, he repeats the command but with some explanation (v. 7). The explanation suggests but does not state a further message, that Elijah is to take a long journey. The prophet again obeys, and the food and water sustain him for the forty days and nights of the trip (v. 8). Only in the final note do we hear of the destination, "Horeb the mount of God."

In addition to the parallels with the journeys of Jacob noted above, the account recalls the flight of Moses to the wilderness and his encounter with God there (Exod. 2:15–4:31). Moreover, like the people of Israel in the wilderness, who also travel to and from the mount of God, Elijah's food and water are provided by the Lord.

Two themes in particular present themselves for theological and homiletical reflection. First, there is the journey and the status of the traveler. Elijah clearly sets out into the wilderness as a fugitive. Has he become, by the end of our passage, a pilgrim? At first he is only going away from danger; in the end he is going to a holy place. But the goal of the journey is not emphasized, nor is any new purpose for the trip mentioned. So the encounters with the divine messenger and the acceptance of the life-sustaining gifts take place on the way, when the prophet does not yet know whether he is a fugitive or a pilgrim.

Second, there is the prophet's experience of fear and despair. There under a bush, praying for his own death, he reminds us of that cantankerous prophet Jonah (Jon. 4:1–5). In the case of Elijah, the only explanation given for the change from triumph to despair is the circumstances. In the moment of his success, Queen Jezebel seems still to have the upper hand. The hearers and readers—both ancient and modern—of the story are expected to identify with Elijah and Elijah's God. They learn that even the majestic man of God of Mt. Carmel is human. Like him, they have experienced both success and failure, triumph and self-doubt, confidence and fear. Such hearers and readers are given to understand that flight does not take them beyond the reach of this God and that fugitives can become pilgrims.

Psalm 34:1–8

Psalm 34 is a thanksgiving psalm intended for use by individuals who had moved through trouble and distress and now enjoyed security on the "redeemed" side of the turmoil. The experience of salvation and redemption is recalled in verses 4–6, which provide a bit of autobiography of the worshiper. This psalm has a long history of association with Communion services in the church because of verse 8.

As we have noted in earlier discussions, one of the major functions of both the thanksgiving rituals and thanksgiving psalms in ancient Israel was the teaching of others through testimonial and admonition. This particular psalm contains not a single word addressed to God. It is teaching material through and through and thus is proclamation and admonition.

Verses 1–3 have the worshiper announce boldly that praise is now the content of the song and call upon others to join in the celebration and praise of Yahweh.

Verses 4 and 5 are autobiographical but only in a very general sense. There is reference to seeking the Lord, to crying out (vv. 4a, 6a), and to the salvation and redemption that occurred (vv. 4b, 6b). The problems plaguing the individual are described in the most general of categories—"my fears" and "my every trouble."

The central affirmation of this section is found in verse 7, which declares that an angel of the Lord encamps around those fearing God and delivers them in time of trouble—a point of contact with the reading from 1 Kings 19:4–8.

Verses 5 and 8 are admonitions calling upon the audience at the thanksgiving service to imitate the worshiper and cast themselves upon the Lord.

Ephesians 4:25–5:2

If chapters 1–3 of the Letter to the Ephesians unfold a richly textured theological tapestry, the final four chapters give us concrete instructions about the life of faith. In the early church, as now, there was the constant need for catechesis. New and old Christians needed to be reminded of the ethical implications of their faith. In the preceding verses, the readers, who were former pagans, are called to renounce their former ways (4:17–24). Ethical options are presented to them in terms of "putting away your old self" and "being clothed with a new self" (vv. 22–23). What makes this possible is an inward transformation: "be renewed in the spirit of your minds" (v. 23).

Today's lection provides a miscellany of ethical instructions. They deal with everyday, ordinary matters, but they are not trivial. It was typical of early Christian instruction, as it was for Jewish and Greco-Roman ethical instruction as well, to provide catalogs of virtues and vices that delineated profiles of acceptable and unacceptable behavior. Although this passage does not fit neatly this scheme of virtue and vice catalogs, it exhibits the same concern to provide concrete guidelines for behavior appropriate to the Christian calling. Our text is quite matter of fact in insisting that life in Christ requires the "putting away" of certain forms of behavior (cf. Col. 3:8; James 1:21; 1 Pet. 2:1).

1. *"Putting away falsehood"* (v. 25). In the words of Zechariah 8:16, the text urges that we "speak the truth to our neighbors." The Decalogue prohibited bearing false witness against a neighbor, especially in a juridical setting (Exod. 20:16). Noteworthy here is the motivation: "for we are members of one another" (cf. Rom. 12:5; 1 Cor. 12:25; Eph. 5:30). Concern for the community of faith now becomes an operative principle in ethics. No longer is it a matter of an individual making these decisions in isolation, as if only the individual's welfare is affected.

2. *"Be angry but do not sin"* (vv. 26–27). Again, this instruction has an Old Testament basis (Ps. 4:4). Jesus insisted that anger was tantamount to murder, for at the bottom of both are active ill will (Matt. 5:22; also 1 John 3:15). Elsewhere, Christians are cautioned to be "slow to anger" (James 1:19–20). Today's text recognizes that anger can easily make one vulnerable to the wiles of Satan (cf. Eph. 6:11; James 4:7; 1 Pet. 5:8–9).

3. *"Thieves must give up stealing"* (v. 28). As did the Mosaic law (Exod. 20:15), so did Christian teaching prohibit thievery. Instead, Christians were expected to "work honestly" as did Paul, who worked with his own hands (Acts 18:3; 20:34; 1 Cor. 4:12; 1 Thess. 2:9; 4:11; 2 Thess. 3:8). Nor was one to work merely for one's sole benefit, but rather to help the needy (cf. Titus 3:14; 1 John 3:17).

4. *"Let no evil talk come out of your mouths"* (v. 29). The speech of Christians was expected to be appropriate to the occasion as well as edifying (Col. 3:16; 4:6). Jesus himself had taught that his disciples would be responsible for their words (Matt. 12:37).

5. *"Do not grieve the Holy Spirit of God"* (v. 30). Once again, the language is borrowed from the Old Testament (Isa. 63:10). Earlier, the readers had been assured that they received the "seal of the promised Holy Spirit" (1:13–14), and here it is said to last until "the day of redemption" (cf. Rom. 3:24; 8:23; 1 Cor. 1:30; Col. 1:14). This injunction may be directly related to the previous caution against evil speech, for blasphemy against the Holy Spirit receives such prominent attention in the Gospel tradition (cf. Matt. 12:31–32 and parallels).

6. Verses 31–32 approximate a vice-virtue catalog (cf. Matt. 15:19; Luke 18:11; Rom. 1:29; 13:13; 2 Cor. 12:20; Gal. 5:19–21; Eph. 5:3–5; Col. 3:5, 8; 1 Tim. 1:9–10; 6:4–5; 2 Tim. 3:2–4; Titus 3:3; 1 Pet. 4:3; Rev. 9:21; 21:8; 22:15; also 4 Macc. 1:26; 2:15). Bitterness, wrath, anger, clamor, and slander—all of which are malicious in their motivation—are to be put away and replaced by kindness, tenderheartedness, and a forgiving spirit (cf. Col. 3:12–13; Matt. 6:14). The latter has a theological motivation: "as God in Christ has forgiven you" (v. 32).

7. *"Be imitators of God"* (5:1). This injunction has a very important qualifier: "as beloved children." Imitation of God, strictly speaking, is impossible because of the unbridgeable gulf between us and God. Nevertheless, Christians are called on to emulate God as children who are the recipients of God's love (cf. Matt. 5:45; 1 Cor. 11:1; Col. 3:12).

8. *"Live in love"* (5:2). The Christian "walk" is to be typified by love, for it is predicated on the love Christ had for us in offering himself as a sacrifice to God (cf. 1 Tim. 2:6; Gal. 1:4; 2:20; Titus 2:14). His was indeed a "fragrant offering" (cf. Gen. 8:21; Exod. 29:18; Lev. 1:9, 13; Heb. 10:10; Phil. 4:18).

Many of these injunctions, as we have seen, have Old Testament roots, and in this respect Christian ethics owed much to Jewish ethics. Nevertheless, there are some striking features in these instructions, such as the concern for the community of believers as the motivation for honesty, or the relation of these ethical instructions to the work of God, Christ, and the

Spirit. They are perhaps most striking for their practicality and concreteness. The preacher should not blithely assume, however, that the Christians to whom he or she speaks have mastered even these seemingly elementary principles of the faith.

John 6:35, 41–51

The Gospel for today comes as an offer of a gift, an offer of bread from heaven that gives to the recipient life eternal. John 6:35, 41–51 continues a theme begun two Sundays ago. Without repeating the details from the commentary on John 6 already given, it is enough to recall here that we have referred to the feeding of the multitude as level one of the narrative. On this level the crowd lives, thinks, and acts. Even its talk of God, its immediate embrace of Jesus, its talk of signs and faith is willful, calculating, and self-serving. That the arena of action and conversation is religion instead of money or physical indulgence should not blind us to the fact that the motivational currents here all move toward self-interest. No one in the crowd is talking commitment or discipleship; the entire focus is upon what God through Jesus can do for us. When this Evangelist talks of "the world," nowhere does he deal with the usual popular images of dissipating sin. On the contrary, he uses the world to describe religious practices, places, rituals, traditions, and creeds that are perverted to self-interest. To Jesus' auditors in John 6, bread was bread, not a sign of anything more or better. The next meal, not new life, was on their minds. Even so, to them Jesus still speaks of the true bread from heaven.

Earlier in the Gospel, Jesus had pointed Nicodemus beyond birth to Birth (chap. 3) and the Samaritan woman beyond water to Water (chap. 4). Here he points his listeners beyond the meal of the evening before, beyond even the manna in the wilderness that their ancestors had eaten (vv. 31, 49), to the true bread that comes down from heaven and gives life to the world (v. 33). The listeners seem to have an appetite for this true bread that gives life (v. 34) until Jesus identifies himself as this Bread (v. 35). At this they murmur, able to think of Jesus as being from Nazareth, son of Joseph and Mary, but certainly not from heaven (vv. 41–42).

In what sense does the Evangelist want us to understand Jesus as the true bread from heaven? It is too early at this point to be thinking of the eucharistic bread. Jesus as the bread that is consumed (eat my flesh) does not become explicitly the meaning of his reference to himself as bread until verse 51, or at least no earlier than verse 50. That will be level three of the narrative. At level one, bread was bread; at level two the bread is the word of God (vv. 32–50). In other words, Jesus is here the life-giving Logos as in the Prologue (1:1–18), the true bread as in the hymn "Break Thou the Bread of Life," which was written to precede not the Eucharist but the sermon. Notice the references to being *taught* of God, of *hearing* and *learning* from God (v. 45). The word that reveals God is life-giving. Deuteronomy 8:3 states, "He humbled you by letting you hunger, then by feeding you with manna, with which neither you nor your ancestors were acquainted, in order to make you understand that one does not live by bread alone, but by every word that comes from the mouth of the LORD." Philo of Alexandria, commenting on this verse, had, prior to John's Gospel, identified the manna, which the people did not know, as the wisdom, or word, of God. "Not by bread alone, but by every word that comes from the mouth of God."

Such an interpretation of Jesus as the life-giving Word from heaven is not only congenial with this Gospel's identification of Jesus as the Word (1:14) but with this Gospel's theological assumption that the fundamental human appetite, the hunger beneath all hungers, is for a word from God. No one has ever seen God (1:18); how then will we know this God whom to know is life eternal (17:3)? As Philip expressed it, "Lord, show us the Father, and we will be satisfied" (14:8). The only Son from the bosom of the Father has revealed God (1:18). Jesus, says our writer, not only speaks the word that proceeds from the mouth of God; Jesus *is* that Word, the Bread which is more than bread, the manna that the people do not know.

There is no famine of the word of God, but at this point in the text the people remain hungry, having refused the Bread.

Proper 15 [20]
(Sunday between August 14 and 20 inclusive)

1 Kings 2:10–12; 3:3–14;
Psalm 111; or
Proverbs 9:1–6;
Psalm 34:9–14;
Ephesians 5:15–20;
John 6:51–58

Today's Old Testament reading from the *Common Lectionary* concludes the cycle of readings pertaining to the Davidic covenant with an account of David's death and Solomon's accession to the throne. God is praised in Psalm 111 as full of majesty and honor and faithful in keeping covenant. Establishing the fear of the Lord as the beginning of wisdom in Psalm 111 echoes Solomon's request for wisdom in the Old Testament reading.

For other lectionaries, personified Wisdom's invitation to those lacking wisdom serves as the Old Testament lesson, and the selection from Psalm 34 is an invitation to fear the Lord.

Today's Gospel reading from John continues Jesus' discourse on the bread from heaven from last week, where he invites those seeking eternal life to receive nourishment from his flesh and blood.

Words to the wise also dominate the Epistle lesson from Ephesians, which envisions Spirit-filled worship that edifies the church.

1 Kings 2:10–12; 3:3–14

The Old Testament reading in the semicontinuous lessons for the season contains two distinct sections. The second (1 Kings 3:3–14) is a summary statement about the beginning of the reign of King Solomon. The first (1 Kings 2:10–12) is part of the very last chapter of the Throne Succession Document, the final verse of which is 1 Kings 2:46b: "So the kingdom was established in the hand of Solomon." As pointed out in the commentary on 2 Samuel 11 (see the discussion at Proper 12 [17] in this volume), one of the major purposes of that document was to show how Solomon, instead of one of the more logical successors, came to David's throne. First Kings 1 describes the final struggle for the succession, with David influenced by Bathsheba and Nathan to have Solomon anointed king. This result had been anticipated at the birth of Solomon, when we were told that "the LORD loved him" (2 Sam. 12:24).

However, the texts assigned for today do not stem from the court historian. They are part of the deuteronomistic history, some of the verses coming from the hand of the editors and others from older traditions. The Books of Deuteronomy, Joshua, Judges, First and Second Samuel, First and Second Kings were edited into their present form by a series of editors whose style and theology were quite similar to that of the Book of Deuteronomy. They relied on a great many sources, both oral and written, including the Throne Succession Document, records or chronicles of the kings, and prophetic traditions, among others. The work was finally completed not long after the last event it describes (2 Kings 25:27–30), that is, ca. 560 BC during the Babylonian Exile.

One major purpose of the history is to explain the disaster of the Exile. The historians have examined the old traditions to discover what went wrong and have concluded that the fault was not Yahweh's, but Israel's. The work, then—with very few exceptions—is a history of sin.

First Kings 2:1–4 states some of the major themes of the history, including the standard by which sin is recognized. Obedience to the statutes, commandments, ordinances, and testimonies of God is required. Moreover, those requirements are written "in the law of Moses" (v. 3), that is, the version of the laws in the Book of Deuteronomy. By that standard the kings in particular are judged, and virtually all of them are found wanting. Here it is applied not only to Solomon but also to his "heirs" (v. 4) and is made the condition for the continuation of the dynasty. By the standard of Deuteronomy none of the northern kings could be approved because they did not respect the single sanctuary in Jerusalem. First Kings 2:1–4 is one of the important deuteronomic editorial summaries. Similar material is found in other speeches, especially at key transitions in the history (see Josh. 1, Deut. 31).

The final note concerning the death and burial of David (1 Kings 2:10–12) is probably also deuteronomistic. The expression "slept with his ancestors" is a common euphemism for death. The "city of David" is Jerusalem, during the monarchy the possession not of one of the tribes but of the crown. These verses mark the transition from the reign of David to that of his son Solomon.

Just as there had been different assessments of the wisdom of Israel's establishment of kingship (see the commentary on 1 Sam. 8 for Proper 5 [10] in this volume), so there were different evaluations of the reign of Solomon. First Kings 11 presents the negative evaluation, while the reading for today (1 Kings 3:3–14) gives the positive appraisal. According to one perspective, that of the royal ideology, kingship—and particularly the Davidic monarchy—is a gift of God for the people of God. God's covenant with David is virtually unconditional. According to the other perspective, the conditional aspects of the promise are emphasized. Kings who are faithful to the law are approved, and those who are disobedient are not. In the deuteronomistic history, only two kings after Solomon, Hezekiah and Josiah, are regarded as faithful.

Because our text for the day presumes Deuteronomy's law for the king (Deut. 17:14–20), it is tempting to attribute the verses to the Deuteronomistic Historian. However, it seems more likely that the editors here had access to somewhat older traditions concerning Solomon's reign.

The passage is framed as the account of a liturgical event. 'Solomon went to sacrifice at Gibeon (v. 4). The Deuteronomic Historian had a problem with this, for the only true place of worship was Jerusalem, but solved it by pointing out (v. 2) that the temple had not yet been built. Remarkably, the section ends with Solomon in Jerusalem before the ark of the covenant, offering sacrifices (v. 15). At the cultic center, probably an open-air sanctuary, Yahweh appears to Solomon at night in a dream vision. The purpose of the dialogue that transpires in the vision is to validate Solomon's kingship and to interpret his reign as an ideal one. Note what does not happen to authorize his rule. Unlike the earlier leaders, including Saul and

David, he is not selected because of skill at war or leadership. Nor is he acclaimed by the representatives of the tribes. His is the first genuinely dynastic accession. The stories leading up to this point had made it clear on the one hand, that, he was king because of a series of events that eliminated the other possibilities and political intrigue on the part of his mother and others, and on the other hand, that God's hand had been at work in such events ("the LORD loved him," 2 Sam. 12:24).

The dialogue begins with a word from God that could be taken as a test: "Ask what I should give you" (3:5). Solomon gives the right answer. First, he acknowledges that God has shown both him and his father "great and steadfast love" (v. 6). Second, with a long prelude that acknowledges the difficulty of the office and his own limitations (vv. 7–8), Solomon asks for one thing, "an understanding mind to govern your people" (v. 9).

In a narrative aside (v. 10) we are informed explicitly that Solomon had made the right response. The remainder of the dream vision is God's reply to Solomon. Because Solomon asked for wisdom to govern, putting the people of God above himself, God grants his request and more. There is the distinct sense of the conferral of the capacities required to rule, specifically, the gifts of wisdom and discernment. Furthermore, because Solomon did not ask for long life, riches, or the death of his enemies (v. 11), God will give him what he has not asked for, and more (v. 13). The address concludes with the conditional interpretation of the royal covenant: Solomon's life will be lengthened if he is obedient to the divine statutes and ordinances (v. 14).

Two important Old Testament traditions are reflected in this unit. One is the tradition of Solomon's legendary wisdom. In one form, this tradition concerns learning and scholarship, particularly in the form of proverbial wisdom. That is the perspective of 1 Kings 5:9–14; 10:1–10, 13, 23. Here, however, wisdom is the capacity for judicious and discerning leadership. The section that follows our reading (3:16–28) will provide the most famous illustration of Solomon's wisdom. The other tradition is the royal, messianic ideal in which the role of the king is to establish justice and righteousness, to provide the proper political structure for the people of God. Similar themes are found in such expressions of hope for the future as Isaiah 11:1–5.

The view of governmental leadership set out here is an ideal one, far beyond what would have been the case in the reign of Solomon. The king—or by extension, any political leader—is a servant, in the biblical sense both of God and of the people. By its very emphasis on wise and judicial capacities as special gifts from God, the text acknowledges that such gifts are rare and remarkable. In any case, this passage provides the occasion for us to reflect on the nature of political leadership and the relationship of concrete instances of political officials to the will of God.

Psalm 111

This psalm was previously discussed as one of the readings for the Fourth Sunday After the Epiphany.

Proverbs 9:1–6

The reading is part of a larger literary context, the collection of poems in Proverbs 1–9. These chapters contain some twelve units, most of them wisdom instructions generally regarded as examples of late Israelite wisdom thought. They are quite different from the remainder of the Book of Proverbs, which is mainly a series of short proverbial sayings, admonitions, and exhortations. Most of the poems in Proverbs 1–9 begin with the address "My child," reflecting the situation of a teacher addressing students. The unit before us today is not such a discourse but a poem that puts the words of invitation and exhortation in the mouth of Wisdom herself, personified as a woman.

Throughout Proverbs 1–9, Wisdom frequently is personified as an attractive woman. In the light of the parallels with the other instructions in Proverbs 1–9, it appears that Wisdom assumes the role of the teacher. She stands in sharp contrast to that other woman of these chapters, variously described as the "loose woman" (5:3), an "adulteress" (5:20), the "the wife of another . . . the adulteress" (6:24), "the woman . . . decked out like a prostitute" (7:10), or "the foolish woman" (9:13). The last of these is the personification of folly, the antithesis of Wisdom. On the surface, most of the warnings about the other woman seem to involve practical moral advice to young men, to avoid certain kinds of women. In the context, however, they reflect a more basic dimension, the contrast between the path of wisdom and the path of folly.

This poem has two distinct parts. Verses 1–3 describe the preparations Wisdom has made for a banquet. She has built her house with seven pillars (v. 1), prepared the meal by slaughtering animals, mixing wine, and setting her table (v. 2), sent out her servant girls (v. 3a)—it is uncertain whether she has dismissed them or sent them out with invitations—and now she issues the invitation. Verses 4–6 contain her invitation to come to the banquet. It is issued to the "simple," "those without sense" (v. 4), that is, those in need of wisdom. These she invites to eat of her bread and drink her wine (v. 5). The invitation concludes with an exhortation to grow up and "walk in the way of insight" (v. 6).

Clearly, the central figure in the poem is the personification of a way of life, the way of wisdom. Because the language is metaphorical, the figures can be heard in various ways. On the one hand, Wisdom sounds like a noblewoman. In her invitation and her exhortations, addressed to the foolish, she parallels the teacher who addresses the student as "my child" in the discourses of Proverbs 1–9. But there are also parallels to the personified Wisdom of chapter 8, whom the Lord created at the beginning (8:22–23), and through whom all things were made:

> When there were no depths I was brought forth,
> > when there were no springs abounding with water.
> Before the mountains had been shaped,
> > before the hills, I was brought forth. (8:24–25)

Read in the light of the preceding chapter, then, the Wisdom of 9:1–6, is the principle by which God created the world. Thus the "house" (v. 1) is the world, with the pillars holding up the vault of the sky. To come to Wisdom's banquet is to savor and appreciate and enjoy and learn from creation.

Wisdom presents the simple and uneducated with a straightforward moral choice, and it is a matter of life and death. To "lay aside immaturity," to accept Wisdom's invitation is to live (v. 6). The choice is a general one; no specific moral injunctions are given. The counterpart of our passage is the invitation from the foolish woman (9:13–18). She is loud and ignorant, and persuasive in offering transitory pleasures, but her way leads to death (v. 18).

The theological interpretation of this moral choice between the way of wisdom and the way of folly is expressed in 9:10:

> The fear of the LORD is the beginning of wisdom,
> and the knowledge of the Holy One is insight.

Obviously, ancient Israel wrestled with the persistent question of the relationship between knowledge and wisdom that could be attained by the study of the world and of tradition and that which was revealed; between the way of the school and the way of the temple; between the way of the sages and the way of the priests. Those who considered this question came to the conclusion that in the last analysis both led to true piety.

Psalm 34:9–14

This reading, a continuation of the psalm lection for Proper 14 [19], constitutes primarily the admonition section of the psalm. The admonitions, with their associated promises and assurances, are very similar to the type of material one finds in such a wisdom book as Proverbs. Like the proverbs, the admonitory instructions in the thanksgiving psalms are cast as insightful truths that might be or have been gained from personal experiences. The teaching, as in Proverbs, is described as the "fear of the LORD" (v. 11).

The rhetorical question in verse 12, which expects the answer "everyone," sets the stage for the instruction that follows. Those who want to live a long life full of good must be willing to commit themselves to the hard-earned lessons of others' experience. The advice that ensues, in verses 13–14, is practical, humanistic, and nontheological: control of the tongue (see Prov. 18:21), avoidance of evil, works that produce good, and the pursuit of peace (shalom). All of these are understood as contributing to the length and enjoyment of one's life.

This psalm exudes confidence in the divine order and promises stability of life and sufficiency for human needs for those who trust in and fear God. (This approach to life works in most cases, but unfortunately does not meet the needs of those who suffer undeservedly.) It is the "holy ones" who are addressed, that is, the believers and the loyal for whom life's problems are solvable by proper attitudes and behavior.

Ephesians 5:15–20

The exhortations contained in today's epistolary reading follow numerous injunctions concerning righteous living (5:3–14). In a sense, they serve as a summary of these several ethical admonitions.

Our text opens with a word of caution: "Be careful then how you live" (v. 15). The readers are called to exercise discrimination concerning their own behavior. They should not adopt a cavalier attitude about the way they have chosen to walk, as if staying on a straight course is obvious and automatic. Rather, they are called to be deliberate, thoughtful, and self-reflective.

Prudence is such a universal virtue that one does not normally consider it necessary to remind people to behave "not as unwise people but as wise" (v. 15). Yet virtually every culture and people possess a tradition that embodies the proven wisdom of the ages. Not surprisingly, Jesus frequently draws on the Jewish wisdom tradition as he instructs his disciples about life in the kingdom of God (cf. Matt. 7:24; 10:16; 25:1–12). In fact, one of the most intriguing stories reported in the Gospels is the parable of the unjust steward whose conduct Jesus commended, most likely because he exercised prudence in a time of crisis (cf. Luke 16:1–13).

This advice is rephrased in even more direct terms in verse 17: "So do not be foolish, but understand what the will of the Lord is." Here, the other side of folly is the ability to be discerning with respect to knowing and doing God's will. This is not a matter of deciphering mysterious hieroglyphics, but rather developing a set of spiritual senses that result from the transformation and renewal of the mind and heart (cf. Rom. 12:2; also Rom. 2:18; Phil. 1:10).

Practically, prudence and discernment will mean "making the most of the time" (v. 16; cf. Col. 4:5). This observation is set within an eschatological framework: "because the days are evil" (cf. Eph. 6:13; Gal. 1:4; also Amos 5:13). The word for "time" here is *kairos* and should perhaps best be rendered "opportunity" (REB: "Use the present opportunity to the full").

Closely connected with the caution against folly is the injunction to avoid getting drunk with wine (v. 18). The Jewish wisdom tradition had long since recognized the folly of drunkenness (Prov. 23:31–35), and Jesus had likewise warned his disciples against "dissipation and drunkenness" (Luke 21:34). Although it is not included in the vice lists earlier in Ephesians (cf. 4:31; 5:3–5), it becomes a stock item in others (cf. Gal. 5:21; 1 Cor. 6:10).

"Being filled with the Spirit" is offered as an alternative to being filled with wine, or drunkenness. It is not the ecstasy of individual inspiration that is in view here, but the spiritual intoxication that occurs in Christian worship (cf. Col. 3:16; 1 Cor. 14:15; Acts 16:25). In this setting, one learns that "at all times and for everything" to give thanks "in the name of our Lord Jesus Christ to God the Father" (v. 20; Col. 3:16; 1 Thess. 5:18). Thankfulness, as it turns out, typifies the Christian outlook, for Christians owe their existence to an uncalculated act of loving grace (5:2). Thanksgiving, then, becomes one of the most frequent forms of prayer, as the opening prayers of many of the letters of the New Testament indicate (cf., e.g., 1 Cor. 1:4–9).

Part of the attraction of this part of the liturgical year is the opportunity it offers the preacher to instruct the church in some of the hard, practical realities of life. Separated from the high liturgical moments such as Christmas and Easter, this period seems fitted for instructions concerning prudence, discernment, and meaningful worship as an alternative to inebriation. These words from Ephesians speak directly to these needs.

John 6:51–58

We can well approach this text by first getting in touch with the language with which our biblical ancestors expressed their most profound experiences: grief, remorse, repentance, devotion, love, and joy of life. We who tend to associate all these emotions with "the heart" encounter the ancient writers' descriptions in terms of bone, breath, flesh, marrow, joints, and stomach. Many of us know how totally the human frame is affected by significant experiences, but we do not express it so fully. The psalmist's sin and remorse reverberate through every bone and sinew (Ps. 102). David's lament over Absalom is total; his whole body joins in a chorus of grief (2 Sam. 18–19). Apparently, some of the Christians addressed in Ephesus were imbibing wine as a way to get the body to join more fully in the joyous expressions of the Spirit-filled life (Eph. 5). The assumption is that eating and drinking, flesh and bone, are not to be separated from the experiences of soul and spirit. In fact, the New Testament knows no more meaningful act for effecting and witnessing to the relationship of Christians with one another and with Christ than eating together. Whoever has removed eating from the list of profoundly religious acts will have great difficulty with our Gospel for today.

The New Testament is filled with images and analogies that express the close relation of believers with Christ. Paul speaks of one body, of union in his death and resurrection, of Christ in us, and of our being in Christ. Ephesians and Revelation will use the image of husband and wife to portray the mutual love of Christ and the church. The Fourth Gospel gives us many of our most familiar expressions of this relationship: shepherd and sheep, vine and branches, abiding in God's house, Christ abiding in God as we abide in Christ. But in John 6:51–58, language is pressed to the limit to express union and full participation of one life in another: "Those who eat my flesh and drink my blood abide in me, and I in them" (v. 56).

If it is the case, as many scholars believe, that this Gospel went through several "editions" in the sense of modifications to meet the theological needs of a changing Christian community, then it is likely that John 6 began with the received tradition of Jesus feeding the multitudes. The story might have been a compassion narrative, as it is in Mark 6:34–44 and Matthew 14:13–21. At some point, as is the case with the Synoptics, the story took on eucharistic implications, as did most if not all the accounts of Jesus' meals with the disciples. That is, one meal, the last supper, affected the way all meals were understood and described. This Evangelist, with his pattern of signs and discourses and in language with double meanings, saw in the event a sign of a greater truth, that Jesus himself is the bread, the word of revelation from God that gives life to the world. We cannot live by bread alone. But the image of Jesus not only providing bread but being the bread was pressed even further, joining it with the common understanding that eating and drinking are the very epitome of intimacy and union. Jesus offers himself as the food and drink. Here, then, is divine self-giving, life for life, and by full participation in Christ's word, his life, and his death, the believer abides in God. Recall that in this Gospel, "to abide" is the term for expressing unhindered trust that neither wavers nor needs supporting signs for reassurance.

As the writer told us at the outset, this is a Passover story (v. 4). In this Gospel, this means that the death of Jesus is an underlying theme of the narrative. According to John, Jesus did not keep the Passover before his death; he *was* the Passover (19:31–37). He did not eat the Passover meal; he *was* the Passover meal, the food and drink. "Those who eat my flesh and drink my blood have eternal life, and I will raise them up on the last day" (v. 54).

Our language is also pressed to the limit to find the bold analogy for expressing the continuing relationship of believers with the living Christ.

Proper 16 [21]
(Sunday between August 21 and 27 inclusive)

1 Kings 8: (1, 6, 10–11) 22–30, 41–43;
Psalm 84; or
Joshua 24:1–2a, 14–18;
Psalm 34:15–22;
Ephesians 6:10–20;
John 6:56–69

For today's *Common Lectionary* Old Testament lesson, we have portions of Solomon's prayer of dedication, praising God for establishing the Davidic lineage and inviting the nations to recognize God's greatness. In the responsorial psalm, the psalmist praises Zion and exults at the thought of worshiping in the house of God.

For the other Old Testament reading, the occasion is the covenant at Shechem, where Joshua enjoins Israel to leave behind their ancestral gods and serve the one God of Israel, and Israel commits itself to faithful service. The concluding verses from Psalm 34 portray the Lord as a faithful ally of the righteous.

The last of several Gospel readings from John, today's Gospel text has Jesus presenting his disciples with a choice similar to that of the Joshua text.

Sobering images dominate the Epistle lesson, the last of the semicontinuous readings from Ephesians, as it enjoins believers to arm for the cosmic battle against evil.

1 Kings 8: (1, 6, 10–11) 22–30, 41–43

Last week's Old Testament lesson in the semicontinuous readings for the season concerned King Solomon's legendary wisdom. Today's reading concerns the outstanding facet of his reign. First Kings 8, as the account of Solomon's dedication of the temple in Jerusalem, lies near the heart of what later generations considered most important about Solomon. Foremost among his many building projects was the magnificent temple. Most of the verses assigned for reading on this day come from the king's dedicatory prayer. The prayer had been preceded by the account of the assembly and the installation of the ark of the covenant in the new building (vv. 1–13), and Solomon's address to the assembly (vv. 14–21). After the prayer (vv. 22–53), the king will address the people again with a sermon (vv. 54–61) and will conclude the ceremony with sacrifices and a feast (vv. 62–66).

Virtually all of the chapter bears the marks of the theology and style of the Book of Deuteronomy and thus stems from the Deuteronomistic Historian or Historians who were responsible for collecting and editing the account of Israel's history from the time of Moses to the Babylonian Exile (Deuteronomy through 2 Kings). Although there are numerous older written and oral sources in the history, and there likely was a pre-exilic edition of it, the work as a whole was completed shortly after the last event it reports (2 Kings 25:27–3), during the Babylonian Exile (ca. 560 BC). Consequently, the report of the dedication of the temple was composed for a people who had lost their land and holy city, and knew that the temple lay in ruins.

Solomon's prayer of dedication is a series of four prayers of petition. The first (vv. 23–26) is a prayer that God confirm the promise to David that one of his sons would always sit on the throne in Jerusalem. The second (vv. 27–30) and fourth (vv. 52–53) are general requests that God hear and respond, and the third (vv. 31–51) contains a series of petitions concerning seven possible future situations.

Our assigned verses contain parts of the narrative framework, the first (vv. 22–26) and second (vv. 27–30) prayers, and the fifth of the petitions concerning future circumstances (vv. 41–43), the one that expects "foreigners" to come to the temple.

Verse 22, as well as its larger context, invites reflection on prayer, particularly public prayer. Some of the liturgical features are obvious here, and others are not. It is assumed that Israel's kings performed important priestly functions as a special link between Yahweh and the people. As the temple is dedicated, Solomon is said to be before the altar and in the presence of the assembled people, but the precise location is difficult to identify. (The parallel account in 2 Chron. 6:13 has him in the courtyard of the temple on an elevated platform.) The posture of prayer is standing with hands outstretched "to heaven" (cf. Exod. 9:29; Isa. 1:15). In view of the fact that gods, like kings, in the ancient Near East generally are pictured as sitting on thrones, the posture of supplication is to stand with outstretched arms. Note, however, that when the prayers are concluded, Solomon is said to have been kneeling before the altar (8:54).

The initial lines of the first prayer (v. 23) invite reflection on several matters central to the biblical faith. First, Yahweh, God of Israel, is addressed as incomparable ("no God like you . . ."). This is not an assertion of monotheism, although it comes close. Rather, it parallels the view of the First Commandment ("you shall have no other gods before me," Exod. 20:3). Devotion to their God, rather than the abstract question of the number of the gods, is the central concern for ancient Israel. Second, Israel's God is trustworthy and loyal, "keeping covenant and steadfast love" to those who are faithful. These two expressions are virtually synonymous, emphasizing the stability of God's relationship with the covenant people.

The second prayer (vv. 27–30) is at the heart of the deuteronomic tradition's understanding of both the centrality and the limitations of the temple. It begins (v. 27) with a disclaimer that acknowledges that God cannot be restricted to the earth, much less a house built by human hands. Against the backdrop of non-Israelite religions whose temples housed images of the gods and were thought to be the residences of those gods, ancient Israel affirms that Yahweh does not live in Solomon's temple. Rather, Solomon prays that the ancient promise (expressed in Deuteronomy 12) be fulfilled—that the Lord will choose to allow his name to dwell in the temple. Thus the temple is a place where that name can be called in prayer, and the Lord will hear the prayer. This deuteronomic theology of the presence of the name contrasts with the priestly tradition of the presence of the Lord's "glory" (see 1 Kings 8:10–11) in the temple's most holy place. Reading this prayer of dedication evokes reflection on the importance and the limitations of holy places.

The petition in verses 41–43 indicates that ancient Israel's concerns reached beyond boundaries of nation and culture. It is an intercessory prayer on behalf of any "foreigner" who comes to pray in the temple. If Yahweh is incomparable, other peoples will hear and come to worship him. Solomon asks that their prayers be heard as well. Although stressing the importance of the temple, the petition acknowledges that God's true dwelling place is "in heaven" (v. 43). The goal is that the Lord's "name"—who he is and what he has done—be known to all peoples (v. 43). The Lord does not actually dwell in the temple, but it is called by his name and is the place where he chooses to "put his name" (Deut. 12:5).

Psalm 84

Two issues dominate this psalm: pilgrimage to Zion and worship in the temple. The psalm can be understood as a composition written for singing as pilgrims journeyed to attend a festival in Jerusalem. (Many scholars, however, understand the psalm as a composition by someone who could not make the trip to Jerusalem. Thus it is a psalm of homesickness for Zion. This interpretation seems unlikely.)

Psalms were no doubt sung by pilgrims on the journey to Jerusalem. Psalm 42:4 speaks of the throng making its way in procession to the house of God "with glad shouts and songs of thanksgiving." Isaiah 30:29, speaking of the good time to come, says: "You shall have a song as in the night when a holy festival is kept; and gladness of heart, as when one sets out to the sound of the flute to go to the mountain of the LORD." Psalms 120–134 are a collection of songs to be sung on pilgrimage.

One might expect that on pilgrimage antiphonal singing might take place. That is, the leader of the pilgrimage group and the pilgrims would engage in singing to lift the spirits, pass the time, and express the "tourist" atmosphere of the occasion as well as genuine religious sentiments. This may help explain some of the variations in address in Psalm 84. The following verses are addressed to the Deity—1, 3–7a, 8-10a, 12—whereas the others speak about the Deity—2, 7b, 10b–11. Perhaps the two types of material in the psalm were sung by two different groups in the pilgrimage party or by the leader, with the pilgrims responding.

Verses 1–2 manifest the temple veneration, almost a mystical devotion to the temple, from two perspectives. Verse 1 appears as an objective assertion, or as an affirmation external to the worshipers: "How lovely is your dwelling place, O LORD of hosts!" The temple was, of course, the "house [home] of God," and here one has the type of accolade that might be made in value-judging a human's place of residence—"What a lovely place you have!" From the external affirmation, the psalm turns to the internal emotion associated with the temple (v. 2). Longing, fainting for, yearning for, singing for joy about are feelings associated with the temple courts. We Christians, and Protestants in particular, may have difficulty sharing or understanding the almost sensual happiness and joy associated with festival observances in the temple. Such observances combined high pageantry, feasting, and dancing, and the sense of the divine presence with the atmosphere of a country fair and community reunion. Old acquaintances were renewed, past experiences shared, and new relationships acquired. At the same time, one participated in the cultic services and sacrifices that were seen as restoring and preserving world order.

Verses 3–4 give expression to this devotion in terms of a fantasied identification. How glorious it must be for the birds who nest in the temple precincts, near the altars! The birds— here sparrows and swallows—did not nest in or even beside the altars (the altar of sacrifice in the courtyard and the altar of incense in the building) but near them. "Those who live in your house" may refer to the birds, but also the phrase could denote the temple servants, some of whom were always in the temple.

Verses 5–7 speak about factors associated with the pilgrimage—finding refuge (strength) in God and contemplating the roadways or pilgrim paths to Jerusalem. The presence of pilgrims in the valley of Baca ("thirst" or "weeping") transforms it into an oasis, just as the early fall rains, which could begin in September before the fall festival, moisten the soil, hot and arid from the rainless summer. As the pilgrims move closer to Jerusalem, their numbers swell ("from strength to strength") as parties from other areas join together.

Verses 8–9 are, in some ways and when analyzed closely, a bit peculiar. Verse 8 contains references in the first person singular ("my"), whereas verse 9 uses the plural ("our"). Again, this may be explained by antiphonal usage. The prayer for the welfare of the king ("your anointed") is not so much out of place if we think in terms of a monarchical society and the close association between the Davidic king and the temple/Deity.

Two analogies are drawn in verse 10 to describe the joy of worship in and a visit to the temple. One day there is better than a thousand somewhere else. Verse 10*b* seems, in Hebrew, to give the following sense: "I would rather serve insecurely at the threshold of the temple than to dwell at ease in the tents of wickedness." Better nothing and servitude in the sanctuary than plenty and wealth elsewhere.

In the last analysis, the psalm turns to praise of God in verses 11–12, for it is because of God that the temple is what it is. It is God who gives and provides and does not withhold.

Joshua 24:1–2*a*, 14–18

This reading consists of selections from the account of the covenant made at Shechem under the leadership of Joshua. In the wider biblical narrative that runs from Genesis through 2 Kings, Joshua 24 is a pivotal chapter. On the one hand it looks back, concluding the account of the fulfillment of the promise of progeny and land to Abraham (Gen. 12:1–4): having become a great nation, the descendants have occupied the promised land. On the other hand, the chapter looks forward, establishing the basis for the life of the people in that land in a covenant with the God who gave it to them. Will Israel be faithful to the God who has been faithful to them? Will they keep their promises as Yahweh has kept his?

Within the Book of Joshua, our lesson is part of a second farewell address by Joshua, the first coming in chapter 23. The setting for both addresses is established by 24:29–31, the account of the death and burial of Joshua. The fact that we have two versions of the last will and testament of Joshua indicates something of the complex literary history of the book. Chapter 23, which comes from the deuteronomistic editors who put together the history contained in the Books of Deuteronomy through 2 Kings, contains a sermon regarding the forms of Israel's worship of Yahweh in the land. Chapter 24, which also bears the marks of deuteronomistic editing, preserves ancient traditions about the establishment of a covenant. Its major concern is Israel's exclusive worship of Yahweh.

The full account of the covenant ceremony includes an introduction (vv. 1–2*a*) in which the people are summoned to Shechem, Joshua's speech recounting Yahweh's saving acts as the basis for Israel's faith (vv. 2*b*–13), Joshua's challenge and the response of the people (vv. 14–24), and the account of the covenant ceremonies, concluding with the dismissal of the people to their assigned territories (vv. 25–28).

Although the text presents itself as an account of an event that happened once just before Joshua died, there is strong evidence that it reflects a rite that was reenacted periodically if not regularly in ancient Israel. Internal evidence for this conclusion consists of the liturgical features of the account, including the solemnity and the location of the gathering, the leader's questions and the people's responses (vv. 15–24), the concluding description of what has happened (v. 25), the setting up of a monument (vv. 26–27), and the dismissal (v. 28). The external evidence that this is the reflection of a recurrent ceremony, the renewal of the Sinai covenant (Exod. 19–24), is seen in the other reports of such events (2 Kings 23; Neh. 9–10), including the parallel report in Joshua 8:30–35 and the covenantal structure of the Book of Deuteronomy.

Joshua begins the ceremony with a recital that is common to covenant rituals, the recital of the history of salvation (vv. 2b–13). The purpose of this account is to identify the God with whom the covenant is made, to indicate that Yahweh has chosen a people and how he chose them, and to testify that this God keeps promises. The shortest form of that history is the prelude to the Decalogue in Exodus 20:1: "I am the LORD your God, who brought you out of the land of Egypt. . . ." Various forms of this confession appear throughout the Old Testament (see esp. Deut. 6:20–25; 26:5–9). The covenant is established with a free decision of the people, affirmed solemnly (vv. 16–18, 21). Like a contractual agreement, it is sealed by witnesses (v. 22; cf. Ruth 4:9–11). The contents of the covenant are the laws (here "statutes and ordinances," v. 25) that define the lives of those bound to Yahweh (Exodus 20–24). Lest there be any doubt about the contents of the laws that bind the people to Yahweh, the covenant is written down (vv. 26–27). The tone of the report of the inscribed stone implies what is explicit in other accounts of covenants: Those who obey will be blessed and those who disobey will be cursed (Josh. 8:34; Deut. 27–28).

Behind this passage stand at least two quite distinct situations for the people of God, corresponding to the final editorial stage and the older covenant traditions. The material was given its final form in the time of the Babylonian Exile, when the descendants of Joshua's generation no longer possessed the promised land, when the blessing had turned to curse. The older traditions relate to an unknown era—and very likely more than one period—after the time of Joshua, perhaps as early as the time of the judges. In both situations, the central point, the most pressing concern, is expressed in Joshua's challenge: "choose this day whom you will serve . . . but as for me and my household, we will serve the LORD" (v. 15).

In the earlier situation, reflecting the crisis for Israel in the land, the people are faced with the choice between Yahweh and the gods of either their ancestors or of the native inhabitants of the land. Behind this language (vv. 2, 14) stands the old perspective that deities are limited geographically and that every land has its god or gods. Joshua insists that the people must renounce allegiance to all other gods for this one, Yahweh. (Verse 14 contains the only reference in the Pentateuch to the gods worshiped in Egypt.) Thus the center of this covenant is the substance of the First Commandment, the radical and uncompromising requirement that worship of Yahweh must be undivided. Moreover, the older traditions indicate that the covenant not only binds people to God but also people to people.

In the time of the Babylonian Exile, when the deuteronomistic history was completed, the call to exclusive and unswerving fidelity to Yahweh would be the same, now heard by people living far beyond the bounds of the land, even in the region from which their ancestors came. They could see around them powerful alternatives to the worship of Yahweh—specifically, the gods of Babylon—and must have wondered if the Lord was present in foreign lands. Beyond that, this text served one of the central themes of the full history of Israel, namely, the explanation of the reasons for the Exile. Like the Book of Deuteronomy, this covenant states faithfulness to Yahweh as the requirement for Israel's continued existence in the land. The Exile is thus understood as punishment for a history of apostasy. Finally, this passage contains good news, even for exiles in Babylon. The covenant can be renewed once again if Israel is willing and responds positively, just as her ancestors did in the time of Joshua.

Psalm 34:15–22

Verses 15–22 of this psalm are much more theological in content than the rest of the psalm and overtly engage in God-talk. Four emphases in these verses are worthy of note and provide perspectives for sermon development. One, however, should be warned that the wisdom answers to life's questions and problems fit a majority but certainly not all cases.

First, God is seen as especially favorably disposed toward the righteous. Such an assurance can be seen as a deduction drawn from long experience with the human condition. Righteousness produces a style of life that is good, long, and full of joy—one that has the special protection of God.

Second, the evil and the wicked may expect the opposition of God and their life to end disastrously. In verse 16, it is the face of the Lord that is against evildoers and that will cut off all remembrance of them from the earth; that is, God is said to oversee their death and their disappearance from memory. Almost the same thing is said in verse 21, except here it is the evil itself that will slay the wicked. This double way of saying something appears rather frequently in the Old Testament: God is described as taking action to destroy the wicked, or wickedness itself is seen as taking its own toll. The first is a theological way of expressing matters; the second is a more humanistic manner of saying things.

Third, God is described as having a special concern for the downtrodden and the calamity-struck. The brokenhearted and those crushed in spirit are the ones God is nearest (v. 18). Another way of making a similar point is to say that the brokenhearted and the crushed in spirit can be more open to God in their lives. Throughout the Old Testament, narrative after narrative shows how God intervenes for the poor and the unpromising and reverses the fate of their lives. Many of the biblical narratives have a Cinderella quality about them.

Finally, this psalm assumes that the righteous in life will not be immune to suffering. Not an absence of suffering is promised but rather compassion and help when suffering comes. Note the following references to the distress of the righteous: "their cry" (v. 15), "cry for help," "their troubles" (v. 17), and "afflictions" (v. 19). What the psalm promises is divine help to see it through.

Ephesians 6:10–20

In this final lection from Ephesians, we are urged to "be strong in the Lord and in the strength of his power" (v. 10). This was the apostle's prayer (3:16). The source of lasting strength is located "in the Lord," who has been exalted to a position of heavenly dominion "far above all rule and authority and power and dominion (1:21). Such empowering strength is his to give.

The Christian "walk" has been the topic of discussion, especially in chapters 4–6. This final exhortation is realistic in the way it envisions life in Christ as a serious struggle, comparable to waging warfare. The imagery is bold and powerful. The Christian is portrayed as putting on the gear of warfare worn by soldiers. The image of the soldier was commonplace in antiquity, so the metaphor used here had immediate impact. But the images are not drawn merely from everyday experience. They are already firmly entrenched in the Old Testament, where Yahweh is similarly clothed (Isa. 59:16–17; esp. Wisd. of Sol. 5:17–23). Closely associated with this is the image of Yahweh as the Divine Warrior (cf. Isa. 13, 34; also Ezek. 7). Given this background, we are to take quite literally the injunction "Put on the whole armor of God" (v. 11; also v. 13). We are asked to put on the very armor God wears!

The apostle insists that Christians are not engaged in a conflict between themselves and other human beings: "our struggle is not against enemies of blood and flesh" (v. 12). This does not mean, however, that ours is simply a psychological battle fought within ourselves, in the recesses of our own minds. It is rather "against the authorities, against the cosmic powers of this present darkness, against the spiritual forces of evil in the heavenly places" (v. 12; cf. Eph. 1:21; 2:2; 3:10; Rom. 8:38; 1 Cor. 15:24; Col. 1:13, 16; 2:10, 15; 1 Pet. 3:22; Heb. 2:5; 2 Pet. 2:10). The contest is one in which superhuman forces are pitted against one another (cf. Rom. 13:12; 2 Cor. 6:7; 10:4). The earth is viewed as the arena in which the contest is carried out, but the conflict actually engages cosmic forces, seen here as under the dominion of Satan himself (cf. Eph. 4:14, 27; 1 Pet. 5:8–9; James 4:7).

We recognize this as the Jewish apocalyptic imagery, but this should not obscure the central truth that the conflict between good and evil in every age, ours included, involves forces that surpass our own human understanding and limitations. Whether we choose to depict the powers of good and evil this way, our text reminds us that questions or morality should not be reduced to the level of human transaction, with good and evil serving simply as the sum total of individual actions. Today's text recognizes that the Christian soldier may finally emerge as victor, but not without serious struggle. This alone should caution us against adopting a naive optimism toward critical issues facing us.

What is striking about the individual pieces of armor is that they symbolize qualities of God, not ordinary human virtues: truth, righteousness, peace, faith, salvation, the word of God. This in itself is suggestive, for it reminds us that it is not within our human capacity to equip ourselves for a battle of such magnitude. It is rather a matter of embodying within ourselves those theological realities and attributes that God uses to achieve the divine purpose within the world.

Some comments on the individual pieces of equipment may be helpful. "Fasten the belt of truth around your waist" (v. 14) recalls the image of the messiah, who is girded with righteousness and faithfulness (Isa. 11:5; cf. also Exod. 12:11; 1 Kings 18:46; Nah. 2:1; Luke 12:35; 1 Pet. 1:13). The "breastplate of righteousness" (v. 14) recalls God's own character (Isa. 59:17; Wisd. of Sol. 5:18; cf. also 1 Thess. 5:8). Footwear that "will make you ready to proclaim the gospel of peace" (v. 14) recalls the image of the courier bearing the good tidings of peace (Isa. 52:7; Nah. 1:15). This is a salutary reminder that even in waging war metaphorically, the Christian's central message is the good news of "peace" (Acts 10:36; also Luke 2:14; Eph. 2:17). The "shield of faith" (v. 16) enables one to deflect Satan's fiery darts (cf. Wisd. of Sol. 5:19, 21; 1 Thess. 5:8). The "helmet of salvation" (v. 17), again, recalls the description of Yahweh (Isa. 59:17; also 1 Thess. 5:8). The only offensive weapon included is the "sword of the Spirit" (v. 17), identified as the word of God, suggesting the image of words being sharp and penetrating in their effect (Isa. 49:2; Hos. 6:5; Heb. 4:12).

The final section of the passage includes an exhortation to "pray in the Spirit at all times" (v. 18; cf. Matt. 26:41 and parallels; Col. 4:2; Jude 20), combined with a call for alert perseverance (Mark 13:33; Luke 21:36). Finally, the apostle enlists the prayers of the readers in his behalf (Rom. 15:30; Col. 4:3; 1 Thess. 5:25; 2 Thess. 3:1; Heb. 13:18). His desire is to speak boldly the mystery of the gospel of Christ (cf. Luke 21:15; Col. 4:3; also Acts 4:13, 29, 31; 28:31). As a prisoner (3:1; 4:1), he regards himself as an "ambassador in chains" (v. 20; cf. 2 Cor. 5:20), hoping to be able to speak boldly or in a manner appropriate to the message and task.

It may be that some find the militaristic images used in this passage unsuitable to the message of the gospel. But they are just that—images. What should be noticed is that the "weapons of warfare" depicted here are those things that bring about justice and peace—righteousness, truth, and salvation. Christians are challenged by these words to be vigilant in their struggle to bring about peace and justice. In the words of Betty Williams Perkins, winner of the 1977 Nobel Peace Prize for her work in Northern Ireland, "Without peace there is no justice; without justice, there is no peace." Our text reminds us that they do not happen automatically, or even naturally, but occur as the result of our acting aggressively in their behalf. When such warfare is done "in the Lord," it attests the "strength of God's might."

John 6:56–69

Today we conclude John's narrative of the feeding of the multitude and the sermon on bread. Perhaps we should say *sermons* (plural), because Jesus as the Bread of Heaven is presented along two lines: Jesus is the Bread in the sense of being the Word proceeding from God, and the Bread in the sense of the Eucharist consumed by the believing community in whom he abides.

The sermon by Jesus in the synagogue at Capernaum (v. 59) is rejected by two groups: the Jews and many Christians. That the former group did not accept Jesus' message is not surprising, given the "Jesus vs. Jews" perspective of most of this Gospel. This viewpoint reflects a time and place in which the writer was much involved in church-synagogue tensions (15:21–16:4). Our responsibility to the text demands, however, that we not assume uncritically that tension and generalize on it but rather examine the grounds for the Jews' rejection of Jesus' sermon.

No doubt one point of offense was the language "eat my flesh, drink my blood" (vv. 51–58). These words not only disturbed those in the audience committed to food laws that forbade eating human flesh and the blood of any living thing, but also many who were numbered among Jesus' disciples. "This teaching is difficult; who can accept it?" (v. 60). Apparently, the Johannine church took a position on the Eucharist not shared by all Christian groups. It is unrealistic when reading the New Testament to think of only two groups, Jews and Christians. As Judaism contained different groups such as Pharisees, Sadducees, and Essenes, so the early church consisted of communities that understood the gospel according to the traditions received, usually finding their identity in an apostle or other outstanding leader. At times this practice became divisive (1 Cor. 3). In the verses before us (vv. 60–66) one observes the crumbling of a group referred to as "disciples," some leaving because of theological dissent and one by betrayal (vv. 64–66). The honesty of the passage in allowing us to see inside the church as well as inside the synagogue should relieve us of prejudging all Jews and idealizing all Christians.

A second stumbling block for the Jewish audience (and possibly some disciples) was Jesus' refusal to accept the crowd's confession of him as the promised one, the one like Moses whom God would raise up (v. 14; Deut. 18:18). Some Christians would be content with that as a confession of faith, a way of saying that Jesus was the promised messiah. In fact, this was indeed preached in some quarters of the church (Acts 3:22–23). But for this Gospel, such an acknowledgement was not adequate. This is not to say that Jesus rejected outright the designation of "the prophet like Moses," but rather that he is qualitatively more than was expected. Where a messiah was expected, the expectation tended to become defined not by what God would do for the people but by what people wanted from God. "When the messiah comes" is an expression that may unleash a shopping list of the things we desire. So even the category "messiah" can become corrupted to the point that a confession that Jesus is the Messiah, that he is the one we have been waiting for, is inappropriate to Jesus' own understanding of himself and his mission. To say this is not to comment solely on Jesus' listeners in the synagogue at Capernaum but on ourselves as well.

John 6 elaborates on a theme running through the entire Gospel: the fundamental offense in the words and work of Jesus is the offense of grace. It is sometimes stated gently: we have life from the bread that God gives. It is sometimes stated bluntly, so as to offend all our claims of free will and self-determination: no one can come to me unless that person has been drawn of God (vv. 37–40, 44, 65). This is truly the hard saying, but the issue is clear. Do we preside over life, demanding that Jesus do as Moses did, calling for signs as proof so we can decide whether or not to believe, electing Jesus king by our acclamation? Or do we accept the gift from heaven? The bread in the wilderness was a gift; the bread as the word from heaven was and is a gift; the bread of the Eucharist is a gift. Take, eat, and live.

For all who do not walk away, Simon Peter speaks: "Lord, to whom can we go? You have the words of eternal life. We have come to believe and know that you are the Holy One of God" (vv. 68–69).

Proper 17 [22]
(Sunday between August 28 and September 3 inclusive)

Song of Solomon 2:8–13;
Psalm 45:1–2, 6–9; or
Deuteronomy 4:1–2, 6–9;
Psalm 15;
James 1:17–27;
Mark 7:1–8, 14–15, 21–23

Images of springtime and young lovers liven today's Old Testament lesson from the Song of Solomon in the *Common Lectionary*. This is matched by the wedding images from Psalm 45, where the king is praised in lavish terms.

In the Old Testament reading from other lectionary traditions, we hear Moses enjoining Israel to be diligent in keeping God's commands, confident that doing so would commend them to other nations as a wise, discerning people. In Psalm 15, moral uprightness is presented as a prerequisite for admission to the people of God.

For the Gospel reading, we return to Mark, where Jesus echoes the sentiments of Deuteronomy 4 and Psalm 15 by insisting on moral uprightness as the central demand of the law and criticizing traditional interpretations that circumvent the law's true purpose.

Today's Epistle lesson is the first of five semicontinuous readings from the Epistle of James, which begins by turning our attention to God as the source of "every generous act of giving."

Song of Solomon 2:8–13

The Song of Solomon, also called Song of Songs or Canticles, contains some of the most beautiful and evocative poetry in the Bible. The book is not a single poem but a composition or collection of some two dozen poems or parts of poems. The consistent theme of the book is human love, and human sexual love in particular, stated most concisely in the concluding chapter:

> Set me as a seal upon your heart,
>   as a seal upon your arm;
> for love is strong as death,
>   passion fierce as the grave. (8:6)

For the most part, the book contains a series of songs in which the woman and the man alternate in praising the physical beauty of the other. The language is highly metaphorical, but it is also very graphic and sensual, especially as each lover describes the body of the other.

The presence of such a book in the Bible has troubled many commentators, leading to a wide range of interpretations of the literal language of sexual love. Both in Judaism and in the Christian church, the poetry was taken symbolically and allegorically. In Judaism, it was understood to express the love of the Lord for Israel (cf. Hos. 2:16–19). In Christianity, the partners were Christ and his church; precedent for the metaphor of the church as the bride of Christ can be seen in Revelation 21:2–9.

Modern critical commentators have focused on the literal meaning of the Song of Songs, and many have seen the book as a collection of wedding songs. Some have seen here mythic expressions stemming from the fertility religions of Israel's neighbors and have interpreted the female figure praised in the songs as one or another goddess of love. Regardless of the possible symbolic meanings or mythological background, there is no doubt that the explicit and literal sense of the book's poetry concerns human sexual love.

In the reading assigned for today, the woman speaks first concerning her beloved (vv. 8–10a) and then quotes his words to her (vv. 10b–13). The reader is invited to see and hear the man from the perspective of the woman. Speaking from her room, she reports hearing the voice of her beloved and then imagining his approach, like that of a gazelle or young stag bounding over the hills toward her. He takes his place outside her window and then speaks, calling for her to arise and come away with him, for spring has arrived. Clearly, the song speaks of courtship and not marriage. The partners are separated; he comes to her house and asks her to go away with him. She hears him calling her "my love, my fair one" (vv. 10, 13). Most of the lines in his address to her concern the time of year, the arrival of spring: "the winter is past, the rain is over and gone" (v. 11). He describes the sights, sounds, and smells of the new season: flowers, singing, the voice of the returning turtledove, fruitful fig trees, and the fragrance of blossoms.

If the song concerns only human sexual love, the attraction of the man for the woman and the woman for the man, it is love understood profoundly, deeply connected with all of reality. Human love springs forth like the revival of the earth in springtime. So it is not just fertility religion but also the biblical faith that has a place for the appreciation of and admiration for fecundity and sexual attraction. These two lovers joyfully celebrate one another. To celebrate with them is to celebrate God's good creation of the physical universe.

Psalm 45:1–2, 6–9

Tradition has long associated this psalm with Christ and the incarnation. No doubt written by some court composer—a poet laureate at the Jerusalem court—the psalm is addressed to humans, to the reigning king and his bride-to-be. After an opening introduction (v. 1), the king (vv. 2–9) and the bride (vv. 10–15) are addressed in order before the king is extolled in the concluding words (vv. 16–17).

References to the king and the bride in the text have been generally approached in one of four ways.

1. One line of interpretation is what might be called the metaphorical approach. This assumes that the marriage described is simply a conventional wedding. The normal, everyday groom is described in metaphorical language as a "king" and the bride as a "princess."

2. A second approach can be called the mythological. This assumes that the wedding partners are actually the male deity, played by the king, and the female goddess, played by the queen.

3. A third approach is the allegorical. The king in the text stands for Yahweh, and the bride is God's chosen people. What is said in the text is not to be taken literally but allegorically. The association of this psalm with Song of Solomon 2:8–13 is based on this sort of allegorical reading.

4. A fourth interpretation is the historical. This assumes that the text was composed for an actual wedding for an actual ancient Israelite or Judean king. Because the text refers to Tyre, it has sometimes been assumed that the psalm was composed for the marriage of King Ahab of Israel to the Phoenician princess Jezebel, who hailed from the city of Tyre.

The praise of the king in verses 6–9 opens with a statement that addresses the king as God (*'elohim*). For years most English translations put this reading in the footnote or margins, but the NRSV correctly reads the text "your [the king's] throne, O God, endures forever and ever." Verses 6*b* and 7*a* highlight the king's commitment to justice and equity and the hatred of wickedness.

Verses 7*a*–9 emphasize the special relationship the king has to Yahweh, his royal dress, lavish palaces, royal harem, and the queen (or bride-to-be) decked out in golden attire.

Deuteronomy 4:1–2, 6–9

The Book of Deuteronomy as a whole is structured as the account of the last words and deeds of Moses. The situation is pictured as the end of Israel's wandering in the wilderness between Egypt and the promised land. As the life of Moses comes to an end, the Israelites are camped on the plains of Moab. Most of Deuteronomy consists of lengthy addresses attributed to Moses. These addresses constitute the last will and testament of the one who led Israel out of Egypt and facilitated their covenant with the Lord at Mt. Sinai (called Mt. Horeb in Deuteronomy).

The book was written centuries after the death of Moses and gives evidence of several stages of composition. It contains ancient traditions, including laws and possibly also stories that go back to the earliest period in Israel's history. These laws were in turn used as the texts for sermons as priestly teachers interpreted and reinterpreted the law to apply to changed social and economic circumstances. For example, Deuteronomy 15:1–18 is a series of homiletical instructions on the sabbatical year, applying what had been rules for letting the land lie fallow to debts and debt slavery. A major turning point in the development of the book was the written book of the law, associated with the reform of Josiah (ca. 621 BC). This book of the law probably consisted of at least the present chapters 12–26. The final stage in the development of the book came when it became the first chapter in the long deuteronomistic history work, the account of Israel's history from the time of Moses to the Babylonian Exile (Deuteronomy through 2 Kings). At that point the introductory (at least Deut. 1–4) and concluding chapters were added.

Thus our reading for the day comes from the hand of the Deuteronomistic Historians. They would have given final shape to these verses during the Babylonian Exile (ca. 560 BC), and most likely in Babylon.

Chapter 4 is the concluding section of Moses' first long speech. Like the other addresses in the book, it is in the second person as the leader speaks directly to the assembled people. Its style is hortatory, as Moses, like a preacher, tries to lay the law on the hearts of the people, giving them every possible reason for obedience. In the preceding section, Moses had reminded the people of the history of the Lord's saving actions and of their frequent rebellion against the Lord in the wilderness. The subject of the section before us is not a particular law, but the law itself, recalled in the context of the covenant established at Horeb (4:10–14). Obedience is urged upon the people standing before Moses for their sake and for the sake of future generations ("to your children and your children's children"). These verses thus serve as a fitting general introduction to the subsequent parts of the book in which specific "statutes and ordinances" will be presented.

Just as Moses had recalled the past, now he looks to the future, promising Israel that if Israel heeds the statutes and ordinances they will live to occupy the land that the Lord is giving them. The expression "statutes and ordinances" stands for the divine law as a whole, and there is no distinction between religious and secular laws. In the covenant, the law defines what it means for the people to be the people of God. This law is revealed by God: "what I command you . . . the commandments of the LORD your God with which I am charging you" (v. 2).

All the reasons for obedience given here are positive. Obedience leads to life and the occupation of the promised land (v. 1). Obedience will demonstrate Israel's "wisdom and discernment" before all the foreign nations, who will marvel at this people whose god is so near, and also wonder that no other nation has such statutes and ordinances as Israel (vv. 6–8). This concern for the respect and admiration by the other nations is particularly poignant in the era of the Babylonian Exile, when Israel was a captive of such a nation.

The vocabulary for the people's attention to the law is rich. They are urged to "give heed" (v. 1), "keep the commandments" (v. 2), "observe them diligently" (v. 6), "take care and watch yourself closely" (v. 9), and "neither forget . . . nor let them slip from your mind" (v. 9). In Deuteronomy, the opposite of forgetting is remembering, an active process of calling to mind and acting in accordance with both the history of the Lord's saving acts and the law. Moses is said to have prohibited any change in the statutes and ordinances: "You must neither add anything to what I command you nor take away anything from it" (v. 2). This is particularly remarkable given the fact that the sermons on the law in the Book of Deuteronomy constantly reinterpret—and even revise—the ancient laws for contemporary situations. Thus one may—indeed must—reinterpret the law in the spirit of the law for the sake of future generations.

Psalm 15

Psalm 15 was originally used as an entrance liturgy by pilgrims entering the sanctuary. Paralleling the reading from Deuteronomy, Psalm 15 offers a series of qualities characteristic of the ideal worshiper.

The psalm opens with a question, perhaps asked by pilgrims as they reached the temple gates: Who can enter the sacred precincts? It is asked here in a graphic and metaphorical form, as if access was to be permanent (v. 1). Admittance to the courts of the temple is the concern of the questions.

The remainder of the psalm is an answer to the question, probably spoken by cultic officials (the Levites? the priests?) inside the precincts. The requirements for entry are given in a series of ten characteristics. It should be noted that, in antiquity, temples did not operate on the principle "Everyone welcome, all come." Certain persons (cripples and the deformed, those with improper parentage) and persons at certain times (when unclean from contact with some pollutant, women during menstruation, persons with certain skin ailments) were not admitted into the sanctuary (see Deut. 23:1–8).

The characteristics of those who might enter were probably proclaimed to the worshipers as the proper qualities of life; pilgrims couldn't be checked on an individual basis, and some of the characteristics noted are as much attitudes as action. Two features about the requirements in the psalm are noteworthy. First, the requirements articulated all fall into the category of what we would today call moral qualities and interpersonal attitudes. None of the characteristics would fit into the category of purity laws and regulations, such as having recently touched a dead body or eaten unkosher food. (Note how the two are intermingled in Ezek. 18). Second, the qualifications given in the psalm are ten in number. (Ten was a round figure, and lists of ten could be memorized by ticking off the list on one's fingers. The Ten Commandments may once have been used in such gate or entrance liturgies, perhaps being written on two stone slabs or the posts of the temple gates.)

The following is a listing of the ten requirements:

1. Walks blamelessly and does what is right (behaves according to the accepted mores and standards of the society)

2. Speaks truth from the heart (shows integration of the internal will and external actions; does what one says and says what one thinks)

3. Does not slander with one's tongue (does not attack others verbally and falsely so as to destroy them)

4. Does no evil to a friend (does not physically harm a fellow human being)

5. Does not take up a reproach against the neighbor (does not participate in or perpetuate gossip or spread rumors)

6. Despises a reprobate (dislikes those who turn their back upon God or society)

7. Honors those who fear God (the positive counterpart to the preceding negative)

8. Swears to one's own hurt and does not change (one's word and oath are kept, even if keeping them brings injury and cost to oneself)

9. Does not put out money at interest (does not use another person's need to one's advantage; see Deut. 23:19–20)

10. Does not take a bribe against the innocent (would not do wrong even if paid; see Exod. 23:8; Lev. 19:15; Deut. 16:19)

Those who live up to such standards are declared blessed, unshakable, immovable (v. 5c). This final formulation is interesting. The focus of the conclusion is no longer on such a person who has access to the holy place but on such a person who has the quality of life and integration of social characteristics that make for stability of life.

James 1:17–27

Today begins a series of five lections taken from the Letter of James. According to tradition, the letter is attributed to James, the brother of the Lord, but this is doubtful. It is remarkable how little explicit Christian teaching it contains. For example, it contains only two references to Jesus (1:1; 2:1). Old Testament figures and examples are much more decisive in informing the author. The letter bears many similarities to the Jewish wisdom tradition, and with some qualification could be thought of as a Christian wisdom book. In these five weeks, the readings from James are juxtaposed with Old Testament readings from the Jewish wisdom writings, and both sets of readings may be profitably explored for their similarity in outlook and approach to the religious life.

Like the Jewish wisdom writings, James defies outlining. Often sayings are clustered in a topical arrangement, but just as often they may be scattered. For this reason, today's lection will be treated in terms of recurrent themes rather than verse-by-verse.

The lection opens with a theological assertion: God is the source of every good gift. This in itself is worth noting, for wisdom literature in general, and the Letter of James in particular, are often pilloried as being practical in their outlook but with no deep theological underpinnings. Yet here God is said to be the "Father of lights" (v. 17), probably a reference to God's creation of the heavenly lights (Gen. 1:14–18; also Ps. 136:7). In other texts, God is actually identified with light (1 John 1:5; cf. 1 Pet. 2:9). The qualifying phrase is difficult: "with whom there is no variation or shadow due to change" (v. 17, NRSV). Other translations may be consulted with profit, but the fundamental assertion appears to be one of God's invariability (cf. Heb. 1:12; Ps. 102:27).

God is not only the source of "every generous act of giving," but of Christian existence as well (vv. 17–18). We have been brought into being by a divine begetting (1 Pet. 1:23; John 3:3, 5), accomplished through the creative power of the "word of truth" (Eph. 1:13; Col. 1:5–6; 2 Tim. 2:5; Ps. 119:43). With its power to engender life, it is a "living Word" (Heb. 4:12), not a human word but that of God (1 Thess. 2:13; also 1:6; Acts 8:14; 17:11). Later, in verse 21, it is said to be an "implanted word that has the power to save your souls" (cf. Luke 8:11). Meekness is a precondition for such reception (cf. Sir. 3:17). The planting metaphor is extended in the description of us as "a kind of first fruits of his creatures" (vv. 18; Rev. 14:4; also Rom. 16:5).

Having established that God is the source of all that we have and are, the author now turns to practical religion.

One theme that emerges has to do with the emotion of anger and the attendant forms of speech: "Let everyone be quick to listen, slow to speak, slow to anger" (v. 19). This advice echoes Sirach 5:11: "Be quick to hear, and be deliberate in answering" (cf. Eccles. 5:1–2). The Jewish wisdom tradition also knew the advantage of thoughtful speech (Prov. 15:1–2; Sir. 5:12–13), as well as recognizing that anger usually causes us to say things we later regret. Consequently, wisdom dictated that anger should be curbed (Eccles. 7:9). Later in the passage (v. 26), bridling the tongue is seen as a prerequisite to being religious (Ps. 34:13). This theme receives even fuller treatment later in the letter (3:1–12).

A second theme concerns "hearing and doing" (vv. 22–25). The Book of James is especially well known for the way in which its emphasis on "faith that works" (2:14–26) provides a counterpoint to the Pauline emphasis on faith alone (Rom. 1:17). The author first notices that there is a distinction between "hearing the word" and "doing it," but this is not his unique observation (cf. Matt. 7:21–27; 21:29; Luke 6:46; Rom. 2:13; 1 John 3:18). His illustration of the man looking in the mirror suggests that "hearing" is a deliberate act that requires concentration and memory. Consequently, to "look into the perfect law, the law of liberty," (v. 25) requires careful attention and perseverance before appropriate action results. The author seems to have had experience with the self-styled religious person who hears but does not allow the commandment of the Lord to enlighten the eyes (Ps. 19:8).

A third, closely related, theme concerns "religion that is pure and undefiled" (v. 27). This is actually an extension of the second theme, for it illustrates in concrete terms what is involved in a "religion that does." Singled out for attention here is care for orphans and widows (cf. Exod. 22:21–24; Ps. 10:10, 18). This teaching echoes the sentiments of Jesus' teaching concerning practical discipleship (Matt. 25:31–46). The insistence of this text is that "keeping oneself unstained by the world" (v. 27) occurs as a result of practical acts of Christian charity rather than from ritual purification (cf. 2 Pet. 3:14).

If one wishes to preach about practical Christianity, one could do worse than begin with this lection from the Book of James. To begin with, today's lection illustrates that Christian practice begins with the fundamental recognition of God as the source of every gift, including our own Christian birthright. But then it moves on to the practical plane of Christian living, insisting that the truly "implanted word" received with meekness will produce disciples who are long on obedience and short on words.

Mark 7:1–8, 14–15, 21–23

We return to Mark for the Gospel lesson and, with the exception of the Sunday of Christ the King and All Saints, will continue with Mark until the beginning of Advent. The portion of Mark to which we return is the large block of material beginning at 4:1, which presents Jesus as extremely popular as a teacher and healer, traveling with his disciples to both sides of the Sea of Galilee and ministering to both Jews and Gentiles. This same body of material portrays the Twelve as continuing in their inability to understand Jesus, the climax coming at 8:31 with Jesus' introduction of his coming passion and his instruction of the disciples.

That today's reading consists of three pieces out of a larger unit (7:1–23) may create some suspicion of editorial violation of Mark in the pursuit of a theme or doctrine. Closer examination, however, reveals that this is not the case. We have had several occasions earlier to notice that a structural characteristic of this Gospel is the writer's insertion of material within material. Within 7:1–23 are at least two insertions by the writer. Verses 3–4 explain to the reader the ritual cleansing practices of Judaism. We can only assume that Mark here is explaining to Gentile Christians the background practices with which they were not familiar. Verses 9–13 focus on the practice of Corban as an example of permitting a tradition (oral law) to set aside a command of God as fundamental as honoring one's father and mother. This Corban discussion, which does not necessarily refer to the cleansing practices being argued, probably was brought from another context to serve the writer's point here.

Another characteristic of Mark's structure is the division of a narrative into portions addressed to different audiences. Usually this consists of Jesus' speaking to the crowd and then explaining his words to the disciples in private (4:1–12; 9:14–29; 10:1–10; 13:1–8).

Our reading fits that pattern. In fact, attention to audiences explains what seems at first a fragmented lection: the Pharisees and scribes are addressed in verses 1–8; the crowd in verses 14–15; the disciples in verses 21–23. At the center of the entire narrative is the pronouncement by Jesus: "There is nothing outside a person that by going in can defile, but the things that come out are what defile" (v. 15).

In form, then, our text is very similar to other pronouncement stories in Mark, such as the one recorded in 3:23–28. First, there is a charge against Jesus' disciples. That it is the disciples who are criticized and Jesus who comes to their defense reflects the condition of the early church facing accusations from the synagogue that Christians violate tradition and misinterpret Scripture. A common defense by the church was to present Jesus' response to such charges. Second, there is the countercharge, and in this case, an illustration supporting the countercharge. Third, Jesus makes the pronouncement and again explains the pronouncement to the Twelve.

And what issue is at stake here? Jesus' statement that it is not what one puts in the stomach but what proceeds from the heart that determines defilement or cleanliness was not a new or unique criticism of Jewish rituals. Judaism had strong prophetic voices and movements of self-criticism. Many Jews would agree with Jesus and the early church on the matter as long as the issue was not oversimplified, tossing away the stomach in favor of the heart. In proper perspective, the stomach, too, is involved in genuine spirituality. But Mark, by having Jesus address confused disciples, was able to have Jesus meet the needs of two groups in the church. Converts from a Gentile background needed to have both an answer for Jewish critics of church practices and a defense against being lured into legalism and ritualism. The other group consisted of Jewish Christians who probably never totally lost the tug toward their past with its rich traditions, authoritative voices, and familiar rituals. After all, none of us ever outgrows the need to hear Jesus confirm anew that the path of discipleship is liberating and life-giving. Old habits tend to live long past the convictions that gave them birth.

Proper 18 [23]
(Sunday between September 4 and 10 inclusive)

Proverbs 22:1–2, 8–9, 22–23;
Psalm 125; or
Isaiah 35:4–7*a*;
Psalm 146;
James 2:1–10 (11–13) 14–17;
Mark 7:24–37

What all the verses selected from Proverbs 22 have in common is their cautious stance toward riches and their sympathy for the poor. Read alongside the Old Testament lesson from the *Common Lectionary*, Psalm 125 commends the upright life as exemplary.

For the first lesson in other lectionaries, Isaiah's message is full of hope: a God who vindicates the cause of the just, human disease healed, and withering weather reversed. Similar confidence in God's impressive power is echoed in Psalm 146.

Today's Gospel text presents Jesus as healer, first of the Syrophoenician woman's daughter, then a deaf man with a speech impediment.

Respectful treatment of the poor is called for in today's epistolary lesson from James, which calls for faith that works to supply the physical needs of the hungry and naked.

Proverbs 22:1–2, 8–9, 22–23

With the exception of the concluding poem on the ideal wife, Proverbs 10–31 is a large collection of short wisdom sayings. There is little systematic organization in the collection, though some sayings are grouped according to content and others according to form or simply linked by catchwords. Most are quite brief, consisting of a single two-part sentence.

There is no way to determine the date and authorship of the individual sayings. The attribution of the book as a whole and of the collection in Proverbs 10:1–22:16 is based on the tradition of Solomon's legendary wisdom. The final form of the book is relatively late, reflecting the literary activity of the wisdom teachers such as ben Sirah (Sir. 51:23). But in the collections, old and new sayings appear side by side. Some of the forms of the proverbs and doubtless many of the individual sayings come from folk wisdom; others may have been composed by teachers as they reflected on the meaning of life and sought the most apt and memorable way of expressing their conclusions.

The sayings come in various forms and styles and serve different ends. They are different from the formal instructions, such as the ones in Proverbs 1–9 (see the commentary on Prov. 9:1–6 for Proper 15 [20] in this volume). Some simply draw a conclusion from experience and state it as a general truth. The purpose is to make sense of reality, especially of human relationships in society. Others express a value judgment about some aspect of experience and indicate directions for conduct: "Whoever loves pleasure will suffer want; whoever loves wine and oil will not be rich" (Prov. 21:17). Typical themes of such sayings are the differences between wisdom and foolishness, the values of hard work, and the merits of prudent behavior. Still other sayings go a step farther and give explicit directions for conduct in the form of commands, prohibitions, exhortations, or admonitions: "Do not rob the poor because they are poor, or crush the afflicted at the gate" (Prov. 22:22). Although they are similar to the Old Testament laws, their force is different because their authority rests not upon divine revelation but on the persuasiveness of the directions themselves.

Proverbs 22:1 is a saying of the second type. It states a value based on experience and leaves it to the hearer to draw the obvious conclusions about conduct. Reputation ("a good name") and goodwill ("favor") are better than wealth. Consequently, one should act at all times with integrity. There is no real connection between verses 1 and 2 beyond the catchwords "riches"/ "the rich." Verse 2 is a simple statement of "fact." It does not inculcate a value or suggest a course of action, although a certain value may be taken for granted. It is to be observed and described, but not fully comprehended, that society consists of both rich and poor, and Yahweh obviously made them all. The social order rests in creation. It is a conclusion that generates further reflection, including our own. Does this saying simply recognize and approve of the status quo? Or does the affirmation that all are created by the Lord suggest equality? Whatever the intention of the saying itself, we certainly can use the theological interpretation of human life as we analyze our society and consider courses of action.

Verse 8 is a statement of "fact," but it is presented in such a way that a course of action is commended to the hearer. The one who acts unjustly will suffer; his deeds will bring him retribution. (Read the second half of the verse with NEB: "and the end of his work will be the rod.") This proverb states the view, frequently encountered in wisdom literature and elsewhere in the Old Testament, that the unrighteous suffer and the righteous prosper. Expression of that perspective is not only moralism, to encourage proper behavior, it is also confirmed by experience. Those who sow the wind do in fact often reap the whirlwind (Hos. 8:7). But, as the Books of Job and Ecclesiastes point out, it is a limited view. The righteous do indeed suffer, and the race is not always to the swift, bread to the wise, or riches to the intelligent, "but time and chance happen to them all" (Eccles. 9:11).

Verse 9 clearly states and inculcates a value, generosity to the poor. It should not be taken as the positive side of what was stated in the previous verse. Blessing does not come as a reward to the one who looks kindly upon others ("are generous") and shares bread with the poor. Generosity and concern for others is its own reward in that with it comes peace of heart.

Verses 22–23 contain an exhortation, explicit directions for behavior. The parallel lines articulate the same understanding of social justice found in the early prophets. The exhortation urges against stealing from the poor or abusing the weak in the law court ("at the gate"), and then gives a reason for following the exhortation: the Lord will act as the attorney ("pleads their cause") for the poor and afflicted, and will judge those who abuse them (v. 23).

Psalm 125

This psalm falls into two parts. The first, in verses 1–3, consists of statements and descriptions of confidence. The second, in verses 4–5, consists of a prayer for the blessing of those who are good and a declaration that evildoers will be led away.

Two motives are given for the expressions of confidence. First, "those who trust in the LORD" have the same type of security and divine protection as the city of Zion, the site of the temple. Zion is described as immovable, abiding forever. A basic tenet of Hebrew thought about Zion asserted that it was unconquerable and inviolable (see Pss. 46, 48, 76). The eternal durability of Zion was associated, in later Judaism, with the idea of the navel or center of the universe. The sacred rock over which the temple was constructed was considered to mark the navel of the world and thus the meeting place of the heavenly world and the underworld.

The security of the faithful ones is declared assured, for God is round about the people like the mountains that encircle Zion (v. 2). Among the mountains encircling Jerusalem are Mount Scopus and the Mount of Olives, both of which are higher in elevation than the mountain spur on which Jerusalem was built.

Verse 3 is difficult to interpret. The text seems to promise that foreign oppressors or evil rulers ("the scepter of wickedness") will not rule over the holy land ("the land allotted to the righteous"). That they will not rule is to ensure that the righteous will not depart from the proper path; that is, local citizens will not become collaborators with the foreign power. Throughout much of Israel's history, the land was ruled by outsiders, and the local citizens were constantly tempted to cooperate with the occupying troops or even to give up their ancestral ways and religious practices, that is, to cease being Jewish.

Verse 4 is an intercessory prayer that God will do good to those who are good and who are upright in their hearts; in other words, those who are loyal to God externally ("those who are good") and internally ("upright in their hearts").

Verse 5 is not a prayer but a declaration that those who turn aside—the apostates, the unfaithful, the renegades—will be led away—into exile.

The psalm thus begins with a description of those who trust in God—they are firmly anchored and immovable—and concludes with a description of those who in their crookedness act corruptly—they are not fixed but insecure, and their future is to be moved away.

Isaiah 35:4–7*a*

This reading presents a vision of the reign of God over the land, and especially the wilderness. What had been viewed as hostile is now envisioned as a supportive environment for human beings. In Isaiah 35, the wider context of our lesson, Zion is the goal of a pilgrimage of the elect through lands that once were dangerous and threatening.

Because of its similarities to the poetry in Isaiah 40–55, some commentators have attributed Isaiah 35 to the same prophet, Second Isaiah, who wrote those words in 539 BC. On closer examination, however, it appears that the author of Isaiah 35 knew and depended upon Second Isaiah, and thus was even later than the prophet of the end of the Babylonian Exile. He frequently cites but often reinterprets expressions from the prophet whose words are found in Isaiah 40–55: "highway" (v. 8) from 40:3, "streams in the desert" (v. 6) from 43:19, the appearance of the "glory of the LORD" (v. 2) from 40:3, 5, and more. However, where Second

Isaiah had announced the return of the Judean exiles from Babylon along a highway in the desert, the poet of chapter 35 expects even more. The dispersed of Israel from throughout the world will return to Zion, and the desert will become a fertile garden. The vision in our passage is even more cosmic and eschatological than that of Second Isaiah. Because it depends upon Second Isaiah, the chapter can be dated to the postexilic age, and perhaps relatively late in the Persian period.

The question of the place of this chapter in its context in the book is closely related to the issue of its date of composition. Isaiah 35 stands in sharp contrast to the immediately preceding chapter, a harsh prophecy of judgment with almost apocalyptic overtones against Edom, Judah's neighbor. Isaiah 36–39 is an appendix to the prophetic collection containing narrative accounts concerning Isaiah of Jerusalem. It thus seems likely that at one stage in the growth of the book, our chapter stood either as the conclusion to the work of Isaiah of Jerusalem or as the transition to the words of Second Isaiah in chapters 40–55.

The poem from which our verses for today have been taken closely resembles a prophetic announcement of salvation, but its themes and language are more apocalyptic in character. Its two main parts, linked by their attention to wonderful changes in nature, present distinct but closely related themes.

1. Verses 1–6a, with all the language about the transformation of the desert, concerns the coming of "the glory of the LORD" (v. 2). The words actually seem to be addressed to the Lord's messenger or messengers, urging them to call for the wilderness to celebrate and the desert to bloom (vv. 1–2). The messengers also are to encourage the weak (vv. 3–4). There are echoes here of the old tradition about the theophany, the arrival of God and the dramatic and terrifying effect his coming has on nature, but here nature is transformed by the coming of God's glory, and then the sick are healed (vv. 5–6).

2. Verses 6b–10, on the other hand, concern the return of the redeemed, that is, the dispersed people of Israel, to Zion. Here, too, nature is transformed, made into a well-watered land, and fitted with a highway called "the Holy Way" (v. 8). The familiar threats to travelers in the desert—dry land, wild beasts, and enemies—no longer exist. The final lines of the unit (v. 10) catch the tone of the entire poem: joy and gladness, for "sorrow and sighing shall flee away." And that is the contribution of this text for Christian proclamation. Those who experience their lives as exile, those who pass through a wilderness, those who are weak may shout for joy, for God will transform all things.

Psalm 146

This psalm is the first in a small collection (Pss. 146–150) all of which begin and end with a call to praise, hallelujah ("Praise the Lord!"). The psalm praises God, describing the divine character and divine activity, while simultaneously contrasting the Divine with the human. The composition could be aptly described as a theological synopsis summarizing aspects of Israel's belief about God.

Verses 3–4 warn against placing one's faith in humans even if the humans are extraordinary and exceptional ("princes"). Humans are ultimately helpless; they all die, and with death their planning ceases and their thinking terminates. Such death-oriented creatures are not proper objects of trust.

On the other hand, God is a worthy object of trust and one who brings blessedness and happiness in his train. A series of four characteristics of God are presented as supporting the contention that "happy is the one whose help and hope is in God." First, appeal is made to God as creator. As the one who made heaven, earth, and sea—that is, the totality of the universe—God is not bound by the structures and limitations of creaturehood. As creator, God is owner and ruler. Second, appeal is made to the fidelity and constancy of the Creator "who keeps faith forever" (v. 6). Unlike humans, whose plans and programs die with them, God and divine help endure forever. Unlike humans, God is not threatened by the possibility of nonbeing. Third, God is the one who is not only concerned for but also executes (guarantees) justice for the oppressed. In this affirmation and throughout verses 7–9, one finds a consistent emphasis of the Old Testament: God takes a special interest in and acts in behalf of the downtrodden, the powerless, and the despairing. Fourth, the satisfaction of physical needs is also the concern of God, who "gives food to the hungry." As the maker of heaven and earth, God does not will that humans be oppressed nor that they should suffer from hunger.

Following these four divine characteristics, the psalmist speaks of seven activities of God in which the Divine acts to alleviate human distress and to defend those without rights. Most of those noted as the object of God's care are persons without full authority and potential to assume responsibility for and to exercise rights for their own welfare: the prisoners (at the mercy of the legal system or perhaps in slavery), the blind (at the mercy of the seeing), those who are bowed down or with bent backs (in debt or oppressed by others, thus carrying burdens not their own), the righteous (the innocent in the legal system who however were at the mercy of the upholders of justice), the sojourners (foreign settlers or visitors, not members of the native culture and thus aliens), and the widow and fatherless (who were without the support of a male patriarch in a male-dominated culture). God is declared to be committed to the care of all these while at the same time seeing to it that the wicked come to their just reward—ruin.

The psalmist here obviously presents the basic nature and character of God but does not claim that conditions and circumstances conform to this idealized divine will. In the list of attributes, God is primarily contrasted with human leaders (vv. 3–4 over against vv. 5–9). Verse 10 adds an eschatological note to the text and perhaps points to the future as the time when the intervention of God in behalf of society's rejects and subjects will occur.

In preaching from this psalm, attention should be focused on its attempt to define the divine disposition as in favor of the downtrodden and the destitute, the powerless living at the peripheries of society, in the basements of humanity's houses.

James 2:1–10 (11–13) 14–17

In spite of their seeming unrelatedness, all three texts from today's epistolary lection reflect a common theme—merciful treatment of the poor.

The first passage opens with a memorable scene depicting a rich man receiving deferential treatment in finding a seat in the synagogue, whereas a poor man is politely given standing room only or seated on the floor. It is a scene we all know and likely have experienced in one form or another. The author's sympathy is with the poor man, as seen in the remarks that follow (vv. 5–7). We are reminded that God's choice lies with the poor who turn out to be "rich in faith" and the real "heirs of the kingdom." By contrast, the author has little use for the rich who, in his experience, turn out to be those who oppress the poor, take them to court, and blaspheme the "excellent name," probably Christian.

This unequivocal sympathy with the poor and judgment against the rich is reminiscent of the first Lukan beatitude and woe: "Blessed are the poor; woe to the rich" (Luke 6:20, 24). In fact, it fits well with the overall depiction of the rich and poor in Luke-Acts. Indeed, earlier (1:9), the "believer who is lowly" is enjoined to "boast in being raised up," whereas the rich is ordered to boast in his humiliation. Although the author's viewpoint is not grounded in the prophetic tradition, it could well have been, for his protest against the rich's treatment of the poor echoes the sentiments of the Old Testament prophets (cf. Amos 4:1; 5:10–13; 8:4–6).

That such discrimination against the poor actually occurred in the early church, even within worship settings, is seen in 1 Corinthians 11:17–22. A close reading of the text suggests that distinctions based on socioeconomic status were being made within the fellowship, and Paul sharply condemns those who "humiliate those who have nothing" (v. 22), literally, the "have-nots." This fits with his remarks that some were eating and drinking to excess while others were going hungry.

The scene in the Book of James is depicted to make a single point: Christians should not show favoritism (v. 1). It is this theme that connects verses 1–7 with the verses that follow, where loving one's neighbor as oneself (Lev. 19:18; Matt. 22:39; Rom. 13:9; Gal. 5:14) is set over against showing favoritism, which is treated as a grave offense. In fact, to show favoritism is an offense liable to conviction under the Mosaic law, although there it cuts both ways: "You shall not render an unjust judgment; you shall not be partial to the poor or defer to the great: with justice you shall judge your neighbor" (Lev. 19:15; also cf. Exod. 23:3; Deut. 1:17; Sir. 7:6). The text recognizes that some readers will regard this as a relatively trivial matter, and thus it emphasizes that breaking a single point of the law, however minor it may seem, renders one guilty of breaking the whole law (cf. Matt. 5:19; Gal. 5:3).

No attempt is made in our text to defend the principle of impartiality by appealing to God's impartial nature. But this is certainly an axiomatic principle in Scripture and one well worth noting in this connection (cf. Acts 10:34; Rom. 2:11; Gal. 2:6; Eph. 6:9; Col. 3:25; 1 Pet. 1:17; also 2 Chron. 19:7; Sir. 35:12–13).

The parenthetical verses in today's text merely reinforce the point that we are responsible for the full demands of the law. We are warned that the merciless will be treated mercilessly.

The second main part of today's lection (vv. 14–17) treats the well-known theme of "faith without works." The text ends climactically with the emphatic assertion "So faith by itself, if it has no works, is dead" (v. 17). This principle may be profitably contrasted with the Pauline doctrine of justification by faith; but given the juxtaposition of this text with the other selections from the chapter, it will be more to the point to notice that the central example has to do with the proper care of the poor. Thus, to the hungry and scantily clothed, a warm greeting and a hollow prayer will not do. "What good is it?" The point echoes the teaching of Jesus concerning the hungry and poor (Matt. 25:35–36) and also relates to a similar problem in the Johannine community (1 John 3:17).

Neither of these texts spells out a well-developed social ethic, but their basic point cannot be ignored. Insofar as this is done at all in the New Testament, it is done best by Luke-Acts. Rather, what we have here is direct, hard-hitting teaching about the evil and seriousness of discrimination and, by extension, neglect of the poor. We are told that deference toward the rich and denigration of the poor are unacceptable behaviors for those who "really believe in our glorious Lord Jesus Christ" (v. 1); that showing favoritism in these matters is a grievous wrong; and, finally, that the needs of the poor and hungry are not met by proclaiming that we have faith, or even by proclaiming the faith. Rather, they are met by the simple gesture of giving a cup of cold water.

This, according to the Book of James, constitutes genuine faith.

Mark 7:24–37

Today's Gospel tells of two healings, both occurring to the north and northeast (see below for a discussion of the uncertain itinerary of Jesus) of Galilee. It is as if Jesus, having presented his teaching on clean and unclean (7:1–23), moves now to implement and underscore that teaching in his own work. He is here ministering to the "unclean."

Jesus travels north of Galilee to a region with the ancient name of Phoenicia, which is, at the time of this event, the westernmost part of Syria. Tyre was an important coastal city. Seeking privacy, but again the victim of his own fame, Jesus is found by a Phoenician (Matthew says "Canaanite," 15:22) woman. She is humble, she pleads, but she is also tenacious. Jesus puts her off with a painful proverb about Jews (children) and Gentiles (dogs). She will not relent: if I am a dog, treat me as a dog and give me the crumbs from your table. Because of what she said, an unusual but gripping claim on the compassion of Jesus, her plea is heard, her prayer answered.

No one misses the seeming harsh tone of Jesus. Some commentators seek to soften it by explaining that Jesus is testing her faith, but that is not quite satisfying. Perhaps Jesus is still struggling with the idea of a Gentile mission. The apostles certainly did (Acts 15), and racial and ethnic barriers still hinder the church. Perhaps it is a better view of the story to say that a woman, and a Gentile woman at that, wrestled and would not turn loose till Jesus blessed her, reminding us all that faith is a lively, vigorous, and insisting power that does not give up easily.

The story in verses 31–37 is not unusual in its format, conforming in general to other miracle stories and in particular to the one recorded in the next chapter (8:22–26). Frequently in Mark, persons with special needs are brought to Jesus (2:3; 7:32; 8:22; 9:20; 10:13). The methods of healing attributed to Jesus were common to healers and practitioners of magic arts. In the case before us, the deaf mute is taken aside for privacy, the afflicted parts are touched, spittle is applied, the healer looks heavenward, groans, and gives the healing command. Keeping the power word *Ephphatha* in the original Aramaic (cf. also 5:41) not only keeps the sense of mystery but may also reflect the church's practice of preserving traditional healing formulas. Following the healing, Jesus again calls for secrecy, the charge to secrecy is disobeyed by the zealous preaching of the witnesses, and the account closes with a general expression of astonishment.

If Mark offers any commentary at all on this miracle, it is in verse 37b: "He even makes the deaf to hear and the mute to speak." This description of the ministry of Jesus very likely was intended to recall Isaiah's grand vision of Zion's future in the day of salvation: the blind see, the deaf hear, the mute speak, and the lame leap for joy (35:5–6). But beyond this story's witness to the end time and the presence of God's kingdom, is Mark saying anything else?

Mark often interprets by the location of a narrative. Where an event occurs geographically and where it is placed within the Gospel are both forms of interpretation and deserve the reader's careful attention.

Geographically, the two healings occur in Gentile territory. The preceding story took place in the region of Tyre. From there Mark describes a most improbable itinerary by Jesus. For example, he says Jesus went from Tyre to Sidon to the Sea of Galilee "in the midst of" (translated "from the region of," NRSV) the Decapolis (v. 31). Sidon is north of Tyre, and the Sea of Galilee does not lie in the midst of Decapolis. Whatever may have been Mark's knowledge of the country or whatever his sources, there is no doubt about his intention: Jesus made a wide-ranging journey in Gentile territory and healed, exorcized, taught, and preached there (5:1–20; 6:53–56; 7:24–30; 7:31–37). The message and blessing of Jesus Christ were being taken to geographical and ethnic limits. Apparently, the Christian community Mark addressed needed to know that, or be reminded of it. Jesus' own ministry authorized the Gentile mission of Mark's church.

The literary context for these two stories also serves an interpretive purpose. In the cycle of stories in chapters 6–7, Jesus feeds, exorcizes demons, and heals, with great receptions at the fringes of his country but with criticism by Jewish leaders and with misunderstanding by his disciples. The signs of the kingdom are there for those who would perceive and believe. The crowds applaud; the critics continue in hardened opposition. But what of Jesus' disciples; where are they? Not with the applauding crowd, not with the hounding critics. Have they seen and heard enough to be ready for the next word from Jesus: the Son of Man must suffer, be rejected, and be killed? If Jesus' own followers miss the point, who will continue his work?

Proper 19 [24]
(Sunday between September 11 and 17 inclusive)

Proverbs 1:20–33;
Psalm 19 or Wisdom of Solomon 7:26–8:1; or
Isaiah 50:4–9*a*;
Psalm 116:1–9;
James 3:1–12;
Mark 8:27–38

In today's Old Testament lesson from the *Common Lectionary* we hear Wisdom prophesying in the streets, scolding fools for their refusal to heed her advice. Apart from its view that the heavens display God's glory, Psalm 19 also extols the law of the Lord for, among other things, making the simple wise.

The first half of the third Servant Song from Isaiah 50 provides the Old Testament lesson for other lectionaries today. Among other things, the servant has received the gift of comforting speech from the Lord. The prayer of Psalm 116 depicts a thankful worshiper whom the Lord has healed.

Revelation and misunderstanding occur side by side at Caesarea Philippi, the pivotal episode in Mark's Gospel, which serves as the Gospel lesson for today.

The sins of the tongue are treated in the epistolary lesson from James, which in itself exemplifies the power of graphic speech.

Proverbs 1:20–33

The reading from Proverbs 1 is the second in a series of twelve extended addresses or speeches in Proverbs 1–9. All of them are instructions concerning wisdom or speeches by Wisdom herself. Unlike the almost random collections of individual sayings in Proverbs 10–30, each of these addresses is a carefully crafted composition that probably arose among Israel's sages for the purpose of teaching their students.

The unit is organized clearly into two parts. First (vv. 20–21) is the more-or-less narrative introduction of Wisdom and her speech. The only other instances such as this in which personified Wisdom speaks out are Proverbs 8–9 (see the commentary on the reading from these chapters for the Easter Vigil in this volume) and Sirach 24. Her address is public, "in the streets," "the squares," "the busiest corner," and "at the entrance of the city gates." She does not wait for students to come to her but goes out and seeks those who need wisdom.

The second part, or the body of the unit, is the speech itself (vv. 22–33). It begins in the form of a direct address (vv. 22–27 are in the second person), but in verses 28–33 it shifts, referring to the addressees impersonally in the third person. In some respects the address is similar to the other discourses in Proverbs 1–9, in which the speaker quite clearly is a wisdom teacher addressing students ("my child," 2:1; 3:1; etc.). There are admonitions, exhortations, and instructions that call for the listener to learn the way of wisdom, and the way of wisdom is contrasted with the way of stupidity. On the other hand, the discourse has some affinities with prophetic speeches. The warnings of disaster for refusal to pay heed to Wisdom's words are quite strong (vv. 27–28), and some of the language is quite similar to that found in prophetic literature. The expression "have stretched out my hand" (v. 24) recalls the outstretched hand of the Lord in Isaiah 5:25; 9:12, 17, 21; 10:4, and verse 28 recalls Amos 8:11–12. More specifically, Wisdom's reliance on the authority of Yahweh in verse 29 resembles the prophetic appeal to the word of Yahweh. The sages, on the other hand, base their instructions on knowledge acquired through experience and tradition.

Although it has affinities with both the wisdom instruction and the prophetic address, the speech is best understood as a sermon. Its goal is to change the hearts and minds of the hearers, to persuade them in every possible way to follow in the path of wisdom. There are rhetorical questions (v. 22) that invite the "simple" to recognize who they are, direct admonitions to listen (v. 23), and warnings of the danger of failing to heed Wisdom's call (vv. 24–27, 28–33). Most of the warnings are threatening, pointing out the dangerous results of stupidity. The speech concludes, however, with the positive side, the promise of security and peace of mind to those who do listen.

There is almost no specific statement of the substance of the way of wisdom, of what it means in particular to be wise. The sages seem to take for granted what it means to act wisely, and it certainly would have included diligent study of the traditions they handed down. One has to look elsewhere, such as the remainder of the Book of Proverbs, for details.

One of the most troubling themes of this passage for most modern readers is the apparently direct correlation between actions and their consequences in verses 29–33. This is stated in the wisdom manner and not like the prophets would state it. The dominant voice in the prophetic literature speaks of divine intervention to judge sin. The sages see actions as leading to their own consequences: Those who fail to heed the call of Wisdom "shall eat the fruit of their way and be sated with their own devices" (v. 31). Complacency has its own reward, destruction (v. 32). The Book of Proverbs reiterates this point over and over:

> A little sleep, a little slumber,
>   a little folding of the hands to rest,
> and poverty will come upon you like a robber,
>   and want, like an armed warrior. (24:33–34)

Certainly, human experience regularly confirms the judgment that actions have their consequences, that wise and discerning actions bring better results than stupid ones. But that point of view has its limitations. True, laziness may lead to poverty, but it is potentially destructive to reason back in every case from the "effect" to a "cause"; for example, to conclude that because someone is poor, they have been stupid or lazy. And the Book of Job is a profound and ringing challenge to the view that human suffering is always the result of human sin.

Psalm 19

This psalm was previously discussed as one of the readings for the Third Sunday in Lent.

Wisdom of Solomon 7:26-8:1

Both the reading from Proverbs and this lection from The Wisdom of Solomon praise Wisdom, depicted as a female. The depiction of the female is not that of a mother who envelops and succours the adherent with motherly care and advice nor that of a helpless girl who seeks care and protection from another. Instead of these images, Wisdom is presented as an inviting, tempting, and alluring female who possesses the clues for right living and success in the world. This Wisdom entices humans to cleave to her and does so in rather sensual terms.

Wisdom is, of course, identified with the true knowledge of how the world operates and how the Divine is related to the world in general and humanity in particular. Wisdom also involves "scientific" considerations and the ability to understand the course of history. Wisdom 7:17-21 notes some of the intellectual and spiritual gifts that Wisdom bestows, and 7:22-23 lists her 21 (7×3) attributes.

In the reading for today, Wisdom is considered a reflection and mirror of God (v. 26), who enters or is given to holy souls. In verse 28, one sees declared a view that became highly influential in Judaism, namely, that wisdom, learning, and education are valued by God so that study becomes a means of service and devotion to God. Wisdom knows no darkness; against her evil cannot prevail. At the same time, Wisdom has a universal quality, for it is she who orders all things.

Isaiah 50:4-9a

This text is the Old Testament lesson for Passion/Palm Sunday and has been discussed at that point in this volume.

Psalm 116:1-9

This psalm, portions of which are a lection for Holy Thursday in all three years, gives expression to the theme of "escape from death." Although frequently interpreted as expressing a belief in the resurrection (so similarly Ps. 16; see Acts 2:25-31), the psalm was originally composed to be used in a thanksgiving ritual following recovery from sickness.

Thanksgiving rituals, in ancient Israel, as in most cultures, were intent on two goals: (1) celebration of the new or renewed status of the person/group/community and (2) offering testimony to the one who had granted the status being celebrated. Both of these goals focus more on the human situation than on gaining the attention of the Divine. (This is unlike the lamenting situation, where exactly the opposite is the case.)

Thus, in this psalm the addressee is fundamentally the human audience. (God is addressed only in vv. 16–17 and possibly in v. 8. In v. 7, the worshiper engages in self-address and self-assurance.)

The condition of trouble or the state of distress from which the worshiper has been saved is depicted in various ways throughout the psalm: snares of death, pangs of Sheol, distress and anguish, brought low, death, tears, stumbling. All of these illustrate the marginal state of existence into which sickness had thrown the person.

The worshiper's actions, in taking to God the predicament of illness, is noted in v. 4 as calling "on the name of the LORD" or simply praying for help. The recovered or assured worshiper even provides a summary of the prayer spoken on that earlier occasion (see v. 4*b*).

The divine aid granted by God is also described in various ways: has heard, inclined his ear, saved me, delivered my soul, my eyes, my feet.

Verse 7, in which the worshiper's own soul is addressed, could suggest that the person's illness or disease is still present and that the worshiper has only been assured of recovery rather than actually having recovered.

James 3:1–12

Contrary to what we might expect, today's epistolary text begins with a discouraging word to teachers. We all recognize the need for teachers, especially good teachers, and we are prone to encourage others to pursue teaching. But James is more cautious. He thinks teachers are held to a higher standard: "we who teach will be judged with greater strictness" (v. 1). As a result, he does not think teaching is for everyone.

Why? Because to teach is to make a living with the tongue, and the tongue is a dangerous thing. He knows full well that whoever speaks makes mistakes. We speak too many words not to blunder occasionally. So he concedes, "All of us make many mistakes" (v. 2). The perfect speaker is not to be found. But it is not fine grammatical speaking that he is worried about, but something more sinister that happens when the tongue strikes a match.

For one thing, James knows that small things can do great harm. Size is not the main measure of power. The tongue is like a ship's rudder or a horse's bridle—tiny by comparison with ship or horse, but highly leveraged. Moving the rudder just slightly at the beginning of a voyage is the difference between docking in England or in Spain. A small metal rod properly pulled can control a raging stallion. That is the power of the tongue—small, often hidden from view, but the controlling rudder, the bridling bit.

James also knows about fires. Big fires often begin with a small match, and they can rage for days, destroy acres and acres, defying legions of firefighters. So it is with the tongue. Its words are like sparks of flint, setting fire to woods that have been carefully nurtured for years. Relationships slowly built are savagely destroyed by the wrong words said in the wrong way. Jealousies are created with no more than a word or two, wrongly uttered, even if rightly meant. And so it goes. The whole range of emotions—hatreds, jealousies, ill will, raging like a forest fire set by the tongue.

Especially vile are words maliciously spoken. These are perhaps what James has in mind when he speaks of the tongue as "a restless evil, full of deadly poison" (v. 8). Capable of blessing and cursing, the tongue that curses condemns, belittles, abuses, intimidates, waging its war with words like Sherman marching to the sea—destroying everything in sight. It would come as no surprise to James that so many laws are laws against words—slander, contempt, perjury.

Yet we do well to remember that his instructions began with teachers, those entrusted with the responsibility of transmitting traditions. We all know how access to knowledge and esoteric wisdom gives us a way with words, and our words give us advantage over others. Specialized knowledge easily intimidates generalized ignorance. And so it is that teachers can become arrogant and intimidating, using speech that is both intemperate and abusive, all in the interest of furthering knowledge, so we say.

If this is the way it works with secular knowledge, the excesses may be even more bizarre with religious knowledge, which, after all, represents the highest form of esoteric learning. Not without reason does religion produce more than its share of fanatics, teachers expert in using words, preachers as skillful wordsmiths, who let their language get away from them. Qualifiers soon disappear, along with ambiguities. Before long, words are whittling away like a freshly sharpened Boker Tree Brand knife, and truth lies a bleeding victim. This is why James insists that not everyone should become teachers, especially religious teachers.

Mark 8:27–38

Because Mark 8:27–38 is a turning point in the Gospel in that Jesus introduces his coming passion to his disciples and begins to move toward Jerusalem, we need to take a moment to back away and see this text in perspective. It is part of a larger body of material beginning at 8:27 and ending at 10:45. This larger unit is bracketed by stories of healing the blind (8:22–26; 10:46–52). The governing theme is Jesus' predictions of his passion (8:31; 9:31; 10:32–34) and the disciples' total inability to understand or to accept what Jesus said. As Jesus moves toward his destination, the recurring phrase "on the way" gives unity to the narrative (8:27; 9:33; 10:17; 10:32).

Our lection consists of three parts: the confession of Peter (vv. 27–30), Jesus' prediction of his passion (vv. 31–33), and the instructions to the crowd about discipleship (vv. 34–38). Verses 31–33 govern the whole and give the passage its critical importance. The exchanges between Jesus and Peter give to verses 27–30 and 31–33 a kind of unity, a narrative consisting of three brief episodes. All three episodes focus on who Jesus is.

The first consists of Jesus' inquiry about public opinion and the disciples' response (vv. 27–28). The several expressions of the Galileans' views of Jesus all say one thing: they think of Jesus as the forerunner of the messiah. Jesus' announcement of the approaching kingdom and his words and deeds of power have heightened anticipation but have not persuaded them that he is the fulfillment of that anticipation. They have, as we all have, an image of the coming messiah, but Jesus does not fit it. After all, it is easier to believe that a messiah *will* come than to believe one *has* come. Messiah as future keeps one's image intact and makes no demands; messiah as present calls for an altered image and demands an altered self.

The second episode consists of another view of Jesus, followed by a sharp rebuke and charge to silence (vv. 29–30). Simon Peter makes it clear that the disciples differ with the crowds in their view of Jesus. You are not the forerunner of the messiah, says Peter; you *are* the Messiah. One is tempted here to slip over into Matthew and hear Jesus bless Simon for this confession (Matt. 16:17), but in Mark, Jesus neither approves nor disapproves; he only charges them to silence. Remember that for Mark, Jesus cannot properly be understood prior to the passion. Until the cross redefines "messiah" it cannot properly be applied to Jesus. After the cross and resurrection, the disciples can proclaim it (9:9).

The third episode offers yet another view of Jesus, followed by an exchange of rebukes (vv. 31–33). Jesus presents himself as the suffering, rejected, crucified, and risen Son of Man. Peter's rebuke is a dramatic expression of the disciples' resistance to such an impossible image of a Christ. Jesus' counter rebuke means that Jesus recognizes in Peter the voice of Satan, the adversary of God. The language of rebuke is the same used to silence demons in the exorcism stories, and so these two friends verbalize the clash of good and evil. The wrong thinking of Peter is no less crippling than the other diseases encountered by Jesus. Let the preacher ponder what it means for the locus of satanic power to be in the heart of a disciple and friend who seeks to save life, not lose it; to defend Jesus, not oppose him. Is there a route to the kingdom that bypasses Golgotha?

Verses 34–38 are editorially joined to the preceding narrative. This is evident in Mark's having the multitudes join the disciples, even though the scene is far north from the places of Jesus' ministry and it is clearly a private meeting between Jesus and the Twelve. The editorial hand is even more evident in that the words to the crowd not only indicate that the crowd knew what Jesus had said to the Twelve about his own passion but also assume that they knew that the form of his death was crucifixion. Jesus had not mentioned the cross. This postpassion material is appropriate at this point, however, because the call to self-denial and cross bearing belongs with Jesus' description of his own fate. And the path of self-denial is not for the Twelve alone; it is for all who would follow. The five sayings of Jesus in these verses have probably been gathered from other contexts, for each has its own integrity and meaning. When joined in one place, however, and placed in the shadow of Jesus' words about his own passion, the terms of discipleship are made inescapably clear.

Proper 20 [25]
(Sunday between September 18 and 24 inclusive)

Proverbs 31:10–31;
Psalm 1; or
Wisdom of Solomon 1:16–2:1, 12–22 or Jeremiah 11:18–20;
Psalm 54;
James 3:13–4:3, 7–8*a*;
Mark 9:30–37

There is hardly a more well-known passage in Proverbs than today's praise of the capable wife, which serves as the Old Testament lesson for the *Common Lectionary*. Similar rectitude toward the law of the Lord is also held out as an ideal in Psalm 1, which serves as introduction to the entire Psalter.

Other lectionaries offer a choice for the first lesson. The verses from The Wisdom of Solomon criticize the ungodly for their cynical outlook and their unholy alliance against the cause of the righteous. One of Jeremiah's personal laments, in which he calls on God for protection, serves as the alternate Old Testament reading. Similar sentiments are echoed in Psalm 54, where the psalm calls on God to vindicate his cause against ruthless enemies.

Mark's second passion prediction and Jesus' teaching about true greatness illustrated by embracing a child provide the Gospel reading.

Yet another selection from James serves as the epistolary text, which pursues the question of the true identity of the wise person.

Proverbs 31:10–31

Until the publication of the *Revised Common Lectionary*, this text had not found its way into the lectionaries of the church, except, of course, for its traditional use on Mother's Day. On the surface it has usually seemed to many readers and preachers to be a straightforward lesson, the affirmation and praise of the "good wife." But on deeper reflection, and from different perspectives, it turns out that this poem is not so unambiguous after all. Read in the wider biblical context, it has both its positive and its potentially destructive implications.

There is a kind of symmetry to the fact that the poem concludes the Book of Proverbs, which began with poems concerning both wisdom and folly personified as women. The bridge from the long collection of individual sayings in Proverbs 10–30 to this unit is the "oracle" of

King Lemuel's mother (31:1–9), which includes warnings against giving one's "strength to women" (31:3).

The poem is an acrostic; that is, each verse begins with a successive letter of the Hebrew alphabet. Because this more-or-less mechanical principle rather than thematic development determined the organization of the poem, its outline is somewhat haphazard. What holds it together is the catalog of the admirable characteristics and activities of the "capable wife." The poem begins with a rhetorical question that asserts that it is difficult to find such a capable wife. She is more rare and thus more precious than jewels (v. 10). Her husband trusts her because she is productive (v. 11), and she does him good and not harm (v. 12). She works with her mind and her hands (v. 13), going as far as necessary to get food and arising before daylight to "provide food for her household and tasks for her servant girls" (v. 15). She works tirelessly (vv. 17–19, 27), takes good care of her household (v. 21), and does not fear the future because she has prepared for it (v. 25). Moreover, she is a wise teacher (v. 26) and is generous to the poor and needy (v. 20). Her beauty is more than skin deep, and she fears the Lord (v. 30). No wonder that her husband is respected in the city gate (v. 23) and that he and her children bless and praise her (vv. 28–29)!

Clearly, this picture is drawn from the perspective of the husband, and one who lives in a patriarchal society. And herein lies the potential for harm in this text—that the wife is seen in terms of what good she can do for her husband and that the expectations are set so high. Virtually anyone fails when measured against this list of accomplishments and sterling traits. She is pictured as fulfilling all of the "traditional" household duties, such as preparing food and clothing for her family; but in addition she manages the family business affairs. So this poem, in praising the "capable wife," presents an ideal set of expectations or demands. The husband of such a wife is able to spend his days in the city gate among the elders (v. 23). Behind these wishes stands the common human desire to be taken care of—to be sure, a desire shared by male and female. Reflecting on this text can help to make us aware of such wishes, how we may misuse others when we act upon them, but also how they may represent our awareness of our own limitations and needs.

Moreover, although this text emerges from a patriarchal society, it entails a remarkable critique of some aspects of such societies. In expressing praise for the capable wife, the poem attributes exceptional power and authority to her. Above all, she is by no means limited to traditional roles within the family, for she has significant public and economic roles. She is a capable merchant (v. 14) and businesswoman (vv. 18–19, 24), both producing and selling goods. She invests in real estate and improves it (v. 16). In short, virtually the only significant role she does not fulfill in her society is to sit with the elders in the gate (v. 23).

Psalm 1

This psalm has been previously discussed as one of the readings for the Seventh Sunday of Easter.

Wisdom of Solomon 1:16–2:1, 12–22

For an analysis of this section of The Wisdom of Solomon, see the commentary in this volume on the overlapping reading (1:13–15; 2:23–24) assigned for Proper 8 [13]. As a part of the book's exhortations to lead the life that is immortal, this reading gives an argument for faithfulness. The text contrasts immortality with death, setting both into a moral context. Righteousness is life. Those who are righteous live. Because God's righteousness is eternal, those who live out of that image of God will live eternally.

Jeremiah 11:18–20

This reading is the beginning section of the first of a series of prayers generally identified as the laments of Jeremiah. The section that begins in 11:18 runs through 12:6. Although the exact number and identification are debated, the others are generally considered to be Jeremiah 15:10–21; 17:14–18; 18:18–23; 20:7–13; 20:14–18. It is more accurate to identify these prayers as complaints than as laments; a lament is a funeral song, and these units are prayers that express the prophet's grievances against God and ask for help.

In terms of genre, these prayers in the Book of Jeremiah closely parallel the individual complaint psalms that make up approximately one third of the Book of Psalms. In these complaints, an individual in trouble addresses God to complain about the circumstances and to ask for help. Typically, the complaint psalms include the invocation of the name of God, complaints in which the speaker tells God of the trouble and reproaches God for failing to respond or for allowing it to continue, and a plea or petition for help. Sometimes they also include assertions of confidence in God and vows of offerings to be performed when the trouble ends. The center of these prayers is the plea for help, and all other elements serve to support that petition. When the supplicant confesses sin, it is because the suffering is seen as punishment. If the sin can be forgiven, then the trouble can end. But frequently the person in trouble confesses or asserts innocence:

> Hear a just cause, O Lord; attend to my cry;
>   give ear to my prayer from lips free of deceit.
>   (Ps. 17:1)

Such confessions of innocence or complaints of unjust suffering make it clear that in ancient Israel no emotion—not even anger against God—was inappropriate in prayer.

Moreover, although the individual complaint psalms are highly personal, speaking of pain, illness, and the fear of death, it has been recognized in recent years that they too, like other liturgical literature, were not simply expressions of personal piety but had their place in corporate worship. Such prayer services would not have necessarily taken place in the temple precincts, but could have been in the homes of the sick. They would have involved the victim's family, neighbors, and friends, but also ritual specialists who knew the words and acts to lead the service.

Jeremiah's complaints reflect an awareness of this liturgical tradition of prayer in ancient Israel. The heart of the reading for today is verse 20:

> But you, O Lord of hosts, who judge righteously,
>   who try the heart and the mind,
> let me see your retribution upon them,
>   for to you I have committed my cause.

The invocation of God's name and the plea for help are explicit. The plea is supported by expression of confidence in the God who judges fairly, who knows human hearts and minds, and in whom Jeremiah places his confidence. This plea had been preceded in verses 18–19 by an account of the trouble. Jeremiah perceives his problem to be threats to his life from enemies. This, too, is a common theme in the individual complaint psalms.

The complaint psalm in 11:18–20 is followed by an account of God's response to the prayer. The prophet hears God's word of judgment on those enemies of Jeremiah, because they have tried to stand in the way of the word of God. Next (12:1–6) comes another complaint psalm, or the completion of the one begun in 11:18. In this case, the sense of unjust suffering is stronger, and the challenge of or charge against God more explicit:

> Why does the way of the guilty prosper?
> Why do all who are treacherous thrive? (Jer. 12:1)

Certainly, these passionate pleas for help relate to Jeremiah's particular situation, and even to his personality. He encountered resistance and threats to his life more than once, and he suffered through the awareness that he, too, stood under the announcement of judgment he pronounced against the people of Judah. However, the fact that his complaints stand in a liturgical tradition suggests that they reflect corporate understandings of how one may speak to God, that they are not simply individualistic notes. The sense of being abandoned by God, or even of being tricked by God, is not limited to a few sensitive prophetic personalities, but is common. Moreover, in the biblical tradition it was—and is—not only acceptable but sometimes necessary to complain vigorously to God.

Psalm 54

The Old Testament readings for this proper focus on the actions of the impious against the godly and the righteous. The psalm fits this interest and reflects the prayer of one persecuted wrongly. In the synagogue, this psalm was associated with Saul's persecution of David and was understood as the prayer the latter might have uttered while in flight (see the subscription to the psalm and 2 Sam. 23:15–19).

Most of the psalm is direct address to God and is thus prayer. Only verses 4–5a and 7 are human-to-human address. These latter verses are statements confessing confidence in God (vv. 4–5a), asserting that God will help or else asserting that God has helped (v. 7). Verse 7 may indicate that the priest officiating in worship assured the supplicant that God had heard the request, or else it may indicate that the worshiper had become so convinced that God would aid that an affirmation could be made asserting that aid had already been given.

The other components of the psalm are appeals to God for aid (vv. 1–2), a statement of the distress (v. 3), a prayer for the destruction of the enemy (v. 5b), and a vow (v. 6).

The distress is described in very general terms—"outsiders" (NRSV = "insolent") and "cruel ones" (NRSV = "the ruthless") are set on destroying the one praying. In the last line of verse 3, the opponents are described as atheists; they have no regard for God. But this may be simply an exaggerated statement meaning "I am the one who trusts in God."

The appeal for attention from God and a hearing in verses 1–2 could imply that the one praying was charged with some wrongdoing. The desire that God listen to the supplication and vindicate the intercessor point in the same direction.

The psalm expresses, as does Jeremiah 11:20, a desire that the enemy would be destroyed (v. 5b). Such a destruction is described as an act of God's faithfulness (see v. 7).

The worshiper vows to repay God's favor with a freewill sacrifice once the condition of distress has been alleviated and to offer thanks, probably in the form of a public testimony or the public recital of a thanksgiving psalm (v. 6).

James 3:13–4:3, 7–8a

Whereas Job 28:20–28 insists on the inscrutability of wisdom as an exclusive property of God, the New Testament reading from the Book of James envisions the possibility that wisdom and understanding can become visibly embodied in the conduct of the righteous. When our text asks, "Who is wise and understanding among you?" (v. 13), the question is not rhetorical. In keeping with the positive evaluation of good works made earlier (2:18), our text points to one's "good life" as the concrete manifestation of the "gentleness born of wisdom." This emphasis on public good deeds is also found in the Jewish wisdom tradition (Sir. 3:17). Elsewhere they become an occasion for acceptability among the people of God (1 Pet. 2:12).

Our text distinguishes between two types of wisdom: that which does not come down "from above" (vv. 14–16) and that which is "from above" (v. 17). The former is designated as "earthly, unspiritual, devilish" (v. 15). Here, the possibility is allowed that wisdom may be sabotaged by evil forces and desires (cf. Jude 19) and corrupted by persons whose outlook and motives are selfish. The language here—"unspiritual"—recalls that of Paul in 1 Corinthians 2:14, when he speaks of the "unspiritual" man as being unable to discern spiritual realities.

In particular, what undermines wisdom, according to today's text, are "bitter envy and selfish ambition" (vv. 14 and 16). Elsewhere, jealousy and strife are regarded as expressions of immature faith (1 Cor. 3:3; cf. 2 Cor. 12:20), works of the flesh (Gal. 5:20), and evil works to be put away (Eph. 4:31). These are also linked with arrogance: "do not be boastful and false to the truth" (v. 14). Paul is especially insistent that boasting that does not glorify the Lord is impermissible (1 Cor. 1:31; also 3:20).

It may be that these comments about wisdom and understanding should be seen in light of the opening verses of chapter 3, where the topic concerns the proper qualifications of teachers. If so, today's text is stressing the importance of proper conduct for one who aspires to teach, the "wise and understanding," and disallows those qualities that undermine effective teaching, such as boasting, selfish ambition, and being false to the truth.

Against this negative portrait can be seen the positive side: "wisdom from above" (vv. 17–18). It is said to be "pure, then peaceable, gentle, willing to yield, full of mercy and good fruits, without a trace of partiality or hypocrisy." Wisdom of this kind is seen to be a gift from God (1:5; also Prov. 2:3–6). The description of wisdom here is a veritable catalog of qualifications for the effective, and memorable, teacher. It could profitably be explored in a sermon, or any other setting, where the characteristics of the model teacher are being discussed. This portrait concludes with a reference to the "harvest of righteousness" that is "sown in peace by those who make peace" (v. 18). When wisdom comes to be embodied in those who exhibit these characteristics, then righteousness can be extended in the earth (cf. Prov. 3:9; 11:30; Amos 6:2; Gal. 5:22; Phil. 1:11; Heb. 12:11). And if the "wisdom from above" excludes boasting, jealousy, and selfish ambition, peace will be sown (Prov. 10:10; Heb. 12:14; also Matt. 5:9).

In many ways, this description of the one who embodies heavenly wisdom is summarized in Isaiah 32:8: "Those who are noble plan noble things, and by noble things they stand."

In the second part of today's text, the source of "conflicts and disputes" among believers is explored. Perhaps the relationship between this subject and the preceding verses is that strife and conflict often run rampant among those with pretensions to wisdom and understanding. Yet today's text traces these divisive impulses to our inordinate desires. Wanting something we cannot get causes us to kill. Or, coveting what belongs to someone else causes us to fight and quarrel. The source of these troubles is located in our inability to ask properly. It is not so much that we do not ask, but that our asking stems from the wrong motives.

The final two verses suggest that God's proximity to us is directly proportional to our proximity to God. God is as near to us as we are to God. Wisdom dictates that we pursue God singlemindedly and urges that a devil resisted is a devil in flight.

Mark 9:30–37

Last week we introduced Mark 8:27–10:45 as the block of material to which our Gospel lections for six Sundays belong; therefore we can proceed directly to our text, Mark 9:30–37.

Jesus and the Twelve are not only passing through Galilee (v. 30); they are "on the way" (vv. 33–34). This phrase in Mark refers to the way of Jesus, culminating in the cross, and to the path of discipleship defined by Jesus' own life of service and death. Jesus is seeking privacy because he is instructing the Twelve about his passion. Such time alone with his disciples characterizes this section of Mark, but is not confined to it (4:10; 7:17). A common description of this privacy is with the expression "when he was in the house" (v. 33; 7:17), that is, out of the public arena.

We have already noted that Mark 8:27–10:45 is dominated by three predictions of the passion. At each of these three points Mark has the same threefold cluster of material. First, Jesus predicts his suffering, rejection, death, and resurrection (8:31; 9:31; 10:33–34). Second, the disciples respond with misunderstanding, confusion, and an inability to accept his message (8:32; 9:32–34; 10:35–41). Third, Jesus gives instruction on discipleship (8:34–38; 9:35–37; 10:42–45). Our Gospel for today is the second of these clusters of prediction-response-instruction.

As to the prediction, it is worth noticing that the primary attention is given to suffering and death and not to the resurrection. This is true in all three predictions even though the wording varies. The resurrection is stated in all three, to be sure, but one has but to read the predictions to understand where the accent is placed. This emphasis upon the cross and its attending abuses and humiliation is appropriate to the entire Gospel, which moves to its climax at the crucifixion. The resurrection is reported in 16:1–8 by the empty tomb and a young man in a white robe, but there is no appearance of the risen Christ. By this attention to the cross, Mark is not only defining the nature of Jesus' messiahship but also describing the terms of following Jesus "on the way."

The response of the Twelve is stated as one of misunderstanding and fear (v. 32). But their problem is deeper, for when Jesus was teaching them about his approaching death, they were involved in a discussion on who was the greatest (vv. 33–34). Their obsession with position and power rendered them incapable of comprehending, much less of accepting, Jesus' word about himself. Understanding is a matter not only of intelligence but also of character. But we should be careful about using this and other texts to berate the disciples. A church that offers three glorious services on Easter but none on Good Friday may be in the same camp, claiming the promises of resurrection but avoiding the demands of the cross.

Notice with what deliberate intent Jesus follows the response of the Twelve with instruction on discipleship: "He sat down, called the twelve, and said to them" (v. 35). The instruction itself (v. 35) is an aphorism preserved in different forms in different contexts (Mark 10:43–44; Matt. 20:26–27; 23:11; Luke 9:48; 22:26). No teaching of Jesus more frequently or more directly addresses the love of position and prestige, which has never ceased to infect the church's leadership from then until now. As though his point were not clear enough, Jesus elaborates, adding vividness to his words by holding a child in his arms. The child is the classic image of the powerless, those without claim and without capacity to reward or repay. And yet the disciple of Jesus attends to even these, welcoming them, serving them (vv. 36–37). To serve the least is to find one's reason not in the return of such service, but in the understanding that this is the life of the kingdom, the life that God has affirmed by the resurrection of Jesus, servant of us all.

Proper 21 [26]
(Sunday between September 25 and October 1 inclusive)

Esther 7:1–6, 9–10; 9:20–22;
Psalm 124; or
Numbers 11:4–6, 10–16, 24–29;
Psalm 19:7–14;
James 5:13–20;
Mark 9:38–50

These selected verses from today's *Common Lectionary* Old Testament reading rehearse Esther's request for Haman's life, his death on the gallows he had prepared for Mordecai, and the decree establishing the feast of Purim. In Psalm 124 the Lord is praised for delivering Israel from its enemies.

Those using other lectionaries have as their Old Testament lesson passages from Numbers recalling Israel's murmuring in the wilderness, and the Lord's appointment of seventy elders to assist Moses in leading the people. As a response, verses from the latter half of Psalm 19 praise God's law as supremely illuminating.

In the Gospel reading from Mark, we hear Jesus teaching the disciples not to be too exclusive, to be attentive to weaker members of the community, and to be prepared for trials.

Pastoral concerns are prominent in the Epistle lesson, the last of the semicontinuous readings from James.

Esther 7:1–6, 9–10; 9:20–22

This is the only reading from the Book of Esther in the entire three years of the lectionary. It is a well-chosen selection, for this collection of verses brings the reader into the plot of the book as a whole, as well as an understanding of the traditional liturgical use of this book in Judaism. As indicated in the verses from chapter 9, the book purports to explain the origin of the Jewish festival of Purim (taken from *pur*, the casting of lots mentioned in 3:7–15). Thus the book has been read aloud in the synagogue at that feast since antiquity.

The verses from chapter 7 come from the climax of one of the two main lines of the story's plot and are best understood in that wider context. In this book, basically a novella or short story, the author sacrifices characterization to plot. Three main characters, Esther, Mordecai, and Haman, and two lesser ones, King Ahasuerus and Queen Vashti, populate the story. The author

420

deals only in passing with the motivations and feelings of the actors. They are almost caricatures. Haman is evil incarnate, whereas Esther and Mordecai are synonymous with beauty, wisdom, and the good. The reader is given no opportunity to sympathize with Haman and none to criticize or question Mordecai and Esther. The king is shown to be something of a buffoon, always acting on the spur of the moment, at the mercy of his emotions and whims.

Some attention is given to the description of the scenery of the actions. There are particularly detailed accounts of the pomp, circumstance, wealth, and bureaucracy of the Persian royal court. It seems that a great deal happens in the palace at the frequent banquets held by the king.

The book gives the story of an unsuccessful attempt to kill the Jews living in the Persian Empire during the reign of a certain Ahasuerus, probably meant to be Xerxes I (485–464 BC). The threat was averted by the courage and shrewdness of Esther and her cousin Mordecai, with the aid of a series of fortuitous circumstances. It is a relatively simple story of the triumph of good over evil, but the author keeps the outcome in suspense as long as possible. The tale does not unfold without irony and humor.

There are two distinct but closely related threads to the plot—the one concerning the threat to the life of Mordecai and the other the threat to the survival of the Jewish people as a whole. The first begins when Mordecai refuses to bow down before Haman (3:1–3), thus disobeying one of the laws of the king. The story does not state directly why Mordecai put his life in danger, but it implies that it is because he is a Jew. When Haman learns of Mordecai's refusal (3:4–6), he vows to kill all the Jews, thus setting into motion the other thread of the plot. Then Haman schemes to accomplish his goal, bribing the king to proclaim the destruction of the Jews (3:7–15) on a date set by the casting of lots (*pur*, hence the festival is called Purim). The first thread of the plot is brought to a climax when King Ahasuerus, finding Haman in what he takes to be a compromising position with Esther, decrees Haman's death (7:1–10). It was not just Esther's appeal to the king but a chance encounter that brought the enemy's downfall. The irony is that Haman dies on the gallows he had built for Mordecai.

But the lives of the Jews still hang in the balance, for the king's edict against them has gone out and cannot be called back. As the book stresses more than once, royal proclamations cannot be changed (1:19; 3:12–15; 8:8). But Ahasuerus can allow another edict to be circulated, this one authorizing the Jews to defend themselves. When this document is circulated (8:11–14), the main plot has reached its resolution. What follows, including the extermination of the enemies of the Jews, is the working out of the results of that climax.

The book's theme is one of the favorites of oppressed and persecuted people everywhere—that their powerful but foolish persecutors are defeated by their own hostile plans. From the perspective of the Book of Esther, good triumphs over evil as long as the good are—like Esther and Mordecai—shrewd, courageous, and fortunate. What can a tale filled with such violence teach us? On the one hand, the story gives encouragement to those who see themselves threatened by hostile oppressors; on the other hand, it teaches those who wield authority over the weak how contemptible they are in the eyes of the powerless.

Psalm 124

Psalms 120–134 are called "Songs of Ascents." Perhaps a better translation would be "Songs of Pilgrimage." This collection, or booklet, of psalms was put together to be sung by pilgrims as they made their way from various towns throughout Palestine to Jerusalem for the great festivals. According to Exodus 23:14–17, every male was required to participate in the three great festivals held every year. These festivals were the Feast of Unleavened Bread (also called Passover) in the early spring, the feast of harvest (our Pentecost) in early summer, and the feast of ingathering (also called Tabernacles) in the early fall. These were great national celebrations. The most important of these was the fall festival, which marked the end of the old year and the beginning of the new. It also celebrated the creation of the world and Yahweh's establishment and preservation of order in the universe.

The Mishnah, a collection of rabbinic materials from the days of the early church, tells us a bit about how pilgrims made their journey to Jerusalem. People from a district would assemble in the main city of the district. The pilgrims spent the night in the district capital. The night was spent sleeping outdoors to avoid any contamination that would make them unclean and thus unable to make the pilgrimage. For example, sleeping outside avoided being in a house when someone died. Everyone in the house became unclean for seven days when a death occurred.

The pilgrims left town early in the morning under the direction of a pilgrim leader. The journey to Jerusalem might take several days, depending on the distance.

Psalm 124 is a thanksgiving psalm that offers thanks for God's care during the past. Thus it is the type of psalm that would have been appropriate for the occasion when pilgrims looked back over the past year.

Probably the opening of the psalm was sung by the pilgrim leader, who then called upon all the pilgrims to join the song. This explains why verse 2a repeats verse 1a and why verse 1b says, "Let Israel now say." The remainder of the psalm may have been sung by the leader line by line and then repeated by the pilgrims.

The psalm offers thanks for having survived the past; we would say for having survived the alienation and anarchy of life. Two main images are employed to give expressions to the concepts—overwhelming waters (vv. 3–5) and bird traps (vv. 6–7). The opponents of the worshipers are simply described as "enemies" (v. 2b) and "their" (v. 6b). The actual opponents are not as significant as the sentiments expressed. The psalm allows the worshipers to express their feelings and give vent to their emotions.

The sense of alienation and being overwhelmed by life are described with strong pictures: swallowed up, anger kindled, floods sweeping, torrents overcoming, and "raging waters." Obviously, the idea is that of people struggling to retain their bearings and some stability in life. The threat is that of absolutely losing control. The minister could preach on this psalm and deal with the human effort required to stay in control of life. Much of every person's life is spent fighting anarchy. Paying bills, meeting schedules, and a whole range of activities are undertaken merely to clear a little space in which we feel at home. Sickness, and in this case, the actions of others, always are potential "waters" that threaten to engulf life.

Verses 6–7 pay tribute to God's care. Just as verses 1–5 proclaim that having God on one's side gives life some tranquillity, so God is here blessed for having offered rescue in the time of need. Again strong metaphors appear. The NJPSV translates these verses:

> Blessed is the Lord, who did not let us
>   be ripped apart by their teeth.
> We are like a bird escaped from the fowler's trap;
>   the trap broke and we escaped.

Here, as is observed so frequently in the psalms, the speakers seem to be paranoid to a certain extent. Whether or not this seems to reflect a situation bordering on the psychotic or not would depend on how one experiences and interprets life. There is a legitimate extent to which all people occasionally experience the world as a very hostile place, as if life were lived on a beachhead. At least, ancient Israel allowed its worshipers to give expression to this sense of life as enemy territory.

The psalm, or course, does not begin or end on a pessimistic note. At the beginning, one encounters the assuring word that God is on our side before meeting a description of life's problems. At the end, the psalm concludes with a strong affirmation. After all, if God who made heaven and earth is on our side, then we have hope. In the psalm, people offer thanksgiving for this bedrock of faith in the Divine.

Numbers 11:4–6, 10–16, 24–29

The lesson from Numbers is selected because of its parallel with the Gospel lection, particularly in that Moses rebukes Joshua (v. 29) for similar reasons that Jesus rebukes John (Mark 9:39–41). But this collection of verses adds up to a complex reading. In many ways, it summarizes the main themes of the traditions about Israel's wandering in the wilderness between the Exodus and the entrance into the promised land.

Two themes recur repeatedly throughout the account of the wandering in the wilderness: God's gracious care for the people and their rebellion, or murmuring, against God and Moses. Our text begins with an account of the people's murmuring, or rebellion, moves to report Moses' own complaints against Yahweh, and finally reports how the Lord cared for the people in a particular way. The larger story of this particular rebellion begins in 11:3 and concludes in 11:35. As is often the case, the complaint concerns food. The people are tired of the regular diet of manna and ask for meat (11:4); not only that, they long for the diverse and well-flavored menu they had in Egypt. In response to the complaining of the people, Moses protests to God (11:10–15), whose response in turn concerns both the problem of the people's desire for meat and Moses' grievance about the burdens of leadership. The answer to the people's complaint is the divine vow to give them so much meat that they will become sick of it. The concluding verses concerning the distribution of the spirit (vv. 24–29) is the reaction to Moses' struggle with his burdens.

The context for the account of the distribution of the spirit is the report of Moses' frustrations with the strains of dealing with this rebellious people. When Moses complains that he cannot bear the burden of this people alone, God commands him to select seventy from the twelve tribes (v. 16) who are elders and officers and bring them to the tent where God will take some of the spirit that is on Moses and put it on them so that "they shall bear the burden of the people" along with Moses (v. 17). Our text reports how these instructions and promises were carried out. In its concern for the allocation of authority and responsibility, the text is similar to Exodus 18.

There is no new appearance of the divine spirit when Moses brings the seventy to the tent, but the distribution of God's spirit that already had been given to Moses. Note also that the gift of the spirit entails both responsibility and authority. The elders are to share Moses' authority and to help him bear the burdens. The structure is hierarchical; that is, the seventy do not communicate directly with Yahweh, and their authority is derived from that of Moses. Still, the spirit is spread more widely among the people.

Already in the account of the giving of the spirit to the elders there is a hint of controversies to follow. When the spirit rested upon them, the elders prophesied, but only once. That they "did not do so again" (v. 25) indicates some uneasiness in the tradition either with the dilution of Moses' authority or with widespread prophecy.

The latter concern comes to the fore in the report of the outbreak of prophecy, not before the tent, but back in the camp by Eldad and Medad (v. 26). The flow of the narrative suggests that these two were numbered among the seventy ("registered") but stayed in the camp. Joshua, concerned about any challenge to the authority of Moses, reports this irregular behavior and asks Moses to put an end to it (v. 28). But Moses rebukes him with the famous words "Would that all the LORD's people were prophets, and that the LORD would put his spirit on them!" (v. 29).

As this part of the story began, the distribution of the spirit meant the distribution of authority and responsibility, but as it concludes, the gift of the spirit leads to prophecy. Prophecy in this case will have referred to some kind of ecstatic behavior that could have been observed by others, including Joshua. More fundamentally, prophecy meant the capacity to mediate between God and the people, to understand and interpret the will of God. But can anyone besides Moses do such a thing? In that respect, the account touches on the issue posed in Deuteronomy 18:15–22, the question of prophets whom God will raise up after the death of Moses. Certainly, the biblical tradition knows, such figures will be needed. But can they be trusted? How will one test the spirits?

The appearance of the spirit is controversial, and that is because it will not be confined to the "authorized" or the familiar structures. It is powerful and often perceived as dangerous. In Numbers 11 the controversy is related to the concern that these prophetic figures have usurped the authority of Moses. Joshua knew that the spirit of prophecy threatened established authority. Moses, on the other hand, is reported to have welcomed and encouraged such an outbreak of the spirit. So the text encourages its readers not to fear the appearance of the spirit of God.

This is one of the many Old Testament accounts of the divine spirit. It is the spirit as the breath of life that makes the human being a living being (Gen. 2:7). Frequently, the spirit of the Lord "falls upon" someone to empower them to accomplish God's will, as in the case of Saul (1 Sam. 11:6) and David (1 Sam. 16:13). The spirit empowers leaders, and it inspires prophetic activity (1 Sam. 10:10). The Hebrew term for it is *ruach*, which means both "spirit" and "wind," as well as other things. This dual meaning ties the account of the distribution of the spirit in our chapter with the story of the rebellion, for in 11:31, it is the "wind" (*ruach*) sent by God that brings flocks of quails that land outside the camp. Like the wind, the spirit of God cannot be seen, it is powerful, its effects can be perceived, and its coming and going cannot be predicted.

Psalm 19:7–14

This psalm was previously discussed as one of the readings for the Third Sunday in Lent.

James 5:13–20

Everyday needs are addressed in today's epistolary text, which envisions a community in which people suffer and pray, rejoice and sing, become sick and get well, sin and are forgiven. Such a broad spectrum of activities reflects congregational life as we know it—

people with all kinds of needs looking to the community of faith for help. And what is instructive here is that the church offers help in ways that are genuinely appropriate and effective.

For the most part, we meet here people in need, but not exclusively. For in the midst of suffering and sickness, we find cheer. Perhaps it is cheer that comes from alleviated pain or restored health, but it is cheer all the same. Or there may be the recognition that within every community tears of joy exist alongside tears of pain. On the same Sunday that we hear someone old has died, we also hear a child has been born.

In either case, our text recognizes that prayer and singing belong together, whether the circumstances are seemingly desperate, as was the case when Paul and Silas were imprisoned at midnight (Acts 16:25), or in Gethsemane (Matt. 26:30). Or the circumstances may be normal services of worship, where singing hymns exhibits its power to buoy hopes (Eph. 5:19; Col. 3:16).

Praying is seen to take many forms. As we would expect, the sick themselves pray for their own recovery, a reminder that prayers of self-interest are sometimes in order. But the sick are sometimes too sick to pray. Or even if not, they turn to the community of faith for healing, in this case, to "the elders of the church" (v. 14) or those in the church especially appointed to a ministry of healing. And those so appointed are expected to go to the sick, pray for them, anoint them with the oil of healing. In doing so, they stand in the tradition of Jesus' disciples, who went out to the sick, cast out their demons, anointed them with oil, and made them well (Mark 6:13; also, cf. 16:18); or of the good Samaritan, who reached out to the wounded traveler, bandaged his wounds, anointing them with soothing oil and wine (Luke 10:34).

Our text speaks not only of sickness, but of sin as well. Confessing our sins to one another is closely linked with praying for one another. Praying for health is mentioned alongside the assurance that sins will be forgiven. There is no explicit indication here that God sends physical sickness as punishment for sin, hence no cause-effect relationship between sin and sickness. Yet our text seems to recognize what we know all too well—that sickness and sin are sometimes related. Certainly, the psychological effects of sin are well known, and every pastor knows how closely a sense of being forgiven is related to a sense of health. And it may very well be that the reason our text so emphatically reassures us that "anyone who has committed sins will be forgiven" (v. 15) is that precisely the opposite was assumed—that some sins cannot be forgiven.

Thus, what is presented in today's text is a community of faith where the connection between sin and sickness is recognized, where prayer and confession go together with forgiveness and health. It may remind us of the debilitating effects of separating the healing profession so sharply from the counseling profession.

As if to counter the suspicion that prayer is a mind-game, our text reassures us of the effective power of prayer. As elsewhere in the New Testament (e.g., Luke 4:25), the remarkable ministry of Elijah is recalled (1 Kings 17–18). Assured that he was a "human being like us" (v. 17; cf. Acts 14:15), we are reminded of his fervent prayer that first had negative effects and finally had positive effects. The hope is that although our prayers may not be able to keep it from raining for three and a half years or, just as dramatically, to bring rains that yield rich harvests, at the very least they will be able to effect change in our own, far less dramatic situations.

The connection between healthy communities and healthy souls is once again underscored in the concluding remarks, where we are urged to retrieve those who have "wandered from the truth" and travel the highways of sin. The need to effect reconciliation within the community of faith is well known (cf. Matt. 18:15–20), as is the difficulty of doing so. Although it is not said here, as it is said elsewhere (1 Pet. 4:8; citing Prov. 10:12)—that love covers a multitude of sins—the willingness to reach out and restore meaningful relationships is nothing if not a gesture of love. Those so rescued may expect to experience the blessedness of which the psalmist speaks: "Happy are those whose transgression is forgiven, whose sin is covered" (Ps. 32:1).

Mark 9:38–50

The Gospel reading for today poses for the interpreter-preacher two immediate problems: what is the relationship of Mark 9:38–50 to the preceding material, and what gives to Mark 9:38–50 any internal unity? These cannot be regarded as questions only for the academic study of the text if the preacher is to treat these verses in sermons.

If it is any comfort, Matthew and Luke, although often following Mark as a primary source, encounter difficulties here. Matthew, for example, omits altogether the story of the strange exorcist (vv. 38–39), places Mark 9:40 in another context and in a stronger form (12:30), joins Mark 9:37 and 41 in one passage (10:40–42), and scatters in the Sermon on the Mount many of the sayings in Mark 9:42–50 (5:13; 29–30). Luke, on the other hand, preserves the story of the strange exorcist (9:49–50) without Mark's verse 41, and, like Matthew, scatters to other points the sayings on conduct (14:34–35; 17:1–2). We must conclude that the present arrangement of Mark 9:38–50 is the writer's own, gathering to this place stories and sayings for which we have no original context.

We can only conjecture, but there are clues in the text that point us toward Mark's intention in these verses. First, instruction on what it means to be a disciple was introduced earlier in verses 33–37. Verses 38–50 do not really depart from that, for they treat the questions of who really is a disciple (vv. 38–40), hospitality among disciples (v. 41), taking care not to offend new disciples (v. 42), the moral earnestness of the life of a disciple (vv. 43–49), and the call to unity among disciples (v. 50). Second, behavior "in the name" of Christ is introduced in verse 37. This is to say, living and acting in Christ's name is clearly a signal that all this material is addressed to the post-Easter church. During his ministry, Jesus did not teach his followers to wear or use his name. In fact, Jesus himself did not accept the name of Christ (v. 41) prior to his passion (14:61–62). The repetition of the phrase referring to Christ's name (vv. 37, 38, 39, 41) therefore joins this apparently divergent material as early Christian teaching on discipleship. Third, the use of a child for instruction in humble service (vv. 36–37) might have prompted the inclusion here of the unit of teaching that begins, "If any of you put a stumbling block before one of these little ones who believe in me" (v. 42). This association of "child" and "little ones" could have been made even though the addition of the modifier "who believe" indicates that "little ones" of verse 42 refers to disciples, very likely new to the community, and not to children as such. In keeping with this idea of instructing new believers is the suggestion that the sayings in verses 43–50 may have been taken from a catechism. Catchwords and phrases such as parts of the body, "it is better," salt, and fire hold these unrelated statements together. These could have served the catechumens as memory devices.

What, then, is being said in Mark 9:38–50? At least four areas of instruction are embedded here. (1) "Not being one of us" is not an adequate criterion for determining that a person is not a Christian. Granted, standards for discerning who was and who was not a disciple were a serious problem for the early church, especially in the case of itinerant exorcists (v. 38), healers, and prophets. Ethical conduct, said Matthew (7:16, 21–23); doctrinal confession, said John (1 John 4:2); confession of Jesus as Lord and service to others, said Paul

(1 Cor. 12:1–7). But not being in our circle, at least in Mark's church, was no ground for exclusion. (2) Hospitality was to be practiced freely and with minimal requirements. Even a cup of cold water given and received (v. 41) was not unnoticed or unrewarded. (3) New converts are to be accorded special care and consideration (v. 42). Causing one of them to stumble was as grave a sin for Mark as for Paul (1 Cor. 8:7–13). (4) The life of a disciple must be morally earnest inasmuch as our present behavior has eternal consequences (vv. 43–50). Nowhere in the Gospels is the language of Jesus more vivid and emphatic than in these calls to self-discipline and to arms against temptation.

Proper 22 [27]
(Sunday between October 2 and 8 inclusive)

Job 1:1; 2:1–10;
Psalm 26; or
Genesis 2:18–24;
Psalm 8;
Hebrews 1:1–4; 2:5–12;
Mark 10:2–16

As a way of introducing a four-week cycle of readings from Job that serve as the Old Testament lessons in the *Common Lectionary,* today's text consists of the brief characterization of Job in the first verse of the book and the fateful debate within the heavenly council between God and Satan that sets the story on its course. One could well imagine Psalm 26, which presents the faithful and upright worshiper of God calling for vindication, on the lips of Job.

God's creation of woman as a way of making man fully human serves as the Old Testament reading for other lectionaries today. The elevated status of human beings as God's supreme creation is celebrated in Psalm 8.

Today's epistolary reading, the first of seven semicontinuous readings from the Letter to the Hebrews, combines the majestic opening paragraph of the Book of Hebrews and the christological reflection based on Psalm 8.

In the Gospel reading, we hear Jesus affirming marriage, making explicit appeal to Genesis 2:24, and embracing children as he gives instruction about life in the kingdom.

Job 1:1; 2:1–10

This lesson begins a series of three readings from the Book of Job, taking us from the beginning of the book through Job's complaints against God (23:1–9, 16–17) to God's response to those complaints (38:1–7, 34–41).

It has become commonplace in studies of the Book of Job to distinguish between the major sections of the work in terms of prose and poetry. It begins (1:1–2:13) and ends (42:7–17) with prose narratives, while the remainder of the book is a series of poetic dialogues. So our reading for the day is part of the prose prologue.

Together, the prose prologue and epilogue tell a rather straightforward story, set long ago and far away in the land of Uz. The story first (1:1–5) introduces Job as the epitome of piety, "blameless and upright" (v. 1). Then the scene shifts to the heavenly court and a discussion between Yahweh and Satan, one of the heavenly beings. When presented with Job as a paragon of righteousness, Satan argues that of course Job fears God and is righteous, because God has blessed him in every way. Yahweh accepts this as a challenge and allows Satan to take away all that Job has—family and property—but without laying a hand on Job himself. This episode (1:6–22) ends with Job bereft and mourning, but maintaining his piety.

And there begins the body of the reading for today (2:1–10). Again, in the heavenly court, Yahweh repeats to Satan what he had said earlier about Job: "Have you considered my servant Job? There is no one like him on the earth, a blameless and upright man who fears God and turns away from evil. He still persists in his integrity, although you incited me against him, to destroy him for no reason" (2:3). Satan issues another challenge: If you "touch his bone and his flesh, . . . he will curse you to your face" (v. 5). So Yahweh allows Satan to heap sores upon Job "from the sole of his foot to the crown of his head" (v. 7). As he sits among the ashes scraping his sores, his wife ridicules him for his integrity, recommending that he "curse God, and die" (v. 9).

The concluding lines of the lesson focus the issues posed by the prologue, and the problems considered by the book as a whole. Clearly, a major—if not the central—question of the book is the suffering of the righteous. Job's wife is right: it is his very integrity that has brought these disasters upon Job, for if he had not been so righteous he would not have become the bone of contention between Yahweh and Satan. In slightly different terms, this is the problem of arbitrary human suffering. Yahweh himself rebukes Satan for inciting him to destroy Job "for no reason" (2:3). Yet another way to think of the issue is in terms of the justice of God. Why does God allow suffering—or at least the suffering of the righteous—to take place? Insofar as that is the question, the response of this part of the book is less than satisfactory. At one level, the story of Satan's challenge to God and God's acceptance is a monstrous game, a joke at the expense of Job. Yahweh seems to be defending his own honor at a high price, literally taking it out of Job's hide.

But there is another question, or set of questions, the ones explicitly posed by Yahweh and Satan in the heavenly council and the one taken up by Job in the concluding verse of our lesson (2:10): Why is Job—or anyone, for that matter—righteous? Satan asserts that one is righteous because of the rewards one receives from God. Job says, "Shall we receive the good at the hand of God, and not receive the bad?" (v. 10). If his family and fortune come from God, so does his suffering. If he affirms that it is the Lord who gives, then he will affirm that it is the Lord who takes away. Thus he accepts the order as it is. His integrity is defined by his consistency. That is a kind of answer that serves for the moment and sets the stage for the lengthy series of dialogues. It does make clear that in addition to the question of suffering and the justice of God, the book is concerned as well with the question of human integrity.

Psalm 26

This text is best understood as a composition used to claim and affirm innocence when the falsely accused was charged with some crime or breach of sacral obligation. Three elements characterize the psalm: the desire to be judged, the affirmation of innocence, and the certainty of the outcome. The psalm thus makes a good parallel to Job's insistence on living in his integrity.

The opening section appeals to God for a legal decision or personal assessment ("Vindicate me . . . Prove me . . . try me . . . test my heart and mind" [literally, "my kidneys and heart"]). Such terminology may suggest an actual religious court context, or it may be used metaphorically ("acknowledge my righteousness . . . see for yourself"), although the former seems more likely. The presence of a phrase referring to God in the third person in the context of direct address to God (v. 1c) can probably best be explained as a technical expression, "to trust in the LORD," which came more easily than "to trust in you."

The statement of innocence found in verses 4–8 refers to the types of person whom the worshiper avoids. Verses 6–7 refer to what must have been part of the ritual involved in asserting innocence, washing the hands and walking around the altar, and to the events associated with being cleared of charges—a song (psalm) of thanksgiving and public testimony.

Verse 8 affirms the worshiper's devotion to Yahweh. The rather peculiar expression "I love the house in which you dwell" (or "the dwelling-place of Your glory," NJPSV) may be a circumlocution for saying, "I love Yahweh." The psalm composers did not have the worshipers frequently refer to loving Yahweh (see Pss. 31:23; 97:10; 116:1; 145:20) but used such expressions as to love God's name (Pss. 5:11; 69:36), God's law (Pss. 119:47, 48, 97, 113, 119, 127, 159, 163), or God's salvation (Pss. 40:16; 70:5). In Deuteronomy, where "to love God" is frequently employed, the expression seems to mean, primarily, to obey God's will.

Although it probably reads into the psalm more than was originally structured into it, the person's claims in the protestation of innocence can be seen as tenfold:

1. Walking in integrity (1a)

2. Trusting in the Lord (1b)

3. Remembering divine love (3a)

4. Walking in faithfulness (3b)

5. Not sitting with the worthless (probably idolaters) (4a)

6. Not consorting with hypocrites (probably members of some secret cult) (4b)

7. Hating evildoers (5a)

8. Not associating with the wicked (5b)

9. Proper worshiping of God (6–7)

10. Loving the temple (8)

Genesis 2:18–24

Genesis 2:18–24 is a crucial part of the Yahwistic account of creation and the Fall (Gen. 2:4b–3:24). In contrast to the Priestly Writer's account of creation (Gen. 1:1–2:4a), in which the activity of God is central, this one focuses upon the human situation. The purpose of the narrative in 2:4b–24 is to account for human existence as it was intended to be. Chapter 3 then accounts for human existence as it is experienced, full of ambiguities, pains, and troubles.

The Yahwistic story of creation reports how Yahweh made the first human being from the "dust of the ground, and breathed into his nostrils the breath of life" (Gen. 2:7), and then established all the conditions necessary for fully human existence. Those factors were (1) life itself as a gift of God, (2) a supportive environment (2:8–9), (3) work as both physical labor (2:15) and intellectual endeavor (2:19–20), (4) freedom ("freely eat," 2:16) and limits ("but of the tree . . . you shall not eat," 2:17), which together leave the creature with moral decisions to make, and (5) community, if only in the presence of a single other (2:18–25). The situation described is not paradise as popularly understood, but, as the concluding verse indicates, things were right, as they should be; the first pair had no shame (2:25). The features described here are always present, however much they are obscured by evil, pain, and suffering. The final verse also prepares us for the next episode, when things change.

The story of the creation of woman is a lively and compelling one. At the end, the writer provides us with an interpretation of the events in the form of a narrative aside (v. 24). The account is not without humor. After observing that "it is not good that the man should be alone" (v. 18), Yahweh creates the animals, acknowledging that not one of them is sufficient to solve the problem. Then after creating woman, Yahweh, like the father of the bride, leads her to the man, who exclaims his pleasure in poetic lines (v. 23).

Several points in the text call for particular comment. The term translated "helper" (vv. 18, 20) by no means indicates the subordination of the woman to the man. The same Hebrew word frequently applies to God (Exod. 18:4; Ps. 121:1–2). In this context it is better translated "partner." The "deep sleep" (v. 21) is not some divine anesthesia, but is for the purpose of concealing the creative act from the man. The creation of woman is a mystery that he must not observe.

The man's poetic reaction (v. 23) includes a play on words and is a popular explanation of the fact that the terms for "woman" and "man" are similar. More important, it expresses that fundamental identification of the sexes with one another also expressed in the next verse. Both verses are responses to a deep question: How does one explain the attraction between male and female, an attraction so strong that they leave the homes of their parents to be together? Answer: They were originally one flesh. "One flesh" here does not refer to a romantic or spiritual union of the two, but is quite concrete. Two persons do indeed become one, specifically in sexual union and its results, children.

The main point of the narrative is clear and unambiguous. The union of male and female—marriage as such is not mentioned—is both good and necessary. Full humanity, by implication, is found only in community. Moreover, human sexuality is affirmed without qualification. It is neither the cause nor the result of the Fall, but part of God's good creation.

Psalm 8

This psalm was discussed previously as one of the readings for January 1.

Hebrews 1:1–4; 2:5–12

The first part of this lection serves as the epistolary reading for Christmas, Proper 3, in all three years, and the reader may want to consult our remarks in that liturgical context. But because our epistolary readings for the next several weeks are taken from Hebrews, some preliminary remarks about the epistle are in order here.

Even though the Letter to the Hebrews was for a long time associated with Paul, it is in fact anonymous. It is now generally agreed that the letter was not written by Paul. To call it a letter is something of a misnomer, for it bears little formal resemblance to other New Testament letters. It lacks a formal greeting that mentions the author and addressees. Only at the end of the letter (13:22–25) does it really resemble other New Testament letters. It is more in the nature of an essay, or treatise, although it is clearly sermonic. By its own definition, it is a "word of exhortation" (13:22).

The concern throughout the letter is to bolster the readers' faith by demonstrating the incomparable superiority of Christ. In terms of its style and literary composition, it is a finely crafted work, demonstrating an excellent command of Greek and rhetorical sensitivity.

In many ways, the preface (vv. 1–4), which serves as the first part of today's lection, sets the tone of the work with its clear christological focus. The finality and fullness of the revelation of Christ is contrasted with the partial revelation of the past. The author does not deny that God has spoken effectively in times past "to our ancestors . . . by the prophets" (cf. Hos. 12:10; Luke 1:55). But he does insist that a new stage of God's revelation has begun "in these last days" (cf. Jer. 23:20; Heb. 9:26; 1 Pet. 1:20). There is the clear conviction that a new age has dawned and that if one wants to hear God's new revelation, one must do so through Christ.

Packed into these few verses are numerous claims about Christ, and they are quite staggering. Some scholars have seen in these opening verses an early Christian hymn, and this may account for the confessional nature of these christological claims.

1. Christ is "a Son . . . appointed heir of all things" (v. 2). A few verses later, Christ is identified with the "Son" of Psalm 2:7 (v. 5), and in this capacity obviously becomes the Father's heir (Matt. 21:38).

2. Christ is God's assistant in creation (v. 2). Here the author is influenced by the Jewish wisdom tradition in which Wisdom had become personified, elevated to preexistent status, and given a role as God's agent in creation (Wisd. of Sol. 9:2). Christ is similarly depicted elsewhere in the New Testament (John 1:3; 1 Cor. 8:6; Col. 1:16–17; Rev. 3:14).

3. He is a reflection of the glory, or radiance, of God, and also the imprint of God's nature (v. 3). Here again the language is drawn from the wisdom tradition in which Wisdom is said to be "a reflection of eternal light . . . an image of [God's] goodness" (Wisd. of Sol. 7:26). The image suggested by the text is that of Christ as a ray of dazzling light from which the radiance of God emanates (cf. 2 Cor. 3:18; Rom. 8:29; Col. 1:15).

4. Christ "sustains all things by his powerful word" (v. 3). Christ has both creative and sustaining power, or in the words of Colossians 1:17, "in him all things hold together." The creative power attributed to God's word is now extended to Christ through whose "powerful word" the universe holds together (cf. Wisd. of Sol. 9:1).

5. Christ "made purification for sins" (v. 3). In these few words, the atoning work of Christ is summarized (cf. Heb. 9:14, 26; cf. Job 7:21).

6. His resurrection is seen as an exaltation to the right hand of God (v. 3). The image is more specific. Christ is said to be seated at the "right hand of the Majesty on high" (cf. Ps. 110:1; 113:5; Heb. 8:1; 10:12; 12:2; Eph. 1:20; Mark 16:19).

7. His exalted position beside God renders Christ superior to the angels (v. 4). The theme of Christ's superiority to the angels is developed further in the remainder of chapter 1. The "name" is doubtless that of "Son" (cf. v. 5; cf. Eph. 1:21; Phil. 2:9; 1 Pet. 3:22).

The second part of the lection relates to the preface thematically with its reference to Jesus, made "lower than the angels" (v. 9). This, of course, is a reference to Psalm 8:5 (cf. Heb. 2:7). But here the emphasis shifts to his incarnate status as one who received glory through his suffering and death. However, some new images are introduced: Jesus whom God made the pioneer of our salvation (cf. Heb. 12:2; Acts 3:15) through his suffering (cf. Heb. 5:8–9). Also, he is the one who sanctifies us (cf. Heb. 9:13; 13:12; also John 17:19; cf. Exod. 31:13). The image here is Jesus as the perfect sacrifice through which our purification is achieved (cf. Heb. 10:10, 14, 29, 13:12; cf. 1 Thess. 4:3).

With the wealth of christological images packed into these verses, today's epistolary lection obviously offers a cornucopia of christological possibilities. Any one of these images might be fruitfully explored homiletically. Or one might wish to address the theological question of the finality of God's revelation in Christ and the way modern Christians might appropriate this in our pluralistic world.

Mark 10:2–16

With striking and, to many preachers, welcome unity, all the lections for today focus on primary human relationships, and they do so by affirming God's purpose in creation. In fact, in the Gospel reading Jesus quotes a portion of the Old Testament lesson (Gen. 2:24).

Mark 10:2–16 belongs to the larger block of material, 8:27–10:45, which we have characterized in earlier comments. This text falls between the second and third predictions of the passion. Jesus and the Twelve are "on the way," literally and theologically, to Jerusalem. The location has changed (10:1), but the pattern in the narrative is familiar: Jesus is teaching, crowds have gathered. Pharisees raise a question touching the interpretation of Scripture; Jesus responds; and then in private ("in the house") he further instructs the Twelve. The rubrics of public and private teaching (4:1–12; 7:14–23; 9:14–29; 13:1–8) enable Mark to present the tradition from Jesus and then interpret it for his church. Mark 10:2–12 falls, then, into two parts, verses 2–9 and 10–12. To the discussion of marriage Mark joins a story about children, variations of which are found elsewhere (Mark 9:36; Matt. 19:13–15; 18:3; Luke 18:15–17).

That the question about divorce was raised not for information but to test Jesus should not lessen for the reader the importance of the inquiry or of the response. The issue is divorce, and the Pharisees quote the law (Deut. 24:1–4), which permitted a man who found something unseemly in his wife to give her a bill of divorce and send her away. Jesus shifts the issue from what the law allows, which Jesus judged to be a concession to human weakness (v. 5), to what God intends. The subject, then, is not divorce, but marriage, in support of which Jesus also quotes Scripture, from the two creation stories (Gen. 1:27; 2:24). God's act and God's intent are not negated or superseded by legal permissions.

Jesus' shift of attention to marriage and God's creation of "one flesh" leaves the disciples with the lingering question of divorce. Here Mark places a statement from the sayings of Jesus to the effect that divorce and remarriage constitute adultery (vv. 11–12). That the saying assumes that either spouse may divorce the other indicates that Jesus' teaching has already been adjusted to fit the possibilities in the Greco-Roman society of Mark's church. The Judaism of Jesus' time made no provision for a wife to divorce her husband. But Mark's church is not alone in seeking to address a problem in its membership in a way that honored Jesus' teaching that marriage, not divorce, expressed God's will. Matthew (5:32; 19:9) allowed for divorce on grounds of adultery. Paul, although adhering to the tradition from Jesus, offered the Corinthians a different interpretation for marriage in which only one partner was a Christian (1 Cor. 7:10–11). The church from that time until now has been most wise when continuing in the way of the New Testament writers, struggling with God's will in each situation rather than quoting the particular Scripture that seems to smile most favorably upon one's preference.

It may seem surprising that the same disciples who were taught about the kingdom by Jesus as he held a child before them (9:35–37) would here rebuke those bringing children to Jesus (v. 13). But these are the men who argued over greatness and who had keen appetites for power. Thinking of the kingdom in terms of place and power, they had no time for children. After all, children could not march, organize, plan, lead, or provide financial support. But that, says Jesus, is just the point. A child can receive the kingdom without offering, without claim, without calculation. Such is a clear transaction of grace. The preacher will want to avoid, therefore, the fruitless and questionable exhortations about how we should all be like children. Equally inappropriate are those pink and blue lists of children's qualities that we are to emulate. If children *qualified* for the kingdom, then what happens to grace? And if we imitate children in order to *qualify*, what happens to us? Children are brought to receive Jesus' blessing, and so are we.

Proper 23 [28]
(Sunday between October 9 and 15 inclusive)

Job 23:1–9, 16–17;
Psalm 22:1–15; or
Amos 5:6–7, 10–15;
Psalm 90:12–17;
Hebrews 4:12–16;
Mark 10:17–31

J ob's bitter complaint against an elusive, terrifying God serves as the Old Testament lesson in the *Common Lectionary* for today. Job's sense of forsakenness is echoed in the selection from Psalm 22, a desperate cry for help.

Threats against an Israel who prefers falsehood over truth and who oppresses the poor rather than caring for them are heard in the Old Testament reading from Amos. In response, this concluding section of Psalm 90 is a petition for God to show favor on Israel and reverse its fortunes.

Amos's critique of avarice becomes personalized in the Markan account of the law-abiding but ungenerous rich man, and Jesus' instructions about wealth and discipleship.

The epistolary lesson continues the readings from Hebrews, here focusing on the penetrating power of the word of God and Jesus, the sympathetic high priest.

Job 23:1–9, 16–17

B etween last week's reading from Job 2 and today's lesson a great deal has transpired. That lesson from the prose narrative of the prologue had concluded with Job refusing to relinquish his integrity and piety because he had lost family, fortune, and health: "Shall we receive the good at the hand of God, and not receive the bad?" (2:10). Following those words, the three friends gather first to mourn silently with Job and then to engage him in dialogue. For the most part, they argue that God is just and therefore Job must be suffering because of sins that he should confess. When Job needed friends, what he got was theologians. Or, in showing how the friends failed to stand with Job, the poet shows that "it is better to suffer with a friend than to defend his God" (Habel).

Our reading for today comes from Job's response to Eliphaz in the third cycle of interchanges. Job previously had responded quite directly to his friends, but here he speaks obliquely. Nor does he address God directly but rather reflects in tones similar to the soliloquy with which

435

the poetic part of the book began in chapter 3. His full address occupies two chapters. Chapter 23 is concerned with Job's desire to face God, and chapter 24 deals with the problem of justice more broadly.

But chapter 23 has already prepared the way for the more wide-ranging consideration of justice. One of the leading themes of this unit is Job's desire for a fair trial. Our lesson is full of the language of the law court. Job begins by explicitly identifying his presentation as a "complaint" (v. 2), that is, a legal case. Moreover, it is a "rebellious" one (reading with the Hebrew; see NRSV footnote). The speech includes a great deal of the technical language of the juridical process in ancient Israel. He wants to present the "arguments" of his "case" (v. 4), and he wants God to "answer" him (v. 5), that is, respond as in court. To "contend" (v. 6) and to "reason" (v. 7) describe the process of legal discourse. In short, Job's goal is to "be acquitted forever by my judge" (v. 7). Job is convinced that he has been treated unjustly, and is certain that if he were given a fair trial he could convince God. Justice here is understood both as the substance of the issue—Job's arbitrary suffering—and as due process.

The other leading theme of this reading, however, is the absence of God, the one judge who could hear the arguments and declare Job to be righteous, "upright" (v. 7). Even before Job asks for a fair hearing in court, he bemoans the fact that he does not know where to find God (v. 3), even expressing his willingness to go to God's "dwelling" (v. 3) if only he knew where it was. How can he issue a summons if he cannot find the other party to the suit? The language of verses 8–9 is particularly strong and graphic. On the one hand (v. 8), Job seems to confess his own human limitations: No matter where I go I cannot perceive him. But on the other hand (v. 9), he blames God for the difficulty: No matter where I turn I cannot see him because "he hides." This language, and the experience it expresses, echoes the individual complaint psalms in which the suffering individual feels abandoned by God.

The concluding verses of the lesson show just where the experience of the absence of God can lead. Job asserts that it is God himself who has made his "heart faint," who has "terrified" him, so he stands on the brink of despair, wishing he could simply disappear:

> If only I could vanish in darkness,
> and thick darkness would cover my face! (v. 17)

The profound despair certainly has its roots in suffering, but even more, it comes from the failure of justice and the sense of being alone. If there is no justice, then where is the meaning of life? And if God will not even listen to the complaints of one who suffers, then it might be preferable to disappear.

This text, like most of the Book of Job, provokes more questions than answers, more reflection than solutions. One of its contributions to our reflections is to enable us to understand more fully and perhaps even appreciate the experience of the absence of God. Moreover, read in its fuller context, it shows how easy answers to deep problems and experiences can be harmful. Job, to be sure, wanted answers. But more than that he wanted responses, both from God and from his friends. Even the awareness of having a hearing would bring some relief. Instead he was left to stand alone, with none to identify with and understand his suffering.

Psalm 22:1–15

This psalm was previously discussed as one of the readings for Good Friday.

Amos 5:6–7, 10–15

Amos is the earliest of the prophets whose words were saved in a book by his name. He was active not long before 745 BC, in the last peaceful era for the Northern Kingdom. It is important to remember that he was an outsider, a shepherd from Judah (1:1; 7:15) who was called to proclaim the word of Yahweh in the north. He must have been active for only a short time, for he was forced by Amaziah the priest of Bethel to leave the country (7:10–17). The original power of the words of Amos was in their oral presentation. As those oral words were collected and written down, later generations, beyond the fall of Israel in 722/21 BC and even the Babylonian Exile, knew that the words in written form could speak to their times as well.

In many respects, this selection is not typical of the speeches in the Book of Amos. Most of the prophet's addresses are indictments or announcements of punishment against the neighboring nations (1:3–2:5), Israel, a group (the wealthy women of Samaria, 4:1–3), or an individual (Amaziah the priest of Bethel, 7:16–17). A typical address is 4:1–3, which moves from a call to attention that specifies the addressees and indicts them for their sins (v. 1) to the announcement of a day when the city will be captured and the addressees carried away (vv. 2–3). Amos indicts the people for social injustice and religious arrogance, and proclaims that Yahweh has determined to bring total destruction upon the nation (9:1–4) in the form of military disaster and exile.

In the passage before us today, however, Amos holds out the possibility that the disaster may be averted. The reading contains admonitions calling for the people to change their behavior and indicates that Yahweh may yet "be gracious" (5:15). Admonitions such as this are limited to a few verses in chapter 5; in addition to our reading, they are 5:4–5 and 21–24. How do these speeches relate to the prophet's otherwise uncompromising message of doom? Was this his message when he first began, and he became more and more negative as Israel failed to respond? Or is this his last word, that there is always the possibility that Yahweh will change his plans if the people return, as in Ezekiel 18 and 33? It is impossible to know. However, one should not resolve the problem by denying that Amos originated these words, for they are otherwise consistent with his style and his indictment of Israel for social injustice.

The reading contains three distinct units, verses 6–7, 10–13, and 14–15. Verses 8–9, omitted from the lection, contain one of the three short doxologies, or hymnic fragments (the others are 4:13 and 9:5–6), that likely were added to the book as it was used in worship during the exilic or postexilic period. All three of our units are speeches of the prophet in which he does not cite the words of Yahweh directly. Amos 5:4–5 is similar to 5:6–7 except that in it Yahweh himself issues the call.

The key word in the first and third speeches is "seek" (vv. 6, 14). The word, a plural imperative, is addressed to the people as a whole, referring to a corporate rather than an individualistic action. Cultic activity seems to stand in the background. In 5:4–6, seeking Yahweh is contrasted with seeking Bethel, Gilgal, and Beer-sheba, probably meaning centers of worship. Second Chronicles 15:12, in a context that concerns foreign gods and the renewal of the covenant, notes that failure "to seek the Lord" made one liable to the death penalty. "To seek" Yahweh in some cases meant consulting a prophet or priest for the divine will. In our context, it is clear that "seeking the Lord" is not simply an internal, spiritual matter, but entails faithfulness in the stipulations of the covenant that established justice.

Amos has a great deal to teach us about justice and righteousness (vv. 7, 15), mainly through his accusations concerning injustice. Often he bemoans the absence of the simple procedural justice of the law court. Trials, both criminal and civil, were held "in the gate" (vv. 10, 12, 15) of the city. The courts are corrupt. One who presents a case ("reproves") or tells the truth (v. 10) is rejected, people take bribes, and the needy are turned away (v. 12). Distributive justice, as the equitable division of resources, has failed, and that strikes at the heart of the purpose of law in Israel, to protect the weak from the strong. The rich trample the poor and charge them too much in order to build fine houses and vineyards for themselves (v. 11). Finally, the prophet's concerns about social inequity rest on ancient Israel's understanding of the substance of justice. The people are expected to treat one another with justice because the Lord is just. Consequently, those who trample the poor are threatened with disaster. To seek the Lord and live, and to seek the good is to establish justice in society.

Psalm 90:12–17

This psalm is a communal lament in which the community offers its complaint to the Deity about the transience and the brevity, the toil and the trouble of life.

Two basic contrasts are drawn in the psalm between the Deity and humanity. The one contrast, and the most overt, is that between the eternal, everlasting nature of God and the transitory, dying character of humankind. The second contrast is that between the holy God, who reacts with anger and wrath against disobedience, and humanity, with its overt iniquity and secret sin, its unholiness and rebellion.

There is a certain undercurrent of animosity toward God in this psalm. Although it doesn't stand out starkly revealed, nonetheless it is there. The psalm writer must have felt, even if he did not say it, that there seems to be some injustice to the way things are. On the one hand, God exists forever and is in no way conditioned by the calendar or subservient to time. On the other hand, human life is so fleeting, so time-bound, so insubstantial. In spite of this disparity between the human and the Divine, the psalmist, however, is not led to despair. Instead, the writer sees the one eternal God as the dwelling place for the endless generations of human beings (v. 1) and asks for divine assistance in coming to terms with the length and shape of human existence (v. 12).

In spite of the psalmist's rather dark and pessimistic (realistic?) reading of life, the writer does not end in absolute discouragement or counsel despair or contemplate suicide or encourage hedonistic abandonment. Verse 12 is, of all things, an appeal for instruction. To be taught! As if life itself were not a lesson hard enough! The psalmist prays for wisdom so we will be able to number our days, to calculate our calendars, to live aright so that we may not die awry.

The remainder of the psalm calls on God to show favor, to be gracious, and to reverse the fate of the worshipers. The hope is that God would make the people glad for as long as they had suffered under divine wrath.

Hebrews 4:12–16

Earlier in the chapter, we are reminded that the message of God must be met with responsive hearts, and this introduces the central theme of verses 12–13: the living and active word of God. We miss the significance of these words if we equate the word of God with a book. Rather, what is in view here is the spoken word in all its dynamic force, illustrated, for example, in the creation (Gen. 1:3–31; cf. Wisd. of Sol. 9:1). The powerful force of the spoken word is rightly compared with a sharp sword, as for example, in Isaiah 49:2, when the prophet says that the Lord "made my mouth like a sharp sword." The same metaphor is used in The Wisdom of Solomon in a description of God's visitation of the Egyptians in the Exodus: "For while gentle silence enveloped all things, and night in its swift course was now half gone, thy all-powerful word leaped from heaven, from the royal throne, into the midst of the land that was doomed, a stern warrior carrying the sharp sword of thy authentic command, and stood and filled all things with death, and touched heaven while standing on the earth" (18:14–16).

It is against this background that our author speaks of the word of God as "living and active," having the capacity to penetrate the very soul and spirit of human beings. The final image is particularly graphic as it depicts every creature as naked before "the eyes of the one to whom we must render an account" (cf. 1 Enoch 9:5; Ps. 139; Rev. 1:14).

The second part of today's lection (vv. 14–16) serves as part of the traditional epistolary reading for Good Friday, which has been treated earlier. In that liturgical setting, quite obviously we tend to focus on Jesus' full identification with humanity as it is expressed in this passage. Other notes are sounded in the passage, however, and it is appropriate here to listen to them.

The passage actually unfolds in a two-part structure. It opens with a bold and dramatic statement about Christ, the exalted high priest (v. 14), but then speaks of his priestly capacity to identify with human suffering (vv. 15–16). In both instances, it is the image of Christ, the "great high priest," exalted as the Son of God, that is in view. But what is worth noting is that he sits on the heavenly "throne of grace," listening to our prayers, not as one who has known only heavenly exaltation but earthly temptation as well. Even though in his exalted state, he has no needs, in his earthly life he too had occasion to ask for "help in time of need." And this ability to listen as one who is able to identify with the petitioner's experience is the critical difference.

First, let us consider his exaltation. Jesus as the "great high priest" is a recurrent christological image developed in the Book of Hebrews (2:17; 3:1; 5:5, 10; 6:20; 7:26; 8:1; 9:11; 10:21). In the following chapter, which is treated in next week's epistolary lection, this high priest image is linked directly with the figure of Melchizedek. But here the emphasis is on the "great high priest who has passed through the heavens," indeed, who has been "exalted above the heavens" (7:26). In fact, there is no distinction here, as there is in Luke-Acts, between his resurrection and his ascension, as if there were a two-stage exaltation. It is viewed rather as a single, pioneering journey through the heavens, where he is finally "seated at the right hand of the throne of the Majesty in the heavens" (8:1; cf. Eph. 4:10). Moreover, it is "Jesus, the Son of God," who is interpreted as the object of Yahweh's words in Psalm 2:7: "You are my Son, today I have begotten you" (1:5; 5:5; also cf. 6:6; 7:3; 10:29). The perspective throughout is post-Easter. Christ's exaltation is treated as axiomatic, "Since, then, we have . . . " (v. 14). And it is this Easter conviction that becomes the basis of the exhortation "Let us hold fast to our confession" (v. 14; cf. 3:6; 10:23). The exhortation to fidelity is grounded in the Easter faith. At the heart of the confession lies the triumph of Easter.

But our text then moves from exaltation to temptation, with emphasis on Jesus as the "one who in every respect has been tested as we are" (v. 15). Most immediately, the wording here recalls the Gospel accounts of Jesus' temptation (Matt. 4:1–11 and parallels), although the experience of Gethsemane is not far away (cf. Matt. 26:41; also Luke 22:28). In trying to understand what is implied by "in every respect," we do well to use the Gospel accounts of

Jesus' temptation as the interpretive device, for there the three temptations are clearly seen as tests of his vocation. That Jesus "had to become like his brothers and sisters in every respect" is affirmed by a variety of New Testament witnesses (2:17; Rom. 8:3; Phil. 2:7; Col. 1:22). Yet, just as uniformly, the New Testament conviction is also that in spite of his full participation in humanity, he did so without sinning (7:26; John 8:46; 2 Cor. 5:21; 1 Pet. 2:22; 3:18; 1 John 3:5). Again, the clue to what this means is provided by the Gospel accounts of the temptation: he was fully faithful to his divine vocation. The passion narrative even further reinforces this as it depicts his obedience to the will of the Father (Mark 14:36 and parallels).

His full humanity, and in particular the way in which he identified with human suffering by suffering himself, enables him to be sympathetic with our weaknesses. "Because he himself was tested by what he suffered, he is able to help those who are being tested" (2:18). Consequently, just as the first part of our passage concluded with an exhortation, so does the second part. But this time, it is not an appeal to "hold fast to our confession" (v. 14). It is rather an appeal to "approach the throne of grace with boldness" (v. 16), or, in other words, an exhortation to confident confession. Elsewhere, the author stresses that such drawing near is possible with the fullest assurance of faith (10:22; cf. 10:19, 35; also 1 John 2:28; 3:21; 4:17; 5:14; Rom. 5:1–2).

What emerges, then, from today's epistolary lection is a twofold exhortation: to confess the creed and to confess our sins. We are urged that both can be done in full confidence: the first because Christ, our high priest, has been exalted; the second because he has also been tested—fully exalted, fully tested.

Mark 10:17–31

Last Sunday in the Gospel lesson, Jesus was asked a question by persons looking to the law of Moses, and Jesus set them before God. The subject was marriage and divorce. Today a man asks Jesus a question about eternal life. The man knows and has kept the law of Moses and, unsatisfied, comes to Jesus, the Good Teacher, for an answer. He, too, is set before God. Neither Moses' law nor Jesus' wisdom gives life; life is a gift of God. Between the gift of eternal life and this seeker lies a problem—wealth. As in last Sunday's text, Jesus and the Twelve are on the way to Jerusalem and the cross. Mark has already prepared us to expect in these journey narratives radical demands from Jesus and confusion from the Twelve.

Mark 10:17–31 consists of four parts joined by Mark to create not only a description of an event in Jesus' ministry but out of it a clear word to the church. The first part, verses 17–22, is a complete unit, telling the story of Jesus and a man seeking eternal life. The man is unnamed; that he was Saul of Tarsus is the creation of a novelist. In fact, our identification of him as "the rich young ruler" is possible only by borrowing "young" from Matthew's account (19:20) and "ruler" from Luke's (18:18). The man's sincerity appears in his kneeling (v. 17) and his frustration in his contradictory question "What must I *do* to *inherit*?" (v. 17). Jesus responds in a clearly discernible process. He first sets the man before God as the giver of eternal life (v. 18). Jesus wants the man to understand that what he seeks only God can give (Christians who become so Jesus-centered as to forget God should take note). Second, Jesus sets the man within his own faith tradition (v. 19). The Commandments cited are rather randomly drawn from the second half of the Decalogue and even include a new one, "Do not defraud." All of them have to do with human relationships (Matthew adds the love-of-neighbor command from Lev. 19; Matt. 19:19). Finally, Jesus leads the man to complete what is lacking: go, sell, give, come, follow (v. 21). Here Jesus is not adding anything to be done by a man who has been doing his religion since his youth. On the contrary, Jesus is calling him to cast aside all other dependencies and in radical trust stand bare before the God who gives. In other words, this is an invitation to discipleship. There is here no praise of poverty or an attack on the wealthy. The world's goods can be passed around without love or trust in God, and many plans for such have been devised. But here stands a person whose life has been defined by wealth, and sadly, he will not accept a new definition of himself—a man rich before God (v. 21). In a very rare use of the word "love" in Mark (here and 12:29–31), the writer says, "Jesus loved him" (v. 21). The man asked a big question and he got a big answer; small answers to ultimate questions are insulting. He was allowed to say no to Jesus. Where there is no room to say no, a yes is meaningless.

The second part of Mark 10:17–31 consists of verses 23–27, which contain, in addition to the portrait of the disciples as amazed at Jesus' words (v. 24), a group of sayings related to wealth. Mark has appropriately placed these sayings after the story of the rich man who sought eternal life. By the typical pattern of having Jesus elaborate to the Twelve on the teachings given others (v. 23), Mark is able to say to the church that what Jesus said back then he is still saying to us. The message is clear: riches constitute a formidable obstacle to persons who seek discipleship. But the difficulty is not an impossibility. The good news does not lie in changing "camel" to "rope" (a very similar word in Greek) or in interpreting "the needle's eye" as a small gate through which kneeling, unburdened camels could barely pass. Such interpretive efforts to make the kingdom humanly possible are out of order. "For mortals it is impossible, but not for God; for God all things are possible" (v. 27; Gen. 18:17; Job 42:2). That is the good news; and just as Jesus looked intently at the rich man (v. 21), so does he look at his church when he speaks (v. 27).

The third part of our text, verses 28–30, is a word of assurance to Peter, to the Twelve, and to the church. Those who leave everything for Jesus and the gospel (v. 29; also 8:35) will be vindicated. Even amid persecution (v. 30), they will have life now and, in the age to come, life eternal. The rich man asked about eternal life, and Jesus answered not only him but us as well.

The fourth part, a single verse (v. 31), is what is commonly called a "floating saying" of Jesus, so termed because it is found in a variety of settings and as the conclusion to a number of Jesus' teachings (Matt. 19:30; 20:16; Luke 13:30). Here it functions as a warning against calculating one's rewards in the kingdom. Having promised returns to all who sacrifice for the gospel, Jesus reminds his hearers that even so, rewards are God's to give. God determines who enters eternal life, and in what order.

Proper 24 [29]
(Sunday between October 16 and 22 inclusive)

Job 38:1–7 (34–41);
Psalm 104:1–9, 24, 35c; or
Isaiah 53:4–12;
Psalm 91:9–16;
Hebrews 5:1–10;
Mark 10:35–45

Whereas last week, in the *Common Lectionary*'s Old Testament reading, we heard Job's protest, today we hear the Lord's response—a reminder of God's unique creative capacities. So also do we hear God's creative work praised in the verses selected from Psalm 104.

Perhaps the most well-known Servant Song, Isaiah 53 supplies the Old Testament lesson for other lectionaries today. The concluding portion of Psalm 91, which serves as today's responsorial psalm, praises God as the one who protects the faithful.

Just as it was the lot of God's Servant to suffer, so are Jesus' disciples promised, in today's Gospel text from Mark, that suffering will be inevitable for them, even as it was for the Son of Man.

Jesus as a high priest in the tradition of the enigmatic Melchizedek serves as the predominant image in today's epistolary lesson from Hebrews.

Job 38:1–7 (34–41)

For a commentary on this lesson, see the discussion of Job 38 for Proper 7 [12] in this volume.

Psalm 104:1–9, 24, 35c

An ancient Egyptian pharaoh, Akhenaton (ca. 1380–1363 BC), composed or had composed a hymn to the sun god Aten, which praised Aten as the only god (other than the pharaoh, who claimed divinity). This ancient hymn has many parallels to Psalm 104. Whether the Hebrews copied this text from the Egyptians or not cannot be known. Perhaps the contemplation of aspects of creation in both cultures led to similar perspectives and parallel descriptions.

The various stanzas in the psalm, excluding the summarizing depiction and the conclusion in verses 27–35, focus on the various wonders of creation: the sky (vv. 2b–4), the earth (vv. 5–9), the water (vv. 10–13), the vegetation (vv. 14–18), the moon and sun (vv. 19–23), and the sea (vv. 24–26). (It is instructive to compare these with the structure and characterization of the six days of creation in Gen. 1.)

This Sunday's psalm reading focuses on the portion of the psalm that deals with the creation of the sky and the earth (vv. 2b–9), which parallels the reading from Job 38. The sky is spread out like a tent, and the beams upholding it are anchored in the waters beneath the earth and at its outer extremities. Underneath the sky, the clouds, wind, and lightning serve the purposes of God and manifest divine movement and activity.

The earth is pictured as emerging from the watery chaos but firmly anchored on unshakable foundations. The turbulent waters above and beneath are set within a boundary so that they cannot ultimately threaten creation except at the explicit will of God.

Isaiah 53:4–12

This reading is part of the fourth Servant Song in Second Isaiah (Isa. 52:13–53:12). The entire song is the traditional and most appropriate Old Testament reading for Good Friday. No other passage in the Hebrew Scriptures more clearly describes the messiah as a suffering servant of God, one who was obedient to death, and one whose suffering and death were vicarious. The song, more than any other in the Old Testament, enabled the earliest Christians to understand and to communicate to one another and to the world at large the meaning of the death of Jesus (see Acts 8:34; Rom. 5:25; 1 Cor. 15:4).

The structure of the poem as a whole is relatively easy to recognize if one is attentive to the shifts in the speakers. It has three parts, and in none of them does the servant himself speak: (1) at the beginning (52:13–15), God speaks to proclaim the exaltation of the servant before the astonished response of nations and kings; (2) in the central section (53:1–11a), some unidentified group speaks to report on the life and death of the servant and their response to it; and (3) finally (53:11b–12), God speaks again to confirm the meaning and effect of the servant's suffering; he will be exalted because "he bore the sin of many."

Although the poem is quite distinctive in terms of style and literary genre, it probably was written by the same prophet who wrote Isaiah 40–55, and it has some affinities with other Old Testament literature. The account of the servant's suffering is similar to the cultic tradition of individual complaints such as Psalms 22 and 35. However, in such songs it is usually the individual in trouble who gives an account of that suffering and, in the songs of thanksgiving, of deliverance. Here the suffering of a third person is described. There are words of confession by the unnamed speakers (v. 4–6), suggesting a service of penitence. Finally, the direct quotation of the words of God at the beginning and the end is like that in prophetic speeches.

It seems unlikely that the question of the identity of the servant in the poem's original historical context can be resolved decisively. Analysis of the form, however, suggests an answer to part of the eunuch's question in Acts 8:34: "About whom, may I ask you, does the prophet say this, about himself or about someone else?" He speaks about another. It is also clear from Isaiah 52:13–15 that he is speaking of the same one introduced in the first Servant Song (Isa. 42:1–4). But whereas the context of the first song takes the servant to be the people of Israel, this one clearly speaks of an individual. Commentators who interpret the servant of all the songs as Israel take the personal language of Isaiah 52:13–53:12 metaphorically to mean that Israel's suffering and humiliation through the Exile were on behalf of the world, so she shall be vindicated. Far more important, however, than the historical identity of the servant is the meaning of his life and death.

All of the major themes of the poem as a whole are expressed in the part that forms our reading. (1) The basic message is stated at the outset and reiterated in the conclusion (53:12a): God will vindicate and exalt his Suffering Servant. That point, not only in the original context but in all others, is a reversal of expectations, including those of the disciples in Mark 10:43–45. God's power and authority are manifested in weakness; God acts through one whose suffering made him repulsive to all who saw him. (2) We are asked to identify with the life of the innocent sufferer, recounted here from youth (53:2) through a trial and death (53:7–8). (3) The servant's life of suffering and humiliation is both vicarious and efficacious. It is on behalf of others, and it effectively removes their sin (53:6, 8, 12). (4) Not only will the servant be vindicated before the whole world, but also his suffering is on behalf of the transgressions of all ("the many," 53:12).

The association of this text with the New Testament readings for the day certainly will emphasize its understanding of the messiah. But the Markan and Hebrews lections also call attention to the reaction of believers to their encounter with the servant. In Isaiah 53:1–11b it is those who have seen the Suffering Servant who acknowledge and accept the fact that his suffering was for them. Mark goes further, with Jesus rebuking ambitions for glory, telling the disciples that they too must suffer like he will and that the last shall be first. Those who follow the servant of God will also become servants.

Psalm 91:9–16

In some respects, this psalm is an enigma for scholars. In what context did it originate? Who is being spoken to and about in the psalm? A breakdown of the psalm may help answer these questions. Verses 1–8 seem to be a brief sermonette addressed to a "you" but spoken in reasonably general terms. The thrust of these verses is to assure the worshiper of divine care and preservation in the face of a forthcoming situation of grave danger. In verses 9–13, the address to the worshiper becomes a little more personal, a little more directly assuring. Reading these verses, one gets the feeling of a particular "thou," an actual human person being spoken to. Verses 14–16 shift from human-human speech to divine-human speech. In God's address, in these verses, the "thou" has become a "he" or a "she"; the person earlier spoken to has become the person spoken about.

One way of interpreting this psalm is to see it as originally used in a worship service in which the king was the central figure (see Pss. 20–21). The king was perhaps facing the dangers of a forthcoming war. (If not about a king going to war, then perhaps the context was a situation in which an ordinary person was confronting a major but dangerous undertaking—a long journey, a dangerous job, military service. At any rate, the psalm was to launch one forth with confidence and chutzpah.)

The verses for this lection contain the positive words addressed to the worshiper, perhaps by the priest (vv. 9–13), but also by God, the words probably delivered as divine address by the priest (vv. 14–16). The basis of confidence is expounded in verse 9 (cf. vv. 1–2), namely, the worshiper's willingness to seek refuge with and take recourse in God. The consequences of such protection are stated negatively and then positively. Negatively, the person will not fall victim to any evil or scourge (two general terms, the first perhaps denoting evil in the sense of moral wrong and the latter signifying amoral ill fortune). Positively, the worshiper is assured that God's angels (or messengers; the Hebrew and Greek words mean both) will be guards for the person, watching over even such small matters as the foot stumbling against a stone. Playing off the imagery of the foot, the writer declares that the worshiper can tread on snakes and trample beasts underfoot.

The divine speech that finishes off the psalm uses language that is both calming and consoling. There is no longer reference to snakes, thousands dying on every hand, pestilence in the darkness, and "things that go 'bump' in the night." There is, however, the repetition of the causal relationship, as in verses 1–2 and 9: "Those who love me" (v. 14). These final verses are dominated by a focus on the Divine: in God's speech, the first person pronoun or suffix occurs twelve times in Hebrew. The divine "I" hovers over the sentiments of the psalm and is the source of the promises of protection.

Read in conjunction with Isaiah 53:4–12, the sentiments of Psalm 91:14–16 and those of Isaiah 53:13–14 overlap and interpenetrate. (The NRSV's reading of the plural "those who" rather than the masculine singular "he who" tends to mitigate the connections somewhat.) Both sections speak of life and purpose beyond danger and calamity.

Hebrews 5:1–10

In last week's lesson, we noted how the author treated Jesus, the "great high priest." Now he elaborates more fully on the Levitical priesthood.

First, he notes that the Levitical priest is "put in charge of things pertaining to God" (v. 1). He is, in other words, a mediator between humans and God, commissioned to act on behalf of his constituents. Though the term is not used here, "advocate" (*parakletos*) comes close to expressing the thought. The roles of both Jesus and the Holy Spirit come to be interpreted in this way (John 14:16; 15:26; 1 John 2:1). The work of the high priest in this respect is adequately described by Jethro, the father-in-law of Moses, when he said to Moses, "You should represent the people before God, and you should bring their cases before God" (Exod. 18:19; also cf. Exod. 4:16). Or, as the author earlier writes, the high priest acts "in the service of God, to make a sacrifice of atonement for the sins of the people" (2:17). This obviously involved the offering of "gifts and sacrifices" for sins (cf. 8:3). It is interesting to note that similar language is used by Paul in describing his own apostolic ministry, when he speaks of working "in the priestly service of the gospel of God" and calls his work among the Gentiles "work for God" (Rom. 15:16–17).

Second, our text speaks of the humanity and vulnerability of the Levitical high priest: "He himself is subject to weakness" (v. 2; 7:28). In spite of the fact that the standards for becoming a high priest were quite rigorous, he was nevertheless human, and therefore subject to sin. Accordingly, in the various descriptions of his work, it is usually stressed that he must offer sacrifices not only for the people but for his own sins as well (7:27; 9:7; Lev. 9:7; 16:6, 15–16). But our text is quite specific in noting that his task is to deal with "the ignorant and wayward" (v. 2), or more literally, "those who do not know and who wander off." The Mosaic law took a hard line on sins committed deliberately, or in the words of the Old Testament, "acting high-handedly" (cf. Num. 15:30; Deut. 17:12; Ps. 19:12–13). By contrast, those who committed "unwitting sins" were dealt with mercifully (cf. Num. 15:27–29; Lev. 4:2).

The language of today's text is closely related to that used in Jesus' parable of the sheep gone astray (Matt. 18:10–14; Luke 15:3–7). One also thinks of numerous New Testament references concerning those who act "in ignorance" (Acts 3:17; 13:27; 17:30; Luke 23:34; 1 Tim. 1:13). Because each of us, at one time or another, has behaved in a way that is "ignorant and wayward," this phrase may be a useful avenue to explore homiletically.

From the human weakness of the high priest, the author finally turns to the nature of his appointment. Even the Levitical high priest was divinely appointed (Exod. 28:1), and in this respect Christ was no different, for he was not self-appointed as a high priest, but received his appointment from God (cf. John 3:27). The author interprets Psalm 2:7, "You are my Son; today I have begotten you," as words spoken by Yahweh directly to Christ, his Son. Originally, this psalm celebrated the coronation of the king, but was appropriated by Christians early on to express their conviction that Christ, the Son of God, had been exalted to a position of divine kingship (cf. 1:5; Acts 13:33). In addition, the words of Psalm 110:4, "You are a priest forever according to the order of Melchizedek," were similarly appropriated to underscore the permanent nature of Christ's appointment to the high priesthood of God. Christ's similarity with the priesthood of Melchizedek receives full elaboration in chapter 7 (cf. also 1 Macc. 14:41).

The other part of today's lection (vv. 7–10), which stresses Jesus' full identification with human pain and suffering, is treated more fully in connection with the Fifth Sunday in Lent in Year B and Good Friday in all three years. We refer the reader to our discussion earlier in the volume.

Mark 10:35–45

The lections for today speak of the suffering of God's servant and of the meaning of that suffering for the people. Against such a backdrop, the request by James and John for positions in the kingdom is a most discordant note. But the inappropriateness of their request is no less evident when placed in the context Mark has provided.

Between last Sunday's Gospel and the reading before us is Mark's account of the third and last prediction of the passion (10:32–34). With that prediction and the story of James and John, this entire section of Mark (8:27–10:45) comes to a close. Following Jesus' first prediction (8:31), Simon Peter strongly objects and rebukes Jesus. Following the second (9:31), the Twelve engage in a discussion as to who is the greatest. And now, after the third and most detailed of the predictions, James and John ask for the favored positions in glory. With their request, the blindness, not only of the Twelve but of the inner circle (Peter, James, John) in particular, is complete. Also complete is the vast difference between Jesus and his followers on the nature of the messianic mission. In the crisis, they will abandon him (14:50). Some scholars believe Mark has taken a position over against the Twelve and the church they represent. More likely, Mark is addressing a church that, though having the advantage of hindsight, has not embraced the cross as the definition not only of the messiah but of discipleship as well.

The story of James and John is told in verses 35–40. Matthew, who follows Mark closely otherwise (20:20–28), has the request come from the mother rather than James and John. That this is editing by Matthew, perhaps protecting the two apostles, is evident in that Jesus answers not her but James and John, exactly as in Mark (Matt. 20:22; Mark 10:38). Luke, for whom the apostles are the guarantee of the church's continuity with Jesus, omits the story altogether and relocates the dispute that follows (vv. 41–45) in the upper room at the Last

Supper (22:24–27). In response to the request of James and John, Jesus promises suffering but cannot guarantee positions in glory. To describe that suffering, Jesus uses two Old Testament metaphors: the cup of wrath (Isa. 51:17; 22; Lam. 4:21) and baptism in the overwhelming flood (Ps. 42:7; 69:1–2; Isa. 43:2). Here Jesus may be drawing on current views of the messianic woes that would initiate the eschatological age.

In verses 41–44, the indignation of the ten toward James and John provides the occasion for Jesus to instruct the group on the matter of service in the kingdom. In these sayings, Jesus separates true greatness from the exercise of authority over others and reverses the usual categories of service and greatness. That all four Gospels repeatedly record this instruction (Matt. 20:24–27; 23:11; Mark 9:35; Luke 9:48; 22:24–27; John 12:24–26; 13:12–16; 15:20) is not only an argument that these sayings represent an authentic tradition from Jesus, but it also testifies to the widespread and persistent condition of a church that remained enamored of power and position. And Jesus' words continue to be difficult to hear and to obey.

Verse 45 closes not only this lection but also this entire section of Mark. It is appropriate to the immediate context in that it presents Jesus as the Son of Man whose entire mission is to serve, not to be served. However, this verse transcends the context in that Jesus' giving of himself has salvific value, unlike the serving and dying of his disciples. The death of Jesus, says Mark, is a ransom; that is, his death sets free captives and hostages. The statement launches, but does not contain within itself, elaborate theories of atonement. Almost as significant as the content of verse 45 is its location in the Gospel. Predictions of the passion are past; instructions about discipleship are past. With Jerusalem and Golgotha now within view, past teaching and impending fate are joined in one statement about Jesus' entire purpose: to serve, to die, to set free.

Proper 25 [30]
(Sunday between October 23 and 29 inclusive)

Job 42:1–6, 10–17;
Psalm 34:1–8 (19–22); or
Jeremiah 31:7–9;
Psalm 126;
Hebrews 7:23–28;
Mark 10:46–52

Job's candid, but penitent, reply to the Lord, his last in the Book of Job, and the conclusion of the book depicting Job's restoration comprise the Old Testament reading for today in the *Common Lectionary*. Faith in a God who answers the prayers of the needy and rescues them from affliction is expressed in verses from Psalm 34 that serve as the responsorial psalm.

Those using other lectionaries have as an Old Testament lection Jeremiah's announcement that Israel would receive salvation by being returned from exile. Psalm 126, with its prayers for restoration and cries of celebration, directly continues and responds to both the content and mood of the Jeremiah passage.

Salvation comes to Bartimaeus in the Gospel text from Mark, as the blind beggar exhibits faith sufficient to regain his sight.

In the epistolary reading, Jesus' high priesthood is compared with the Levitical priesthood and is found to be unique.

Job 42:1–6, 10–17

These verses from Job 42 confront us in a direct way with the complicated problem of the meaning of the book as a whole. Do we now have, after all the dialogues and speeches, the poet's final word on the issue of the suffering of the righteous? These verses include the last of the poetic lines. They have the ring of finality, and it is a good literary principle that "the last shall be first"; that is, the most important point is the last one.

The tone and content of Job's final speech are quite different from his others, and the issue of the differences cannot be resolved by treating this passage as a secondary addition. It is essential to the book. The problem is that Job seems to acknowledge that he was wrong; he even "repents" of what he said. Does that mean we can now forget everything that has transpired earlier? By no means.

The book resists simple formulations of its meaning. Does one find the poet's perspective expressed in Job's speeches (and if so, which ones?), in the Yahweh speeches, or in the words of the friends? All are presented with equal poetic power, and there is something to be said even for the insensitive advice of the friends, who in the face of real pain offer conventional theology.

Throughout the book, Job insists upon his innocence, questions the conventional answers, and angrily demands that God vindicate him and give him some answers. In the end, when God does grant him his wish for a direct encounter, Job's charges are not addressed directly. Yahweh does not vindicate Job, and he raises even more questions, demonstrating that knowledge of the order of the cosmos is beyond human ken or control.

Then Job in genuine humility acknowledges his finitude and the limits of his wisdom. What has brought about the change? Above all, it is the fact that he has experienced the divine revelation, God in the whirlwind. Given the turmoil of the book, that imagery makes good sense. Job now stands in awe before God. Does the encounter with God convince him that there is order and meaning, and purpose, even if he cannot fully comprehend them?

Job's repentance (v. 6) does not mean that he regrets what he said. It indicates that his perspective is now changed, moved in another direction. What he confesses as wrong is his attempt to know what only God can know. Moreover, in verse 7, the poet has God approve of what Job said all along, in contrast to what the friends had said. Job told the truth, he was innocent, and even his angry insistence on a hearing was "right."

Job's final speech is an affirmation of trust in the power and wisdom of God and a recognition of human limitations. Set into the context of the book, three further observations are called for: (1) if one comes to such a point of faith, it is through the struggle, including the struggle with God; (2) Job was right to be angry, to quarrel with God, and to challenge the conventional theological formulations; the God of Job expects honest prayers and is not destroyed by our questions or our anger; and (3) these final words of Job may in the last analysis be all we can say in the face of innocent suffering, to stand in humble acknowledgment that God can do all things and that we can never fully comprehend God's purposes. Still, such words might very well be wrong as one's immediate response to persons in suffering—righteous or otherwise. To do so could place one in the posture of Job's friends, who offered theology when friendship was called for.

Psalm 34:1–8 (19–22)

This psalm has been previously discussed as one of the readings of Propers 14 [19], 15 [20], and 16 [21].

Jeremiah 31:7–9

Even the *Revised Common Lectionary*, with its expanded list of Old Testament readings, includes surprisingly few readings from the Book of Jeremiah in contrast, for example, with the Book of Isaiah. And the reading for this day is very similar in style and content to the material in Second Isaiah (chaps. 40–55). There is not sufficient evidence to determine authorship, but it probably came, like Isaiah 40–55, from the time of the Babylonian

Exile (597–538 BC). The prophet Jeremiah was active from about 627 BC until at least 586 BC, the decades immediately preceding the first and second Babylonian invasions.

Jeremiah 31:7–9 is a part of what has been called "the book of consolation" (Jer. 30–31), a collection consisting mainly of announcements of salvation. Within that collection it stands as a distinct and independent unit of tradition. Certainly, there are similarities of theme with what precedes and follows, but the opening formula in verse 7 signals a new unit, as does the summons to hear in verse 10.

As the messenger formula that begins it shows, the unit is a prophetic speech, one in which the prophet conveys not his own words but those of the Lord. The speech itself is a prophecy of salvation with three distinct parts. (1) In verse 7—except for the introductory formula—Yahweh gives instructions to an unidentified addressee. That the imperatives are in the plural indicates that he addresses the people as a whole. The Lord calls for them to shout for joy and then tells them what to say: "Save, O LORD, your people, the remnant of Israel" (cf. Isa. 40). (2) Yahweh then announces what he will do for the people, those now scattered from the land (vv. 8–9b). He will bring them back, including the blind, lame, and pregnant women, even those in labor who have difficulty traveling. The road back will be smooth, and water will be easy to find. (3) Finally, Yahweh gives his reason for what he plans to do and the reason why he can be trusted to do it—"for I have become a father to Israel, and Ephraim is my firstborn" (v. 9).

The prophetic books, especially the earlier ones, are filled with prophetic announcements, usually of punishment. Such speeches generally have Yahweh speak to indict Israel for her sins, and the indictment functions to give the reasons for the punishment that is on the horizon. Prophecies of salvation often give no reason at all for the Lord's graceful action. If they do, it is in terms similar to the ones used here. The "reason" lies in God's free decision, out of love for the people. The metaphor of Yahweh as parent and Israel as a child is not uncommon (see Isa. 1:2–3; Hos. 11:1–9).

The speech is unqualified good news. Several features remind us, however, of the dark backdrop of the proclamation, that these are words of hope to the hopeless. The "remnant of Israel" (v. 7) are those left after the disaster, the ones who have been through the fire. The words are for those presently scattered to the "land of the north," even "the farthest parts of the earth" (v. 8). The latter expression may be poetic hyperbole, or it may reflect the awareness that the people are dispersed from Babylonia to Egypt. Moreover, the glorious description of the road home (v. 9) reminds us that it was anything but smooth and easy.

The vision of the future is based on that worldly spirituality of the Old Testament. The Lord is a saving God whose gifts include a place to live, and whose people—"a great company" (v. 8)—include the blind, the lame, the pregnant women, and the women in labor.

Psalm 126

This psalm has been selected as a companion reading to Jeremiah 31:7–9 because of the assumed connection of the psalm with the return from exile that is predicted in the prophetic text. The association of the psalm with the Exile appears to be a secondary development, however. The psalm was probably originally written for use in the fall festival, which fell just before the autumn rains and the fall planting. The theme of the psalm—the reversal of fortune—fits nicely, however, with the Jeremiah text. For a full discussion of this psalm, see the lections for the Third Sunday of Advent.

Hebrews 7:23–28

These verses conclude the discussion of the priesthood of Melchizedek, a theme introduced earlier (5:6, 10) and developed more fully in the first part of chapter 7. As far as
our author is concerned, the only real analogy for Jesus' priesthood supplied by the Old
Testament is that provided by Melchizedek, the mysterious king of Salem and "priest of
the Most High God" (7:1; Gen. 14:17–20). That he had "neither beginning of days nor end
of life" (v. 3) supplied the point of contact with Christ, the Son of God, who had become a
"priest forever" (v. 3).

The fact that Jesus was not of Levitical descent (v. 14) was of no consequence. Neither
was Melchizedek a Levitical priest; yet according to Scripture, Abraham clearly acknowledged
the superiority of Melchizedek's priestly status by paying tithes to him (v. 4). This clearly
shows that genealogical descent has nothing to do with establishing the relative value of one's
priesthood. Thus Jesus has become a priest "not through a legal requirement concerning physical descent, but through the power of an indestructible life" (v. 16). Convinced that Christ,
through his resurrection, now lives forever, the author sees no one else to whom the words of
Psalm 110:4 can be applied, "You are a priest forever, according to the order of Melchizedek"
(v. 17). But the author also saw the two preceding lines of the psalm as especially significant:
"The Lord has sworn and will not change his mind" (v. 21). For him, this constituted a divine
oath. It meant not only that Christ was a high priest forever, but that his status had been
confirmed by an oath from God.

Jesus, then, was "the guarantee of a better covenant" (v. 22). The superiority of the "new
covenant" is a major theme of the Book of Hebrews (8:6–10; 9–15–20; 12:24; cf. Luke 22:20;
2 Cor. 3:7–18). But, in precisely what respects is it better? Today's epistolary lection supplies
the answer.

First, Christ's priesthood is permanent (vv. 23–25). The Levitical priesthood could only
survive through a succession of high priests. Because the priests were mortal, replacements
had to be found when they died. There could be continuity of office, but no continuity of
person. With this setup, the Levitical priesthood was subject to all the vagaries of human institutions that are passed on from one person to another. As we all know, with each new president, boss, CEO, or dean, we have to begin negotiations all over again. Policies change with
the person.

By contrast, the priesthood of the new covenant has only one occupant, Jesus, who
"continues forever" (v. 24; 5:6). To deal with one high priest, as opposed to a succession of
them, offers distinct advantages, not the least of which is permanent availability: "He is able
for all time to save those who approach God through him" (v. 25). He is always on call: "He
always lives to make intercession for them" (v. 25; cf. 9:24; Rom. 8:34). Not only does he hold
office permanently, but he remains unvarying: "Jesus Christ is the same yesterday and today
and forever" (13:8).

Second, the moral character of Christ far exceeds that of any given Levitical high priest.
Earlier in the letter, in noting the humanity of Christ, the author stressed his identification
with human weakness. Here, however, there is a vast chasm between Christ the high priest
and the Levitical priests. Among other things, Christ is "holy, blameless, undefiled, separated
from sinners, and exalted above the heavens" (v. 26). By contrast, Levitical priests are men
"subject to weakness" (v. 28). The contrast is clear and the difference broad: Christ is everything they are not.

The imperfection of the Levitical priests is shown by the fact that they must offer sacrifices for their own sins, according to the Mosaic law (5:3; 9:7; Lev. 16:6, 11, 15). The sacrifices they offer are "continual" (Exod. 29:38–46; Num. 28:3–31), and this in itself attests their relative ineffectiveness. Were they of permanent value, they would only need to be offered "once for all," as was the case with Christ's sacrifice. In his case, once was enough, and this stress on the absolute finality of the sacrificial death of Christ further extends the remarks made in the preface to the letter (1:1–4; 9:12, 26–28; 10:10; also Rom 6:10; 1 Pet. 3:18).

Third, Christ's status as high priest was sealed with a divine oath. As noted above, the crucial Old Testament phrase has already been introduced from Psalm 110:4 (v. 21). And the obvious point has been drawn: Levitical priests were installed without an oath. By contrast, Christ's appointment as high priest was secured by God's own vow, one that superseded the law (v. 28).

Quite clearly, the outlook throughout this passage is confessional. The author's exegesis of the Old Testament, his interpretation and appropriation of the Melchizedek story, and his assessment of the many shortcomings of the Levitical priesthood all hold only because of his unwavering faith in the "indestructible life" of Christ (v. 16). But, given this as a hermeneutical principle, the priesthood of Christ is seen to be a "better covenant" (v. 22). Numerous themes suggest themselves for homiletical appropriation, not the least of which is the permanence of Christ's high priesthood. This becomes all the more attractive in view of the way in which we moderns know and experience change.

Mark 10:46–52

Mark 10:46–52 joins Jeremiah 31:7–9 and Psalm 126 in the mood of joy as the blind, lame, and sorrowing shout and sing their way up to Zion. By placing the story of the healing of blind Bartimaeus immediately prior to Jesus' entry into Jerusalem, Mark has made this healing a prelude to that festive occasion and in a sense has put Bartimaeus in that parade. However, to find the meaning of this story one must, as with other Markan texts, look in two directions: within the account itself and in the location of the narrative in the Gospel as a whole.

Internally, Mark 10:46–52 is a healing story, bearing some traits common to other such stories in the Gospel, but with other familiar characteristics missing. It is an "on the way" story with the usual cast of characters: Jesus, the Twelve, a huge crowd, and a person in need. In this case, the one in need is named, perhaps an indication that Bartimaeus was known to the Markan church. Bartimaeus is the very image of one without anything to offer, anything to claim; he is a blind beggar. In his call for help, Bartimaeus addressed Jesus as "Son of David" (v. 47). By including a messianic title that he dislikes, is Mark simply passing along an unedited tradition, or is he implying that such a title for Jesus is something a blind man would say? In Jerusalem, the crowds will shout, "Blessed is the coming kingdom of our ancestor David" (11:10). It is difficult to know what either Bartimaeus or Mark intended here. The attempt to silence Bartimaeus recalls the response of the disciples to the approach of the woman with the blood flow (5:30–32) and to those who brought children to Jesus (10:13–16). But persistence wins (7:25–29), the blind man makes his plea to Jesus, and Jesus pronounces him healed by faith. Although released to go his own way, the healed Bartimaeus chooses to follow Jesus "on the way" (v. 52). Noticeably absent are the attempts to find privacy for the healing and the charge to silence. Apparently, the last healing story in Mark belongs not with the itinerant ministry marked by Jesus' repeated demands for silence, but with the Jerusalem ministry in which Jesus even acknowledged to the Jewish court that he was the Christ (14:61–62). Events in Jerusalem will reveal the meaning of Galilee's secret.

Perhaps Mark's location of this healing story just prior to the entry into Jerusalem helps the reader understand why it differs so noticeably from the account of healing a blind man in 8:22–26. We noted in an earlier lesson that the block of material, 8:27–10:45, is governed internally by three predictions of the passion and is bracketed on either side by stories of Jesus healing the blind (8:22–26; 10:46–52). The earlier healing is performed with great difficulty, in private, followed by Jesus' charge that the one healed not return to tell what happened. In the stories that follow, the disciples are given inside information about Jesus' fate but repeatedly show themselves to be blind. With that instruction of the Twelve now concluded, Mark tells of the healing of another blind man, but this time the healing is without difficulty, without privacy, and without a charge to secrecy. In fact, the blind man who now sees becomes a disciple.

Whatever a preacher may make of Mark's dramatic arrangement of his narrative, one thing is clear: there is no room here for any sense of superiority over the characters in the text. The crowd tried to silence a blind beggar whose cries for help were an annoyance to their triumphant parade with Jesus. But who among us has not done the same? And the Twelve, insiders all the way and privy to Jesus' painful disclosures about his approaching passion, heard all and heard nothing, saw all and still were blind. Both pulpit and pew still ask, "Lord, is it I?" In John 9 there is a story of Jesus healing a blind man. It is not at all parallel to Mark in content or in style, but it concludes with a comment that is fitting here: the blind see, the seeing are blind.

Proper 26 [31]
(Sunday between October 30 and November 5 inclusive)

Ruth 1:1–18;
Psalm 146; or
Deuteronomy 6:1–9;
Psalm 119:1–8;
Hebrews 9:11–14;
Mark 12:28–34

The introduction to the Book of Ruth, culminating in Ruth's speech expressing her resolute commitment to remain with Naomi, serves as the Old Testament reading for the *Common Lectionary*. In Psalm 146, the Lord is praised as both creator and sustainer. A thematic connection with the reading from Ruth is the assurance that God watches over strangers and cares for widows and orphans.

In the Old Testament reading from Deuteronomy 6, Israel is urged to observe the statutes and commandments. These include the Shema, which enjoins Israel to love God exclusively and absolutely. The law is held in equally high esteem in the opening verses of Psalm 119, the lengthy psalm of meditation on Torah.

For the Gospel text, Mark's version of Jesus' teaching about the Great Commandment, we hear Jesus quoting the Shema and insisting that obedience is more important than sacrifice.

The epistolary selection from Hebrews continues the christological mediation on Jesus as high priest, insisting on the effectual power of Christ's sacrifice to purify our conscience.

Ruth 1:1–18

The preacher who chooses to proclaim the texts from Ruth in Christian worship would do well to follow Jewish practice and read the book in its entirety, at least in preparation for preaching. Although the individual scenes often are compelling and some individual lines are powerful, the book is a total composition that is meant to be read or heard in its entirety. The messages of the story are carried by the plot as a whole.

The Book of Ruth is a carefully crafted literary creation, the work of a skillful and sensitive author. It is best identified as a historical novella or short story. Its setting, circumstances, characters, and plot are entirely plausible, and its author captures and holds the readers' attention by creating and eventually resolving tension at several levels. It shares features in common with several other Old Testament stories, including the Books of Esther, Judith, Tobit, Jonah, and the story of Joseph in Genesis 37–50. Although there are differences—for example, some of the others contain legendary features not found in Ruth—all these are deeply interested in the development of the human characters, and they intend to be both entertaining and edifying.

There is considerable disagreement among students of the book concerning its date of composition. Because of the similarity of perspective to that of some early works, such as the Yahwistic Document of the Pentateuch and the court history of David (2 Sam. 9–20; 1 Kings 1–2), some scholars date it as early as the tenth century BC. Because of its similarity to later literature such as Esther and Tobit, as well as the fact that its heroine is a foreigner, others have seen it as a postexilic document written in opposition to Ezra and Nehemiah's prohibitions against keeping foreign wives (Ezra 10:1–5; Neh. 13:23–27). Whether it arose in such circumstances or not, the book certainly could have been used to advocate the same kind of appreciation of foreigners that the Book of Jonah commends as well. It would be helpful to know when and where the book was written, but that is not possible. Finally, however, the important world is the one the story itself assumes and creates.

At every turn, the book is the story of women making their way in a man's world—the patriarchal society as known in general throughout all of ancient Israel's history, and in particular as it was in the time before the monarchy. Thus, to say that it is a story of women is to say that it is about the socially and economically weak, if not oppressed. Its characters are ordinary people, some of whom have extraordinary qualities, such as wisdom, loyalty, devotion, and courage. Its main characters are scrupulous about following the law, due process, and custom, but there are those who go beyond duty. In the end, it is a tale of the triumph of justice against strong odds. It turns out to have a happy ending, but the grace in the end is not cheap, nor won without great risk.

Our reading for today contains most of the first episode of the story, which runs through the end of chapter 1. The two distinct parts are verses 1–5 and 6–19a. By giving the time, place, circumstances, and main characters, verses 1–5 provide the setting of the actual story that will unfold. In a time of famine in Judah, Elimelech, his wife Naomi, and their two sons left Bethlehem for Moab. Elimelech died, his two sons married Moabite wives, Orpah and Ruth, and ten years later both of these sons died. By the end of the introduction, which is the point of the real story's beginning, three widows stand before us. What took years to develop is told quickly, leading to a dangerous predicament. The narrator considers it unnecessary to tell the reader that widows in that world have no means of support. How they will survive is the question that leads the story on.

If the introduction compresses time, the next scene (vv. 6–18) is occupied with a single moment in time, a conversation between Naomi and her two daughters-in-law as they set out to return to Judah. Naomi urges the others to return to their maternal homes with her blessing and prayer that they find husbands, but they both refuse to separate from her (vv. 8–9). Naomi urges them a second time, pointing out that they have no hope for husbands through her, for she has no other sons to give and no prospects for marriage at her age (vv. 11–13). This time Orpha bids Naomi farewell, "but Ruth clung to her" (v. 14). Once again Naomi insists that Ruth return to her own people, and Ruth, going beyond what law and custom require, declines in terms that Naomi cannot refuse.

Ruth's speech to her mother-in-law contains some of the best-known lines of the Bible, often applied to romantic circumstances:

> "Where you go, I will go;
>   Where you lodge, I will lodge;
> your people shall be my people,
>   and your God my God." (v. 16)

The young woman has thrown her lot in with the older one in total solidarity, even beyond death (v. 17). She has chosen separation from homeland and family and risked her life and future. Why does Ruth put herself in such jeopardy? The narrator gives no direct answer but shows us the feelings and motives of the characters only by their words and actions. By the time the story is ended, we will know that Ruth is a woman of courage, wisdom, and compassion. Now we know only that she has chosen to go with Naomi, who otherwise would be alone. Thus she becomes for us a model of one who goes beyond what law and custom require to stand with the one in need.

Where is the hand of God in these affairs? The narrator gives no direct answer, allowing the tragedies of the famine and the deaths of the three men to transpire without explanation. However, Naomi has her view, expressed in the language of complaint: "It has been far more bitter for me than for you, because the hand of the LORD has turned against me" (v. 13; cf. also 1:21). Whether the author shares Naomi's interpretation or not, he or she—it is quite possible that the book arose among women storytellers—knows that Naomi has every right to complain and that such complaints are not inconsistent with faith in God.

Psalm 146

This psalm has been previously discussed as one of the readings for Proper 18 [23].

Deuteronomy 6:1–9

Virtually the entire Book of Deuteronomy is presented as the farewell speech of Moses to the assembled people of God. (The exceptions are narrative introductions or transitions such as 1:1–4; 4:41–43; 10:6–9, and the account of Moses' final deeds and his death in chap. 31.) Although there are differences in style and form in various parts of the book that indicate a long history of growth and composition, almost everything is second person address and hortatory or homiletical in style. The law and the saving history are interpreted, explained, and laid on the heart of the addressees.

Deuteronomy 6:1–9 consists of two distinct parts, verses 1–3 and 4–9. Read together, the first paragraph will serve as the introduction to the second; but in the composition of the book, 6:1–3 actually concludes one section concerned with the law, and 6:4 begins a new one.

Verses 1–3 are in that repetitious, hortatory language common to the book. The preacher seeks every possible way to urge the law upon the hearers and to persuade them to obey. He holds out the promises of possession of the good land, long life, and well-being to faithful Israel. Elsewhere, threats will also be used, but here the view that rewards follow faithfulness is presented warmly: be obedient so that Yahweh can do what he desires to do, fulfill his promises.

The crux of the reading, and of the book as a whole, is verses 4–9. The passage is known in Judaism by its first word, "Hear" (in Hebrew, *shema'*). In Judaism, the term describes a distinct section for liturgical and devotional use, variously including only verse 4, verses 4–5, or verses 4–9. Its beginning imperative, "Hear," is more than a call to attention; it is a summons to listen actively and respond. We may take that summons as a directive to consider seriously the meaning of the words in their original context, without rejecting the rich history of liturgical use and theological reflection in synagogue and church.

What follows the initial imperative in verse 4 is a statement in the indicative. The Hebrew of the statement can be legitimately translated in various ways, as comparison of translations or even a look at the NRSV footnotes will reveal. When Hebrew philology, grammar, and syntax leave several possibilities, the context must be decisive, and in this case the context is the book as a whole and the covenantal traditions here reflected. On those grounds, the NRSV alternative is the most appropriate: "The LORD is our God, the LORD alone." Neither monotheism nor the unity of God is the meaning, but undivided allegiance to Yahweh. The covenant and the Decalogue stand behind this verse, and undivided devotion is the point of the First Commandment (Deut. 5:7; Exod. 20:3). Moreover, the problem that Deuteronomy repeatedly, almost constantly, addresses is not the more-or-less abstract one of monotheism, but the danger of worshiping false gods, the possibility of corrupting the faith with Canaanite beliefs and practices. The fact that Israel's God is a single one, Yahweh, is the foundation not only for the Decalogue but also for all of life.

Verse 5 is in the imperative form of a command. In substance, it is the positive form of the First Commandment, "You shall have no other gods before me" (Deut. 5:7; Exod. 20:3), but the injunction to "love the LORD your God" makes it distinctive. In the context of the covenant and the law, "love" is not simply a feeling but a total response of devotion and obedience, with the emphasis on its permanence. "Heart," "soul," and "might" stress that love is to entail all of one's faculties and abilities. The foundation of this command is Yahweh's love for his people: "The LORD set his heart in love on your fathers alone and chose you, their descendants after them, out of all the peoples, as it is today" (Deut. 10:15; see also 4:37; 6:7; 7:7; and elsewhere).

In view of the Great Commandment's addition, with Jewish tradition, of the command to love one's neighbor, we should point out that such concern is by no means lacking in Deuteronomy. The love of God, through obedience to the law, expresses itself in love and concern for others, including slaves, the poor, foreigners, the widow, and the orphan (see Deut. 10:18; 15:7–18; 16:11; 24:17–18).

The remainder of the reading (vv. 6–9) urges obedience and provides guidance for the way it is to be done. Take the words to heart, teach them to your children, speak of them at all times in your everyday conversation. Love of God must become a habit of heart and mind. The injunction to talk of the law "when you lie down and when you rise" (v. 7) led to the twice-daily recital of the *Shema* in Judaism, and the binding of the words as a sign led to the practice of wearing phylacteries, copies of the Shema worn in small leather containers. The fundamental concern of these verses is that the tradition remains vital and is passed on through the generations, lest it be forgotten (Deut. 6:12).

The two points here that cry out for proclamation and interpretation in the context of worship are singleness of devotion to God and the love of God. Concerning the first, it is easy to name false gods, but we must struggle with the complexity of the matter in our own time. At one level, it was simple for the preachers of Deuteronomy as for the prophets and even the priests: worship only the Lord, not the Canaanite deities. But it was also complicated for them: to what extent can we follow the customs of the culture and still be faithful? The authors of Deuteronomy took a radical course, setting out to destroy all vestiges of foreign religion and centralize worship in Jerusalem. They did not do that, however, without constant attention to the concern that faith in the God who had brought them out of slavery in Egypt must be acted out day to day in society.

The command to love God is even more difficult. How can one command such a thing? Love cannot be coerced. Two mutually supportive directions are suggested by Deuteronomy 6:1–9. (1) How does anyone learn to love? Only by being loved can one respond in kind. That is why Deuteronomy will constantly remind the congregations of Israel—and ours as well—that obedience in love is the response to being chosen and loved by God. (2) One's actions, emotions, and even passions are affected by training, habit, practice, and education. We are shaped by what we hear, read, discuss, and do. That is why Deuteronomy insists that the command and its foundation be taught, discussed, and kept constantly before one's eyes.

Psalm 119:1–8

The 176 verses of this psalm divide into twenty-two stanzas of eight lines each. In each individual stanza, all eight lines begin with the same Hebrew letter, working through the alphabet in order. In each of the stanzas there is a play on a series of synonyms for the law or the will of the Deity. Generally, there are eight such synonyms per stanza, and generally the same eight are used throughout the entire psalm. In verses 1–8, the eight terms referring to the Torah are "law," "decrees," "ways," "precepts," "statutes," "commandments," "ordinances," and "statutes" (repeated).

Verses 1–8 reflect a rather interesting pattern insofar as speaker-audience is concerned. Verses 1–3 contain two benedictions pronouncing blessedness upon the obedient. The benedictions are thus composed to be addressed to a general human audience. Verses 4–8 are a prayer addressed directly to the Deity. The prayer, running throughout the remainder of the psalm, is thus the response to the benedictions.

In the prayer of verses 1–8, the worshiper asks to be obedient and observant of God's Torah. Running through these verses are both negative and positive strands. The positive aspects are reflected in references such as "be steadfast," "keep," "eyes fixed," "praise," "learn," and "observe." The negative aspect—that is, the inability to keep the law and obey the commandments—is also present. The worshiper prays "not to be put to shame" and that God "not utterly forsake me." On the human level, the fear is that of failure; on the divine-human level, it is the fear of being forsaken by the Divine.

Shame, which is noted frequently in the Bible, is a common human emotion. It is often, as here, associated with the failure to measure up, the failure to be what one aspires to be, the failure to achieve one's goal. Shame is, however, an emotion that does not necessarily arise from public awareness or disclosure. One doesn't have to be found out in order to suffer shame. The ancient rabbis noted that it is the heart that puts a person to shame because the heart knows what it has done and is ashamed of itself.

Hebrews 9:11–14

This passage from Hebrews serves as the epistolary reading for Monday in Holy Week in all three years. The reader is referred to our discussion of this text earlier in this volume, as well as in the other volumes treating that liturgical setting.

Mark 12:28–34

The lections for today join in permitting, or rather urging, continuity between Christianity and Judaism by focusing on the heart of both: love of God and love of neighbor. As Paul expressed it, the commandments "are summed up in this word, 'Love your neighbor as yourself'" (Rom. 13:9). In fact, the Old Testament readings remind us that not every Israelite experienced the law as oppressive, breeding despair and hypocritical displays of religion. And our Gospel reminds us that even in contexts of disputes with Jewish leaders, Jesus claimed and affirmed the fundamental tenets of his tradition. Too often Christians forget this, creating generalized and largely false dichotomies between law and gospel, work and faith, act and motive.

Mark 12:28–34 is a complete story, only lightly tied to its present context (v. 28a) and rounded off at the end (v. 34b). It could effectively be placed in any context without loss of meaning. In fact, Luke, who recasts the story, places it earlier in his narrative (10:25–28). Mark, and Matthew after him (22:34–40), has located this exchange between Jesus and a scribe in the block of material that presents Jesus in Jerusalem, teaching and debating, and in general pronouncing God's judgment upon a Judaism gone awry (11:1–13:37). The time sequences in the events we traditionally place in Holy Week are impossible to recover. Mark has framed this material upon a series of visits to the temple by Jesus (11:11, 15, 27; 12:35, 41; 13:1). It is probably because the scribe responds to Jesus by saying that love of God and neighbor are "much more important than all whole burnt offerings and sacrifices" (v. 33) that Mark sets the story in the temple. At any rate, in the institution that was the heart of Judaism, Jesus and a scribe go straight to the heart of their common tradition.

The scribe who approaches Jesus with a question is presented in a positive light. Of the nineteen references to scribes in Mark, this one is alone in that regard. Matthew (20:35) and Luke (10:25) portray the questioner as a lawyer seeking to test Jesus, but the preacher must not let that influence how our text is heard. Mark's story is most refreshing. After a series of entrapment questions from Pharisees, Herodians, and Sadducees (12:13–27), the sincerity and perception of this scribe are welcomed. His question was appropriate to Judaism's continued reflection upon its tradition and faith in the effort to keep perspective and not to stray from the center. And Jesus' answer was not original with him. Rabbis before him had joined the Shema ("Hear, O Israel, . . . ," Deut. 6:45) and the command to love one's neighbor (Lev. 19:18b) in a capsule statement of Israel's faith and ethic. It would be totally inaccurate, therefore, to portray Jesus as the first to understand the point of Judaism. In fact, by his citations from Deuteronomy and Leviticus and by his agreement with the scribe that these take precedence over rituals, Jesus places himself in the prophetic tradition that included Isaiah, Jeremiah, and Amos. Law can lose its heart; ritual can lose its reason; a relationship can lose its love. But both Mark and we know all to well that Judaism has no monopoly on such distortions of faith.

The scribe agrees with Jesus, and Jesus agrees with the scribe. It is a rare and pleasant moment. But agreeing is not enough. The scribe is "not far from the kingdom of God" (v. 34). Like the rich man in an earlier story (10:17–22), the scribe is lacking something. For Mark, it is following Jesus on the way and all the way to the cross. The kingdom of God is not agreeing on the right answers, important as the search for truth is. It is rather living, doing, and relating in ways that the love of God and love of neighbor inspire, inform, and discipline.

Proper 27 [32]
(Sunday between November 6 and 12 inclusive)

Ruth 3:1–5; 4:13–17;
Psalm 127; or
1 Kings 17:8–16;
Psalm 146;
Hebrews 9:24–28;
Mark 12:38–44

For the *Common Lectionary*'s Old Testament reading, a second passage from Ruth is used: Naomi's instructions for Ruth to go to Boaz, the marriage of Ruth and Boaz, and the birth of Obed, who became the grandfather of David. A home dedicated to the Lord and blessed with many children is the object of reflection in Psalm 127.

The other Old Testament lesson from 1 Kings 17 records the story of the widow of Zarephath who feeds Elijah from a jar of meal and a jug of oil that are never depleted. Psalm 146 speaks about the righteous poor and God's execution of justice for the oppressed and concern with the feeding of the hungry.

Another widow figures in the Gospel text from Mark. She too is both poor and generous, and her exemplary behavior is used by Jesus to censure greedy religious readers.

As our reading through the Letter to the Hebrews continues, today's epistolary passage continues its emphasis on the sacrificial work of Christ, especially as it culminates in his second coming.

Ruth 3:1–5; 4:13–17

With this reading we come to the close of the story of Ruth, the final resolution of the tensions established at the outset: How will two widows survive in their patriarchal society?

In the homeland of Ruth's mother-in-law, the relationship between Ruth, young and poor, and Boaz, an older man of substance, flourished. We notice that Boaz was attracted to Ruth entirely because of her character, epitomized in her devotion to her mother-in-law and her hard work in the fields. Naomi recognized the hand of Yahweh in these events—that he has led Ruth to Boaz as the means of caring for the widows (2:20–21)—so she encouraged Ruth to do her part to ensure the success of the divine plan (2:22–23). The third episode (chap. 3) reports how Ruth did just that, meeting Boaz on the threshing floor and inviting him to exercise the right of the next of kin toward her. That scene contains the main climax of the story, when Boaz affirmed his intention to exercise the right of the "next of kin" (3:10–13).

Ruth 4:1–12 gives the fourth episode of the story, set at the gate of Bethlehem where legal matters were to be resolved, and the report of the aftermath of the drama follows (4:13–22). The actions in the fourth episode concern civil law and the rights and responsibilities of relatives to one another. Boaz goes to the city gate to accomplish what he promised Ruth the night before, but there is one possible impediment to the plans—a relative who is closer to the family of Ruth's father-in-law than he. Boaz calls this "next of kin" and convenes what is in effect a civil court, before ten elders of the city.

Two legal considerations stand behind the scene in the court, one involving the "redemption" of land and another concerning the perpetuation of the name of dead males by the next of kin. Boaz invites the unnamed next of kin to purchase the parcel of land that belonged to Elimelech. A parallel to this practice is noted in Jeremiah 32, in the story of the prophet's purchase of land that belonged to his relative. The purpose of this practice was to respect and protect the allocation of land according to families. If it had to be sold, a near relative should keep it in the family. Tension rises in the scene at the gate when the "next of kin" readily agrees to buy the land.

But at that point Boaz calls attention to the other legal concern, linking it to the redemption of the land: "The day you acquire the field from the hand of Naomi, you are also acquiring Ruth the Moabite, the widow of the dead man, to maintain the dead man's name on his inheritance" (4:5). What Boaz has in view is the so-called levirate marriage (Deut. 25:5–10; Lev. 25:25; 27:9–33), although that usually involved a brother of the widow's husband (see also Gen. 38). What fear or concern motivates the next of kin's reluctance is unclear.

Our narrator then reports in precise terms how Boaz fulfilled all the legal obligations and followed due process to take possession of the property and to marry Ruth. There is reference to the symbolic removal of a sandal to seal the transaction (vv. 8–9) and the account of the formal notarizing of the agreement. This was done orally, with the elders affirming that they were witnesses (vv. 10–11), but it would have been no less binding than a written contract. The elders go further to pronounce a blessing on the new family (vv. 11–12).

As the story had begun with trouble and tragedy, so it ends with the happiest of reports, that of the birth of a child. Not only is the welfare of Naomi and Ruth secure; now there is a future for the family that seemed doomed. The child is surrounded by mother, grandmother, and the women of the town, who bless Naomi and name the child (vv. 14–17).

It is highly significant that this child is the father of Jesse, the father of King David. Ordinary people, but people who go beyond what the law requires to act with compassion for others, are the ancestors of kings. There is another remarkable fact here. As the narrator points out over and over again, Ruth is a Moabite, a foreign woman of unusual courage and loyalty. This foreigner is the grandmother of Israel's greatest king, who founded a dynasty that lasted in Judah until the Babylonian Captivity. Whether or not the story of Ruth is a polemic against narrow nationalism, it certainly strikes a blow for the acceptance of foreigners.

Psalm 127

Two themes, the building of a house and children as a blessing, dominate this psalm and thus parallel some of the interests of the readings from Ruth.

In the heading of the composition, the psalm is associated with Solomon. Such an association reflects the attempt of late Hebrew exegetes to connect the psalms with various personages and events. Two features probably led to connecting the psalm with Solomon: (1) the reference to the building of a house was taken as a reference to the temple constructed by Solomon, and (2) the word for "beloved" in verse 2 is the same as the name given Solomon by the prophet Nathan in 2 Samuel 12:25.

Verses 1–2 proclaim the futility of labor, unless it has Yahweh's blessing. Building a house, watching a city, early to work, late to bed, working hard for bread—none are of consequence unless God is somehow part of the picture. (The last line of verse 2 is difficult to interpret; it seems to mean that it is God who is the source of rest at night, not the diligence of our labor nor our commitment to our effort.) Although stated negatively, this text has many similarities to Jesus' affirmation that the flowers of the field and the birds of the air possess something that labor and effort cannot give; that is, one should "hang loose" in life and trust the beneficence of the Creator and the creation.

Verses 3–5 affirm the benefit of progeny, especially males. Again, the source of the blessing is seen as Yahweh. The author, like people in all generations, recognizes that there is always an uncertainty about childbearing. Taking thought and taking action do not an offspring insure. Sons are here seen as a source of authority in the gate. A person with a retinue of sons possessed clout in public places. Social protection, personal welfare, social security, survival assurance, continuity of the name, inheritance insurance, comradeship in life, all of these were involved in male progeny. In ancient society, much would be lost without them.

1 Kings 17:8–16

This Old Testament reading is one episode in the stories of the prophet Elijah found in 1 Kings 17:1–19:21; 2 Kings 1. The setting of the stories is the Northern Kingdom during the reign of Ahab (874–852 BC) of the dynasty of Omri. The Elijah stories are an old collection doubtless handed down in prophetic circles before they were incorporated by the Deuteronomistic Historians into their account of Israel's past. Such stories were particularly important to the deuteronomistic writers because of their conviction that history was set on its course by the word of God through prophets.

Elijah had appeared on the scene abruptly and without introduction, announcing to Ahab that there would be "neither dew nor rain these years, except by my word" (1 Kings 17:1). The word of the Lord then led him first to a brook east of the Jordan to be fed by ravens (1 Kings 17:2–7) and then to Zarephath to be fed by a widow.

In the background of the story in 1 Kings 17:8–16, then, is the conflict between prophet and king, but that is set aside for the moment. More immediately there is the drought. The story is complete and self-contained, although it is followed by the account of Elijah's miraculous raising of the widow's dead son.

It is the drought that provides the narrative tension, the uncertainty that creates suspense. That suspense is heightened by Yahweh's command that it is to be a widow who will feed him, and even more by the revelation that she is so poor that her life and that of her son are threatened (v. 12). It is not the greatness of the man of God that will save them all, but the power of the word of Yahweh through him. "Do not be afraid," he says, and not as simple reassurance but as an oracle of salvation. Then in typically prophetic form he announces the word of God concerning the future: "The jar of meal will not be emptied and the jug of oil will not fail until the day that the LORD sends rain upon the earth" (v. 14). And that is the way it turned out.

The episode is a miracle story with legendary and folkloristic features. It is told, however, not to glorify Elijah, but to show how the power of God, in the form of the prophetic word, was made manifest through him. Although the Bible contains more dramatic miracle stories than this one, we are still meant to be astonished. To provide a rationalistic explanation—for example, the generosity of the widow moved her neighbors to bring meal and oil—may serve only to reduce the astonishment that the divine word could solve such a problem.

Especially when this story is considered in connection with Mark 12:38–44, the role of the widow becomes crucial. That the widow was poor is not surprising. In ancient Israelite society, economic well-being generally required a male head of the household. Even all the Old Testament texts that express God's concern for the widow and the fatherless indicate that there was need for such concern. She is not only poor; she is a foreigner. All the more dramatic then is her willingness to be generous with what little she had, trusting that the prophet's word was indeed the word of God.

Psalm 146

This psalm has been previously discussed as one of the readings for Proper 18 [23].

Hebrews 9:24–28

In last week's epistolary reading from Hebrews, the high priesthood of Christ was compared with the Levitical priesthood and found to be superior. Today's passage continues this comparison, but advances it even further.

Christ is said to have entered a sanctuary "not . . . made by human hands, a mere copy of the true one, but . . . into heaven itself" (v. 24). In the preceding verse, the author speaks of the vessels of the tabernacle as "sketches of the heavenly things." Earlier in the chapter, the author mentions the "greater and perfect tent (not made with hands, that is, not of this creation)" that Christ entered (9:11). All these references presuppose the discussion earlier in the letter where the author contrasts the earthly tabernacle in the wilderness with the heavenly tabernacle (8:1–6).

Underlying this comparison appears to be a Platonic outlook that conceived of two worlds, or levels of reality. The world we experience is the world of things perceived with the senses, the phenomenal world, and it has as its counterpart the world of ideas perceived with the mind, the noumenal world. Each "thing" in the real world has its counterpart in the ideal world, in fact may be regarded as a "shadow" or "type" of its corresponding "idea." Of the two worlds, the world of ideas is the more "real," more basic, for every "thing" in the real world is thought to have been derived from its corresponding "idea" in the noumenal world. Thus the world of ideas is the "unseen world," but is not for that reason imaginary. It is both more basic and more permanent in every respect.

Drawing on this outlook, our author conceives of the earthly tabernacle as a "sketch and shadow" (8:5) of the heavenly tabernacle. Of the two, the latter is "the true tent" (8:2). Thus, in today's text, he insists that the sanctuary Christ entered was not "a sanctuary made by human hands" (9:24) or some "thing" manufactured, modeled, or handcrafted from an original. It was no mere "copy," but was itself "the true one." The heavenly tabernacle where Christ carries out his priestly work is far more original and is closer to the actual presence of God, for "he entered into heaven itself, now to appear in the presence of God on our behalf" (v. 24). In one sense, God's presence had dwelt in the Holy Place of the earthly sanctuary by proxy; it was there, but only as an extension of God's heavenly presence. But now, in the heavenly tabernacle, Christ officiates in the very presence of God, not in an earthly tabernacle far removed in distance from the realm of "true" reality.

At this point, our text resumes points of contrast treated in previous epistolary lections. Basically, there are two: (1) the Levitical priesthood involved repeated, or "continual," offerings, whereas Christ's priesthood involved a single offering made "once for all"; and (2) the Levitical high priest offered blood not his own, that is, the blood of bulls and goats (9:12, 19; 10:4), whereas Christ, "by the sacrifice of himself" (v. 26), offered his own blood. In each of these respects, the form of Christ's priesthood is found to be superior. The "continual" offerings of the Levitical priests merely attested their ineffectiveness (10:1–3). Had Christ's offering been of the same kind, it would have been necessary for him to have made an annual offering "since the foundation of the world" (v. 26). This is obviously absurd.

The author's Christology is aptly summarized in verse 26: "He has appeared." This is a clear reference to his incarnation. The same word is used, and elaborated, in 1 Timothy 3:16, an early Christian confession: "He was revealed in flesh."

"Once for all." This phrase is typically used by the author to express the absolute finality of the work of Christ (7:27; 9:12; 10:10; cf. 1 Pet. 3:18). Christ is the "last word" God has spoken (1:2).

"At the end of the age." The phrase expresses the Christian conviction that Christ's coming to the earth signaled the final stage of salvation history (Matt. 13:39–40, 49; 24:3; 28:20; 1 Cor. 10:11; 1 Pet. 1:20; 4:7; 1 John 2:18; also Gal. 4:4; 1 Enoch 16:1; 4 Esdras 7:113).

"To remove sin by the sacrifice of himself." The death of Christ is seen as the ultimate sacrifice through which purification for the sins of humanity was achieved (1:3; cf. 1 John 3:5; also Testament of Levi 8:9). He was "offered once to bear the sins of many" (v. 28; 9:6; 10:12, 14; also Rom. 6:10; 1 Pet. 2:24; 3:18).

At the conclusion of our passage there is a shift in the argument. Up to this point the author has been contrasting the work of Christ with that of the Levitical priesthood. Here, however, he sees a similarity between that which all humans experience and that which Christ experiences (vv. 27–28). The argument seems to be that just as everyone of us experiences death "once" and from death passes to another stage (in our case, "judgment"), so Christ experienced death "once" and from death passed to another stage of his work. The final stage of his work was not judgment, however, but salvation. At his second coming, his task will no longer be to "deal with sin," because that was accomplished once and for all in his sacrificial death. Rather, it will be to "save those who are eagerly waiting for him" (v. 28).

Obviously, our text provides additional material for preaching on the work of Christ as presented in the Book of Hebrews. One may wish to explore the intercessory work of Christ in the "heavenly sanctuary" as it occurs "in the presence of God" and relate this to other New Testament passages, such as Romans 8:34. Or the eschatological theme introduced at the conclusion of today's lection might be fruitful to explore, especially because it resonates with themes and texts used in the All Saints service.

Mark 12:38–44

Today's Gospel lesson continues the selected teachings and events within Mark's larger unit, 11:1–13:37, a body of material set within Jerusalem and primarily in the temple. This setting provides not only a context for dispute with Jewish leaders over the proper understanding of life before God, but also a backdrop for instructing the disciples in what constitutes good and bad models of leadership. In the text before us, those instructions are drawn from observing the scribes at work and a widow at worship.

Mark 12:38–44 consists of two distinct parts: verses 38–40, which warn against the influence of scribes, and verses 41–44, which praise the example of a widow. The first part is clearly intended by Mark as only one sample of what Jesus taught: "And as he taught, he said" (v. 38a). Verse 40 is rather awkwardly joined to what precedes and may have existed earlier in another context. Part two, verses 41–44, is an independent story with its own introduction and conclusion. It is absent from Matthew and is preserved in briefer form in Luke (21:1–4). How can one account for these two units being placed together here in Mark? Several possibilities suggest themselves. Because the widow story is set in the temple (v. 41), it is congenial to a context of many temple events. It may also be the case that the reference to widows in verse 40 attracted the poor widow story. This may seem a reason without substance, but in oral cultures ease of memory may take precedence over logic. (Was a similar principle at work in the lectionary for today, with other readings having to do with poor widows joining this one?) A more practical reason may lie in Mark's desire to place before the church two contrasting models of behavior: scribes who are proud and greedy, and a widow who is humble and generous.

The behavior of the scribe in last Sunday's Gospel (Mark 12:28–34) makes it clear that the indictment in today's text did not apply to all scribes but to those whose behavior is described in verses 38–40. In a community centered in its regard for the Torah, its interpretation and application, the scribe was an important and duly honored person. But places of honor tend to attract persons who are not honorable, and regrettably, this applies also to the field of religion. And as positions in the worlds of politics and commerce provide temptations to greed and self-aggrandizement, so does the world of the spirit. In fact, history has demonstrated that power and greed can be unusually demonic here, given the naïveté and simple trust of many of the faithful who do not realize what transactions are taking place beneath ·robes, prayers, and sacred texts. The "greater condemnation" (v. 40) that comes to such leaders is calculated on a simple formula: greater knowledge means greater responsibility; from the one to whom more is given, more is expected. As the Epistle of James states it: "Not many of you should become teachers, my brothers and sisters, for you know that we who teach will be judged with greater strictness" (3:1).

The brief story in verses 41–44 is so dramatic and evocative of emotion that the reader has to be attentive to avoid missing its point. The principal character is a figure of pathos in that culture—a poor widow. And her small act, unnoticed except by Jesus, is performed among the rich pouring out abundant gifts, a fact that would have further diminished her offering, except for Jesus. It is he who properly evaluates her two lepta, the smallest coins in circulation, because it is he who knows this is all she has. The canon by which Jesus weighs her gift is not sentiment, but the comparison of one's gift to what one has remaining for oneself. He does not inveigh against large gifts or romanticize small ones. He simply notes that some, after giving large amounts, still have abundance, whereas the widow, after her gift, has nothing—nothing, that is, except complete trust in God. No wonder that Jesus, who earlier had taken a child in his arms and taught the Twelve, again calls his disciples to him and says in effect, "You have been very interested in greatness. Look at her; she has done something great."

In a world in which widows were victimized, we have a story of one who took initiative in her life. Perhaps her poverty is the result of some scribe taking advantage of her grief, her lack of skill in handling financial matters until now the business of her husband, and her increased tear-stained devotion to religion. Even so, she does not whine nor retreat in bitterness. Rather, she takes the small remainder and acts, taking responsibility for her life. Unknowingly, she receives a blessing no one can take from her.

Proper 28 [33]
(Sunday between November 13 and 19 inclusive)

1 Samuel 1:4–20;
1 Samuel 2:1–10; or
Daniel 12:1–3;
Psalm 16;
Hebrews 10:11–14 (15–18) 19–25;
Mark 13:1–8

Two texts from 1 Samuel supply the Old Testament reading and the responsorial song in the *Common Lectionary*. In the first, Hannah's prayer for a child is answered in the birth of Samuel, and the song of Hannah from 1 Samuel 2 serves as the prayer of response.

For other lectionaries, the Old Testament reading from Daniel sketches a vision of the last days, when the dead are raised to everlasting life. Though it does not contain an explicit reference to resurrection, as is the case in the Daniel text, Psalm 16 praises God, who will not allow the faithful to be given up to Sheol.

Daniel's vision has its counterpart in the apocalyptic vision from Mark's text, which portrays the cosmic turbulence that will accompany the end of time.

Today we have the last of the semicontinuous readings from Hebrews, which envisions Christ exalted to the right hand of God.

1 Samuel 1:4–20

The story of the birth of Samuel comes at a key turning point in the history of Israel. In the semicontinuous readings from the Old Testament, this lesson follows two readings from the Book of Ruth, which makes sense both because Ruth precedes 1 Samuel in the Christian canons and also because both the readings from Ruth and from 1 Samuel 1 focus attention on women. But in the Hebrew canon from which the Christian Bible is derived, the Book of Ruth is found in the Writings, so the Book of Judges is followed directly by 1 Samuel.

That is the sequence that reveals the importance of the events reported in 1 Samuel. The story of the judges had concluded on a bad note. After describing chaos, warfare among the tribes of Israel, the brutal death of the Levite's concubine, the last word concerning the time of the judges was "In those days there was no king in Israel; all the people did what was right in their own eyes" (Judg. 21:25). From the longer perspective of the way history developed, one purpose of the last part of the Book of Judges was to show the need for the monarchy.

From that same perspective, the story of the birth of Samuel is part of the history of the rise of the monarchy. Samuel will be the last of the judges—inspired leaders of Israel. But he will also act as a priestly and a prophetic figure. And from the point of view of political history, his role will be to designate both the first king, Saul, and the second one, David. The first part of the Book of 1 Samuel will chronicle the rise of kingship and the struggle about its religious legitimacy. The key figure in that process is Samuel.

So this reading is the account of the birth of Samuel. Like many other great figures, his birth will be dramatic, unusual, and attended by divine intervention. The story shows that there was doubt about his birth in the first place—his mother was barren—and it will also begin to account for his power and importance as a religious leader—he was dedicated to God even before he was born.

But the central figure in this story is no king, prophet, priest, nor even a husband—although all of these are present to some degree. At the center of the story is a woman, Hannah, wife of Elkanah and mother of Samuel. It is the story of her pain and suffering, of her devotion, and of her vindication.

First, the background or situation is set out in terms of both family life and religious institutions (1:1–8). We are introduced first to Elkanah. The most important facts about him are that he has two wives and that every year he goes to Shiloh to worship. One of the wives, Peninnah, has children, but the other, Hannah, is barren. Elkanah's special love for Hannah is seen in his giving her a double portion of the sacrifice. But Peninnah makes Hannah's life miserable, "because the LORD had closed her womb" (v. 6). Elkanah's efforts to comfort Hannah, although well-meaning, are clumsy. He encourages her to cheer up, for, "Am I not more to you than ten sons" (v. 8). In addition to revealing that he is self-centered or needs to be assured of his importance to her, the remark shows that he is unwilling to sympathize with Hannah.

So Hannah turns to the Lord. First (vv. 9–11), there in the temple at Shiloh she presents her burden to the Lord, weeping bitterly and asking for help. In support of her petition, she makes a dramatic vow: If the Lord will give her a son, she will dedicate him to the Lord as a nazirite from birth (v. 11). (Relatively little is known of nazirites beyond the information provided here; that is, that they refrain from wine and do not cut their hair. As the story of that other famous nazirite, Samson, shows, a nazirite need not necessarily be pious.) Second (vv. 12–18), Hannah continues to pray in the temple because she has had no assurance that the Lord has heard her. Now another man, this time the priest Eli, fails to understand her. Seeing her agitation—praying silently but moving her lips—he reproaches her for being drunk (vv. 12–14). But when she tells him the depth of her trouble and the content of her prayer, he gives the priestly response, the assurance that God has heard and will answer her prayer: "Go in peace; the God of Israel grant the petition you have made to him" (v. 17). With those words the story has reached its resolution. Hannah will have her son.

In the final episode of our reading (vv. 19–20), Hannah and her husband worship one last time in the temple at Shiloh and return home, where the Lord "remembered" her, and in due time she bears a son, whom she names Samuel. The readers have no doubt about how the story will turn out, but the final action of the mother is delayed. At the time of the next yearly sacrifice (v. 21), Elkanah and his household return to Shiloh, but Hannah does not go. She promises that as soon as he is old enough to be weaned she will dedicate him forever to the service of the Lord. And so she did, when the time was right.

Although it is a story of divine power and authority—the Lord who had closed Hannah's womb opened it and gave her a son—it is also a story of human authority as well. Without the persistence and passion of this abused and misunderstood woman, there would have been no Samuel, and some other way would have had to be found to establish Israel and the monarchy. Moreover, this woman knew that she had the power and authority to give God a good gift: "Therefore I have lent him to the LORD; as long as he lives, he is given to the LORD" (v. 28).

1 Samuel 2:1–10

Hannah's song was not originally a part of the story of the birth and dedication of Samuel but has been added subsequently, functioning for the readers of the book in much the same way that responsorial psalms serve us in worship. Apart from the narrative introduction, nothing in the song refers specifically to the situation of Hannah or Samuel, though there is the reference to barrenness and birth (v. 5). Moreover, the mention of the "king" in verse 10 is anachronistic for the story of Samuel's beginnings, and the song as a whole corresponds to later psalms that were used in the temple. Consequently, exegesis of this passage should be attentive to the meaning of the song on at least three levels: (1) the song in its present literary context, (2) its meaning in itself independent of the narrative, and (3) its appropriation and interpretation in the early church as reflected in texts such as Luke 1:39–57.

1. In the Book of 1 Samuel the song is part of Hannah's act of worship when she brings her son Samuel to the sanctuary at Shiloh to loan him to the Lord (1 Sam. 1:28). It is preceded by the story of Hannah's barrenness, her prayer for a child, and her vow that he would be dedicated to Yahweh (1 Sam. 1). In every respect she is a woman of faith, presented as a model to all who hear her story. She is also a woman of destiny, for the account of Hannah and her son Samuel is an important key in the history of the people as a whole. It comes at a decisive turning point, between the chaos of the period of the judges—"In those days there was no king in Israel; all the people did what was right in their own eyes," (Judg. 21:25)—and the rise of the monarchy, first with Saul and then David, both of whom Samuel anointed. Samuel's birth heralds a new age, and his mother is more than a passive participant.

2. Hannah's song itself is a thanksgiving psalm with many elements of a hymn of praise. It begins with the declaration of intent to praise God (v. 1) and then affirms that Yahweh is the incomparable God who knows all (vv. 2–3). Next (vv. 4–9), God is praised as the one who protects and cares for the weak, who is indeed Lord of life and death, and who executes justice. The song concludes (v. 10) on a distinctly messianic and cosmic note: Yahweh will defeat those who oppose him, judge the entire earth, and elevate his anointed.

3. In the early church context, it was not only the parallels between Hannah and Mary that were picked up but also the fundamental point of the song. It is God who acts to save the weak, the lowly, the poor, and the needy. The God of justice, who sets the world on its pillars (v. 8), chooses to be known through humanity at its most vulnerable stages, a baby just weaned from his mother's milk, or even one yet unborn.

Daniel 12:1-3

This passage is one of only two or three Old Testament texts that directly express belief in resurrection from the dead. The perspective in Daniel 12, however, is not quite the same as that in the New Testament, and our interpretation should take note of the differences. The most important contribution this passage can make to Christian preaching and teaching is to set the biblical understanding of resurrection into its proper frame of reference. First, however, we should review the passage in its literary and historical context.

Because of the historical allusions and perspective of the contents, there is general agreement among scholars concerning the date of the final composition of the Book of Daniel and of this section of it in particular. It was written during the Maccabean revolt against the Hellenistic ruler Antiochus Epiphanes IV, after he had taken the Jerusalem temple in 167 BC and before it had been recaptured and rededicated by the Maccabeans in December, 164 BC. It was a time of military struggle against what appeared to be superior forces, but—equally important—it was a period of religious conflict between faith and culture, between faithful adherence to the ancient traditions on the one hand and acceptance of new Hellenistic customs and practices on the other. Tensions such as these are reflected in sectarian divisions within Judaism during the period. One of the main purposes of the Book of Daniel was to encourage the faithful to resist both the military threat and the temptations to follow foreign practices.

Daniel 12:1-4 is the concluding paragraph of a lengthy apocalyptic vision that begins in Daniel 10:1. Like the other vision reports in the book, this one consists of a revelation of the future to the seer, a future that leads from one kingdom to another to culminate in the final age. History unfolds as a struggle between the righteous Jews and those who oppose them, including both foreign kings and faithless Jews. Through Daniel 11:39, the revelation concerned the past, at least from the actual perspective of the writer. Daniel 11:40-45 is a prophecy of events that will transpire on the plane of history, leading to the death of the evil king whom we now identify as Antiochus Epiphanes IV. Daniel 12:1-3 gives the vision of the final events, including the historical plane but also transcending it. Daniel 12:4 signals the end of the vision with the instructions to Daniel to seal up the book until the right time for its disclosure, which actually was the time of its composition in the second century BC.

A great deal is compressed into the three verses before us today. The introductory formula "At that time" refers to a specific date, but does not say which one. The writer clearly has in view a time in the near future, a time when all things will be transformed. The time has already been characterized as one of serious trouble for the faithful, and now that is stated explicitly (v. 1). The description of what follows is similar in many ways to a judgment scene, with Michael, the patron saint of Israel, standing up as a judge, checking records in "the book," and determining rewards and punishments for those who stand before him. The events include more than a trial, however, for Michael as the agent of the divine will is warrior as well as judge. The events of the end time transpire in three steps: First, Michael arises in victory and delivers the nation ("your people," v. 1). Second, there is the resurrection of "many . . . who sleep in the dust of the earth," some to eternal life and some to "everlasting contempt" (v. 2). Third, there is the exaltation of "those who are wise," "who lead many to righteousness" (v. 3).

Partly because this vision of the end is such a new and bold theological stroke, the meaning of several points is unclear. "The many" who will arise do not include all who have ever died, but who are they? They are not just the faithful Israelites who have fallen in the current war, for some will be raised in order to be punished. The writer seems to have in view those in his time who have not received their just rewards. Who are "those who are wise" (*maskilim*), who "shall shine like the brightness of the sky"? They probably are not the same as the many who will be raised to eternal life, but some group of leaders within the community. That they have died in the process of turning "many to righteousness" recalls the Suffering Servant of Isaiah 52:12–53:13.

What stands in the center of the proclamation is not the promise of resurrection, but the promise of the deliverance and vindication of the people of God, by God acting through the angel Michael. All of those people will be vindicated, both those living at the time of the divine intervention and those who have already died. Our writer could not believe that God would forget those who had died in the struggle. Resurrection is part of a larger drama, the triumph of God's justice and righteousness in a transformation of all things.

That, then, is the biblical frame of reference for belief in the resurrection of the dead: the hope for and confidence in the eventual triumph of God's will, even in and through and beyond the most terrible of circumstances. In the biblical view—not only here but in the New Testament as well—resurrection is never a natural phenomenon. Human beings do not live forever because of some innate force or power. However, God may raise even the dead to life, everlasting life. Thus the foundation for the resurrection hope is confidence in God. The specific frame of reference is the apocalyptic view of the world and history. Such a view includes a corporate, communal understanding of the hope. Individuals are raised as part of the people of God. To live with that hope is to live in confidence and trust, and also with the urgency that the light of God's kingdom is already shining in the present age.

Psalm 16

This psalm was previously discussed as one of the readings for the Easter Vigil.

Hebrews 10:11–14 (15–18) 19–25

Further contrast between the Levitical priests and Christ is seen in the respective posture they adopted for officiating. The Levitical priests stood before God to minister to him (Num. 16:9; Deut. 10:8; 18:7), whereas Christ made a sacrifice "once for all" and then "sat down at the right hand of God" (vv. 12; 1:3, 13; 8:1; Ps. 110:1; Matt. 22:44; Acts 2:34–35; Rev. 3:21). The Levitical priests' standing position is itself a symbol of impermanence. The image of Christ "seated at the right hand of the throne of the Majesty in the heavens" (8:1) symbolizes, by contrast, that his work has been completed. So effective was the single sacrifice that he offered, no work remains to be done in this respect. All that is left is for him to await the final subjugation of his enemies (v. 13). His task now is one of intercession with God on behalf of those who "approach God through him" (7:25; 9:24).

Themes echoed earlier in the epistle continue here. The Levitical sacrifices were offered repeatedly, and their very repetition is a sign of their ineffectiveness. The only conclusion our author can draw from this is that such sacrifices "can never take away sins" (v. 11). They never get through to the "conscience of the worshiper" (9:9). Because annual sacrifices do not succeed in cleansing the conscience of the worshiper, they only serve as a "reminder of sin year after year" (10:2–3). This leads to the inevitable conclusion: "It is impossible for the blood of bulls and goats to take away sins" (10:4; cf. 7:18–19; 9:9, 13–14).

By contrast, Christ made a "single sacrifice for sins," and it was done "once for all" (vv. 12; 7:27; 9:28; Rom. 6:10; 1 Pet. 2:24; 3:18). In doing so, he achieved full sanctification for those who worshiped him (1:3, 10:10, 29; 13:12; 1 Thess. 4:3). Whereas "the law made nothing perfect" (7:19), Christ's sacrifice made it possible for us to be "perfected for all time" (v. 14). He was able to do in a single sacrifice what the Levitical priests were unable to do through hundreds of years of annual sacrifices—offer genuine forgiveness of sins.

To clinch this point, the author cites the well-known promise of Jeremiah that was introduced earlier in the epistle (8:8–12). Here he quotes only parts of the longer passage that bear directly on his argument, noting by way of introduction that the witness of the Holy Spirit bears him out (cf. 3:7). First, the new covenant of which Jeremiah spoke promised an inward law written on the hearts and minds (v. 16; Jer. 31:33). Second, it offered the hope that sins and misdeeds would be remembered no more (v. 17; Jer. 31:34). True forgiveness would mean no more annual reminders. Thus, "where there is forgiveness of these [sins], there is no longer any offering for sin" (v. 18).

The second main part of the epistolary lection (vv. 19–25) occurs as part of the epistolary lection for Good Friday (Heb. 10:16–25) in all three years and has been treated in more detail in that connection in this as well as the other volumes. The reader is referred to those discussions.

Because today's epistolary lection concludes the readings taken from the Letter to the Hebrews, it may be useful to make some summary comments. As we have seen, the image of Christ as our high priest receives extensive and elaborate treatment. In numerous ways, the author contrasts the Levitical priesthood with that of Christ and consistently finds the latter superior. In one sense, this translates into a denigration of the Levitical priesthood, but in another sense this form of comparison only attests the richness of the set of metaphors provided by the tabernacle and priesthood.

As a way of setting our author's exegetical work into context, it should be noted that other authors of the period, such as Philo and Josephus, conceived of a cosmic tabernacle corresponding to the one on earth. From this they developed an elaborate symbolic interpretation of the tabernacle and Levitical priesthood. The author of Hebrews is working in this same hermeneutical tradition, but with the chief difference made by the Easter faith. It was the conviction that Christ had risen and was seated at the right hand of God that helped our author reinterpret the priestly cultus. Accordingly, Christ was for him a "priest forever." Because he did his intercessory work in the very presence of God, in the "heavenly tabernacle," it was efficacious in a way that the Levitical sacrifices could never be. By the very fact that theirs was "earth-bound," it had temporary value. Above all, the way in which it dealt with the most pressing and persistent human need—sin and its forgiveness—was finally ineffective. What was needed was a sacrifice to end all sacrifices, one that could bring about full and final purification and forgiveness of sins. The testimony of the Book of Hebrews is that Christ "by a single offering . . . has perfected for all time those who are sanctified" (10:14).

Mark 13:1–8

Mark 13:1–8 drops the reader down in terrain remarkably different from the biographical-type narrative of the remainder of the Gospel. Were the material not identified as Markan, one would guess it to be from Daniel or Revelation, for like those two books, Mark 13 is apocalyptic in nature. An apocalypse is an unveiling, a revealing, a vision that grants its recipient a glimpse beyond what is going on to what is really going on. Half-revealed, half-concealed in language that is dramatic, filled with symbolic images and numbers, apocalyptic literature speaks of what God is doing and will do both by means of and apart from historical events. Scenes are painted on cosmic canvas, including heaven and earth, nature and human history, past, present, and future. God's judging and redeeming activity will be so critical, so important, so final that to speak of it is to stretch and to burst the bounds of ordinary speech. It is a kind of religious literature embraced by persons in dire straits, who, seeing no relief from sinful social, religious, and political institutions, cling desperately to their faith and look to heaven for vindication. From one point of view, Mark 13 sits awkwardly where it is, and the reader of the Gospel could without loss of continuity move from chapter 12 to chapter 14. But from another point of view, this apocalyptic discourse of Jesus could hold a key position in the entire narrative. Many find the Gospel coming to an unsatisfactory conclusion, emphasizing the cross, having no resurrection appearance, calling the disciples to reassemble with Jesus in Galilee, and describing frightened women fleeing silent from the tomb. If there is an incompleteness, perhaps the answer is in chapter 13: the final climactic events are yet to occur. Let us move in for a closer reading.

Jesus entered Jerusalem (11:1), went to the temple, looked around, and the next day (?) went again to the temple, this time to cleanse it in an act that signaled the end of its function. Now in 13:1, for the final time Jesus leaves the temple and predicts its complete destruction. He is seated on the Mount of Olives opposite the temple. Notice the language: Jesus is seated "opposite" the temple, the location itself being described in such a way as to alert the reader that what follows will be the end of the temple system and the vindication of Jesus' life and work. Jesus is asked by the first four disciples whom he had called (v. 3) when this destruction would occur and what signs would announce it. In the discourse that follows, the end of the temple, the end of all things, and the glorious coming of the Son of Man to gather his own (the Parousia) are interwoven themes. But perhaps clarity will be served by looking at the passage as a response to the two questions of the disciples: When? What signs?

Jesus' response begins at verse 5 and continues through verse 37. The portion for today extends only through verse 8, but the preacher may want to review the discussion of verses 24–37 at the First Sunday of Advent. Jesus begins with a word of warning about false leaders and about misreading the signs of the end time. In desperate times desperate people will rally around those who seem to possess power and charisma. This is especially true if such would-be leaders invoke the name of Jesus and even say, "I am" (v. 6), an expression sometimes used by Jesus that, by implication, associated him with God (Yahweh, I am). Such a claim by anyone would be, in effect, a claim to be Jesus resurrected or Jesus returned. Messianic claims (see also vv. 21–22) were indeed made by revolutionary figures during the outbreaks of violence against Roman rule beginning in the forties and extending until early in the second century, the time of the rise and fall of Simon bar Cochba (Son of the Star). One mark of these false claimants, said Jesus, was the assertion that the end time is here. To be sure, Jesus shared the general view of Jewish apocalyptists that certain messianic woes would precede the end of history as it now is and the beginning of God's reign: convulsions in the natural world, violence in the social world. However, these crises are not the end but "the beginning of the birthpangs" (v. 8). Something marvelous that God is doing is yet to arrive, to be born. In other words, keep your belief in the final act of God, do not despair in these violent times, and do not be led by false teachers to abandon the mission. Be watchful and alert, to be sure, but endure in the task given to the church: "The good news must first be proclaimed to all nations" (v. 10).

Proper 29 [34]
(Christ the King or Reign of Christ; Sunday between November 20 and 26 inclusive)

2 Samuel 23:1–7;
Psalm 132:1–12 (13–18); or
Daniel 7:9–10, 13–14;
Psalm 93;
Revelation 1:4b–8;
John 18:33–37

The Feast of Christ the King was instituted by Pius XI in 1925 to celebrate the kingship of Christ as a way of combating the destructive forces of this age. Originally, it was celebrated on the last Sunday of October and was seen as prelude to the celebration of All Saints' Day. This was fitting symbolism because the triumphant Christ was seen to have motivated the saints and lived on in the church's memory of their noble deeds. The feast is now celebrated, however, on the last Sunday of the liturgical year as the climax toward which the celebration of the year moves and toward which individual Christians orient their own lives. Its eschatological dimension should be duly noted, as did Vatican II in acknowledging the significance of this feast at the end of the liturgical year by celebrating the Lord of glory as "the goal of human history, the focal point of the desires of history and civilization, the center of mankind, the joy of all hearts, and the fulfillment of all aspirations. . . . Animated and drawn together in his Spirit we press onward toward the consummation of history which fully corresponds to the plan of his love: 'to unite all things in him, things in heaven and things on earth' (Eph. 1:10)" (*Pastoral Constitution on the Church in the Modern World*, cited in A. Adam, *The Liturgical Year* [New York: Pueblo Publishing, 1981], 179).

All of the texts in the various lectionary traditions celebrate, in one way or another, the kingly reign of Christ.

In the *Common Lectionary*, the Old Testament lesson comes from 2 Samuel 23, which records the "last words of David," a psalm heralding God's everlasting covenant. As a response, the verses from Psalm 132 recall God's establishment of the Davidic dynasty.

For other lectionaries, the Old Testament reading is the well-known Danielic vision of "one like a human being" being given dominion by the Ancient One. The complementary psalm of response is Psalm 93, which celebrates the enthronement of Yahweh.

The Gospel reading for today is the Johannine account of the memorable confrontation between Pilate and Jesus, where Johannine irony makes it clear who is the real king.

The epistolary lesson is supplied by Revelation 1:4b–8, which praises God as king forever and Christ as "ruler of the kings of the earth."

2 Samuel 23:1–7

Before turning to 2 Samuel 23:1–7 itself, we should first remind ourselves of its literary context. After the death of Absalom and David's grief (2 Samuel 18–19:8*a*), David's troubles continued. There was an outbreak of sectional strife, reflecting the old tribal organization and the division between Judah and Israel. The occasion appears to have been David's return to Jerusalem, and the issue that of which tribes would be the first to welcome him (2 Samuel 19:9–43). Some of the old tribes revolted under the leadership of a "scoundrel" (2 Sam. 20:1) named Sheba, but once again Joab ended the threat (2 Samuel 20). There was a famine, believed to be Yahweh's punishment for Saul's treatment of the Gibeonites, so members of Saul's family were sacrificed to end the danger (2 Sam. 21:1–14). There were further wars with the Philistines, and David was judged too old to go into battle (2 Sam. 21:15–22). Immediately before the last words of David stands a hymn of praise (2 Samuel 22).

As a theological explanation of the dynasty of David, and the foundation for future messianic expectations, the last words of David are almost as significant as the promise reported in 2 Samuel 7. The latter comes at the pinnacle of David's career, the former at its end. Both concern the office of the king and the basis for the dynasty in Yahweh's election, and both contain old traditions. Many scholars consider most of 2 Samuel 23:1–7 to be quite ancient.

The narrative introduction at the beginning ("Now these are the last words of David") recalls the last will and testament of Moses (Deut. 33), the last words of Isaac (Gen. 27:1–2), and the blessing of Jacob (Gen. 49). In ancient Israel, as in most cultures, last words and wills carried great significance. David's "last words" themselves are comprised of a self-introduction in which he claims divine inspiration (vv. 1*b*–3*a*), the body of the will concerning the just king and the dynasty (vv. 3*b*–5), and concluding remarks about the fate of the godless (vv. 6–7).

The self-introduction begins with words of self-praise. David is the one "raised on high" (with the *NRSV* footnote), "anointed of the God of Jacob," and the "favorite of the Strong One of Israel" (v. 1). What appears at first glance as self-praise actually praises God: David is the recipient of God's actions of elevation and anointing. Moreover, this language concerns the office of the king more than the individual. The remainder of the introduction (vv. 2–3*a*) is unusual, more appropriate for a prophet than a king. David affirms that it is the "spirit of the LORD" that speaks through him. On the one hand, this reflects the older, premonarchical view that Yahweh chose individual leaders by having his spirit fall upon them. On the other hand, the just king was believed to rule through divine guidance (see 1 Kings 3:5; Isa. 11:2).

The body of the king's will, what David leaves to his successors, is the "everlasting covenant" (v. 5) made by God and reminders of the effects of just and pious rule. Two similies are used to characterize those effects—the morning sun and the rain. The choice of those images is not accidental; they emphasize the cosmic as well as corporate dimensions of justice. If the king, ruling by divine designation, acts justly and "in the fear of God" (v. 3), then the people as a whole are blessed, and God smiles through nature. If the promise to David in 2 Samuel 7 linked the dynasty to the history of salvation, especially to the exodus traditions, then this text at least implicitly connects the Davidic covenant to creation.

The final words (vv. 6–7) are similar to Psalm 1 in that they contrast the fate of the wicked with that of the righteous. Probably they concern those who oppose the divinely ordained king, but it is possible that they could apply to the king who does not rule justly.

The primary focus of theological and homiletical reflection in this reading will be the question of the relationship between faith and politics. Analogies between the Old Testament situation and modern conditions should be drawn cautiously. There are significant differences between a theocratic monarchy, in which the religion and the state are virtually coterminous, and a modern democracy, in which there is separation of church and state. Still, who could quarrel with the affirmation of this text, that there is a direct relationship between just rule—also linked with true piety—and the health of the body politic? Moreover, in a democracy it is not just a king but every citizen who is responsible for just rule.

Psalm 132:1–12 (13–18)

Like the Old Testament reading, a portion of this selection from the psalm focuses on the continuing rule of the family of David. Two features about this continuing rule are stressed: (1) the covenant between David and God is pictured as a sure oath and (2) the promise that David's descendants would rule after him, however, is made conditional on their obedience to the will of Yahweh.

Other aspects of this reading are its emphases upon Zion as the chosen dwelling place of God (vv. 12–16) and the promise to bless David (vv. 17–18). This bipolar, or double, focus on Zion and David is what one finds so frequently in the Old Testament. Sacred city and chosen dynasty are commonly so intricately interwoven as to comprise a single theological tapestry. The reasons for this are based on the fact that David was the conqueror of Jerusalem (Zion), which prior to his day had been no part of Israel or Judah. With the establishment of the political capital there, the Davidic monarch was in a special way the ruler over Jerusalem. This is why the town could be called "the city of David." It was the personal property of the Davidic family by right of conquest.

When Jerusalem was made into the religious capital for the people, this added a new dimension to the city. Zion was understood as the special home of God, who "resided" in Jerusalem in a way that was not the case any place else. The special presence of Yahweh in Jerusalem thus supported the claims of the Davidic family. The kings of the line of David were the defenders of Yahweh's city. At the same time, as the Deity of the city, Yahweh defended David and the rule of his descendants.

The content of Psalm 132 suggests that the psalm was used in a major recurring ritual celebration. Some scholars, however, have argued that the psalm was written for and used on the single occasion when David brought the ark to Jerusalem (2 Sam. 6). The differences between this psalm and the account of the bringing of the ark to Jerusalem as well as the reference to David's sons as rulers suggest that the psalm was not composed for that specific occasion. (Note that there is no material in 2 Sam. 6 similar to David's oath in Ps. 132:1–4.)

The psalm is set up so that the oath of David sworn to God, in verses 3–5 (which has no parallel in any of the narratives about David), is counterbalanced by the oath of God sworn to David, in verses 11b–12. If one preaches on this psalm reading, the parallel oaths and their stipulations should be noted—the human oath balanced by the divine.

The oath of God to David in verses 11b–12 actually has two emphases. There is, first, the assurance that one of David's sons would sit on his throne after him. One can understand this affirmation in relationship to Solomon. In fact, such a divine promise to David could be seen as theological justification for the rule of Solomon, who usurped the throne from his older brother, Adonijah, under rather shady and questionable circumstances. Second, the eternal rule ("forever") of subsequent Davidic descendants on the throne is promised but is hedged about with a major condition: they must keep the covenant and testimonies of God. There was no blank check made out to the house of David making payable an eternal rule without strings attached. The rights of dominion are tempered by the requirements of discipleship.

In verses 13–16, the emphases of the text focus on the role of Zion and God's special association and attachment to the city. The unique relationship between God and Zion—understood as the consequence of God's election of the city and his habitation in his house (temple) in its environs (v. 13)—is given expression in the form of a direct quote from God (vv. 14–16). Such a divine saying must have originated in the form of a prophetic oracle similar to those attributed to Nathan in 2 Samuel 7.

Zion is described as God's resting place (see 2 Sam. 7:4–8) and dwelling. Both verses 13 and 14 speak of God's desiring Zion, as if to stress the divine enthusiastic fervor for the place. David's bringing of the ark to Zion (vv. 6–7) thus fulfills the yearning and pleasure of God. The city (vv. 15–16) and the Davidic rulers (vv. 17–18) are to be blessed by the Deity, who dwells in Zion. The psalm thus stresses not only the blessing bestowed upon David and his descendants but also the blessing of the city and its inhabitants. There is thus no overemphasis on the royal elite in the psalm. The city is promised abundant provisions (food) for its livelihood and bread for its poor. As a consequence or parallel, the priests will be clothed in salvation, and the city's saints (inhabitants? cultic ministers?) will shout for joy. Thus the divine promise encompasses both physical and spiritual concerns.

The final two verses of the psalm revert to the theme of the Davidic family, although the theme is linked to the material on Zion by the reference to "there" in verse 17. Two images are used to speak of the royal descendants: a horn and a lamp. The horn was a symbol of strength and rulership (see Dan. 7:7–8). The lamp is a frequent figure used for the monarch (see 2 Sam. 21:17), no doubt because of the significance of the lamp in providing light and thus a perspective from which to view life. Finally, the Davidic monarch is promised that his enemies will be humiliated, whereas his own stature and importance, represented by the crown, will only increase in luster. In the international politics of antiquity, a ruler's success was built on the humiliation of others.

Three factors in the psalm may be noted in summary. First, the psalm illustrates the central role played by Zion in Israelite life, thus allowing one to appreciate why Jewish hopes and Zionism have always been intertwined. Second, the stress on the obedience of the Davidic rulers as a condition for God's support reflects an interpretation of history in which the downfall of the state was associated with the disobedience of the ruler (see 1 Sam. 12:13–15). Third, the stress on the eternal rule of the anointed (the messiah) from the house of David fed the expectations of a coming ruler who would reign as the ideal figure, the true Messiah.

Daniel 7:9–10, 13–14

Chapter 7 occupies a central place in the Book of Daniel, which was written during the Maccabean revolt, when faithful Jews were being persecuted by the Seleucid ruler Antiochus Epiphanes IV (167–164 BC). Much of the symbolism of the book relates directly to that situation. (For further commentary, see the discussion of Dan. 12:1–3 for Proper 28 [33] in this volume.)

Daniel 7 is the first of four vision reports in the book. Although similar in superficial ways to earlier prophetic visions, the apocalyptic visions are quite distinctive. Like most prophetic visions, they report a vision and then give its interpretation, and often the visionary sees himself in the revelation. But apocalyptic visions are much longer, and their symbolism is striking, bizarre, and detailed. The more significant contrast is that although prophetic visions generally concerned the immediate future, apocalyptic visions set the immediate situation of the visionary into the framework of world history as a whole and its imminent radical transformation. The writer of Daniel thus believed that the events of the wars and persecutions were the last throes of the forces of evil and that God would soon act to establish his reign.

Our lesson should be read in the context of Daniel 7 as a whole. The first and last verses provide a narrative framework. The remainder consists of the report of what was seen (vv. 2–14) and its interpretation (vv. 15–27), which at points reverts to the description of the scene before Daniel. Everything is recounted in the first person, that is, from the perspective of the visionary. Today's reading thus is the second part of the description of the revelation. It was preceded by the appearance of four great and horrible beasts out of the sea, finally focusing on the little horn of the last beast to appear.

The vision of the appearance of "an Ancient One" (v. 9) contrasts dramatically with the foregoing scene. But the dark backdrop of terror is not forgotten. As myriads of worshipers come before the glorious throne, the sound of the little horn can still be heard (v. 11).

The scene in Daniel 7:9–14 includes three distinct movements. First (vv. 9–10), there is the vision of the appearance of the Ancient One and his court. This is doubtless a description of God and is remarkable in its visual detail. In the Old Testament, God is never described so specifically. Other features of the description, however, are indebted to traditions found elsewhere in the Old Testament. Prophets and others often envisioned God's heavenly court (1 Kings 22:19; Job 1:6; Ezek. 1; Isa. 6; Ps. 82). The fiery throne with wheels appears in Ezekiel 1–3. The "court" may be simply the reflection of a royal throne room, but here it is juridical, for "judgment" (v. 10). Second (vv. 11–12), judgment is executed on "the beast," apparently the last one with the horns. This amounts to a death sentence upon the Greek Empire, including its Seleucid descendants. Third (vv. 13–14), "one like a human being" appears before the Ancient One and is granted dominion and glory, a kingdom that shall not end.

The "one like a human being" is not named, and his identity has been a lively question in the history of the interpretation and application of the text. A very similar expression, "son of man," occurs numerous times in the Book of Ezekiel, as the form of address when Yahweh speaks to the prophet. There it means simply "human being." The phrase is used this way in Daniel 8:17 in an address to Daniel, but in 8:15, one "having the appearance of a man" means an angelic figure. Because his kingdom will not pass away (v. 14), and the same thing is said of the kingdom given to the "saints of the Most High," some have taken "the one like a human being" as a collective reference to the "saints," the righteous faithful worshipers. But the expression here must have in view an angelic, messianic figure. To be "like a human being" must mean not human but having some human characteristics or appearance. It is easy to see why such vocabulary became important in expressing the meaning of the incarnation of God in Jesus, both fully human and fully divine.

The purpose of this text in the framework of chapter 7 is to communicate and publish a divine revelation concerning the course and end of history, which will be the reign of God in justice. God will put an end to the worldly enemy and set up a kingdom in which the faithful will participate. Even suffering under bestial powers has meaning, and it will last for only a while.

The proclamation of apocalyptic texts is not easy, but such texts lie at the heart of the Christian faith. God's dominion has already come, but it is not yet consummated. We live, said the earliest Christians with the Book of Daniel, already in the light of the New Age that is dawning upon us. The vision of that age must inform all we say and do. One way to proclaim such texts is to look for signs of that reign of God around us. Here the hungry are fed. There people live together in peace. Here a family is reconciled. None of these is the kingdom. But the kingdom of God is like that.

Psalm 93

This psalm was discussed previously as one of the readings for the Ascension of the Lord.

Revelation 1:4*b*–8

It would be difficult to find a text more suitable for the occasion than today's epistolary lection, with its powerful images of vindication and triumph, its stress on Christ as "the ruler of the kings of the earth" (v. 5), and its eschatological motif (v. 7). First, however, it should be noted that in form it is an epistolary greeting from "John to the seven churches that are in Asia" (1:4*a*). Typical of the way many New Testament letters begin, the Book of Revelation as a letter begins with a prayer addressed to the readers. Perhaps it is even more appropriate that the final epistolary lection of the liturgical year is in the form of a prayer that magnificently addresses those in whom the hopes of every Christian lie: God "who is and who was and who is to come" (4:8; 11:17; 16:5; Exod. 3:14; Isa. 41:4); the Holy Spirit here conceived as "the seven spirits of God" (3:1; 4:5; 5:6; cf. esp. Isa. 11:2–3); and Christ, who is given multiple acclamations that we will note later. Though not fully Trinitarian as the term later came to be understood by the church, the opening greeting at least pays homage to the fullness of Christian Deity.

The centerpiece of the prayer, however, is Christ, who is acclaimed with a veritable cluster of rich and powerful images, any one of which the preacher could profitably explore on this final Sunday of the liturgical year:

Faithful witness (v. 5). Taken one way, the Greek wording may actually imply two acclamations: "the witness," or literally "the martyr" (*martys*), and "the faithful one." Jesus as a martyr figure who was slain is obviously a dominant image of the Book of Revelation (cf. 5:9; 13:8) and one that doubtless heartened the readers who themselves were being persecuted, and in some cases martyred (6:9–10; 20:4–6). This might be developed along with the emphasis in the passion narrative of the Gospel of Luke, where Christ's death is portrayed especially as that of a martyred figure, an innocent prophet unjustly convicted and killed. But not only was he a "martyr"; he was one who demonstrated absolute fidelity to his calling. He is thus the "faithful and true witness" (3:14; also 19:11; cf. Ps. 89:1–2; Jer. 42:5). It may be that the phrase "faith of Jesus Christ" (Rom. 3:22) is a reference to such fidelity on his part, that is, the faithfulness that Christ demonstrated in his sacrificial death. In any case, the example of Christ emphasizes the exhortation to these readers, "Be faithful until death, and I will give you the crown of life" (2:10).

Firstborn of the dead (v. 5). By his resurrection, Christ became the "first fruits of those who have died" (1 Cor. 15:20), or to use another metaphor, the "firstborn from the dead" (cf. Col. 1:18). As the "first child" of the resurrected life, he enjoys the status and esteem that rightly falls to the firstborn, and, therefore, oldest child (Ps. 89:27; also 2:7).

Ruler of the kings of the earth (v. 5). Just as David had been described as the "leader and commander for the peoples" (Isa. 55:4), so Christ as David's heir enjoys the rank of the "kings' king" (cf. Luke 1:32–33), or in the words of our author, "Lord of lords and King of kings" (17:14; 19:16; also 1 Tim. 6:15).

After these words of acclamation about Christ, the prayer turns to the work of Christ and what he has done on our behalf. First, it is noted that he "loves us and freed us from our sins by his blood" (v. 5). The language here recalls earlier epistolary lections, such as Ephesians 5:1: "Christ loved us and gave himself up for us." His sacrificial death and redemption achieved through the shedding of his blood call to mind the epistolary lections from Hebrews that have just been concluded (cf. Heb. 9:14), but can also be related to a host of other biblical readings (1 John 1:7; also Isa. 40:2; Ps. 130:7–8).

Not only did he effect true and lasting forgiveness for us; he also elevated us to priestly status, making us "priests serving his God and Father" (v. 6), thereby fulfilling the prophetic hope (Isa. 61:6; also 1 Pet. 2:5, 9). But priestly service also implies sharing in his kingly reign. Israel was called to the service of Yahweh as "a priestly kingdom and a holy nation" (Exod. 19:6), and this double honor Christ has made possible for us (5:10). Those who remain faithful are promised to be made "priests of God and of Christ" and to "reign with him a thousand years" (20:6).

Because of what he has made possible on our behalf, his is "glory and dominion forever and ever" (v. 6). Such universal adoration is typically given to both God and Christ throughout the Book of Revelation (4:11; 5:13; 7:10, 12; 11:15, 17; 12:10; 15:3–4; 19:1–2, 5, 6–7). Other New Testament doxologies similarly acknowledge their preeminent position (Rom. 11:36; 16:27; Gal. 1:5; Eph. 3:21; Phil. 4:20; 1 Tim. 1:17; 2 Tim. 4:18; Heb. 13:21; 1 Pet. 4:11; 2 Pet. 3:18; Jude 25).

With verse 7, there is emphatic stress on the eschatological work of Christ as the one who "is coming with the clouds" (cf. Dan. 7:13; also Matt. 24:30 and parallels). His coming will be universally visible (cf. Zech. 12:10), especially to those who were party to his crucifixion (cf. John 19:37). Judgment will be handed out to "all the tribes of the earth," and "on his account" they "will wail."

After the conclusion of the prayer, the Lord God proclaims, "I am the Alpha and the Omega . . . who is and who was and who is to come, the Almighty" (v. 8). Standing at the beginning and end of time and all things (cf. Isa. 44:6), God encompasses all time: past, present, and future (21:6; 22:13; also 4:8; 11:17; 16:5). As the victor of time, God is unquestionably "the Almighty" (4:8; 11:17; 15:3; 16:7, 14; 19:6, 15; 21:22; also 2 Cor. 6:18; cf. 2 Sam. 7:8, Amos 3:13; 4:13).

With this multifaceted text, rich with christological symbolism and packed with powerful confessional statements, the preacher will find it difficult to decide what not to explore. Almost any single element of the passage could serve as the springboard for the sermon on this occasion.

John 18:33–37

The Season of Pentecost concludes with the service of Christ the King. The Gospel proclamation for this service draws on Jesus' response to Pilate's question "Are you the King of the Jews?" (John 18:33). In order to hear the response properly, we need first to attend to the occasion that prompted the question.

Many efforts to reconstruct the trial of Jesus use the Synoptics primarily, inserting from John any phases of the procedure not reported by the other Evangelists. Unique to the Fourth Gospel is the interrogation by Annas (18:13, 19–24), high priest and father-in-law of Caiaphas, who was functioning as "high priest that year" (18:13). Because the high priesthood was for life, the reference to Caiaphas as high priest "that year" is probably the writer's caustic comment on the power of Roman politics to determine even the religious institution. But using John to supplement the Synoptics is hardly a proper way to read this Gospel. The fact is, John has an entirely different perspective on the trial, as he does on the entire ministry of Jesus.

In the Gospel of John, Jesus is from God, is going again to God, and is, throughout his ministry, aware of this origin and destiny. He carries out God's will according to "his hour" and is not determined in word or deed by outside forces. In 12:23, Jesus says, "The hour has come for the Son of Man to be glorified," and the reader senses that all the subsequent events will unfold to that end. Judas, the soldiers, the priests, Pilate: all are responsible for their actions; but for this Evangelist what really needs to be seen is the purpose of God at work through all the contingencies of historical events. From this perspective, Jesus is presented clear-eyed, firm, and totally in control while all about him other characters are running around filling their roles in the drama.

With this in mind, let us notice more closely the trial scenes. The interrogation by religious leaders occupies verses 13–27. The appearance before Annas is sketchily presented, Annas being high priest but not really high priest. Caiaphas is mentioned four times, but there is not one word about his encounter with Jesus. After all, Caiaphas is high priest but not really high priest. Of the four brief paragraphs, two are devoted to Simon Peter (vv. 15–18, 25–27). Why? Because that is where the real trial is taking place, outside by the charcoal fire. Inside, Jesus is being questioned, but it is meaningless; Jesus moves with firm purpose to his own glorification. But outside, Simon Peter (and the disciples, and the church) is being questioned, and that trial is not going well at all. The Evangelist proves himself as much the preacher as the historian.

The trial before Pilate is, unlike the Synoptics, very lengthily told (18:29–19:16). Our lection records the second of seven episodes (18:29–32, 33–38a, 38b–40; 19:1–3, 47, 8–11, 12–16) in that trial during which Pilate is portrayed as a tragi-comical figure who shuttles back and forth between the Jews outside and Jesus inside. He claims the power of the state, not knowing that his power has been given to him from above (19:11). He shouts his authority but performs in confusion and fear, submitting to petty politics and prejudice. He says he is in charge, but it is obvious that Jesus is in charge. Jesus counters Pilate's question with a question (v. 34), offers logical proof that his kingdom is not of this world ("not from this world" does not mean otherworldly but that his kingdom is not determined by or grounded in the values and strategies of the world), and tells Pilate the reason he cannot understand this (v. 37). In the two-level drama of this Gospel, the writer and reader understand what the characters in the story do not.

Pilate can ask, "So you are a king?" (v. 37), but he cannot understand the answer. But the church did, and does. The church stood and stands before powers and authorities, being interrogated. And in that hour the church recalls this scene. "So you are a king?" Yes, but not because of the world's authorities or in spite of them. Because human hands did not place the crown on his head, human hands cannot remove it.

All Saints, November 1, or on First Sunday in November

Wisdom of Solomon 3:1–9 or Isaiah 25:6–9;
Psalm 24;
Revelation 21:1–6*a*;
John 11:32–44

On All Saints' Day, we remember those who have preceded us in the life of faith. We recall their noble lives as examples of courage and fidelity, and we celebrate the heavenly hope to which they aspired. In doing so, we find ourselves linked with them as sharers of a common hope and destiny.

The *Common Lectionary* offers two options for the Old Testament reading. With assurance that the souls of the righteous are in the hands of God, the text from the Wisdom of Solomon captures the celebratory spirit of All Saints. The eschatological vision of Isaiah sketches the fulfilled hopes of the righteous. Psalm 24 responds by offering assurance that the faithful will ascend Zion and have a place in God's presence.

The epistolary reading sketches the eschatological vision of "a new heaven and a new earth," a vision that has captured the imagination of saints in every century. They have been drawn to it and motivated by it, even as we are.

In recounting the story of the raising of Lazarus, the Gospel reading from John brings to the fore themes of resurrection and eternal life.

Wisdom of Solomon 3:1–9

The Wisdom of Solomon is attributed to Israel's third king on the grounds of the tradition of his great wisdom. But the book most likely was written in the Hellenistic period by a pious and learned Jew living outside Palestine. It almost certainly was originally written not in Hebrew—like virtually all of the Hebrew canon—but in Greek, probably in Alexandria, and in the first century before Jesus. The book as a whole, addressed to Jews in a pagan world, is an extraordinary argument for faithfulness to the ancient covenant. The author both polemicizes against and is influenced by various aspects of the dominant Hellenistic culture.

The assigned verses from chapter 3 express the main themes of the first section of the book, chapters 1–5. Those chapters contain a series of exhortations to live the life that is immortal. They are part of the book's larger argument for faithfulness. The main concerns of this initial series of exhortations are immortality and death. The views articulated on those issues go far beyond those in the Hebrew Scriptures, but at the same time the writer makes explicit connections with ancient biblical traditions.

Both in terms of mood and contents, this is a highly appropriate reading for All Saints' Day. On this day we remember and celebrate those of the faithful throughout the centuries who have died. This text is explicitly concerned with "the righteous" (v. 1), whose souls are in the hand of God, God's "holy ones" (v. 9) whom God watches over. Whereas other parts of this section of The Wisdom of Solomon contain exhortations and arguments to live the life that is eternal, these verses joyfully celebrate those who have lived and now are "at peace" (v. 3).

Unlike Daniel 12:1–3, in which the expectation is the resurrection of the dead, this text celebrates immortality, the eternal life of those who have died. It is only in "the eyes of the foolish" that they seemed to have died (v. 2). It seemed that their death was a disaster, but they are at peace (v. 3). Death was not a punishment, for they had hope for immortality (v. 4). In fact, the lives of the saints were tested to see if they would be worthy of immortality (v. 5).

But there is just a glimpse of a more apocalyptic view, a look even beyond the death of the saints to a time when the reign of God will be established (vv. 7–8). Those who have been tried in the furnace and then accepted by God (v. 6) "will govern nations and rule over peoples, and the Lord will reign over them forever" (v. 8). That is, while celebrating the eternal life of the saints, these lives still look to the establishment of the reign of God in righteousness.

This text, like the biblical tradition as a whole, emphasizes that immortal life is in the hands of God. Like life itself, it is a gift of God. It is connected with the life of faith ("those who trust in him," v. 9), love, grace, and mercy (v. 9). And because eternal life is a gift of God, these words from The Wisdom of Solomon can sound out as a hymn of praise and thanksgiving to God for all the saints.

Isaiah 25:6–9

For a discussion of this text, see the commentary on the texts assigned for Easter Day in this volume.

Psalm 24

This psalm has been previously discussed in this volume (see Proper 10 [15]). Its connection with All Saints' Day is made possible by a certain spiritualizing and Christianizing of the text.

The psalm was part of an entrance liturgy used when the doors to the temple precincts were opened to allow entry of pilgrims who had come to Jerusalem to celebrate a festival. The employment of this text on All Saints' Day can be seen in the following associations: (1) the object of entry, the temple precincts, referred to in the psalm as the "hill of the LORD" and "his holy place" (v. 3), is understood as the abode of God or the other world, the heavenly destiny; (2) those entering are understood to be the deceased, the dead who were entering the other world; and (3) the ethical requirements for entering the temple (in v. 4) are interpreted as the ethical standards by which the dead are judged.

Psalm 24 was also used in the early church for understanding Jesus' descent into Hades. In addition, the psalm was used as an interpretive text for expounding his ascent into heaven.

It may have been this latter usage that was then adopted to the "entry" of the saints into the heavenly world of glory.

Revelation 21:1–6a

The vision of "a new heaven and a new earth" in Revelation 21:1–6a should not be viewed in isolation. It is only one in a series of visions in which the seer has been shown the victorious Christ (19:11–21), the binding of Satan and the millennial reign of the martyrs (20:1–6), the loosing of Satan and the Great Assize (20:7–15). Today's passage is actually the first segment of the lengthy vision of the new Jerusalem (21:1–22:5). This broader literary context is worth noting because today's passage makes no explicit mention of the saints who inhabit the new Jerusalem. They are in view, however, as the larger context makes clear. The seer has been shown those saints martyred for the faith who have been raised to share in the millennial reign (20:4–6). He also describes the inhabitants of the new Jerusalem as "those who are written in the Lamb's book of life" (21:27).

The vision opens with a cosmic transformation in which the "first heaven and the first earth" have "passed away" (v. 1; cf. 2 Pet. 3:7). In apocalyptic thought, the created order is subject to the more powerful sway of the divine will and may be said to "vanish" or "flee" (6:14; 16:20; 20:11). But even in the pictorial language of the psalms, the created order is similarly viewed (Ps. 114:3, 7). The disappearance of the sea indicates that it is a complete transformation. The primeval waters that serve as the home of dragons and beasts no longer separate heaven and earth (13:1; 17:1). This vision of the new heaven and earth is informed by the prophetic vision of Isaiah (65:17–18; 66:22).

Descending from heaven is "the holy city, the new Jerusalem" (v. 2; cf. 3:12; also Gal. 4:26; Heb. 11:16; 12:22). It became proverbial to speak of Jerusalem as "the holy city" (Isa. 48:2; Dan. 9:24; Neh. 11:1, 18; Matt. 4:5; 27:53; Rev. 11:2; 21:10; 22:19). So closely was the city identified with Israel itself that the city could virtually signify the people of God, whose character was expected to be consonant with the holy character of the city (Isa. 52:1). This emphasis on moral purity as a prerequisite for admission to the temple is seen in today's psalm. To compare the "holy city" with "a bride adorned for her husband" (v. 2) only serves to reinforce this image of wholeness and purity. It also introduces the image of the messianic feast, which is frequently used as an eschatological image (19:9, 17; 21:9; Matt. 9:15; 18:23; 22:2; Isa. 61:10).

The reference to "the voice from the throne" (v. 3) recalls an earlier vision where God sits enthroned on a "great white throne" (20:11; cf. 16:7; 19:5). The message of the voice is that God's presence is now fully realized. God's dwelling, or literally his "tent," is now pitched "with mortals," thereby fulfilling Old Testament hopes (Lev. 26:11–12; Ezek. 37:27; 1 Kings 8:27; also Zech. 2:13; cf. John 1:14; Rev. 13:6). To experience the full presence of God is to become identified as God's people (v. 3; cf. Isa. 8:10; Jer. 31:1, Ps. 95:7).

Especially striking about this new world is what is not there: tears, death, mourning, crying, pain (v. 4). Each of these should be understood as having specific reference to the martyrs who have been mentioned earlier (cf. 7:17). Yet this eschatological vision also expresses the realization of prophetic hopes (Isa. 25:8; Jer. 31:16).

In the final words of today's lection, the seer is reassured that this is a genuinely new reality: "See, I am making all things new" (v. 5). The new creation begun in the Christ-event (2 Cor. 5:17) has now come to full fruition. He is also assured that these revelatory words are "trustworthy and true" (v. 5). This has been the confident hope of every believer who has lived and died for the faith. Finally, there is the declaration "It is done!" (v. 6a). The work of God has now been completed fully and finally. And the one who has brought history to its end is "the Alpha and the Omega, the beginning and the end" (v. 6a). To speak of God in this way is more than a claim that God brackets time and history on both ends. It is rather a way of saying that God is both the source and purpose of history.

As we have seen, today's text has in mind in particular the saints who have been martyred for the faith. On All Saints' Day we remember the acts of Christian martyrs, as well as the deeds and works of "canonized" saints. But we also celebrate the lives of all the faithful, living and dead, for whom the new Jerusalem is their ultimate destiny. The words of the preface in the festal Mass are especially appropriate: "Today we keep the festival of your holy city, the heavenly Jerusalem, our mother. Around your throne the saints, our brothers and sisters, sing your praise for ever. Their glory fills us with joy, and their communion with us in your Church gives us inspiration and strength as we hasten on our pilgrimage of faith, eager to meet them" (cited in A. Adam, *The Liturgical Year* [New York: Pueblo Publishing, 1981], 229).

John 11:32–44

T he celebration of All Saints' Day reminds us that God is a God of the living and not of the dead. Texts appropriate to that affirmation announce resurrection, life eternal, and the inheritance of the faithful among the saints in light. For this reason, we return to the Gospel that proclaims Jesus as the resurrection and the life, and to the chapter of that Gospel which says this most dramatically.

John 11:32–44 is the story of the raising of Lazarus, but the story begins in 11:1, and so a review of the entire account is necessary for understanding today's text. Even in the sermon proper, the preacher would do well to move the listener through the entire drama. Sometimes we assume that people recall more of a biblical story than they in fact do. But even so, those familiar with a text appreciate being confirmed in what they know. Such a recital would be especially appropriate to John 11:1–44 because, even though this is one of the many sign stories, this one is unique in a literary sense. In the preceding sign stories the pattern is fairly consistent: the sign is performed, followed by a discourse or dispute. Here, however, the sign comes at the end, after the gradual heightening of dramatic tension.

To say that John 11:32–44 is part of a sign story is to say that Jesus will act according to "his time" and not in response to requests or pressure ("he stayed two days longer in the place where he was," v. 6). Recall Jesus' response to his mother at Cana (2:4). Being a sign also means that what Jesus does will be a revelatory act, an act making God known. In this case, we are told that what is to transpire will be for the glory of God (v. 4). But the reader is also told that the event that follows will result in the glorifying of the Son of God (v. 4). This is Johannine language for the elevation of Jesus upon the cross and his exaltation to the presence of God (12:23–26, 32). In other words, Jesus' act in relation to Lazarus will effect Jesus' own death, which in fact was the case, according to verses 45–57. Neither Mary (v. 32) nor Martha (v. 21) could, of course, know the price that Jesus would pay for raising their brother. They could not know that this act would set in motion the political machinery for Jesus' death (vv. 47–48; 12:9–11), that Lazarus' release from the tomb would mean Jesus had to enter it.

But the reader knows, being given clues all along, not only in verse 4 but in the story itself: a tomb near Jerusalem; the tomb a cave covered by a large stone; the stone rolled away; Jesus troubled; Jesus cried out; the grave cloth. In fact, the descriptions of Jesus as "greatly disturbed in spirit and deeply moved" (v. 33), weeping (v. 35), and "again greatly disturbed" (v. 38) may be understood as a Johannine Gethsemane, all evidences of agony or grief being absent in John's account of the garden scene itself. Because this is a sign narrative, therefore, the reader knows that the text is not dealing only with a family crisis in Bethany but with the crisis of the world, not only with the death and resurrection of Lazarus but with the death and resurrection of Jesus, not only with what two sisters want but with what the world needs. Jesus will give life not to Lazarus alone but to all who believe.

The key to the entire narrative was stated in the words of Jesus to Martha: "I am the resurrection and the life. Those who believe in me, even though they die, will live; and everyone who lives and believes in me will never die" (vv. 25–26). Martha expressed faith in a resurrection at the end time (v. 24), but obviously thinking of eternal life only in terms of the hereafter was small comfort to her in a time of grief. Jesus not only corrects her faith but enlarges her hope by moving eternal life from the end time alone to the time of faith in Christ. Christ is the eschatological event; he is the point where death ends and life begins; he provides life on both sides of the grave, here and hereafter. But the story does not have its fulfillment when the sign is understood. Jesus did not ask Martha, "Do you understand this?" Rather, he asked her what the entire Gospel asks the reader (20:31). "Do you *believe* this?"

Thanksgiving Day

Joel 2:21–27;
Psalm 126;
1 Timothy 2:1–7;
Matthew 6:25–33

All the texts for this day can help the worshiping community express its thanks to God. Joel 2:21–27 calls for rejoicing and celebration in view of God's promises, including material blessings such as food to eat. Moreover, the Lord promises to be present with the people. Psalm 126, though not one of thanksgiving, contains harvest motifs. It is a prayer that those who sow in tears shall reap in joy, "carrying their sheaves" (v. 6). First Timothy 2:1–7 exhorts the faithful to offer prayers, including ones of thanksgiving, for kings and others in high places, in order "that we may lead a quiet and peaceable life" (v. 2). The Gospel lection contains the teaching of Jesus about anxiety for food and clothing.

Joel 2:21–27

The Book of Joel is a liturgical work in two parts. In the first part (Joel 1:2–2:17), the prophet directs the community to convene a service of complaint and petition to God, initially because of the threat of a plague of locusts (1:4–20) and then because of the terrifying prospect of the day of the Lord. In the second part (Joel 2:18–3:21), the mood changes dramatically because the people have repented. God promises salvation and over and over again assures the people that their prayers have been heard. The day of the Lord has become a day of salvation because the people trust in their God.

Although there is no superscription that dates the book, the political and religious references fit the Persian period, probably about 400 BC. Joel is an example of a prophet who participated directly, and probably in an officially recognized fashion, in the services of worship in the second temple. We hear him giving the call to prayer and fasting, ordering the priests to gather the people, giving instructions in proper prayer, and then proclaiming the divine response to the people's genuine contrition.

In terms of form, the passage before us is a series of announcements of salvation. In verses 21–23 the prophet is the speaker, proclaiming words of assurance to nature. The land itself is called to rejoice. Then (v. 24) similar calls to celebrate are spoken to the people because God has given the rain. Verses 24–25 amount to a reversal of the bad fortune described in the first part of the book. The Lord promises that there will be plenty of grain, wine, and oil, and that he will restore the losses caused by the locusts. In a final announcement of salvation (vv. 26–27), the bounty of nature is related to the joy of worship and the continuing presence of God among the people. When all these things happen, the people will be assured that there is no other God but Yahweh.

On the occasion of Thanksgiving, this reading calls attention to the bounty of nature—the land, animals, pastures, trees, vines, rain—and provides the language for celebration in humble thanks. Experience confirms that there are countless reasons for thanks. But even more, it calls attention to the God from whom we receive all things necessary for life. With the material gifts comes the presence of the Giver, the very one who made and sustains all those things. In that way the reading coincides with the reading from Matthew: "Strive first for the kingdom of God and his righteousness . . ." (Matt. 6:33).

Psalm 126

This psalm has been previously discussed in the present volume (see the Third Sunday of Advent). A few comments at this point will be made about the possible use of this psalm in connection with Thanksgiving. The selection of this psalm for this season of the year is based on the psalm's employment of harvest imagery.

The polarities found in the psalm—weeping/shouting, tears/joy, going forth/coming home, sowing/reaping—might be the departure point for developing a sermon. Thanksgiving, of course, embodies one of the poles of human existence, namely, joy and extravagance. In a way, all festival times should be periods when normal sentiments and feelings are heightened, intensified, and celebrated to the breaking point. For example, the two dominant characteristics of the Thanksgiving Season are a thankful spirit and a gluttonous indulgence. At this season, we intensify our sense of being dependent and therefore thankful for life's gifts, and we gorge our appetites and stuff our stomachs. Both activities are quite appropriate—they are the way in which we interrupt the ordinary flow of life with the insertion of the extraordinary. Tears, sowing, going forth, weeping are pushed into the background, and we give full vent to the other pole of human existence. In preaching from this text, the minister should find ways to affirm both the thanksgiving and the extravagance of the season.

1 Timothy 2:1–7

This epistolary lection has been chosen as a text for Thanksgiving Day because it urges "thanksgivings" as one form of prayer to be offered on behalf of everyone (v. 1). Actually, this passage is part of a larger set of instructions concerning the protocol of Christian worship, and it should be read beside other passages urging us to be vigilant and constant in prayer (Acts 2:42; Rom. 12:12; Eph. 6:18; Phil. 4:6; Col. 4:2; 1 Thess. 5:17). By including "thanksgivings" with "supplications, prayers, [and] intercessions," today's text teaches us that in prayer we must learn not only to ask but also to acknowledge.

What is striking about these instructions is that they urge us to cast our net widely as we pray. We are instructed to pray "for everyone" (v. 1). In its insistence that we pray for all of humanity, our text recognizes that we tend to pray for our own kind and thus urges that we break through such narrowness. And why should Christian prayers be concerned for all humanity? Because this is the scope of God's concern. God, after all, "desires everyone to be saved and to come to the knowledge of the truth" (v. 4). As the prophet Ezekiel put it, God takes no pleasure in the death of the wicked (Ezek. 18:23, 32; 33:11; cf. Wisd. of Sol. 11:26). Or in the words of Second Peter, God wants no one to perish (2 Pet. 3:9; cf. Rom. 11:32).

To clinch his point, it looks as if the author cites part of a primitive Christian confession in verses 5–6 (cf. Nestle, 26th ed.; printed strophically in NRSV, though not in REB and NJB). If these words are creedal, we are reminded that what we confess in worship bears this out; namely, that "there is one God; there is also one mediator between God and humankind, Christ Jesus, himself human, who gave himself a ransom for all" (vv. 5–6). At the heart of our faith are exclusive claims: one God (1 Cor. 8:4, 6; 12:5–16; Rom. 3:30; Eph. 4:5–6; Mal. 2:10) and one mediator, Christ Jesus (Heb. 8:6; 9:15; 12:24). Yet their saving grace is all-embracing, for God through Christ intended to ransom all (Matt. 20:28 and parallels; 2 Cor. 5:5; Gal. 1:4; 2:20; Eph. 5:2, 25; Titus 2:14; cf. Ps. 49:8). Just as their salvation was universal in scope, so should our prayers reach beyond ourselves to all humanity.

We might notice the similarity between the sentiments of our text and the teaching of Jesus in Matthew 5:43–48. There, the point is put more sharply as Jesus challenges his disciples to love their enemies and pray for their persecutors. And why? Because God has the capacity to send sunshine and rain on the good and the bad, the just and the unjust. Like our text, Matthew insists that in deciding whom to pray for, Christians should take their cue from God.

But our text goes further in urging us to pray for "kings and all who are in high positions" (v. 2). As before, it seems to recognize that this too will be difficult for us at times because of apathy or because of passionate disagreement. In this respect, our text echoes other New Testament passages that urge us to be prayerful for civil authorities (Rom. 13:1–7; Titus 3:1; 1 Pet. 2:13–15; cf. Ezra 6:10; Bar. 1:11–12; Jer. 29:7). Nor are the reasons selfless, for our text quite frankly urges this on the grounds that stable governments make it possible to "lead a quiet and peaceable life" (v. 2; cf. 1 Thess. 4:11; 2 Thess. 3:12). Obviously, we should not allow this text to blind us to the realities of corrupt governments, and we do well to balance this picture with the one in the Book of Revelation, where oppressive rulers are depicted as beasts to be resisted rather than gods to be obeyed.

Our text, then, opens on a note of thanksgiving, but quickly introduces to us dilemmas of our faith. We confess the one God and the one mediator, Jesus Christ, and in doing so separate ourselves from those who cannot and will not confess likewise. Yet our text will not allow us to become a Christian ghetto where we pray only to ourselves and for ourselves. As squarely as we stand within our confession, we nonetheless are bound to see beyond it. To the degree that we are able to do this, we become like God. And to this extent, we can learn to say prayers of thanksgiving.

Matthew 6:25–33

The Gospel reading for a Thanksgiving Day service reminds us that gratitude is not simply a generalized orientation but is properly gratitude *to God* who provides for our needs, relieving us of a consuming anxiety about material things.

Matthew 6:25–33 is one of several units of teachings of Jesus common to Matthew and Luke but absent from Mark. Scholars have come to assume a sayings-source back of these two Gospels that is, for lack of a better term, called Q from the German *Quelle*, "source." But even with a common source, each Evangelist determined the location of the sayings within his own narrative. Luke places the teachings in today's lesson at 12:22–34, immediately after the parable of the rich fool. Matthew sets them within the Sermon on the Mount immediately after sayings on earthly treasures and service to God and mammon.

This lection from Matthew consists of sayings, maxims, and proverbs and, therefore, presents Jesus as the sage, the teacher of wisdom. If the source common to Matthew and Luke portrayed Jesus primarily in the wisdom tradition, that image has been preserved more by Matthew than by Luke. That the form and to a large extent the content of this material were found among the rabbis' instructions to the faith community does not argue convincingly that these are not authentic sayings of Jesus. Matthew says that Jesus, after teaching in parables, told his disciples, "Therefore every scribe who has been trained for the kingdom of heaven is like the master of a household who brings out of his treasure what is new and what is old" (13:52).

Matthew provides no description of those to whom Jesus addressed these teachings about anxiety. History has proven them equally appropriate for the wealthy and the poor, for anxiety about money seems to afflict both those who have it and those who do not. Because, however, the concerns here are as elementary as food and clothing, and given the general socioeconomic status of Jesus' listeners, very likely he was speaking to the poor.

The subject matter is anxiety, obsessive and debilitating worry, over material things. Jesus' instruction is not overspiritualized and unrealistic. As to food, clothing, and shelter, Jesus states clearly "your heavenly Father knows that you need all these things" (v. 32). What he does say, however, is that anxiety is totally futile (v. 27). Excessive worry does not solve problems, reach goals, overcome difficulties. No one by means of anxiety has added one cubit (yard) to one's life span (stature?). A more fruitful alternative is to take one's mind off oneself and look around at the bounty of God's providence. Studying the face of nature and drawing lessons from observing animals, plants, earth, and sky were characteristics common to sages and teachers of wisdom. In this case, Jesus points to birds of the air and lilies of the field, all of them free of the burdens of laboring men (toil) and women (spin) and yet fed and clothed by a God who cares for every creature. If then, argues Jesus from the lesser to the greater, God cares for birds and flowers, is it not reasonable to trust that no less care will be shown to us?

The words of Jesus on the subject of anxiety about things are a part of his teachings about the kingdom. The call is for radical trust and single-minded service. That which is uncompromisingly primary is orienting one's life to the approaching reign of God (v. 33). After all, life is qualified by what one seeks. If relative, created values are made absolute, there is no release from anxiety with their attainment. The promise is impoverished in its fulfillment, and anxiety returns. But when absolute values (God's kingdom and righteousness) are made absolute, the relative values and creature needs will take their proper place, and with satisfaction. And lest seeking God's kingdom become in itself a new cause of anxiety, Luke concludes this section with "Do not be afraid, little flock, for it is your Father's good pleasure to give you the kingdom" (12:32).

Presentation of the Lord, February 2

Malachi 3:1–4;
Psalm 84 or Psalm 24:7–10;
Hebrews 2:14–18;
Luke 2:22–40

This day is the celebration of the event reported in the Gospel reading, the presentation of Jesus in the temple in Jerusalem in accordance with Jewish law. Either of the psalms is highly appropriate, for both enable the church at worship to recreate the scene at the temple. Psalm 84 is a pilgrim hymn in praise of Zion, and Psalm 24:7–10 is an entrance liturgy that praises the King of glory. The christological reflections in Hebrews 2:14–18 show a fully human Lord as high priest in service of God. Malachi 3:1–4 is the promise of a messenger of the covenant, who will come like a "refiner's fire," after which the offerings—such as those mentioned in the Gospel—will be acceptable to God.

Malachi 3:1–4

The Book of Malachi originated in the postexilic period, between 520 BC, when the temple was rebuilt, and 400 BC, when the law was instituted by Ezra. Sacrifices and offerings in the temple seem to have become a regular part of the life of worship. Judah would have been a province of the Persian Empire, with its own "governor" (Mal. 1:8).

Nothing is known about the life of the prophet himself, not even his name. "Malachi" is not a proper name but the title "my messenger," apparently taken from the passage before us (3:1). The person responsible for the book continues the ancient prophetic tradition of speaking in the name of the Lord concerning the immediate future, and he is willing to challenge current beliefs and practices. He was deeply interested in priestly matters and likely was identified with the Levites (Mal. 2:4–9).

The reading for today is part of a unit that begins in 2:17 and concludes with 3:5. It is a disputation between the prophet, speaking on behalf of the Lord, and persons whose words he quotes. They have "wearied" the Lord by saying, "All who do evil are good in the sight of the LORD, and he delights in them," and by asking, "Where is the God of justice?" (2:17). In short, because evildoers prosper, these opponents question the presence of a God of justice.

Malachi 3:1–4 is the prophetic response to such objections. The prophet hears the Lord announcing the arrival of a messenger, the messenger of the covenant, who will prepare for the appearance of the Lord himself in the temple. The day of arrival, elsewhere called the day of the Lord, will be a terrible time, for no one can stand before him. It will be a day of refining and purification, particularly of the Levites, who will then present offerings that "will be pleasing to the LORD" (v. 4).

Next, the Lord himself will appear in judgment, punishing "all who do evil" (2:17), including sorcerers, adulterers, and those who deal unjustly with the weak, such as hirelings, widows, orphans, and resident aliens (3:5). Where is the God of justice? God is sending a messenger to prepare the way, cleansing the priesthood and the temple worship, and then God himself will approach as judge. Sinners may prosper, but not for long.

The passage has reverberated in various ways throughout Christian tradition. Mark took the messenger to be John the Baptist and quoted the initial line of verse 1 to introduce the account of John's appearance and his baptism of Jesus. On the commemoration of Presentation, read with Luke 2:22–40, the ambiguities of verse 1 take on added significance. Is Jesus the messenger, or the Lord himself, who "will suddenly come to his temple?" The somber, apocalyptic tone of the passage from Malachi underscores the threatening aspects of the presentation of Jesus in the temple (Luke 2:34–35). Behind this serious note, however, the good news of Malachi is unmistakable. God will establish justice, and the arrival of his messenger will restore the means of communion with God (3:4).

Psalm 84

The two psalms selected for reading in celebration of Jesus' presentation at the temple are concerned with devotion to the temple (for a full discussion of Psalm 84, see above at Proper 16 [21]). Psalm 84 may have been once used in conjunction with pilgrimages made to Jerusalem at festival time, although verse 9 seems to suggest it was used by the king. Psalm 24 contains words spoken at the time when pilgrims entered the sanctuary precincts.

Psalm 84:5–7 probably talks about the route to Zion taken by pilgrims as they made their way along the roads to the city. At the time of the fall festival, some of the early autumn rains may already have fallen, reviving the parched land. "Strength to strength" (v. 7) could be translated "stronghold to stronghold"; that is, the people move from one village outpost to another.

The piety of the worshiper and the psalm composer can be seen in various ways in the text. One way of analyzing the materials is to note the three groups whom the writer declares "blessed" (or "happy," which is a better translation of the Hebrew word used in all three cases).

1. First, happy are the birds that dwell continuously in the temple (vv. 3–4). The sparrows and swallows that nest in the sacred precincts have the advantage of constantly dwelling in the house of God, where they can sing God's praise forever.

2. Happy are those who go on pilgrimage to Jerusalem (vv. 5–7). To visit the temple and Zion is to experience happiness and to see "the God of gods."

3. Happy are those who trust in God (v. 12), who find their confidence in him. Here we have a sort of generalizing pronouncement that moves beyond the specificity of temple piety.

Verse 10 may be taken as embodying the overall sentiment of the psalm: to visit the temple and worship in its courts were some of the supreme experiences for the ancient Hebrews.

Psalm 24:7–10

Of all the psalms, Psalm 24 probably illustrates most clearly the fact that the psalms were used as the spoken part of cultic rituals (see also Proper 10 [15]). Throughout verses 3–10, the material is comprised of a series of questions and answers probably recited by pilgrims and priests.

The psalm opens (vv. 1–2) with a hymnic praise of Yahweh that identifies the God of Israel as the possessor of the world and all that is in it. The ownership of the terrestrial kingdom is Yahweh's by right of creation. Yahweh is the one who anchored the earth in the midst of the seas and established it firmly upon the rivers (or streams) of the deep that ancients believed lay underneath the dry land. (Such a belief is partially based on the presence of springs and wells that suggest that water lies beneath the earth.)

The questions in verse 3 were addressed by the pilgrims to the priests inside the temple as the pilgrims arrived at the gates of the temple. The questions concern the qualifications demanded of those allowed to enter the sacred precincts: "Who shall ascend the hill of the LORD [who can enter the temple precincts]? And who shall stand in his holy place [in the temple in the presence of God]?" The priestly answer in this catechism of admission (vv. 4–5) brings together two paris of ethical qualifications: purity of outward deeds (clean hands) and purity of thought or inward truthfulness (pure heart) followed by purity of religious practice or unadulterated faith (not lifting up the soul to what is vain) and purity in speaking (not swearing deceitfully). These four principles in themselves provide a rather comprehensive perspective of ethical demands and requirements. If such demands as these were made as part of the worship, then one surely cannot accuse ancient worship services of being devoid of ethical interests and demands.

Verse 6 provides the worshipers' response to the requirements for entrance: "Those are the kind of people we are." Thus they claim the promises of verse 5—blessing and vindication from God.

With verse 7, the focus shifts from humankind and the moral values of living to God himself. The pilgrims or choir outside the sanctuary address the temple gates demanding that they be lifted up so that the King of glory may come in. But how could God enter the sanctuary? No doubt, the ark, the symbol of God's presence, had been carried out of the temple to reenter with the pilgrims on a high holy festival day. The choir or priests within offer a response in the form of a question. "Who is this King of glory?" (v. 8). God is then described as the one strong and mighty, mighty in battle. Perhaps part of the festival involved the proclamation of God's triumph over the forces of evil.

Hebrews 2:14–18

At one time, especially in the Western church, this feast day was oriented toward Mary, and this was reflected in its name, "Purification of the Blessed Virgin Mary." But because this appeared to threaten the doctrine of the sinlessness of Mary, in modern times the Roman church reverted to the more ancient understanding of the Eastern church, which celebrated this day as the "Presentation of the Lord." This more nearly conformed to its various designations in the East: "Coming of the Son of God into the Temple" (Armenian); "Presentation of the Lord in the Temple" (Egyptian); "The Meeting of the Lord" (Byzantine). The shift in title reflects a shift in emphasis: it is intended to be a feast of the Lord and not a feast honoring Mary.

With this focus on the presentation of the Lord, which, according to scriptural prescription, took place forty days after his birth (Lev. 12:2–8), this feast day has an incarnational cast. Celebrated on February 2, the fortieth day after Christmas, it serves to mark the end of the Christmas Season. Although the Gospel reading provides an account of the Lukan story of the presentation of Jesus in the temple (Luke 2:22–40), the epistolary reading serves to anchor the redemptive work of Christ in his incarnation. This text should not be forced into a false harmony with the Gospel reading, for each reflects a different theological interest. Nevertheless, there is a certain irony in the fact that the child who is presented in the temple "according to the law of Moses" finally becomes the merciful and faithful high priest officiating in the heavenly temple, making expiation for the sins of the people.

Several features of today's epistolary lection are worth noting.

First is the solidarity between Christ, "the one who sanctifies," and all humanity, "those who are sanctified" (v. 11). In the previous verses, several Old Testament texts are placed on the lips of Christ to show that he identifies completely with all of God's children (Ps. 22:22; Isa. 8:17–18). As such, he was born a member of the human family, sharing completely in our nature as "flesh and blood" (v. 14; Rom. 8:3, 29; Phil. 2:7). Just as it is the lot of every member of the human family to die, so did he experience death.

The effects of his death, however, were far from ordinary. For one thing, it was God "for whom and through whom all things exist" who made Jesus the "pioneer . . . perfect through sufferings" (v. 10). In addition, through death he passed through the heavens and became the exalted Son of God (Heb. 4:14). Because his death was both uniquely exemplary and triumphant, he destroyed death as the stronghold of Satan (v. 14; John 12:31; Rom. 6:9; 1 Cor. 15:55; 2 Tim. 1:10; Rev. 12:10). In his death, he delivered "those who all their lives were held in slavery by the fear of death" (v. 15). The incarnation of Christ eventually meant the freedom of all humanity from the fear of death.

The second feature of our lection is Christ as the merciful and faithful high priest (3:1; 4:14; 5:5, 10; 6:20; 7:26; 8:1; 9:11; 10:21). Because of his complete obedience, he demonstrated his true fidelity as the Son of God (5:8–9; cf. 1 Sam. 2:35). Because of his complete identification with the entire human family through his becoming "flesh and blood," he can be thoroughly sympathetic with the human condition. His own suffering and testing qualifies him to assist us in our sufferings and testing (v. 18; 5:2; cf. Matt. 4:1–11 and parallels; 26:36–46 and parallels).

In his role as high priest, Christ makes expiation for our sins (v. 17). His unique experience as one of God's earthly children makes it possible for him to plead in our behalf (5:1; Rom. 3:25; 1 John 2:2; 4:10; cf. Exod. 4:16).

Christ as a heavenly high priest, officiating in the heavenly temple and pleading in our behalf, can easily become a lofty image, far removed from the world we know and live in. Oddly enough, Christians have always found it easier to worship such an elevated Christ, enthroned high above the heavens. It is far more difficult for us to envision a Christ who became like us in every respect (v. 17). Yet today's epistolary text makes this unqualified claim about Christ, who was concerned not with angels but with the descendants of Abraham (v. 16). Given a choice between the company of angels and the company of humans, Christ plumps for flesh and blood. Why shouldn't we?

Because Hebrews 2:10–18 serves as the epistolary reading for the First Sunday After Christmas in Year A, the reader may also want to consult our comments in the earlier volume in connection with that day.

Luke 2:22–40

The text that provides a Gospel basis for the service of the presentation of Jesus is found only in Luke (2:22–40). In fact, Luke places between the nativity (2:1–20) and Jesus' beginning his public life at age thirty (3:23) three stories: the circumcision and naming when the child was eight days old (2:21; see the special service for January 1); the presentation in the temple when he was about forty days old (2:22–40; Lev. 12:1–4); and the visit to the temple at age twelve (2:41–52). All this is to say that the Jesus who began his ministry at age thirty was thoroughly grounded and rooted in his tradition, that observance of the law and attendance to temple duties were very important, and that although he was a Galilean, neither he nor his disciples scorned Jerusalem. In fact, says Luke alone, Jesus' disciples were to remain in Jerusalem after his ascension and from Jerusalem were to launch their mission (24:47–48). "And [they] returned to Jerusalem with great joy; and they were continually in the temple blessing God" (24:52–53). It is no wonder that Jesus, the true Israelite, went to the synagogue on the sabbath, "as was his custom" (4:16). Jesus and some of the religious leaders disputed over the tradition, to be sure, but it was a tradition he knew and kept from childhood.

When one looks at the presentation account itself, it is evident that there is the story line (2:22–24, 39–40) into which two substories have been inserted: that of Simeon (vv. 25–35) and that of Anna (vv. 36–38). The principal story line seems to have as its basic purpose the demonstration that in the life of the Christ Child the law of Moses had been meticulously observed (vv. 22, 23, 24, 27, 39). In the course of making that point, Luke has conflated two regulations: a mother was to be ceremonially purified after childbirth (Lev. 12:1–4; in cases of poverty, Lev. 12:6–8 was applied), and a firstborn male was to be dedicated to God (Exod. 13:2, 12–16). Of course, provision was made for parents to redeem their son from the Lord (Num. 18:15–16) so they could keep him as their own. Luke says nothing about the redemption of Jesus; perhaps his silence serves to prepare the reader for the next story in which Jesus in the temple at age twelve said to his parents, "Did you not know that I must be in my Father's house?" (v. 49). That story, along with verses 40 and 52, makes it evident that Luke is echoing the story of the boy Samuel, who was dedicated to God and who lived in the temple (1 Sam. 1–2).

In the persons of Simeon (vv. 25–35) and Anna (vv. 36–38) Luke tells how the Israel that is true, believing, hoping, devout, and temple-attending responded to Jesus. Simeon's acknowledgment of Jesus as "the Lord's Messiah" was inspired by the Holy Spirit (v. 26), and Anna's was that of a true prophet who fasted and prayed continually (vv. 36–37). Simeon longed for "the consolation of Israel" (v. 25), a phrase referring to the messianic age. The Nunc Dimittis (vv. 29–32) may have been a portion of a Christian hymn familiar to Luke and his readers. Simeon's words make it clear that Israel's consolation would not be a time of uninterrupted joy; hostility and death would be aroused by the appearance of the deliverer. Good news always has its enemies. Mary herself would pay a heavy price: "and a sword will pierce your own soul too" (v. 35). Devout and obedient Israel, as portrayed in the old prophet Anna, also saw in Jesus "the redemption of Jerusalem" (v. 38). Her thanks to God and her witness concerning Jesus provide a model of the Israel that accepted Jesus and saw in him the fulfillment of ancient hopes. Luke will write later of that portion of Israel that rejected Jesus and turned a deaf ear to the preaching of the early church. But in Luke's theology, they are thereby rejecting their own tradition and their own prophets as it was interpreted to them by one who was a true Israelite, Jesus of Nazareth. He kept the law, held Jerusalem in great affection (13:34), and was faithful to the synagogue. Moreover, his teaching was in keeping with all that was written in Moses, the prophets, and the writings (24:44). No prophet is so powerful and so disturbing as the one who arises out of one's own tradition and presents to the people the claims of that tradition.

Annunciation, March 25

Isaiah 7:10–14;
Psalm 45 or Psalm 40:5–10;
Hebrews 10:4–10;
Luke 1:26–38

The Feast of the Annunciation of the Lord occurs on March 25, nine months prior to the celebration of his birth at Christmas on December 25. When the feast first began to be celebrated in the fifth century, it was done in close connection with Christmas, but eventually it was shifted to the spring. It was variously celebrated as a feast of the Lord and as a feast of Mary, as its different names attest: "The Annunciation of the Lord," "Conception of Christ," "Incarnation of Christ," "The Annunciation of Mary." Because it is observed on a fixed date, it may occur during the Season of Lent, when the mood is somber and penitential. But it may occur as late as Easter Week, when the joy of resurrection life is the central focus. Thus it can become an occasion of joy that breaks the penitential mood of Lent or one that complements the joyous celebration of the risen Lord. In either case, when we think of the announcement of Christ's birth, it can only be an occasion of joy.

This day is the liturgical commemoration of the events reported in Luke 1:26–38, the angel Gabriel's announcement to Mary that she will give birth to the Messiah. Though it is not quoted in the Lucan passage, Isaiah's promise of the birth of Immanuel as a sign certainly stands in the background. Messianic themes occur in Psalm 45, a royal psalm on the occasion of the king's wedding. The selection from Psalm 40 meets the Gospel lection at two points: the expression of one who delights in doing the will of God and the proclamation of "the glad news of deliverance" (v. 9). The epistolary reading from Hebrews is chosen because of its incarnational emphasis.

Isaiah 7:10–14

This passage from the Book of Isaiah provides important background for the Lucan account of the Annunciation. Central here is the prophecy of a birth as a sign of God's intentions toward God's people. Moreover, the name of that child, "Immanuel," which means "God is with us," is an interpretation of the Lord's will. Although we now recognize that Isaiah had in view a particular woman and child in his own time, and not Mary and her son Jesus, the ancient promise still has its contribution to make to Christian worship and to the Christian life.

Some of the literary and historical questions concerning our passage can be answered with relative certainty. It is one of a number of reports of encounters in Jerusalem between Isaiah and King Ahaz at a particularly critical moment in the history of Judah. The historical situation is summarized in Isaiah 7:1–2 and spelled out further in 2 Kings 16:1–20. When the Assyrian king Tiglath-pileser III started to move against the small states of Syria and Palestine, the leaders of those states began to form a coalition to oppose him. Apparently because Ahaz of Judah refused to join them, the kings in Damascus and Samaria moved against Jerusalem (ca. 734 BC) to topple Ahaz and replace him with someone more favorable to their policies. In the passage (7:1–9) that immediately precedes our reading, Isaiah counseled nonresistence based on faith in the ancient promise to David that one of his sons would always occupy the throne in Jerusalem. The fact that our unit begins with the expression "Again the LORD spoke to Ahaz" (v. 10) indicates that it is a continuation of the prophet's actions in the same situation.

Isaiah 7:10–14 is good news in the form of a prophetic symbolic action, especially to the king but also thereby to the people as a whole. Note that the entire section is presented as if the Lord himself is speaking directly to King Ahaz, but it would have been the prophet who conveyed the message. In the previous unit, Ahaz had been afraid; here he refuses even to inquire of the Lord, even when Isaiah instructs him to do so (vv. 11–12). It was common for kings or other leaders to inquire of the Lord, often through prophets, before deciding to go to battle (see 2 Kings 13:14–19). When Ahaz refuses to ask for a sign, the prophet becomes impatient and says that the Lord himself will give a sign: "Look, the young woman is with child and shall bear a son, and shall name him Immanuel" (v. 14). He goes on to interpret the sign, promising that before the child knows how to "refuse the evil and choose the good"— that is, within a short time—the present military threat will have ended. Although the means are not stated, the prophet promises that God will intervene to save his people.

Few textual and translation problems in the Old Testament have generated more controversy than those of Isaiah 7:14. However, there can be little doubt about the meaning or translation of the crucial word. The Hebrew word 'almah is correctly rendered by the NRSV and almost all other modern translations "young woman." The term is neutral with regard to her marital status. It was the Greek translation of the Book of Isaiah, the Septuagint, that read "virgin" (Greek *parthenos*), thus setting the stage for the particular messianic interpretation of the passage expressed in the New Testament. The bridge between the eighth century and the early church is thus yet another historical and theological context, that of the translation of the Hebrew Scriptures for Jews in a Hellenistic, pre-Christian culture. It is equally clear that the Book of Isaiah originally read here "young woman" and that the Evangelists inherited a translation of Isaiah that read "virgin."

As in most other prophetic announcements or symbolic actions, Isaiah has the immediate future in view, and thus the woman and child are his contemporaries. As the NRSV (see also REB) indicates, he indicates to the king a woman who is already pregnant. But the identity of the woman is difficult if not impossible to establish. In view of a context that stresses the significance of the Davidic dynasty, many commentators have taken the child to be the crown prince, and the woman as the wife of Ahaz. Others, seeing the passage in some ways parallel to Isaiah 8:1–4, have argued that the woman was the wife of the prophet, and the child his son. It is quite likely, however, that the "young woman" was simply a pregnant woman whom Isaiah saw as he was addressing the king.

One of the keys to the meaning of this passage is the word "sign" (Hebrew 'oth). It is the same word used in the tradition about the "signs and wonders" performed in Egypt before the Exodus and thus has come to be associated in our minds with the so-called miraculous. However, such signs may be ordinary events as well as extraordinary ones. The decisive point in the Old Testament view is that a "sign" is revelatory, that it communicates God's word or will or nature. Thus it is not remarkable that in Isaiah 7 something as common—and also as wonderful—as the birth of a baby boy is a message from God, and for the future. The name embodies the promise of God's saving presence.

To be sure, it is hardly possible for Christians to hear this passage and not think of the coming of Jesus. But in addition to directing our attention to the incarnation, Isaiah 7:10–14 has its own good news. It is a message that sees pregnancy and birth—even when not understood as miraculous—as signs of God's concern for God's people. Furthermore, this message is directed to a people living in chaos and fear, faced with such specific problems as international politics and the threat of destruction. Even in such a situation, the word of God offers hope.

Psalm 45

Psalm 45 is clearly a wedding psalm. The references to the king and the bride in the text, however, are the source of differences in interpretation. Four approaches are worthy of note.

1. One line of interpretation is what might be called the metaphorical approach. This assumes that the marriage described is simply a conventional wedding. The normal, everyday groom is described in metaphorical language as a "king" and the bride as a "princess."

2. A second approach can be called the mythological. This assumes that the wedding partners are actually the male deity, played by the king, and the female goddess, played by the queen.

3. A third approach is the allegorical. The king in the text stands for Yahweh, and the bride is his chosen people. What is said in the text is not to be taken literally but allegorically.

4. A fourth interpretation is the historical. This assumes that the text was composed for an actual wedding for an actual ancient Israelite or Judean king. Because the text refers to Tyre, it has sometimes been assumed that the psalm was composed for the marriage of King Ahab of Israel to the Phoenician princess Jezebel, who was from the city of Tyre.

The association of this text with the Annunciation strains any reading of the text unless one wants to understand the king in the text as God and the bride as the virgin Mary. The more common Christian interpretation is to relate the figure of the king to that of Jesus, as is already done in Hebrews 1:8–9. If Jesus is identified with the groom, the bride, however, is best understood as the church, not as Mary. At any rate, any exegesis of the text that Christianizes the interpretation forces the imagery considerably.

Of the four interpretations noted above, the most likely original reading is that which sees the psalm as a composition from an actual wedding of a Hebrew king, though it is doubtful if we can identify which king was the groom.

The following is the outline of the psalm: (1) a statement about the poet and the purpose of the poem (v. 1), (2) the glorification and praise of the king (vv. 2–9), (3) the glorification and praise of the bride (vv. 10–15), and (4) a statement to the king that promises him great and famous progeny (vv. 16–17). The psalm allows us some insight into the opulence of the royal court and a glimpse at some of the flattery of the king that must have characterized court life.

Although the poet praises and flatters the king, he may also have engaged in some "preaching" to the monarch by making frequent reference to the king's responsibilities. The ruler is described as the fairest of men, one blessed with grace. The king, gloriously garbed in regal splendor with girded sword, can be visualized in the imagery of verse 3. The king, whose arrows destroy his enemies, is portrayed as the defender of the right and the cause of truth. The throne of the king is proclaimed as eternal and his rule as one of equity and righteousness. The status and well-being of the king are reflected in the perfumes that scent his royal robes, in the ivory palaces where he is entertained by instrumental music, in the daughters of royalty who inhabit his mansion, and in the golden splendor of his queen.

The bride is addressed and admonished to forget her family and country (Tyre) and to give her affection and attention to her new husband. The bride in her wedding finery and her attendants and ladies-in-waiting are described as being led in procession to the palace of the king.

The psalm concludes, like many modern Near Eastern weddings, with a statement expressing the hope and assurance of numerous offspring. Because fertility—numerous offspring—was considered a blessing from God (see Ps. 127:3–5), such a promise or blessing was especially appropriate for the king, whose offspring would share in the rule of the Davidic dynasty to whom God had promised eternal rulership.

Psalm 40:5–10

This lection is excerpted from the thanksgiving portion of a psalm probably originally used by the king. Verses 5–10 comprise the worshiper's thanksgiving spoken directly to the Deity in response to having been redeemed from some great distress (described in vv. 1–3). The association of this text with and its appropriateness for the Annunciation are its emphasis on willingly submitting to the divine will (see esp. v. 8), as was the case with Mary.

Several statements in the text require explanation. Verse 6 declares that God does not desire sacrifice. Four different types of sacrifice are referred to, some of the freewill type and others mandatory. What the verse intends to emphasize, however, is that what God really requires is a faithful, hearing attitude. The expression "ears thou hast dug for me" probably was a proverbial way of saying, "I am really hearing you."

The book referred to in verse 7 may have been the Book of the Law, especially if this was written for use by the king (see Deut. 17:14–17), perhaps an official record or court document, or maybe a heavenly book in which it was believed were recorded all the activities of a person's life. At least, the book seems to give a favorable opinion of the worshiper (see v. 8).

In verses 9–10, the worshiper testifies to having proclaimed the salvation of God. In these verses, the same point is made with two positive affirmations (vv. 9a, 10b) and three denials (vv. 9b, 10a, 10c). The psalmist declares that the story he or she made known in public worship in the life of the congregation has thus borne testimony to God's salvation.

Hebrews 10:4–10

With its mention of the time "when Christ came into the world" (v. 5), the epistolary reading is especially fitting to the occasion. To elaborate on Christ's incarnation, the writer of Hebrews uses the language of Psalm 40:6–8, where the psalmist speaks of "coming" to do the will of God. This psalm quotation is part of one of the psalm selections for this day, and thus the readings from the Psalm and the Epistle can be related directly to each other. We should note, however, that the author of Hebrews puts the words of the psalm on the lips of Christ himself and uses them to explain Christ's own vocation. In doing so, he has given the psalm an explicit incarnational interpretation when he has Christ say, "See, God, I have come to do your will, O God" (v. 7). This emphasis on the incarnate Christ coming to the world to do the will of God echoes a major Johannine emphasis (John 4:34; 5:30; 6:38). We may recall that in response to the raising of Lazarus and Christ's discourse concerning the resurrection and the life, Martha confessed, "Yes, Lord, I believe that you are the Messiah, the Son of God, the one coming into the world" (John 11:27). Here we see an explicit connection between Easter and incarnation. Even if we separate them liturgically, they eventually come together in Christian confession.

Because of the prominence of sacrificial language in today's epistolary reading and the emphasis on Christ as the ultimate sacrifice that is to be preferred to that of "bulls and goats" (v. 4; cf. 7:18–19; 9:12, 19), the text may be appropriated within the context of Lenten observance. This is clearly the case in the final verse: "And it is by God's will that we have been sanctified through the offering of the body of Jesus Christ once for all" (v. 10; cf. 10:14, 29; 13:12; also 1 Thess. 4:3; Eph. 5:2).

Like the author of Hebrews, we can only reflect on Christ's incarnation, and more specifically on the announcement of his conception, from a post-Easter perspective. In doing so, we think of it as the moment that began a life of filial obedience committed to doing the will of God. We see it as a life that ended with the ultimate sacrifice, "the offering of the body of Jesus Christ once for all" (v. 10), through which we have been sanctified or become dedicated to doing the will of the Father.

Luke 1:26–38

I t would be a mistake to think that the early church's sole interest in the calendar was in various attempts to ascertain the time of the end and the return of Christ. Although such calculations have waxed and waned throughout the life of the church, the calendar has held other interests for Christians. Quite early there was a desire to structure the disciplines of worship and prayer on the significant hours and days in the life of Christ. Christian calendars were developed and framed primarily around the seasons of central importance, Easter and Christmas. Once a date was set for the celebration of Jesus' birth, it was only a matter of time until the day nine months earlier would be observed as the Annunciation, the day of Gabriel's visit to Mary. By thus observing March 25, the church was able to focus upon the beautiful text of Luke 1:26–38 outside the already rich and full season of Advent.

Luke says that Mary received the word of God's favor from the messenger (the meaning of the word "angel") Gabriel. In later Judaism, angels, both in the service of God and in the service of Satan, came to figure prominently in theology and in popular religion. Such beings were common in religions of Persia and may have found a welcome in Jewish thought in a time when the distance between a transcendent God and human beings required mediators. Angels carried messages and performed other functions in God's dealings with creation. In some literature, important angels were given names, Gabriel being one of the most familiar (Dan. 9:21). In the New Testament, Luke's stories are the most populated with angels, with the obvious exception of the heavenly scenes in the Apocalypse. Christians have differed in their ways of appropriating the conversation between Mary and an angel: some literally, others by means of literary, psychological, or sociological categories. The story has survived all interpretations.

Luke apparently has no need to speculate on the choice of Mary as the mother of the Christ. The point is, God has chosen her, and as in any act of divine grace, the reasons are enfolded in God's purposes and not in the recipient. The angel's message that Mary's child will be Son of God and son of David is a composite of phrases and lines from Isaiah, Genesis, 2 Samuel, Micah, Hosea, and Daniel. It is possible that this hymnlike expression of praise (vv. 32–33) came to Luke from an early Christian liturgy. Many scholars believe that the church quite early put together Old Testament verses that were useful in worship, preaching, and teaching new members.

Mary wonders, quite naturally, how she, without a husband, can conceive and bear a son. She is given no answer that approaches biology. Rather, she is given an announcement and a bit of information that functioned as a sign of the truth of the promise. The announcement was that the birth would be the work of the Holy Spirit and the power of the Most High (v. 35). In other words, Jesus of Nazareth is God's act of grace and power. The information that encourages Mary's faith is that her kinswoman Elizabeth, old and barren, is in her sixth month of pregnancy. Echoed in the Elizabeth story is that of Abraham and Sarah (Gen. 18:14). But behind the stories of Mary's, Elizabeth's, and Sarah's conceptions is the creed beneath and behind all other creeds: "For nothing will be impossible with God" (v. 37). It is to this word that Mary responds in trust and in obedience.

Visitation, May 31

1 Samuel 2:1–10;
Psalm 113;
Romans 12:9–16b;
Luke 1:39–57

The lections for use in commemorating Mary's visit to Elizabeth (Luke 1) focus on Mary and, through Mary as representative, on all the lowly and humble who serve God. Luke uses the Song of Hannah (1 Sam. 2) in the song of Mary, and both Psalm 113 and Romans 12 speak of God as helper of those who do chores for which they get little attention and less praise. By keeping the attention on Mary as God's servant, the preacher will avoid making this a premature Advent service.

1 Samuel 2:1–10

This lesson has been discussed with the readings for Proper 28 [33] in this volume.

Psalm 113

Three general considerations about this psalm should be noted initially: (1) It, along with Psalms 114–118, was employed in both temple services (at the time of the slaughter of the lambs) and home celebrations (as part of the meal ritual) during the Passover festival; thus the imagery of the psalm came to be associated with the events of the Exodus, which was commemorated in the Passover ritual. (2) The psalm has many similarities to the Song of Hannah in 1 Samuel 2:1–10, with which it may profitably be compared; the similarity of both of these to Mary's Magnificat in Luke 1:46–55 has led to their connection with Visitation. (3) The psalm shares in a common biblical motif, which might be called the "reversal of fate" or the "from rags to riches" sentiment.

The genre and structure of the psalm are clear. It is a hymn used to express and instill faith and particular beliefs by and in the congregation. The initial verses (vv. 1–4) are a summons to praise God, temporally in all time and forever (v. 2), and geographically in all places and everywhere (v. 3). Verses 5–9 provide the motivations, the reasons why God should be praised. These are presented in the form of a question (vv. 5–6) and an answer (vv. 7–9).

The psalm develops a dialectic in the Divine and thus speaks about God in contrasting ways. In the question (vv. 5–6), God is highly exalted; God sits above and looks far down upon earth and even far down upon the heavens. If such a transcendent God must squint to see the earth, then surely the course of events and the status of individual persons must be beyond divine purview. The answer given to "Who is like Yahweh?" comes, however, as unexpected in its content. Yahweh is the one who reverses the fate of the unfortunate, who transforms the status of those whom society judges as failures. Yahweh is not an unconcerned transcendent Deity but the caretaker of the dispossessed and the unpossessing. The heavenly Lord is involved in earthly human existence.

Verses 7–8 concern the reversal of status of the male. The poor and the needy would have been those condemned by fate and fortune to marginal participation in the life of the community. These would have been forced to live in poverty at the peripheries of society. Perhaps they had gotten in that condition by the accident of birth, misfortune, poor harvests, illness, or debt. The dust and the ash heap refer to the city garbage dump, where the dispossessed and unpossessing as well as the sick and leprous (see Lam. 4:5; Job 2:8; Lev. 13:45–46) made their domicile, grubbed for survival, begged for a handout, and got food and clothing from family and friends if they had any. Such places of last resort are similar to modern old folks' homes and public shelters as well as dump hovels where the world's refugees congregate. A male living under such conditions in ancient times would have been without social standing and without self-respect and confidence. So much for verse 7, the "before" in the psalmic commercial.

The "after" we find in verse 8. The ones suffering deprivation and ostracism are made to sit with the nobles/princes, that is, with the rich and the powerful. To "sit with" implies acceptance by others and self-assurance by the new participant. (Remember the difference between standing integration and sitting integration in the South. "Sit-ins" marked a new state in the civil rights movement because to "sit with" is to share.) For the ideal of one who sits with the nobles, see Job 29:1–25.

The transformation of the unfortunate female is noted in verse 9. The mother was not really "at home" in the extended family of her husband; that is, she had no real security or sense of fully belonging and participating until she and her children created their own space and place in the family. The wife, always brought into the husband's family, was an outsider to her in-laws until children transformed her into an insider and made her "at home." It must have been lonely in such a situation for the barren wife, so much so, that barrenness could be understood as a disgrace, if not a curse from God (see Gen. 16:2; 20:18; 1 Sam. 1:5; Luke 1:25). Many of the matriarchs of Israel, however, were barren (Sarah, Rachel, Hannah) for a long time before they produced a child viewed as the result of divine intervention.

Romans 12:9–16b

This text is included in the epistolary reading for Proper 17 [22] in Year A (Rom. 12:9–21), and the reader may want to consult additional remarks made there. Because the same texts are used for Visitation in all three years, the reader may want to consult our remarks made in connection with Years A and C.

On the occasion celebrating Mary's visit to Elizabeth, it is the Gospel reading from Luke that sets the liturgical agenda. The tradition of Mary's "visitation" is recorded only in Luke, and it is the Magnificat that sets the tone for the observance of this day. One of the primary notes sounded in this passage is the exaltation of the lowly. Mary, the humble handmaiden of God, is raised to an exalted position as the one through whom the promise of God will be fulfilled. It is the reversal of roles we come to expect in Luke: God dethroning the mighty and enthroning the lowly in their place.

What makes today's epistolary reading appropriate in this setting is its insistence that we "not be haughty, but associate with the lowly" (v. 16). We miss the full force of this injunction if we read it as an ethic of politeness. It is more than a call for us not to be conceited in our attitude toward those of low estate. It is a mandate to identify with them, to be with them in their lowliness. In a similar fashion, the Magnificat is quite revolutionary in its social outlook. It calls for the reversal of the normal social order and reminds us that Yahweh's concern is to feed the hungry and send the rich away empty. In its boldest form, it envisions a radical redistribution of resources.

So does today's epistolary text call for radical identification with the earth's lowly. Only in this way can the charge to "love one another with mutual affection" (v. 10) be carried out seriously. What is being called for here is a level of Christian fellowship that transcends all barriers—social, racial, sexual. It is a form of community that expresses itself concretely in displays of genuine hospitality (v. 13), where financial contributions are made as expressions of Christian love. In view here are the "needs of the saints" (v. 13), and the primary focus of this instruction is internal. Yet this urge to transcend self-interest in reaching out to the needs of others extends beyond the Christian circle (cf. Gal. 6:10).

As it turns out, hating "what is evil, [and holding] fast to what is good" (v. 9) may result in self-exposure. That which is evil may very well be our refusal to "associate with the lowly" in any genuine sense of identification and empathy. What it may expose are those subtle forms of discrimination that are masked by other forms of religiosity, even prayer and worship. We may find ourselves being religious in one sense, but discriminatory in another, much more sinister, sense. We want to come to God without fully identifying with all of God's creatures: high and low, exalted and humble, franchised and disenfranchised, rich and poor.

"Holding fast to what is good" may mean clinging to those from whom all signs of good are ostensibly absent, in whom good no longer appears to reside, for whom there is no more good, who are indeed regarded by us, by the church, and by society as "no good." Only in this way can all signs and expressions of haughtiness and conceit be removed from the Christian fellowship. Only in this way can "love be genuine" (v. 9).

Luke 1:39–57

The service of Visitation recalls Mary's visit to her kinswoman Elizabeth in the hill country of Judah. This celebration not only provides the occasion for the church to anticipate Christmas yet six months away, but also the opportunity to hear Luke sing and expound on that beautiful moment. Before the births of either John or Jesus, the reader of Luke is made privy, through their mothers, to the profound Christian themes yet to be lived out and proclaimed.

Elizabeth and Mary are not nameless and faceless women who are no more than the wombs that carry great sons. They are persons with names, addresses, beliefs, hopes, and joy in service. Such is Luke's treatment of women in the Gospel story. Mary will reappear in trust and devotion (Acts 1:14), as will other women who join in the mission (Luke 8:1–3), and to them is entrusted the one sustained hallelujah of the Christian faith: He is risen (Luke 24:1–12).

Mary's visit to Elizabeth provides the occasion for the two women to celebrate the angel's word to Mary, which was also the angel's word to Abraham and Sarah: "For nothing will be impossible with God" (1:37; Gen. 18:14). As Paul was to express it, God gives life to the dead and calls into existence things that do not exist (Rom. 4:17). It does not matter whether it is a case of an old and barren couple or a virgin without a husband. The Visitation is, therefore, a double celebration of the power of God to give life.

The Visitation is also a study in contrasts. Elizabeth is old, the wife of a priest who was part of an ancient order of things in Israel. Having a child in her old age is a reminder of the past: Abraham and Sarah, Manoah and his wife, Elkanah and Hannah, from whom came Isaac and Samson and Samuel. The promises of God survived and continued through the unlikely births to the old and barren. But Mary was young, a life new, virgin, and all promise. She and her child do not remind one of the past; in fact, in them begins a new history. Mary's child is continuous with the past, to be sure, the fulfillment of a promise, but in him God is doing a new thing. So radically new is this act of God that the only appropriate means was a woman young, and a virgin.

The Visitation is also a beautiful reflection, through the women, of the futures of their unborn sons. As Elizabeth is humbled by the visit of "the mother of my Lord" (v. 43), so John was witness and servant to Jesus. As John leaped in Elizabeth's womb when Mary entered the house (vv. 41, 44), so John's joy was that of a groomsman when the bridegroom arrived (John 3:29–30). As Elizabeth blessed Mary not only for her child but also because Mary believed the word of God (vv. 42–45), so John would come calling for faith in Jesus as the means of life in the kingdom. There is never any question for Luke that Jesus and not John is the Messiah, but neither is there any question that both Elizabeth and Mary are servants of God's purpose, both their sons are gifts of God, and both sons have appointed ministries in God's plan for the ingathering of the nations.

The Visitation is also a preview of reversals yet to come. The ordinary structures of history, the usual cause and effect sequences of events, could not sustain or contain what God would be doing. The empty will be full and the full, empty; the poor will be rich and the rich, poor; the powerless will reign and the powerful will be dethroned. In a close approximation of the Song of Hannah (1 Sam. 2:1–10), Mary sings of the eschatological reversal of stations and fortunes in the realm where and when God's love and justice rule supreme.

Holy Cross, September 14

Numbers 21:4b–9;
Psalm 98:1–5 or Psalm 78:1–2, 34–38;
1 Corinthians 1:18–24;
John 3:13–17

The imagery is strange and striking, with all the appearances of "foolishness" (1 Cor. 1:18): Jesus lifted up on the cross "as Moses lifted up the serpent in the wilderness" (John 3:14). However, when we examine more closely the story of the serpent in the wilderness, the meaning of the metaphor and the theological logic of the New Testament typology become apparent. The selection of Psalm 78 is the more direct response to the Old Testament reading itself. Psalm 98:1–5 celebrates God's victory and vindication of the faithful.

Numbers 21:4b–9

Like many other Old Testament readings for special days, this one has been connected with the particular occasion on the basis of typological exegesis. The association of this passage from Numbers with the cross of Jesus comes from New Testament times. "Just as Moses lifted up the serpent in the wilderness, so must the Son of Man be lifted up" (John 3:14). It continues to be instructive to reflect on the ways the story of the serpent in the wilderness is like the story of the cross.

It seems as if Moses had nothing but trouble from the people of Israel in the wilderness. On other occasions in the readings for this season, we have encountered those people complaining against Moses and the Lord, even objecting to the burdens of their election, the fact that they were set free from slavery in Egypt.

Although this story of complaint begins like most of the others, its results are quite different from the previous ones. There is the general observation that the people "became impatient on the way" (v. 4). The reader familiar with the story of Israel's travels from Egypt will already find this remarkable; they had been impatient and dissatisfied almost from the first day! Then follows the grumbling that is a summary of all the things they have complained about from the beginning. They grumble against God and Moses about being in the wilderness, about the lack of food and water, and—inconsistently—about the food they do have. This doubtless is an objection to the manna, never especially appealing, but certainly boring after the traditional forty years in the desert.

Usually what has happened at this point in the stories of Israel's complaints is Moses' intercession with the Lord, who graciously meets the needs of the people, either for food, water, or security. But we hear without explanation that the Lord sent "fiery serpents among the people and they bit the people, so that many people of Israel died" (v. 6). Now the people do two things: they confess their sin of rebellion against the Lord and the leadership of Moses, and they ask Moses to intercede with the Lord to remove the serpents (v. 7).

When Moses prays for the people, the Lord responds but does not "take away the serpents." Instead, the Lord instructs Moses to make a fiery serpent and set it on a pole so that those who are bitten may look at it and live (v. 8). Moses did as instructed, setting up a bronze serpent, and it functioned as promised (v. 9).

The religious background of the traditions in this passage are complex. The belief is widespread that the image of a dangerous animal can function as protection against it, and the image of the snake in particular is associated with healing rituals in various religions. But does not the very fashioning of such an image violate the Second Commandment (Exod. 20:4) and thus threaten to violate the First Commandment (Exod. 20:3)? Perhaps that is why the text mentions cautiously that the people were only to "look at" the bronze serpent. It is not an idol but a gift of the Lord. There must have been such an image in the temple in Jerusalem, for 2 Kings 18:4 reports that when Hezekiah purified the worship, he destroyed "the bronze serpent that Moses had made." Even healing symbols can become objects of idolatry.

Theologically, the most important factor here is the pattern of sin, punishment, and God's means of grace. Once the people sin, experience the punishment, confess their sin, and pray for relief, the Lord responds. On the one hand, it appears that the Lord was eager to respond almost before they asked. On the other hand, the prayer is not granted in the form requested. Sin has—and will continue to have—its effects. The dangers remain, and the people continue to suffer from the potentially death-dealing snakes. However, now there is healing from the Lord, although the scars of the snake bites—the effects of sin—doubtless will remain.

Psalm 98:1–5

One of the enthronement hymns, Psalm 98 praises Yahweh as the sovereign reigning over the world of creation and as the special benefactor of the house of Israel. Thus both the universal and the particular domains of Yahweh are noted.

Much of this psalm consists of calls or summons to praise/worship as well as reasons why God should be worshiped and praised. Those called upon to praise God are the community of Israel (implied; vv. 1–3), all the earth (all humanity; vv. 4–6), and various elements in the world of nature (sea, world, their inhabitants, floods, and hills; vv. 7–9). The ancient rabbis, in commenting on verse 8, noted that there are only three references in Scripture (Old Testament) to the clapping of hands: the peoples clapping hand in hand (Ps. 47:1), the trees of the field clapping branch against branch (Isa. 55:2), and the floods clapping against the banks of the river (Ps. 98:8).

The reasons for praise in the first section (vv. 1–3) are all associated with the word "victory." God has won victory for himself (v. 1), God has made known his victory (v. 2), and the ends of the earth have seen his victory (v. 3). The marvelous things God has done, which are not spelled out, are related to his vindication ("His triumph"; NJPSV) in the sight of the nations and to the manifestation of his steadfast love and faithfulness to Israel. The reason for praise in the second section (vv. 4–9) is the coming of God to judge the world, not simply to judge but to judge with (establish) righteousness and equity (v. 9).

For a fuller discussion of this psalm, see the readings for Christmas, Third Proper.

Psalm 78:1–2, 34–38

This psalm is a long composition offering a recital of the historical epochs of Israel's past. The following epochs are covered: (1) the patriarchal period (vv. 5–11), (2) the Exodus and wilderness wanderings (vv. 12–53), (3) the settlement in the land of Canaan (vv. 54–66), and (4) the election of David and Zion (vv. 67–72). These epochs and the events associated with them are used as points of departure for preaching and proclamation. In this psalm, most of the past is interpreted as times of disobedience and is used to engender a sense of guilt and shame from those addressed in the psalm.

The two sections selected for this lection are part of the introduction (vv. 1–2) and a portion of the psalmist's interpretation and preaching on the wilderness theme (vv. 34–38). The opening verses present the historical synopsis and interpretation that follow as a teaching or a parable, that is, not as a pure recital of history but as an interpretative reading of the past intended to speak to the present.

Verses 34–38 are a portion of the homily on Israel's behavior in the wilderness. Although cared for, preserved, and fed in the desert, the Hebrews are described as having constantly sinned. The people are depicted as demurring and demanding, unappreciative and uncooperative. Over and over again, God has to act to reprimand them. Verses 34–38 proclaim two things about the people. First, they were not repentant until they were punished; they did not turn toward God until God had turned against them. Their repentance was the product of divine coercion. Second, their devotion was superficial and temporary. Their mouths and their tongues were committed to religious expression, not their hearts. Flattery and lies, not fidelity and loyalty, were their hallmarks.

In spite of the people's behavior and their transient faith, they depicted God as their refuge and redeemer (v. 35). Long-suffering and forbearing, God forgave and did not destroy; God withheld his anger and did not give vent to his wrath (v. 38).

1 Corinthians 1:18–24

Because 1 Corinthians 1:18–31 serves as the epistolary lection for Tuesday in Holy Week in all three years, the reader may want to consult the remarks made about it earlier in this volume and in the other volumes. Even so, for a special day of celebration devoted to the cross, this passage from Paul is singularly appropriate, for it is a *locus classicus* for his theology of the cross. As he remarks later in writing to the Corinthian church, "Jesus Christ, and him crucified" formed the center of his proclamation (1 Cor. 2:2). Nor did this serve merely as the object of his preaching. As is well known, the "crucified Christ" became the mold into which he cast his own personal existence, so much so that he could claim that he had been "crucified with Christ" (Gal. 2:19). It is not as if Christ's death on the cross served as some external model over against which he patterned his life, although this was true to a certain extent. Rather, the language here is that of true participation. He has actually reenacted the crucifixion in his own life, not as an event that occurred "back there" in his conversion, but as an act that continued to shape his identity and apostolic vocation (2 Cor. 4:7–12).

Central to today's epistolary reading is Paul's claim that the message of the cross is foolishness (v. 18). In Paul's own experience, he found this message disquieting and unnerving to Jews and Greeks alike. The former saw it as a "stumbling block," the latter as "foolishness" (v. 23).

For most first-century Jews, a crucified messiah was not only a contradiction in terms, but a violation of Scripture. When they read Deuteronomy 21:22–23, they concluded that to be hung on a tree was a sure sign of criminality. They could draw no other conclusion than that "Jesus crucified" bore the stigma of scriptural condemnation. Quite simply, he died under the curse of the Torah. Greeks, by contrast, found the message incredible, not because of troubling passages from the Hebrew Scriptures but because they had difficulty reconciling the message of a crucified hero with their expectations of savior-figures. To be sure, many of them saw the death of Socrates as a noble death for a noble cause. And they also knew myths of dying and rising gods from the mystery religions. Even so, the death of a Jewish messianic pretender did not strike them as particularly commendable as an event through which they might experience salvation and eternal life.

This, at least, was Paul's own experience. Yet he saw that consistent rejection of his preaching of the "crucified Christ" as a clear instance of human presumption. For him, it was an unassailable axiom of faith that in Christ God had acted to justify humanity. This, after all, was his own saving experience. Above all else, Paul had experienced God in Christ (2 Cor. 5:19). For anyone to interpret the Christ-event otherwise was to call God into question. Consequently, in our passage Paul assails God's detractors as those who would dare to put God in the dock. How can humans subject God to a test (v. 20)?

What emerges is Paul's understanding of the cross as paradox. Ostensibly, it looks foolish. But, to whom? To human beings who pretend to be wise. Yet true wisdom is God's domain, and it is revealed in this instance in what appears to be an act of consummate folly. But so be it, for it is precisely in such unexpected ways that God has acted in the past. The Corinthians' own conversion was perhaps the most immediate example of this, for they had very little to commend themselves before God, yet God performed the miracle of creation in them (vv. 26–31).

Paul recognizes full well that for one to see the cross as a display of God's wisdom is a confessional act. It is the power of God "to us who are being saved" (v. 18). It presupposes that we are "called" (v. 24). Then, as now, the best perspective on the cross is found by those who have experienced saving power through the crucified God.

John 3:13–17

As a magnet, the subject of the cross has been held over the text for the day, drawing to itself those verses pertaining directly to that event. Fairness to the subject and to the text demands, however, that verses 13–17 be set back into the context in order to extract them again.

John 3:1–21 is usually regarded as a conversation between Jesus and Nicodemus. However, where the Evangelist ends the conversation and where his own comments begin is not clear. One has but to look at different red-letter editions to see this uncertainty illustrated: Do Jesus' words end at verse 15, at 16, or at 21? The question is, however, a moot one, because the text reveals clearly that John is doing more than reporting a conversation. Such a shift begins at verse 7, with a change from the singular to the plural "you." The message from Jesus, says the writer, is to all and not to Nicodemus alone. The plural continues in verses 11 and 12. In addition, at verse 11 the "conversation" becomes more openly a debate between the church and the synagogue over the subject of life in the kingdom. Note the "we" versus "you" (plural). Furthermore, at verse 13 the passage becomes even more obviously a post-Easter Christian message by the statement in the past tense: "No one has ascended into heaven except the one who descended from heaven, the Son of Man." The earthly sojourn of the Savior is viewed as a completed event. It would be unfair, therefore, to treat this text within the confines of a private conversation at the beginning of Jesus' ministry, and it would be grossly unfair to be critical of Nicodemus for not understanding it. The Evangelist, by means of Nicodemus, is addressing the reader.

And what is the Evangelist saying to the reader? Let us confine ourselves to the bearing of the text on our subject, the cross of Christ. If the cross is not mentioned in verses 13–17, how is it to be discerned here? To be sure, in traditional church art, music, and theology, John 3:16 is associated with Golgotha. It is as though it were to be translated, "For God so loved the world that he gave his only Son *on the cross.*" That the cross is a part of the Johannine understanding of salvation is beyond question. Jesus lays down his life for the sheep (10:11); he lays down his life for his friends (15:13); he dies as the Passover lamb providing the freedom of a new exodus for the people of God (19:31–37). But the cross in this Gospel is the means of glorifying the Son (12:23–28), that is, of returning the Son to the presence of God. Hence the double meaning of being "lifted up" (v. 14; 8:28; 12:34)—up on the cross and up into glory. This being lifted up is as surely an act of God's grace and love as was the provision for salvation in the camp of Israel when they suffered God's judgment and punishment for their unbelief and disobedience (v. 14; Num. 21). Jesus' being lifted up was an act of love from God toward the world; and to be understood as this Evangelist presents it, that act needs to be seen in the full movement of the descending and the ascending of the Son of Man (v. 13).

In summary fashion, John's message may be stated this way: the Son came into the world to reveal God (1:18), whom to know is life eternal (17:3). That revelation is not only in signs and discourses but also in the cross.

The God revealed in the Son is a God who loves, who loves the whole world, and who desires none to perish but that all have life eternal. God does not simply wish this; God sends the only Son to offer this life as a gift.

However, the cross refers not only to Jesus' death but to his being lifted up to God. This also is a part of the salvation event in that the glorified Christ sends the Holy Spirit to his church (7:39): "Nevertheless I tell you the truth: it is to your advantage that I go away, for if I do not go away, the Advocate will not come to you; but if I go, I will send him to you" (16:7).

Index